# AMERICAN
# INCOMES

# AMERICAN INCOMES

*Demographics of Who Has Money*

BY THE EDITORS OF NEW STRATEGIST PUBLICATIONS  3rd EDITION

New Strategist Publications, Inc.
Ithaca, New York

New Strategist Publications, Inc.

P.O. Box 242, Ithaca, New York 14851

800/848-0842

www.newstrategist.com

ISBN 1-885070-24-1

Printed in the United States of America

# Contents

# List of Tables

## Chapter 2. Men's Income

### Men's Income Trends

**Men's Income, 1997**

## Chapter 3. Women's Income

### Women's Income Trends

**Women's Income, 1997**

**Chapter 4. Discretionary Income**

## Chapter 5.  Wealth

## Chapter 6.  Poverty

### Poverty Trends

### Poverty, 1997

# List of Illustrations

## Chapter 3. Women's Income

## Chapter 4. Discretionary Income

## Chapter 5. Wealth

**Chapter 6. Poverty**

American Incomes

# Introduction

The Affluent Nineties—that's how we may remember this decade in the years ahead. The economy is booming. Unemployment is at a 30-year low. The stock market is setting records. And never before have there been so many affluent households.

The third edition of *American Incomes: The Demographics of Money* explores and explains our affluence. Since we published the first edition of *American Incomes* in 1993 (titled *The Offical Guide to American Incomes*), our economy has emerged from recession and grown at a faster rate than at any time in the past three decades. Technological and social changes are transforming the workplace, family life, and the roles of men and women. *American Incomes* explores the economic consequences of these changes, revealing who is pulling ahead and who is falling behind. Armed with these facts, business researchers and public policymakers can better position themselves to keep the good times rolling.

Since we first published *American Incomes*, dramatic technological change has reshaped the demographic reference industry. The government's detailed income data, once widely available to all in printed reports, is now accessible only to Internet users or in unpublished tables obtained by calling the appropriate government agency with a specific request. The government's web sites, which house enormous spreadsheets of data, are of great value to researchers with the time and skills to first download and then extract the important nuggets of information. The shift from printed reports to web sites—while convenient for number-crunchers—has made income analysis a bigger chore. For researchers, it has become more time-consuming than ever to get no-nonsense answers to their questions about the economic status of Americans.

*American Incomes* has the answers. It has the numbers and the stories behind them. Thumbing through its pages, you can gain more insight into the economic well-being of Americans than you could by spending all afternoon surfing databases on the Internet. By having it on your bookshelf, you can get the answers to your questions even faster than you could with the fastest modem.

## How to Use This Book

*American Incomes* is designed for easy use. It is divided into six chapters, each of which provides an abundance of data about Americans and their money. The chapters are Household Income, Men's Income, Women's Income, Discretionary Income, Wealth, and Poverty.

✘ **Household Income** Chapter 1 examines trends in household income over the past three decades. It also presents current household income statistics by age of householder, race and Hispanic origin of householder, type of household, and other important demographic characteristics.

✘ **Men's Income**  The trends in men's incomes are examined in chapter 2. Recent income statistics for men are also shown by a variety of demographic characteristics.

✘ **Women's Income**  Chapter 3 examines trends and the current status of women's income, which has become increasingly important to economic well-being over the past few decades.

✘ **Discretionary Income**  Unique to *American Incomes*, the statistics in chapter 4 show that most American households have money to spend after paying taxes and buying necessities.

✘ **Wealth**  The statistics shown in chapter 5 provide a comprehensive portrait of the wealth of American households.

✘ **Poverty**  Despite our growing affluence, poverty remains. Chapter 6 shows who is poor and how the characteristics of the poor are changing.

Most of the tables in *American Incomes* are based on data from the March 1998 Current Population Survey (CPS). In this annual survey, the Census Bureau interviews the occupants of about 50,000 households, asking them for their demographic characteristics and their income in the preceding year. The Current Population Survey is the best source of up-to-date, reliable information on the incomes of Americans. While most of the CPS data published here are produced by the Census Bureau, the tables in *American Incomes* are not reprints of Census Bureau spreadsheets—as is the case in many other reference books. Instead, each of the book's tables was individually compiled and created by New Strategist's editors, with calculations designed to reveal the stories behind the statistics. A page of text accompanies most of the tables, analyzing the data and highlighting the trends.

The discretionary income statistics in chapter 4 of *American Incomes* were produced by Thomas G. Exter and and Vladislav Balaban of Compusearch Micromarketing Data and Systems. The wealth statistics in chapter 5 are from the Federal Reserve Board's 1995 Survey of Consumer Finances. This survey, taken every three years, provides the most comprehensive and reliable portrait of the wealth of Americans. The data shown in chapter 5 are the latest available until the 1998 survey results are released in late 1999 or early 2000.

*American Incomes* contains a lengthy table list to help you locate the information you need. For a more detailed search, use the index at the back of the book. Also at the back of the book is the glossary, which defines the terms commonly used in the tables and text. A list of telephone and web site contacts also appears at the end of the book, allowing researchers to access government specialists and web sites.

*American Incomes* is a snapshot of America at its best. With this book on your desktop, prosperity is at hand.

# Chapter 1

# Household Income

Household income stands at a record high today, with the median reaching $37,005 in 1997. Nearly one in ten households had an income of $100,000 or more—also a record. While the booming economy is one factor behind our affluence, another factor is the aging of the baby-boom generation into its peak earning years. Boomers spanned the ages of 33 to 51 in 1997.

Typically, householders aged 45 to 54 have the highest incomes, and this is even more true today than in the past. Not only are 45-to-54-year-olds at the height of their career, but middle-aged households are more likely to have two or more earners today than in the past, boosting incomes even higher.

The affluence of American households will continue to rise as the entire baby-boom generation fills the peak-earning age groups. Expect to see especially strong income growth among householders aged 55 to 64 as early retirement becomes less common. Among full-time workers, those aged 55 to 64 make more money than 45-to-54-year-olds.

✘ With boomers remaining on the job longer than today's older generation, household affluence will grow for at least another decade.

# Household Income Trends

# Affluence Is at Record Level

**The proportion of households with incomes of $100,000 or more has tripled during the past 30 years.**

Never before have so many households enjoyed such affluence. In 1997, 9.4 percent of American households had incomes of $100,000 or more, up from just 2.8 percent in 1967, after adjusting for inflation. The proportion of households with incomes of $50,000 or more rose from 22 to 37 percent during those years.

The number of affluent households has grown enormously during the past 30 years. In 1967, fewer than 2 million households had incomes of $100,000 or more (in 1997 dollars). By 1997, the number had soared to nearly 10 million—more than five times the 1967 figure. The number of households with incomes of $50,000 or more grew from 13 million to 36 million during those years.

As the ranks of the affluent have expanded, the ranks of the not-so-well-off have shrunk. The proportion of households with incomes below $25,000 fell from 39 to 34 percent during the past three decades. The middle class is also getting smaller. The share of households with incomes between $25,000 and $49,999 fell from 39 to 30 percent between 1967 and 1997. While the proportions of households with low and middle incomes have shrunk, their numbers have increased. The number of households with incomes below $25,000

## Big rise in high-income households

*(percent of households with incomes of $100,000 or more, 1967 to 1997; in 1997 dollars)*

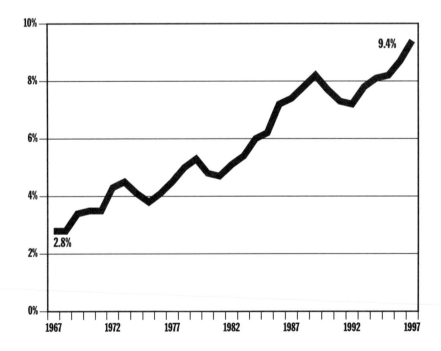

rose from 24 million to 35 million between 1967 and 1997. At the same time, the number of households with incomes between $25,000 and $49,999 rose from 24 million to 30 million.

Both blacks and whites are enjoying record levels of affluence. Fully 21 percent of black households had incomes of $50,000 or more in 1997, up from just 9 percent in 1967, after adjusting for inflation. The number of black households with incomes of $50,000 or more climbed from fewer than 1 million to 2.6 million during those years. Black household incomes are rising as blacks' career opportunities expand and their educational attainment increases.

Trends for Hispanics have not been as positive. While the share of Hispanic households with incomes of $50,000 or more has grown since 1972 (the earliest year for which data by Hispanic origin are available), the proportion of households with incomes below $25,000 has also grown. While many Hispanics are educated professionals, a large share are poorly educated immigrants. The number of Hispanic households with incomes of $50,000 or more rose from fewer than 500,000 in 1972 to 1.8 million in 1997. At the same time, the number of Hispanic households with incomes below $25,000 grew from 1.2 million to 4.1 million.

✘ Behind today's record level of affluence is the aging of the dual-income couples of the baby-boom generation into their peak-earning years. Expect household incomes to rise for another ten years.

✘ While millions of households have affluent incomes, they earned their money the hard way—with both spouses in the labor force. Hard-working two-income couples are not only busy, they are also cautious spenders, making the marketer's task more difficult than ever.

# Distribution of Households by Income, 1967 to 1997: Total Households

*(number and percent distribution of households by income, 1967 to 1997; in 1997 dollars; households in thousands as of the following year)*

| | total households | total | under $15,000 | $15,000– $24,999 | $25,000– $34,999 | $35,000– $49,999 | $50,000– $74,999 | $75,000– $99,999 | $100,000 or more |
|---|---|---|---|---|---|---|---|---|---|
| 1997 | 102,528 | 100.0% | 19.1% | 14.9% | 13.3% | 16.3% | 18.1% | 9.0% | 9.4% |
| 1996 | 101,018 | 100.0 | 19.9 | 15.1 | 13.6 | 16.1 | 18.2 | 8.4 | 8.7 |
| 1995 | 99,627 | 100.0 | 19.8 | 15.3 | 14.0 | 16.7 | 17.7 | 8.3 | 8.2 |
| 1994 | 98,990 | 100.0 | 20.7 | 15.6 | 13.8 | 16.5 | 17.1 | 8.2 | 8.1 |
| 1993 | 97,107 | 100.0 | 21.1 | 15.5 | 14.1 | 16.3 | 17.3 | 7.9 | 7.8 |
| 1992 | 96,426 | 100.0 | 21.0 | 15.2 | 14.1 | 16.6 | 17.9 | 7.9 | 7.2 |
| 1991 | 95,669 | 100.0 | 20.2 | 15.3 | 13.9 | 17.1 | 17.8 | 8.3 | 7.3 |
| 1990 | 94,312 | 100.0 | 19.5 | 14.8 | 13.8 | 17.7 | 18.2 | 8.3 | 7.7 |
| 1989 | 93,347 | 100.0 | 18.8 | 14.8 | 13.7 | 17.1 | 18.7 | 8.8 | 8.2 |
| 1988 | 92,830 | 100.0 | 19.5 | 14.8 | 13.3 | 17.1 | 18.8 | 8.7 | 7.8 |
| 1987 | 91,124 | 100.0 | 19.6 | 14.6 | 13.5 | 17.4 | 18.6 | 8.8 | 7.4 |
| 1986 | 89,479 | 100.0 | 20.0 | 14.9 | 13.3 | 17.6 | 18.7 | 8.3 | 7.2 |
| 1985 | 88,458 | 100.0 | 20.5 | 15.1 | 14.1 | 17.9 | 17.9 | 8.2 | 6.2 |
| 1984 | 86,789 | 100.0 | 20.5 | 15.9 | 14.0 | 17.9 | 18.0 | 7.6 | 6.0 |
| 1983 | 85,290 | 100.0 | 21.0 | 16.3 | 14.5 | 18.0 | 17.6 | 7.2 | 5.4 |
| 1982 | 83,918 | 100.0 | 21.3 | 16.0 | 14.8 | 18.0 | 17.7 | 7.1 | 5.1 |
| 1981 | 83,527 | 100.0 | 21.0 | 16.5 | 14.0 | 18.5 | 18.2 | 7.2 | 4.7 |
| 1980 | 82,368 | 100.0 | 20.6 | 15.8 | 14.0 | 19.2 | 18.4 | 7.2 | 4.8 |
| 1979 | 80,776 | 100.0 | 19.8 | 15.5 | 14.1 | 18.5 | 19.4 | 7.4 | 5.3 |
| 1978 | 77,330 | 100.0 | 19.9 | 15.5 | 13.7 | 19.2 | 19.2 | 7.5 | 5.0 |
| 1977 | 76,030 | 100.0 | 20.6 | 15.7 | 14.3 | 19.1 | 19.0 | 6.8 | 4.5 |
| 1976 | 74,142 | 100.0 | 20.7 | 15.9 | 14.3 | 19.8 | 18.7 | 6.5 | 4.1 |
| 1975 | 72,867 | 100.0 | 21.3 | 15.9 | 15.3 | 19.4 | 18.3 | 6.1 | 3.8 |
| 1974 | 71,163 | 100.0 | 20.0 | 15.7 | 15.3 | 19.9 | 18.5 | 6.6 | 4.1 |
| 1973 | 69,859 | 100.0 | 20.0 | 14.9 | 14.7 | 19.7 | 19.4 | 6.8 | 4.5 |
| 1972 | 68,251 | 100.0 | 20.5 | 14.7 | 14.9 | 20.2 | 18.9 | 6.4 | 4.3 |
| 1971 | 66,676 | 100.0 | 21.4 | 15.4 | 15.6 | 21.0 | 17.7 | 5.5 | 3.5 |
| 1970 | 64,778 | 100.0 | 20.9 | 15.1 | 16.1 | 21.1 | 17.7 | 5.5 | 3.5 |
| 1969 | 63,401 | 100.0 | 20.7 | 15.0 | 16.3 | 21.6 | 17.7 | 5.3 | 3.4 |
| 1968 | 62,214 | 100.0 | 21.4 | 15.3 | 17.7 | 21.2 | 16.9 | 4.6 | 2.8 |
| 1967 | 60,813 | 100.0 | 22.7 | 16.2 | 17.3 | 21.9 | 14.9 | 4.3 | 2.8 |

*Source: Bureau of the Census, Money Income in the United States: 1997, Current Population Reports, P60-200, 1998*

## Distribution of Households by Income, 1967 to 1997: Black Households

*(number and percent distribution of black households by income, 1967 to 1997; in 1997 dollars; households in thousands as of the following year)*

|  | total households | total | under $15,000 | $15,000–$24,999 | $25,000–$34,999 | $35,000–$49,999 | $50,000–$74,999 | $75,000–$99,999 | $100,000 or more |
|---|---|---|---|---|---|---|---|---|---|
| 1997 | 12,474 | 100.0% | 31.9% | 17.9% | 14.2% | 14.9% | 13.1% | 4.6% | 3.3% |
| 1996 | 12,109 | 100.0 | 34.1 | 17.6 | 13.9 | 14.1 | 12.6 | 4.7 | 3.1 |
| 1995 | 11,577 | 100.0 | 34.1 | 18.0 | 14.3 | 14.6 | 11.9 | 4.4 | 2.8 |
| 1994 | 11,655 | 100.0 | 35.5 | 18.2 | 13.3 | 13.3 | 12.1 | 4.3 | 3.3 |
| 1993 | 11,281 | 100.0 | 38.0 | 17.9 | 13.8 | 12.6 | 11.0 | 3.8 | 2.9 |
| 1992 | 11,269 | 100.0 | 39.1 | 16.7 | 13.7 | 13.4 | 11.1 | 3.5 | 2.6 |
| 1991 | 11,083 | 100.0 | 37.3 | 17.4 | 13.2 | 14.1 | 11.4 | 4.0 | 2.5 |
| 1990 | 10,671 | 100.0 | 37.1 | 16.5 | 13.0 | 15.0 | 11.5 | 4.3 | 2.6 |
| 1989 | 10,486 | 100.0 | 35.2 | 17.3 | 13.8 | 14.2 | 11.6 | 5.1 | 2.7 |
| 1988 | 10,561 | 100.0 | 37.8 | 16.7 | 13.4 | 12.7 | 12.1 | 4.6 | 2.8 |
| 1987 | 10,192 | 100.0 | 37.3 | 17.4 | 14.3 | 13.1 | 11.4 | 4.0 | 2.5 |
| 1986 | 9,922 | 100.0 | 37.5 | 17.5 | 13.1 | 13.9 | 11.7 | 3.7 | 2.5 |
| 1985 | 9,797 | 100.0 | 37.1 | 18.3 | 13.6 | 14.1 | 11.1 | 4.0 | 1.6 |
| 1984 | 9,480 | 100.0 | 38.2 | 19.7 | 13.2 | 13.5 | 10.3 | 3.6 | 1.6 |
| 1983 | 9,243 | 100.0 | 39.8 | 19.0 | 13.2 | 13.3 | 10.2 | 3.2 | 1.2 |
| 1982 | 8,916 | 100.0 | 38.7 | 19.6 | 13.6 | 14.2 | 10.4 | 2.3 | 1.2 |
| 1981 | 8,961 | 100.0 | 39.6 | 19.7 | 13.0 | 13.5 | 10.3 | 3.0 | 0.9 |
| 1980 | 8,847 | 100.0 | 38.1 | 19.2 | 13.3 | 14.7 | 10.5 | 3.1 | 1.1 |
| 1979 | 8,586 | 100.0 | 36.2 | 19.8 | 13.6 | 14.4 | 11.6 | 3.2 | 1.2 |
| 1978 | 8,066 | 100.0 | 48.6 | 18.8 | 13.8 | 15.2 | 11.1 | 3.8 | 1.2 |
| 1977 | 7,977 | 100.0 | 36.2 | 20.8 | 14.2 | 14.4 | 10.2 | 3.0 | 1.1 |
| 1976 | 7,776 | 100.0 | 36.7 | 19.6 | 13.9 | 15.7 | 10.4 | 2.7 | 0.9 |
| 1975 | 7,489 | 100.0 | 38.1 | 18.8 | 15.9 | 14.3 | 9.8 | 2.4 | 0.8 |
| 1974 | 7,263 | 100.0 | 36.0 | 20.9 | 15.2 | 14.5 | 10.4 | 2.2 | 0.7 |
| 1973 | 7,040 | 100.0 | 35.7 | 20.2 | 15.3 | 15.1 | 9.9 | 2.7 | 1.1 |
| 1972 | 6,809 | 100.0 | 36.3 | 20.1 | 15.5 | 13.6 | 11.2 | 2.2 | 1.1 |
| 1971 | 6,578 | 100.0 | 37.3 | 21.0 | 15.7 | 14.6 | 8.6 | 2.1 | 0.7 |
| 1970 | 6,180 | 100.0 | 36.5 | 20.9 | 15.8 | 14.5 | 9.2 | 2.2 | 0.8 |
| 1969 | 6,053 | 100.0 | 36.4 | 21.9 | 16.3 | 14.7 | 8.2 | 1.9 | 0.6 |
| 1968 | 5,870 | 100.0 | 38.1 | 22.0 | 16.3 | 13.4 | 7.7 | 1.8 | 0.5 |
| 1967 | 5,728 | 100.0 | 40.8 | 22.6 | 15.1 | 12.9 | 6.1 | 1.7 | 0.9 |

*Source: Bureau of the Census,* Money Income in the United States: 1997, *Current Population Reports, P60-200, 1998*

## Distribution of Households by Income, 1972 to 1997: Hispanic Households

*(number and percent distribution of Hispanic households by income, 1972 to 1997; in 1997 dollars; households in thousands as of the following year)*

| | total households | total | under $15,000 | $15,000–$24,999 | $25,000–$34,999 | $35,000–$49,999 | $50,000–$74,999 | $75,000–$99,999 | $100,000 or more |
|---|---|---|---|---|---|---|---|---|---|
| 1997 | 8,590 | 100.0% | 27.5% | 19.7% | 15.0% | 16.6% | 12.2% | 5.0% | 4.1% |
| 1996 | 8,225 | 100.0 | 28.7 | 20.8 | 14.9 | 15.0 | 12.5 | 4.4 | 3.7 |
| 1995 | 7,939 | 100.0 | 30.7 | 21.0 | 15.2 | 14.1 | 12.1 | 3.9 | 3.0 |
| 1994 | 7,735 | 100.0 | 30.3 | 19.1 | 15.1 | 15.2 | 11.9 | 4.7 | 3.5 |
| 1993 | 7,362 | 100.0 | 29.5 | 19.9 | 16.3 | 15.1 | 11.7 | 4.5 | 3.0 |
| 1992 | 7,153 | 100.0 | 29.2 | 19.6 | 16.5 | 14.8 | 12.8 | 4.2 | 3.1 |
| 1991 | 6,379 | 100.0 | 27.9 | 18.9 | 15.6 | 16.2 | 13.2 | 4.6 | 3.4 |
| 1990 | 6,220 | 100.0 | 27.7 | 18.5 | 15.7 | 17.1 | 12.9 | 4.9 | 3.2 |
| 1989 | 5,933 | 100.0 | 25.5 | 18.9 | 15.2 | 16.3 | 15.1 | 5.2 | 3.9 |
| 1988 | 5,910 | 100.0 | 27.1 | 18.9 | 15.4 | 16.2 | 14.1 | 4.7 | 3.7 |
| 1987 | 5,642 | 100.0 | 27.9 | 18.4 | 15.8 | 16.0 | 13.7 | 4.8 | 3.5 |
| 1986 | 5,418 | 100.0 | 28.0 | 19.5 | 14.1 | 16.7 | 13.3 | 5.5 | 2.8 |
| 1985 | 5,213 | 100.0 | 29.4 | 18.6 | 15.3 | 16.9 | 12.7 | 4.9 | 2.2 |
| 1984 | 4,883 | 100.0 | 29.1 | 19.5 | 14.2 | 17.3 | 13.3 | 4.0 | 2.5 |
| 1983 | 4,666 | 100.0 | 30.2 | 19.3 | 16.1 | 16.4 | 12.2 | 4.1 | 1.9 |
| 1982 | 4,085 | 100.0 | 30.0 | 19.1 | 16.8 | 15.7 | 12.6 | 3.8 | 2.0 |
| 1981 | 3,980 | 100.0 | 26.2 | 19.9 | 16.6 | 17.7 | 13.5 | 4.1 | 1.9 |
| 1980 | 3,906 | 100.0 | 26.6 | 20.2 | 16.5 | 17.1 | 13.6 | 3.9 | 2.1 |
| 1979 | 3,684 | 100.0 | 24.1 | 20.7 | 16.1 | 18.5 | 13.8 | 4.4 | 2.4 |
| 1978 | 3,291 | 100.0 | 24.5 | 20.2 | 16.5 | 18.7 | 14.4 | 3.9 | 1.9 |
| 1977 | 3,304 | 100.0 | 25.4 | 20.5 | 18.2 | 18.1 | 12.6 | 3.5 | 1.7 |
| 1976 | 3,081 | 100.0 | 27.8 | 20.7 | 16.9 | 18.0 | 12.7 | 2.5 | 1.4 |
| 1975 | 2,948 | 100.0 | 27.7 | 21.8 | 17.2 | 18.7 | 10.8 | 2.5 | 1.3 |
| 1974 | 2,897 | 100.0 | 24.5 | 21.5 | 17.4 | 19.6 | 12.2 | 3.1 | 1.5 |
| 1973 | 2,722 | 100.0 | 22.9 | 21.5 | 18.6 | 18.1 | 14.3 | 3.2 | 1.3 |
| 1972 | 2,655 | 100.0 | 23.9 | 20.8 | 20.3 | 19.2 | 11.4 | 2.7 | 1.5 |

*Source: Bureau of the Census,* Money Income in the United States: 1997, *Current Population Reports, P60-200, 1998*

# Distribution of Households by Income, 1967 to 1997: White Households

*(number and percent distribution of white households by income, 1967 to 1997; in 1997 dollars; households in thousands as of the following year)*

| | total households | total | under $15,000 | $15,000–$24,999 | $25,000–$34,999 | $35,000–$49,999 | $50,000–$74,999 | $75,000–$99,999 | $100,000 or more |
|---|---|---|---|---|---|---|---|---|---|
| 1997 | 86,106 | 100.0% | 17.3% | 14.6% | 13.2% | 16.5% | 18.8% | 9.5% | 10.2% |
| 1996 | 85,059 | 100.0 | 17.8 | 14.9 | 13.7 | 16.4 | 19.0 | 8.8 | 9.3 |
| 1995 | 84,511 | 100.0 | 17.8 | 15.1 | 14.0 | 17.0 | 18.5 | 8.8 | 8.9 |
| 1994 | 83,737 | 100.0 | 18.6 | 15.3 | 13.9 | 16.9 | 17.8 | 8.7 | 8.7 |
| 1993 | 82,387 | 100.0 | 18.7 | 15.2 | 14.1 | 16.8 | 18.2 | 8.4 | 8.4 |
| 1992 | 81,795 | 100.0 | 18.6 | 15.0 | 14.2 | 17.0 | 18.9 | 8.4 | 7.8 |
| 1991 | 81,675 | 100.0 | 17.9 | 15.1 | 14.1 | 17.6 | 18.7 | 8.8 | 7.8 |
| 1990 | 80,968 | 100.0 | 17.3 | 14.6 | 14.0 | 18.1 | 19.1 | 8.8 | 8.2 |
| 1989 | 80,163 | 100.0 | 16.6 | 14.5 | 13.7 | 17.4 | 19.6 | 9.3 | 8.8 |
| 1988 | 79,734 | 100.0 | 17.0 | 14.6 | 13.4 | 17.8 | 19.8 | 9.1 | 8.4 |
| 1987 | 78,519 | 100.0 | 17.3 | 14.3 | 13.5 | 18.0 | 19.6 | 9.4 | 8.0 |
| 1986 | 77,284 | 100.0 | 17.8 | 14.5 | 13.3 | 18.1 | 19.7 | 8.8 | 7.7 |
| 1985 | 76,576 | 100.0 | 18.5 | 14.8 | 14.1 | 18.4 | 18.8 | 8.7 | 6.8 |
| 1984 | 75,328 | 100.0 | 18.3 | 15.5 | 14.2 | 18.5 | 18.9 | 8.1 | 6.4 |
| 1983 | 74,170 | 100.0 | 18.6 | 16.0 | 14.8 | 18.6 | 18.5 | 7.7 | 5.9 |
| 1982 | 73,182 | 100.0 | 19.2 | 15.6 | 15.0 | 18.6 | 18.6 | 7.6 | 5.6 |
| 1981 | 72,845 | 100.0 | 18.8 | 16.1 | 14.1 | 19.1 | 19.1 | 7.7 | 5.1 |
| 1980 | 71,872 | 100.0 | 18.5 | 15.4 | 14.1 | 19.7 | 19.4 | 7.6 | 5.2 |
| 1979 | 70,766 | 100.0 | 17.7 | 15.1 | 14.2 | 19.1 | 20.3 | 7.9 | 5.7 |
| 1978 | 68,028 | 100.0 | 18.1 | 15.1 | 13.7 | 19.6 | 20.2 | 7.8 | 5.4 |
| 1977 | 66,934 | 100.0 | 18.7 | 15.1 | 14.3 | 19.7 | 20.1 | 7.2 | 4.9 |
| 1976 | 65,353 | 100.0 | 18.8 | 15.5 | 14.4 | 20.2 | 19.7 | 7.0 | 4.5 |
| 1975 | 64,392 | 100.0 | 19.4 | 15.6 | 15.2 | 20.0 | 19.3 | 6.5 | 4.1 |
| 1974 | 62,984 | 100.0 | 18.1 | 15.1 | 15.3 | 20.5 | 19.4 | 7.1 | 4.5 |
| 1973 | 61,965 | 100.0 | 18.1 | 14.3 | 14.6 | 20.3 | 20.5 | 7.2 | 4.9 |
| 1972 | 60,618 | 100.0 | 18.7 | 14.0 | 14.9 | 21.0 | 19.8 | 6.9 | 4.7 |
| 1971 | 59,463 | 100.0 | 19.6 | 14.8 | 15.7 | 21.7 | 18.6 | 5.9 | 3.8 |
| 1970 | 57,575 | 100.0 | 19.2 | 14.5 | 16.1 | 21.8 | 18.6 | 5.9 | 3.8 |
| 1969 | 56,248 | 100.0 | 18.9 | 14.2 | 16.2 | 22.4 | 18.8 | 5.6 | 3.7 |
| 1968 | 55,394 | 100.0 | 19.6 | 14.5 | 17.9 | 22.1 | 17.9 | 4.9 | 3.0 |
| 1967 | 54,188 | 100.0 | 20.8 | 15.5 | 17.6 | 22.8 | 15.8 | 4.5 | 3.0 |

*Source: Bureau of the Census,* Money Income in the United States: 1997, *Current Population Reports, P60-200, 1998*

## Distribution of Households by Income, 1972 to 1997: Non-Hispanic White Households

*(number and percent distribution of non-Hispanic white households by income, 1972 to 1997; in 1997 dollars; households in thousands as of the following year)*

|  | total households | total | under $15,000 | $15,000–$24,999 | $25,000–$34,999 | $35,000–$49,999 | $50,000–$74,999 | $75,000–$99,999 | $100,000 or more |
|---|---|---|---|---|---|---|---|---|---|
| 1997 | 77,936 | 100.0% | 16.2% | 14.0% | 13.0% | 16.4% | 19.5% | 10.0% | 10.8% |
| 1996 | 77,240 | 100.0 | 16.8 | 14.3 | 13.5 | 16.6 | 19.7 | 9.3 | 9.9 |
| 1995 | 76,932 | 100.0 | 16.5 | 14.5 | 13.9 | 17.3 | 19.1 | 9.2 | 9.4 |
| 1994 | 77,004 | 100.0 | 17.6 | 15.0 | 13.8 | 17.1 | 18.3 | 9.1 | 9.2 |
| 1993 | 75,697 | 100.0 | 17.7 | 14.8 | 13.9 | 17.0 | 18.8 | 8.8 | 8.9 |
| 1992 | 75,107 | 100.0 | 17.7 | 14.6 | 14.0 | 17.2 | 19.4 | 8.8 | 8.2 |
| 1991 | 75,625 | 100.0 | 17.1 | 14.7 | 14.0 | 17.7 | 19.1 | 9.2 | 8.2 |
| 1990 | 75,035 | 100.0 | 16.4 | 14.3 | 13.8 | 18.2 | 19.6 | 9.1 | 8.6 |
| 1989 | 74,495 | 100.0 | 16.0 | 14.2 | 13.6 | 17.5 | 20.0 | 9.6 | 9.2 |
| 1988 | 74,067 | 100.0 | 16.2 | 14.2 | 13.2 | 17.9 | 20.2 | 9.5 | 8.8 |
| 1987 | 73,120 | 100.0 | 16.6 | 14.0 | 13.3 | 18.1 | 20.0 | 9.7 | 8.3 |
| 1986 | 72,067 | 100.0 | 17.1 | 14.2 | 13.2 | 18.2 | 20.1 | 9.1 | 8.1 |
| 1985 | 71,540 | 100.0 | 17.8 | 14.5 | 14.0 | 18.5 | 19.2 | 9.0 | 7.1 |
| 1984 | 70,586 | 100.0 | 17.7 | 15.2 | 14.2 | 18.5 | 19.3 | 8.4 | 6.7 |
| 1983 | 69,648 | 100.0 | 17.9 | 15.8 | 14.7 | 18.7 | 18.9 | 7.9 | 6.1 |
| 1982 | 69,214 | 100.0 | 18.5 | 15.4 | 14.9 | 18.7 | 18.9 | 7.8 | 5.8 |
| 1981 | 68,996 | 100.0 | 18.3 | 15.9 | 13.9 | 19.2 | 19.4 | 7.9 | 5.3 |
| 1980 | 68,106 | 100.0 | 18.0 | 15.2 | 14.0 | 19.9 | 19.7 | 7.8 | 5.4 |
| 1979 | 67,203 | 100.0 | 17.5 | 14.8 | 14.1 | 19.1 | 20.6 | 8.1 | 5.9 |
| 1978 | 64,836 | 100.0 | 17.8 | 14.8 | 13.6 | 19.7 | 20.5 | 8.0 | 5.6 |
| 1977 | 63,721 | 100.0 | 18.4 | 14.8 | 14.1 | 19.7 | 20.5 | 7.4 | 5.1 |
| 1976 | 62,365 | 100.0 | 18.3 | 15.2 | 14.2 | 20.3 | 20.0 | 7.2 | 4.6 |
| 1975 | 61,533 | 100.0 | 19.1 | 15.3 | 15.1 | 20.0 | 19.6 | 6.7 | 4.2 |
| 1974 | 60,164 | 100.0 | 17.8 | 14.8 | 15.2 | 20.6 | 19.8 | 7.2 | 4.6 |
| 1973 | 59,236 | 100.0 | 18.0 | 14.0 | 14.4 | 20.4 | 20.7 | 7.4 | 5.1 |
| 1972 | 58,005 | 100.0 | 18.5 | 13.7 | 14.6 | 21.1 | 20.2 | 7.0 | 4.9 |

*Source: Bureau of the Census,* Money Income in the United States: 1997, *Current Population Reports, P60-200, 1998*

# The Rich Are Getting Richer

## The richest households are capturing a growing share of the nation's income.

A common way to examine the distribution of income is to divide the total number of households into fifths—or quintiles—based on their income and determine how much of the total household income accrues to each fifth. This calculation reveals that a growing share of the nation's income is controlled by the richest households.

In 1967, households in the top quintile of the income distribution controlled 44 percent of aggregate household income. By 1997, they controlled an even larger 49 percent. Even more telling, households in the top 5 percent of the household income distribution captured 22 percent of aggregate household income in 1997, up from 18 percent in 1967. The share of income controlled by the bottom four fifths of households declined from 56 to 51 percent during those years.

Hispanics have experienced the most dramatic shift in income distribution over the past few decades, while blacks have seen little change. In 1972, the poorest three-fifths of Hispanic households controlled 34 percent of Hispanic household income. By 1997, they controlled a smaller 27 percent. The top 5 percent of Hispanic households captured 22 percent of Hispanic household income in 1997, up from just 16 percent in 1972.

✗ As well-educated dual-income couples of the baby-boom generation continue to fill the peak-earning age groups, the richest households will soon control over half of the nation's household income.

### Poorest households control a smaller share of income

*(percent of household income accruing to households in the top and bottom fifth of the household income distribution, 1967 and 1997)*

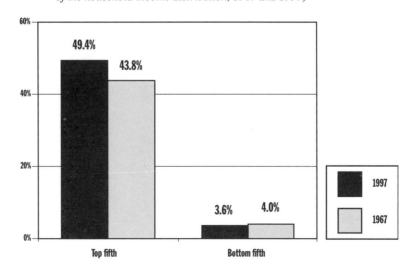

## Share of Aggregate Income Received by Each Fifth and
## Top 5 Percent of Households, 1967 to 1997: Total Households

*(distribution of aggregate income by household income quintile for total households, 1967 to 1997; households in thousands as of the following year)*

|  | total households | total | bottom fifth | second fifth | third fifth | fourth fifth | top fifth | top 5 percent |
|---|---|---|---|---|---|---|---|---|
| 1997 | 102,528 | 100.0% | 3.6% | 8.9% | 15.0% | 23.2% | 49.4% | 21.7% |
| 1996 | 101,018 | 100.0 | 3.7 | 9.0 | 15.1 | 23.3 | 49.0 | 21.4 |
| 1995 | 99,627 | 100.0 | 3.7 | 9.1 | 15.2 | 23.3 | 48.7 | 21.0 |
| 1994 | 98,990 | 100.0 | 3.6 | 8.9 | 15.0 | 23.4 | 49.1 | 21.2 |
| 1993 | 97,107 | 100.0 | 3.6 | 9.0 | 15.1 | 23.5 | 48.9 | 21.0 |
| 1992 | 96,426 | 100.0 | 3.8 | 9.4 | 15.8 | 24.2 | 46.9 | 18.6 |
| 1991 | 95,669 | 100.0 | 3.8 | 9.6 | 15.9 | 24.2 | 46.5 | 18.1 |
| 1990 | 94,312 | 100.0 | 3.9 | 9.6 | 15.9 | 24.0 | 46.6 | 18.6 |
| 1989 | 93,347 | 100.0 | 3.8 | 9.5 | 15.8 | 24.0 | 46.8 | 18.9 |
| 1988 | 92,830 | 100.0 | 3.8 | 9.6 | 16.0 | 24.3 | 46.3 | 18.3 |
| 1987 | 91,124 | 100.0 | 3.8 | 9.6 | 16.1 | 24.3 | 46.2 | 18.2 |
| 1986 | 89,479 | 100.0 | 3.9 | 9.7 | 16.2 | 24.5 | 45.7 | 17.5 |
| 1985 | 88,458 | 100.0 | 4.0 | 9.7 | 16.3 | 24.6 | 45.3 | 17.0 |
| 1984 | 86,789 | 100.0 | 4.1 | 9.9 | 16.4 | 24.7 | 44.9 | 16.5 |
| 1983 | 85,290 | 100.0 | 4.1 | 10.0 | 16.5 | 24.7 | 44.7 | 16.4 |
| 1982 | 83,918 | 100.0 | 4.1 | 10.1 | 16.6 | 24.7 | 44.5 | 16.2 |
| 1981 | 83,527 | 100.0 | 4.2 | 10.2 | 16.8 | 25.0 | 43.8 | 15.6 |
| 1980 | 82,368 | 100.0 | 4.3 | 10.3 | 16.9 | 24.9 | 43.7 | 15.8 |
| 1979 | 80,776 | 100.0 | 4.2 | 10.3 | 16.9 | 24.7 | 44.0 | 16.4 |
| 1978 | 77,330 | 100.0 | 4.3 | 10.3 | 16.9 | 24.8 | 43.7 | 16.2 |
| 1977 | 76,030 | 100.0 | 4.4 | 10.3 | 17.0 | 24.8 | 43.6 | 16.1 |
| 1976 | 74,142 | 100.0 | 4.4 | 10.4 | 17.1 | 24.8 | 43.3 | 16.0 |
| 1975 | 72,867 | 100.0 | 4.4 | 10.5 | 17.1 | 24.8 | 43.2 | 15.9 |
| 1974 | 71,163 | 100.0 | 4.4 | 10.6 | 17.1 | 24.7 | 43.1 | 15.9 |
| 1973 | 69,859 | 100.0 | 4.2 | 10.5 | 17.1 | 24.6 | 43.6 | 16.6 |
| 1972 | 68,251 | 100.0 | 4.1 | 10.5 | 17.1 | 24.5 | 43.9 | 17.0 |
| 1971 | 66,676 | 100.0 | 4.1 | 10.6 | 17.3 | 24.5 | 43.5 | 16.7 |
| 1970 | 64,778 | 100.0 | 4.1 | 10.8 | 17.4 | 24.5 | 43.3 | 16.6 |
| 1969 | 63,401 | 100.0 | 4.1 | 10.9 | 17.5 | 24.5 | 43.0 | 16.6 |
| 1968 | 62,214 | 100.0 | 4.2 | 11.1 | 17.5 | 24.4 | 42.8 | 16.6 |
| 1967 | 60,813 | 100.0 | 4.0 | 10.8 | 17.3 | 24.2 | 43.8 | 17.5 |

*Source: Bureau of the Census, Internet web site <http://www.census.gov/hhes/income/histinc/index.html>*

# Share of Aggregate Income Received by Each Fifth and
# Top 5 Percent of Households, 1967 to 1997: Black Households

*(distribution of aggregate income by household income quintile for black households, 1967 to 1997; households in thousands as of the following year)*

| | total households | total | bottom fifth | second fifth | third fifth | fourth fifth | top fifth | top 5 percent |
|---|---|---|---|---|---|---|---|---|
| 1997 | 12,474 | 100.0% | 3.2% | 8.5% | 15.1% | 24.5% | 48.7% | 19.1% |
| 1996 | 12,109 | 100.0 | 3.1 | 8.0 | 14.5 | 23.7 | 50.7 | 21.7 |
| 1995 | 11,577 | 100.0 | 3.2 | 8.2 | 14.8 | 24.2 | 49.6 | 20.2 |
| 1994 | 11,655 | 100.0 | 3.0 | 7.9 | 14.3 | 24.3 | 50.5 | 20.1 |
| 1993 | 11,281 | 100.0 | 3.0 | 7.7 | 14.3 | 23.7 | 51.3 | 21.1 |
| 1992 | 11,269 | 100.0 | 3.1 | 7.8 | 14.7 | 24.8 | 49.7 | 19.1 |
| 1991 | 11,083 | 100.0 | 3.1 | 7.8 | 15.0 | 25.2 | 48.9 | 18.3 |
| 1990 | 10,671 | 100.0 | 3.1 | 7.9 | 15.0 | 25.1 | 49.0 | 18.5 |
| 1989 | 10,486 | 100.0 | 3.2 | 8.0 | 15.0 | 24.9 | 48.9 | 18.2 |
| 1988 | 10,561 | 100.0 | 3.3 | 7.7 | 14.6 | 24.7 | 49.7 | 18.7 |
| 1987 | 10,192 | 100.0 | 3.3 | 7.9 | 14.8 | 24.4 | 49.7 | 19.3 |
| 1986 | 9,922 | 100.0 | 3.2 | 8.0 | 15.0 | 25.1 | 48.8 | 18.2 |
| 1985 | 9,797 | 100.0 | 3.5 | 8.3 | 15.2 | 25.0 | 48.0 | 17.5 |
| 1984 | 9,480 | 100.0 | 3.6 | 8.4 | 15.0 | 24.7 | 48.3 | 17.4 |
| 1983 | 9,243 | 100.0 | 3.6 | 8.3 | 15.2 | 25.2 | 47.8 | 16.9 |
| 1982 | 8,916 | 100.0 | 3.6 | 8.6 | 15.3 | 25.5 | 47.0 | 16.9 |
| 1981 | 8,961 | 100.0 | 3.8 | 8.6 | 15.3 | 25.4 | 46.9 | 16.1 |
| 1980 | 8,847 | 100.0 | 3.7 | 8.7 | 15.4 | 25.3 | 46.9 | 16.6 |
| 1979 | 8,586 | 100.0 | 3.9 | 8.8 | 15.5 | 25.4 | 46.3 | 16.1 |
| 1978 | 8,066 | 100.0 | 4.0 | 8.7 | 15.6 | 25.3 | 46.4 | 16.3 |
| 1977 | 7,977 | 100.0 | 4.2 | 9.2 | 15.5 | 24.9 | 46.3 | 16.7 |
| 1976 | 7,776 | 100.0 | 4.3 | 9.2 | 15.8 | 25.5 | 45.2 | 15.7 |
| 1975 | 7,489 | 100.0 | 4.2 | 9.1 | 16.0 | 25.5 | 45.3 | 15.9 |
| 1974 | 7,263 | 100.0 | 4.2 | 9.4 | 16.2 | 25.2 | 45.0 | 15.7 |
| 1973 | 7,040 | 100.0 | 4.1 | 9.4 | 16.0 | 25.1 | 45.5 | 16.6 |
| 1972 | 6,809 | 100.0 | 3.9 | 9.2 | 15.8 | 24.9 | 46.2 | 16.9 |
| 1971 | 6,578 | 100.0 | 4.0 | 9.4 | 16.1 | 25.1 | 45.4 | 16.4 |
| 1970 | 6,180 | 100.0 | 3.7 | 9.3 | 16.3 | 25.2 | 45.5 | 16.4 |
| 1969 | 6,053 | 100.0 | 3.9 | 9.7 | 16.5 | 25.1 | 44.7 | 15.9 |
| 1968 | 5,870 | 100.0 | 4.0 | 9.8 | 16.3 | 25.1 | 44.9 | 15.9 |
| 1967 | 5,728 | 100.0 | 3.8 | 9.3 | 15.9 | 24.3 | 46.7 | 18.2 |

*Source: Bureau of the Census, Internet web site <http://www.census.gov/hhes/income/histinc/index.html>*

## Share of Aggregate Income Received by Each Fifth and
## Top 5 Percent of Households, 1972 to 1997: Hispanic Households

*(distribution of aggregate income by household income quintile for Hispanic households, 1972 to 1997; households in thousands as of the following year)*

|      | total households | total | bottom fifth | second fifth | third fifth | fourth fifth | top fifth | top 5 percent |
|------|------------------|-------|--------------|--------------|-------------|--------------|-----------|---------------|
| 1997 | 8,590 | 100.0% | 3.6% | 8.9% | 14.9% | 23.1% | 49.5% | 21.5% |
| 1996 | 8,225 | 100.0 | 3.8 | 9.0 | 14.7 | 23.1 | 49.5 | 21.5 |
| 1995 | 7,939 | 100.0 | 3.8 | 8.9 | 14.8 | 23.3 | 49.3 | 20.8 |
| 1994 | 7,735 | 100.0 | 3.7 | 8.7 | 14.8 | 23.3 | 49.6 | 21.0 |
| 1993 | 7,362 | 100.0 | 3.9 | 9.1 | 15.1 | 23.1 | 48.7 | 20.4 |
| 1992 | 7,153 | 100.0 | 4.0 | 9.4 | 15.7 | 24.1 | 46.9 | 18.1 |
| 1991 | 6,379 | 100.0 | 4.0 | 9.4 | 15.8 | 24.3 | 46.5 | 17.7 |
| 1990 | 6,220 | 100.0 | 4.0 | 9.5 | 15.9 | 24.3 | 46.3 | 17.9 |
| 1989 | 5,933 | 100.0 | 3.8 | 9.5 | 15.7 | 24.4 | 46.6 | 18.1 |
| 1988 | 5,910 | 100.0 | 3.7 | 9.3 | 15.6 | 24.2 | 47.2 | 19.0 |
| 1987 | 5,642 | 100.0 | 3.7 | 9.1 | 15.5 | 24.1 | 47.6 | 19.2 |
| 1986 | 5,418 | 100.0 | 4.0 | 9.5 | 15.9 | 24.8 | 45.8 | 16.5 |
| 1985 | 5,213 | 100.0 | 4.1 | 9.5 | 16.1 | 24.8 | 45.6 | 16.5 |
| 1984 | 4,883 | 100.0 | 3.9 | 9.5 | 16.2 | 25.0 | 45.3 | 16.6 |
| 1983 | 4,666 | 100.0 | 4.2 | 9.7 | 16.3 | 24.9 | 44.9 | 16.0 |
| 1982 | 4,085 | 100.0 | 4.2 | 9.6 | 16.2 | 24.7 | 45.3 | 16.7 |
| 1981 | 3,980 | 100.0 | 4.5 | 10.3 | 16.7 | 24.8 | 43.6 | 15.3 |
| 1980 | 3,906 | 100.0 | 4.4 | 10.2 | 16.4 | 24.9 | 44.1 | 16.0 |
| 1979 | 3,684 | 100.0 | 4.6 | 10.5 | 16.6 | 24.6 | 43.7 | 15.9 |
| 1978 | 3,291 | 100.0 | 4.7 | 10.7 | 16.9 | 24.9 | 42.8 | 15.4 |
| 1977 | 3,304 | 100.0 | 4.9 | 10.8 | 16.9 | 24.7 | 42.8 | 15.4 |
| 1976 | 3,081 | 100.0 | 4.7 | 10.5 | 16.9 | 25.1 | 42.8 | 15.2 |
| 1975 | 2,948 | 100.0 | 4.8 | 10.7 | 16.9 | 24.9 | 42.9 | 15.8 |
| 1974 | 2,897 | 100.0 | 5.2 | 10.9 | 17.2 | 24.7 | 42.0 | 15.1 |
| 1973 | 2,722 | 100.0 | 5.1 | 11.1 | 17.1 | 24.7 | 42.0 | 15.0 |
| 1972 | 2,655 | 100.0 | 5.3 | 11.2 | 17.2 | 24.0 | 42.3 | 16.2 |

*Source: Bureau of the Census, Internet web site <http://www.census.gov/hhes/income/histinc/index.html>*

# Share of Aggregate Income Received by Each Fifth and Top 5 Percent of Households, 1967 to 1997: White Households

*(distribution of aggregate income by household income quintile for white households, 1967 to 1997; households in thousands as of the following year)*

| | total households | total | bottom fifth | second fifth | third fifth | fourth fifth | top fifth | top 5 percent |
|---|---|---|---|---|---|---|---|---|
| 1997 | 86,106 | 100.0% | 3.8% | 9.1% | 15.0% | 23.0% | 49.1% | 21.7% |
| 1996 | 85,059 | 100.0 | 3.9 | 9.2 | 15.2 | 23.2 | 48.4 | 21.1 |
| 1995 | 84,511 | 100.0 | 4.0 | 9.3 | 15.3 | 23.3 | 48.1 | 20.7 |
| 1994 | 83,737 | 100.0 | 3.8 | 9.2 | 15.1 | 23.2 | 48.6 | 21.1 |
| 1993 | 82,387 | 100.0 | 3.9 | 9.3 | 15.3 | 23.3 | 48.2 | 20.7 |
| 1992 | 81,795 | 100.0 | 4.1 | 9.7 | 15.9 | 24.1 | 46.2 | 18.4 |
| 1991 | 81,675 | 100.0 | 4.1 | 9.9 | 16.0 | 24.1 | 45.8 | 17.9 |
| 1990 | 80,968 | 100.0 | 4.2 | 10.0 | 16.0 | 23.9 | 46.0 | 18.3 |
| 1989 | 80,163 | 100.0 | 4.1 | 9.8 | 16.0 | 23.8 | 46.3 | 18.7 |
| 1988 | 79,734 | 100.0 | 4.1 | 10.0 | 16.2 | 24.1 | 45.6 | 18.0 |
| 1987 | 78,519 | 100.0 | 4.1 | 10.0 | 16.3 | 24.2 | 45.5 | 17.9 |
| 1986 | 77,284 | 100.0 | 4.1 | 10.1 | 16.4 | 24.3 | 45.1 | 17.2 |
| 1985 | 76,576 | 100.0 | 4.2 | 10.2 | 16.5 | 24.4 | 44.7 | 16.8 |
| 1984 | 75,328 | 100.0 | 4.3 | 10.3 | 16.6 | 24.6 | 44.2 | 16.2 |
| 1983 | 74,170 | 100.0 | 4.4 | 10.4 | 16.6 | 24.6 | 44.1 | 16.1 |
| 1982 | 73,182 | 100.0 | 4.4 | 10.4 | 16.8 | 24.6 | 43.9 | 15.9 |
| 1981 | 72,845 | 100.0 | 4.5 | 10.5 | 17.0 | 24.8 | 43.2 | 15.3 |
| 1980 | 71,872 | 100.0 | 4.5 | 10.6 | 17.1 | 24.7 | 43.1 | 15.5 |
| 1979 | 70,766 | 100.0 | 4.4 | 10.6 | 17.0 | 24.6 | 43.4 | 16.2 |
| 1978 | 68,028 | 100.0 | 4.5 | 10.6 | 17.1 | 24.6 | 43.2 | 16.1 |
| 1977 | 66,934 | 100.0 | 4.5 | 10.6 | 17.2 | 24.7 | 43.0 | 15.8 |
| 1976 | 65,353 | 100.0 | 4.6 | 10.7 | 17.3 | 24.7 | 42.8 | 15.9 |
| 1975 | 64,392 | 100.0 | 4.6 | 10.8 | 17.2 | 24.7 | 42.7 | 15.7 |
| 1974 | 62,984 | 100.0 | 4.6 | 11.0 | 17.2 | 24.6 | 42.6 | 15.7 |
| 1973 | 61,965 | 100.0 | 4.4 | 10.8 | 17.3 | 24.5 | 43.1 | 16.4 |
| 1972 | 60,618 | 100.0 | 4.3 | 10.8 | 17.2 | 24.3 | 43.4 | 16.8 |
| 1971 | 59,463 | 100.0 | 4.3 | 11.0 | 17.4 | 24.4 | 43.0 | 16.5 |
| 1970 | 57,575 | 100.0 | 4.2 | 11.1 | 17.5 | 24.3 | 42.9 | 16.5 |
| 1969 | 56,248 | 100.0 | 4.3 | 11.3 | 17.6 | 24.3 | 42.5 | 16.4 |
| 1968 | 55,394 | 100.0 | 4.4 | 11.4 | 17.6 | 24.3 | 42.3 | 16.5 |
| 1967 | 54,188 | 100.0 | 4.1 | 11.2 | 17.4 | 24.0 | 43.3 | 17.3 |

*Source: Bureau of the Census, Internet web site <http://www.census.gov/hhes/income/histinc/index.html>*

# Older Householders Have Seen Biggest Gains

**The median income of householders aged 65 or older rose 70 percent between 1967 and 1997, after adjusting for inflation.**

The substantial rise in the median income of the oldest householders during the past three decades has occurred as better educated and more affluent generations have entered the age group. Income gains have been much smaller for householders under age 65. Nevertheless, the economic fortunes of householders in all but the youngest age group have improved since 1967—thanks to America's rising standard of living. Since 1990, householders aged 35 to 44 are the only ones who have experienced a decline in income.

The 9 percent decline in the median income of householders under age 25 can be partly explained by the growing propensity of young adults to go to college. College students are likely to work only part-time or not at all. Consequently, the incomes of young adults have fallen as more have chosen to go to school. After graduation, college graduates will earn much more than those who did not continue their education.

✘ Because fewer people in their fifties and early sixties will opt for early retirement in the years ahead, the incomes of householders aged 55 to 64 should rise substantially.

## Incomes of youngest householders have declined

*(percent change in median household income by age of householder, 1967 to 1997; in 1997 dollars)*

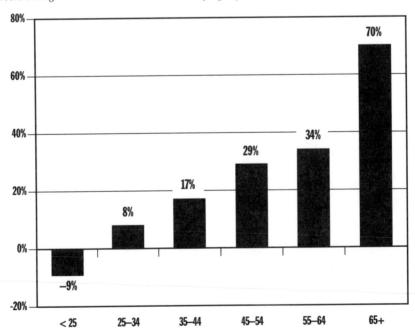

# Median Income of Households by Age of Householder, 1967 to 1997

*(median household income by age of householder, 1967 to 1997; percent change for selected years; in 1997 dollars)*

| | total households | under 25 | 25 to 34 | 35 to 44 | 45 to 54 | 55 to 64 | aged 65 or older | | |
| | | | | | | | total | 65 to 74 | 75 or older |
|---|---|---|---|---|---|---|---|---|---|
| 1997 | $37,005 | $22,583 | $38,174 | $46,359 | $51,875 | $41,356 | $20,761 | $25,292 | $17,079 |
| 1996 | 36,306 | 21,930 | 36,711 | 45,439 | 51,630 | 40,729 | 19,894 | 23,948 | 16,362 |
| 1995 | 35,887 | 22,094 | 36,545 | 45,775 | 50,612 | 40,101 | 20,111 | 24,255 | 16,157 |
| 1994 | 34,942 | 20,945 | 35,902 | 45,125 | 51,183 | 38,156 | 19,597 | 23,200 | 15,954 |
| 1993 | 34,700 | 21,474 | 34,745 | 45,387 | 51,323 | 37,180 | 19,717 | 23,670 | 15,914 |
| 1992 | 35,047 | 20,206 | 35,737 | 45,591 | 50,834 | 38,887 | 19,602 | 23,304 | 15,581 |
| 1991 | 35,501 | 21,580 | 36,345 | 46,369 | 51,557 | 39,246 | 20,004 | 23,643 | 16,419 |
| 1990 | 36,770 | 22,107 | 37,281 | 47,353 | 51,480 | 39,744 | 20,698 | 24,919 | 16,148 |
| 1989 | 37,415 | 24,157 | 38,602 | 48,713 | 53,746 | 39,891 | 20,413 | 24,540 | 15,663 |
| 1988 | 36,937 | 23,119 | 38,542 | 49,594 | 51,844 | 39,213 | 20,246 | 23,706 | 16,017 |
| 1987 | 36,820 | 23,237 | 38,099 | 49,711 | 52,565 | 38,938 | 20,406 | 24,191 | 15,948 |
| 1986 | 36,460 | 22,420 | 37,925 | 48,014 | 52,221 | 39,211 | 20,275 | – | – |
| 1985 | 35,229 | 22,448 | 37,418 | 46,339 | 49,557 | 38,122 | 19,770 | – | – |
| 1984 | 34,626 | 21,670 | 36,665 | 46,009 | 48,684 | 37,219 | 19,771 | – | – |
| 1983 | 33,655 | 21,597 | 35,043 | 44,603 | 48,911 | 36,706 | 18,883 | – | – |
| 1982 | 33,864 | 23,195 | 35,728 | 44,272 | 46,983 | 37,061 | 18,536 | – | – |
| 1981 | 33,978 | 23,589 | 36,541 | 45,218 | 48,175 | 37,481 | 17,641 | – | – |
| 1980 | 34,538 | 24,789 | 37,711 | 46,077 | 48,991 | 38,120 | 17,125 | – | – |
| 1979 | 35,703 | 25,838 | 39,481 | 47,924 | 49,989 | 38,902 | 17,089 | – | – |
| 1978 | 35,819 | 26,189 | 39,238 | 47,384 | 50,364 | 38,111 | 16,837 | – | – |
| 1977 | 34,467 | 24,306 | 38,284 | 45,905 | 49,209 | 36,344 | 16,119 | – | – |
| 1976 | 34,278 | 23,945 | 37,815 | 45,180 | 47,728 | 36,239 | 16,109 | – | – |
| 1975 | 33,699 | 23,241 | 37,489 | 44,386 | 46,614 | 35,656 | 15,950 | – | – |
| 1974 | 34,627 | 25,086 | 38,415 | 46,035 | 47,541 | 35,471 | 16,365 | – | – |
| 1973 | 35,745 | 25,490 | 40,241 | 47,480 | 47,881 | 36,986 | 15,584 | – | – |
| 1972 | 35,053 | 25,525 | 39,319 | 45,865 | 47,445 | 36,272 | 15,070 | – | – |
| 1971 | 33,619 | 24,507 | 37,526 | 43,257 | 44,746 | 34,796 | 14,199 | – | – |
| 1970 | 33,942 | 25,917 | 37,657 | 43,257 | 44,353 | 34,610 | 13,594 | – | – |
| 1969 | 34,173 | 25,908 | 37,990 | 43,718 | 44,553 | 33,676 | 13,561 | – | – |
| 1968 | 32,964 | 25,663 | 36,579 | 41,832 | 41,602 | 32,479 | 13,538 | – | – |
| 1967 | 31,751 | 24,827 | 35,425 | 39,776 | 40,227 | 30,760 | 12,203 | – | – |

**Percent change**

| | | | | | | | | | |
|---|---|---|---|---|---|---|---|---|---|
| 1990–1997 | 0.6% | 2.2% | 2.4% | –2.1% | 0.8% | 4.1% | 0.3% | 1.5% | 5.8% |
| 1967*–1997 | 16.5 | –9.0 | 7.8 | 16.6 | 29.0 | 34.4 | 70.1 | 4.6 | 7.1 |

*\* Or earliest year available.*
*Note: (–) means data not available.*
*Source: Bureau of the Census, Internet web site, <http://www.census.gov/hhes/income/histinc/index.html>; calculations by New Strategist*

# Women Who Live Alone Have Gained the Most

## Male-headed households have seen the smallest income gains.

The median income of American households rose 7 percent between 1980 and 1997, after adjusting for inflation. The incomes of women who live alone, married couples, and female-headed families rose faster than average, while those of households headed by men rose at a below-average rate.

Women who live alone have seen a 19 percent rise in median income since 1980. Behind this rise is the entry of a more affluent generation into the 55-and-older age group, which accounts for the majority of women who live alone. The incomes of female-headed families grew as better educated women commanded higher salaries, while married couples made gains because nowadays more of them are two-income couples.

Households headed by men—both family and nonfamily—have not fared as well. Behind men's slower gains, and even declines during the 1990s, is the erosion in the earning power of younger men over the past few decades. Not only has the stagnation in men's income hurt the economic status of households headed by men, but it has made two incomes a necessity for most married couples.

✘ The rapid income gains made by married couples since 1980 should continue for the next few years because the well-educated dual-income couples of the baby-boom generation are now in their peak earning years.

## Households headed by women have made big gains

*(percent change in household income by household type, 1980 to 1997; in 1997 dollars)*

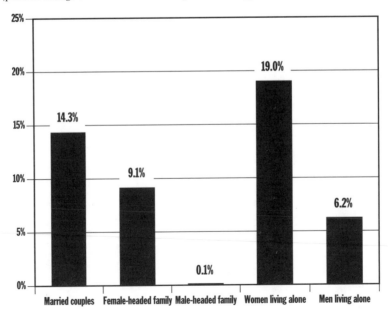

# Median Income of Households by Type of Household, 1980 to 1997

*(median income of households by household type, 1980 to 1997; percent change in income for selected years; in 1997 dollars)*

| | | family households | | | nonfamily households | | | |
| | | | | | women | | men | |
| | total households | married couples | female hh, no spouse present | male hh, no spouse present | total | living alone | total | living alone |
|---|---|---|---|---|---|---|---|---|
| 1997 | $37,005 | $51,681 | $23,040 | $36,634 | $17,613 | $15,530 | $27,592 | $23,871 |
| 1996 | 36,306 | 51,002 | 22,059 | 36,476 | 16,774 | 14,962 | 27,892 | 24,602 |
| 1995 | 35,887 | 49,634 | 22,483 | 35,316 | 16,737 | 15,093 | 27,406 | 23,786 |
| 1994 | 34,942 | 48,779 | 21,521 | 33,001 | 16,189 | 14,546 | 26,634 | 22,977 |
| 1993 | 34,700 | 47,905 | 20,598 | 33,154 | 16,531 | 14,434 | 27,466 | 23,738 |
| 1992 | 35,047 | 48,008 | 21,010 | 34,674 | 16,517 | 14,795 | 26,438 | 22,856 |
| 1991 | 35,502 | 48,403 | 21,170 | 36,543 | 16,883 | 15,124 | 27,129 | 23,873 |
| 1990 | 36,770 | 49,115 | 22,189 | 38,746 | 17,314 | 15,409 | 27,617 | 24,516 |
| 1989 | 37,415 | 50,045 | 22,500 | 39,266 | 17,804 | 15,778 | 29,023 | 25,391 |
| 1988 | 36,937 | 49,433 | 21,777 | 38,859 | – | 15,768 | – | 24,806 |
| 1987 | 36,820 | 49,383 | 21,871 | 37,730 | – | 15,143 | – | 24,010 |
| 1986 | 36,460 | 48,144 | 20,995 | 38,517 | – | 14,609 | – | 24,116 |
| 1985 | 35,229 | 46,481 | 21,354 | 36,327 | – | 14,579 | – | 24,332 |
| 1984 | 34,626 | 45,858 | 20,812 | 37,925 | – | 14,890 | – | 23,483 |
| 1983 | 33,655 | 44,039 | 19,722 | 36,873 | – | 14,730 | – | 22,754 |
| 1982 | 33,864 | 43,763 | 19,950 | 35,619 | – | 13,695 | – | 23,197 |
| 1981 | 33,978 | 44,723 | 20,380 | 36,593 | – | 13,191 | – | 22,867 |
| 1980 | 34,538 | 45,205 | 21,120 | 36,615 | – | 13,047 | – | 22,480 |
| **Percent change** | | | | | | | | |
| 1990–1997 | 0.6% | 5.2% | 3.8% | –5.5% | 1.7% | 0.8% | –0.1% | –2.6% |
| 1980*–1997 | 7.1 | 14.3 | 9.1 | 0.1 | –1.1 | 19 | –4.9 | 6.2 |

*\* Or earliest year available.*

*Note: (–) means data not available.*

*Source: Bureau of the Census, Internet web site, <http://www.census.gov/hhes/income/histinc/index.html>; calculations by New Strategist*

# Black Household Incomes Are Rising Rapidly

## Hispanic household incomes are falling.

Since 1967, the median income of black households has grown 31 percent, after adjusting for inflation—nearly double the 17 percent gain in the median income of the average household. Behind this rapid growth is social change that has created more opportunities for blacks. During the 1990s, black household income has continued to grow rapidly, posting a 9 percent gain.

In contrast to the strong gains made by blacks, Hispanic households have lost economic ground. The median income of Hispanic households fell 4 percent between 1972 and 1997, after adjusting for inflation. Behind this decline is the entry of millions of unskilled Hispanic immigrants into the United States during the past few decades.

The median household income of Asian Americans declined 4 percent between 1990 and 1997. Nevertheless, Asians have a higher median household income than any other racial or ethnic group, including non-Hispanic whites. In 1997, the median income of households headed by Asian Americans stood at $45,249.

✘ Black household income should continue to grow rapidly as better-educated generations replace older, less-skilled blacks in the work force.

### Asians have seen incomes decline during the 1990s

*(percent change in median household income by race and Hispanic origin of householder, 1990 to 1998; in 1997 dollars)*

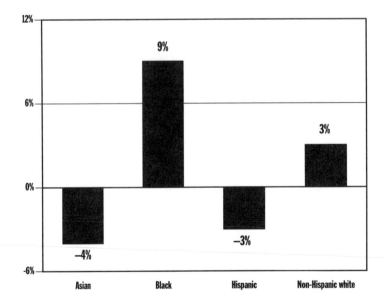

# Median Income of Households by Race and Hispanic Origin, 1967 to 1997

*(median income of households by race and Hispanic origin of householder, 1967 to 1997; percent change in income for selected years; in 1997 dollars)*

| | total households | Asian | black | Hispanic | white | non-Hispanic white |
|---|---|---|---|---|---|---|
| 1997 | $37,005 | $45,249 | $25,050 | $26,628 | $38,972 | $40,577 |
| 1996 | 36,306 | 44,269 | 24,021 | 25,477 | 38,014 | 39,677 |
| 1995 | 35,887 | 42,773 | 23,583 | 24,075 | 37,667 | 39,154 |
| 1994 | 34,942 | 43,842 | 22,772 | 25,365 | 36,852 | 38,041 |
| 1993 | 34,700 | 42,593 | 21,696 | 25,420 | 36,610 | 37,957 |
| 1992 | 35,047 | 43,243 | 21,455 | 25,850 | 36,846 | 38,083 |
| 1991 | 35,501 | 42,952 | 22,162 | 26,739 | 37,201 | 38,090 |
| 1990 | 36,770 | 47,217 | 22,934 | 27,421 | 38,352 | 39,229 |
| 1989 | 37,415 | 46,729 | 23,406 | 28,374 | 39,356 | 40,203 |
| 1988 | 36,937 | 43,777 | 22,260 | 27,621 | 39,048 | 40,124 |
| 1987 | 36,820 | – | 22,142 | 27,319 | 38,794 | 39,861 |
| 1986 | 36,460 | – | 22,083 | 26,875 | 38,331 | 39,202 |
| 1985 | 35,229 | – | 22,105 | 26,051 | 37,154 | 37,989 |
| 1984 | 34,626 | – | 20,809 | 26,248 | 36,529 | 37,287 |
| 1983 | 33,655 | – | 20,029 | 25,632 | 35,294 | – |
| 1982 | 33,864 | – | 20,093 | 25,482 | 35,453 | 36,047 |
| 1981 | 33,978 | – | 20,145 | 27,255 | 35,900 | 36,418 |
| 1980 | 34,538 | – | 20,992 | 26,622 | 36,437 | 37,083 |
| 1979 | 35,703 | – | 21,978 | 28,287 | 37,433 | 37,960 |
| 1978 | 35,819 | – | 22,377 | 28,065 | 37,236 | 37,937 |
| 1977 | 34,467 | – | 21,388 | 27,039 | 36,245 | 36,963 |
| 1976 | 34,278 | – | 21,351 | 25,856 | 35,907 | 36,639 |
| 1975 | 33,699 | – | 21,156 | 25,317 | 35,241 | 35,507 |
| 1974 | 34,627 | – | 21,536 | 27,542 | 36,213 | 36,522 |
| 1973 | 35,745 | – | 22,052 | 27,693 | 37,462 | 37,792 |
| 1972 | 35,053 | – | 21,465 | 27,751 | 36,774 | 37,298 |
| 1971 | 33,619 | – | 20,772 | – | 35,165 | – |
| 1970 | 33,942 | – | 21,518 | – | 35,353 | – |
| 1969 | 34,173 | – | 21,558 | – | 35,664 | – |
| 1968 | 32,964 | – | 20,239 | – | 34,322 | – |
| 1967 | 31,583 | – | 19,123 | – | 32,936 | – |
| **Percent change** | | | | | | |
| 1990–1997 | 0.6% | –4.2% | 9.2% | –2.9% | 1.6% | 3.4% |
| 1967*–1997 | 17.2 | 3.4 | 31.0 | –4.0 | 18.3 | 8.8 |

*\* Or earliest year available.*
*Note: (–) means data not available.*
*Source: Bureau of the Census, Internet web site, <http://www.census.gov/hhes/income/histinc/index.html>; calculations by New Strategist*

# The Value of a College Degree Is Growing

**Incomes of households headed by college graduates top those of high school graduates by a growing margin.**

No wonder so many young adults are choosing to get a college degree. The incomes of college graduates are rising, while those of high school graduates are falling. In 1991, the median income of households headed by people with a bachelor's degree was $23,826 greater than that of households headed by people with only a high school diploma. By 1997, the gap had grown to $25,269.

Between 1991 and 1997, the median income of households headed by people without a high school diploma fell, while that of high school graduates was flat, after adjusting for inflation. In contrast, the median income of households headed by people with a bachelor's degree grew 3 percent and that of householders with master's degrees was up 5 percent.

✘ Because the returns on an investment in education are great, expect a growing proportion of young adults to pursue a college degree. Many older adults, as well, are likely to return to school to gain the credentials that will help them earn higher salaries.

## College graduates make much more

*(median income of householders aged 25 or older by educational attainment, 1997)*

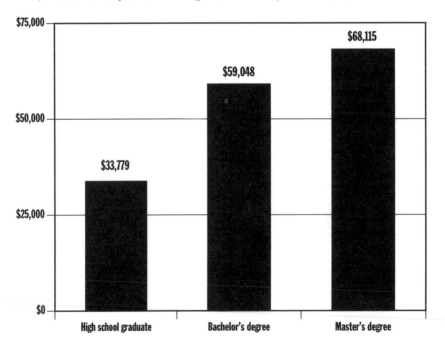

# Median Income of Households by Education of Householder, 1991 to 1997

*(median income of households by educational attainment of householder aged 25 or older; 1991 to 1997; in 1997 dollars)*

| | total households | less than 9th grade | 9th to 12th grade | high school graduate | some college | associate's degree | bachelor's degree or more | | | | |
| --- | --- | --- | --- | --- | --- | --- | --- | --- | --- | --- | --- |
| | | | | | | | total | bachelor's degree | master's degree | professional degree | doctoral degree |
| 1997 | $38,190 | $15,541 | $19,851 | $33,779 | $40,015 | $45,258 | $63,292 | $59,048 | $68,115 | $92,228 | $87,232 |
| 1996 | 37,354 | 15,729 | 20,103 | 33,036 | 39,279 | 45,530 | 61,354 | 56,402 | 65,353 | 92,417 | 83,021 |
| 1995 | 37,108 | 15,843 | 19,271 | 33,044 | 39,131 | 44,357 | 61,137 | 55,666 | 68,413 | 86,369 | 84,257 |
| 1994 | 36,265 | 15,460 | 18,999 | 32,567 | 38,857 | 43,599 | 62,207 | 56,717 | 66,111 | 84,476 | 84,644 |
| 1993 | 35,728 | 15,461 | 19,955 | 31,878 | 39,120 | 43,966 | 62,330 | 57,180 | 67,022 | 97,373 | 83,030 |
| 1992 | 36,149 | 15,352 | 19,816 | 33,085 | 40,309 | 43,787 | 61,684 | 56,491 | 66,061 | 96,913 | 80,099 |
| 1991 | 36,569 | 15,580 | 20,663 | 33,569 | 41,421 | 46,783 | 61,596 | 57,395 | 65,017 | 91,856 | 82,861 |
| **Percent change** | | | | | | | | | | | |
| 1991–1997 | 4.4% | –0.3% | –3.9% | 0.6% | –3.4% | –3.3% | 2.8% | 2.9% | 4.8% | 0.4% | 5.3% |

*Source: Bureau of the Census, Internet web site, <http://www.census.gov/hhes/income/histinc/index.html>; calculations by New Strategist*

# Biggest Gains for Smallest Households

**The median income of single-person households has grown 81 percent since 1967, after adjusting for inflation.**

Behind the substantial rise in the median income of single-person households are the improving economic fortunes of the nation's older Americans. The majority of single-person households are headed by people aged 55 or older. As better-educated and more affluent generations filled the older age group during the past 30 years, the incomes of single-person households have grown.

The largest households have seen the smallest rise in median income since 1967. The median income of households with six or more persons grew less than 20 percent between 1967 and 1997, after adjusting for inflation. Many larger households are headed by immigrants, who typically have lower-paying jobs than native-born Americans.

✘ The incomes of households with one or two people should grow faster than those of larger households in the years ahead as boomers become empty nesters and the affluence of older Americans continues to rise.

## Incomes up for single-person households

*(median income of single-person households, 1967 to 1997; in 1997 dollars)*

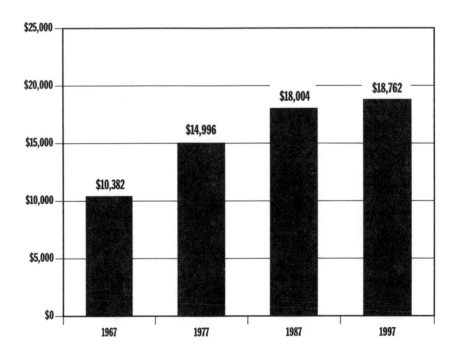

# Median Income of Households by Size, 1967 to 1997

*(median income of households by size of household, 1967 to 1997; percent change in income for selected years; in 1997 dollars)*

| | total households | one person | two persons | three persons | four persons | five persons | six persons | seven or more |
|---|---|---|---|---|---|---|---|---|
| 1997 | $37,005 | $18,762 | $39,343 | $47,115 | $53,165 | $50,407 | $46,465 | $42,343 |
| 1996 | 36,306 | 18,308 | 38,138 | 45,841 | 52,584 | 48,939 | 43,412 | 41,263 |
| 1995 | 35,887 | 17,970 | 37,597 | 44,489 | 52,164 | 48,139 | 46,616 | 41,087 |
| 1994 | 34,942 | 17,568 | 36,773 | 44,449 | 50,638 | 47,798 | 46,226 | 39,661 |
| 1993 | 34,700 | 17,844 | 36,025 | 43,778 | 50,079 | 46,918 | 45,644 | 36,787 |
| 1992 | 35,047 | 17,640 | 36,397 | 44,162 | 50,354 | 48,214 | 42,437 | 37,933 |
| 1991 | 35,501 | 18,196 | 36,791 | 45,067 | 50,735 | 48,070 | 43,476 | 40,226 |
| 1990 | 36,770 | 18,842 | 38,508 | 45,148 | 50,929 | 48,230 | 46,859 | 44,341 |
| 1989 | 37,415 | 19,194 | 38,652 | 46,955 | 52,737 | 50,844 | 45,696 | 42,253 |
| 1988 | 36,937 | 18,970 | 38,017 | 46,055 | 52,491 | 48,873 | 50,078 | 42,975 |
| 1987 | 36,820 | 18,004 | 37,472 | 45,823 | 52,352 | 50,483 | 47,299 | 44,033 |
| 1986 | 36,458 | 17,799 | 37,039 | 45,401 | 50,754 | 50,032 | 48,075 | 40,763 |
| 1985 | 35,229 | 17,727 | 35,601 | 44,237 | 48,781 | 47,370 | 46,376 | 42,154 |
| 1984 | 34,626 | 17,782 | 34,933 | 43,142 | 47,938 | 47,616 | 43,734 | 40,609 |
| 1983 | 33,655 | 17,318 | 33,943 | 41,425 | 47,033 | 45,167 | 43,329 | 37,745 |
| 1982 | 33,863 | 16,762 | 33,913 | 41,040 | 46,365 | 45,625 | 45,650 | 39,818 |
| 1981 | 33,978 | 16,372 | 33,682 | 42,040 | 46,891 | 46,547 | 47,997 | 43,746 |
| 1980 | 34,538 | 15,917 | 34,140 | 42,389 | 47,604 | 48,474 | 47,614 | 45,500 |
| 1979 | 35,703 | 15,948 | 34,926 | 43,916 | 48,757 | 50,729 | 49,462 | 49,013 |
| 1978 | 35,819 | 15,857 | 34,366 | 43,214 | 48,654 | 49,938 | 49,477 | 48,069 |
| 1977 | 34,467 | 14,996 | 33,197 | 41,565 | 47,381 | 48,414 | 48,447 | 43,848 |
| 1976 | 34,278 | 14,496 | 32,981 | 40,906 | 46,294 | 47,888 | 47,685 | 44,389 |
| 1975 | 33,699 | 13,725 | 31,903 | 40,219 | 45,263 | 47,090 | 46,099 | 41,761 |
| 1974 | 34,627 | 14,018 | 32,521 | 40,320 | 46,332 | 48,311 | 47,479 | 45,348 |
| 1973 | 35,745 | 13,823 | 32,685 | 41,390 | 46,990 | 48,898 | 48,983 | 46,028 |
| 1972 | 35,057 | 12,909 | 31,717 | 40,855 | 46,643 | 47,622 | 46,972 | 42,930 |
| 1971 | 33,616 | 12,185 | 30,257 | 38,583 | 43,495 | 44,672 | 44,352 | 41,008 |
| 1970 | 33,942 | 12,063 | 30,522 | 39,052 | 43,432 | 44,921 | 44,831 | 41,481 |
| 1969 | 34,173 | 12,017 | 30,686 | 39,188 | 43,600 | 44,561 | 44,162 | 41,608 |
| 1968 | 32,964 | 11,448 | 29,269 | 38,035 | 41,905 | 42,198 | 41,334 | 39,691 |
| 1967 | 31,751 | 10,382 | 27,670 | 36,897 | 39,754 | 40,479 | 39,864 | 36,875 |
| **Percent change** | | | | | | | | |
| 1990–1997 | 0.6% | −0.4% | 2.2% | 4.4% | 4.4% | 4.5% | −0.8% | −4.5% |
| 1967–1997 | 16.5 | 80.7 | 42.2 | 27.7 | 33.7 | 24.5 | 16.6 | 14.8 |

*Source: Bureau of the Census, Internet web site, <http://www.census.gov/hhes/income/histinc/index.html>; calculations by New Strategist*

# Two-Earner Households Have Growing Incomes

## Households with only one earner have lost ground since 1987.

The median income of two-earner households has grown 5 percent since 1987, after adjusting for inflation. In contrast, the median income of households with only one earner fell 2 percent between 1987 and 1997.

Behind these divergent trends are the rising incomes of women and the stagnant or declining incomes of men. Typically, households with two earners are dual-income couples, who are benefiting from the rapidly growing incomes of women. Men are the breadwinners in most one-earner households, and men's incomes are barely keeping pace with inflation.

In response to these economic trends, the number of two-earner households grew 32 percent between 1987 and 1997. Households with one earner grew only 19 percent during those years. In 1997, the nation's 36 million two-earner households slightly outnumbered the 35 million with only one earner.

✗ Look for the incomes of two-earner households to expand in the years ahead as the baby-boom generation fills the peak-earning age groups.

### Incomes of two-earner households are growing fastest

*(percent change in median household income by number of earners in household, 1990 to 1997; in 1997 dollars)*

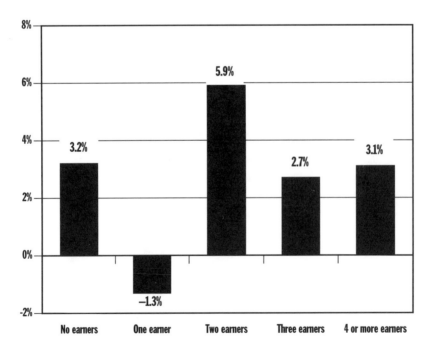

# Median Income of Households by Number of Earners, 1987 to 1997

*(median income of households by number of earners, 1987 to 1997; in 1997 dollars)*

| | total | no earners | one earner | two earners | three earners | four or more earners |
|---|---|---|---|---|---|---|
| 1997 | $37,005 | $14,142 | $29,780 | $54,192 | $67,182 | $84,816 |
| 1996 | 36,306 | 13,626 | 28,535 | 53,619 | 63,860 | 80,305 |
| 1995 | 35,887 | 13,798 | 29,032 | 52,658 | 66,550 | 78,189 |
| 1994 | 34,942 | 13,185 | 28,385 | 51,696 | 65,436 | 80,441 |
| 1993 | 34,700 | 13,114 | 28,390 | 51,605 | 63,614 | 80,241 |
| 1992 | 35,047 | 13,111 | 28,890 | 51,012 | 64,166 | 79,168 |
| 1991 | 35,501 | 13,564 | 29,265 | 50,712 | 65,295 | 81,507 |
| 1990 | 36,770 | 13,703 | 30,178 | 51,154 | 65,402 | 82,276 |
| 1989 | 37,415 | 13,857 | 30,817 | 52,047 | 66,694 | 84,395 |
| 1988 | 36,937 | 13,472 | 30,578 | 51,852 | 66,536 | 86,916 |
| 1987 | 36,820 | 13,448 | 30,495 | 51,542 | 66,932 | 85,260 |
| **Percent change** | | | | | | |
| 1990–1997 | 0.6% | 3.2% | –1.3% | 5.9% | 2.7% | 3.1% |
| 1987–1997 | 0.5 | 5.2 | –2.3 | 5.1 | 0.4 | –0.5 |

*Source: Bureau of the Census, Internet web site <http://www.census.gov/hhes/income/histinc/index.html>; calculations by New Strategist*

# Biggest Gains for Households without Children

**The median household income of married couples without children at home has grown 25 percent since 1974, after adjusting for inflation.**

Households without children have seen their incomes grow significantly faster than households with children over the past two decades. The older age of householders without children explains this difference, since the incomes of older householders have been growing much faster than those of younger adults.

The median income of married couples with children under age 18 at home grew 18 percent between 1974 and 1997, after adjusting for inflation—well below the 25 percent gain for married couples without children at home. Female-headed families without children at home have seen their median income grow 11 percent since 1974, while those with children at home experienced a 7 percent gain. Male-headed families have fared the worst. While the median income of those without children at home grew 9 percent, those with children at home experienced a 13 percent decline in median income.

✘ As baby boomers become empty nesters, these income trends will intensify. The incomes of married couples without children at home are likely to grow much faster than the incomes of those with children.

## Bigger gains for the child-free

*(percent change in median household income by type of household and presence of children under age 18 at home, 1974 to 1997; in 1997 dollars)*

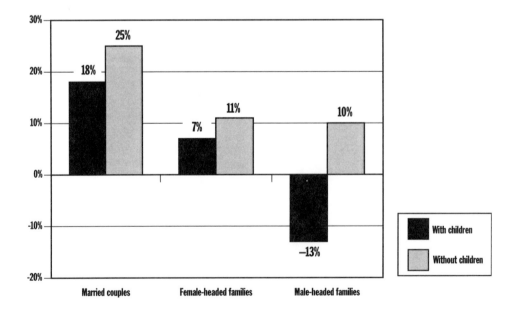

## Median Income of Families by Type and Presence of Children, 1974 to 1997

*(median income of family households by type and presence of related children under age 18 at home, 1974 to 1997; percent change in income for selected years; in 1997 dollars)*

| | total families | | married-couple families | | female householder, no spouse present | | male householder, no spouse present | |
|---|---|---|---|---|---|---|---|---|
| | *no children* | *with children* | *no children* | *with children* | *no children* | *with children* | *no children* | *with children* |
| 1997 | $45,624 | $43,545 | $48,588 | $54,395 | $31,038 | $17,256 | $41,483 | $28,668 |
| 1996 | 45,048 | 41,925 | 48,013 | 52,956 | 31,246 | 16,765 | 40,740 | 27,109 |
| 1995 | 43,442 | 42,143 | 46,671 | 52,625 | 30,002 | 17,098 | 36,555 | 28,425 |
| 1994 | 42,944 | 41,073 | 45,688 | 51,165 | 30,586 | 16,139 | 34,737 | 26,092 |
| 1993 | 42,040 | 40,208 | 44,755 | 50,591 | 30,194 | 14,964 | 35,033 | 24,823 |
| 1992 | 43,114 | 40,649 | 45,345 | 50,555 | 31,378 | 15,178 | 39,018 | 25,416 |
| 1991 | 43,534 | 41,233 | 46,056 | 50,099 | 30,770 | 15,334 | 38,090 | 28,483 |
| 1990 | 44,870 | 42,035 | 46,976 | 50,667 | 33,181 | 16,077 | 41,557 | 30,959 |
| 1989 | 45,344 | 43,307 | 47,688 | 51,768 | 33,374 | 16,799 | 41,443 | 32,043 |
| 1988 | 44,658 | 42,933 | 47,111 | 51,327 | 32,831 | 16,110 | 41,452 | 31,028 |
| 1987 | 43,969 | 43,571 | 46,231 | 51,466 | 32,079 | 16,057 | 38,143 | 32,775 |
| 1986 | 43,351 | 42,912 | 46,013 | 50,284 | 29,745 | 14,880 | – | – |
| 1985 | 41,415 | 41,326 | 43,948 | 48,253 | 29,712 | 15,030 | – | – |
| 1984 | 41,067 | 40,632 | 43,683 | 47,487 | 28,604 | 15,089 | – | – |
| 1983 | 40,030 | 39,197 | 42,454 | 45,386 | 26,668 | 14,750 | – | – |
| 1982 | 39,143 | 39,539 | 41,433 | 45,571 | 27,043 | 15,028 | – | – |
| 1981 | 39,277 | 40,481 | 41,707 | 46,707 | 26,243 | 16,406 | – | – |
| 1980 | 40,170 | 41,666 | 42,286 | 47,401 | 28,182 | 16,506 | – | – |
| 1979 | 40,800 | 43,810 | 42,932 | 49,054 | 28,888 | 17,779 | – | – |
| 1978 | 40,318 | 43,252 | 42,343 | 48,530 | 28,462 | 16,728 | 39,122 | 34,773 |
| 1977 | 38,906 | 42,121 | 40,752 | 47,353 | 27,534 | 16,512 | 38,294 | 34,756 |
| 1976 | 38,212 | 41,960 | 40,379 | 46,540 | 25,723 | 16,055 | 34,375 | 35,415 |
| 1975 | 37,163 | 40,670 | 38,708 | 44,911 | 26,463 | 15,664 | 39,460 | 33,608 |
| 1974 | 37,323 | 41,764 | 38,761 | 46,100 | 27,860 | 16,133 | 37,895 | 33,068 |
| **Percent change** | | | | | | | | |
| 1990–1997 | 1.7% | 3.6% | 3.4% | 7.4% | –6.5% | 7.3% | –0.2% | –7.4% |
| 1974–1997 | 22.2 | 4.3 | 25.4 | 18.0 | 11.4 | 7.0 | 9.5 | –13.3 |

*Note: (–) means data not available.*
*Source: Bureau of the Census, Internet web site, <http://www.census.gov/hhes/income/histinc/index.html>; calculations by New Strategist*

# Dual-Earner Couples Enjoy Rising Incomes

## The incomes of single-earner couples are falling.

Because it takes two incomes to make ends meet, dual earners now are the majority of married couples. Among the nation's 54 million couples, 33 million are dual earners—meaning both husband and wife are in the labor force.

Since 1987, the median income of married couples in which the husband works full-time and the wife does not work has fallen 3 percent, to $48,510, after adjusting for inflation. In contrast, the median income of couples in which the husband works full-time and the wife also works rose 3 percent, to $64,902. The income gap between dual-earner and single-earner couples grew from $12,684 to $16,392 between 1987 and 1997.

✘ The incomes of single-earner couples have been falling because of the stagnation and even decline in men's incomes over the past few decades. In contrast, dual-income couples have made gains because of women's growing earning power.

### Dual earners are gaining ground

*(median income of married couples in which the husband works full-time by work status of wife, 1987 and 1997; in 1997 dollars)*

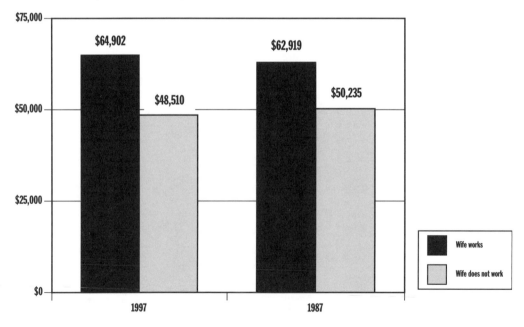

# Median Income of Married Couples by Work Status, 1987 to 1997

*(median income of married couples by work status of husband and wife, 1987 to 1997; in 1997 dollars)*

| | total married couples | husband worked | | | | husband worked full-time, year round | | | | husband did not work | | | |
|---|---|---|---|---|---|---|---|---|---|---|---|---|---|
| | | total | wife worked | | wife did not work | total | wife worked | | wife did not work | total | wife worked | | wife did not work |
| | | | total | full-time | | | total | full-time | | | total | full-time | |
| 1997 | $51,591 | $57,794 | $61,837 | $67,053 | $43,482 | $61,495 | $64,902 | $69,507 | $48,510 | $27,639 | $37,239 | $44,548 | $24,986 |
| 1996 | 50,848 | 56,903 | 61,206 | 65,753 | 41,940 | 60,465 | 63,662 | 67,644 | 46,014 | 26,755 | 34,909 | 41,193 | 24,702 |
| 1995 | 49,563 | 55,647 | 60,030 | 65,511 | 41,810 | 59,246 | 63,061 | 67,700 | 45,420 | 27,100 | 36,500 | 42,638 | 24,438 |
| 1994 | 48,690 | 55,314 | 59,419 | 65,396 | 41,430 | 59,063 | 62,684 | 67,538 | 45,561 | 25,729 | 34,088 | 40,895 | 23,445 |
| 1993 | 47,767 | 54,925 | 58,307 | 64,301 | 41,632 | 58,723 | 62,220 | 67,433 | 46,402 | 25,689 | 33,467 | 38,499 | 23,311 |
| 1992 | 47,921 | 54,234 | 58,397 | 64,199 | 42,001 | 58,855 | 62,323 | 67,595 | 47,095 | 26,306 | 34,192 | 39,992 | 24,090 |
| 1991 | 48,309 | 54,201 | 57,952 | 64,095 | 42,706 | 59,029 | 62,111 | 67,278 | 47,747 | 27,203 | 33,651 | 40,394 | 25,473 |
| 1990 | 48,991 | 54,457 | 58,126 | 64,645 | 43,621 | 58,423 | 61,756 | 67,624 | 47,994 | 27,413 | 34,102 | 40,082 | 25,551 |
| 1989 | 49,894 | 55,413 | 59,213 | 65,968 | 45,563 | 59,694 | 62,921 | 68,592 | 49,833 | 26,454 | 34,012 | 39,295 | 24,558 |
| 1988 | 49,370 | 55,259 | 59,050 | 66,071 | 44,391 | 59,412 | 63,029 | 69,043 | 49,039 | 27,081 | 35,869 | 42,457 | 24,467 |
| 1987 | 49,279 | 55,105 | 59,009 | 65,392 | 45,327 | 59,597 | 62,919 | 69,073 | 50,235 | 27,163 | 36,245 | 43,483 | 24,406 |
| **Percent change** | | | | | | | | | | | | | |
| 1990–1997 | 5.3% | 6.1% | 6.4% | 3.7% | -0.3% | 5.3% | 5.1% | 2.8% | 1.1% | 0.8% | 9.2% | 11.1% | -2.2% |
| 1987–1997 | 4.7 | 4.9 | 4.8 | 2.5 | -4.1 | 3.2 | 3.2 | 0.6 | -3.4 | 1.8 | 2.7 | 2.4 | 2.4 |

*Source: Bureau of the Census, Internet web site, <http://www.census.gov/hhes/income/histinc/index.html>; calculations by New Strategist*

# Midwest Is Making Gains

**Household incomes in the Midwest have been growing faster than those in other regions since 1990.**

Median household income grew much faster in the Northeast, South, and West than in the Midwest between 1975 and 1997. The biggest gain in median household income came in the South—up 14 percent. The West saw a 12.5 percent gain in median household income during those years, while median household income in the Northeast grew 10.5 percent. Median household income grew only 7 percent in the Midwest between 1975 and 1997.

More recently, the fortunes of the Midwest have improved. Since 1990, median household income has grown fastest in the Midwest—up more than 4 percent, after adjusting for inflation. Median household income grew nearly 4 percent in the South during those years, while the West saw a tiny 0.4 percent gain. In the Northeast, median household income fell 3 percent between 1990 and 1997, after adjusting for inflation.

✗ The bi-coastal economy of the 1980s has given way to a Midwestern boom in the 1990s. In the years ahead, expect continued ups and downs by region as technological change interacts with regional infrastructure to determine household income growth.

## Midwest is the leader in the 1990s

*(percent change in household income by region, 1990 to 1997; in 1997 dollars)*

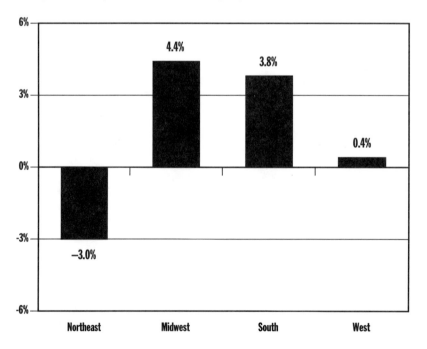

# Median Income of Households by Region, 1975 to 1997

*(median income of households by region, 1975 to 1997; percent change in income for selected years; in 1997 dollars)*

|  | total households | Northeast | Midwest | South | West |
|---|---|---|---|---|---|
| 1997 | $37,005 | $38,929 | $38,316 | $34,345 | $39,162 |
| 1996 | 36,306 | 38,264 | 37,418 | 33,166 | 37,977 |
| 1995 | 35,887 | 38,030 | 37,744 | 32,587 | 37,891 |
| 1994 | 34,942 | 37,825 | 35,203 | 32,513 | 37,311 |
| 1993 | 34,700 | 37,484 | 34,877 | 31,590 | 37,475 |
| 1992 | 35,047 | 37,750 | 35,239 | 31,584 | 38,122 |
| 1991 | 35,501 | 39,438 | 35,266 | 32,027 | 38,007 |
| 1990 | 36,770 | 40,126 | 36,714 | 33,085 | 39,003 |
| 1989 | 37,415 | 42,252 | 37,213 | 33,485 | 40,236 |
| 1988 | 36,937 | 41,278 | 37,364 | 33,385 | 39,122 |
| 1987 | 36,820 | 39,792 | 36,430 | 33,863 | 39,376 |
| 1986 | 36,460 | 38,798 | 36,392 | 33,064 | 39,541 |
| 1985 | 35,229 | 38,014 | 35,130 | 31,917 | 38,457 |
| 1984 | 34,626 | 36,379 | 34,890 | 31,857 | 37,780 |
| 1983 | 33,655 | 35,159 | 33,950 | 31,239 | 35,801 |
| 1982 | 33,864 | 34,764 | 34,954 | 31,212 | 35,579 |
| 1981 | 33,978 | 35,315 | 35,077 | 30,890 | 36,418 |
| 1980 | 34,538 | 35,478 | 35,714 | 31,784 | 37,071 |
| 1979 | 35,703 | 36,577 | 37,537 | 32,464 | 37,839 |
| 1978 | 35,819 | 36,877 | 37,267 | 32,469 | 36,882 |
| 1977 | 34,467 | 36,143 | 36,239 | 31,508 | 35,503 |
| 1976 | 34,278 | 35,326 | 36,972 | 30,968 | 35,229 |
| 1975 | 33,699 | 35,239 | 35,910 | 30,098 | 34,810 |
| **Percent change** | | | | | |
| 1990–1997 | 0.6% | –3.0% | 4.4% | 3.8% | 0.4% |
| 1975–1997 | 9.8 | 10.5 | 6.7 | 14.1 | 12.5 |

*Source: Bureau of the Census, Internet web site, <http://www.census.gov/hhes/income/histinc/index.html>; calculations by New Strategist*

# Household Income Growth Varies by State

## Nationally, median household income barely grew between 1987 and 1997.

While median household income stagnated in the nation as a whole between 1987 and 1997, it grew more than 10 percent in ten states, after adjusting for inflation. Median household income grew fastest in geographically dispersed states ranging from Indiana (up 22 percent, after adjusting for inflation) to Colorado and Washington (up 16 percent) and Alabama (up 15 percent). Median household income fell in 21 states and the District of Columbia during the past decade, and the greatest declines came in Hawaii (down 17 percent), Wyoming (down 14 percent), and Arizona (down 13 percent).

The economic well-being of households is closely tied to local economies. The recession of the early 1990s affected most parts of the country, while recovery from the recession has been much stronger in some states than in others. A few of the nation's poorest states, such as Alabama and West Virginia, have gained relative to other states during the past ten years. At the same time, already well-off states such as Colorado have pulled even farther ahead.

✗ As technological change allows more people to work at well-paying jobs no matter where they live, income disparities by state may shrink.

### Biggest gainer and loser: Indiana and Hawaii

*(percent change in median household income by state, 1987 to 1997; in 1997 dollars)*

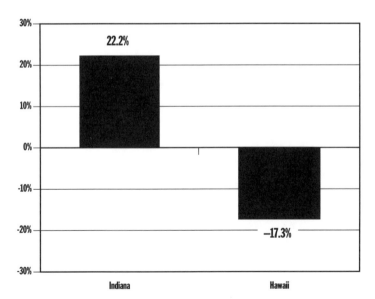

# Median Income of Households by State, 1987 to 1997

*(median income of households by state, 1987 to 1997; percent change in income for selected years; in 1997 dollars)*

| | 1997 | 1996 | 1995 | 1994 | 1993 | 1992 | 1991 | 1990 | 1989 | 1988 | 1987 | percent change 1990–97 | 1987–97 |
|---|---|---|---|---|---|---|---|---|---|---|---|---|---|
| **United States** | **$37,005** | **$36,306** | **$35,887** | **$34,942** | **$34,700** | **$35,047** | **$35,501** | **$36,770** | **$37,415** | **$36,937** | **$36,714** | **0.6%** | **0.8%** |
| Alabama | 31,939 | 30,997 | 27,372 | 29,453 | 27,859 | 29,524 | 28,690 | 28,682 | 27,549 | 27,064 | 27,881 | 11.4 | 14.6 |
| Alaska | 47,994 | 53,990 | 50,503 | 49,132 | 47,685 | 47,821 | 47,858 | 48,258 | 46,605 | 44,912 | 46,953 | -0.5 | 2.2 |
| Arizona | 32,740 | 32,363 | 32,503 | 33,890 | 33,888 | 33,585 | 36,221 | 35,887 | 36,956 | 35,865 | 37,792 | -8.8 | -13.4 |
| Arkansas | 26,162 | 27,745 | 27,186 | 27,687 | 25,590 | 27,320 | 27,616 | 27,981 | 27,742 | 27,368 | 26,600 | -6.5 | -1.6 |
| California | 39,694 | 39,703 | 38,976 | 38,263 | 37,846 | 39,928 | 39,670 | 40,880 | 42,725 | 41,091 | 42,592 | -2.9 | -6.8 |
| Colorado | 43,233 | 41,890 | 42,870 | 40,973 | 38,307 | 37,161 | 37,119 | 37,740 | 34,696 | 35,565 | 37,407 | 14.6 | 15.6 |
| Connecticut | 43,985 | 43,085 | 42,382 | 44,508 | 43,891 | 46,721 | 49,675 | 47,732 | 54,778 | 49,131 | 46,429 | -7.9 | -5.3 |
| Delaware | 43,033 | 40,211 | 36,784 | 38,850 | 40,057 | 40,815 | 38,399 | 37,827 | 41,507 | 41,387 | 41,317 | 13.8 | 4.2 |
| District of Columbia | 31,860 | 32,699 | 32,382 | 32,616 | 30,327 | 34,602 | 35,217 | 33,637 | 34,627 | 36,280 | 38,790 | -5.3 | -17.9 |
| Florida | 32,455 | 31,344 | 31,326 | 31,725 | 31,711 | 31,287 | 32,114 | 32,769 | 33,763 | 34,469 | 34,599 | -1.0 | -6.2 |
| Georgia | 36,663 | 33,242 | 35,911 | 34,079 | 35,169 | 32,943 | 32,067 | 33,845 | 35,649 | 36,043 | 37,743 | 8.3 | -2.9 |
| Hawaii | 40,934 | 42,730 | 45,129 | 45,762 | 47,386 | 48,176 | 43,891 | 47,795 | 45,348 | 44,804 | 49,481 | -14.4 | -17.3 |
| Idaho | 33,404 | 35,505 | 34,413 | 34,153 | 34,444 | 31,693 | 30,775 | 31,075 | 31,911 | 31,815 | 29,324 | 7.5 | 13.9 |
| Illinois | 41,283 | 40,462 | 40,094 | 37,993 | 36,495 | 36,094 | 37,573 | 39,962 | 40,513 | 40,056 | 38,266 | 3.3 | 7.9 |
| Indiana | 38,889 | 35,953 | 35,159 | 30,170 | 32,739 | 32,638 | 31,922 | 33,068 | 33,521 | 35,672 | 31,816 | 17.6 | 22.2 |
| Iowa | 33,783 | 33,971 | 37,407 | 35,824 | 31,837 | 32,881 | 33,647 | 33,510 | 33,996 | 32,975 | 31,351 | 0.8 | 7.8 |
| Kansas | 36,471 | 33,333 | 31,954 | 30,673 | 33,066 | 34,715 | 34,522 | 36,738 | 34,769 | 34,686 | 36,145 | -0.7 | 0.9 |
| Kentucky | 33,452 | 33,157 | 31,394 | 28,802 | 27,075 | 26,866 | 28,004 | 30,430 | 30,136 | 27,008 | 29,208 | 9.9 | 14.5 |
| Louisiana | 33,260 | 30,956 | 29,434 | 27,807 | 29,225 | 29,102 | 29,813 | 27,513 | 29,590 | 27,809 | 30,163 | 20.9 | 10.3 |
| Maine | 32,772 | 35,492 | 35,658 | 32,832 | 30,476 | 33,881 | 32,840 | 33,726 | 36,528 | 35,820 | 33,343 | -2.8 | -1.7 |
| Maryland | 46,685 | 45,002 | 43,222 | 42,451 | 44,361 | 42,559 | 43,545 | 47,717 | 46,617 | 49,591 | 49,407 | -2.2 | -5.5 |
| Massachusetts | 42,023 | 40,400 | 40,624 | 43,861 | 41,168 | 41,594 | 42,086 | 44,511 | 46,708 | 45,061 | 45,552 | -5.6 | -7.7 |
| Michigan | 38,742 | 40,125 | 38,362 | 38,212 | 36,279 | 36,913 | 37,847 | 36,763 | 39,834 | 39,985 | 39,139 | 5.4 | -1.0 |
| Minnesota | 42,564 | 41,932 | 39,949 | 36,436 | 37,412 | 35,442 | 34,738 | 38,639 | 39,070 | 39,463 | 39,676 | 10.2 | 7.3 |
| Mississippi | 28,499 | 27,289 | 27,948 | 27,508 | 24,648 | 23,532 | 22,950 | 24,779 | 25,780 | 24,646 | 26,156 | 15.0 | 9.0 |

*(continued)*

*(continued from previous page)*

| | | | | | | | | | | | | percent change | |
|---|---|---|---|---|---|---|---|---|---|---|---|---|---|
| | **1997** | **1996** | **1995** | **1994** | **1993** | **1992** | **1991** | **1990** | **1989** | **1988** | **1987** | **1990–97** | **1987–97** |
| Missouri | 36,553 | 35,051 | 36,676 | 32,696 | 31,858 | 31,300 | 32,908 | 33,564 | 34,297 | 31,806 | 33,513 | 8.9% | 9.1% |
| Montana | 29,212 | 29,342 | 29,232 | 29,924 | 29,401 | 30,344 | 29,256 | 28,705 | 30,666 | 30,161 | 28,927 | 1.8 | 1.0 |
| Nebraska | 34,692 | 34,794 | 34,679 | 34,433 | 34,441 | 34,374 | 34,821 | 33,748 | 34,066 | 34,134 | 32,874 | 2.8 | 5.5 |
| Nevada | 38,854 | 39,424 | 38,002 | 38,848 | 39,780 | 36,502 | 38,813 | 39,324 | 37,976 | 37,965 | 37,975 | -1.2 | 2.3 |
| New Hampshire | 40,998 | 40,311 | 41,253 | 38,170 | 42,168 | 45,114 | 42,461 | 50,109 | 48,580 | 46,976 | 45,689 | -18.2 | -10.3 |
| New Jersey | 48,021 | 48,557 | 46,259 | 45,789 | 44,984 | 44,615 | 47,194 | 47,565 | 50,635 | 49,231 | 48,377 | 1.0 | -0.7 |
| New Mexico | 30,086 | 25,662 | 27,372 | 29,138 | 29,721 | 29,583 | 31,275 | 30,748 | 29,255 | 26,179 | 29,328 | -2.2 | 2.6 |
| New York | 35,798 | 36,222 | 34,783 | 34,546 | 35,207 | 35,522 | 37,466 | 38,794 | 40,767 | 39,230 | 37,277 | -7.7 | -4.0 |
| North Carolina | 35,840 | 36,418 | 33,679 | 32,613 | 32,011 | 31,769 | 31,644 | 32,332 | 34,179 | 33,124 | 32,157 | 10.8 | 11.5 |
| North Dakota | 31,661 | 32,192 | 30,635 | 30,625 | 31,231 | 30,840 | 30,511 | 31,024 | 32,655 | 32,686 | 31,897 | 2.1 | -0.7 |
| Ohio | 36,134 | 34,852 | 36,798 | 34,499 | 34,749 | 35,925 | 35,105 | 36,856 | 37,563 | 37,635 | 36,413 | -2.0 | -0.8 |
| Oklahoma | 31,351 | 28,067 | 27,709 | 29,231 | 29,168 | 28,924 | 30,005 | 29,944 | 30,633 | 32,109 | 30,646 | 4.7 | 2.3 |
| Oregon | 37,247 | 36,306 | 38,307 | 34,067 | 36,807 | 36,524 | 35,576 | 35,957 | 36,927 | 37,646 | 35,375 | 3.6 | 5.3 |
| Pennsylvania | 37,517 | 35,700 | 36,359 | 34,727 | 34,427 | 34,184 | 35,785 | 35,618 | 37,135 | 36,281 | 35,920 | 5.3 | 4.4 |
| Rhode Island | 34,797 | 37,835 | 37,238 | 34,578 | 37,219 | 34,814 | 36,338 | 39,257 | 38,991 | 40,487 | 39,972 | -11.4 | -12.9 |
| South Carolina | 34,262 | 35,460 | 30,616 | 32,323 | 28,938 | 31,549 | 32,363 | 35,287 | 30,803 | 34,641 | 35,391 | -2.9 | -3.2 |
| South Dakota | 29,694 | 30,203 | 31,150 | 32,201 | 30,808 | 30,040 | 29,035 | 30,173 | 31,204 | 30,247 | 29,883 | -1.6 | -0.6 |
| Tennessee | 30,636 | 31,496 | 30,557 | 31,016 | 27,881 | 27,819 | 28,816 | 27,743 | 29,267 | 28,296 | 29,923 | 10.4 | 2.4 |
| Texas | 35,075 | 33,831 | 33,742 | 33,308 | 31,908 | 31,978 | 32,681 | 34,664 | 33,506 | 33,868 | 34,927 | 1.2 | 0.4 |
| Utah | 42,775 | 37,888 | 38,419 | 38,680 | 39,748 | 39,182 | 33,014 | 37,014 | 39,759 | 35,699 | 37,482 | 15.6 | 14.1 |
| Vermont | 35,053 | 33,100 | 35,622 | 38,773 | 34,505 | 37,471 | 34,357 | 38,188 | 40,507 | 39,329 | 35,908 | -8.2 | -2.4 |
| Virginia | 42,957 | 40,111 | 38,147 | 40,772 | 40,467 | 43,698 | 42,584 | 43,070 | 44,161 | 44,294 | 42,380 | -0.3 | 1.4 |
| Washington | 44,562 | 37,518 | 37,458 | 36,316 | 39,603 | 38,781 | 40,031 | 39,434 | 41,369 | 43,859 | 38,598 | 13.0 | 15.5 |
| West Virginia | 27,488 | 25,826 | 26,202 | 25,520 | 24,904 | 23,190 | 27,277 | 27,184 | 28,058 | 26,257 | 24,311 | 1.1 | 13.1 |
| Wisconsin | 39,595 | 40,919 | 43,132 | 38,325 | 35,283 | 38,104 | 36,688 | 37,713 | 37,696 | 40,125 | 37,255 | 5.0 | 6.3 |
| Wyoming | 33,423 | 31,663 | 33,205 | 35,890 | 32,702 | 34,558 | 34,233 | 36,177 | 38,211 | 35,843 | 38,981 | -7.6 | -14.3 |

*Source: Bureau of the Census, Internet web site, <http://www.census.gov/hhes/income/histinc/index.html>; calculations by New Strategist*

# Household Income, 1997

# Married Couples Have the Highest Incomes

## One in seven married couples has an income of $100,000 or more.

The majority of the nation's married couples have household incomes of $50,000 or more. Married couples are by far the most affluent household type. Behind the higher incomes of married couples is the fact that most are dual earners. Male-headed families rank second in income among household types, with a median of $36,634. Female-headed families have a much lower median of $23,040. Women who live alone have the lowest incomes, with a median of just $15,530 in 1997.

The median income of black households is only 64 percent as high as that of white households, $25,050 versus $38,972 in 1997. Differences in the composition of black and white households explain most of this gap. The majority of white households are headed by married couples. In contrast, only 31 percent of black households are headed by couples, while an equal share are female-headed families—one of the poorest household types. The overall household median income of blacks is lowered by the incomes of female-headed families.

Hispanic married couples have much lower incomes than both white and black couples, with a median of $34,317 in 1997. Hispanic couples have relatively low incomes because they are less likely to be dual-earner couples than whites and blacks and because many Hispanics are recent immigrants.

✘ The incomes of women who live alone will rise in the future as working baby-boom women, with pensions of their own, head a growing share of single-person households.

## Women who live alone have the lowest incomes

*(median income of households by household type, 1997)*

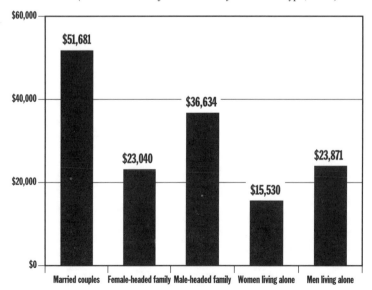

# Distribution of Households by Income and Household Type, 1997: Total Households

*(number and percent distribution of households by household income and household type, 1997; households in thousands as of 1998)*

| | | family households | | | nonfamily households | | | |
| | | | | | female householder | | male householder | |
| | total | married couples | female hh, no spouse present | male hh, no spouse present | total | living alone | total | living alone |
|---|---|---|---|---|---|---|---|---|
| **Total households** | **102,528** | **54,317** | **12,652** | **3,911** | **17,516** | **15,317** | **14,133** | **11,010** |
| Under $5,000 | 3,531 | 593 | 985 | 120 | 1,111 | 1,055 | 723 | 672 |
| $5,000–$9,999 | 7,765 | 878 | 1,619 | 152 | 3,671 | 3,598 | 1,444 | 1,367 |
| $10,000–$14,999 | 8,326 | 2,085 | 1,564 | 262 | 2,907 | 2,805 | 1,508 | 1,366 |
| $15,000–$19,999 | 7,837 | 2,783 | 1,375 | 307 | 1,972 | 1,802 | 1,400 | 1,218 |
| $20,000–$24,999 | 7,406 | 3,102 | 1,202 | 299 | 1,488 | 1,342 | 1,315 | 1,091 |
| $25,000–$29,999 | 6,913 | 3,156 | 1,094 | 405 | 1,192 | 1,023 | 1,065 | 861 |
| $30,000–$34,999 | 6,673 | 3,316 | 880 | 306 | 1,044 | 894 | 1,128 | 911 |
| $35,000–$39,999 | 6,111 | 3,377 | 715 | 272 | 798 | 637 | 949 | 718 |
| $40,000–$44,999 | 5,667 | 3,458 | 605 | 238 | 612 | 458 | 753 | 515 |
| $45,000–$49,999 | 4,920 | 3,145 | 490 | 200 | 485 | 337 | 600 | 394 |
| $50,000–$54,999 | 4,864 | 3,295 | 393 | 210 | 413 | 307 | 552 | 335 |
| $55,000–$59,999 | 3,864 | 2,698 | 292 | 193 | 306 | 203 | 376 | 244 |
| $60,000–$64,999 | 3,751 | 2,710 | 310 | 142 | 215 | 134 | 373 | 221 |
| $65,000–$69,999 | 3,298 | 2,380 | 238 | 149 | 226 | 156 | 305 | 182 |
| $70,000–$74,999 | 2,754 | 2,122 | 138 | 110 | 146 | 85 | 238 | 154 |
| $75,000–$79,999 | 2,399 | 1,816 | 141 | 88 | 141 | 60 | 213 | 143 |
| $80,000–$84,999 | 2,251 | 1,753 | 79 | 110 | 120 | 40 | 189 | 115 |
| $85,000–$89,999 | 1,702 | 1,394 | 88 | 42 | 68 | 36 | 110 | 46 |
| $90,000–$94,999 | 1,509 | 1,236 | 68 | 40 | 85 | 47 | 82 | 36 |
| $95,000–$99,999 | 1,325 | 1,042 | 56 | 49 | 90 | 55 | 89 | 41 |
| $100,000 or more | 9,661 | 7,976 | 321 | 220 | 424 | 241 | 720 | 380 |
| Median income | $37,005 | $51,681 | $23,040 | $36,634 | $17,613 | $15,530 | $27,592 | $23,871 |
| **Percent distribution** | | | | | | | | |
| **Total households** | **100.0%** | **100.0%** | **100.0%** | **100.0%** | **100.0%** | **100.0%** | **100.0%** | **100.0%** |
| Under $25,000 | 34.0 | 17.4 | 53.3 | 29.1 | 63.7 | 69.2 | 45.2 | 51.9 |
| $25,000–$49,999 | 29.5 | 30.3 | 29.9 | 36.3 | 23.6 | 21.9 | 31.8 | 30.9 |
| $50,000–$74,999 | 18.1 | 24.3 | 10.8 | 20.6 | 7.5 | 5.8 | 13.0 | 10.3 |
| $75,000–$99,999 | 9.0 | 13.3 | 3.4 | 8.4 | 2.9 | 1.6 | 4.8 | 3.5 |
| $100,000 or more | 9.4 | 14.7 | 2.5 | 5.6 | 2.4 | 1.6 | 5.1 | 3.5 |

*Source: Bureau of the Census, Internet web site, <http://www.census.gov/cps/ads/sdata.htm>; calculations by New Strategist*

## Distribution of Households by Income and Household Type, 1997: Black Households

*(number and percent distribution of black households by household income and household type, 1997; households in thousands as of 1998)*

| | | family households | | | nonfamily households | | | |
| | | | | | female householder | | male householder | |
| | total | married couples | female hh, no spouse present | male hh, no spouse present | total | living alone | total | living alone |
|---|---|---|---|---|---|---|---|---|
| **Total households** | **12,474** | **3,921** | **3,926** | **562** | **2,190** | **1,982** | **1,876** | **1,594** |
| Under $5,000 | 925 | 64 | 431 | 35 | 222 | 219 | 171 | 161 |
| $5,000 to $9,999 | 1,747 | 122 | 653 | 25 | 590 | 574 | 357 | 339 |
| $10,000 to $14,999 | 1,316 | 176 | 581 | 56 | 264 | 250 | 240 | 222 |
| $15,000 to $19,999 | 1,175 | 247 | 450 | 49 | 239 | 212 | 190 | 166 |
| $20,000 to $24,999 | 1,062 | 243 | 382 | 45 | 189 | 173 | 203 | 182 |
| $25,000 to $29,999 | 934 | 254 | 308 | 92 | 140 | 123 | 139 | 116 |
| $30,000 to $34,999 | 832 | 265 | 258 | 43 | 148 | 121 | 119 | 102 |
| $35,000 to $39,999 | 689 | 248 | 174 | 47 | 114 | 92 | 106 | 81 |
| $40,000 to $44,999 | 642 | 317 | 150 | 27 | 66 | 56 | 83 | 65 |
| $45,000 to $49,999 | 528 | 279 | 116 | 19 | 59 | 45 | 55 | 38 |
| $50,000 to $54,999 | 444 | 242 | 90 | 19 | 41 | 37 | 53 | 37 |
| $55,000 to $59,999 | 398 | 237 | 60 | 25 | 49 | 31 | 26 | 13 |
| $60,000 to $64,999 | 294 | 208 | 57 | 8 | 7 | 3 | 15 | 11 |
| $65,000 to $69,999 | 304 | 182 | 58 | 14 | 27 | 21 | 23 | 15 |
| $70,000 to $74,999 | 197 | 143 | 29 | 11 | 5 | 1 | 9 | 6 |
| $75,000 to $79,999 | 140 | 89 | 21 | 5 | 0 | 0 | 24 | 17 |
| $80,000 to $84,999 | 162 | 118 | 18 | 6 | 7 | 3 | 12 | 6 |
| $85,000 to $89,999 | 111 | 66 | 23 | 8 | 8 | 8 | 7 | 3 |
| $90,000 to $94,999 | 78 | 56 | 13 | 4 | 1 | 1 | 3 | 3 |
| $95,000 to $99,999 | 79 | 54 | 16 | 6 | 0 | 0 | 3 | 0 |
| $100,000 or more | 415 | 312 | 38 | 16 | 12 | 8 | 36 | 11 |
| Median income | $25,050 | $45,372 | $17,962 | $28,593 | $15,341 | $13,738 | $19,459 | $17,139 |

| **Percent distribution** | | | | | | | | |
|---|---|---|---|---|---|---|---|---|
| **Total households** | **100.0%** | **100.0%** | **100.0%** | **100.0%** | **100.0%** | **100.0%** | **100.0%** | **100.0%** |
| Under $25,000 | 49.9 | 21.7 | 63.6 | 37.4 | 68.7 | 72.0 | 61.9 | 67.1 |
| $25,000 to $49,999 | 29.1 | 34.8 | 25.6 | 40.6 | 24.1 | 22.0 | 26.8 | 25.2 |
| $50,000 to $74,999 | 13.1 | 25.8 | 7.5 | 13.7 | 5.9 | 4.7 | 6.7 | 5.1 |
| $75,000 to $99,999 | 4.6 | 9.8 | 2.3 | 5.2 | 0.7 | 0.6 | 2.6 | 1.8 |
| $100,000 or more | 3.3 | 8.0 | 1.0 | 2.8 | 0.5 | 0.4 | 1.9 | 0.7 |

*Source: Bureau of the Census, Internet web site, <http://www.census.gov/cps/ads/sdata.htm>; calculations by New Strategist*

# Distribution of Households by Income and Household Type, 1997: Hispanic Households

*(number and percent distribution of Hispanic households by household income and household type, 1997; households in thousands as of 1998)*

| | | family households | | | nonfamily households | | | |
| | | | | | female householder | | male householder | |
| | total | married couples | female hh, no spouse present | male hh, no spouse present | total | living alone | total | living alone |
|---|---|---|---|---|---|---|---|---|
| **Total households** | **8,590** | **4,804** | **1,612** | **545** | **754** | **617** | **875** | **623** |
| Under $5,000 | 473 | 121 | 167 | 18 | 87 | 82 | 80 | 64 |
| $5,000 to $9,999 | 968 | 202 | 331 | 45 | 242 | 238 | 148 | 137 |
| $10,000 to $14,999 | 916 | 430 | 240 | 54 | 99 | 90 | 93 | 80 |
| $15,000 to $19,999 | 840 | 417 | 210 | 58 | 65 | 51 | 89 | 74 |
| $20,000 to $24,999 | 851 | 498 | 142 | 62 | 49 | 34 | 100 | 71 |
| $25,000 to $29,999 | 672 | 403 | 107 | 51 | 51 | 34 | 61 | 40 |
| $30,000 to $34,999 | 618 | 372 | 96 | 46 | 40 | 23 | 64 | 39 |
| $35,000 to $39,999 | 534 | 356 | 69 | 35 | 22 | 20 | 52 | 31 |
| $40,000 to $44,999 | 490 | 333 | 60 | 40 | 26 | 13 | 31 | 18 |
| $45,000 to $49,999 | 404 | 268 | 48 | 33 | 23 | 10 | 32 | 17 |
| $50,000 to $54,999 | 310 | 225 | 30 | 27 | 10 | 3 | 19 | 12 |
| $55,000 to $59,999 | 226 | 168 | 17 | 15 | 9 | 5 | 18 | 8 |
| $60,000 to $64,999 | 216 | 166 | 21 | 6 | 2 | 1 | 20 | 9 |
| $65,000 to $69,999 | 152 | 109 | 18 | 10 | 2 | 2 | 13 | 2 |
| $70,000 to $74,999 | 142 | 98 | 17 | 7 | 4 | 2 | 16 | 8 |
| $75,000 to $79,999 | 130 | 95 | 10 | 10 | 9 | 1 | 6 | 1 |
| $80,000 to $84,999 | 106 | 83 | 4 | 7 | 4 | 2 | 8 | 6 |
| $85,000 to $89,999 | 70 | 58 | 4 | 3 | 1 | 0 | 3 | 1 |
| $90,000 to $94,999 | 70 | 63 | 0 | 3 | 0 | 0 | 4 | 0 |
| $95,000 to $99,999 | 53 | 48 | 3 | 0 | 0 | 0 | 2 | 0 |
| $100,000 or more | 351 | 292 | 19 | 13 | 10 | 6 | 17 | 5 |
| Median income | $26,628 | $34,317 | $16,393 | $28,249 | $11,485 | $9,666 | $21,059 | $16,524 |
| **Percent distribution** | | | | | | | | |
| **Total households** | **100.0%** | **100.0%** | **100.0%** | **100.0%** | **100.0%** | **100.0%** | **100.0%** | **100.0%** |
| Under $25,000 | 47.1 | 34.7 | 67.6 | 43.5 | 71.9 | 80.2 | 58.3 | 68.4 |
| $25,000 to $49,999 | 31.6 | 36.1 | 23.6 | 37.6 | 21.5 | 16.2 | 27.4 | 23.3 |
| $50,000 to $74,999 | 12.2 | 15.9 | 6.4 | 11.9 | 3.6 | 2.1 | 9.8 | 6.3 |
| $75,000 to $99,999 | 5.0 | 7.2 | 1.3 | 4.2 | 1.9 | 0.5 | 2.6 | 1.3 |
| $100,000 or more | 4.1 | 6.1 | 1.2 | 2.4 | 1.3 | 1.0 | 1.9 | 0.8 |

*Source: Bureau of the Census, Internet web site, <http://www.census.gov/cps/ads/sdata.htm>; calculations by New Strategist*

## Distribution of Households by Income and Household Type, 1997: White Households

*(number and percent distribution of white households by household income and household type, 1997; households in thousands as of 1998)*

| | | family households | | | nonfamily households | | | |
| | | | | | female householder | | male householder | |
| | total | married couples | female hh, no spouse present | male hh, no spouse present | total | living alone | total | living alone |
|---|---|---|---|---|---|---|---|---|
| **Total households** | **86,106** | **48,066** | **8,308** | **3,137** | **14,871** | **12,980** | **11,725** | **9,018** |
| Under $5,000 | 2,415 | 481 | 519 | 79 | 842 | 800 | 494 | 455 |
| $5,000 to $9,999 | 5,773 | 708 | 922 | 116 | 2,991 | 2,937 | 1,036 | 985 |
| $10,000 to $14,999 | 6,716 | 1,797 | 934 | 192 | 2,573 | 2,497 | 1,221 | 1,112 |
| $15,000 to $19,999 | 6,436 | 2,443 | 881 | 239 | 1,698 | 1,554 | 1,174 | 1,017 |
| $20,000 to $24,999 | 6,114 | 2,743 | 790 | 243 | 1,278 | 1,152 | 1,058 | 865 |
| $25,000 to $29,999 | 5,738 | 2,784 | 753 | 296 | 1,028 | 884 | 877 | 702 |
| $30,000 to $34,999 | 5,612 | 2,920 | 591 | 250 | 875 | 760 | 974 | 787 |
| $35,000 to $39,999 | 5,166 | 2,975 | 519 | 208 | 657 | 530 | 807 | 612 |
| $40,000 to $44,999 | 4,803 | 2,997 | 440 | 200 | 515 | 381 | 650 | 433 |
| $45,000 to $49,999 | 4,201 | 2,733 | 367 | 166 | 417 | 283 | 518 | 337 |
| $50,000 to $54,999 | 4,278 | 2,950 | 299 | 185 | 360 | 261 | 485 | 292 |
| $55,000 to $59,999 | 3,312 | 2,349 | 218 | 157 | 249 | 164 | 339 | 221 |
| $60,000 to $64,999 | 3,277 | 2,382 | 238 | 122 | 191 | 123 | 345 | 199 |
| $65,000 to $69,999 | 2,861 | 2,107 | 170 | 121 | 193 | 130 | 271 | 163 |
| $70,000 to $74,999 | 2,462 | 1,906 | 96 | 97 | 141 | 84 | 222 | 146 |
| $75,000 to $79,999 | 2,150 | 1,642 | 111 | 79 | 137 | 56 | 181 | 120 |
| $80,000 to $84,999 | 1,998 | 1,574 | 52 | 94 | 111 | 36 | 168 | 105 |
| $85,000 to $89,999 | 1,509 | 1,260 | 63 | 34 | 52 | 25 | 100 | 43 |
| $90,000 to $94,999 | 1,363 | 1,130 | 47 | 33 | 84 | 46 | 69 | 27 |
| $95,000 to $99,999 | 1,163 | 921 | 39 | 35 | 83 | 49 | 85 | 41 |
| $100,000 or more | 8,762 | 7,262 | 260 | 191 | 397 | 226 | 651 | 354 |
| Median income | $38,972 | $52,199 | $25,670 | $38,511 | $17,997 | $15,818 | $30,009 | $25,415 |

| **Percent distribution** | | | | | | | | |
|---|---|---|---|---|---|---|---|---|
| **Total households** | **100.0%** | **100.0%** | **100.0%** | **100.0%** | **100.0%** | **100.0%** | **100.0%** | **100.0%** |
| Under $25,000 | 31.9 | 17.0 | 48.7 | 27.7 | 63.1 | 68.9 | 42.5 | 49.2 |
| $25,000 to $49,999 | 29.6 | 30.0 | 32.1 | 35.7 | 23.5 | 21.9 | 32.6 | 31.8 |
| $50,000 to $74,999 | 18.8 | 24.3 | 12.3 | 21.7 | 7.6 | 5.9 | 14.2 | 11.3 |
| $75,000 to $99,999 | 9.5 | 13.6 | 3.8 | 8.8 | 3.1 | 1.6 | 5.1 | 3.7 |
| $100,000 or more | 10.2 | 15.1 | 3.1 | 6.1 | 2.7 | 1.7 | 5.6 | 3.9 |

*Source: Bureau of the Census, Internet web site, <http://www.census.gov/cps/ads/sdata.htm>; calculations by New Strategist*

# Household Income Peaks in the 45-to-54 Age Group

## The median income of householders aged 45 to 54 surpasses $50,000.

The median income of all households stood at $37,005 in 1997. Household income peaks in the 45-to-54 age group at a much higher $51,875. Household incomes are highest in middle age because people in their forties and fifties are usually at the height of their careers. Fully 16 percent of householders aged 45 to 54—or one in six—have incomes of $100,000 or more. Income rises with age as people develop job skills, then falls after retirement. Householders under age 25 had a median income of $22,583 in 1997, while those aged 75 or older had a median income of $17,079.

Among whites, median household income peaks at $54,879. Black household income peaks at a much lower $33,761, while Hispanic household income tops out at just $32,074. The median household income of blacks, at its peak, is just 62 percent as high as that of whites, while the Hispanic peak is just 58 percent of the white peak. Behind the gap in incomes are the differing lifestyles and characteristics of whites, blacks, and Hispanics. Black households are much less likely to be headed by married couples than white households, and married couples are by far the most affluent household type. Hispanic couples are less likely to be dual earners, and many are recent immigrants with little education and few job skills.

✘ The affluence of householders aged 55 to 64 is likely to grow in the years ahead as well-educated two-income baby-boom couples enter the age group and fewer men in their fifties opt for early retirement .

## Incomes are lowest for older householders

*(median income of households by age of householder, 1997)*

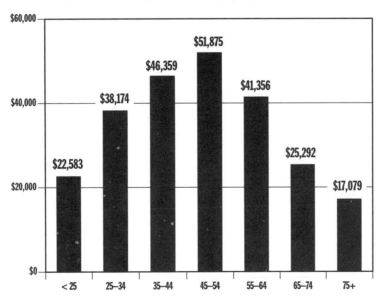

## Distribution of Households by Income and Age of Householder, 1997: Total Households

*(number and percent distribution of households by household income and age of householder, 1997; households in thousands as of 1998)*

| | total | 15–24 | 25–34 | 35–44 | 45–54 | 55–64 | 65 or older total | 65–74 | 75 or older |
|---|---|---|---|---|---|---|---|---|---|
| **Total households** | **102,528** | **5,435** | **19,033** | **23,943** | **19,547** | **13,072** | **21,497** | **11,272** | **10,226** |
| Under $5,000 | 3,531 | 445 | 720 | 680 | 538 | 484 | 667 | 306 | 361 |
| $5,000–$9,999 | 7,765 | 697 | 915 | 1,008 | 780 | 955 | 3,409 | 1,420 | 1,990 |
| $10,000–$14,999 | 8,326 | 595 | 1,302 | 1,181 | 876 | 871 | 3,501 | 1,381 | 2,119 |
| $15,000–$19,999 | 7,837 | 637 | 1,266 | 1,278 | 955 | 873 | 2,829 | 1,370 | 1,460 |
| $20,000–$24,999 | 7,406 | 586 | 1,418 | 1,425 | 993 | 837 | 2,150 | 1,102 | 1,049 |
| $25,000–$29,999 | 6,913 | 505 | 1,398 | 1,540 | 997 | 756 | 1,717 | 961 | 756 |
| $30,000–$34,999 | 6,673 | 447 | 1,549 | 1,460 | 1,100 | 783 | 1,335 | 835 | 500 |
| $35,000–$39,999 | 6,111 | 314 | 1,367 | 1,560 | 1,082 | 722 | 1,065 | 671 | 394 |
| $40,000–$44,999 | 5,667 | 303 | 1,301 | 1,429 | 1,070 | 770 | 795 | 500 | 294 |
| $45,000–$49,999 | 4,920 | 193 | 1,153 | 1,330 | 932 | 678 | 635 | 416 | 218 |
| $50,000–$54,999 | 4,864 | 175 | 1,114 | 1,330 | 1,045 | 703 | 498 | 327 | 169 |
| $55,000–$59,999 | 3,864 | 136 | 818 | 1,192 | 827 | 471 | 421 | 278 | 141 |
| $60,000–$64,999 | 3,751 | 60 | 826 | 1,212 | 938 | 407 | 309 | 186 | 123 |
| $65,000–$69,999 | 3,298 | 54 | 756 | 929 | 876 | 387 | 295 | 218 | 77 |
| $70,000–$74,999 | 2,754 | 37 | 548 | 917 | 720 | 331 | 201 | 134 | 67 |
| $75,000–$79,999 | 2,399 | 49 | 436 | 776 | 631 | 309 | 197 | 149 | 49 |
| $80,000–$84,999 | 2,251 | 48 | 439 | 665 | 583 | 296 | 220 | 148 | 72 |
| $85,000–$89,999 | 1,702 | 15 | 253 | 518 | 499 | 265 | 152 | 109 | 43 |
| $90,000–$94,999 | 1,509 | 4 | 217 | 466 | 492 | 243 | 86 | 45 | 41 |
| $95,000–$99,999 | 1,325 | 13 | 186 | 421 | 419 | 183 | 102 | 65 | 39 |
| $100,000 or more | 9,661 | 125 | 1,054 | 2,629 | 3,193 | 1,747 | 913 | 650 | 263 |
| Median income | $37,005 | $22,583 | $38,174 | $46,359 | $51,875 | $41,356 | $20,761 | $25,292 | $17,079 |

| **Percent distribution** | | | | | | | | | |
|---|---|---|---|---|---|---|---|---|---|
| **Total households** | **100.0%** | **100.0%** | **100.0%** | **100.0%** | **100.0%** | **100.0%** | **100.0%** | **100.0%** | **100.0%** |
| Under $25,000 | 34.0 | 54.5 | 29.5 | 23.3 | 21.2 | 30.8 | 58.4 | 49.5 | 68.2 |
| $25,000–$49,999 | 29.5 | 32.4 | 35.6 | 30.6 | 26.5 | 28.4 | 25.8 | 30.0 | 21.1 |
| $50,000–$74,999 | 18.1 | 8.5 | 21.3 | 23.3 | 22.5 | 17.6 | 8.0 | 10.1 | 5.6 |
| $75,000–$99,999 | 9.0 | 2.4 | 8.0 | 11.9 | 13.4 | 9.9 | 3.5 | 4.6 | 2.4 |
| $100,000 or more | 9.4 | 2.3 | 5.5 | 11.0 | 16.3 | 13.4 | 4.2 | 5.8 | 2.6 |

*Source: Bureau of the Census, Internet web site, <http://www.census.gov/cps/ads/sdata.htm>; calculations by New Strategist*

# Distribution of Households by Income and Age of Householder, 1997: Black Households

*(number and percent distribution of black households by household income and age of householder, 1997; households in thousands as of 1998)*

| | total | 15–24 | 25–34 | 35–44 | 45–54 | 55–64 | 65 or older | | |
| | | | | | | | total | 65–74 | 75 or older |
|---|---|---|---|---|---|---|---|---|---|
| **Total households** | **12,474** | **935** | **2,752** | **3,096** | **2,371** | **1,441** | **1,878** | **1,123** | **755** |
| Under $5,000 | 925 | 158 | 242 | 202 | 144 | 84 | 96 | 57 | 39 |
| $5,000–$9,999 | 1,747 | 199 | 276 | 309 | 173 | 228 | 561 | 289 | 274 |
| $10,000–$14,999 | 1,316 | 108 | 304 | 265 | 145 | 167 | 325 | 181 | 145 |
| $15,000–$19,999 | 1,175 | 90 | 245 | 302 | 215 | 123 | 200 | 128 | 73 |
| $20,000–$24,999 | 1,062 | 89 | 256 | 278 | 189 | 92 | 160 | 106 | 54 |
| $25,000–$29,999 | 934 | 67 | 201 | 305 | 175 | 89 | 96 | 70 | 27 |
| $30,000–$34,999 | 832 | 49 | 222 | 192 | 164 | 106 | 98 | 65 | 32 |
| $35,000–$39,999 | 689 | 27 | 166 | 199 | 148 | 81 | 68 | 58 | 11 |
| $40,000–$44,999 | 642 | 20 | 189 | 153 | 118 | 88 | 74 | 48 | 26 |
| $45,000–$49,999 | 528 | 18 | 101 | 190 | 112 | 76 | 32 | 21 | 10 |
| $50,000–$54,999 | 444 | 24 | 136 | 93 | 109 | 52 | 30 | 14 | 16 |
| $55,000–$59,999 | 398 | 32 | 85 | 124 | 108 | 23 | 26 | 10 | 17 |
| $60,000–$64,999 | 294 | 2 | 80 | 70 | 94 | 32 | 16 | 3 | 13 |
| $65,000–$69,999 | 304 | 5 | 97 | 72 | 80 | 33 | 18 | 16 | 2 |
| $70,000–$74,999 | 197 | 7 | 26 | 77 | 57 | 25 | 6 | 3 | 3 |
| $75,000–$79,999 | 140 | 5 | 28 | 41 | 42 | 15 | 8 | 8 | 0 |
| $80,000–$84,999 | 162 | 7 | 33 | 52 | 45 | 20 | 4 | 4 | 0 |
| $85,000–$89,999 | 111 | 8 | 4 | 32 | 45 | 14 | 7 | 7 | 0 |
| $90,000–$94,999 | 78 | 0 | 2 | 20 | 41 | 7 | 7 | 4 | 3 |
| $95,000–$99,999 | 79 | 0 | 13 | 24 | 25 | 12 | 6 | 2 | 3 |
| $100,000 or more | 415 | 17 | 48 | 95 | 145 | 72 | 39 | 30 | 8 |
| Median income | $25,050 | $15,056 | $26,149 | $27,710 | $33,761 | $27,350 | $14,241 | $16,287 | $12,101 |
| **Percent distribution** | | | | | | | | | |
| **Total households** | **100.0%** | **100.0%** | **100.0%** | **100.0%** | **100.0%** | **100.0%** | **100.0%** | **100.0%** | **100.0%** |
| Under $25,000 | 49.9 | 68.9 | 48.1 | 43.8 | 36.5 | 48.2 | 71.5 | 67.8 | 77.5 |
| $25,000–$49,999 | 29.1 | 19.4 | 31.9 | 33.6 | 30.2 | 30.5 | 19.6 | 23.3 | 14.0 |
| $50,000–$74,999 | 13.1 | 7.5 | 15.4 | 14.1 | 18.9 | 11.5 | 5.1 | 4.1 | 6.8 |
| $75,000–$99,999 | 4.6 | 2.1 | 2.9 | 5.5 | 8.4 | 4.7 | 1.7 | 2.2 | 0.8 |
| $100,000 or more | 3.3 | 1.8 | 1.7 | 3.1 | 6.1 | 5.0 | 2.1 | 2.7 | 1.1 |

*Source: Bureau of the Census, Internet web site, <http://www.census.gov/cps/ads/sdata.htm>; calculations by New Strategist*

# Distribution of Households by Income and Age of Householder, 1997: Hispanic Households

*(number and percent distribution of Hispanic households by household income and age of householder, 1997; households in thousands as of 1998)*

| | total | 15–24 | 25–34 | 35–44 | 45–54 | 55–64 | 65 or older total | 65–74 | 75 or older |
|---|---|---|---|---|---|---|---|---|---|
| **Total households** | **8,590** | **780** | **2,303** | **2,316** | **1,386** | **889** | **916** | **566** | **350** |
| Under $5,000 | 473 | 57 | 125 | 106 | 57 | 59 | 68 | 32 | 36 |
| $5,000–$9,999 | 968 | 112 | 171 | 183 | 118 | 115 | 268 | 141 | 128 |
| $10,000–$14,999 | 916 | 114 | 242 | 211 | 123 | 81 | 144 | 98 | 47 |
| $15,000–$19,999 | 840 | 121 | 225 | 210 | 110 | 84 | 90 | 49 | 41 |
| $20,000–$24,999 | 851 | 101 | 249 | 219 | 123 | 79 | 81 | 57 | 25 |
| $25,000–$29,999 | 672 | 62 | 226 | 182 | 103 | 50 | 51 | 37 | 14 |
| $30,000–$34,999 | 618 | 60 | 181 | 167 | 109 | 58 | 45 | 28 | 16 |
| $35,000–$39,999 | 534 | 57 | 155 | 159 | 88 | 48 | 27 | 23 | 4 |
| $40,000–$44,999 | 490 | 31 | 154 | 135 | 95 | 45 | 29 | 18 | 11 |
| $45,000–$49,999 | 404 | 16 | 115 | 137 | 68 | 31 | 37 | 25 | 12 |
| $50,000–$54,999 | 310 | 21 | 86 | 96 | 52 | 47 | 8 | 6 | 1 |
| $55,000–$59,999 | 226 | 7 | 58 | 82 | 45 | 27 | 7 | 5 | 2 |
| $60,000–$64,999 | 216 | 2 | 71 | 64 | 44 | 27 | 7 | 6 | 1 |
| $65,000–$69,999 | 152 | 1 | 41 | 50 | 31 | 21 | 9 | 5 | 4 |
| $70,000–$74,999 | 142 | 5 | 34 | 54 | 32 | 8 | 9 | 5 | 4 |
| $75,000–$79,999 | 130 | 2 | 33 | 46 | 25 | 19 | 3 | 3 | 0 |
| $80,000–$84,999 | 106 | 2 | 38 | 34 | 16 | 10 | 4 | 4 | 0 |
| $85,000–$89,999 | 70 | 4 | 12 | 20 | 14 | 18 | 3 | 3 | 0 |
| $90,000–$94,999 | 70 | 0 | 19 | 17 | 19 | 10 | 5 | 5 | 0 |
| $95,000–$99,999 | 53 | 0 | 12 | 32 | 8 | 2 | 0 | 0 | 0 |
| $100,000 or more | 351 | 3 | 55 | 117 | 105 | 51 | 20 | 17 | 3 |
| Median income | $26,628 | $19,341 | $27,519 | $31,148 | $32,074 | $27,648 | $14,168 | $15,885 | $11,015 |

| **Percent distribution** | | | | | | | | | |
|---|---|---|---|---|---|---|---|---|---|
| **Total households** | **100.0%** | **100.0%** | **100.0%** | **100.0%** | **100.0%** | **100.0%** | **100.0%** | **100.0%** | **100.0%** |
| Under $25,000 | 47.1 | 64.7 | 43.9 | 40.1 | 38.3 | 47.0 | 71.1 | 66.6 | 79.1 |
| $25,000–$49,999 | 31.6 | 29.0 | 36.1 | 33.7 | 33.4 | 26.1 | 20.6 | 23.1 | 16.3 |
| $50,000–$74,999 | 12.2 | 4.6 | 12.6 | 14.9 | 14.7 | 14.6 | 4.4 | 4.8 | 3.4 |
| $75,000–$99,999 | 5.0 | 1.0 | 5.0 | 6.4 | 5.9 | 6.6 | 1.6 | 2.7 | 0.0 |
| $100,000 or more | 4.1 | 0.4 | 2.4 | 5.1 | 7.6 | 5.7 | 2.2 | 3.0 | 0.9 |

*Source: Bureau of the Census, Internet web site, <http://www.census.gov/cps/ads/sdata.htm>; calculations by New Strategist*

# Distribution of Households by Income and Age of Householder, 1997: White Households

*(number and percent distribution of white households by household income and age of householder, 1997; households in thousands as of 1998)*

| | total | 15–24 | 25–34 | 35–44 | 45–54 | 55–64 | 65 or older total | 65–74 | 75 or older |
|---|---|---|---|---|---|---|---|---|---|
| **Total households** | **86,106** | **4,242** | **15,344** | **19,761** | **16,400** | **11,163** | **19,196** | **9,917** | **9,279** |
| Under $5,000 | 2,415 | 257 | 424 | 436 | 375 | 380 | 541 | 233 | 308 |
| $5,000–$9,999 | 5,773 | 460 | 596 | 660 | 584 | 697 | 2,776 | 1,103 | 1,672 |
| $10,000–$14,999 | 6,716 | 452 | 929 | 841 | 683 | 680 | 3,132 | 1,179 | 1,952 |
| $15,000–$19,999 | 6,436 | 524 | 962 | 941 | 696 | 722 | 2,590 | 1,216 | 1,375 |
| $20,000–$24,999 | 6,114 | 473 | 1,104 | 1,092 | 760 | 723 | 1,961 | 983 | 978 |
| $25,000–$29,999 | 5,738 | 418 | 1,121 | 1,190 | 782 | 640 | 1,588 | 875 | 713 |
| $30,000–$34,999 | 5,612 | 379 | 1,273 | 1,209 | 886 | 651 | 1,215 | 757 | 458 |
| $35,000–$39,999 | 5,166 | 275 | 1,136 | 1,275 | 887 | 619 | 974 | 598 | 376 |
| $40,000–$44,999 | 4,803 | 264 | 1,076 | 1,215 | 890 | 649 | 710 | 448 | 262 |
| $45,000–$49,999 | 4,201 | 167 | 1,000 | 1,079 | 782 | 576 | 596 | 388 | 208 |
| $50,000–$54,999 | 4,278 | 142 | 943 | 1,214 | 894 | 634 | 452 | 299 | 152 |
| $55,000–$59,999 | 3,312 | 101 | 695 | 1,008 | 696 | 429 | 383 | 260 | 123 |
| $60,000–$64,999 | 3,277 | 52 | 703 | 1,058 | 822 | 355 | 287 | 177 | 110 |
| $65,000–$69,999 | 2,861 | 42 | 633 | 799 | 765 | 350 | 273 | 200 | 73 |
| $70,000–$74,999 | 2,462 | 30 | 490 | 807 | 653 | 292 | 188 | 130 | 59 |
| $75,000–$79,999 | 2,150 | 43 | 384 | 695 | 570 | 286 | 175 | 130 | 44 |
| $80,000–$84,999 | 1,998 | 39 | 383 | 599 | 513 | 261 | 203 | 142 | 61 |
| $85,000–$89,999 | 1,509 | 7 | 225 | 453 | 435 | 248 | 141 | 100 | 42 |
| $90,000–$94,999 | 1,363 | 4 | 202 | 413 | 443 | 230 | 71 | 35 | 37 |
| $95,000–$99,999 | 1,163 | 13 | 159 | 382 | 355 | 162 | 92 | 59 | 31 |
| $100,000 or more | 8,762 | 101 | 907 | 2,396 | 2,930 | 1,580 | 848 | 605 | 244 |
| Median income | $38,972 | $24,423 | $40,477 | $49,695 | $54,879 | $43,053 | $21,374 | $26,363 | $17,410 |

**Percent distribution**

| | total | 15–24 | 25–34 | 35–44 | 45–54 | 55–64 | 65 or older total | 65–74 | 75 or older |
|---|---|---|---|---|---|---|---|---|---|
| **Total households** | 100.0% | 100.0% | 100.0% | 100.0% | 100.0% | 100.0% | 100.0% | 100.0% | 100.0% |
| Under $25,000 | 31.9 | 51.1 | 26.2 | 20.1 | 18.9 | 28.7 | 57.3 | 47.5 | 67.7 |
| $25,000–$49,999 | 29.6 | 35.4 | 36.5 | 30.2 | 25.8 | 28.1 | 26.5 | 30.9 | 21.7 |
| $50,000–$74,999 | 18.8 | 8.7 | 22.6 | 24.7 | 23.4 | 18.5 | 8.2 | 10.7 | 5.6 |
| $75,000–$99,999 | 9.5 | 2.5 | 8.8 | 12.9 | 14.1 | 10.6 | 3.6 | 4.7 | 2.3 |
| $100,000 or more | 10.2 | 2.4 | 5.9 | 12.1 | 17.9 | 14.2 | 4.4 | 6.1 | 2.6 |

*Source: Bureau of the Census, Internet web site, <http://www.census.gov/cps/ads/sdata.htm>; calculations by New Strategist*

# The Most Affluent Householders Are Middle-Aged Married Couples

## Married couples aged 45 to 54 had a median income of $66,192 in 1997.

As is true for all households, the incomes of married couples peak in middle age. The majority of couples aged 35 to 64 had incomes of $50,000 or more in 1997, with those aged 45 to 54 having the highest incomes. Fully 23 percent of couples in the 45-to-54 age group had an income of $100,000 or more. A substantial 19 percent of couples aged 55 to 64 and 16 percent of those aged 35 to 44 had incomes that high.

The youngest and oldest married couples have the lowest incomes. Married couples aged 75 or older had a median income of $26,558 in 1997, slightly less than the $27,756 of couples under age 25. Incomes are relatively low for young couples because many people in the age group are still in school.

The incomes of married couples peak in the 45-to-54 age group for blacks, Hispanics, and whites. Black couples in the age group had a median income of $56,950, fully 85 percent as much as the $67,249 median of their white counterparts. Hispanic couples aged 45 to 54 had a median income of just $41,999, only 62 percent as high as that of whites. Not only are Hispanic couples less likely to be dual earners than white couples, but many Hispanics are recent immigrants with little earning power.

✘ The income gap between black and white couples will continue to narrow as younger, better-educated blacks replace older, less-educated generations. But the income gap between Hispanics and whites is not likely to disappear until immigrants become a much smaller share of the Hispanic population.

### Incomes of couples peak in the 45-to-54 age group

*(median income of married couples aged 45 to 54 by race and Hispanic origin, 1997)*

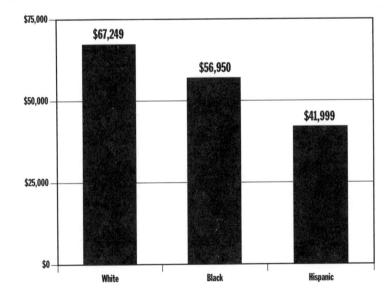

# Distribution of Married Couples by Household Income and Age of Householder, 1997: Total Married Couples

*(number and percent distribution of married couples by household income and age of householder, 1997; married couples in thousands as of 1998)*

| | total | 15–24 | 25–34 | 35–44 | 45–54 | 55–64 | 65 or older total | 65–74 | 75 or older |
|---|---|---|---|---|---|---|---|---|---|
| Total couples | 54,317 | 1,373 | 9,886 | 14,180 | 11,734 | 7,936 | 9,208 | 5,841 | 3,368 |
| Under $5,000 | 593 | 28 | 105 | 113 | 96 | 129 | 122 | 85 | 37 |
| $5,000–$9,999 | 878 | 57 | 133 | 159 | 118 | 162 | 248 | 150 | 98 |
| $10,000–$14,999 | 2,085 | 153 | 361 | 309 | 222 | 258 | 782 | 408 | 374 |
| $15,000–$19,999 | 2,783 | 159 | 447 | 416 | 279 | 352 | 1,130 | 582 | 548 |
| $20,000–$24,999 | 3,102 | 197 | 542 | 512 | 331 | 390 | 1,130 | 635 | 495 |
| $25,000–$29,999 | 3,156 | 163 | 596 | 585 | 415 | 425 | 974 | 580 | 394 |
| $30,000–$34,999 | 3,316 | 148 | 710 | 691 | 506 | 425 | 837 | 537 | 300 |
| $35,000–$39,999 | 3,377 | 119 | 727 | 811 | 576 | 442 | 704 | 487 | 217 |
| $40,000–$44,999 | 3,458 | 101 | 824 | 885 | 605 | 530 | 515 | 350 | 165 |
| $45,000–$49,999 | 3,145 | 69 | 739 | 854 | 617 | 469 | 399 | 280 | 119 |
| $50,000–$54,999 | 3,295 | 54 | 750 | 968 | 672 | 525 | 325 | 241 | 85 |
| $55,000–$59,999 | 2,698 | 43 | 557 | 897 | 569 | 354 | 278 | 205 | 73 |
| $60,000–$64,999 | 2,710 | 15 | 585 | 912 | 689 | 308 | 201 | 122 | 79 |
| $65,000–$69,999 | 2,380 | 16 | 531 | 717 | 623 | 296 | 197 | 147 | 52 |
| $70,000–$74,999 | 2,122 | 6 | 425 | 746 | 526 | 264 | 154 | 114 | 40 |
| $75,000–$79,999 | 1,816 | 16 | 305 | 621 | 492 | 253 | 130 | 102 | 28 |
| $80,000–$84,999 | 1,753 | 12 | 298 | 559 | 479 | 239 | 165 | 113 | 52 |
| $85,000–$89,999 | 1,394 | 1 | 176 | 447 | 420 | 236 | 116 | 93 | 23 |
| $90,000–$94,999 | 1,236 | 0 | 147 | 404 | 417 | 211 | 57 | 41 | 16 |
| $95,000–$99,999 | 1,042 | 5 | 139 | 343 | 344 | 149 | 61 | 45 | 17 |
| $100,000 or more | 7,976 | 11 | 792 | 2,233 | 2,738 | 1,519 | 682 | 526 | 156 |
| Median income | $51,681 | $27,756 | $48,331 | $59,237 | $66,192 | $53,527 | $31,239 | $34,450 | $26,558 |

**Percent distribution**

| | total | 15–24 | 25–34 | 35–44 | 45–54 | 55–64 | 65 or older total | 65–74 | 75 or older |
|---|---|---|---|---|---|---|---|---|---|
| Total couples | 100.0% | 100.0% | 100.0% | 100.0% | 100.0% | 100.0% | 100.0% | 100.0% | 100.0% |
| Under $25,000 | 17.4 | 43.3 | 16.1 | 10.6 | 8.9 | 16.3 | 37.1 | 31.8 | 46.1 |
| $25,000–$49,999 | 30.3 | 43.7 | 36.4 | 27.0 | 23.2 | 28.9 | 37.2 | 38.2 | 35.5 |
| $50,000–$74,999 | 24.3 | 9.8 | 28.8 | 29.9 | 26.2 | 22.0 | 12.5 | 14.2 | 9.8 |
| $75,000–$99,999 | 13.3 | 2.5 | 10.8 | 16.7 | 18.3 | 13.7 | 5.7 | 6.7 | 4.0 |
| $100,000 or more | 14.7 | 0.8 | 8.0 | 15.7 | 23.3 | 19.1 | 7.4 | 9.0 | 4.6 |

*Source: Bureau of the Census, Internet web site, <http://www.census.gov/cps/ads/sdata.htm>; calculations by New Strategist*

## Distribution of Married Couples by Household Income and Age of Householder, 1997: Black Married Couples

*(number and percent distribution of black married couples by household income and age of householder, 1997; married couples in thousands as of 1998)*

| | total | 15–24 | 25–34 | 35–44 | 45–54 | 55–64 | 65 or older total | 65–74 | 75 or older |
|---|---|---|---|---|---|---|---|---|---|
| **Total couples** | **3,921** | **111** | **858** | **1,066** | **884** | **485** | **518** | **369** | **149** |
| Under $5,000 | 64 | 5 | 9 | 18 | 10 | 11 | 10 | 8 | 2 |
| $5,000–$9,999 | 122 | 7 | 14 | 26 | 13 | 24 | 37 | 28 | 9 |
| $10,000–$14,999 | 176 | 2 | 26 | 33 | 11 | 22 | 83 | 44 | 39 |
| $15,000–$19,999 | 247 | 17 | 41 | 67 | 35 | 25 | 63 | 45 | 18 |
| $20,000–$24,999 | 243 | 16 | 69 | 60 | 35 | 19 | 43 | 41 | 2 |
| $25,000–$29,999 | 254 | 15 | 45 | 84 | 40 | 28 | 43 | 32 | 10 |
| $30,000–$34,999 | 265 | 10 | 72 | 55 | 41 | 42 | 45 | 27 | 18 |
| $35,000–$39,999 | 248 | 4 | 57 | 47 | 64 | 28 | 47 | 41 | 6 |
| $40,000–$44,999 | 317 | 10 | 89 | 71 | 65 | 49 | 34 | 20 | 13 |
| $45,000–$49,999 | 279 | 5 | 70 | 104 | 48 | 39 | 14 | 10 | 3 |
| $50,000–$54,999 | 242 | 0 | 92 | 70 | 52 | 26 | 2 | 2 | 0 |
| $55,000–$59,999 | 237 | 12 | 56 | 74 | 66 | 15 | 15 | 7 | 8 |
| $60,000–$64,999 | 208 | 1 | 64 | 54 | 62 | 19 | 8 | 1 | 7 |
| $65,000–$69,999 | 182 | 0 | 61 | 52 | 42 | 17 | 11 | 9 | 2 |
| $70,000–$74,999 | 143 | 0 | 19 | 59 | 40 | 19 | 5 | 1 | 3 |
| $75,000–$79,999 | 89 | 5 | 15 | 21 | 27 | 15 | 8 | 8 | 0 |
| $80,000–$84,999 | 118 | 0 | 20 | 41 | 37 | 16 | 4 | 4 | 0 |
| $85,000–$89,999 | 66 | 0 | 0 | 23 | 28 | 7 | 7 | 7 | 0 |
| $90,000–$94,999 | 56 | 0 | 0 | 15 | 32 | 6 | 4 | 4 | 0 |
| $95,000–$99,999 | 54 | 0 | 13 | 20 | 14 | 5 | 2 | 2 | 0 |
| $100,000 or more | 312 | 1 | 28 | 75 | 124 | 52 | 33 | 25 | 8 |
| Median income | $45,372 | $26,918 | $45,431 | $48,133 | $56,950 | $44,562 | $27,588 | $28,142 | $26,076 |

| **Percent distribution** | | | | | | | | | |
|---|---|---|---|---|---|---|---|---|---|
| **Total couples** | **100.0%** | **100.0%** | **100.0%** | **100.0%** | **100.0%** | **100.0%** | **100.0%** | **100.0%** | **100.0%** |
| Under $25,000 | 21.7 | 42.3 | 18.5 | 19.1 | 11.8 | 20.8 | 45.6 | 45.0 | 47.0 |
| $25,000–$49,999 | 34.8 | 39.6 | 38.8 | 33.9 | 29.2 | 38.4 | 35.3 | 35.2 | 33.6 |
| $50,000–$74,999 | 25.8 | 11.7 | 34.0 | 29.0 | 29.6 | 19.8 | 7.9 | 5.4 | 13.4 |
| $75,000–$99,999 | 9.8 | 4.5 | 5.6 | 11.3 | 15.6 | 10.1 | 4.8 | 6.8 | 0.0 |
| $100,000 or more | 8.0 | 0.9 | 3.3 | 7.0 | 14.0 | 10.7 | 6.4 | 6.8 | 5.4 |

*Source: Bureau of the Census, Internet web site, <http://www.census.gov/cps/ads/sdata.htm>; calculations by New Strategist*

# Distribution of Married Couples by Household Income and Age of Householder, 1997: Hispanic Married Couples

*(number and percent distribution of Hispanic married couples by household income and age of householder, 1997; married couples in thousands as of 1998)*

| | total | 15–24 | 25–34 | 35–44 | 45–54 | 55–64 | 65 or older | | |
| | | | | | | | total | 65–74 | 75 or older |
|---|---|---|---|---|---|---|---|---|---|
| **Total couples** | **4,804** | **300** | **1,345** | **1,427** | **812** | **507** | **412** | **282** | **130** |
| Under $5,000 | 121 | 13 | 34 | 25 | 8 | 16 | 25 | 14 | 11 |
| $5,000–$9,999 | 202 | 27 | 41 | 51 | 25 | 21 | 36 | 22 | 15 |
| $10,000–$14,999 | 430 | 57 | 117 | 103 | 52 | 36 | 62 | 46 | 17 |
| $15,000–$19,999 | 417 | 41 | 131 | 108 | 51 | 36 | 51 | 29 | 22 |
| $20,000–$24,999 | 498 | 51 | 151 | 134 | 67 | 41 | 54 | 38 | 17 |
| $25,000–$29,999 | 403 | 30 | 150 | 109 | 45 | 35 | 33 | 22 | 10 |
| $30,000–$34,999 | 372 | 30 | 116 | 100 | 62 | 37 | 26 | 18 | 8 |
| $35,000–$39,999 | 356 | 27 | 97 | 122 | 56 | 33 | 22 | 21 | 1 |
| $40,000–$44,999 | 333 | 5 | 110 | 93 | 76 | 28 | 21 | 13 | 8 |
| $45,000–$49,999 | 268 | 8 | 69 | 100 | 50 | 20 | 22 | 12 | 9 |
| $50,000–$54,999 | 225 | 4 | 56 | 80 | 38 | 40 | 7 | 4 | 1 |
| $55,000–$59,999 | 168 | 1 | 39 | 62 | 40 | 20 | 6 | 5 | 1 |
| $60,000–$64,999 | 166 | 0 | 59 | 41 | 36 | 27 | 4 | 3 | 1 |
| $65,000–$69,999 | 109 | 0 | 26 | 35 | 26 | 16 | 6 | 5 | 2 |
| $70,000–$74,999 | 98 | 1 | 24 | 41 | 18 | 6 | 9 | 5 | 4 |
| $75,000–$79,999 | 95 | 1 | 25 | 33 | 19 | 14 | 1 | 1 | 0 |
| $80,000–$84,999 | 83 | 1 | 30 | 27 | 13 | 8 | 3 | 3 | 0 |
| $85,000–$89,999 | 58 | 1 | 7 | 20 | 13 | 15 | 3 | 3 | 0 |
| $90,000–$94,999 | 63 | 0 | 16 | 15 | 18 | 10 | 4 | 4 | 0 |
| $95,000–$99,999 | 48 | 0 | 8 | 30 | 8 | 2 | 0 | 0 | 0 |
| $100,000 or more | 292 | 1 | 39 | 97 | 94 | 43 | 17 | 16 | 1 |
| Median income | $34,317 | $21,117 | $31,668 | $38,243 | $41,999 | $38,992 | $22,522 | $24,059 | $19,973 |

**Percent distribution**

| | total | 15–24 | 25–34 | 35–44 | 45–54 | 55–64 | 65 or older | | |
| | | | | | | | total | 65–74 | 75 or older |
|---|---|---|---|---|---|---|---|---|---|
| **Total couples** | **100.0%** | **100.0%** | **100.0%** | **100.0%** | **100.0%** | **100.0%** | **100.0%** | **100.0%** | **100.0%** |
| Under $25,000 | 34.7 | 63.0 | 35.2 | 29.5 | 25.0 | 29.6 | 55.3 | 52.8 | 63.1 |
| $25,000–$49,999 | 36.1 | 33.3 | 40.3 | 36.7 | 35.6 | 30.2 | 30.1 | 30.5 | 27.7 |
| $50,000–$74,999 | 15.9 | 2.0 | 15.2 | 18.1 | 19.5 | 21.5 | 7.8 | 7.8 | 6.9 |
| $75,000–$99,999 | 7.2 | 1.0 | 6.4 | 8.8 | 8.7 | 9.7 | 2.7 | 3.9 | 0.0 |
| $100,000 or more | 6.1 | 0.3 | 2.9 | 6.8 | 11.6 | 8.5 | 4.1 | 5.7 | 0.8 |

*Source: Bureau of the Census, Internet web site, <http://www.census.gov/cps/ads/sdata.htm>; calculations by New Strategist*

## Distribution of Married Couples by Household Income and Age of Householder, 1997: White Married Couples

*(number and percent distribution of white married couples by household income and age of householder, 1997; married couples in thousands as of 1998)*

| | total | 15–24 | 25–34 | 35–44 | 45–54 | 55–64 | 65 or older total | 65–74 | 75 or older |
|---|---|---|---|---|---|---|---|---|---|
| **Total couples** | **48,066** | **1,221** | **8,557** | **12,382** | **10,324** | **7,125** | **8,456** | **5,338** | **3,118** |
| Under $5,000 | 481 | 24 | 83 | 86 | 82 | 107 | 101 | 70 | 30 |
| $5,000–$9,999 | 708 | 50 | 103 | 119 | 103 | 132 | 201 | 116 | 85 |
| $10,000–$14,999 | 1,797 | 150 | 305 | 242 | 199 | 229 | 671 | 352 | 320 |
| $15,000–$19,999 | 2,443 | 133 | 386 | 331 | 234 | 311 | 1,049 | 525 | 524 |
| $20,000–$24,999 | 2,743 | 169 | 458 | 423 | 273 | 358 | 1,063 | 584 | 480 |
| $25,000–$29,999 | 2,784 | 143 | 511 | 485 | 358 | 377 | 911 | 537 | 373 |
| $30,000–$34,999 | 2,920 | 137 | 610 | 599 | 434 | 368 | 772 | 499 | 274 |
| $35,000–$39,999 | 2,975 | 112 | 646 | 711 | 469 | 395 | 641 | 437 | 204 |
| $40,000–$44,999 | 2,997 | 85 | 715 | 773 | 498 | 457 | 471 | 325 | 147 |
| $45,000–$49,999 | 2,733 | 64 | 636 | 703 | 544 | 405 | 381 | 266 | 115 |
| $50,000–$54,999 | 2,950 | 52 | 630 | 881 | 586 | 487 | 315 | 231 | 84 |
| $55,000–$59,999 | 2,349 | 30 | 471 | 779 | 485 | 326 | 258 | 196 | 63 |
| $60,000–$64,999 | 2,382 | 14 | 501 | 796 | 607 | 274 | 189 | 117 | 72 |
| $65,000–$69,999 | 2,107 | 16 | 452 | 625 | 555 | 275 | 184 | 135 | 49 |
| $70,000–$74,999 | 1,906 | 6 | 382 | 663 | 476 | 238 | 143 | 110 | 32 |
| $75,000–$79,999 | 1,642 | 11 | 274 | 560 | 452 | 231 | 113 | 86 | 27 |
| $80,000–$84,999 | 1,574 | 12 | 268 | 508 | 419 | 210 | 156 | 109 | 47 |
| $85,000–$89,999 | 1,260 | 1 | 162 | 395 | 372 | 225 | 106 | 84 | 23 |
| $90,000–$94,999 | 1,130 | 0 | 142 | 364 | 378 | 199 | 48 | 32 | 16 |
| $95,000–$99,999 | 921 | 5 | 118 | 310 | 299 | 135 | 53 | 40 | 13 |
| $100,000 or more | 7,262 | 10 | 701 | 2,031 | 2,502 | 1,389 | 630 | 487 | 142 |
| Median income | $52,199 | $28,046 | $48,574 | $60,312 | $67,249 | $54,303 | $31,449 | $34,858 | $26,525 |
| **Percent distribution** | | | | | | | | | |
| **Total couples** | **100.0%** | **100.0%** | **100.0%** | **100.0%** | **100.0%** | **100.0%** | **100.0%** | **100.0%** | **100.0%** |
| Under $25,000 | 17.0 | 43.1 | 15.6 | 9.7 | 8.6 | 16.0 | 36.5 | 30.9 | 46.2 |
| $25,000–$49,999 | 30.0 | 44.3 | 36.4 | 26.4 | 22.3 | 28.1 | 37.6 | 38.7 | 35.7 |
| $50,000–$74,999 | 24.3 | 9.7 | 28.5 | 30.2 | 26.2 | 22.5 | 12.9 | 14.8 | 9.6 |
| $75,000–$99,999 | 13.6 | 2.4 | 11.3 | 17.3 | 18.6 | 14.0 | 5.6 | 6.6 | 4.0 |
| $100,000 or more | 15.1 | 0.8 | 8.2 | 16.4 | 24.2 | 19.5 | 7.5 | 9.1 | 4.6 |

*Source: Bureau of the Census, Internet web site, <http://www.census.gov/cps/ads/sdata.htm>; calculations by New Strategist*

# Many Female-Headed Families Are Doing Well

## The youngest householders are the poorest.

The median income of female-headed families was just $23,040 in 1997—meaning half such families had incomes below $23,040 and the other half had incomes above that amount.

Female family householders under age 35 have below-average incomes, with the median income of those under age 25 was just $13,307 in 1997. In contrast, families headed by women aged 45 or older have above-average incomes. Those headed by women aged 45 to 54 have a relatively high median income of $32,297. Most families headed by young women include children. Many of these households include only one or even no earner, which explains their low incomes. Many families headed by older women include other adults—such as grown children or siblings. These households often include two or more earners, which explains their higher incomes.

The poorest female-headed families are those headed by young black women. Black families with a female householder under age 25 had a median income of just $10,191 in 1997. Among whites, the poorest female-headed families are headed by women under age 25, with a median of just $16,633. Among Hispanic female-headed families, the poorest are those headed by 25-to-34-year-olds, with a median income of $12,452.

✗ With the aging of the baby-boom generation, an increasing share of female-headed families will be headed by older women. Consequently, the incomes of female-headed families are likely to rise in the years ahead.

### Older female family heads have highest incomes

*(median income of female-headed families by age of householder, 1997)*

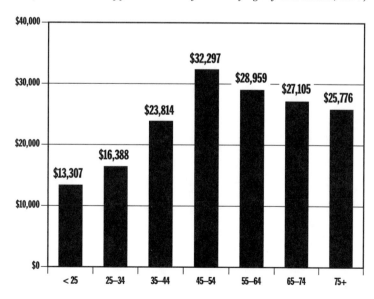

## Distribution of Female-Headed Families by Household Income and Age of Householder, 1997: Total Female-Headed Families

*(number and percent distribution of female-headed families by household income and age of householder, 1997; female-headed families in thousands as of 1998)*

| | total | 15–24 | 25–34 | 35–44 | 45–54 | 55–64 | 65 or older total | 65–74 | 75 or older |
|---|---|---|---|---|---|---|---|---|---|
| **Total female-headed families** | **12,652** | **1,095** | **2,887** | **3,637** | **2,260** | **1,099** | **1,676** | **938** | **738** |
| Under $5,000 | 985 | 173 | 368 | 275 | 96 | 47 | 25 | 15 | 10 |
| $5,000–$9,999 | 1,619 | 265 | 510 | 448 | 146 | 105 | 144 | 82 | 63 |
| $10,000–$14,999 | 1,564 | 139 | 467 | 403 | 221 | 118 | 215 | 121 | 94 |
| $15,000–$19,999 | 1,375 | 143 | 318 | 411 | 177 | 99 | 229 | 127 | 102 |
| $20,000–$24,999 | 1,202 | 90 | 292 | 350 | 192 | 106 | 174 | 85 | 89 |
| $25,000–$29,999 | 1,094 | 59 | 231 | 370 | 187 | 97 | 149 | 90 | 59 |
| $30,000–$34,999 | 880 | 45 | 177 | 252 | 216 | 74 | 117 | 81 | 35 |
| $35,000–$39,999 | 715 | 40 | 108 | 227 | 144 | 71 | 127 | 73 | 53 |
| $40,000–$44,999 | 605 | 33 | 98 | 155 | 140 | 76 | 106 | 59 | 46 |
| $45,000–$49,999 | 490 | 20 | 60 | 161 | 109 | 56 | 84 | 50 | 33 |
| $50,000–$54,999 | 393 | 18 | 46 | 103 | 98 | 57 | 70 | 30 | 40 |
| $55,000–$59,999 | 292 | 13 | 31 | 82 | 85 | 33 | 46 | 24 | 22 |
| $60,000–$64,999 | 310 | 3 | 43 | 116 | 86 | 26 | 35 | 18 | 17 |
| $65,000–$69,999 | 238 | 6 | 39 | 59 | 83 | 24 | 28 | 23 | 6 |
| $70,000–$74,999 | 138 | 11 | 14 | 38 | 51 | 16 | 6 | 3 | 3 |
| $75,000–$79,999 | 141 | 2 | 5 | 55 | 51 | 8 | 21 | 12 | 8 |
| $80,000–$84,999 | 79 | 6 | 19 | 18 | 12 | 12 | 11 | 3 | 8 |
| $85,000–$89,999 | 88 | 3 | 16 | 17 | 29 | 14 | 9 | 6 | 4 |
| $90,000–$94,999 | 68 | 0 | 6 | 9 | 29 | 9 | 15 | 3 | 12 |
| $95,000–$99,999 | 56 | 2 | 5 | 7 | 15 | 14 | 11 | 2 | 9 |
| $100,000 or more | 321 | 24 | 32 | 79 | 91 | 40 | 54 | 30 | 24 |
| Median income | $23,040 | $13,307 | $16,388 | $23,814 | $32,297 | $28,959 | $26,528 | $27,105 | $25,776 |

**Percent distribution**

| **Total female-headed families** | **100.0%** | **100.0%** | **100.0%** | **100.0%** | **100.0%** | **100.0%** | **100.0%** | **100.0%** | **100.0%** |
|---|---|---|---|---|---|---|---|---|---|
| Under $25,000 | 53.3 | 74.0 | 67.7 | 51.9 | 36.8 | 43.2 | 47.0 | 45.8 | 48.5 |
| $25,000–$49,999 | 29.9 | 18.0 | 23.3 | 32.0 | 35.2 | 34.0 | 34.8 | 37.6 | 30.6 |
| $50,000–$74,999 | 10.8 | 4.7 | 6.0 | 10.9 | 17.8 | 14.2 | 11.0 | 10.4 | 11.9 |
| $75,000–$99,999 | 3.4 | 1.2 | 1.8 | 2.9 | 6.0 | 5.2 | 4.0 | 2.8 | 5.6 |
| $100,000 or more | 2.5 | 2.2 | 1.1 | 2.2 | 4.0 | 3.6 | 3.2 | 3.2 | 3.3 |

*Source: Bureau of the Census, Internet web site, <http://www.census.gov/cps/ads/sdata.htm>; calculations by New Strategist*

## Distribution of Female-Headed Families by Household Income and Age of Householder, 1997: Black Female-Headed Families

*(number and percent distribution of black female-headed families by household income and age of householder, 1997; female-headed families in thousands as of 1998)*

| | total | 15–24 | 25–34 | 35–44 | 45–54 | 55–64 | 65 or older total | 65–74 | 75 or older |
|---|---|---|---|---|---|---|---|---|---|
| **Total female-headed families** | **3,926** | **429** | **1,084** | **1,146** | **607** | **314** | **345** | **214** | **131** |
| Under $5,000 | 431 | 90 | 161 | 120 | 48 | 9 | 3 | 0 | 3 |
| $5,000–$9,999 | 653 | 122 | 190 | 186 | 37 | 45 | 73 | 38 | 34 |
| $10,000–$14,999 | 581 | 65 | 194 | 149 | 72 | 41 | 59 | 50 | 9 |
| $15,000–$19,999 | 450 | 47 | 120 | 137 | 81 | 28 | 37 | 22 | 15 |
| $20,000–$24,999 | 382 | 28 | 95 | 131 | 69 | 20 | 39 | 19 | 20 |
| $25,000–$29,999 | 308 | 12 | 93 | 114 | 38 | 31 | 21 | 16 | 5 |
| $30,000–$34,999 | 258 | 12 | 67 | 61 | 59 | 26 | 32 | 24 | 8 |
| $35,000–$39,999 | 174 | 6 | 40 | 65 | 31 | 18 | 14 | 9 | 5 |
| $40,000–$44,999 | 150 | 6 | 40 | 37 | 20 | 29 | 18 | 12 | 6 |
| $45,000–$49,999 | 116 | 5 | 9 | 49 | 31 | 15 | 7 | 7 | 0 |
| $50,000–$54,999 | 90 | 11 | 24 | 17 | 14 | 8 | 14 | 3 | 12 |
| $55,000–$59,999 | 60 | 7 | 6 | 23 | 17 | 2 | 6 | 2 | 4 |
| $60,000–$64,999 | 57 | 0 | 8 | 14 | 18 | 8 | 8 | 2 | 6 |
| $65,000–$69,999 | 58 | 5 | 10 | 8 | 23 | 10 | 4 | 4 | 0 |
| $70,000–$74,999 | 29 | 3 | 5 | 7 | 11 | 3 | 1 | 1 | 0 |
| $75,000–$79,999 | 21 | 0 | 2 | 14 | 5 | 0 | 0 | 0 | 0 |
| $80,000–$84,999 | 18 | 4 | 5 | 5 | 3 | 3 | 0 | 0 | 0 |
| $85,000–$89,999 | 23 | 0 | 4 | 4 | 10 | 5 | 0 | 0 | 0 |
| $90,000–$94,999 | 13 | 0 | 2 | 0 | 9 | 2 | 0 | 0 | 0 |
| $95,000–$99,999 | 16 | 0 | 0 | 0 | 5 | 7 | 3 | 0 | 3 |
| $100,000 or more | 38 | 6 | 10 | 7 | 6 | 6 | 3 | 2 | 0 |
| Median income | $17,962 | $10,191 | $14,918 | $19,215 | $24,653 | $28,083 | $19,997 | $19,185 | $21,700 |

| **Percent distribution** | | | | | | | | | |
|---|---|---|---|---|---|---|---|---|---|
| **Total female-headed families** | **100.0%** | **100.0%** | **100.0%** | **100.0%** | **100.0%** | **100.0%** | **100.0%** | **100.0%** | **100.0%** |
| Under $25,000 | 63.6 | 82.1 | 70.1 | 63.1 | 50.6 | 45.5 | 61.2 | 60.3 | 61.8 |
| $25,000–$49,999 | 25.6 | 9.6 | 23.0 | 28.4 | 29.5 | 37.9 | 26.7 | 31.8 | 18.3 |
| $50,000–$74,999 | 7.5 | 6.1 | 4.9 | 6.0 | 13.7 | 9.9 | 9.6 | 5.6 | 16.8 |
| $75,000–$99,999 | 2.3 | 0.9 | 1.2 | 2.0 | 5.3 | 5.4 | 0.9 | 0.0 | 2.3 |
| $100,000 or more | 1.0 | 1.4 | 0.9 | 0.6 | 1.0 | 1.9 | 0.9 | 0.9 | 0.0 |

*Source: Bureau of the Census, Internet web site, <http://www.census.gov/cps/ads/sdata.htm>; calculations by New Strategist*

# Distribution of Female-Headed Families by Household Income and Age of Householder, 1997: Hispanic Female-Headed Families

*(number and percent distribution of Hispanic female-headed families by household income and age of householder, 1997; female-headed families in thousands as of 1998)*

| | total | 15–24 | 25–34 | 35–44 | 45–54 | 55–64 | 65 or older total | 65–74 | 75 or older |
|---|---|---|---|---|---|---|---|---|---|
| **Total female-headed families** | **1,612** | **179** | **435** | **461** | **284** | **135** | **117** | **78** | **39** |
| Under $5,000 | 167 | 16 | 63 | 48 | 25 | 11 | 4 | 1 | 3 |
| $5,000–$9,999 | 331 | 50 | 102 | 93 | 45 | 22 | 17 | 13 | 3 |
| $10,000–$14,999 | 240 | 28 | 78 | 57 | 31 | 26 | 20 | 13 | 6 |
| $15,000–$19,999 | 210 | 26 | 48 | 67 | 37 | 18 | 16 | 11 | 5 |
| $20,000–$24,999 | 142 | 17 | 44 | 33 | 27 | 14 | 8 | 4 | 3 |
| $25,000–$29,999 | 107 | 7 | 24 | 31 | 29 | 4 | 12 | 10 | 2 |
| $30,000–$34,999 | 96 | 7 | 20 | 26 | 28 | 7 | 10 | 5 | 4 |
| $35,000–$39,999 | 69 | 14 | 15 | 15 | 15 | 5 | 4 | 1 | 3 |
| $40,000–$44,999 | 60 | 6 | 14 | 22 | 8 | 4 | 5 | 4 | 1 |
| $45,000–$49,999 | 48 | 1 | 7 | 15 | 7 | 5 | 12 | 9 | 3 |
| $50,000–$54,999 | 30 | 1 | 5 | 7 | 10 | 3 | 2 | 2 | 0 |
| $55,000–$59,999 | 17 | 0 | 3 | 9 | 0 | 3 | 1 | 0 | 1 |
| $60,000–$64,999 | 21 | 0 | 4 | 13 | 5 | 0 | 0 | 0 | 0 |
| $65,000–$69,999 | 18 | 1 | 4 | 9 | 3 | 1 | 1 | 1 | 0 |
| $70,000–$74,999 | 17 | 4 | 0 | 5 | 8 | 0 | 0 | 0 | 0 |
| $75,000–$79,999 | 10 | 0 | 0 | 2 | 3 | 2 | 2 | 2 | 0 |
| $80,000–$84,999 | 4 | 0 | 1 | 2 | 1 | 0 | 0 | 0 | 0 |
| $85,000–$89,999 | 4 | 0 | 0 | 0 | 1 | 3 | 0 | 0 | 0 |
| $90,000–$94,999 | 0 | 0 | 0 | 0 | 0 | 0 | 0 | 0 | 0 |
| $95,000–$99,999 | 3 | 0 | 1 | 2 | 0 | 0 | 0 | 0 | 0 |
| $100,000 or more | 19 | 1 | 0 | 7 | 3 | 5 | 3 | 1 | 2 |
| Median income | $16,393 | $13,670 | $12,452 | $17,215 | $20,780 | $17,054 | $21,157 | $20,461 | $23,050 |

**Percent distribution**

| Total female-headed families | 100.0% | 100.0% | 100.0% | 100.0% | 100.0% | 100.0% | 100.0% | 100.0% | 100.0% |
|---|---|---|---|---|---|---|---|---|---|
| Under $25,000 | 67.6 | 76.5 | 77.0 | 64.6 | 58.1 | 67.4 | 55.6 | 53.8 | 51.3 |
| $25,000–$49,999 | 23.6 | 19.6 | 18.4 | 23.6 | 30.6 | 18.5 | 36.8 | 37.2 | 33.3 |
| $50,000–$74,999 | 6.4 | 3.4 | 3.7 | 9.3 | 9.2 | 5.2 | 3.4 | 3.8 | 2.6 |
| $75,000–$99,999 | 1.3 | 0.0 | 0.5 | 1.3 | 1.8 | 3.7 | 1.7 | 2.6 | 0.0 |
| $100,000 or more | 1.2 | 0.6 | 0.0 | 1.5 | 1.1 | 3.7 | 2.6 | 1.3 | 5.1 |

*Source: Bureau of the Census, Internet web site, <http://www.census.gov/cps/ads/sdata.htm>; calculations by New Strategist*

# Distribution of Female-Headed Families by Household Income and Age of Householder, 1997: White Female-Headed Families

*(number and percent distribution of white female-headed families by household income and age of householder, 1997; female-headed families in thousands as of 1998)*

| | total | 15–24 | 25–34 | 35–44 | 45–54 | 55–64 | 65 or older total | 65–74 | 75 or older |
|---|---|---|---|---|---|---|---|---|---|
| **Total female-headed families** | **8,308** | **613** | **1,725** | **2,371** | **1,551** | **748** | **1,301** | **710** | **591** |
| Under $5,000 | 519 | 79 | 196 | 141 | 46 | 36 | 22 | 15 | 6 |
| $5,000–$9,999 | 922 | 130 | 311 | 252 | 101 | 58 | 71 | 44 | 27 |
| $10,000–$14,999 | 934 | 70 | 265 | 234 | 136 | 75 | 154 | 68 | 86 |
| $15,000–$19,999 | 881 | 89 | 187 | 266 | 83 | 68 | 188 | 102 | 87 |
| $20,000–$24,999 | 790 | 61 | 188 | 212 | 113 | 83 | 134 | 66 | 69 |
| $25,000–$29,999 | 753 | 47 | 133 | 246 | 134 | 67 | 127 | 73 | 54 |
| $30,000–$34,999 | 591 | 32 | 102 | 185 | 145 | 44 | 83 | 56 | 27 |
| $35,000–$39,999 | 519 | 30 | 63 | 151 | 113 | 51 | 111 | 64 | 48 |
| $40,000–$44,999 | 440 | 23 | 58 | 115 | 116 | 43 | 87 | 47 | 39 |
| $45,000–$49,999 | 367 | 13 | 51 | 112 | 73 | 42 | 76 | 43 | 33 |
| $50,000–$54,999 | 299 | 6 | 22 | 86 | 84 | 47 | 53 | 25 | 29 |
| $55,000–$59,999 | 218 | 4 | 25 | 58 | 64 | 27 | 37 | 19 | 18 |
| $60,000–$64,999 | 238 | 0 | 33 | 92 | 67 | 18 | 27 | 16 | 11 |
| $65,000–$69,999 | 170 | 1 | 30 | 46 | 56 | 14 | 22 | 18 | 4 |
| $70,000–$74,999 | 96 | 8 | 9 | 27 | 40 | 7 | 5 | 2 | 3 |
| $75,000–$79,999 | 111 | 2 | 3 | 40 | 39 | 7 | 18 | 12 | 6 |
| $80,000–$84,999 | 52 | 0 | 14 | 12 | 9 | 9 | 7 | 3 | 4 |
| $85,000–$89,999 | 63 | 3 | 11 | 13 | 19 | 9 | 7 | 5 | 3 |
| $90,000–$94,999 | 47 | 0 | 2 | 6 | 19 | 7 | 14 | 3 | 10 |
| $95,000–$99,999 | 39 | 2 | 5 | 7 | 9 | 7 | 8 | 2 | 6 |
| $100,000 or more | 260 | 16 | 16 | 69 | 86 | 26 | 47 | 27 | 20 |
| Median income | $25,670 | $16,633 | $17,375 | $26,773 | $35,682 | $28,871 | $27,977 | $29,157 | $26,537 |

**Percent distribution**

| **Total female-headed families** | **100.0%** | **100.0%** | **100.0%** | **100.0%** | **100.0%** | **100.0%** | **100.0%** | **100.0%** | **100.0%** |
|---|---|---|---|---|---|---|---|---|---|
| Under $25,000 | 48.7 | 70.0 | 66.5 | 46.6 | 30.9 | 42.8 | 43.7 | 41.5 | 46.5 |
| $25,000–$49,999 | 32.1 | 23.7 | 23.6 | 34.1 | 37.5 | 33.0 | 37.2 | 39.9 | 34.0 |
| $50,000–$74,999 | 12.3 | 3.1 | 6.9 | 13.0 | 20.1 | 15.1 | 11.1 | 11.3 | 11.0 |
| $75,000–$99,999 | 3.8 | 1.1 | 2.0 | 3.3 | 6.1 | 5.2 | 4.2 | 3.5 | 4.9 |
| $100,000 or more | 3.1 | 2.6 | 0.9 | 2.9 | 5.5 | 3.5 | 3.6 | 3.8 | 3.4 |

*Source: Bureau of the Census, Internet web site, <http://www.census.gov/cps/ads/sdata.htm>; calculations by New Strategist*

# Male-Headed Families Have Average Incomes

## The median income of male-headed families almost equals the national median.

Male-headed families are the least common household type. In 1997, there were only 3.9 million of them, compared to 12.7 million families headed by women. Male-headed families account for fewer than 4 percent of the nation's households. The median income of male-headed families stood at $36,634 in 1997, 59 percent higher than the median income of female-headed families and close to the $37,005 national median.

The income of male-headed families peaks in the 45-to-54 age group, at a relatively high $45,321. Male family heads under age 25 have the lowest incomes, a median of $29,419 in 1997. Many younger men who head families are raising children, while older ones live with adult relatives such as siblings or parents. Because of these differences in household composition, families headed by older men are more likely to have two earners than those headed by younger men, which accounts in part for the income differences.

The small number of black and Hispanic families headed by men show an income pattern different from that of families headed by whites. Income for black male-headed families peaks in the 25-to-34 age group, while it peaks in the 65-and-older age group among Hispanics. For whites, the income peak is in the 45-to-54 age group.

✗ With the incomes of women rising over the past few decades and the incomes of men stagnating, it is likely that the income gap between male- and female-headed families will shrink in the years ahead.

### Among male-headed families, whites have highest incomes

*(median income of male-headed families by race and Hispanic origin, 1997)*

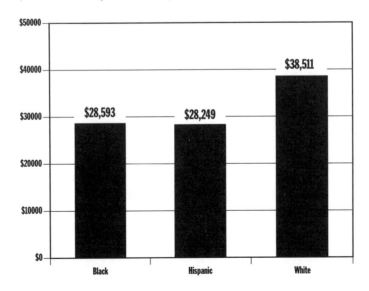

# Distribution of Male-Headed Families by Household Income and Age of Householder, 1997: Total Male-Headed Families

*(number and percent distribution of male-headed families by household income and age of householder, 1997; male-headed families in thousands as of 1998)*

| | total | 15–24 | 25–34 | 35–44 | 45–54 | 55–64 | 65 or older | | |
| | | | | | | | total | 65–74 | 75 or older |
|---|---|---|---|---|---|---|---|---|---|
| **Total male-headed families** | **3,911** | **551** | **866** | **1,055** | **700** | **352** | **386** | **210** | **176** |
| Under $5,000 | 120 | 30 | 18 | 29 | 27 | 7 | 8 | 4 | 4 |
| $5,000–$9,999 | 152 | 40 | 36 | 33 | 23 | 13 | 7 | 3 | 4 |
| $10,000–$14,999 | 262 | 51 | 63 | 59 | 40 | 27 | 23 | 7 | 15 |
| $15,000–$19,999 | 307 | 56 | 64 | 81 | 40 | 22 | 43 | 25 | 18 |
| $20,000–$24,999 | 299 | 46 | 69 | 64 | 58 | 21 | 41 | 28 | 13 |
| $25,000–$29,999 | 405 | 60 | 79 | 147 | 53 | 29 | 38 | 10 | 27 |
| $30,000–$34,999 | 306 | 27 | 77 | 94 | 38 | 27 | 42 | 33 | 10 |
| $35,000–$39,999 | 272 | 34 | 66 | 82 | 33 | 29 | 27 | 10 | 17 |
| $40,000–$44,999 | 238 | 30 | 55 | 85 | 37 | 10 | 20 | 9 | 11 |
| $45,000–$49,999 | 200 | 25 | 55 | 50 | 29 | 27 | 15 | 8 | 7 |
| $50,000–$54,999 | 210 | 39 | 46 | 54 | 37 | 21 | 13 | 9 | 3 |
| $55,000–$59,999 | 193 | 36 | 45 | 37 | 46 | 18 | 12 | 5 | 6 |
| $60,000–$64,999 | 142 | 6 | 42 | 40 | 32 | 9 | 14 | 9 | 5 |
| $65,000–$69,999 | 149 | 10 | 38 | 37 | 30 | 21 | 14 | 9 | 6 |
| $70,000–$74,999 | 110 | 8 | 18 | 35 | 33 | 11 | 5 | 0 | 5 |
| $75,000–$79,999 | 88 | 4 | 21 | 19 | 25 | 6 | 13 | 8 | 5 |
| $80,000–$84,999 | 110 | 14 | 31 | 21 | 18 | 7 | 19 | 12 | 6 |
| $85,000–$89,999 | 42 | 8 | 3 | 11 | 10 | 4 | 5 | 4 | 1 |
| $90,000–$94,999 | 40 | 1 | 5 | 8 | 11 | 9 | 5 | 1 | 5 |
| $95,000–$99,999 | 49 | 3 | 3 | 12 | 20 | 8 | 2 | 2 | 0 |
| $100,000 or more | 220 | 21 | 33 | 56 | 60 | 28 | 22 | 13 | 9 |
| Median income | $36,634 | $29,419 | $36,333 | $35,931 | $45,321 | $41,613 | $34,109 | $34,242 | $33,755 |

**Percent distribution**

| | total | 15–24 | 25–34 | 35–44 | 45–54 | 55–64 | total | 65–74 | 75 or older |
|---|---|---|---|---|---|---|---|---|---|
| **Total male-headed families** | **100.0%** | **100.0%** | **100.0%** | **100.0%** | **100.0%** | **100.0%** | **100.0%** | **100.0%** | **100.0%** |
| Under $25,000 | 29.1 | 40.5 | 28.9 | 25.2 | 26.9 | 25.6 | 31.6 | 31.9 | 30.7 |
| $25,000–$49,999 | 36.3 | 31.9 | 38.3 | 43.4 | 27.1 | 34.7 | 36.8 | 33.3 | 40.9 |
| $50,000–$74,999 | 20.6 | 18.0 | 21.8 | 19.2 | 25.4 | 22.7 | 15.0 | 15.2 | 14.2 |
| $75,000–$99,999 | 8.4 | 5.4 | 7.3 | 6.7 | 12.0 | 9.7 | 11.4 | 12.9 | 9.7 |
| $100,000 or more | 5.6 | 3.8 | 3.8 | 5.3 | 8.6 | 8.0 | 5.7 | 6.2 | 5.1 |

*Source: Bureau of the Census, Internet web site, <http://www.census.gov/cps/ads/sdata.htm>; calculations by New Strategist*

## Distribution of Male-Headed Families by Household Income and Age of Householder, 1997: Black Male-Headed Families

*(number and percent distribution of black male-headed families by household income and age of householder, 1997; male-headed families in thousands as of 1998)*

| | total | 15–24 | 25–34 | 35–44 | 45–54 | 55–64 | 65 or older total | 65–74 | 75 or older |
|---|---|---|---|---|---|---|---|---|---|
| **Total male-headed families** | **562** | **91** | **112** | **140** | **103** | **62** | **53** | **24** | **28** |
| Under $5,000 | 35 | 9 | 10 | 1 | 10 | 0 | 4 | 4 | 0 |
| $5,000–$9,999 | 25 | 2 | 7 | 5 | 8 | 2 | 2 | 0 | 2 |
| $10,000–$14,999 | 56 | 15 | 2 | 12 | 3 | 15 | 9 | 0 | 9 |
| $15,000–$19,999 | 49 | 3 | 18 | 11 | 9 | 3 | 6 | 6 | 0 |
| $20,000–$24,999 | 45 | 8 | 8 | 3 | 9 | 10 | 7 | 3 | 4 |
| $25,000–$29,999 | 92 | 18 | 7 | 42 | 16 | 5 | 5 | 0 | 5 |
| $30,000–$34,999 | 43 | 4 | 11 | 10 | 7 | 6 | 6 | 5 | 2 |
| $35,000–$39,999 | 47 | 7 | 14 | 15 | 7 | 3 | 1 | 1 | 0 |
| $40,000–$44,999 | 27 | 1 | 11 | 10 | 0 | 0 | 3 | 0 | 3 |
| $45,000–$49,999 | 19 | 0 | 7 | 6 | 4 | 3 | 0 | 0 | 0 |
| $50,000–$54,999 | 19 | 5 | 0 | 2 | 4 | 5 | 3 | 3 | 0 |
| $55,000–$59,999 | 25 | 6 | 2 | 5 | 5 | 2 | 5 | 0 | 5 |
| $60,000–$64,999 | 8 | 0 | 1 | 0 | 3 | 4 | 0 | 0 | 0 |
| $65,000–$69,999 | 14 | 0 | 10 | 5 | 0 | 0 | 0 | 0 | 0 |
| $70,000–$74,999 | 11 | 3 | 0 | 2 | 5 | 0 | 0 | 0 | 0 |
| $75,000–$79,999 | 5 | 0 | 0 | 0 | 5 | 0 | 0 | 0 | 0 |
| $80,000–$84,999 | 6 | 3 | 3 | 0 | 0 | 0 | 0 | 0 | 0 |
| $85,000–$89,999 | 8 | 6 | 0 | 1 | 0 | 2 | 0 | 0 | 0 |
| $90,000–$94,999 | 4 | 0 | 0 | 4 | 0 | 0 | 0 | 0 | 0 |
| $95,000–$99,999 | 6 | 0 | 0 | 0 | 6 | 0 | 0 | 0 | 0 |
| $100,000 or more | 16 | 0 | 4 | 8 | 2 | 2 | 0 | 0 | 0 |
| Median income | $28,593 | $28,487 | $33,799 | $29,475 | $27,360 | $26,323 | $23,272 | $23,167 | $25,071 |

| **Percent distribution** | | | | | | | | | |
|---|---|---|---|---|---|---|---|---|---|
| **Total male-headed families** | **100.0%** | **100.0%** | **100.0%** | **100.0%** | **100.0%** | **100.0%** | **100.0%** | **100.0%** | **100.0%** |
| Under $25,000 | 37.4 | 40.7 | 40.2 | 22.9 | 37.9 | 48.4 | 52.8 | 54.2 | 53.6 |
| $25,000–$49,999 | 40.6 | 33.0 | 44.6 | 59.3 | 33.0 | 27.4 | 28.3 | 25.0 | 35.7 |
| $50,000–$74,999 | 13.7 | 15.4 | 11.6 | 10.0 | 16.5 | 17.7 | 15.1 | 12.5 | 17.9 |
| $75,000–$99,999 | 5.2 | 9.9 | 2.7 | 3.6 | 10.7 | 3.2 | 0.0 | 0.0 | 0.0 |
| $100,000 or more | 2.8 | 0.0 | 3.6 | 5.7 | 1.9 | 3.2 | 0.0 | 0.0 | 0.0 |

*Source: Bureau of the Census, Internet web site, <http://www.census.gov/cps/ads/sdata.htm>; calculations by New Strategist*

# Distribution of Male-Headed Families by Household Income and Age of Householder, 1997: Hispanic Male-Headed Families

*(number and percent distribution of Hispanic male-headed families by household income and age of householder, 1997; male-headed families in thousands as of 1998)*

| | total | 15–24 | 25–34 | 35–44 | 45–54 | 55–64 | 65 or older total | 65–74 | 75 or older |
|---|---|---|---|---|---|---|---|---|---|
| **Total male-headed families** | **545** | **147** | **164** | **114** | **70** | **33** | **18** | **12** | **6** |
| Under $5,000 | 18 | 9 | 1 | 1 | 3 | 3 | 0 | 0 | 0 |
| $5,000–$9,999 | 45 | 20 | 9 | 6 | 6 | 3 | 1 | 1 | 0 |
| $10,000–$14,999 | 54 | 7 | 17 | 13 | 13 | 0 | 3 | 2 | 1 |
| $15,000–$19,999 | 58 | 30 | 13 | 4 | 5 | 7 | 0 | 0 | 0 |
| $20,000–$24,999 | 62 | 20 | 13 | 16 | 11 | 2 | 1 | 0 | 1 |
| $25,000–$29,999 | 51 | 8 | 17 | 17 | 7 | 3 | 0 | 0 | 0 |
| $30,000–$34,999 | 46 | 7 | 15 | 14 | 5 | 2 | 3 | 2 | 2 |
| $35,000–$39,999 | 35 | 12 | 12 | 4 | 3 | 2 | 1 | 1 | 0 |
| $40,000–$44,999 | 40 | 12 | 7 | 11 | 4 | 5 | 1 | 1 | 0 |
| $45,000–$49,999 | 33 | 2 | 15 | 7 | 7 | 0 | 2 | 2 | 0 |
| $50,000–$54,999 | 27 | 10 | 9 | 5 | 2 | 1 | 0 | 0 | 0 |
| $55,000–$59,999 | 15 | 5 | 8 | 1 | 0 | 0 | 0 | 0 | 0 |
| $60,000–$64,999 | 6 | 0 | 4 | 2 | 0 | 0 | 0 | 0 | 0 |
| $65,000–$69,999 | 10 | 0 | 6 | 0 | 0 | 1 | 2 | 0 | 2 |
| $70,000–$74,999 | 7 | 0 | 1 | 5 | 1 | 0 | 0 | 0 | 0 |
| $75,000–$79,999 | 10 | 1 | 5 | 3 | 1 | 0 | 0 | 0 | 0 |
| $80,000–$84,999 | 7 | 1 | 1 | 1 | 0 | 2 | 2 | 2 | 0 |
| $85,000–$89,999 | 3 | 3 | 0 | 1 | 0 | 0 | 0 | 0 | 0 |
| $90,000–$94,999 | 3 | 0 | 1 | 0 | 1 | 0 | 1 | 1 | 0 |
| $95,000–$99,999 | 0 | 0 | 0 | 0 | 0 | 0 | 0 | 0 | 0 |
| $100,000 or more | 13 | 0 | 8 | 3 | 0 | 2 | 0 | 0 | 0 |
| Median income | $28,249 | $21,180 | $33,281 | $29,957 | $23,660 | $28,759 | $34,646 | $38,249 | $33,852 |

| **Percent distribution** | | | | | | | | | |
|---|---|---|---|---|---|---|---|---|---|
| **Total male-headed families** | **100.0%** | **100.0%** | **100.0%** | **100.0%** | **100.0%** | **100.0%** | **100.0%** | **100.0%** | **100.0%** |
| Under $25,000 | 43.5 | 58.5 | 32.3 | 35.1 | 54.3 | 45.5 | 27.8 | 25.0 | 33.3 |
| $25,000–$49,999 | 37.6 | 27.9 | 40.2 | 46.5 | 37.1 | 36.4 | 38.9 | 50.0 | 33.3 |
| $50,000–$74,999 | 11.9 | 10.2 | 17.1 | 11.4 | 4.3 | 6.1 | 11.1 | 0.0 | 33.3 |
| $75,000–$99,999 | 4.2 | 3.4 | 4.3 | 4.4 | 2.9 | 6.1 | 16.7 | 25.0 | 0.0 |
| $100,000 or more | 2.4 | 0.0 | 4.9 | 2.6 | 0.0 | 6.1 | 0.0 | 0.0 | 0.0 |

*Source: Bureau of the Census, Internet web site, <http://www.census.gov/cps/ads/sdata.htm>; calculations by New Strategist*

## Distribution of Male-Headed Families by Household Income and Age of Householder, 1997: White Male-Headed Families

*(number and percent distribution of white male-headed families by household income and age of householder, 1997; male-headed families in thousands as of 1998)*

| | total | 15–24 | 25–34 | 35–44 | 45–54 | 55–64 | 65 or older total | 65–74 | 75 or older |
|---|---|---|---|---|---|---|---|---|---|
| **Total male-headed families** | **3,137** | **436** | **683** | **851** | **579** | **272** | **315** | **174** | **141** |
| Under $5,000 | 79 | 18 | 6 | 27 | 17 | 7 | 4 | 0 | 4 |
| $5,000–$9,999 | 116 | 36 | 27 | 25 | 15 | 11 | 3 | 2 | 1 |
| $10,000–$14,999 | 192 | 30 | 59 | 44 | 36 | 10 | 13 | 7 | 4 |
| $15,000–$19,999 | 239 | 54 | 44 | 64 | 27 | 19 | 32 | 14 | 18 |
| $20,000–$24,999 | 243 | 37 | 54 | 61 | 46 | 10 | 33 | 24 | 9 |
| $25,000–$29,999 | 296 | 40 | 67 | 102 | 34 | 24 | 31 | 10 | 20 |
| $30,000–$34,999 | 250 | 19 | 64 | 79 | 31 | 21 | 36 | 28 | 8 |
| $35,000–$39,999 | 208 | 26 | 49 | 60 | 26 | 23 | 23 | 6 | 17 |
| $40,000–$44,999 | 200 | 29 | 37 | 74 | 37 | 7 | 16 | 9 | 8 |
| $45,000–$49,999 | 166 | 25 | 41 | 38 | 25 | 22 | 15 | 8 | 7 |
| $50,000–$54,999 | 185 | 31 | 46 | 52 | 31 | 16 | 9 | 6 | 3 |
| $55,000–$59,999 | 157 | 30 | 39 | 26 | 40 | 14 | 7 | 5 | 2 |
| $60,000–$64,999 | 122 | 6 | 35 | 36 | 29 | 5 | 11 | 6 | 5 |
| $65,000–$69,999 | 121 | 8 | 26 | 22 | 30 | 21 | 14 | 9 | 6 |
| $70,000–$74,999 | 97 | 5 | 18 | 31 | 28 | 11 | 5 | 0 | 5 |
| $75,000–$79,999 | 79 | 4 | 17 | 19 | 19 | 6 | 13 | 8 | 5 |
| $80,000–$84,999 | 94 | 11 | 24 | 20 | 17 | 5 | 16 | 12 | 4 |
| $85,000–$89,999 | 34 | 3 | 2 | 11 | 10 | 2 | 5 | 4 | 1 |
| $90,000–$94,999 | 33 | 1 | 3 | 4 | 11 | 8 | 5 | 1 | 5 |
| $95,000–$99,999 | 35 | 3 | 0 | 10 | 11 | 8 | 2 | 2 | 0 |
| $100,000 or more | 191 | 19 | 24 | 44 | 57 | 25 | 22 | 13 | 9 |
| Median income | $38,511 | $30,349 | $36,549 | $36,561 | $49,429 | $46,134 | $36,402 | $35,878 | $36,867 |

**Percent distribution**

| | total | 15–24 | 25–34 | 35–44 | 45–54 | 55–64 | 65 or older total | 65–74 | 75 or older |
|---|---|---|---|---|---|---|---|---|---|
| **Total male-headed families** | **100.0%** | **100.0%** | **100.0%** | **100.0%** | **100.0%** | **100.0%** | **100.0%** | **100.0%** | **100.0%** |
| Under $25,000 | 27.7 | 40.1 | 27.8 | 26.0 | 24.4 | 21.0 | 27.0 | 27.0 | 25.5 |
| $25,000–$49,999 | 35.7 | 31.9 | 37.8 | 41.5 | 26.4 | 35.7 | 38.4 | 35.1 | 42.6 |
| $50,000–$74,999 | 21.7 | 18.3 | 24.0 | 19.6 | 27.3 | 24.6 | 14.6 | 14.9 | 14.9 |
| $75,000–$99,999 | 8.8 | 5.0 | 6.7 | 7.5 | 11.7 | 10.7 | 13.0 | 15.5 | 10.6 |
| $100,000 or more | 6.1 | 4.4 | 3.5 | 5.2 | 9.8 | 9.2 | 7.0 | 7.5 | 6.4 |

*Source: Bureau of the Census, Internet web site, <http://www.census.gov/cps/ads/sdata.htm>; calculations by New Strategist*

# Women Living Alone Have Lowest Incomes

**Most women who live alone are aged 55 or older, which accounts for their low incomes.**

Single-person households are the second most common household type in the United States. They outnumber married couples with children under age 18 at home and are second only to married couples without children at home. Single-person households headed by women are far more numerous than those headed by men—15 million versus 11 million.

Women who live alone have much lower incomes than their male counterparts. The median income of women who live alone stood at just $15,530 in 1997—the lowest income of any household type and only 65 percent as high as the median income of men who live alone. But there is great variation by age in the incomes of women who live alone. Sixty-three percent of women who live alone are aged 55 or older, and 49 percent are aged 65 or older. Most are widows who never worked or are no longer in the work force, which explains their low incomes. In contrast, younger women who live alone have relatively high incomes. Women aged 25 to 34 who live alone have higher incomes than their male counterparts— a median of $27,739 for women versus $27,124 for men in 1997.

Hispanic women who live alone have extremely low incomes at almost any age. Only those aged 25 to 34 had a median income above $20,000 in 1997.

✘ The incomes of older women who live alone should rise rapidly as baby-boom women—with their own pensions, retirement savings, and Social Security benefits—enter the 55-and-older age group.

## Young women who live alone have higher incomes

*(median household income of women who live alone, by age, 1997)*

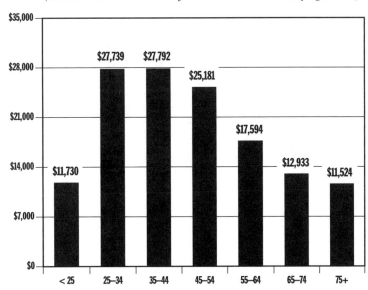

## Distribution of Women Living Alone by Household Income and Age of Householder, 1997: Total Women Living Alone

*(number and percent distribution of women living alone by household income and age of householder, 1997; women living alone in thousands as of 1998)*

| | total | 15–24 | 25–34 | 35–44 | 45–54 | 55–64 | 65 or older total | 65–74 | 75 or older |
|---|---|---|---|---|---|---|---|---|---|
| **Total women living alone** | **15,317** | **528** | **1,457** | **1,498** | **2,109** | **2,148** | **7,577** | **2,987** | **4,590** |
| Under $5,000 | 1,055 | 70 | 104 | 116 | 146 | 200 | 418 | 160 | 259 |
| $5,000–$9,999 | 3,598 | 155 | 81 | 128 | 272 | 458 | 2,504 | 943 | 1,561 |
| $10,000–$14,999 | 2,805 | 82 | 106 | 132 | 223 | 298 | 1,963 | 643 | 1,321 |
| $15,000–$19,999 | 1,802 | 74 | 154 | 104 | 228 | 244 | 999 | 429 | 571 |
| $20,000–$24,999 | 1,342 | 67 | 175 | 167 | 178 | 212 | 543 | 242 | 301 |
| $25,000–$29,999 | 1,023 | 19 | 185 | 162 | 175 | 135 | 349 | 160 | 188 |
| $30,000–$34,999 | 894 | 21 | 198 | 144 | 167 | 168 | 195 | 105 | 90 |
| $35,000–$39,999 | 637 | 19 | 143 | 114 | 154 | 91 | 115 | 43 | 72 |
| $40,000–$44,999 | 458 | 8 | 93 | 95 | 115 | 63 | 84 | 51 | 33 |
| $45,000–$49,999 | 337 | 3 | 56 | 60 | 75 | 60 | 83 | 48 | 34 |
| $50,000–$54,999 | 307 | 4 | 49 | 59 | 83 | 57 | 55 | 24 | 32 |
| $55,000–$59,999 | 203 | 2 | 29 | 50 | 49 | 27 | 45 | 25 | 19 |
| $60,000–$64,999 | 134 | 0 | 10 | 27 | 40 | 24 | 33 | 18 | 15 |
| $65,000–$69,999 | 156 | 0 | 16 | 32 | 55 | 22 | 31 | 21 | 11 |
| $70,000–$74,999 | 85 | 0 | 5 | 10 | 28 | 12 | 29 | 10 | 19 |
| $75,000–$79,999 | 60 | 0 | 12 | 13 | 15 | 7 | 11 | 10 | 1 |
| $80,000–$84,999 | 40 | 0 | 2 | 8 | 10 | 13 | 7 | 7 | 0 |
| $85,000–$89,999 | 36 | 0 | 9 | 12 | 5 | 1 | 10 | 3 | 7 |
| $90,000–$94,999 | 47 | 0 | 3 | 19 | 11 | 11 | 3 | 0 | 3 |
| $95,000–$99,999 | 55 | 0 | 2 | 14 | 12 | 2 | 24 | 11 | 12 |
| $100,000 or more | 241 | 3 | 26 | 33 | 65 | 39 | 76 | 35 | 41 |
| Median income | $15,530 | $11,730 | $27,739 | $27,792 | $25,181 | $17,594 | $11,937 | $12,933 | $11,524 |

**Percent distribution**

| | | | | | | | | | |
|---|---|---|---|---|---|---|---|---|---|
| **Total women living alone** | **100.0%** | **100.0%** | **100.0%** | **100.0%** | **100.0%** | **100.0%** | **100.0%** | **100.0%** | **100.0%** |
| Under $25,000 | 69.2 | 84.8 | 42.6 | 43.2 | 49.6 | 65.7 | 84.8 | 80.9 | 87.4 |
| $25,000–$49,999 | 21.9 | 13.3 | 46.3 | 38.4 | 32.5 | 24.1 | 10.9 | 13.6 | 9.1 |
| $50,000–$74,999 | 5.8 | 1.1 | 7.5 | 11.9 | 12.1 | 6.6 | 2.5 | 3.3 | 2.1 |
| $75,000–$99,999 | 1.6 | 0.0 | 1.9 | 4.4 | 2.5 | 1.6 | 0.7 | 1.0 | 0.5 |
| $100,000 or more | 1.6 | 0.6 | 1.8 | 2.2 | 3.1 | 1.8 | 1.0 | 1.2 | 0.9 |

*Source: Bureau of the Census, Internet web site, <http://www.census.gov/cps/ads/sdata.htm>; calculations by New Strategist*

# Distribution of Women Living Alone by Household Income and Age of Householder, 1997: Black Women Living Alone

*(number and percent distribution of black women living alone by household income and age of householder, 1997; women living alone in thousands as of 1998)*

| | | | | | | | 65 or older | | |
|---|---|---|---|---|---|---|---|---|---|
| | *total* | *15–24* | *25–34* | *35–44* | *45–54* | *55–64* | *total* | *65–74* | *75 or older* |
| **Total women living alone** | **1,982** | **100** | **238** | **267** | **379** | **335** | **663** | **359** | **304** |
| Under $5,000 | 219 | 18 | 33 | 31 | 31 | 38 | 68 | 37 | 31 |
| $5,000–$9,999 | 574 | 42 | 25 | 25 | 48 | 97 | 337 | 171 | 166 |
| $10,000–$14,999 | 250 | 6 | 5 | 24 | 41 | 47 | 128 | 61 | 67 |
| $15,000–$19,999 | 212 | 12 | 35 | 35 | 46 | 43 | 40 | 25 | 16 |
| $20,000–$24,999 | 173 | 12 | 32 | 27 | 37 | 26 | 39 | 24 | 15 |
| $25,000–$29,999 | 123 | 6 | 22 | 23 | 38 | 18 | 16 | 14 | 3 |
| $30,000–$34,999 | 121 | 0 | 32 | 32 | 30 | 21 | 5 | 5 | 0 |
| $35,000–$39,999 | 92 | 4 | 30 | 24 | 23 | 11 | 0 | 0 | 0 |
| $40,000–$44,999 | 56 | 0 | 3 | 15 | 24 | 3 | 12 | 10 | 2 |
| $45,000–$49,999 | 45 | 0 | 4 | 6 | 20 | 10 | 4 | 4 | 0 |
| $50,000–$54,999 | 37 | 0 | 2 | 0 | 13 | 11 | 10 | 6 | 4 |
| $55,000–$59,999 | 31 | 0 | 5 | 15 | 11 | 0 | 0 | 0 | 0 |
| $60,000–$64,999 | 3 | 0 | 0 | 0 | 2 | 1 | 0 | 0 | 0 |
| $65,000–$69,999 | 21 | 0 | 5 | 2 | 8 | 3 | 3 | 3 | 0 |
| $70,000–$74,999 | 1 | 0 | 0 | 0 | 1 | 0 | 0 | 0 | 0 |
| $75,000–$79,999 | 0 | 0 | 0 | 0 | 0 | 0 | 0 | 0 | 0 |
| $80,000–$84,999 | 3 | 0 | 0 | 0 | 2 | 1 | 0 | 0 | 0 |
| $85,000–$89,999 | 8 | 0 | 0 | 5 | 3 | 0 | 0 | 0 | 0 |
| $90,000–$94,999 | 1 | 0 | 0 | 1 | 0 | 0 | 0 | 0 | 0 |
| $95,000–$99,999 | 0 | 0 | 0 | 0 | 0 | 0 | 0 | 0 | 0 |
| $100,000 or more | 8 | 0 | 4 | 0 | 2 | 2 | 0 | 0 | 0 |
| Median income | $13,738 | $7,830 | $23,765 | $22,888 | $22,476 | $12,521 | $8,805 | $9,066 | $8,549 |

**Percent distribution**

| | | | | | | | | | |
|---|---|---|---|---|---|---|---|---|---|
| **Total women living alone** | **100.0%** | **100.0%** | **100.0%** | **100.0%** | **100.0%** | **100.0%** | **100.0%** | **100.0%** | **100.0%** |
| Under $25,000 | 72.0 | 90.0 | 54.6 | 53.2 | 53.6 | 74.9 | 92.3 | 88.6 | 97.0 |
| $25,000–$49,999 | 22.0 | 10.0 | 38.2 | 37.5 | 35.6 | 18.8 | 5.6 | 9.2 | 1.6 |
| $50,000–$74,999 | 4.7 | 0.0 | 5.0 | 6.4 | 9.2 | 4.5 | 2.0 | 2.5 | 1.3 |
| $75,000–$99,999 | 0.6 | 0.0 | 0.0 | 2.2 | 1.3 | 0.3 | 0.0 | 0.0 | 0.0 |
| $100,000 or more | 0.4 | 0.0 | 1.7 | 0.0 | 0.5 | 0.6 | 0.0 | 0.0 | 0.0 |

*Source: Bureau of the Census, Internet web site, <http://www.census.gov/cps/ads/sdata.htm>; calculations by New Strategist*

## Distribution of Women Living Alone by Household Income and Age of Householder, 1997: Hispanic Women Living Alone

*(number and percent distribution of Hispanic women living alone by household income and age of householder, 1997; women living alone in thousands as of 1998)*

| | total | 15–24 | 25–34 | 35–44 | 45–54 | 55–64 | 65 or older total | 65–74 | 75 or older |
|---|---|---|---|---|---|---|---|---|---|
| **Total women living alone** | **617** | **25** | **75** | **71** | **75** | **115** | **256** | **127** | **129** |
| Under $5,000 | 82 | 5 | 9 | 8 | 8 | 24 | 27 | 10 | 18 |
| $5,000–$9,999 | 238 | 4 | 1 | 7 | 19 | 48 | 159 | 75 | 84 |
| $10,000–$14,999 | 90 | 8 | 3 | 14 | 17 | 7 | 40 | 25 | 14 |
| $15,000–$19,999 | 51 | 3 | 9 | 8 | 3 | 10 | 17 | 6 | 9 |
| $20,000–$24,999 | 34 | 0 | 7 | 3 | 4 | 11 | 9 | 9 | 0 |
| $25,000–$29,999 | 34 | 1 | 14 | 3 | 6 | 5 | 3 | 1 | 2 |
| $30,000–$34,999 | 23 | 1 | 6 | 6 | 4 | 3 | 2 | 0 | 2 |
| $35,000–$39,999 | 20 | 0 | 8 | 4 | 7 | 2 | 0 | 0 | 0 |
| $40,000–$44,999 | 13 | 2 | 5 | 0 | 3 | 2 | 0 | 0 | 0 |
| $45,000–$49,999 | 10 | 0 | 3 | 7 | 0 | 0 | 0 | 0 | 0 |
| $50,000–$54,999 | 3 | 0 | 2 | 0 | 1 | 0 | 0 | 0 | 0 |
| $55,000–$59,999 | 5 | 0 | 1 | 3 | 1 | 0 | 0 | 0 | 0 |
| $60,000–$64,999 | 1 | 0 | 0 | 1 | 0 | 0 | 0 | 0 | 0 |
| $65,000–$69,999 | 2 | 0 | 2 | 0 | 0 | 0 | 0 | 0 | 0 |
| $70,000–$74,999 | 2 | 0 | 0 | 1 | 0 | 1 | 0 | 0 | 0 |
| $75,000–$79,999 | 1 | 0 | 0 | 1 | 0 | 0 | 0 | 0 | 0 |
| $80,000–$84,999 | 2 | 0 | 2 | 0 | 0 | 0 | 0 | 0 | 0 |
| $85,000–$89,999 | 0 | 0 | 0 | 0 | 0 | 0 | 0 | 0 | 0 |
| $90,000–$94,999 | 0 | 0 | 0 | 0 | 0 | 0 | 0 | 0 | 0 |
| $95,000–$99,999 | 0 | 0 | 0 | 0 | 0 | 0 | 0 | 0 | 0 |
| $100,000 or more | 6 | 0 | 2 | 2 | 1 | 0 | 0 | 0 | 0 |
| Median income | $9,666 | $11,399 | $27,808 | $18,214 | $11,876 | $7,482 | $7,424 | $8,342 | $6,930 |
| **Percent distribution** | | | | | | | | | |
| **Total women living alone** | **100.0%** | **100.0%** | **100.0%** | **100.0%** | **100.0%** | **100.0%** | **100.0%** | **100.0%** | **100.0%** |
| Under $25,000 | 80.2 | 80.0 | 38.7 | 56.3 | 68.0 | 87.0 | 98.4 | 98.4 | 96.9 |
| $25,000–$49,999 | 16.2 | 16.0 | 48.0 | 28.2 | 26.7 | 10.4 | 2.0 | 0.8 | 3.1 |
| $50,000–$74,999 | 2.1 | 0.0 | 6.7 | 7.0 | 2.7 | 0.9 | 0.0 | 0.0 | 0.0 |
| $75,000–$99,999 | 0.5 | 0.0 | 2.7 | 1.4 | 0.0 | 0.0 | 0.0 | 0.0 | 0.0 |
| $100,000 or more | 1.0 | 0.0 | 2.7 | 2.8 | 1.3 | 0.0 | 0.0 | 0.0 | 0.0 |

*Source: Bureau of the Census, Internet web site, <http://www.census.gov/cps/ads/sdata.htm>; calculations by New Strategist*

## Distribution of Women Living Alone by Household Income and Age of Householder, 1997: White Women Living Alone

*(number and percent distribution of white women living alone by household income and age of householder, 1997; women living alone in thousands as of 1998)*

| | total | 15–24 | 25–34 | 35–44 | 45–54 | 55–64 | 65 or older total | 65–74 | 75 or older |
|---|---|---|---|---|---|---|---|---|---|
| **Total women living alone** | **12,980** | **396** | **1,153** | **1,179** | **1,667** | **1,778** | **6,807** | **2,577** | **4,230** |
| Under $5,000 | 800 | 45 | 67 | 79 | 115 | 158 | 337 | 116 | 221 |
| $5,000–$9,999 | 2,937 | 100 | 52 | 95 | 221 | 353 | 2,118 | 751 | 1,368 |
| $10,000–$14,999 | 2,497 | 67 | 94 | 102 | 165 | 242 | 1,827 | 579 | 1,248 |
| $15,000–$19,999 | 1,554 | 60 | 107 | 68 | 178 | 192 | 950 | 399 | 550 |
| $20,000–$24,999 | 1,152 | 55 | 140 | 133 | 137 | 187 | 501 | 219 | 283 |
| $25,000–$29,999 | 884 | 13 | 162 | 138 | 137 | 114 | 321 | 139 | 182 |
| $30,000–$34,999 | 760 | 21 | 162 | 108 | 133 | 144 | 189 | 100 | 90 |
| $35,000–$39,999 | 530 | 15 | 107 | 87 | 126 | 81 | 114 | 42 | 71 |
| $40,000–$44,999 | 381 | 8 | 88 | 72 | 81 | 60 | 72 | 41 | 31 |
| $45,000–$49,999 | 283 | 3 | 47 | 54 | 50 | 50 | 78 | 43 | 34 |
| $50,000–$54,999 | 261 | 4 | 39 | 59 | 69 | 45 | 45 | 18 | 27 |
| $55,000–$59,999 | 164 | 2 | 24 | 32 | 38 | 27 | 42 | 22 | 19 |
| $60,000–$64,999 | 123 | 0 | 7 | 24 | 37 | 23 | 33 | 18 | 15 |
| $65,000–$69,999 | 130 | 0 | 11 | 27 | 44 | 19 | 28 | 18 | 11 |
| $70,000–$74,999 | 84 | 0 | 5 | 10 | 28 | 12 | 29 | 10 | 19 |
| $75,000–$79,999 | 56 | 0 | 11 | 13 | 14 | 7 | 8 | 7 | 1 |
| $80,000–$84,999 | 36 | 0 | 2 | 8 | 7 | 12 | 7 | 7 | 0 |
| $85,000–$89,999 | 25 | 0 | 6 | 7 | 3 | 1 | 10 | 3 | 7 |
| $90,000–$94,999 | 46 | 0 | 3 | 18 | 11 | 11 | 3 | 0 | 3 |
| $95,000–$99,999 | 49 | 0 | 0 | 14 | 9 | 2 | 24 | 11 | 12 |
| $100,000 or more | 226 | 3 | 19 | 33 | 61 | 37 | 73 | 35 | 39 |
| Median income | $15,818 | $13,304 | $28,501 | $28,881 | $25,527 | $18,713 | $12,282 | $13,564 | $11,795 |
| **Percent distribution** | | | | | | | | | |
| **Total women living alone** | **100.0%** | **100.0%** | **100.0%** | **100.0%** | **100.0%** | **100.0%** | **100.0%** | **100.0%** | **100.0%** |
| Under $25,000 | 68.9 | 82.6 | 39.9 | 40.5 | 49.0 | 63.7 | 84.2 | 80.1 | 86.8 |
| $25,000–$49,999 | 21.9 | 15.2 | 49.1 | 38.9 | 31.6 | 25.3 | 11.4 | 14.2 | 9.6 |
| $50,000–$74,999 | 5.9 | 1.5 | 7.5 | 12.9 | 13.0 | 7.1 | 2.6 | 3.3 | 2.2 |
| $75,000–$99,999 | 1.6 | 0.0 | 1.9 | 5.1 | 2.6 | 1.9 | 0.8 | 1.1 | 0.5 |
| $100,000 or more | 1.7 | 0.8 | 1.6 | 2.8 | 3.7 | 2.1 | 1.1 | 1.4 | 0.9 |

*Source: Bureau of the Census, Internet web site, <http://www.census.gov/cps/ads/sdata.htm>; calculations by New Strategist*

# Incomes Are Low for Men Living Alone

## The median income of men who live alone was well below the national average in 1997.

Both men and women who live alone have below-average incomes, but the median income of men who live alone is considerably higher than that of women living alone—$23,871 versus $15,530 in 1997. The income gap by age is much smaller, however. In fact, the median income of men aged 25 to 34 who live alone is less than that of their female counterparts—$27,124 versus $27,739. The incomes of men who live alone peak in the 45-to-54 age group at $30,554. Those aged 65 or older have a median income of just $16,634.

Most of the income gap between men and women who live alone is explained by their differing ages. While nearly half (49 percent) the women who live alone are aged 65 or older, half the men who live alone are under age 45. Most women who live alone are not in the labor force—they are elderly widows who either never worked or are now retired. Most men who live alone have jobs, which is why their median income is substantially higher.

Black and Hispanic men who live alone have much lower incomes than their white counterparts. The median income of black men who live alone was just $17,139 in 1997, while the figure was an even lower $16,524 for Hispanics. The median income of white men who live alone was a much higher $25,415. Among men aged 65 or older who live alone, the median income of whites was more than double that of Hispanics.

✗ In the years ahead, the incomes of older men who live alone will rise as fewer opt for early retirement.

## Among men who live alone, income peaks in 45-to-54 age group

*(median household income of men who live alone, by age, 1997)*

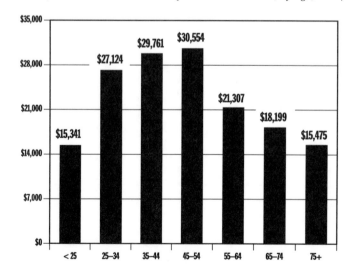

# Distribution of Men Living Alone by Household Income and Age of Householder, 1997: Total Men Living Alone

*(number and percent distribution of men living alone by household income and age of householder, 1997; men living alone in thousands as of 1998)*

| | total | 15–24 | 25–34 | 35–44 | 45–54 | 55–64 | 65 or older total | 65–74 | 75 or older |
|---|---|---|---|---|---|---|---|---|---|
| **Total men living alone** | **11,010** | **723** | **2,222** | **2,555** | **2,011** | **1,153** | **2,345** | **1,111** | **1,234** |
| Under $5,000 | 672 | 113 | 103 | 136 | 145 | 90 | 86 | 37 | 49 |
| $5,000–$9,999 | 1,367 | 121 | 138 | 214 | 209 | 207 | 477 | 234 | 243 |
| $10,000–$14,999 | 1,366 | 121 | 260 | 223 | 133 | 136 | 492 | 189 | 304 |
| $15,000–$19,999 | 1,218 | 94 | 209 | 222 | 200 | 117 | 376 | 174 | 201 |
| $20,000–$24,999 | 1,091 | 80 | 237 | 280 | 184 | 74 | 237 | 99 | 136 |
| $25,000–$29,999 | 861 | 63 | 251 | 210 | 114 | 51 | 171 | 95 | 76 |
| $30,000–$34,999 | 911 | 80 | 276 | 240 | 144 | 63 | 111 | 54 | 56 |
| $35,000–$39,999 | 718 | 14 | 172 | 234 | 146 | 74 | 78 | 50 | 27 |
| $40,000–$44,999 | 515 | 8 | 114 | 136 | 121 | 75 | 60 | 27 | 33 |
| $45,000–$49,999 | 394 | 11 | 89 | 131 | 70 | 47 | 45 | 19 | 26 |
| $50,000–$54,999 | 335 | 8 | 65 | 97 | 109 | 24 | 31 | 23 | 9 |
| $55,000–$59,999 | 244 | 0 | 59 | 77 | 51 | 25 | 33 | 12 | 20 |
| $60,000–$64,999 | 221 | 3 | 60 | 52 | 63 | 31 | 14 | 9 | 5 |
| $65,000–$69,999 | 182 | 5 | 34 | 59 | 46 | 19 | 18 | 16 | 2 |
| $70,000–$74,999 | 154 | 2 | 30 | 41 | 60 | 14 | 7 | 7 | 0 |
| $75,000–$79,999 | 143 | 0 | 46 | 38 | 26 | 15 | 19 | 14 | 4 |
| $80,000–$84,999 | 115 | 0 | 22 | 41 | 30 | 7 | 16 | 11 | 6 |
| $85,000–$89,999 | 46 | 0 | 7 | 9 | 19 | 2 | 8 | 0 | 8 |
| $90,000–$94,999 | 36 | 0 | 10 | 9 | 10 | 1 | 5 | 0 | 5 |
| $95,000–$99,999 | 41 | 0 | 4 | 17 | 12 | 6 | 2 | 2 | 0 |
| $100,000 or more | 380 | 0 | 37 | 89 | 118 | 75 | 61 | 37 | 24 |
| Median income | $23,871 | $15,341 | $27,124 | $29,761 | $30,554 | $21,307 | $16,634 | $18,199 | $15,475 |

**Percent distribution**

| | total | 15–24 | 25–34 | 35–44 | 45–54 | 55–64 | 65 or older total | 65–74 | 75 or older |
|---|---|---|---|---|---|---|---|---|---|
| **Total men living alone** | **100.0%** | **100.0%** | **100.0%** | **100.0%** | **100.0%** | **100.0%** | **100.0%** | **100.0%** | **100.0%** |
| Under $25,000 | 51.9 | 73.2 | 42.6 | 42.1 | 43.3 | 54.1 | 71.1 | 66.0 | 75.6 |
| $25,000–$49,999 | 30.9 | 24.3 | 40.6 | 37.2 | 29.6 | 26.9 | 19.8 | 22.1 | 17.7 |
| $50,000–$74,999 | 10.3 | 2.5 | 11.2 | 12.8 | 16.4 | 9.8 | 4.4 | 6.0 | 2.9 |
| $75,000–$99,999 | 3.5 | 0.0 | 4.0 | 4.5 | 4.8 | 2.7 | 2.1 | 2.4 | 1.9 |
| $100,000 or more | 3.5 | 0.0 | 1.7 | 3.5 | 5.9 | 6.5 | 2.6 | 3.3 | 1.9 |

*Source: Bureau of the Census, Internet web site, <http://www.census.gov/cps/ads/sdata.htm>; calculations by New Strategist*

## Distribution of Men Living Alone by Household Income and Age of Householder, 1997: Black Men Living Alone

*(number and percent distribution of black men living alone by household income and age of householder, 1997; men living alone in thousands as of 1998)*

| | total | 15–24 | 25–34 | 35–44 | 45–54 | 55–64 | 65 or older total | 65–74 | 75 or older |
|---|---|---|---|---|---|---|---|---|---|
| **Total men living alone** | **1,594** | **102** | **342** | **366** | **343** | **176** | **266** | **142** | **124** |
| Under $5,000 | 161 | 29 | 25 | 30 | 44 | 22 | 10 | 7 | 2 |
| $5,000–$9,999 | 339 | 22 | 36 | 61 | 64 | 56 | 101 | 50 | 51 |
| $10,000–$14,999 | 222 | 19 | 71 | 38 | 17 | 29 | 47 | 26 | 21 |
| $15,000–$19,999 | 166 | 5 | 24 | 35 | 41 | 17 | 45 | 23 | 22 |
| $20,000–$24,999 | 182 | 16 | 44 | 49 | 38 | 8 | 28 | 17 | 10 |
| $25,000–$29,999 | 116 | 8 | 30 | 39 | 28 | 4 | 6 | 4 | 2 |
| $30,000–$34,999 | 102 | 2 | 30 | 30 | 23 | 7 | 8 | 5 | 4 |
| $35,000–$39,999 | 81 | 0 | 12 | 29 | 17 | 17 | 6 | 6 | 0 |
| $40,000–$44,999 | 65 | 0 | 38 | 10 | 6 | 7 | 3 | 3 | 0 |
| $45,000–$49,999 | 38 | 0 | 5 | 16 | 8 | 2 | 7 | 0 | 7 |
| $50,000–$54,999 | 37 | 0 | 9 | 6 | 23 | 0 | 0 | 0 | 0 |
| $55,000–$59,999 | 13 | 0 | 0 | 4 | 7 | 2 | 0 | 0 | 0 |
| $60,000–$64,999 | 11 | 0 | 6 | 0 | 6 | 0 | 0 | 0 | 0 |
| $65,000–$69,999 | 15 | 0 | 3 | 5 | 3 | 3 | 0 | 0 | 0 |
| $70,000–$74,999 | 6 | 0 | 2 | 4 | 0 | 0 | 0 | 0 | 0 |
| $75,000–$79,999 | 17 | 0 | 4 | 7 | 6 | 0 | 0 | 0 | 0 |
| $80,000–$84,999 | 6 | 0 | 3 | 3 | 0 | 0 | 0 | 0 | 0 |
| $85,000–$89,999 | 3 | 0 | 0 | 0 | 3 | 0 | 0 | 0 | 0 |
| $90,000–$94,999 | 3 | 0 | 0 | 0 | 0 | 0 | 3 | 0 | 3 |
| $95,000–$99,999 | 0 | 0 | 0 | 0 | 0 | 0 | 0 | 0 | 0 |
| $100,000 or more | 11 | 0 | 0 | 0 | 8 | 0 | 3 | 3 | 0 |
| Median income | $17,139 | $10,048 | $21,682 | $22,524 | $20,484 | $10,956 | $12,120 | $12,198 | $11,995 |

**Percent distribution**

| | total | 15–24 | 25–34 | 35–44 | 45–54 | 55–64 | 65 or older total | 65–74 | 75 or older |
|---|---|---|---|---|---|---|---|---|---|
| **Total men living alone** | **100.0%** | **100.0%** | **100.0%** | **100.0%** | **100.0%** | **100.0%** | **100.0%** | **100.0%** | **100.0%** |
| Under $25,000 | 67.1 | 89.2 | 58.5 | 58.2 | 59.5 | 75.0 | 86.8 | 86.6 | 85.5 |
| $25,000–$49,999 | 25.2 | 9.8 | 33.6 | 33.9 | 23.9 | 21.0 | 11.3 | 12.7 | 10.5 |
| $50,000–$74,999 | 5.1 | 0.0 | 5.8 | 5.2 | 11.4 | 2.8 | 0.0 | 0.0 | 0.0 |
| $75,000–$99,999 | 1.8 | 0.0 | 2.0 | 2.7 | 2.6 | 0.0 | 1.1 | 0.0 | 2.4 |
| $100,000 or more | 0.7 | 0.0 | 0.0 | 0.0 | 2.3 | 0.0 | 1.1 | 2.1 | 0.0 |

*Source: Bureau of the Census, Internet web site, <http://www.census.gov/cps/ads/sdata.htm>; calculations by New Strategist*

# Distribution of Men Living Alone by Household Income and Age of Householder, 1997: Hispanic Men Living Alone

*(number and percent distribution of Hispanic men living alone by household income and age of householder, 1997; men living alone in thousands as of 1998)*

| | | | | | | | 65 or older | | |
|---|---|---|---|---|---|---|---|---|---|
| | *total* | *15–24* | *25–34* | *35–44* | *45–54* | *55–64* | *total* | *65–74* | *75 or older* |
| **Total men living alone** | **623** | **53** | **156** | **159** | **94** | **65** | **95** | **55** | **40** |
| Under $5,000 | 64 | 9 | 14 | 17 | 10 | 3 | 10 | 8 | 3 |
| $5,000–$9,999 | 137 | 10 | 14 | 21 | 18 | 20 | 53 | 28 | 25 |
| $10,000–$14,999 | 80 | 7 | 20 | 18 | 9 | 11 | 17 | 10 | 7 |
| $15,000–$19,999 | 74 | 11 | 17 | 24 | 12 | 7 | 4 | 2 | 2 |
| $20,000–$24,999 | 71 | 3 | 21 | 26 | 9 | 6 | 6 | 4 | 2 |
| $25,000–$29,999 | 40 | 1 | 14 | 13 | 8 | 1 | 3 | 3 | 0 |
| $30,000–$34,999 | 39 | 5 | 13 | 7 | 7 | 4 | 2 | 2 | 0 |
| $35,000–$39,999 | 31 | 1 | 10 | 11 | 6 | 3 | 0 | 0 | 0 |
| $40,000–$44,999 | 18 | 2 | 9 | 2 | 2 | 4 | 0 | 0 | 0 |
| $45,000–$49,999 | 17 | 0 | 9 | 3 | 2 | 1 | 0 | 0 | 0 |
| $50,000–$54,999 | 12 | 3 | 5 | 0 | 1 | 2 | 0 | 0 | 0 |
| $55,000–$59,999 | 8 | 0 | 1 | 3 | 2 | 2 | 0 | 0 | 0 |
| $60,000–$64,999 | 9 | 0 | 2 | 6 | 0 | 0 | 1 | 1 | 0 |
| $65,000–$69,999 | 2 | 0 | 0 | 2 | 0 | 0 | 0 | 0 | 0 |
| $70,000–$74,999 | 8 | 0 | 4 | 0 | 3 | 0 | 0 | 0 | 0 |
| $75,000–$79,999 | 1 | 0 | 0 | 1 | 0 | 0 | 0 | 0 | 0 |
| $80,000–$84,999 | 6 | 0 | 0 | 4 | 2 | 0 | 0 | 0 | 0 |
| $85,000–$89,999 | 1 | 0 | 1 | 0 | 0 | 0 | 0 | 0 | 0 |
| $90,000–$94,999 | 0 | 0 | 0 | 0 | 0 | 0 | 0 | 0 | 0 |
| $95,000–$99,999 | 0 | 0 | 0 | 0 | 0 | 0 | 0 | 0 | 0 |
| $100,000 or more | 5 | 0 | 0 | 3 | 2 | 0 | 0 | 0 | 0 |
| Median income | $16,524 | $15,106 | $22,136 | $20,174 | $19,289 | $14,212 | $8,279 | $8,757 | $7,410 |

| **Percent distribution** | | | | | | | | | |
|---|---|---|---|---|---|---|---|---|---|
| **Total men living alone** | **100.0%** | **100.0%** | **100.0%** | **100.0%** | **100.0%** | **100.0%** | **100.0%** | **100.0%** | **100.0%** |
| Under $25,000 | 68.4 | 75.5 | 55.1 | 66.7 | 61.7 | 72.3 | 94.7 | 94.5 | 97.5 |
| $25,000–$49,999 | 23.3 | 17.0 | 35.3 | 22.6 | 26.6 | 20.0 | 5.3 | 9.1 | 0.0 |
| $50,000–$74,999 | 6.3 | 5.7 | 7.7 | 6.9 | 6.4 | 6.2 | 1.1 | 1.8 | 0.0 |
| $75,000–$99,999 | 1.3 | 0.0 | 0.6 | 3.1 | 2.1 | 0.0 | 0.0 | 0.0 | 0.0 |
| $100,000 or more | 0.8 | 0.0 | 0.0 | 1.9 | 2.1 | 0.0 | 0.0 | 0.0 | 0.0 |

*Source: Bureau of the Census, Internet web site, <http://www.census.gov/cps/ads/sdata.htm>; calculations by New Strategist*

# Distribution of Men Living Alone by Household Income and Age of Householder, 1997: White Men Living Alone

*(number and percent distribution of white men living alone by household income and age of householder, 1997; men living alone in thousands as of 1998)*

| | total | 15–24 | 25–34 | 35–44 | 45–54 | 55–64 | 65 or older total | 65–74 | 75 or older |
|---|---|---|---|---|---|---|---|---|---|
| **Total men living alone** | **9,018** | **576** | **1,728** | **2,113** | **1,613** | **939** | **2,050** | **951** | **1,099** |
| Under $5,000 | 455 | 74 | 63 | 94 | 88 | 65 | 72 | 27 | 45 |
| $5,000–$9,999 | 985 | 95 | 97 | 152 | 138 | 137 | 366 | 183 | 183 |
| $10,000–$14,999 | 1,112 | 95 | 174 | 180 | 113 | 107 | 444 | 161 | 283 |
| $15,000–$19,999 | 1,017 | 86 | 173 | 185 | 146 | 99 | 329 | 151 | 179 |
| $20,000–$24,999 | 865 | 58 | 175 | 222 | 142 | 61 | 206 | 80 | 126 |
| $25,000–$29,999 | 702 | 50 | 202 | 160 | 82 | 43 | 165 | 91 | 74 |
| $30,000–$34,999 | 787 | 75 | 237 | 201 | 119 | 53 | 101 | 50 | 52 |
| $35,000–$39,999 | 612 | 13 | 145 | 199 | 129 | 57 | 68 | 41 | 27 |
| $40,000–$44,999 | 433 | 6 | 75 | 117 | 110 | 67 | 57 | 24 | 33 |
| $45,000–$49,999 | 337 | 9 | 74 | 111 | 61 | 45 | 38 | 19 | 19 |
| $50,000–$54,999 | 292 | 8 | 54 | 92 | 87 | 24 | 27 | 19 | 9 |
| $55,000–$59,999 | 221 | 0 | 53 | 69 | 44 | 21 | 33 | 12 | 20 |
| $60,000–$64,999 | 199 | 0 | 50 | 50 | 56 | 29 | 14 | 9 | 5 |
| $65,000–$69,999 | 163 | 5 | 27 | 54 | 43 | 15 | 18 | 16 | 2 |
| $70,000–$74,999 | 146 | 2 | 25 | 37 | 60 | 14 | 7 | 7 | 0 |
| $75,000–$79,999 | 120 | 0 | 37 | 31 | 20 | 13 | 19 | 14 | 4 |
| $80,000–$84,999 | 105 | 0 | 16 | 38 | 30 | 7 | 15 | 9 | 6 |
| $85,000–$89,999 | 43 | 0 | 7 | 9 | 16 | 2 | 8 | 0 | 8 |
| $90,000–$94,999 | 27 | 0 | 10 | 3 | 10 | 1 | 2 | 0 | 2 |
| $95,000–$99,999 | 41 | 0 | 4 | 17 | 12 | 6 | 2 | 2 | 0 |
| $100,000 or more | 354 | 0 | 28 | 89 | 108 | 71 | 58 | 34 | 24 |
| Median income | $25,415 | $16,297 | $28,980 | $31,167 | $33,987 | $24,992 | $17,219 | $18,732 | $15,949 |

| **Percent distribution** | | | | | | | | | |
|---|---|---|---|---|---|---|---|---|---|
| **Total men living alone** | **100.0%** | **100.0%** | **100.0%** | **100.0%** | **100.0%** | **100.0%** | **100.0%** | **100.0%** | **100.0%** |
| Under $25,000 | 49.2 | 70.8 | 39.5 | 39.4 | 38.9 | 49.9 | 69.1 | 63.3 | 74.2 |
| $25,000–$49,999 | 31.8 | 26.6 | 42.4 | 37.3 | 31.1 | 28.2 | 20.9 | 23.7 | 18.7 |
| $50,000–$74,999 | 11.3 | 2.6 | 12.1 | 14.3 | 18.0 | 11.0 | 4.8 | 6.6 | 3.3 |
| $75,000–$99,999 | 3.7 | 0.0 | 4.3 | 4.6 | 5.5 | 3.1 | 2.2 | 2.6 | 1.8 |
| $100,000 or more | 3.9 | 0.0 | 1.6 | 4.2 | 6.7 | 7.6 | 2.8 | 3.6 | 2.2 |

*Source: Bureau of the Census, Internet web site, <http://www.census.gov/cps/ads/sdata.htm>; calculations by New Strategist*

# Below-Average Incomes for Single-Earner Households

## Households with two earners have incomes that are well above average.

The median income of households with one earner stood at $29,780 in 1997, 20 percent below the national median of $37,005. In contrast, the median income of two-earner households was $54,192—46 percent higher than average. Only 5 percent of one-earner households have incomes of $100,000 or more versus 14 percent of households with two earners. Households with no earners had a median income of just $14,142.

Not surprisingly, households with three or more earners have the highest incomes, a median of $71,595. Only 10 percent of households have three or more earners, however. Thirty-five percent of households have two earners, 34 percent have one, and 21 percent have none.

While the median income of black households is just 64 percent as high as that of white households, among two-earner households the black median is 81 percent as high as that of whites. The overall black household median is much lower than the white median because 65 percent of black households have no or only one earner compared to 54 percent of white households. The median income of Hispanic households with two earners was just $37,106 in 1997. Hispanic household incomes are much lower than those of whites because many Hispanics are recent immigrants with low earnings.

✘ The number of households with no earners should surge in another decade as the oldest boomers retire.

### Households with three or more earners have highest incomes

*(median income of households by number of earners, 1997)*

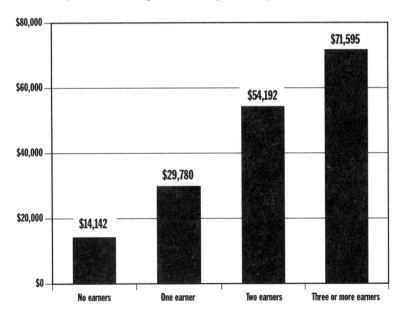

# Distribution of Households by Income and Number of Earners, 1997: Total Households

*(number and percent distribution of households by household income and number of earners, 1997; households in thousands as of 1998)*

| | total | no earners | one earner | two or more earners total | two earners | three or more earners |
|---|---|---|---|---|---|---|
| **Total households** | **102,528** | **21,280** | **35,150** | **46,098** | **36,188** | **9,909** |
| Under $5,000 | 3,531 | 2,185 | 1,206 | 141 | 134 | 7 |
| $5,000–$9,999 | 7,765 | 5,084 | 2,364 | 318 | 301 | 16 |
| $10,000–$14,999 | 8,326 | 3,987 | 3,501 | 837 | 794 | 44 |
| $15,000–$19,999 | 7,837 | 2,819 | 3,683 | 1,335 | 1,236 | 98 |
| $20,000–$24,999 | 7,406 | 1,966 | 3,640 | 1,802 | 1,613 | 188 |
| $25,000–$29,999 | 6,913 | 1,310 | 3,299 | 2,305 | 2,060 | 245 |
| $30,000–$34,999 | 6,673 | 935 | 3,150 | 2,589 | 2,289 | 301 |
| $35,000–$39,999 | 6,111 | 699 | 2,634 | 2,776 | 2,349 | 428 |
| $40,000–$44,999 | 5,667 | 467 | 1,990 | 3,210 | 2,690 | 520 |
| $45,000–$49,999 | 4,920 | 330 | 1,539 | 3,051 | 2,463 | 587 |
| $50,000–$54,999 | 4,864 | 292 | 1,430 | 3,141 | 2,502 | 639 |
| $55,000–$59,999 | 3,864 | 207 | 981 | 2,677 | 2,081 | 595 |
| $60,000–$64,999 | 3,751 | 121 | 905 | 2,725 | 2,165 | 560 |
| $65,000–$69,999 | 3,298 | 129 | 803 | 2,366 | 1,805 | 561 |
| $70,000–$74,999 | 2,754 | 92 | 573 | 2,088 | 1,604 | 483 |
| $75,000–$79,999 | 2,399 | 103 | 475 | 1,822 | 1,284 | 539 |
| $80,000–$84,999 | 2,251 | 84 | 422 | 1,745 | 1,243 | 502 |
| $85,000–$89,999 | 1,702 | 66 | 300 | 1,334 | 944 | 392 |
| $90,000–$94,999 | 1,509 | 29 | 221 | 1,259 | 846 | 415 |
| $95,000–$99,999 | 1,325 | 47 | 194 | 1,083 | 699 | 384 |
| $100,000 or more | 9,661 | 327 | 1,840 | 7,494 | 5,085 | 2,408 |
| Median income | $37,005 | $14,142 | $29,780 | $57,525 | $54,192 | $71,595 |
| **Percent distribution** | | | | | | |
| **Total households** | **100.0%** | **100.0%** | **100.0%** | **100.0%** | **100.0%** | **100.0%** |
| Under $25,000 | 34.0 | 75.4 | 41.0 | 9.6 | 11.3 | 3.6 |
| $25,000–$49,999 | 29.5 | 17.6 | 35.9 | 30.2 | 32.7 | 21.0 |
| $50,000–$74,999 | 18.1 | 4.0 | 13.3 | 28.2 | 28.1 | 28.6 |
| $75,000–$99,999 | 9.0 | 1.5 | 4.6 | 15.7 | 13.9 | 22.5 |
| $100,000 or more | 9.4 | 1.5 | 5.2 | 16.3 | 14.1 | 24.3 |

*Source: Bureau of the Census, Internet web site, <http://www.census.gov/cps/ads/sdata.htm>; calculations by New Strategist*

# Distribution of Households by Income and Number of Earners, 1997: Black Households

*(number and percent distribution of black households by household income and number of earners, 1997; households in thousands as of 1998)*

| | total | no earners | one earner | two or more earners total | two earners | three or more earners |
|---|---|---|---|---|---|---|
| **Total households** | **12,474** | **2,660** | **5,428** | **4,386** | **3,459** | **927** |
| Under $5,000 | 925 | 581 | 335 | 10 | 10 | 0 |
| $5,000–$9,999 | 1,747 | 1,046 | 647 | 55 | 51 | 4 |
| $10,000–$14,999 | 1,316 | 430 | 747 | 139 | 129 | 11 |
| $15,000–$19,999 | 1,175 | 213 | 790 | 173 | 155 | 18 |
| $20,000–$24,999 | 1,062 | 139 | 667 | 257 | 237 | 20 |
| $25,000–$29,999 | 934 | 57 | 554 | 322 | 287 | 35 |
| $30,000–$34,999 | 832 | 58 | 428 | 346 | 308 | 38 |
| $35,000–$39,999 | 689 | 51 | 321 | 317 | 271 | 47 |
| $40,000–$44,999 | 642 | 22 | 243 | 376 | 300 | 76 |
| $45,000–$49,999 | 528 | 11 | 173 | 343 | 279 | 64 |
| $50,000–$54,999 | 444 | 18 | 120 | 305 | 235 | 71 |
| $55,000–$59,999 | 398 | 6 | 104 | 288 | 220 | 69 |
| $60,000–$64,999 | 294 | 9 | 63 | 221 | 164 | 58 |
| $65,000–$69,999 | 304 | 5 | 71 | 226 | 186 | 41 |
| $70,000–$74,999 | 197 | 0 | 29 | 168 | 109 | 60 |
| $75,000–$79,999 | 140 | 0 | 25 | 116 | 75 | 39 |
| $80,000–$84,999 | 162 | 3 | 29 | 131 | 82 | 49 |
| $85,000–$89,999 | 111 | 0 | 25 | 85 | 61 | 24 |
| $90,000–$94,999 | 78 | 3 | 7 | 67 | 48 | 20 |
| $95,000–$99,999 | 79 | 0 | 3 | 76 | 45 | 30 |
| $100,000 or more | 415 | 7 | 47 | 361 | 209 | 152 |
| Median income | $25,050 | $8,172 | $21,319 | $47,602 | $44,728 | $61,234 |
| **Percent distribution** | | | | | | |
| **Total households** | **100.0%** | **100.0%** | **100.0%** | **100.0%** | **100.0%** | **100.0%** |
| Under $25,000 | 49.9 | 90.6 | 58.7 | 14.5 | 16.8 | 5.7 |
| $25,000–$49,999 | 29.1 | 7.5 | 31.7 | 38.9 | 41.8 | 28.0 |
| $50,000–$74,999 | 13.1 | 1.4 | 7.1 | 27.5 | 26.4 | 32.3 |
| $75,000–$99,999 | 4.6 | 0.2 | 1.6 | 10.8 | 9.0 | 17.5 |
| $100,000 or more | 3.3 | 0.3 | 0.9 | 8.2 | 6.0 | 16.4 |

*Source: Bureau of the Census, Internet web site, <http://www.census.gov/cps/ads/sdata.htm>; calculations by New Strategist*

## Distribution of Households by Income and Number of Earners, 1997: Hispanic Households

*(number and percent distribution of Hispanic households by household income and number of earners, 1997; households in thousands as of 1998)*

| | total | no earners | one earner | two or more earners total | two earners | three or more earners |
|---|---|---|---|---|---|---|
| **Total households** | **8,590** | **1,312** | **3,081** | **4,197** | **3,096** | **1,101** |
| Under $5,000 | 473 | 289 | 155 | 29 | 29 | 0 |
| $5,000–$9,999 | 968 | 540 | 355 | 73 | 68 | 4 |
| $10,000–$14,999 | 916 | 211 | 527 | 178 | 165 | 13 |
| $15,000–$19,999 | 840 | 113 | 453 | 274 | 245 | 30 |
| $20,000–$24,999 | 851 | 73 | 402 | 375 | 320 | 56 |
| $25,000–$29,999 | 672 | 30 | 275 | 368 | 308 | 59 |
| $30,000–$34,999 | 618 | 23 | 227 | 368 | 292 | 77 |
| $35,000–$39,999 | 534 | 6 | 186 | 341 | 260 | 83 |
| $40,000–$44,999 | 490 | 12 | 115 | 364 | 253 | 110 |
| $45,000–$49,999 | 404 | 8 | 86 | 311 | 212 | 99 |
| $50,000–$54,999 | 310 | 2 | 61 | 247 | 164 | 83 |
| $55,000–$59,999 | 226 | 0 | 40 | 187 | 107 | 80 |
| $60,000–$64,999 | 216 | 3 | 38 | 175 | 120 | 53 |
| $65,000–$69,999 | 152 | 2 | 31 | 120 | 81 | 39 |
| $70,000–$74,999 | 142 | 0 | 27 | 115 | 84 | 31 |
| $75,000–$79,999 | 130 | 1 | 14 | 115 | 67 | 48 |
| $80,000–$84,999 | 106 | 0 | 23 | 82 | 51 | 31 |
| $85,000–$89,999 | 70 | 0 | 7 | 62 | 33 | 29 |
| $90,000–$94,999 | 70 | 0 | 3 | 67 | 36 | 30 |
| $95,000–$99,999 | 53 | 0 | 3 | 50 | 34 | 16 |
| $100,000 or more | 351 | 0 | 53 | 298 | 169 | 130 |
| Median income | $26,628 | $7,842 | $20,464 | $41,081 | $37,106 | $50,921 |
| **Percent distribution** | | | | | | |
| **Total households** | **100.0%** | **100.0%** | **100.0%** | **100.0%** | **100.0%** | **100.0%** |
| Under $25,000 | 47.1 | 93.4 | 61.4 | 22.1 | 26.7 | 9.4 |
| $25,000–$49,999 | 31.6 | 6.0 | 28.9 | 41.7 | 42.8 | 38.9 |
| $50,000–$74,999 | 12.2 | 0.5 | 6.4 | 20.1 | 18.0 | 26.0 |
| $75,000–$99,999 | 5.0 | 0.1 | 1.6 | 9.0 | 7.1 | 14.0 |
| $100,000 or more | 4.1 | 0.0 | 1.7 | 7.1 | 5.5 | 11.8 |

*Source: Bureau of the Census, Internet web site, <http://www.census.gov/cps/ads/sdata.htm>; calculations by New Strategist*

# Distribution of Households by Income and Number of Earners, 1997: White Households

*(number and percent distribution of white households by household income and number of earners, 1997; households in thousands as of 1998)*

| | | | | two or more earners | | |
|---|---|---|---|---|---|---|
| | total | no earners | one earner | total | two earners | three or more earners |
| **Total households** | **86,106** | **18,104** | **28,332** | **39,670** | **31,256** | **8,414** |
| Under $5,000 | 2,415 | 1,482 | 811 | 122 | 115 | 7 |
| $5,000–$9,999 | 5,773 | 3,911 | 1,614 | 248 | 236 | 11 |
| $10,000–$14,999 | 6,716 | 3,486 | 2,591 | 639 | 613 | 25 |
| $15,000–$19,999 | 6,436 | 2,566 | 2,752 | 1,117 | 1,039 | 78 |
| $20,000–$24,999 | 6,114 | 1,781 | 2,870 | 1,462 | 1,310 | 151 |
| $25,000–$29,999 | 5,738 | 1,226 | 2,623 | 1,889 | 1,688 | 201 |
| $30,000–$34,999 | 5,612 | 842 | 2,614 | 2,156 | 1,904 | 253 |
| $35,000–$39,999 | 5,166 | 633 | 2,217 | 2,317 | 1,967 | 350 |
| $40,000–$44,999 | 4,803 | 438 | 1,678 | 2,687 | 2,277 | 409 |
| $45,000–$49,999 | 4,201 | 318 | 1,286 | 2,596 | 2,094 | 501 |
| $50,000–$54,999 | 4,278 | 269 | 1,281 | 2,728 | 2,186 | 543 |
| $55,000–$59,999 | 3,312 | 196 | 828 | 2,288 | 1,790 | 497 |
| $60,000–$64,999 | 3,277 | 112 | 785 | 2,380 | 1,911 | 468 |
| $65,000–$69,999 | 2,861 | 119 | 706 | 2,037 | 1,558 | 478 |
| $70,000–$74,999 | 2,462 | 92 | 518 | 1,852 | 1,445 | 406 |
| $75,000–$79,999 | 2,150 | 102 | 429 | 1,620 | 1,159 | 461 |
| $80,000–$84,999 | 1,998 | 79 | 374 | 1,545 | 1,121 | 424 |
| $85,000–$89,999 | 1,509 | 63 | 263 | 1,183 | 836 | 346 |
| $90,000–$94,999 | 1,363 | 26 | 202 | 1,136 | 755 | 381 |
| $95,000–$99,999 | 1,163 | 47 | 175 | 942 | 612 | 328 |
| $100,000 or more | 8,762 | 318 | 1,715 | 6,729 | 4,635 | 2,094 |
| Median income | $38,972 | $15,324 | $31,412 | $58,947 | $55,474 | $ 72,862 |

| **Percent distribution** | | | | | | |
|---|---|---|---|---|---|---|
| **Total households** | **100.0%** | **100.0%** | **100.0%** | **100.0%** | **100.0%** | **100.0%** |
| Under $25,000 | 31.9 | 73.1 | 37.5 | 9.0 | 10.6 | 3.2 |
| $25,000–$49,999 | 29.6 | 19.1 | 36.8 | 29.4 | 31.8 | 20.4 |
| $50,000–$74,999 | 18.8 | 4.4 | 14.5 | 28.4 | 28.4 | 28.4 |
| $75,000–$99,999 | 9.5 | 1.8 | 5.1 | 16.2 | 14.3 | 23.1 |
| $100,000 or more | 10.2 | 1.8 | 6.1 | 17.0 | 14.8 | 24.9 |

*Source: Bureau of the Census, Internet web site, <http://www.census.gov/cps/ads/sdata.htm>; calculations by New Strategist*

# Married Couples with Children Have Higher Incomes

### Couples with school-aged children have the highest incomes.

Married couples with children aged 6 to 17 had a median income of $58,871 in 1997, much higher than the median income of couples with younger or no children at home. Behind these income differences are the differing ages of these married couples. Those with school-aged children are generally older and more likely to be in their peak-earning years than those with younger children. Many couples without children at home are empty nesters and retired, which accounts for their lower incomes.

Couples with children aged 6 to 17 have the highest median incomes among black, white, Hispanic, and non-Hispanic white couples. The figure ranges from a low of $40,048 for Hispanic couples to a high of $62,343 for non-Hispanic white couples. Nineteen percent of non-Hispanic white couples with children aged 6 to 17 had incomes of $100,000 or more compared with only 10 percent of black and 7 percent of Hispanic couples.

✘ Because many of the nation's most affluent households are married couples with school-aged children, marketers targeting the affluent should focus on the wants and needs of parents.

### Non-Hispanic white couples with children aged 6 to 17 have the highest incomes

*(median income of married couples with children aged 6 to 17 at home, by race and Hispanic origin, 1997)*

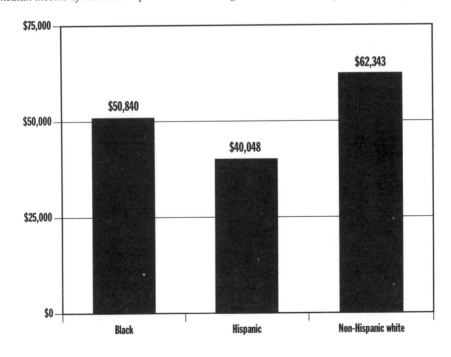

## Distribution of Married Couples by Household Income and Presence of Children, 1997: Total Married Couples

*(number and percent distribution of married couples by household income and presence and age of related children under age 18 at home, 1997; married couples in thousands as of 1998)*

| | | | one or more children under age 18 | | | |
|---|---|---|---|---|---|---|
| | total | no children | total | all under 6 | some < 6, some 6–17 | all 6–17 |
| **Total married couples** | **54,321** | **27,892** | **26,430** | **6,790** | **5,810** | **13,830** |
| Under $5,000 | 595 | 320 | 274 | 77 | 75 | 122 |
| $5,000–$9,999 | 893 | 533 | 360 | 113 | 91 | 156 |
| $10,000–$14,999 | 2,100 | 1,283 | 817 | 258 | 232 | 327 |
| $15,000–$19,999 | 2,787 | 1,774 | 1,013 | 357 | 285 | 371 |
| $20,000–$24,999 | 3,111 | 1,838 | 1,274 | 440 | 323 | 510 |
| $25,000–$29,999 | 3,172 | 1,852 | 1,320 | 368 | 362 | 588 |
| $30,000–$34,999 | 3,325 | 1,816 | 1,509 | 397 | 432 | 681 |
| $35,000–$39,999 | 3,374 | 1,758 | 1,616 | 431 | 409 | 776 |
| $40,000–$44,999 | 3,455 | 1,702 | 1,753 | 522 | 400 | 831 |
| $45,000–$49,999 | 3,148 | 1,434 | 1,715 | 424 | 404 | 887 |
| $50,000–$54,999 | 3,291 | 1,561 | 1,730 | 412 | 303 | 1,015 |
| $55,000–$59,999 | 2,705 | 1,210 | 1,495 | 390 | 298 | 808 |
| $60,000–$64,999 | 2,703 | 1,192 | 1,511 | 378 | 321 | 811 |
| $65,000–$69,999 | 2,388 | 1,056 | 1,331 | 317 | 268 | 747 |
| $70,000–$74,999 | 2,113 | 956 | 1,159 | 281 | 253 | 623 |
| $75,000–$79,999 | 1,827 | 826 | 1,001 | 232 | 184 | 586 |
| $80,000–$84,999 | 1,735 | 845 | 890 | 198 | 166 | 526 |
| $85,000–$89,999 | 1,385 | 699 | 686 | 139 | 114 | 433 |
| $90,000–$94,999 | 1,245 | 642 | 603 | 111 | 113 | 379 |
| $95,000–$99,999 | 1,031 | 535 | 496 | 104 | 97 | 295 |
| $100,000 or more | 7,937 | 4,058 | 3,879 | 840 | 678 | 2,361 |
| Median income | $51,591 | $48,588 | $54,395 | $50,059 | $48,580 | $58,871 |
| **Percent distribution** | | | | | | |
| **Total married couples** | **100.0%** | **100.0%** | **100.0%** | **100.0%** | **100.0%** | **100.0%** |
| Under $25,000 | 17.5 | 20.6 | 14.1 | 18.3 | 17.3 | 10.7 |
| $25,000–$49,999 | 30.3 | 30.7 | 29.9 | 31.5 | 34.5 | 27.2 |
| $50,000–$74,999 | 24.3 | 21.4 | 27.3 | 26.2 | 24.8 | 29.0 |
| $75,000–$99,999 | 13.3 | 12.7 | 13.9 | 11.5 | 11.6 | 16.0 |
| $100,000 or more | 14.6 | 14.5 | 14.7 | 12.4 | 11.7 | 17.1 |

*Source: Bureau of the Census, Internet web site, <http://www.census.gov/cps/ads/sdata.htm>; calculations by New Strategist*

# Distribution of Married Couples by Household Income and Presence of Children, 1997: Black Married Couples

*(number and percent distribution of black married couples by household income and presence and age of related children under age 18 at home, 1997; married couples in thousands as of 1998)*

| | | no | one or more children under age 18 | | | |
| | total | children | total | all under 6 | some < 6, some 6–17 | all 6–17 |
|---|---|---|---|---|---|---|
| **Total married couples** | **3,921** | **1,646** | **2,275** | **522** | **501** | **1,252** |
| Under $5,000 | 64 | 25 | 39 | 12 | 11 | 17 |
| $5,000–$9,999 | 122 | 78 | 44 | 8 | 12 | 25 |
| $10,000–$14,999 | 176 | 113 | 63 | 11 | 14 | 37 |
| $15,000–$19,999 | 251 | 125 | 127 | 39 | 33 | 55 |
| $20,000–$24,999 | 240 | 79 | 161 | 50 | 30 | 79 |
| $25,000–$29,999 | 255 | 118 | 136 | 39 | 30 | 67 |
| $30,000–$34,999 | 265 | 119 | 145 | 26 | 48 | 71 |
| $35,000–$39,999 | 248 | 123 | 124 | 33 | 17 | 73 |
| $40,000–$44,999 | 315 | 126 | 189 | 52 | 39 | 98 |
| $45,000–$49,999 | 279 | 83 | 197 | 38 | 75 | 84 |
| $50,000–$54,999 | 242 | 72 | 169 | 47 | 30 | 91 |
| $55,000–$59,999 | 237 | 88 | 148 | 44 | 23 | 81 |
| $60,000–$64,999 | 207 | 92 | 115 | 32 | 23 | 59 |
| $65,000–$69,999 | 184 | 64 | 119 | 15 | 25 | 80 |
| $70,000–$74,999 | 140 | 29 | 111 | 13 | 28 | 71 |
| $75,000–$79,999 | 89 | 31 | 58 | 8 | 6 | 44 |
| $80,000–$84,999 | 118 | 49 | 70 | 11 | 13 | 46 |
| $85,000–$89,999 | 66 | 26 | 40 | 8 | 7 | 26 |
| $90,000–$94,999 | 56 | 28 | 28 | 0 | 5 | 24 |
| $95,000–$99,999 | 54 | 26 | 28 | 11 | 14 | 3 |
| $100,000 or more | 312 | 150 | 162 | 23 | 16 | 122 |
| Median income | $45,372 | $41,656 | $47,631 | $44,155 | $46,040 | $50,840 |
| **Percent distribution** | | | | | | |
| **Total married couples** | **100.0%** | **100.0%** | **100.0%** | **100.0%** | **100.0%** | **100.0%** |
| Under $25,000 | 21.8 | 25.5 | 19.1 | 23.0 | 20.0 | 17.0 |
| $25,000–$49,999 | 34.7 | 34.6 | 34.8 | 36.0 | 41.7 | 31.4 |
| $50,000–$74,999 | 25.8 | 21.0 | 29.1 | 28.9 | 25.7 | 30.5 |
| $75,000–$99,999 | 9.8 | 9.7 | 9.8 | 7.3 | 9.0 | 11.4 |
| $100,000 or more | 8.0 | 9.1 | 7.1 | 4.4 | 3.2 | 9.7 |

*Source: Bureau of the Census, Internet web site, <http://www.census.gov/cps/ads/sdata.htm>; calculations by New Strategist*

# Distribution of Married Couples by Household Income and Presence of Children, 1997: Hispanic Married Couples

*(number and percent distribution of Hispanic married couples by household income and presence and age of related children under age 18 at home, 1997; married couples in thousands as of 1998)*

| | total | no children | one or more children under age 18 | | | |
|---|---|---|---|---|---|---|
| | | | total | all under 6 | some < 6, some 6–17 | all 6–17 |
| **Total married couples** | **4,804** | **1,511** | **3,293** | **868** | **1,044** | **1,381** |
| Under $5,000 | 123 | 45 | 78 | 26 | 24 | 28 |
| $5,000–$9,999 | 206 | 76 | 130 | 42 | 43 | 45 |
| $10,000–$14,999 | 434 | 129 | 305 | 90 | 104 | 110 |
| $15,000–$19,999 | 420 | 125 | 296 | 90 | 115 | 89 |
| $20,000–$24,999 | 506 | 147 | 359 | 112 | 121 | 126 |
| $25,000–$29,999 | 401 | 104 | 298 | 78 | 124 | 96 |
| $30,000–$34,999 | 376 | 127 | 249 | 48 | 113 | 89 |
| $35,000–$39,999 | 355 | 102 | 254 | 70 | 77 | 106 |
| $40,000–$44,999 | 325 | 97 | 228 | 65 | 61 | 103 |
| $45,000–$49,999 | 268 | 68 | 200 | 27 | 56 | 117 |
| $50,000–$54,999 | 225 | 76 | 149 | 36 | 34 | 79 |
| $55,000–$59,999 | 166 | 46 | 120 | 31 | 21 | 68 |
| $60,000–$64,999 | 164 | 52 | 112 | 22 | 29 | 62 |
| $65,000–$69,999 | 105 | 42 | 61 | 11 | 18 | 32 |
| $70,000–$74,999 | 94 | 35 | 59 | 15 | 14 | 30 |
| $75,000–$79,999 | 96 | 38 | 59 | 20 | 18 | 20 |
| $80,000–$84,999 | 80 | 27 | 53 | 20 | 7 | 26 |
| $85,000–$89,999 | 56 | 21 | 35 | 6 | 9 | 20 |
| $90,000–$94,999 | 63 | 27 | 35 | 7 | 5 | 23 |
| $95,000–$99,999 | 49 | 12 | 36 | 8 | 12 | 17 |
| $100,000 or more | 290 | 114 | 175 | 42 | 37 | 96 |
| Median income | $33,914 | $35,099 | $33,233 | $29,700 | $29,473 | $40,048 |
| | | | | | | |
| **Percent distribution** | | | | | | |
| **Total married couples** | **100.0%** | **100.0%** | **100.0%** | **100.0%** | **100.0%** | **100.0%** |
| Under $25,000 | 35.2 | 34.5 | 35.5 | 41.5 | 39.0 | 28.8 |
| $25,000–$49,999 | 35.9 | 33.0 | 37.3 | 33.2 | 41.3 | 37.0 |
| $50,000–$74,999 | 15.7 | 16.6 | 15.2 | 13.2 | 11.1 | 19.6 |
| $75,000–$99,999 | 7.2 | 8.3 | 6.6 | 7.0 | 4.9 | 7.7 |
| $100,000 or more | 6.0 | 7.5 | 5.3 | 4.8 | 3.5 | 7.0 |

*Source: Bureau of the Census, Internet web site, <http://www.census.gov/cps/ads/sdata.htm>; calculations by New Strategist*

# Distribution of Married Couples by Household Income and Presence of Children, 1997: White Married Couples

*(number and percent distribution of white married couples by household income and presence and age of related children under age 18 at home, 1997; married couples in thousands as of 1998)*

| | | | one or more children under age 18 | | | |
|---|---|---|---|---|---|---|
| | total | no children | total | all under 6 | some < 6, some 6–17 | all 6–17 |
| **Total married couples** | **48,070** | **25,287** | **22,783** | **5,890** | **5,013** | **11,881** |
| Under $5,000 | 483 | 271 | 212 | 63 | 55 | 94 |
| $5,000–$9,999 | 723 | 436 | 286 | 102 | 68 | 116 |
| $10,000–$14,999 | 1,811 | 1,122 | 689 | 230 | 199 | 259 |
| $15,000–$19,999 | 2,440 | 1,612 | 829 | 299 | 236 | 294 |
| $20,000–$24,999 | 2,757 | 1,701 | 1,057 | 369 | 284 | 404 |
| $25,000–$29,999 | 2,799 | 1,672 | 1,127 | 309 | 310 | 507 |
| $30,000–$34,999 | 2,928 | 1,632 | 1,296 | 355 | 371 | 570 |
| $35,000–$39,999 | 2,969 | 1,565 | 1,404 | 379 | 369 | 655 |
| $40,000–$44,999 | 2,994 | 1,515 | 1,479 | 452 | 347 | 679 |
| $45,000–$49,999 | 2,740 | 1,309 | 1,431 | 359 | 309 | 763 |
| $50,000–$54,999 | 2,947 | 1,434 | 1,513 | 355 | 265 | 894 |
| $55,000–$59,999 | 2,357 | 1,091 | 1,266 | 325 | 249 | 690 |
| $60,000–$64,999 | 2,375 | 1,074 | 1,301 | 327 | 284 | 689 |
| $65,000–$69,999 | 2,113 | 968 | 1,145 | 281 | 235 | 629 |
| $70,000–$74,999 | 1,900 | 900 | 1,001 | 245 | 222 | 533 |
| $75,000–$79,999 | 1,649 | 764 | 885 | 197 | 171 | 517 |
| $80,000–$84,999 | 1,559 | 764 | 796 | 185 | 146 | 464 |
| $85,000–$89,999 | 1,252 | 654 | 599 | 127 | 97 | 375 |
| $90,000–$94,999 | 1,135 | 591 | 544 | 99 | 105 | 338 |
| $95,000–$99,999 | 915 | 479 | 436 | 82 | 75 | 278 |
| $100,000 or more | 7,223 | 3,733 | 3,490 | 746 | 614 | 2,130 |
| Median income | $52,098 | $49,219 | $55,232 | $50,321 | $49,298 | $60,073 |
| | | | | | | |
| **Percent distribution** | | | | | | |
| **Total married couples** | **100.0%** | **100.0%** | **100.0%** | **100.0%** | **100.0%** | **100.0%** |
| Under $25,000 | 17.1 | 20.3 | 13.5 | 18.0 | 16.8 | 9.8 |
| $25,000–$49,999 | 30.0 | 30.4 | 29.6 | 31.5 | 34.0 | 26.7 |
| $50,000–$74,999 | 24.3 | 21.6 | 27.3 | 26.0 | 25.0 | 28.9 |
| $75,000–$99,999 | 13.5 | 12.9 | 14.3 | 11.7 | 11.8 | 16.6 |
| $100,000 or more | 15.0 | 14.8 | 15.3 | 12.7 | 12.2 | 17.9 |

*Source: Bureau of the Census, Internet web site, <http://www.census.gov/cps/ads/sdata.htm>; calculations by New Strategist*

# Distribution of Married Couples by Household Income and Presence of Children, 1997: Non-Hispanic White Married Couples

*(number and percent distribution of non-Hispanic white married couples by household income and presence and age of related children under age 18 at home, 1997; married couples in thousands as of 1998)*

| | | | one or more children under age 18 | | | |
|---|---|---|---|---|---|---|
| | total | no children | total | all under 6 | some < 6, some 6–17 | all 6–17 |
| **Total married couples** | **43,427** | **23,839** | **19,588** | **5,046** | **3,990** | **10,552** |
| Under $5,000 | 366 | 226 | 139 | 39 | 31 | 70 |
| $5,000–$9,999 | 525 | 362 | 163 | 61 | 28 | 74 |
| $10,000–$14,999 | 1,389 | 1,000 | 390 | 141 | 95 | 154 |
| $15,000–$19,999 | 2,024 | 1,490 | 534 | 209 | 121 | 205 |
| $20,000–$24,999 | 2,266 | 1,557 | 710 | 259 | 163 | 287 |
| $25,000–$29,999 | 2,411 | 1,572 | 838 | 235 | 190 | 413 |
| $30,000–$34,999 | 2,566 | 1,509 | 1,057 | 310 | 263 | 483 |
| $35,000–$39,999 | 2,630 | 1,468 | 1,162 | 312 | 295 | 556 |
| $40,000–$44,999 | 2,672 | 1,418 | 1,254 | 390 | 287 | 578 |
| $45,000–$49,999 | 2,478 | 1,244 | 1,235 | 332 | 254 | 649 |
| $50,000–$54,999 | 2,732 | 1,367 | 1,365 | 319 | 231 | 815 |
| $55,000–$59,999 | 2,200 | 1,045 | 1,156 | 295 | 233 | 627 |
| $60,000–$64,999 | 2,220 | 1,029 | 1,191 | 306 | 256 | 629 |
| $65,000–$69,999 | 2,009 | 927 | 1,083 | 270 | 216 | 597 |
| $70,000–$74,999 | 1,809 | 865 | 944 | 231 | 209 | 504 |
| $75,000–$79,999 | 1,557 | 729 | 828 | 178 | 153 | 498 |
| $80,000–$84,999 | 1,484 | 739 | 744 | 166 | 139 | 439 |
| $85,000–$89,999 | 1,196 | 632 | 564 | 120 | 88 | 356 |
| $90,000–$94,999 | 1,074 | 564 | 511 | 94 | 100 | 316 |
| $95,000–$99,999 | 867 | 467 | 400 | 74 | 64 | 263 |
| $100,000 or more | 6,950 | 3,628 | 3,322 | 706 | 577 | 2,040 |
| Median income | $54,270 | $50,248 | $58,908 | $53,389 | $55,635 | $62,343 |
| **Percent distribution** | | | | | | |
| **Total married couples** | **100.0%** | **100.0%** | **100.0%** | **100.0%** | **100.0%** | **100.0%** |
| Under $25,000 | 15.1 | 19.4 | 9.9 | 14.1 | 11.0 | 7.5 |
| $25,000–$49,999 | 29.4 | 30.2 | 28.3 | 31.3 | 32.3 | 25.4 |
| $50,000–$74,999 | 25.3 | 22.0 | 29.3 | 28.2 | 28.7 | 30.1 |
| $75,000–$99,999 | 14.2 | 13.1 | 15.6 | 12.5 | 13.6 | 17.7 |
| $100,000 or more | 16.0 | 15.2 | 17.0 | 14.0 | 14.5 | 19.3 |

*Source: Bureau of the Census, Internet web site, <http://www.census.gov/cps/ads/sdata.htm>; calculations by New Strategist*

# The Nation's Most Affluent Households Are Dual-Earner Married Couples

**Both husband and wife work in the majority of married couples.**

Of the nation's 54 million married couples, 33 million—or 60 percent—are dual earners, meaning both husband and wife are in the labor force. The median income of dual-earner couples stood at $61,837 in 1997. In 16 million couples both husband and wife work full-time. These couples account for half of all those in which both spouses work. The median income of dual-earner couples with full-time jobs stood at $69,507 in 1997, 35 percent higher than the median income of all couples.

Among dual-earner couples, those without children under age 18 at home have the highest incomes. Those in which both husband and wife work full-time had a median income of $73,280 in 1997. One in four has an income of $100,000 or more. Behind the higher incomes of working couples without children at home is that they are older than other working couples. Most are empty nesters in their peak earning years.

✗ With the majority of married couples living a dual-earner lifestyle, convenience and simplicity are of paramount concern to the nation's affluent households.

## Working couples without children at home enjoy highest incomes

*(median income of married couples in which both husband and wife work full-time, by presence of children at home, 1997)*

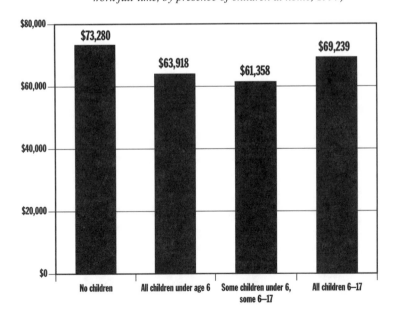

# Distribution of Dual-Income Married Couples by Household Income and Presence of Children, 1997: Husband and Wife Work

*(number and percent distribution of married couples in which both husband and wife work by household income and presence and age of related children under age 18 at home, 1997; married couples in thousands as of 1998)*

| | total | no children | one or more children under age 18 | | | |
|---|---|---|---|---|---|---|
| | | | total | all under 6 | some < 6, some 6–17 | all 6–17 |
| **Total dual-income couples** | **32,834** | **14,020** | **18,814** | **4,822** | **3,708** | **10,284** |
| Under $5,000 | 85 | 34 | 50 | 17 | 16 | 17 |
| $5,000–$9,999 | 122 | 59 | 63 | 30 | 4 | 30 |
| $10,000–$14,999 | 386 | 142 | 245 | 84 | 50 | 111 |
| $15,000–$19,999 | 669 | 249 | 419 | 194 | 105 | 120 |
| $20,000–$24,999 | 976 | 342 | 634 | 230 | 139 | 264 |
| $25,000–$29,999 | 1,292 | 515 | 777 | 242 | 209 | 326 |
| $30,000–$34,999 | 1,644 | 651 | 993 | 290 | 273 | 430 |
| $35,000–$39,999 | 1,850 | 750 | 1,100 | 292 | 256 | 552 |
| $40,000–$44,999 | 2,165 | 885 | 1,280 | 372 | 287 | 621 |
| $45,000–$49,999 | 2,103 | 782 | 1,320 | 324 | 317 | 679 |
| $50,000–$54,999 | 2,268 | 916 | 1,352 | 326 | 226 | 800 |
| $55,000–$59,999 | 1,981 | 755 | 1,226 | 313 | 233 | 680 |
| $60,000–$64,999 | 2,026 | 832 | 1,193 | 284 | 247 | 663 |
| $65,000–$69,999 | 1,770 | 706 | 1,063 | 258 | 186 | 619 |
| $70,000–$74,999 | 1,637 | 685 | 951 | 225 | 198 | 528 |
| $75,000–$79,999 | 1,440 | 608 | 832 | 208 | 124 | 500 |
| $80,000–$84,999 | 1,356 | 616 | 740 | 168 | 128 | 443 |
| $85,000–$89,999 | 1,077 | 528 | 550 | 108 | 80 | 362 |
| $90,000–$94,999 | 1,052 | 530 | 522 | 97 | 93 | 332 |
| $95,000–$99,999 | 846 | 422 | 424 | 80 | 80 | 264 |
| $100,000 or more | 6,090 | 3,012 | 3,078 | 676 | 457 | 1,944 |
| Median income | $61,837 | $65,624 | $59,733 | $55,109 | $54,257 | $63,501 |
| | | | | | | |
| **Percent distribution** | | | | | | |
| **Total dual-income couples** | **100.0%** | **100.0%** | **100.0%** | **100.0%** | **100.0%** | **100.0%** |
| Under $25,000 | 6.8 | 5.9 | 7.5 | 11.5 | 8.5 | 5.3 |
| $25,000–$49,999 | 27.6 | 25.6 | 29.1 | 31.5 | 36.2 | 25.4 |
| $50,000–$74,999 | 29.5 | 27.8 | 30.7 | 29.2 | 29.4 | 32.0 |
| $75,000–$99,999 | 17.6 | 19.3 | 16.3 | 13.7 | 13.6 | 18.5 |
| $100,000 or more | 18.5 | 21.5 | 16.4 | 14.0 | 12.3 | 18.9 |

*Source: Bureau of the Census,* Money Income in the United States: 1997, *Current Population Reports, P60-200, 1998; calculations by New Strategist*

# Distribution of Dual-Income Married Couples by Household Income and Presence of Children, 1997: Husband and Wife Work Full-Time

*(number and percent distribution of married couples in which both husband and wife work full-time, year-round by household income and presence and age of related children under age 18 at home, 1997; married couples in thousands as of 1998)*

| | total | no children | one or more children under age 18 total | all under 6 | some < 6, some 6–17 | all 6–17 |
|---|---|---|---|---|---|---|
| **Total dual-income couples** | **16,244** | **7,392** | **8,852** | **2,047** | **1,594** | **5,211** |
| Under $5,000 | 22 | 7 | 15 | 8 | 3 | 4 |
| $5,000–$9,999 | 10 | 8 | 2 | – | – | 2 |
| $10,000–$14,999 | 48 | 18 | 29 | 8 | 4 | 18 |
| $15,000–$19,999 | 116 | 44 | 72 | 17 | 23 | 32 |
| $20,000–$24,999 | 216 | 97 | 119 | 54 | 24 | 41 |
| $25,000–$29,999 | 356 | 166 | 190 | 61 | 39 | 91 |
| $30,000–$34,999 | 507 | 214 | 293 | 72 | 67 | 154 |
| $35,000–$39,999 | 678 | 295 | 383 | 103 | 77 | 203 |
| $40,000–$44,999 | 949 | 376 | 573 | 161 | 123 | 288 |
| $45,000–$49,999 | 985 | 366 | 619 | 142 | 136 | 341 |
| $50,000–$54,999 | 1,176 | 486 | 690 | 160 | 124 | 406 |
| $55,000–$59,999 | 1,017 | 382 | 635 | 145 | 129 | 361 |
| $60,000–$64,999 | 1,124 | 519 | 605 | 110 | 144 | 351 |
| $65,000–$69,999 | 1,003 | 412 | 591 | 137 | 94 | 360 |
| $70,000–$74,999 | 976 | 415 | 561 | 124 | 113 | 324 |
| $75,000–$79,999 | 875 | 412 | 463 | 113 | 64 | 285 |
| $80,000–$84,999 | 854 | 392 | 462 | 98 | 74 | 290 |
| $85,000–$89,999 | 645 | 339 | 306 | 49 | 47 | 211 |
| $90,000–$94,999 | 649 | 355 | 294 | 54 | 43 | 197 |
| $95,000–$99,999 | 517 | 275 | 242 | 44 | 46 | 151 |
| $100,000 or more | 3,521 | 1,814 | 1,707 | 386 | 221 | 1,101 |
| Median income | $69,507 | $73,280 | $66,477 | $63,918 | $61,358 | $69,239 |
| **Percent distribution** | | | | | | |
| **Total dual-income couples** | **100.0%** | **100.0%** | **100.0%** | **100.0%** | **100.0%** | **100.0%** |
| Under $25,000 | 2.5 | 2.4 | 2.7 | 4.3 | 3.4 | 1.9 |
| $25,000–$49,999 | 21.4 | 19.2 | 23.2 | 26.3 | 27.7 | 20.7 |
| $50,000–$74,999 | 32.6 | 30.0 | 34.8 | 33.0 | 37.9 | 34.6 |
| $75,000–$99,999 | 21.8 | 24.0 | 20.0 | 17.5 | 17.2 | 21.8 |
| $100,000 or more | 21.7 | 24.5 | 19.3 | 18.9 | 13.9 | 21.1 |

*Note: (–) means sample is too small to make a reliable estimate.*
*Source: Bureau of the Census,* Money Income in the United States: 1997, *Current Population Reports, P60-200, 1998; calculations by New Strategist*

# Female-Headed Families without Children Have the Highest Incomes

## Those with preschoolers have the lowest incomes.

The median income of all female-headed families stood at a lowly $21,023 in 1997. Women who are raising children had an even lower median income of $17,256. Those without children had a much higher median of $31,038. Behind this higher income is the fact that female-headed families without children include related adults such as siblings or parents. Many of these households have two wage earners, which boosts their incomes.

Female-headed families with children have low incomes regardless of race or Hispanic origin. Incomes are lowest for Hispanic women whose families include preschoolers as well as school-aged children, with a median income of just $9,637 in 1997. The most affluent female-headed families are those headed by non-Hispanic white women without children at home. They have a median income of $33,323.

✘ The median income of female-headed families may rise in the years ahead as the population ages and a growing share of these families are headed by older women.

### Female-headed families with children have low incomes

*(median income of female-headed families by presence and age of children under age 18 at home, 1997)*

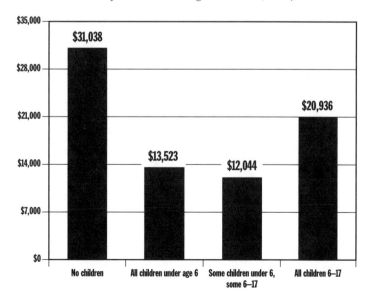

## Distribution of Female-Headed Families by Household Income and Presence of Children, 1997: Total Female-Headed Families

*(number and percent distribution of female-headed families by household income and presence and age of related children under age 18 at home, 1997; female-headed families in thousands as of 1998)*

| | | no children | one or more children under age 18 total | all under 6 | some < 6, some 6–17 | all 6–17 |
|---|---|---|---|---|---|---|
| | total | | | | | |
| **Total female-headed families** | **12,652** | **3,830** | **8,822** | **1,830** | **1,806** | **5,186** |
| Under $5,000 | 1,161 | 91 | 1,070 | 317 | 310 | 445 |
| $5,000–$9,999 | 1,808 | 232 | 1,577 | 411 | 459 | 707 |
| $10,000–$14,999 | 1,661 | 421 | 1,239 | 268 | 284 | 687 |
| $15,000–$19,999 | 1,415 | 387 | 1,028 | 192 | 198 | 639 |
| $20,000–$24,999 | 1,233 | 351 | 882 | 179 | 139 | 564 |
| $25,000–$29,999 | 1,048 | 363 | 684 | 110 | 98 | 476 |
| $30,000–$34,999 | 828 | 311 | 517 | 104 | 86 | 326 |
| $35,000–$39,999 | 668 | 269 | 399 | 56 | 55 | 288 |
| $40,000–$44,999 | 565 | 235 | 331 | 28 | 23 | 279 |
| $45,000–$49,999 | 451 | 215 | 236 | 33 | 35 | 168 |
| $50,000–$54,999 | 370 | 192 | 176 | 22 | 33 | 121 |
| $55,000–$59,999 | 245 | 144 | 101 | 12 | 16 | 71 |
| $60,000–$64,999 | 262 | 135 | 125 | 24 | 15 | 87 |
| $65,000–$69,999 | 189 | 103 | 85 | 7 | 5 | 73 |
| $70,000–$74,999 | 131 | 82 | 49 | 7 | 4 | 39 |
| $75,000–$79,999 | 112 | 50 | 63 | 6 | 9 | 48 |
| $80,000–$84,999 | 66 | 29 | 37 | 7 | 15 | 14 |
| $85,000–$89,999 | 74 | 34 | 40 | 7 | 9 | 23 |
| $90,000–$94,999 | 59 | 39 | 20 | 6 | 4 | 10 |
| $95,000–$99,999 | 50 | 23 | 26 | 6 | 2 | 18 |
| $100,000 or more | 258 | 123 | 135 | 28 | 5 | 101 |
| Median income | $21,023 | $31,038 | $17,256 | $13,523 | $12,044 | $20,936 |

**Percent distribution**

| | | | | | | |
|---|---|---|---|---|---|---|
| **Total female-headed families** | **100.0%** | **100.0%** | **100.0%** | **100.0%** | **100.0%** | **100.0%** |
| Under $25,000 | 57.5 | 38.7 | 65.7 | 74.7 | 77.0 | 58.7 |
| $25,000–$49,999 | 28.1 | 36.4 | 24.6 | 18.1 | 16.4 | 29.6 |
| $50,000–$74,999 | 9.5 | 17.1 | 6.1 | 3.9 | 4.0 | 7.5 |
| $75,000–$99,999 | 2.9 | 4.6 | 2.1 | 1.7 | 2.2 | 2.2 |
| $100,000 or more | 2.0 | 3.2 | 1.5 | 1.5 | 0.3 | 1.9 |

*Source: Bureau of the Census, Internet web site, <http://www.census.gov/cps/ads/sdata.htm>; calculations by New Strategist*

# Distribution of Female-Headed Families by Household Income and Presence of Children, 1997: Black Female-Headed Families

*(number and percent distribution of black female-headed families by household income and presence and age of related children under age 18 at home, 1997; female-headed families in thousands as of 1998)*

| | | | one or more children under age 18 | | | |
| --- | --- | --- | --- | --- | --- | --- |
| | total | no children | total | all under 6 | some < 6, some 6–17 | all 6–17 |
| **Total female-headed families** | **3,926** | **865** | **3,060** | **576** | **808** | **1,676** |
| Under $5,000 | 473 | 24 | 448 | 93 | 145 | 210 |
| $5,000–$9,999 | 696 | 80 | 615 | 114 | 200 | 303 |
| $10,000–$14,999 | 584 | 128 | 456 | 102 | 132 | 222 |
| $15,000–$19,999 | 478 | 93 | 384 | 56 | 76 | 252 |
| $20,000–$24,999 | 387 | 94 | 293 | 59 | 73 | 159 |
| $25,000–$29,999 | 290 | 73 | 216 | 39 | 44 | 133 |
| $30,000–$34,999 | 259 | 67 | 192 | 47 | 49 | 98 |
| $35,000–$39,999 | 157 | 55 | 102 | 11 | 25 | 67 |
| $40,000–$44,999 | 135 | 53 | 82 | 11 | 8 | 65 |
| $45,000–$49,999 | 101 | 35 | 66 | 14 | 21 | 32 |
| $50,000–$54,999 | 86 | 37 | 50 | 14 | 11 | 24 |
| $55,000–$59,999 | 45 | 16 | 30 | 6 | 3 | 21 |
| $60,000–$64,999 | 52 | 27 | 26 | 4 | 1 | 21 |
| $65,000–$69,999 | 49 | 27 | 21 | 6 | 0 | 15 |
| $70,000–$74,999 | 30 | 23 | 7 | 0 | 0 | 7 |
| $75,000–$79,999 | 15 | 6 | 9 | 0 | 2 | 6 |
| $80,000–$84,999 | 17 | 0 | 16 | 3 | 11 | 3 |
| $85,000–$89,999 | 17 | 0 | 16 | 0 | 4 | 13 |
| $90,000–$94,999 | 11 | 4 | 7 | 0 | 2 | 5 |
| $95,000–$99,999 | 16 | 7 | 9 | 0 | 0 | 9 |
| $100,000 or more | 28 | 15 | 13 | 0 | 2 | 11 |
| Median income | $16,879 | $25,772 | $15,111 | $13,998 | $12,167 | $16,711 |

**Percent distribution**

| | total | no children | total | all under 6 | some < 6, some 6–17 | all 6–17 |
| --- | --- | --- | --- | --- | --- | --- |
| **Total female-headed families** | **100.0%** | **100.0%** | **100.0%** | **100.0%** | **100.0%** | **100.0%** |
| Under $25,000 | 66.7 | 48.4 | 71.8 | 73.6 | 77.5 | 68.4 |
| $25,000–$49,999 | 24.0 | 32.7 | 21.5 | 21.2 | 18.2 | 23.6 |
| $50,000–$74,999 | 6.7 | 15.0 | 4.4 | 5.2 | 1.9 | 5.3 |
| $75,000–$99,999 | 1.9 | 2.0 | 1.9 | 0.5 | 2.4 | 2.1 |
| $100,000 or more | 0.7 | 1.7 | 0.4 | 0.0 | 0.2 | 0.7 |

*Source: Bureau of the Census, Internet web site, <http://www.census.gov/cps/ads/sdata.htm>; calculations by New Strategist*

# Distribution of Female-Headed Families by Household Income and Presence of Children, 1997: Hispanic Female-Headed Families

*(number and percent distribution of Hispanic female-headed families by household income and presence and age of related children under age 18 at home, 1997; female-headed families in thousands as of 1998)*

| | | | one or more children under age 18 | | | |
|---|---|---|---|---|---|---|
| | total | no children | total | all under 6 | some < 6, some 6–17 | all 6–17 |
| **Total female-headed families** | **1,612** | **319** | **1,292** | **294** | **336** | **662** |
| Under $5,000 | 198 | 22 | 176 | 46 | 65 | 65 |
| $5,000–$9,999 | 353 | 32 | 322 | 85 | 111 | 125 |
| $10,000–$14,999 | 255 | 44 | 210 | 44 | 47 | 119 |
| $15,000–$19,999 | 216 | 45 | 171 | 24 | 40 | 106 |
| $20,000–$24,999 | 134 | 16 | 118 | 26 | 21 | 71 |
| $25,000–$29,999 | 102 | 26 | 77 | 25 | 11 | 40 |
| $30,000–$34,999 | 89 | 36 | 51 | 12 | 10 | 29 |
| $35,000–$39,999 | 63 | 21 | 42 | 12 | 9 | 21 |
| $40,000–$44,999 | 50 | 18 | 32 | 7 | 3 | 22 |
| $45,000–$49,999 | 41 | 16 | 25 | 4 | 6 | 15 |
| $50,000–$54,999 | 25 | 5 | 19 | 2 | 8 | 9 |
| $55,000–$59,999 | 16 | 9 | 6 | 0 | 1 | 4 |
| $60,000–$64,999 | 10 | 2 | 9 | 2 | 1 | 6 |
| $65,000–$69,999 | 13 | 2 | 11 | 1 | 1 | 9 |
| $70,000–$74,999 | 15 | 9 | 6 | 4 | 0 | 2 |
| $75,000–$79,999 | 8 | 4 | 5 | 0 | 1 | 4 |
| $80,000–$84,999 | 3 | 1 | 2 | 0 | 0 | 2 |
| $85,000–$89,999 | 4 | 4 | 0 | 0 | 0 | 0 |
| $90,000–$94,999 | 0 | 0 | 0 | 0 | 0 | 0 |
| $95,000–$99,999 | 1 | 1 | 0 | 0 | 0 | 0 |
| $100,000 or more | 16 | 5 | 11 | 0 | 1 | 9 |
| Median income | $14,994 | $24,983 | $12,983 | $11,516 | $9,637 | $15,829 |
| **Percent distribution** | | | | | | |
| **Total female-headed families** | **100.0%** | **100.0%** | **100.0%** | **100.0%** | **100.0%** | **100.0%** |
| Under $25,000 | 71.7 | 49.8 | 77.2 | 76.5 | 84.5 | 73.4 |
| $25,000–$49,999 | 21.4 | 36.7 | 17.6 | 20.4 | 11.6 | 19.2 |
| $50,000–$74,999 | 4.9 | 8.5 | 3.9 | 3.1 | 3.3 | 4.5 |
| $75,000–$99,999 | 1.0 | 3.1 | 0.5 | 0.0 | 0.3 | 0.9 |
| $100,000 or more | 1.0 | 1.6 | 0.9 | 0.0 | 0.3 | 1.4 |

*Source: Bureau of the Census, Internet web site, <http://www.census.gov/cps/ads/sdata.htm>; calculations by New Strategist*

# Distribution of Female-Headed Families by Household Income and Presence of Children, 1997: White Female-Headed Families

*(number and percent distribution of white female-headed families by household income and presence and age of related children under age 18 at home, 1997; female-headed families in thousands as of 1998)*

| | total | no children | one or more children under age 18 | | | |
|---|---|---|---|---|---|---|
| | | | total | all under 6 | some < 6, some 6–17 | all 6–17 |
| **Total female-headed families** | **8,308** | **2,806** | **5,502** | **1,204** | **952** | **3,345** |
| Under $5,000 | 651 | 63 | 589 | 212 | 154 | 223 |
| $5,000–$9,999 | 1,061 | 139 | 923 | 287 | 248 | 388 |
| $10,000–$14,999 | 1,023 | 281 | 742 | 163 | 145 | 435 |
| $15,000–$19,999 | 893 | 281 | 613 | 129 | 119 | 365 |
| $20,000–$24,999 | 819 | 249 | 570 | 118 | 64 | 390 |
| $25,000–$29,999 | 728 | 278 | 450 | 70 | 50 | 331 |
| $30,000–$34,999 | 543 | 236 | 307 | 56 | 37 | 215 |
| $35,000–$39,999 | 490 | 205 | 286 | 43 | 30 | 212 |
| $40,000–$44,999 | 415 | 172 | 243 | 18 | 16 | 209 |
| $45,000–$49,999 | 339 | 173 | 166 | 19 | 14 | 134 |
| $50,000–$54,999 | 278 | 154 | 124 | 8 | 21 | 95 |
| $55,000–$59,999 | 186 | 119 | 67 | 6 | 12 | 51 |
| $60,000–$64,999 | 193 | 97 | 96 | 21 | 13 | 62 |
| $65,000–$69,999 | 130 | 70 | 59 | 1 | 5 | 53 |
| $70,000–$74,999 | 89 | 50 | 39 | 4 | 4 | 31 |
| $75,000–$79,999 | 87 | 37 | 50 | 6 | 6 | 38 |
| $80,000–$84,999 | 40 | 22 | 19 | 4 | 3 | 11 |
| $85,000–$89,999 | 55 | 33 | 23 | 7 | 5 | 11 |
| $90,000–$94,999 | 42 | 32 | 11 | 4 | 2 | 5 |
| $95,000–$99,999 | 33 | 15 | 17 | 6 | 2 | 9 |
| $100,000 or more | 209 | 103 | 105 | 25 | 2 | 78 |
| Median income | $22,999 | $32,229 | $18,939 | $13,150 | $12,020 | $23,289 |
| | | | | | | |
| **Percent distribution** | | | | | | |
| **Total female-headed families** | **100.0%** | **100.0%** | **100.0%** | **100.0%** | **100.0%** | **100.0%** |
| Under $25,000 | 53.5 | 36.1 | 62.5 | 75.5 | 76.7 | 53.8 |
| $25,000–$49,999 | 30.3 | 37.9 | 26.4 | 17.1 | 15.4 | 32.9 |
| $50,000–$74,999 | 10.5 | 17.5 | 7.0 | 3.3 | 5.8 | 8.7 |
| $75,000–$99,999 | 3.1 | 5.0 | 2.2 | 2.2 | 1.9 | 2.2 |
| $100,000 or more | 2.5 | 3.7 | 1.9 | 2.1 | 0.2 | 2.3 |

*Source: Bureau of the Census, Internet web site, <http://www.census.gov/cps/ads/sdata.htm>; calculations by New Strategist*

## Distribution of Female-Headed Families by Household Income and Presence of Children, 1997: Non-Hispanic White Female-Headed Families

*(number and percent distribution of non-Hispanic white female-headed families by household income and presence and age of related children under age 18 at home, 1997; female-headed families in thousands as of 1998)*

| | total | no children | one or more children under age 18 | | | |
|---|---|---|---|---|---|---|
| | | | total | all under 6 | some < 6, some 6–17 | all 6–17 |
| **Total female-headed families** | **6,826** | **2,506** | **4,320** | **939** | **641** | **2,740** |
| Under $5,000 | 467 | 44 | 422 | 167 | 91 | 164 |
| $5,000–$9,999 | 738 | 109 | 629 | 210 | 143 | 276 |
| $10,000–$14,999 | 796 | 242 | 555 | 125 | 105 | 325 |
| $15,000–$19,999 | 693 | 237 | 456 | 107 | 80 | 270 |
| $20,000–$24,999 | 694 | 233 | 462 | 94 | 46 | 322 |
| $25,000–$29,999 | 630 | 252 | 378 | 45 | 40 | 293 |
| $30,000–$34,999 | 468 | 200 | 268 | 50 | 31 | 187 |
| $35,000–$39,999 | 428 | 184 | 245 | 31 | 22 | 192 |
| $40,000–$44,999 | 367 | 155 | 212 | 11 | 13 | 187 |
| $45,000–$49,999 | 298 | 157 | 142 | 15 | 8 | 119 |
| $50,000–$54,999 | 253 | 149 | 104 | 6 | 13 | 86 |
| $55,000–$59,999 | 172 | 108 | 63 | 6 | 11 | 47 |
| $60,000–$64,999 | 186 | 95 | 91 | 21 | 13 | 58 |
| $65,000–$69,999 | 119 | 68 | 51 | 0 | 4 | 48 |
| $70,000–$74,999 | 77 | 45 | 33 | 0 | 4 | 29 |
| $75,000–$79,999 | 79 | 33 | 45 | 6 | 6 | 33 |
| $80,000–$84,999 | 37 | 21 | 16 | 4 | 3 | 9 |
| $85,000–$89,999 | 52 | 29 | 23 | 7 | 5 | 11 |
| $90,000–$94,999 | 42 | 32 | 11 | 4 | 2 | 5 |
| $95,000–$99,999 | 32 | 14 | 17 | 6 | 2 | 9 |
| $100,000 or more | 196 | 98 | 98 | 25 | 2 | 71 |
| Median income | $25,188 | $33,323 | $21,022 | $13,792 | $13,816 | $25,217 |
| **Percent distribution** | | | | | | |
| **Total female-headed families** | **100.0%** | **100.0%** | **100.0%** | **100.0%** | **100.0%** | **100.0%** |
| Under $25,000 | 49.6 | 34.5 | 58.4 | 74.9 | 72.5 | 49.5 |
| $25,000–$49,999 | 32.1 | 37.8 | 28.8 | 16.2 | 17.8 | 35.7 |
| $50,000–$74,999 | 11.8 | 18.6 | 7.9 | 3.5 | 7.0 | 9.8 |
| $75,000–$99,999 | 3.5 | 5.1 | 2.6 | 2.9 | 2.8 | 2.4 |
| $100,000 or more | 2.9 | 3.9 | 2.3 | 2.7 | 0.3 | 2.6 |

*Source: Bureau of the Census, Internet web site, <http://www.census.gov/cps/ads/sdata.htm>; calculations by New Strategist*

# Male-Headed Families without Children Have Above-Average Incomes

## Those with preschoolers have the lowest incomes.

The median income of male-headed families was just $32,960 in 1997, well below the all-household median of $37,005. Male-headed families that do not include children under age 18 had a much higher median of $41,483. Men who head families without children live with adult relatives such as siblings or parents. Many of these households have more than one wage earner, which boosts incomes. Of the nation's 3.9 million male-headed families, only 56 percent include children under age 18. A much higher 70 percent of female-headed families have children under age 18 at home.

Male-headed families with preschoolers have the lowest incomes, a median of $21,547 in 1997. Only 24 percent of men who head families are caring for preschoolers.

Among blacks, Hispanics, and whites, incomes of male-headed families with children are much lower than incomes of those without children. White men who head families without children under age 18 have the highest median income, fully $42,436.

✘ Male-headed families are the least common household type, accounting for fewer than 4 percent of households. While this market is not large, it is important to remember that single-parents—whether male or female—share many of the same needs. Marketers targeting single mothers should consider including single fathers in their message.

### Male-headed families with children have lower incomes

*(median income of male-headed families by presence and age of children under age 18 at home, 1997)*

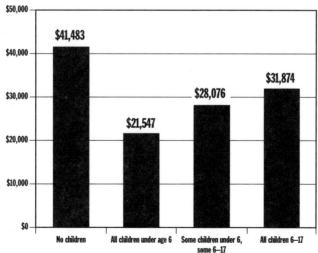

# Distribution of Male-Headed Families by Household Income and Presence of Children, 1997: Total Male-Headed Families

*(number and percent distribution of male-headed families by household income and presence and age of related children under age 18 at home, 1997; male-headed families in thousands as of 1998)*

| | total | no children | one or more children under age 18 | | | |
| --- | --- | --- | --- | --- | --- | --- |
| | | | total | all under 6 | some < 6, some 6–17 | all 6–17 |
| **Total male-headed families** | **3,911** | **1,735** | **2,175** | **663** | **265** | **1,247** |
| Under $5,000 | 172 | 40 | 133 | 61 | 16 | 56 |
| $5,000 to $9,999 | 186 | 44 | 142 | 77 | 11 | 54 |
| $10,000 to $14,999 | 293 | 98 | 194 | 65 | 43 | 87 |
| $15,000 to $19,999 | 349 | 126 | 224 | 96 | 21 | 107 |
| $20,000 to $24,999 | 353 | 138 | 216 | 82 | 22 | 112 |
| $25,000 to $29,999 | 392 | 159 | 232 | 59 | 24 | 150 |
| $30,000 to $34,999 | 315 | 123 | 192 | 47 | 7 | 138 |
| $35,000 to $39,999 | 255 | 99 | 156 | 44 | 25 | 87 |
| $40,000 to $44,999 | 247 | 122 | 126 | 26 | 11 | 89 |
| $45,000 to $49,999 | 191 | 97 | 93 | 23 | 18 | 53 |
| $50,000 to $54,999 | 195 | 94 | 100 | 15 | 21 | 64 |
| $55,000 to $59,999 | 166 | 88 | 78 | 22 | 11 | 45 |
| $60,000 to $64,999 | 138 | 83 | 55 | 6 | 10 | 39 |
| $65,000 to $69,999 | 123 | 67 | 56 | 19 | 9 | 28 |
| $70,000 to $74,999 | 97 | 62 | 35 | 9 | 4 | 21 |
| $75,000 to $79,999 | 68 | 43 | 25 | 1 | 4 | 18 |
| $80,000 to $84,999 | 88 | 61 | 27 | 5 | 3 | 18 |
| $85,000 to $89,999 | 32 | 25 | 7 | 0 | 0 | 7 |
| $90,000 to $94,999 | 32 | 22 | 10 | 3 | 0 | 8 |
| $95,000 to $99,999 | 25 | 16 | 9 | 0 | 0 | 9 |
| $100,000 or more | 196 | 128 | 68 | 5 | 5 | 58 |
| Median income | $32,960 | $41,483 | $28,668 | $21,547 | $28,076 | $31,874 |
| **Percent distribution** | | | | | | |
| **Total male-headed families** | **100.0%** | **100.0%** | **100.0%** | **100.0%** | **100.0%** | **100.0%** |
| Under $25,000 | 34.6 | 25.7 | 41.8 | 57.5 | 42.6 | 33.4 |
| $25,000 to $49,999 | 35.8 | 34.6 | 36.7 | 30.0 | 32.1 | 41.5 |
| $50,000 to $74,999 | 18.4 | 22.7 | 14.9 | 10.7 | 20.8 | 15.8 |
| $75,000 to $99,999 | 6.3 | 9.6 | 3.6 | 1.4 | 2.6 | 4.8 |
| $100,000 or more | 5.0 | 7.4 | 3.1 | 0.8 | 1.9 | 4.7 |

*Source: Bureau of the Census, Internet web site, <http:// www.census.gov/cps/ads/sdata.htm>; calculations by New Strategist*

# Distribution of Male-Headed Families by Household Income and Presence of Children, 1997: Black Male-Headed Families

*(number and percent distribution of black male-headed families by household income and presence and age of related children under age 18 at home, 1997; male-headed families in thousands as of 1998)*

| | total | no children | one or more children under age 18 | | | |
| | | | total | all under 6 | some < 6, some 6–17 | all 6–17 |
|---|---|---|---|---|---|---|
| **Total male-headed families** | **562** | **249** | **312** | **104** | **44** | **165** |
| Under $5,000 | 39 | 16 | 23 | 7 | 0 | 16 |
| $5,000–$9,999 | 35 | 9 | 26 | 17 | 0 | 9 |
| $10,000–$14,999 | 63 | 27 | 37 | 2 | 12 | 23 |
| $15,000–$19,999 | 68 | 20 | 49 | 29 | 3 | 16 |
| $20,000–$24,999 | 63 | 24 | 39 | 18 | 7 | 14 |
| $25,000–$29,999 | 80 | 32 | 49 | 7 | 10 | 32 |
| $30,000–$34,999 | 45 | 13 | 31 | 5 | 3 | 22 |
| $35,000–$39,999 | 35 | 13 | 23 | 5 | 0 | 18 |
| $40,000–$44,999 | 18 | 11 | 7 | 0 | 2 | 5 |
| $45,000–$49,999 | 13 | 8 | 5 | 3 | 0 | 3 |
| $50,000–$54,999 | 25 | 20 | 5 | 4 | 0 | 1 |
| $55,000–$59,999 | 18 | 12 | 6 | 4 | 0 | 2 |
| $60,000–$64,999 | 10 | 6 | 4 | 1 | 0 | 3 |
| $65,000–$69,999 | 9 | 6 | 3 | 0 | 3 | 0 |
| $70,000–$74,999 | 8 | 5 | 3 | 1 | 2 | 0 |
| $75,000–$79,999 | 5 | 5 | 0 | 0 | 0 | 0 |
| $80,000–$84,999 | 6 | 4 | 3 | 0 | 2 | 0 |
| $85,000–$89,999 | 2 | 2 | 0 | 0 | 0 | 0 |
| $90,000–$94,999 | 4 | 4 | 0 | 0 | 0 | 0 |
| $95,000–$99,999 | 3 | 3 | 0 | 0 | 0 | 0 |
| $100,000 or more | 12 | 10 | 2 | 0 | 0 | 2 |
| Median income | $25,654 | $29,526 | $21,815 | $19,596 | $22,292 | $25,735 |
| | | | | | | |
| **Percent distribution** | | | | | | |
| **Total male-headed families** | **100.0%** | **100.0%** | **100.0%** | **100.0%** | **100.0%** | **100.0%** |
| Under $25,000 | 47.7 | 38.6 | 55.8 | 70.2 | 50.0 | 47.3 |
| $25,000–$49,999 | 34.0 | 30.9 | 36.9 | 19.2 | 34.1 | 48.5 |
| $50,000–$74,999 | 12.5 | 19.7 | 6.7 | 9.6 | 11.4 | 3.6 |
| $75,000–$99,999 | 3.6 | 7.2 | 1.0 | 0.0 | 4.5 | 0.0 |
| $100,000 or more | 2.1 | 4.0 | 0.6 | 0.0 | 0.0 | 1.2 |

*Source: Bureau of the Census, Internet web site, <http://www.census.gov/cps/ads/sdata.htm>; calculations by New Strategist*

# Distribution of Male-Headed Families by Household Income and Presence of Children, 1997: Hispanic Male-Headed Families

*(number and percent distribution of Hispanic male-headed families by household income and presence and age of related children under age 18 at home, 1997; male-headed families in thousands as of 1998)*

| | total | no children | one or more children under age 18 | | | |
|---|---|---|---|---|---|---|
| | | | total | all under 6 | some < 6, some 6–17 | all 6–17 |
| **Total male-headed families** | **545** | **221** | **324** | **140** | **53** | **132** |
| Under $5,000 | 30 | 4 | 26 | 16 | 6 | 4 |
| $5,000–$9,999 | 45 | 11 | 33 | 19 | 8 | 7 |
| $10,000–$14,999 | 70 | 18 | 52 | 22 | 14 | 16 |
| $15,000–$19,999 | 70 | 19 | 51 | 21 | 8 | 22 |
| $20,000–$24,999 | 52 | 25 | 27 | 14 | 1 | 10 |
| $25,000–$29,999 | 50 | 22 | 28 | 11 | 1 | 16 |
| $30,000–$34,999 | 48 | 26 | 22 | 8 | 2 | 12 |
| $35,000–$39,999 | 28 | 8 | 21 | 10 | 4 | 8 |
| $40,000–$44,999 | 39 | 24 | 15 | 4 | 1 | 10 |
| $45,000–$49,999 | 29 | 18 | 10 | 8 | 0 | 2 |
| $50,000–$54,999 | 20 | 9 | 11 | 0 | 3 | 7 |
| $55,000–$59,999 | 11 | 5 | 6 | 1 | 0 | 4 |
| $60,000–$64,999 | 4 | 2 | 2 | 0 | 0 | 2 |
| $65,000–$69,999 | 12 | 2 | 10 | 3 | 3 | 3 |
| $70,000–$74,999 | 7 | 3 | 3 | 0 | 0 | 3 |
| $75,000–$79,999 | 8 | 4 | 4 | 1 | 1 | 1 |
| $80,000–$84,999 | 5 | 5 | 0 | 0 | 0 | 0 |
| $85,000–$89,999 | 3 | 3 | 0 | 0 | 0 | 0 |
| $90,000–$94,999 | 2 | 1 | 1 | 0 | 0 | 1 |
| $95,000–$99,999 | 0 | 0 | 0 | 0 | 0 | 0 |
| $100,000 or more | 13 | 9 | 4 | 2 | 0 | 2 |
| Median income | $25,543 | $31,195 | $20,028 | $18,682 | $14,408 | $26,860 |
| **Percent distribution** | | | | | | |
| **Total male-headed families** | **100.0%** | **100.0%** | **100.0%** | **100.0%** | **100.0%** | **100.0%** |
| Under $25,000 | 49.0 | 34.8 | 58.3 | 65.7 | 69.8 | 44.7 |
| $25,000–$49,999 | 35.6 | 44.3 | 29.6 | 29.3 | 15.1 | 36.4 |
| $50,000–$74,999 | 9.9 | 9.5 | 9.9 | 2.9 | 11.3 | 14.4 |
| $75,000–$99,999 | 3.3 | 5.9 | 1.5 | 0.7 | 1.9 | 1.5 |
| $100,000 or more | 2.4 | 4.1 | 1.2 | 1.4 | 0.0 | 1.5 |

*Source: Bureau of the Census, Internet web site, <http://www.census.gov/cps/ads/sdata.htm>; calculations by New Strategist*

# Distribution of Male-Headed Families by Household Income and Presence of Children, 1997: White Male-Headed Families

*(number and percent distribution of white male-headed families by household income and presence and age of related children under age 18 at home, 1997; male-headed families in thousands as of 1998)*

| | total | no children | one or more children under age 18 | | | |
|---|---|---|---|---|---|---|
| | | | total | all under 6 | some < 6, some 6–17 | all 6–17 |
| **Total male-headed families** | **3,137** | **1,362** | **1,774** | **536** | **212** | **1,027** |
| Under $5,000 | 127 | 21 | 106 | 52 | 16 | 39 |
| $5,000 to $9,999 | 138 | 30 | 108 | 57 | 11 | 40 |
| $10,000 to $14,999 | 214 | 62 | 151 | 61 | 29 | 61 |
| $15,000 to $19,999 | 266 | 100 | 167 | 67 | 18 | 82 |
| $20,000 to $24,999 | 277 | 104 | 174 | 61 | 14 | 97 |
| $25,000 to $29,999 | 294 | 121 | 174 | 50 | 15 | 109 |
| $30,000 to $34,999 | 259 | 108 | 151 | 38 | 3 | 110 |
| $35,000 to $39,999 | 203 | 79 | 124 | 36 | 22 | 65 |
| $40,000 to $44,999 | 214 | 99 | 115 | 26 | 10 | 79 |
| $45,000 to $49,999 | 162 | 81 | 81 | 18 | 18 | 45 |
| $50,000 to $54,999 | 159 | 66 | 92 | 11 | 18 | 63 |
| $55,000 to $59,999 | 140 | 68 | 72 | 19 | 10 | 43 |
| $60,000 to $64,999 | 113 | 66 | 49 | 4 | 10 | 34 |
| $65,000 to $69,999 | 105 | 56 | 48 | 17 | 6 | 25 |
| $70,000 to $74,999 | 86 | 56 | 30 | 8 | 0 | 21 |
| $75,000 to $79,999 | 59 | 34 | 25 | 1 | 4 | 18 |
| $80,000 to $84,999 | 72 | 53 | 20 | 3 | 0 | 16 |
| $85,000 to $89,999 | 29 | 22 | 7 | 0 | 0 | 7 |
| $90,000 to $94,999 | 26 | 17 | 10 | 3 | 0 | 7 |
| $95,000 to $99,999 | 18 | 8 | 9 | 0 | 0 | 9 |
| $100,000 or more | 173 | 109 | 64 | 5 | 5 | 54 |
| Median income | $34,802 | $42,436 | $30,201 | $22,029 | $31,594 | $33,760 |
| **Percent distribution** | | | | | | |
| **Total male-headed families** | **100.0%** | **100.0%** | **100.0%** | **100.0%** | **100.0%** | **100.0%** |
| Under $25,000 | 32.6 | 23.3 | 39.8 | 55.6 | 41.5 | 31.1 |
| $25,000 to $49,999 | 36.1 | 35.8 | 36.4 | 31.3 | 32.1 | 39.7 |
| $50,000 to $74,999 | 19.2 | 22.9 | 16.4 | 11.0 | 20.8 | 18.1 |
| $75,000 to $99,999 | 6.5 | 9.8 | 4.0 | 1.3 | 1.9 | 5.6 |
| $100,000 or more | 5.5 | 8.0 | 3.6 | 0.9 | 2.4 | 5.3 |

*Source: Bureau of the Census, Internet web site, <http://www.census.gov/cps/ads/sdata.htm>; calculations by New Strategist*

# Household Incomes Are Highest in the Pacific States

## Incomes are lowest in the East South Central states.

Among the four regions, only the South—which is home to 36 percent of the nation's households—has a median household income below the national average of $37,005. Median household income is slightly above average in the Northeast and Midwest, and it is highest in the West. The gap in median household income between the South and the West amounted to $4,817 in 1997.

Median household income in the Pacific division—which includes Alaska, California, Hawaii, Oregon, and Washington—stood at $40,509 in 1997, 9 percent above the national median. Incomes are almost as high in the Northeast's New England division, at $40,410. In both divisions, one in eight households had an income of $100,000 or more.

The lowest household incomes are found in the East South Central States of Alabama, Kentucky, Mississippi, and Tennessee. Median household income in those states was just $31,237 in 1997, 16 percent below the national figure. The West South Central division (Arkansas, Louisiana, Oklahoma, and Texas) did not fare much better; it had a median household income of $32,770.

✗ As high-tech communications lessens the importance of geography to income, the economic disparities among regions and divisions should disappear.

### West has highest median household income

*(median household income by region, 1997)*

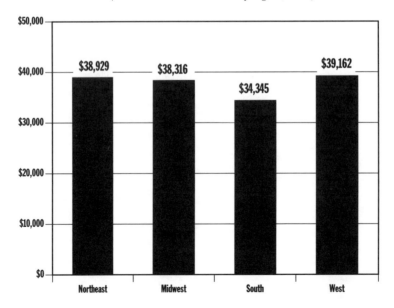

# Distribution of Households by Income, Region, and Division, 1997: Northeast

*(number and percent distribution of households by household income, region, and division, 1997; households in thousands as of 1998)*

| | | Northeast | | |
| | total | total | New England | Middle Atlantic |
|---|---|---|---|---|
| **Total households** | **102,528** | **19,810** | **5,267** | **14,543** |
| Under $5,000 | 3,531 | 741 | 194 | 546 |
| $5,000–$9,999 | 7,765 | 1,653 | 399 | 1,255 |
| $10,000–$14,999 | 8,326 | 1,547 | 384 | 1,163 |
| $15,000–$19,999 | 7,837 | 1,369 | 313 | 1,056 |
| $20,000–$24,999 | 7,406 | 1,278 | 340 | 938 |
| $25,000–$29,999 | 6,913 | 1,166 | 323 | 843 |
| $30,000–$34,999 | 6,673 | 1,208 | 334 | 874 |
| $35,000–$39,999 | 6,111 | 1,141 | 321 | 820 |
| $40,000–$44,999 | 5,667 | 1,034 | 291 | 744 |
| $45,000–$49,999 | 4,920 | 859 | 221 | 638 |
| $50,000–$54,999 | 4,864 | 842 | 226 | 617 |
| $55,000–$59,999 | 3,864 | 733 | 198 | 535 |
| $60,000–$64,999 | 3,751 | 717 | 176 | 542 |
| $65,000–$69,999 | 3,298 | 624 | 176 | 448 |
| $70,000–$74,999 | 2,754 | 617 | 181 | 436 |
| $75,000–$79,999 | 2,399 | 438 | 127 | 311 |
| $80,000–$84,999 | 2,251 | 478 | 135 | 343 |
| $85,000–$89,999 | 1,702 | 357 | 108 | 250 |
| $90,000–$94,999 | 1,509 | 332 | 86 | 246 |
| $95,000–$99,999 | 1,325 | 298 | 96 | 203 |
| $100,000 or more | 9,661 | 2,379 | 643 | 1,736 |
| Median income | $37,005 | $38,929 | $40,410 | $38,363 |
| **Percent distribution** | | | | |
| **Total households** | **100.0%** | **100.0%** | **100.0%** | **100.0%** |
| Under $25,000 | 34.0 | 33.3 | 30.9 | 34.1 |
| $25,000–$49,999 | 29.5 | 27.3 | 28.3 | 26.9 |
| $50,000–$74,999 | 18.1 | 17.8 | 18.2 | 17.7 |
| $75,000–$99,999 | 9.0 | 9.6 | 10.5 | 9.3 |
| $100,000 or more | 9.4 | 12.0 | 12.2 | 12.2 |

*Source: Bureau of the Census, Internet web site, <http://www.census.gov/cps/ads/sdata.htm>; calculations by New Strategist*

# Distribution of Households by Income, Region, and Division, 1997: Midwest

*(number and percent distribution of households by household income, region, and division, 1997; households in thousands as of 1998)*

| | total | Midwest total | East North Central | West North Central |
|---|---|---|---|---|
| **Total households** | **102,528** | **24,236** | **17,022** | **7,214** |
| Under $5,000 | 3,531 | 731 | 505 | 227 |
| $5,000–$9,999 | 7,765 | 1,686 | 1,164 | 522 |
| $10,000–$14,999 | 8,326 | 1,836 | 1,287 | 550 |
| $15,000–$19,999 | 7,837 | 1,865 | 1,272 | 593 |
| $20,000–$24,999 | 7,406 | 1,694 | 1,173 | 521 |
| $25,000–$29,999 | 6,913 | 1,704 | 1,163 | 542 |
| $30,000–$34,999 | 6,673 | 1,574 | 1,106 | 467 |
| $35,000–$39,999 | 6,111 | 1,471 | 1,028 | 443 |
| $40,000–$44,999 | 5,667 | 1,456 | 993 | 463 |
| $45,000–$49,999 | 4,920 | 1,211 | 848 | 362 |
| $50,000–$54,999 | 4,864 | 1,298 | 909 | 388 |
| $55,000–$59,999 | 3,864 | 977 | 715 | 263 |
| $60,000–$64,999 | 3,751 | 900 | 676 | 224 |
| $65,000–$69,999 | 3,298 | 862 | 627 | 235 |
| $70,000–$74,999 | 2,754 | 687 | 468 | 219 |
| $75,000–$79,999 | 2,399 | 606 | 448 | 159 |
| $80,000–$84,999 | 2,251 | 576 | 403 | 173 |
| $85,000–$89,999 | 1,702 | 401 | 275 | 126 |
| $90,000–$94,999 | 1,509 | 415 | 285 | 129 |
| $95,000–$99,999 | 1,325 | 290 | 203 | 88 |
| $100,000 or more | 9,661 | 1,995 | 1,473 | 522 |
| Median income | $37,005 | $38,316 | $38,993 | $36,864 |
| **Percent distribution** | | | | |
| **Total households** | **100.0%** | **100.0%** | **100.0%** | **100.0%** |
| Under $25,000 | 34.0 | 32.2 | 31.7 | 33.4 |
| $25,000–$49,999 | 29.5 | 30.6 | 30.2 | 31.6 |
| $50,000–$74,999 | 18.1 | 19.5 | 19.9 | 18.4 |
| $75,000–$99,999 | 9.0 | 9.4 | 9.5 | 9.4 |
| $100,000 or more | 9.4 | 8.2 | 8.7 | 7.2 |

*Source: Bureau of the Census, Internet web site, <http://www.census.gov/cps/ads/sdata.htm>; calculations by New Strategist*

# Distribution of Households by Income, Region, and Division, 1997: South

*(number and percent distribution of households by household income, region, and division, 1997; households in thousands as of 1998)*

| | total | South total | South Atlantic | East South Central | West South Central |
|---|---|---|---|---|---|
| Total households | 102,528 | 36,578 | 19,001 | 6,468 | 11,108 |
| Under $5,000 | 3,531 | 1,424 | 697 | 240 | 487 |
| $5,000–$9,999 | 7,765 | 3,021 | 1,358 | 647 | 1,018 |
| $10,000–$14,999 | 8,326 | 3,142 | 1,541 | 602 | 999 |
| $15,000–$19,999 | 7,837 | 3,009 | 1,492 | 623 | 895 |
| $20,000–$24,999 | 7,406 | 2,830 | 1,486 | 516 | 828 |
| $25,000–$29,999 | 6,913 | 2,631 | 1,320 | 490 | 822 |
| $30,000–$34,999 | 6,673 | 2,511 | 1,349 | 409 | 753 |
| $35,000–$39,999 | 6,111 | 2,197 | 1,114 | 362 | 720 |
| $40,000–$44,999 | 5,667 | 1,978 | 1,013 | 320 | 645 |
| $45,000–$49,999 | 4,920 | 1,806 | 929 | 334 | 543 |
| $50,000–$54,999 | 4,864 | 1,760 | 905 | 356 | 499 |
| $55,000–$59,999 | 3,864 | 1,292 | 694 | 272 | 328 |
| $60,000–$64,999 | 3,751 | 1,249 | 656 | 218 | 375 |
| $65,000–$69,999 | 3,298 | 1,099 | 618 | 132 | 350 |
| $70,000–$74,999 | 2,754 | 878 | 523 | 128 | 226 |
| $75,000–$79,999 | 2,399 | 775 | 438 | 100 | 237 |
| $80,000–$84,999 | 2,251 | 675 | 387 | 117 | 172 |
| $85,000–$89,999 | 1,702 | 535 | 348 | 61 | 126 |
| $90,000–$94,999 | 1,509 | 450 | 237 | 71 | 142 |
| $95,000–$99,999 | 1,325 | 429 | 227 | 76 | 127 |
| $100,000 or more | 9,661 | 2,884 | 1,670 | 398 | 816 |
| Median income | $37,005 | $34,345 | $36,004 | $31,237 | $32,770 |
| | | | | | |
| **Percent distribution** | | | | | |
| **Total households** | **100.0%** | **100.0%** | **100.0%** | **100.0%** | **100.0%** |
| Under $25,000 | 34.0 | 36.7 | 34.6 | 40.6 | 38.1 |
| $25,000–$49,999 | 29.5 | 30.4 | 30.1 | 29.6 | 31.4 |
| $50,000–$74,999 | 18.1 | 17.2 | 17.9 | 17.1 | 16.0 |
| $75,000–$99,999 | 9.0 | 7.8 | 8.6 | 6.6 | 7.2 |
| $100,000 or more | 9.4 | 7.9 | 8.8 | 6.2 | 7.3 |

*Source: Bureau of the Census, Internet web site, <http://www.census.gov/cps/ads/sdata.htm>; calculations by New Strategist*

# Distribution of Households by Income, Region, and Division, 1997: West

*(number and percent distribution of households by household income, region, and division, 1997; households in thousands as of 1998)*

| | total | West total | West Mountain | West Pacific |
|---|---|---|---|---|
| **Total households** | **102,528** | **21,905** | **6,249** | **15,655** |
| Under $5,000 | 3,531 | 635 | 193 | 443 |
| $5,000–$9,999 | 7,765 | 1,405 | 425 | 979 |
| $10,000–$14,999 | 8,326 | 1,800 | 500 | 1,300 |
| $15,000–$19,999 | 7,837 | 1,592 | 461 | 1,131 |
| $20,000–$24,999 | 7,406 | 1,604 | 499 | 1,105 |
| $25,000–$29,999 | 6,913 | 1,411 | 471 | 940 |
| $30,000–$34,999 | 6,673 | 1,381 | 424 | 957 |
| $35,000–$39,999 | 6,111 | 1,302 | 431 | 871 |
| $40,000–$44,999 | 5,667 | 1,199 | 342 | 858 |
| $45,000–$49,999 | 4,920 | 1,045 | 329 | 716 |
| $50,000–$54,999 | 4,864 | 963 | 291 | 672 |
| $55,000–$59,999 | 3,864 | 862 | 247 | 614 |
| $60,000–$64,999 | 3,751 | 886 | 221 | 664 |
| $65,000–$69,999 | 3,298 | 714 | 188 | 526 |
| $70,000–$74,999 | 2,754 | 572 | 166 | 406 |
| $75,000–$79,999 | 2,399 | 580 | 148 | 433 |
| $80,000–$84,999 | 2,251 | 521 | 139 | 382 |
| $85,000–$89,999 | 1,702 | 408 | 110 | 298 |
| $90,000–$94,999 | 1,509 | 314 | 68 | 246 |
| $95,000–$99,999 | 1,325 | 307 | 74 | 233 |
| $100,000 or more | 9,661 | 2,403 | 521 | 1,882 |
| Median income | $37,005 | $39,162 | $36,572 | $40,509 |
| | | | | |
| **Percent distribution** | | | | |
| **Total households** | **100.0%** | **100.0%** | **100.0%** | **100.0%** |
| Under $25,000 | 34.0 | 32.1 | 33.3 | 31.7 |
| $25,000–$49,999 | 29.5 | 28.9 | 32.0 | 27.7 |
| $50,000–$74,999 | 18.1 | 18.2 | 17.8 | 18.4 |
| $75,000–$99,999 | 9.0 | 9.7 | 8.6 | 10.2 |
| $100,000 or more | 9.4 | 11.0 | 8.3 | 12.0 |

*Source: Bureau of the Census, Internet web site, <http://www.census.gov/cps/ads/sdata.htm>; calculations by New Strategist*

# For Blacks, Household Incomes Are Highest in the West

## Hispanic household income peaks in the Midwest.

In every region, the incomes of white households surpass those of blacks and Hispanics. The median income of white households is highest in the Northeast, at $41,214 in 1997. It is lowest in the South, at $36,681.

Among black households, median income is highest in the West, at $29,998. But fewer than 9 percent of black households live there. Black household incomes are lowest in the Northeast, at $23,312, which is home to 18 percent of black households. The 54 percent majority of black households live in the South, where their median income is $25,074. One factor behind the income gap between blacks and whites are differences in household composition. Black households are much less likely than white households to be headed by married couples, the most affluent household type.

Hispanic household incomes are highest in the Midwest, at a median of $31,009. Only 7 percent of Hispanic householders live in the Midwest, however. In contrast, fully 41 percent of Hispanic households are in the West, where their median income is $27,276. Hispanic household incomes are lowest in the Northeast, at just $24,023 in 1997. Behind the income gap between Hispanics and whites is the fact that poorly educated immigrants make up a large share of the Hispanic population, especially in the West and Northeast.

✘ Regional income disparities by race and Hispanic origin will continue as long as differences in black and white household composition persist and until immigrants make up a smaller share of Hispanics.

### White households in the Northeast have much higher incomes than black or Hispanic households

*(median income of households in the Northeast by race and Hispanic origin, 1997)*

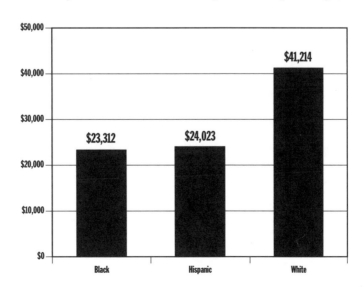

# Distribution of Households by Income, Region, Race, and Hispanic Origin, 1997: Northeast

*(number and percent distribution of households in the Northeast by household income, race, and Hispanic origin, 1997; households in thousands as of 1998)*

| | Northeast | | | |
|---|---|---|---|---|
| | *total* | *black* | *Hispanic* | *white* |
| **Total households** | **19,810** | **2,286** | **1,468** | **16,926** |
| Under $5,000 | 741 | 226 | 113 | 479 |
| $5,000–$9,999 | 1,653 | 350 | 263 | 1,263 |
| $10,000–$14,999 | 1,547 | 227 | 147 | 1,273 |
| $15,000–$19,999 | 1,369 | 219 | 117 | 1,129 |
| $20,000–$24,999 | 1,278 | 177 | 113 | 1,059 |
| $25,000–$29,999 | 1,166 | 128 | 99 | 1,001 |
| $30,000–$34,999 | 1,208 | 167 | 99 | 1,015 |
| $35,000–$39,999 | 1,141 | 126 | 79 | 990 |
| $40,000–$44,999 | 1,034 | 84 | 64 | 916 |
| $45,000–$49,999 | 859 | 81 | 53 | 746 |
| $50,000–$54,999 | 842 | 98 | 41 | 729 |
| $55,000–$59,999 | 733 | 60 | 49 | 652 |
| $60,000–$64,999 | 717 | 41 | 36 | 642 |
| $65,000–$69,999 | 624 | 69 | 20 | 538 |
| $70,000–$74,999 | 617 | 30 | 27 | 565 |
| $75,000–$79,999 | 438 | 9 | 20 | 413 |
| $80,000–$84,999 | 478 | 37 | 20 | 429 |
| $85,000–$89,999 | 357 | 24 | 15 | 325 |
| $90,000–$94,999 | 332 | 13 | 9 | 303 |
| $95,000–$99,999 | 298 | 16 | 17 | 274 |
| $100,000 or more | 2,379 | 105 | 70 | 2,187 |
| Median income | $38,929 | $23,312 | $24,023 | $41,214 |
| **Percent distribution** | | | | |
| **Total households** | **100.0%** | **100.0%** | **100.0%** | **100.0%** |
| Under $25,000 | 33.3 | 52.4 | 51.3 | 30.7 |
| $25,000–$49,999 | 27.3 | 25.6 | 26.8 | 27.6 |
| $50,000–$74,999 | 17.8 | 13.0 | 11.8 | 18.5 |
| $75,000–$99,999 | 9.6 | 4.3 | 5.5 | 10.3 |
| $100,000 or more | 12.0 | 4.6 | 4.8 | 12.9 |

*Source: Bureau of the Census, Internet web site, <http://www.census.gov/cps/ads/sdata.htm>; calculations by New Strategist*

# Distribution of Households by Income, Region, Race, and Hispanic Origin, 1997: Midwest

*(number and percent distribution of households in the Midwest by household income, race, and Hispanic origin, 1997; households in thousands as of 1998)*

| | Midwest | | | |
| --- | --- | --- | --- | --- |
| | total | black | Hispanic | white |
| **Total households** | **24,236** | **2,288** | **644** | **21,465** |
| Under $5,000 | 731 | 170 | 38 | 532 |
| $5,000–$9,999 | 1,686 | 367 | 52 | 1,300 |
| $10,000–$14,999 | 1,836 | 216 | 54 | 1,585 |
| $15,000–$19,999 | 1,865 | 234 | 54 | 1,603 |
| $20,000–$24,999 | 1,694 | 199 | 54 | 1,466 |
| $25,000–$29,999 | 1,704 | 175 | 55 | 1,494 |
| $30,000–$34,999 | 1,574 | 127 | 48 | 1,423 |
| $35,000–$39,999 | 1,471 | 130 | 55 | 1,318 |
| $40,000–$44,999 | 1,456 | 144 | 39 | 1,296 |
| $45,000–$49,999 | 1,211 | 102 | 37 | 1,092 |
| $50,000–$54,999 | 1,298 | 60 | 31 | 1,217 |
| $55,000–$59,999 | 977 | 66 | 19 | 894 |
| $60,000–$64,999 | 900 | 45 | 20 | 838 |
| $65,000–$69,999 | 862 | 47 | 12 | 791 |
| $70,000–$74,999 | 687 | 37 | 9 | 624 |
| $75,000–$79,999 | 606 | 24 | 17 | 565 |
| $80,000–$84,999 | 576 | 25 | 11 | 535 |
| $85,000–$89,999 | 401 | 16 | 4 | 373 |
| $90,000–$94,999 | 415 | 20 | 11 | 388 |
| $95,000–$99,999 | 290 | 14 | 5 | 266 |
| $100,000 or more | 1,995 | 70 | 20 | 1,865 |
| Median income | $38,316 | $23,861 | $31,009 | $40,040 |
| **Percent distribution** | | | | |
| **Total households** | **100.0%** | **100.0%** | **100.0%** | **100.0%** |
| Under $25,000 | 32.2 | 51.8 | 39.1 | 30.2 |
| $25,000–$49,999 | 30.6 | 29.6 | 36.3 | 30.9 |
| $50,000–$74,999 | 19.5 | 11.1 | 14.1 | 20.3 |
| $75,000–$99,999 | 9.4 | 4.3 | 7.5 | 9.9 |
| $100,000 or more | 8.2 | 3.1 | 3.1 | 8.7 |

*Source: Bureau of the Census, Internet web site, <http://www.census.gov/cps/ads/sdata.htm>; calculations by New Strategist*

## Distribution of Households by Income, Region, Race, and Hispanic Origin, 1997: South

*(number and percent distribution of households in the South by household income, race, and Hispanic origin, 1997; households in thousands as of 1998)*

| | Soouth | | | |
|---|---|---|---|---|
| | total | black | Hispanic | white |
| **Total households** | **36,578** | **6,814** | **2,939** | **28,948** |
| Under $5,000 | 1,424 | 489 | 168 | 900 |
| $5,000–$9,999 | 3,021 | 897 | 306 | 2,077 |
| $10,000–$14,999 | 3,142 | 774 | 340 | 2,297 |
| $15,000–$19,999 | 3,009 | 652 | 273 | 2,302 |
| $20,000–$24,999 | 2,830 | 587 | 312 | 2,209 |
| $25,000–$29,999 | 2,631 | 533 | 261 | 2,034 |
| $30,000–$34,999 | 2,511 | 444 | 214 | 2,001 |
| $35,000–$39,999 | 2,197 | 387 | 172 | 1,739 |
| $40,000–$44,999 | 1,978 | 342 | 188 | 1,587 |
| $45,000–$49,999 | 1,806 | 284 | 136 | 1,481 |
| $50,000–$54,999 | 1,760 | 266 | 97 | 1,466 |
| $55,000–$59,999 | 1,292 | 245 | 66 | 1,018 |
| $60,000–$64,999 | 1,249 | 186 | 61 | 1,031 |
| $65,000–$69,999 | 1,099 | 159 | 46 | 922 |
| $70,000–$74,999 | 878 | 90 | 34 | 773 |
| $75,000–$79,999 | 775 | 78 | 40 | 680 |
| $80,000–$84,999 | 675 | 86 | 33 | 572 |
| $85,000–$89,999 | 535 | 62 | 21 | 454 |
| $90,000–$94,999 | 450 | 33 | 25 | 400 |
| $95,000–$99,999 | 429 | 47 | 19 | 373 |
| $100,000 or more | 2,884 | 173 | 126 | 2,631 |
| Median income | $34,345 | $25,074 | $26,207 | $36,681 |
| **Percent distribution** | | | | |
| **Total households** | **100.0%** | **100.0%** | **100.0%** | **100.0%** |
| Under $25,000 | 36.7 | 49.9 | 47.6 | 33.8 |
| $25,000–$49,999 | 30.4 | 29.2 | 33.0 | 30.5 |
| $50,000–$74,999 | 17.2 | 13.9 | 10.3 | 18.0 |
| $75,000–$99,999 | 7.8 | 4.5 | 4.7 | 8.6 |
| $100,000 or more | 7.9 | 2.5 | 4.3 | 9.1 |

*Source: Bureau of the Census, Internet web site, <http://www.census.gov/cps/ads/sdata.htm>; calculations by New Strategist*

# Distribution of Households by Income, Region, Race, and Hispanic Origin, 1997: West

*(number and percent distribution of households in the West by household income, race, and Hispanic origin, 1997; households in thousands as of 1998)*

| | West | | | |
| --- | --- | --- | --- | --- |
| | *total* | *black* | *Hispanic* | *white* |
| **Total households** | **21,905** | **1,086** | **3,539** | **18,767** |
| Under $5,000 | 635 | 42 | 154 | 503 |
| $5,000–$9,999 | 1,405 | 133 | 347 | 1,134 |
| $10,000–$14,999 | 1,800 | 100 | 374 | 1,561 |
| $15,000–$19,999 | 1,592 | 71 | 396 | 1,402 |
| $20,000–$24,999 | 1,604 | 99 | 371 | 1,379 |
| $25,000–$29,999 | 1,411 | 99 | 258 | 1,209 |
| $30,000–$34,999 | 1,381 | 94 | 258 | 1,172 |
| $35,000–$39,999 | 1,302 | 46 | 229 | 1,119 |
| $40,000–$44,999 | 1,199 | 72 | 199 | 1,005 |
| $45,000–$49,999 | 1,045 | 59 | 179 | 882 |
| $50,000–$54,999 | 963 | 21 | 142 | 864 |
| $55,000–$59,999 | 862 | 27 | 93 | 748 |
| $60,000–$64,999 | 886 | 22 | 99 | 767 |
| $65,000–$69,999 | 714 | 28 | 75 | 611 |
| $70,000–$74,999 | 572 | 38 | 72 | 499 |
| $75,000–$79,999 | 580 | 29 | 51 | 492 |
| $80,000–$84,999 | 521 | 14 | 41 | 462 |
| $85,000–$89,999 | 408 | 10 | 29 | 358 |
| $90,000–$94,999 | 314 | 12 | 26 | 273 |
| $95,000–$99,999 | 307 | 2 | 13 | 250 |
| $100,000 or more | 2,403 | 67 | 135 | 2,080 |
| Median income | $39,162 | $29,988 | $27,276 | $39,479 |
| | | | | |
| **Percent distribution** | | | | |
| **Total households** | **100.0%** | **100.0%** | **100.0%** | **100.0%** |
| Under $25,000 | 32.1 | 41.0 | 46.4 | 31.9 |
| $25,000–$49,999 | 28.9 | 34.1 | 31.7 | 28.7 |
| $50,000–$74,999 | 18.2 | 12.5 | 13.6 | 18.6 |
| $75,000–$99,999 | 9.7 | 6.2 | 4.5 | 9.8 |
| $100,000 or more | 11.0 | 6.2 | 3.8 | 11.1 |

*Source: Bureau of the Census, Internet web site, <http://www.census.gov/cps/ads/sdata.htm>; calculations by New Strategist*

# Suburban Households Have the Highest Incomes

**Households in the suburbs of the largest metropolitan areas had a median income of nearly $48,000 in 1997.**

Of the nation's 102.5 million households, 49 percent are located in the suburbs of metropolitan areas—defined as the portion of a metropolitan area outside the central city. Suburban households have the highest incomes, and those outside of the largest metropolitan areas have the highest incomes of all—a median of $47,981 in 1997. Fifteen percent of these households have incomes of $100,000 or more. Households located in the suburbs of smaller metropolitan areas had a median income of $38,581 in 1997.

One in five householders does not live in a metropolitan area. These householders have the lowest incomes, a median of just $30,057 in 1997, 19 percent below the national median of $37,005.

Thirty-one percent of householders live in the central cities of metropolitan areas. Their median income is also below the national figure, at $31,548 in 1997, with little difference by size of metropolitan area.

✗ The income gap between households in suburban and nonmetropolitan areas may narrow in the years ahead as technological change allows a growing share of executives and professionals to work from remote locations.

## Households in nonmetropolitan areas have the lowest incomes

*(median income of households by metropolitan residence, 1997)*

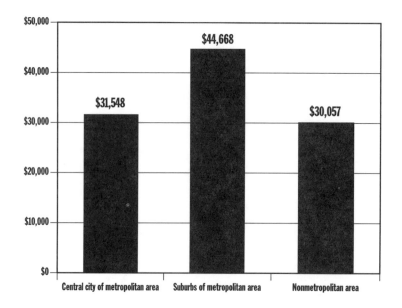

# Distribution of Households by Income and Metropolitan Residence, 1997

*(number and percent distribution of households by household income and metropolitan residence, 1997; households in thousands as of 1998)*

| | | in metropolitan area | | | | | | | not in metropolitan area |
|---|---|---|---|---|---|---|---|---|---|
| | | total | inside central cities | | | outside central cities | | | |
| | total | total | total | 1 million+ | < 1 million | total | 1 million+ | < 1 million | |
| **Total households** | **102,528** | **82,122** | **31,907** | **20,310** | **11,597** | **50,215** | **34,357** | **15,858** | **20,406** |
| Under $5,000 | 3,531 | 2,701 | 1,547 | 1,008 | 539 | 1,154 | 760 | 395 | 830 |
| $5,000–$9,999 | 7,765 | 5,850 | 3,255 | 2,120 | 1,135 | 2,595 | 1,603 | 992 | 1,915 |
| $10,000–$14,999 | 8,326 | 6,085 | 2,926 | 1,817 | 1,108 | 3,159 | 1,958 | 1,201 | 2,241 |
| $15,000–$19,999 | 7,838 | 5,932 | 2,686 | 1,641 | 1,045 | 3,245 | 2,035 | 1,210 | 1,906 |
| $20,000–$24,999 | 7,406 | 5,724 | 2,490 | 1,588 | 902 | 3,233 | 2,081 | 1,152 | 1,682 |
| $25,000–$29,999 | 6,913 | 5,302 | 2,292 | 1,444 | 848 | 3,010 | 1,888 | 1,121 | 1,611 |
| $30,000–$34,999 | 6,674 | 5,223 | 2,068 | 1,264 | 804 | 3,154 | 2,032 | 1,121 | 1,451 |
| $35,000–$39,999 | 6,109 | 4,738 | 1,844 | 1,157 | 686 | 2,895 | 1,901 | 994 | 1,371 |
| $40,000–$44,999 | 5,667 | 4,448 | 1,624 | 1,066 | 558 | 2,824 | 1,854 | 971 | 1,219 |
| $45,000–$49,999 | 4,920 | 3,928 | 1,433 | 866 | 567 | 2,494 | 1,653 | 842 | 992 |
| $50,000–$54,999 | 4,863 | 3,883 | 1,291 | 767 | 524 | 2,592 | 1,758 | 834 | 980 |
| $55,000–$59,999 | 3,864 | 3,183 | 1,027 | 606 | 421 | 2,155 | 1,472 | 683 | 681 |
| $60,000–$64,999 | 3,750 | 3,117 | 1,042 | 688 | 354 | 2,075 | 1,476 | 600 | 633 |
| $65,000–$69,999 | 3,298 | 2,787 | 863 | 582 | 281 | 1,925 | 1,416 | 508 | 511 |
| $70,000–$74,999 | 2,754 | 2,331 | 687 | 450 | 237 | 1,644 | 1,195 | 448 | 423 |
| $75,000–$79,999 | 2,398 | 2,086 | 676 | 438 | 238 | 1,410 | 1,014 | 396 | 312 |
| $80,000–$84,999 | 2,251 | 1,940 | 549 | 361 | 190 | 1,391 | 1,057 | 334 | 311 |
| $85,000–$89,999 | 1,702 | 1,509 | 403 | 243 | 160 | 1,106 | 789 | 317 | 193 |
| $90,000–$94,999 | 1,509 | 1,330 | 346 | 231 | 115 | 984 | 750 | 234 | 179 |
| $95,000–$99,999 | 1,325 | 1,204 | 343 | 242 | 102 | 860 | 632 | 228 | 121 |
| $100,000 or more | 9,661 | 8,820 | 2,512 | 1,732 | 781 | 6,308 | 5,031 | 1,277 | 841 |
| Median income | $37,005 | $39,381 | $31,548 | $31,789 | $31,168 | $44,668 | $47,981 | $38,581 | $30,057 |
| **Percent distribution** | | | | | | | | | |
| **Total households** | **100.0%** | **100.0%** | **100.0%** | **100.0%** | **100.0%** | **100.0%** | **100.0%** | **100.0%** | **100.0%** |
| Under $25,000 | 34.0 | 32.0 | 40.4 | 40.2 | 40.8 | 26.7 | 24.6 | 31.2 | 42.0 |
| $25,000–$49,999 | 29.5 | 28.8 | 29.0 | 28.5 | 29.9 | 28.6 | 27.2 | 31.8 | 32.6 |
| $50,000–$74,999 | 18.1 | 18.6 | 15.4 | 15.2 | 15.7 | 20.7 | 21.3 | 19.4 | 15.8 |
| $75,000–$99,999 | 9.0 | 9.8 | 7.3 | 7.5 | 6.9 | 11.5 | 12.3 | 9.5 | 5.5 |
| $100,000 or more | 9.4 | 10.7 | 7.9 | 8.5 | 6.7 | 12.6 | 14.6 | 8.1 | 4.1 |

*Source: Bureau of the Census, Internet web site, <http://www.census.gov/cps/ads/sdata.htm>; calculations by New Strategist*

# Chapter 2

# Men's Income

While household incomes have been setting records in recent years, the same cannot be said for men's incomes. The median income of men rose only 2 percent during the past three decades, to $24,632 after adjusting for inflation. The incomes of men under age 45 are lower today than they were in 1967, while the biggest gains have been made by the oldest men.

Some men have fared much better than others. The incomes of black men have soared, up an inflation-adjusted 22 percent over the past few decades thanks to expanding educational and job opportunities. Nevertheless, the incomes of black men still lag behind those of whites. The median income of Hispanic men fell 23 percent between 1972 and 1997 because so many unskilled Hispanic immigrants with little earning power arrived in the United States during those years, pulling down the Hispanic median.

✘ If the economy remains strong, men's incomes will rise slowly in the years ahead, but if the economy experiences a downturn, men's incomes may stagnate or even decline.

# Men's Income Trends

# More Men Have High Incomes

## The percentage of men making $75,000 or more is at a record high.

Nearly 8 percent of men with income had an income of $75,000 or more in 1997, up from only 3.5 percent in 1967, after adjusting for inflation. While a growing share of men have been enjoying high incomes, the share of those with middle incomes has fallen as some men—particularly those without a college degree—have found themselves at a disadvantage in the labor market.

Trends in men's incomes differ by race and Hispanic origin. Black men are enjoying rising incomes, and the middle- and upper-income ranks are growing. Trends have not been as positive for Hispanic men. The proportion of Hispanic men with incomes of $50,000 or more rose slightly between 1972 and 1997, but the share with incomes below $15,000 rose much more.

✘ It is likely that men's incomes will continue to polarize, particularly if the economy experiences another recession.

### One-half of men have incomes below $25,000

*(percent distribution of men aged 15 or older by income, 1967 and 1997; in 1997 dollars)*

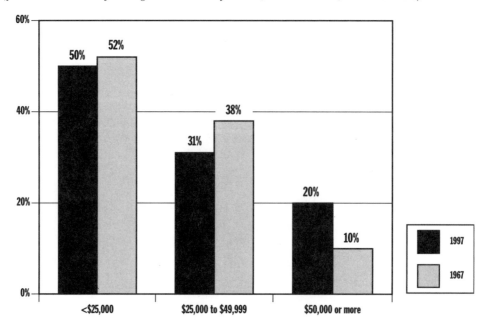

# Distribution of Men by Income, 1967 to 1997: Total Men

*(total number of men aged 15 or older, number with income, and percent distribution by income of men with income, 1967 to 1997; in 1997 dollars; men in thousands as of the following year)*

| | total men | men with income | percent distribution | | | | | | |
|---|---|---|---|---|---|---|---|---|---|
| | | | under $5,000 | $5,000 to $9,999 | $10,000 to $14,999 | $15,000 to $24,999 | $25,000 to $49,999 | $50,000 to $74,999 | $75,000 or over |
| 1997 | 101,123 | 94,168 | 9.1% | 10.2% | 11.4% | 18.9% | 30.9% | 11.6% | 7.9% |
| 1996 | 100,159 | 93,439 | 9.5 | 10.9 | 11.7 | 19.3 | 30.5 | 10.9 | 7.2 |
| 1995 | 98,593 | 92,066 | 10.0 | 10.5 | 11.5 | 19.8 | 30.3 | 10.9 | 7.0 |
| 1994 | 97,704 | 91,254 | 10.3 | 11.1 | 11.6 | 20.0 | 29.7 | 10.3 | 7.1 |
| 1993 | 96,768 | 90,194 | 11.1 | 11.2 | 11.5 | 19.6 | 29.7 | 10.4 | 6.6 |
| 1992 | 95,652 | 90,175 | 11.2 | 11.3 | 11.7 | 19.1 | 30.2 | 10.5 | 6.1 |
| 1991 | 93,760 | 88,653 | 10.6 | 10.9 | 11.2 | 19.8 | 30.8 | 10.5 | 6.3 |
| 1990 | 92,840 | 88,220 | 10.2 | 10.9 | 10.6 | 19.7 | 31.3 | 11.0 | 6.4 |
| 1989 | 91,955 | 87,454 | 9.9 | 10.3 | 10.2 | 19.0 | 31.4 | 12.1 | 7.1 |
| 1988 | 91,034 | 86,584 | 10.4 | 10.5 | 10.1 | 18.7 | 31.8 | 12.0 | 6.6 |
| 1987 | 90,256 | 85,713 | 10.9 | 10.5 | 10.3 | 18.2 | 31.6 | 12.1 | 6.4 |
| 1986 | 89,368 | 84,471 | 11.3 | 10.1 | 10.6 | 18.3 | 31.1 | 12.2 | 6.3 |
| 1985 | 88,478 | 83,631 | 11.7 | 10.6 | 10.8 | 18.5 | 31.1 | 11.5 | 5.9 |
| 1984 | 87,304 | 82,183 | 12.1 | 11.1 | 9.9 | 19.0 | 31.3 | 10.7 | 5.7 |
| 1983 | 86,014 | 80,795 | 13.0 | 11.1 | 10.0 | 19.1 | 31.4 | 10.2 | 5.3 |
| 1982 | 84,955 | 79,722 | 12.3 | 11.1 | 10.2 | 19.1 | 31.6 | 10.5 | 5.3 |
| 1981 | 83,958 | 79,688 | 11.9 | 11.1 | 10.2 | 18.8 | 32.4 | 10.7 | 4.7 |
| 1980 | 82,949 | 78,661 | 11.3 | 11.1 | 9.5 | 18.9 | 33.7 | 10.6 | 4.9 |
| 1979 | 81,947 | 78,129 | 11.1 | 10.6 | 9.4 | 18.2 | 33.8 | 11.5 | 5.4 |
| 1978 | 80,969 | 75,609 | 11.5 | 10.8 | 9.3 | 17.7 | 33.7 | 11.7 | 5.3 |
| 1977 | 79,863 | 74,015 | 11.5 | 10.7 | 9.5 | 17.1 | 34.2 | 11.6 | 5.2 |
| 1976 | 78,782 | 72,775 | 11.7 | 10.7 | 9.8 | 17.8 | 34.5 | 10.9 | 4.7 |
| 1975 | 77,560 | 71,234 | 11.5 | 11.0 | 9.9 | 17.5 | 35.2 | 10.5 | 4.4 |
| 1974 | 76,363 | 70,863 | 11.8 | 10.4 | 8.8 | 18.0 | 35.4 | 10.6 | 5.0 |
| 1973 | 75,040 | 69,387 | 11.5 | 9.7 | 8.6 | 17.1 | 35.9 | 11.9 | 5.3 |
| 1972 | 73,572 | 67,474 | 11.9 | 9.7 | 9.0 | 16.3 | 36.8 | 11.1 | 5.1 |
| 1971 | 72,469 | 66,486 | 12.7 | 10.3 | 9.2 | 17.0 | 37.0 | 9.6 | 4.2 |
| 1970 | 70,592 | 65,008 | 13.1 | 10.1 | 8.5 | 17.2 | 37.5 | 9.4 | 4.2 |
| 1969 | 69,027 | 63,882 | 13.3 | 10.0 | 8.6 | 17.0 | 37.9 | 9.0 | 4.1 |
| 1968 | 67,611 | 62,501 | 13.4 | 9.9 | 8.8 | 17.5 | 38.5 | 8.3 | 3.6 |
| 1967 | 66,519 | 61,444 | 14.2 | 10.5 | 8.7 | 18.9 | 37.5 | 6.9 | 3.5 |

*Source: Bureau of the Census,* Money Income in the United States: 1997, *Current Population Reports, P60-200, 1998*

# Distribution of Men by Income, 1967 to 1997: Black Men

*(total number of black men aged 15 or older, number with income, and percent distribution by income of black men with income, 1967 to 1997; in 1997 dollars; men in thousands as of the following year)*

| | total men | men with income | percent distribution | | | | | | |
|---|---|---|---|---|---|---|---|---|---|
| | | | under $5,000 | $5,000 to $9,999 | $10,000 to $14,999 | $15,000 to $24,999 | $25,000 to $49,999 | $50,000 to $74,999 | $75,000 or over |
| 1997 | 11,283 | 9,671 | 13.0% | 16.6% | 13.1% | 21.3% | 27.3% | 6.6% | 2.2% |
| 1996 | 11,113 | 9,410 | 14.7 | 17.6 | 13.5 | 19.8 | 26.7 | 5.5 | 2.3 |
| 1995 | 10,922 | 9,339 | 16.0 | 16.7 | 13.0 | 22.2 | 24.5 | 5.4 | 2.3 |
| 1994 | 10,825 | 9,119 | 14.8 | 18.5 | 14.1 | 21.0 | 23.6 | 5.7 | 2.3 |
| 1993 | 10,639 | 8,947 | 17.4 | 17.5 | 13.4 | 21.3 | 23.9 | 4.8 | 1.7 |
| 1992 | 10,453 | 9,104 | 18.7 | 18.1 | 13.8 | 19.8 | 23.7 | 4.3 | 1.6 |
| 1991 | 10,252 | 8,943 | 18.3 | 17.5 | 13.4 | 21.4 | 23.1 | 4.8 | 1.5 |
| 1990 | 10,074 | 8,820 | 16.5 | 18.9 | 13.0 | 20.9 | 23.7 | 5.6 | 1.4 |
| 1989 | 9,948 | 8,806 | 15.8 | 17.9 | 12.7 | 22.0 | 24.6 | 5.6 | 1.4 |
| 1988 | 9,809 | 8,610 | 16.9 | 17.7 | 13.2 | 20.2 | 24.7 | 5.3 | 2.0 |
| 1987 | 9,668 | 8,488 | 16.8 | 18.7 | 13.0 | 20.3 | 24.9 | 4.9 | 1.4 |
| 1986 | 9,472 | 8,285 | 17.7 | 17.1 | 14.6 | 20.0 | 24.3 | 4.9 | 1.4 |
| 1985 | 9,309 | 8,127 | 18.3 | 16.6 | 14.1 | 20.8 | 24.7 | 4.3 | 1.2 |
| 1984 | 9,141 | 7,851 | 19.2 | 19.0 | 12.9 | 22.6 | 21.2 | 4.1 | 1.0 |
| 1983 | 8,986 | 7,587 | 20.7 | 17.8 | 12.7 | 21.6 | 22.4 | 4.0 | 0.8 |
| 1982 | 8,757 | 7,290 | 18.3 | 17.8 | 13.5 | 22.4 | 23.8 | 3.4 | 0.8 |
| 1981 | 8,614 | 7,459 | 18.2 | 18.1 | 13.6 | 21.7 | 24.7 | 3.3 | 0.4 |
| 1980 | 8,448 | 7,387 | 18.9 | 18.0 | 11.8 | 21.7 | 24.9 | 4.0 | 0.8 |
| 1979 | 8,292 | 7,288 | 16.5 | 18.2 | 11.8 | 22.0 | 26.4 | 4.2 | 0.9 |
| 1978 | 9,148 | 6,971 | 17.5 | 17.7 | 12.8 | 19.8 | 26.8 | 4.7 | 0.8 |
| 1977 | 8,057 | 6,777 | 17.2 | 16.0 | 14.7 | 21.0 | 26.3 | 3.9 | 1.0 |
| 1976 | 7,914 | 6,651 | 17.6 | 17.4 | 12.8 | 22.2 | 26.0 | 3.3 | 0.8 |
| 1975 | 7,720 | 6,485 | 16.5 | 18.7 | 14.2 | 20.5 | 27.0 | 2.7 | 0.5 |
| 1974 | 7,507 | 6,409 | 16.9 | 17.6 | 11.2 | 23.7 | 26.4 | 3.7 | 0.4 |
| 1973 | 7,415 | 6,394 | 17.2 | 15.3 | 12.3 | 23.1 | 27.9 | 3.6 | 0.7 |
| 1972 | 7,200 | 6,043 | 18.7 | 14.1 | 13.4 | 21.0 | 29.1 | 3.2 | 0.6 |
| 1971 | 7,041 | 6,024 | 19.7 | 15.1 | 13.6 | 22.9 | 26.0 | 2.1 | 0.5 |
| 1970 | 6,796 | 5,844 | 20.6 | 13.7 | 13.2 | 24.3 | 25.6 | 1.9 | 0.5 |
| 1969 | 6,637 | 5,870 | 21.2 | 13.6 | 13.4 | 24.4 | 25.5 | 1.7 | 0.2 |
| 1968 | 6,456 | 5,715 | 21.4 | 13.9 | 13.8 | 24.6 | 24.5 | 1.4 | 0.4 |
| 1967 | 6,318 | 5,572 | 23.3 | 14.2 | 15.4 | 25.5 | 19.8 | 1.2 | 0.5 |

*Source: Bureau of the Census,* Money Income in the United States: 1997, *Current Population Reports, P60-200, 1998*

# Distribution of Men by Income, 1972 to 1997: Hispanic Men

*(total number of Hispanic men aged 15 or older, number with income, and percent distribution by income of Hispanic men with income, 1972 to 1997; in 1997 dollars; men in thousands as of the following year)*

| | total men | men with income | percent distribution | | | | | | |
|---|---|---|---|---|---|---|---|---|---|
| | | | under $5,000 | $5,000 to $9,999 | $10,000 to $14,999 | $15,000 to $24,999 | $25,000 to $49,999 | $50,000 to $74,999 | $75,000 or over |
| 1997 | 10,944 | 9,585 | 11.1% | 15.5% | 19.0% | 24.4% | 22.2% | 5.1% | 2.6% |
| 1996 | 10,627 | 9,305 | 11.8 | 17.0 | 19.2 | 24.1 | 21.4 | 4.6 | 1.8 |
| 1995 | 9,826 | 8,577 | 13.3 | 17.7 | 18.1 | 23.7 | 20.9 | 4.5 | 1.8 |
| 1994 | 9,555 | 8,375 | 12.4 | 19.0 | 17.3 | 24.0 | 20.9 | 4.0 | 2.4 |
| 1993 | 9,312 | 8,208 | 13.6 | 19.1 | 17.5 | 22.7 | 20.9 | 4.3 | 1.9 |
| 1992 | 8,996 | 8,056 | 13.5 | 18.4 | 18.2 | 22.7 | 21.1 | 4.5 | 1.7 |
| 1991 | 7,738 | 6,939 | 11.7 | 17.2 | 18.2 | 23.4 | 23.3 | 4.3 | 1.8 |
| 1990 | 7,502 | 6,767 | 12.9 | 16.4 | 16.9 | 24.6 | 22.9 | 4.4 | 1.9 |
| 1989 | 7,254 | 6,592 | 12.1 | 15.0 | 15.9 | 26.1 | 23.3 | 5.2 | 2.4 |
| 1988 | 7,012 | 6,342 | 12.6 | 15.1 | 15.4 | 25.2 | 24.1 | 5.6 | 2.0 |
| 1987 | 6,768 | 6,102 | 11.7 | 17.0 | 15.5 | 22.5 | 25.5 | 5.7 | 2.1 |
| 1986 | 6,517 | 5,870 | 13.7 | 15.0 | 16.5 | 23.4 | 23.5 | 6.4 | 1.6 |
| 1985 | 6,232 | 5,523 | 13.8 | 15.4 | 16.4 | 21.7 | 25.3 | 5.7 | 1.6 |
| 1984 | 5,809 | 5,174 | 15.1 | 15.8 | 13.9 | 23.1 | 25.4 | 4.9 | 1.8 |
| 1983 | 5,633 | 4,236 | 14.0 | 16.2 | 13.6 | 24.9 | 25.6 | 4.3 | 1.4 |
| 1982 | 4,592 | 4,092 | 13.5 | 15.3 | 14.6 | 24.4 | 25.4 | 5.1 | 1.7 |
| 1981 | 4,557 | 4,131 | 13.2 | 14.6 | 13.9 | 24.5 | 27.0 | 5.3 | 1.3 |
| 1980 | 4,429 | 3,996 | 13.0 | 13.9 | 13.5 | 25.2 | 27.9 | 5.1 | 1.5 |
| 1979 | 4,196 | 3,852 | 13.2 | 13.8 | 11.9 | 25.3 | 28.8 | 5.2 | 1.9 |
| 1978 | 3,880 | 3,447 | 13.2 | 12.4 | 11.9 | 25.8 | 29.6 | 5.6 | 1.6 |
| 1977 | 3,848 | 3,376 | 12.3 | 13.0 | 12.1 | 25.1 | 31.0 | 5.1 | 1.5 |
| 1976 | 3,526 | 3,099 | 14.1 | 13.6 | 12.5 | 24.7 | 29.2 | 4.7 | 1.2 |
| 1975 | 3,415 | 2,945 | 13.6 | 13.1 | 12.6 | 25.3 | 29.9 | 4.4 | 1.0 |
| 1974 | 3,519 | 3,052 | 14.2 | 12.5 | 11.3 | 26.5 | 30.1 | 4.1 | 1.3 |
| 1973 | 3,433 | 2,867 | 13.3 | 10.9 | 10.6 | 26.6 | 33.1 | 4.7 | 0.7 |
| 1972 | 3,204 | 2,709 | 13.5 | 10.8 | 13.0 | 23.6 | 33.5 | 4.0 | 1.5 |

*Source: Bureau of the Census,* Money Income in the United States: 1997, *Current Population Reports, P60-200, 1998*

# Distribution of Men by Income, 1967 to 1997: White Men

*(total number of white men aged 15 or older, number with income, and percent distribution by income of white men with income, 1967 to 1997; in 1997 dollars; men in thousands as of the following year)*

| | total men | men with income | percent distribution | | | | | | |
|---|---|---|---|---|---|---|---|---|---|
| | | | under $5,000 | $5,000 to $9,999 | $10,000 to $14,999 | $15,000 to $24,999 | $25,000 to $49,999 | $50,000 to $74,999 | $75,000 or over |
| 1997 | 85,219 | 80,400 | 8.6% | 9.4% | 11.2% | 18.6% | 31.4% | 12.2% | 8.6% |
| 1996 | 84,540 | 80,041 | 8.8 | 10.1 | 11.4 | 19.3 | 31.1 | 11.5 | 7.8 |
| 1995 | 83,463 | 79,022 | 9.1 | 9.8 | 11.2 | 19.6 | 31.1 | 11.6 | 7.6 |
| 1994 | 82,566 | 78,220 | 9.6 | 10.1 | 11.2 | 19.9 | 30.6 | 10.8 | 7.7 |
| 1993 | 82,026 | 77,650 | 10.3 | 10.3 | 11.2 | 19.5 | 30.5 | 11.1 | 7.1 |
| 1992 | 81,179 | 77,467 | 10.2 | 10.4 | 11.4 | 19.0 | 31.2 | 11.2 | 6.6 |
| 1991 | 80,049 | 76,578 | 9.5 | 10.1 | 11.0 | 19.6 | 31.8 | 11.1 | 6.8 |
| 1990 | 79,555 | 76,480 | 9.3 | 9.9 | 10.2 | 19.6 | 32.3 | 11.7 | 6.9 |
| 1989 | 78,908 | 75,858 | 9.2 | 9.4 | 9.8 | 18.7 | 32.3 | 12.9 | 7.7 |
| 1988 | 78,230 | 75,247 | 9.6 | 9.6 | 9.7 | 18.5 | 32.8 | 12.9 | 7.0 |
| 1987 | 77,743 | 74,647 | 10.1 | 9.5 | 9.9 | 18.1 | 32.5 | 12.9 | 7.0 |
| 1986 | 77,212 | 73,827 | 10.4 | 9.4 | 10.1 | 18.2 | 31.9 | 13.1 | 6.9 |
| 1985 | 76,617 | 73,222 | 10.9 | 9.9 | 10.3 | 18.3 | 31.8 | 12.3 | 6.4 |
| 1984 | 75,487 | 72,162 | 11.3 | 10.2 | 9.7 | 18.7 | 32.5 | 11.4 | 6.2 |
| 1983 | 74,805 | 71,231 | 12.0 | 10.3 | 9.8 | 19.0 | 32.4 | 10.8 | 5.7 |
| 1982 | 74,043 | 70,477 | 11.6 | 10.3 | 9.8 | 18.8 | 32.5 | 11.3 | 5.8 |
| 1981 | 72,449 | 70,351 | 11.3 | 10.4 | 9.8 | 18.6 | 33.3 | 11.6 | 5.2 |
| 1980 | 72,449 | 69,420 | 10.4 | 10.3 | 9.2 | 18.7 | 34.7 | 11.4 | 5.4 |
| 1979 | 71,887 | 69,247 | 10.4 | 9.8 | 9.2 | 17.7 | 34.6 | 12.3 | 6.0 |
| 1978 | 71,308 | 67,273 | 10.9 | 10.1 | 8.9 | 17.4 | 34.5 | 12.4 | 5.7 |
| 1977 | 70,407 | 65,974 | 10.9 | 10.1 | 9.0 | 16.7 | 35.1 | 12.4 | 5.7 |
| 1976 | 69,555 | 64,946 | 11.1 | 10.0 | 9.4 | 17.2 | 35.5 | 11.7 | 5.1 |
| 1975 | 68,573 | 63,629 | 10.9 | 10.3 | 9.4 | 17.2 | 36.1 | 11.4 | 4.8 |
| 1974 | 67,667 | 63,388 | 11.2 | 9.6 | 8.5 | 17.4 | 36.4 | 11.3 | 5.4 |
| 1973 | 66,550 | 62,082 | 11.0 | 9.0 | 8.1 | 16.4 | 36.8 | 12.8 | 5.8 |
| 1972 | 65,385 | 60,565 | 11.2 | 9.2 | 8.5 | 15.8 | 37.7 | 12.0 | 5.6 |
| 1971 | 64,611 | 59,729 | 11.9 | 9.7 | 8.7 | 16.4 | 38.2 | 10.4 | 4.5 |
| 1970 | 63,002 | 58,447 | 12.2 | 9.7 | 8.0 | 16.4 | 38.7 | 10.2 | 4.6 |
| 1969 | 61,645 | 57,343 | 12.5 | 9.7 | 8.0 | 16.2 | 39.3 | 9.8 | 4.5 |
| 1968 | 60,498 | 56,219 | 12.5 | 9.5 | 8.2 | 16.8 | 40.0 | 9.0 | 3.9 |
| 1967 | 59,524 | 55,270 | 13.2 | 10.1 | 8.0 | 18.2 | 39.3 | 7.4 | 3.8 |

*Source: Bureau of the Census,* Money Income in the United States: 1997, *Current Population Reports, P60-200, 1998*

## Distribution of Men by Income, 1972 to 1997: Non-Hispanic White Men

*(total number of non-Hispanic white men aged 15 or older, number with income, and percent distribution by income of non-Hispanic white men with income; 1972 to 1997, in 1997 dollars; men in thousands as of the following year)*

| | total men | men with income | percent distribution | | | | | | |
|---|---|---|---|---|---|---|---|---|---|
| | | | under $5,000 | $5,000 to $9,999 | $10,000 to $14,999 | $15,000 to $24,999 | $25,000 to $49,999 | $50,000 to $74,999 | $75,000 or over |
| 1997 | 74,703 | 71,150 | 8.3% | 8.6% | 10.1% | 17.8% | 32.7% | 13.2% | 9.4% |
| 1996 | 74,349 | 71,084 | 8.5 | 9.2 | 10.4 | 18.7 | 32.3 | 12.4 | 8.6 |
| 1995 | 74,040 | 70,754 | 8.7 | 8.9 | 10.4 | 19.1 | 32.3 | 12.4 | 8.2 |
| 1994 | 74,238 | 70,919 | 9.3 | 9.2 | 10.6 | 19.5 | 31.6 | 11.5 | 8.3 |
| 1993 | 73,580 | 70,179 | 9.9 | 9.4 | 10.5 | 19.1 | 31.5 | 11.8 | 7.7 |
| 1992 | 72,761 | 69,907 | 9.9 | 9.5 | 10.6 | 18.7 | 32.2 | 12.0 | 7.1 |
| 1991 | 72,682 | 69,976 | 9.3 | 9.4 | 10.3 | 19.3 | 32.6 | 11.8 | 7.3 |
| 1990 | 72,352 | 69,987 | 9.0 | 9.3 | 9.6 | 19.1 | 33.2 | 12.4 | 7.4 |
| 1989 | 71,972 | 69,558 | 8.9 | 8.9 | 9.3 | 18.1 | 33.1 | 13.6 | 8.2 |
| 1988 | 71,492 | 69,143 | 9.3 | 9.1 | 9.2 | 17.9 | 33.5 | 13.5 | 7.5 |
| 1987 | 71,224 | 68,762 | 10.0 | 8.8 | 9.5 | 17.7 | 33.1 | 13.5 | 7.4 |
| 1986 | 70,888 | 68,131 | 10.1 | 8.9 | 9.6 | 17.8 | 32.7 | 13.6 | 7.3 |
| 1985 | 70,624 | 67,859 | 10.7 | 9.5 | 9.8 | 18.0 | 32.4 | 12.9 | 6.8 |
| 1984 | 69,835 | 67,126 | 11.1 | 9.8 | 9.4 | 18.3 | 33.0 | 11.9 | 6.6 |
| 1983 | 69,303 | 66,350 | 11.8 | 9.9 | 9.5 | 18.5 | 32.9 | 11.3 | 6.1 |
| 1982 | 69,559 | 66,476 | 11.4 | 10.0 | 9.5 | 18.4 | 32.9 | 11.6 | 6.0 |
| 1981 | 68,849 | 66,327 | 11.2 | 10.1 | 9.6 | 18.2 | 33.7 | 12.0 | 5.4 |
| 1980 | 68,176 | 65,564 | 10.3 | 10.1 | 9.0 | 18.3 | 35.1 | 11.7 | 5.6 |
| 1979 | 67,823 | 65,506 | 10.3 | 9.6 | 9.0 | 17.3 | 35.0 | 12.7 | 6.2 |
| 1978 | 67,528 | 63,916 | 10.8 | 10.0 | 8.8 | 17.0 | 34.8 | 12.8 | 6.0 |
| 1977 | 66,665 | 62,678 | 10.8 | 10.0 | 8.9 | 16.3 | 35.3 | 12.8 | 5.9 |
| 1976 | 66,125 | 61,921 | 10.9 | 9.8 | 9.3 | 16.9 | 35.8 | 12.0 | 5.3 |
| 1975 | 65,251 | 60,755 | 10.8 | 10.1 | 9.3 | 16.8 | 36.4 | 11.7 | 4.9 |
| 1974 | 64,233 | 60,397 | 11.1 | 9.5 | 8.4 | 17.0 | 36.8 | 11.7 | 5.6 |
| 1973 | 63,207 | 59,151 | 10.8 | 8.9 | 8.0 | 15.9 | 37.0 | 13.2 | 6.1 |
| 1972 | 62,273 | 57,870 | 11.0 | 9.1 | 8.3 | 15.5 | 37.9 | 12.4 | 5.8 |

*Source: Bureau of the Census,* Money Income in the United States: 1997, *Current Population Reports, P60-200, 1998*

# Incomes of Young Men Are Down

**The incomes of men under age 45 were lower in 1997 than in 1967, after adjusting for inflation.**

The median income of all men has edged up less than 3 percent since 1967, after adjusting for inflation—reaching $25,212 in 1997. This figure is below men's record median of more than $27,000 achieved back in 1973.

Some men have fared much better than others. Those aged 45 or older have seen their incomes rise over the past 30 years, while men under age 45 earn less money than their counterparts did at their age three decades earlier. The biggest income gain has been for men aged 65 or older. The median income of men in that age group rose a stunning 74 percent between 1967 and 1997, after adjusting for inflation. Behind this rise was the entry of a more affluent generation into the older age groups.

Men aged 25 to 34 experienced the greatest income decline, a 13.5 percent drop between 1967 and 1997. Men in this age group once had a median income 22 percent higher than the median for all men. Today, it is only 3 percent higher.

✘ Younger men have been caught by a changing economy, and their incomes have suffered because of it. The entry of women into the workforce, the rising importance of a college degree, and the disappearance of well-paying manufacturing jobs have affected the earning power of men.

## Older men have gained ground

*(percent change in median income of men by age, 1967 to 1997; in 1997 dollars)*

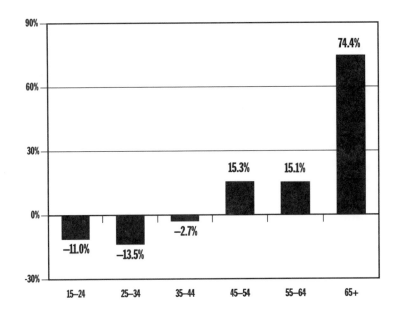

# Median Income of Men by Age, 1967 to 1997

*(median income of men aged 15 or older with income by age, 1967 to 1997; percent change in income for selected years; in 1997 dollars)*

| | total men | 15 to 24 | 25 to 34 | 35 to 44 | 45 to 54 | 55 to 64 | aged 65 or older total | 65 to 74 | 75 or older |
|---|---|---|---|---|---|---|---|---|---|
| 1997 | $25,212 | $7,468 | $25,996 | $32,851 | $37,624 | $31,157 | $17,768 | $19,651 | $15,407 |
| 1996 | 24,381 | 7,120 | 25,757 | 32,905 | 37,063 | 30,203 | 17,067 | 19,032 | 14,827 |
| 1995 | 23,761 | 7,280 | 24,864 | 33,090 | 37,477 | 30,520 | 17,360 | 19,322 | 14,913 |
| 1994 | 23,523 | 7,633 | 24,482 | 33,256 | 37,832 | 29,322 | 16,516 | 17,977 | 14,793 |
| 1993 | 23,439 | 7,141 | 24,355 | 33,702 | 36,825 | 27,923 | 16,642 | 18,089 | 14,908 |
| 1992 | 23,400 | 7,204 | 24,592 | 33,737 | 36,814 | 29,303 | 16,699 | 18,086 | 14,741 |
| 1991 | 24,121 | 7,402 | 25,448 | 34,529 | 37,449 | 30,002 | 16,918 | 18,071 | 15,363 |
| 1990 | 24,920 | 7,760 | 26,271 | 36,561 | 38,077 | 30,459 | 17,417 | 19,609 | 14,344 |
| 1989 | 25,749 | 8,171 | 27,656 | 38,102 | 40,076 | 31,617 | 16,965 | 18,723 | 14,040 |
| 1988 | 25,653 | 7,927 | 28,195 | 38,728 | 40,129 | 30,726 | 16,920 | 18,914 | 13,877 |
| 1987 | 25,129 | 7,710 | 28,154 | 38,206 | 40,248 | 30,917 | 16,851 | 18,949 | 13,702 |
| 1986 | 25,062 | 7,737 | 28,061 | 38,327 | 40,646 | 30,803 | 16,905 | – | – |
| 1985 | 24,330 | 7,451 | 27,837 | 37,825 | 38,551 | 30,216 | 16,259 | – | – |
| 1984 | 24,098 | 7,274 | 27,949 | 37,948 | 37,984 | 30,164 | 16,143 | – | – |
| 1983 | 23,577 | 6,903 | 27,080 | 36,161 | 37,249 | 30,124 | 15,699 | – | – |
| 1982 | 23,420 | 7,432 | 27,560 | 36,346 | 36,168 | 29,931 | 15,425 | – | – |
| 1981 | 24,000 | 5,472 | 28,666 | 37,617 | 37,448 | 30,933 | 14,497 | – | – |
| 1980 | 24,436 | 8,965 | 30,384 | 39,076 | 38,953 | 31,035 | 14,312 | – | – |
| 1979 | 25,548 | 9,231 | 31,822 | 39,787 | 39,507 | 32,595 | 13,953 | – | – |
| 1978 | 26,001 | 8,684 | 31,886 | 39,405 | 39,409 | 32,395 | 14,186 | – | – |
| 1977 | 25,708 | 8,221 | 31,391 | 39,627 | 38,934 | 31,092 | 14,034 | – | – |
| 1976 | 25,469 | 8,028 | 31,660 | 38,709 | 38,082 | 31,135 | 14,302 | – | – |
| 1975 | 25,283 | 8,128 | 31,520 | 38,072 | 37,718 | 30,386 | 14,162 | – | – |
| 1974 | 26,138 | 8,390 | 32,419 | 38,968 | 37,985 | 30,841 | 14,343 | – | – |
| 1973 | 27,394 | – | 34,303 | 40,907 | 39,686 | 32,481 | 13,962 | – | – |
| 1972 | 26,931 | – | 33,322 | 39,890 | 38,936 | 32,180 | 13,541 | – | – |
| 1971 | 25,706 | – | 31,884 | 37,116 | 35,947 | 29,545 | 12,844 | – | – |
| 1970 | 25,921 | – | 32,084 | 36,783 | 35,648 | 29,838 | 11,954 | – | – |
| 1969 | 26,189 | – | 32,483 | 36,846 | 35,110 | 29,652 | 11,520 | – | – |
| 1968 | 25,459 | – | 31,210 | 35,250 | 33,220 | 28,596 | 11,290 | – | – |
| 1967 | 24,553 | – | 30,062 | 33,762 | 32,622 | 27,068 | 10,187 | – | – |
| **Percent change** | | | | | | | | | |
| 1990–97 | 1.2% | –3.8% | –1.0% | –10.1% | –1.2% | 2.3% | 2.0% | 0.2% | 7.4% |
| 1967*–97 | 2.7 | –11.0 | –13.5 | –2.7 | 15.3 | 15.1 | 74.4 | 3.7 | 12.4 |

*\* Or earliest year available.*

*Note: (–) means data not available.*

*Source: Bureau of the Census, Internet web site, <http:// www.census.gov/hhes/income/histinc/index.html>; calculations by New Strategist*

# Incomes Are Growing Fastest for Black Men

## Hispanic men have experienced the greatest losses.

During the past 30 years, the median income of black men rose 22 percent, after adjusting for inflation—rising from just $14,794 to $18,096. While the median income of black men is still far below that of white men, the gap is closing. In 1967, black men made just 57 percent as much as white men. By 1997, they made 69 percent as much as whites.

In contrast to blacks, Hispanic men have lost ground. The median income of Hispanic men fell 22 percent between 1972 and 1997, after adjusting for inflation. In 1972, Hispanic men had a higher median income than black men. Today, Hispanic men have the lowest incomes. Behind this drop is the immigration of millions of poorly educated Hispanic men with little earning power.

Non-Hispanic white men have the highest median income, $27,559 in 1997. Asian men are in second place with a median income of $25,046.

✗ As younger, better-educated generations of men replace older, less-educated men in the black population, the incomes of black men will continue to approach those of whites. In contrast, Hispanic incomes are not likely to rise much until immigrants make up a much smaller share of the Hispanic population.

### Black men narrow the income gap

*(median income of men by race, 1967 and 1997; in 1997 dollars)*

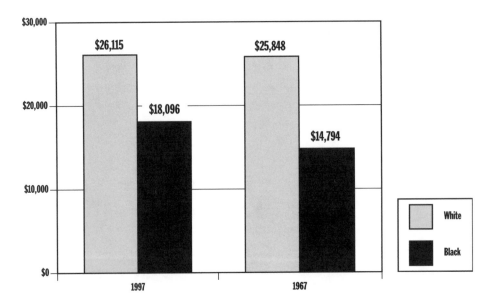

## Median Income of Men by Race and Hispanic Origin, 1967 to 1997

*(median income of men aged 15 or older with income by race and Hispanic origin, 1967 to 1997; percent change in income for selected years; in 1997 dollars)*

| | total men | Asian | black | Hispanic | white | non-Hispanic white |
|---|---|---|---|---|---|---|
| 1997 | $25,212 | $25,046 | $18,096 | $16,216 | $26,115 | $27,559 |
| 1996 | 24,381 | 23,910 | 16,869 | 15,791 | 25,521 | 26,893 |
| 1995 | 23,761 | 23,340 | 16,857 | 15,629 | 25,165 | 26,835 |
| 1994 | 23,523 | 24,790 | 16,225 | 15,703 | 24,550 | 26,124 |
| 1993 | 23,439 | 24,037 | 16,222 | 15,205 | 24,415 | 25,737 |
| 1992 | 23,400 | 22,754 | 14,945 | 15,338 | 24,488 | 25,624 |
| 1991 | 24,121 | 23,130 | 15,275 | 16,283 | 25,212 | 26,130 |
| 1990 | 24,920 | 23,816 | 15,802 | 16,541 | 25,997 | 26,964 |
| 1989 | 25,749 | 26,677 | 16,321 | 17,344 | 27,004 | 28,036 |
| 1988 | 25,653 | 24,993 | 16,340 | 17,678 | 27,079 | 28,088 |
| 1987 | 25,129 | – | 15,845 | 17,279 | 26,710 | 27,825 |
| 1986 | 25,062 | – | 15,848 | 16,888 | 26,447 | 27,636 |
| 1985 | 24,330 | – | 16,062 | 17,055 | 25,523 | 26,390 |
| 1984 | 24,098 | – | 14,595 | 17,148 | 25,437 | 26,194 |
| 1983 | 23,577 | – | 14,450 | 18,174 | 24,818 | – |
| 1982 | 23,420 | – | 14,838 | 17,579 | 24,760 | 25,393 |
| 1981 | 24,000 | – | 15,143 | 18,175 | 25,466 | 26,136 |
| 1980 | 24,436 | – | 15,619 | 18,837 | 25,992 | 26,680 |
| 1979 | 25,548 | – | 16,521 | 19,240 | 26,689 | 27,250 |
| 1978 | 26,001 | – | 16,314 | 19,926 | 27,233 | 27,523 |
| 1977 | 25,708 | – | 15,979 | 19,801 | 26,927 | 27,473 |
| 1976 | 25,469 | – | 16,166 | 19,049 | 26,850 | 27,342 |
| 1975 | 25,283 | – | 15,879 | 19,354 | 26,560 | 27,171 |
| 1974 | 26,138 | – | 16,965 | 19,925 | 27,381 | 27,959 |
| 1973 | 27,394 | – | 17,386 | 21,083 | 28,744 | 29,155 |
| 1972 | 26,931 | – | 17,109 | 20,916 | 28,247 | 28,568 |
| 1971 | 25,706 | – | 16,076 | – | 26,950 | – |
| 1970 | 25,921 | – | 16,163 | – | 27,246 | – |
| 1969 | 26,189 | – | 16,030 | – | 27,558 | – |
| 1968 | 25,459 | – | 15,829 | – | 26,680 | – |
| 1967 | 24,553 | – | 14,794 | – | 25,848 | – |
| **Percent change** | | | | | | |
| 1990–97 | 1.2% | 5.2% | 14.5% | –2.0% | 0.5% | 2.2% |
| 1967*–97 | 2.7 | 0.2 | 22.3 | –22.5 | 1.0 | –3.5 |

*\* Or earliest year available.*
*Note: (–) means data not available.*
*Source: Bureau of the Census, Internet web site, <http:// www.census.gov/hhes/income/histinc/index.html>; calculations by New Strategist*

# Even Educated Men Have Suffered in the 1990s

**During the 1990s, men's incomes have faltered—even for those with college degrees.**

Between 1991 and 1997, the median income of men aged 25 or older rose nearly 4 percent as the recession ended and jobs became more plentiful. But unlike during earlier periods, a college degree has not guaranteed income gains during the 1990s. While high school graduates as well as drop-outs saw little or no income growth between 1991 and 1997, neither did some of the most educated men.

The median income of men with bachelor's degrees fell 1 percent between 1991 and 1997, after adjusting for inflation. Those with professional degrees saw their incomes decline nearly 4 percent as managed care cut the incomes of doctors. Men with associate's degrees or some college also lost ground during those years.

Two groups of men made gains during the 1990s—men with master's degrees and those with doctorates. The biggest gain was for men with doctorates, with a 12 percent rise in median income during the decade. Men with professional degrees continue to surpass all others in income, with a median of $72,274 in 1997.

✗ The labor market pays a premium to highly educated workers, and the stakes appear to be rising. A college degree no longer guarantees financial security. Graduate-level education is becoming increasingly important to economic success.

## A college degree is no guarantee

*(percent change in median income of men by educational attainment, 1991 to 1997; in 1997 dollars)*

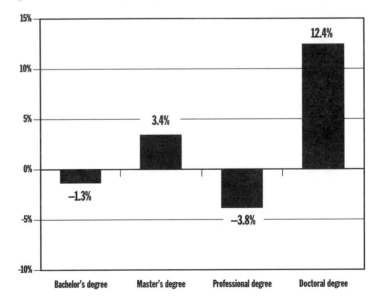

# Median Income of Men by Education, 1991 to 1997

*(median income of men aged 25 or older with income by educational attainment, 1991 to 1997; income in 1997 dollars)*

| | total men | less than 9th grade | 9th to 12th grade | high school graduate | associate's degree | some college | bachelor's degree or more | | | | |
|---|---|---|---|---|---|---|---|---|---|---|---|
| | | | | | | | total | bachelor's degree | master's degree | professional degree | doctoral degree |
| 1997 | $28,919 | $12,157 | $16,818 | $25,453 | $32,930 | $30,536 | $47,126 | $41,949 | $52,530 | $72,274 | $68,643 |
| 1996 | 27,873 | 12,453 | 16,426 | 25,383 | 33,824 | 29,829 | 45,174 | 40,533 | 51,150 | 73,518 | 63,683 |
| 1995 | 27,746 | 12,346 | 16,630 | 24,607 | 32,676 | 29,492 | 45,625 | 41,115 | 51,684 | 69,779 | 60,404 |
| 1994 | 27,578 | 12,264 | 15,794 | 24,245 | 33,186 | 28,990 | 45,515 | 41,913 | 50,506 | 66,863 | 62,248 |
| 1993 | 27,329 | 12,101 | 16,161 | 24,194 | 33,029 | 29,238 | 46,261 | 41,623 | 50,646 | 77,393 | 61,924 |
| 1992 | 27,334 | 11,868 | 16,265 | 24,761 | 32,936 | 30,107 | 46,396 | 42,035 | 50,670 | 78,281 | 59,122 |
| 1991 | 27,912 | 12,160 | 17,365 | 25,390 | 34,596 | 31,335 | 46,904 | 42,502 | 50,819 | 75,113 | 61,095 |
| **Percent change** | | | | | | | | | | | |
| 1991–97 | 3.6% | 0.0% | –3.2% | 0.2% | –4.8% | –2.5% | 0.5% | –1.3% | 3.4% | –3.8% | 12.4% |

*Note: Beginning in 1991, the Census Bureau changed its educational attainment categories, making the new statistics not strictly comparable with those of earlier years.*
*Source: Bureau of the Census, Internet web site, <http://www.census.gov/hhes/income/histinc/index.html>; calculations by New Strategist*

# Men in the South Have Seen the Biggest Income Gains

**In the West, men's incomes have declined sharply.**

Between 1967 and 1997, men in the South saw their median income rise a substantial 23 percent, after adjusting for inflation. By 1997, the median income of men in the region was still lower than the median of men in other regions, but the gap had almost disappeared. The median income of men in the South was only 79 percent as high as the national median in 1967. Thirty years later, it was 95 percent of the national figure.

Men in the West saw their median income fall 10.5 percent between 1967 and 1997, after adjusting for inflation. In 1967 men in the West had a median income that was 13 percent higher than the national median, but it had slipped below the national median by 1997.

The median income of men in both the Northeast and Midwest barely changed over the past 30 years, falling 0.7 percent after adjusting for inflation.

✘ A large share of men in the South are black, and the incomes of black men have been rising rapidly. This is one factor behind the income growth for men in the region. Many Hispanic immigrants with low incomes live in the West, which partly explains why the incomes of men in the region have been falling.

### Stark differences in men's income growth by region

*(percent change in median income of men by region, 1967 to 1997; in 1997 dollars)*

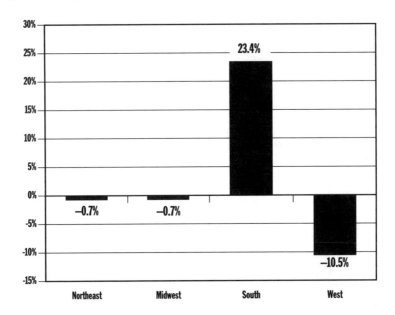

# Median Income of Men by Region, 1967 to 1997

*(median income of men aged 15 or older with income by region, 1967 to 1997; percent change in income for selected years; in 1997 dollars)*

|  | total men | Northeast | Midwest | South | West |
|---|---|---|---|---|---|
| 1997 | $25,212 | $26,378 | $26,285 | $23,896 | $24,832 |
| 1996 | 24,381 | 25,862 | 25,989 | 22,744 | 23,932 |
| 1995 | 23,761 | 25,918 | 25,589 | 22,287 | 23,500 |
| 1994 | 23,523 | 25,677 | 24,124 | 22,031 | 23,857 |
| 1993 | 23,439 | 24,750 | 24,098 | 21,897 | 23,921 |
| 1992 | 23,400 | 25,270 | 23,990 | 21,267 | 24,022 |
| 1991 | 24,121 | 26,336 | 24,241 | 21,770 | 25,421 |
| 1990 | 24,920 | 26,902 | 25,387 | 22,631 | 25,775 |
| 1989 | 25,749 | 28,700 | 25,841 | 23,107 | 26,459 |
| 1988 | 25,653 | 29,229 | 25,989 | 22,756 | 26,362 |
| 1987 | 25,129 | 27,998 | 25,311 | 23,092 | 26,071 |
| 1986 | 25,062 | 27,720 | 25,536 | 22,649 | 26,802 |
| 1985 | 24,330 | 26,224 | 24,429 | 22,278 | 25,940 |
| 1984 | 24,098 | 25,745 | 24,236 | 21,949 | 26,130 |
| 1983 | 23,577 | 24,936 | 23,962 | 21,558 | 25,081 |
| 1982 | 23,420 | 24,417 | 24,495 | 21,523 | 24,543 |
| 1981 | 24,000 | 24,873 | 25,281 | 21,743 | 26,008 |
| 1980 | 24,436 | 25,668 | 26,015 | 22,271 | 26,751 |
| 1979 | 25,548 | 26,370 | 27,428 | 23,179 | 26,790 |
| 1978 | 26,001 | 26,541 | 27,960 | 23,452 | 27,810 |
| 1977 | 25,708 | 26,848 | 27,473 | 22,724 | 26,767 |
| 1976 | 25,469 | 26,804 | 27,628 | 22,556 | 26,550 |
| 1975 | 25,283 | 27,162 | 27,142 | 22,167 | 26,620 |
| 1974 | 26,138 | 28,414 | 28,278 | 22,646 | 27,035 |
| 1973 | 27,394 | 29,213 | 29,801 | 23,096 | 29,213 |
| 1972 | 26,931 | 28,897 | 28,926 | 22,969 | 28,836 |
| 1971 | 25,706 | 27,706 | 27,371 | 21,673 | 27,367 |
| 1970 | 25,921 | 27,965 | 27,693 | 21,767 | 27,685 |
| 1969 | 26,189 | 28,079 | 28,650 | 21,175 | 28,800 |
| 1968 | 25,459 | 26,889 | 27,604 | 20,503 | 28,473 |
| 1967 | 24,632 | 26,551 | 26,476 | 19,362 | 27,740 |
| **Percent change** |  |  |  |  |  |
| 1990–97 | 1.2% | −1.9% | 3.5% | 5.6% | −3.7% |
| 1967–97 | 2.4 | −0.7 | −0.7 | 23.4 | −10.5 |

*Source: Bureau of the Census, Internet web site, <http:// www.census.gov/hhes/income/histinc/index.html>; calculations by New Strategist*

# Little Earnings Growth for Men Working Full-Time

## Men working part-time have seen bigger gains.

Between 1967 and 1997, the median earnings of men who work full-time rose only 6 percent, after adjusting for inflation. In contrast, the median earnings of men who work part-time climbed 35 percent. Those in year-round part-time jobs saw their earnings grow 62 percent. The gains of part-timers did little to boost men's incomes, however, since the average part-timer made less than $5,000 in 1997.

The median earnings of men who work full-time, year-round rose by less than $2,000 during the past 30 years—not much of a difference considering the dramatic social and technological change occurring during that time. This stability masks the growing economic polarization among men, with some faring much better than others.

✗ While a growing share of men are earning good salaries—particularly those with college degrees—many others are falling behind as high-paying manufacturing jobs disappear.

### Big gains for part-timers

*(percent change in median earnings of men by work experience, 1967 to 1997; in 1997 dollars)*

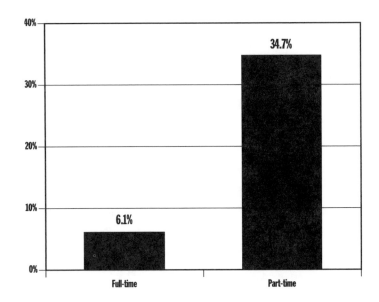

# Median Earnings of Men by Work Experience, 1967 to 1997

*(median earnings of men aged 15 or older with earnings by work experience, 1967 to 1997; percent change in earnings for selected years; in 1997 dollars)*

| | total working men | worked full-time | | worked part-time | |
|---|---|---|---|---|---|
| | | total | year-round | total | year-round |
| 1997 | $26,843 | $30,786 | $33,674 | $4,937 | $8,976 |
| 1996 | 26,377 | 30,283 | 32,882 | 4,484 | 8,761 |
| 1995 | 26,348 | 29,702 | 33,170 | 4,696 | 8,561 |
| 1994 | 25,619 | 29,290 | 33,415 | 4,673 | 8,451 |
| 1993 | 24,928 | 29,139 | 33,774 | 4,334 | 8,038 |
| 1992 | 25,057 | 29,526 | 34,545 | 4,535 | 8,078 |
| 1991 | 25,757 | 30,081 | 34,670 | 4,689 | 8,164 |
| 1990 | 26,429 | 30,505 | 33,989 | 4,840 | 8,434 |
| 1989 | 27,668 | 31,690 | 35,376 | 4,381 | 8,487 |
| 1988 | 27,965 | 31,738 | 36,165 | 4,286 | 8,337 |
| 1987 | 28,000 | 31,319 | 36,658 | 4,004 | 8,317 |
| 1986 | 27,505 | 31,586 | 36,985 | 4,087 | 8,259 |
| 1985 | 26,520 | 30,898 | 36,090 | 4,080 | 8,034 |
| 1984 | 26,301 | 30,914 | 35,866 | 3,887 | 8,144 |
| 1983 | 25,899 | 30,036 | 35,260 | 3,843 | 7,775 |
| 1982 | 25,809 | 29,590 | 35,386 | 4,112 | 8,139 |
| 1981 | 26,829 | 30,438 | 36,090 | 3,994 | 7,899 |
| 1980 | 27,324 | 31,105 | 36,297 | 4,002 | 8,158 |
| 1979 | 28,083 | 32,302 | 36,902 | 4,284 | 8,103 |
| 1978 | 28,850 | 32,309 | 37,402 | 3,888 | 7,830 |
| 1977 | 28,029 | 31,656 | 37,144 | 3,566 | 7,144 |
| 1976 | 27,834 | 31,462 | 36,356 | 3,545 | 6,817 |
| 1975 | 27,628 | 31,180 | 36,435 | 3,438 | 7,000 |
| 1974 | 28,207 | 31,856 | 36,686 | 3,532 | 7,298 |
| 1973 | 29,522 | 33,280 | 38,037 | 3,608 | 6,780 |
| 1972 | 28,886 | 32,422 | 36,879 | 3,557 | 6,330 |
| 1971 | 27,512 | 30,793 | 35,001 | 3,318 | 6,316 |
| 1970 | 27,794 | 30,771 | 34,844 | 3,350 | 6,393 |
| 1969 | 28,104 | 30,992 | 33,514 | 3,353 | 6,172 |
| 1968 | 27,425 | 29,971 | 32,628 | 3,640 | 5,496 |
| 1967 | 26,617 | 29,009 | 31,755 | 3,665 | 5,545 |
| **Percent change** | | | | | |
| 1990–97 | 1.6% | 0.9% | –0.9% | 2.0% | 6.4% |
| 1967–97 | 0.8 | 6.1 | 6.0 | 34.7 | 61.9 |

*Note: Earnings include wages and salaries only.*
*Source: Bureau of the Census, Internet web site, <http:// www.census.gov/hhes/income/histinc/index.html>; calculations by New Strategist*

# Earnings of Black Men Surpass Those of Hispanics

## Hispanic men have seen their earnings plummet.

Among men who work full time, the median earnings of blacks have pulled far ahead of the Hispanic median. In 1972, Hispanic men who worked full-time earned 2 percent more than their black counterparts. By 1997, blacks were ahead by fully 22 percent. Behind this difference are divergent trends: the earnings of black men who work full-time have risen rapidly since 1972, while the earnings of Hispanic men fell during those years. The median earnings of black men are still below those of white men, but the gap has narrowed considerably. Among full-time workers in 1967, black men earned only 65 percent as much as whites. By 1997, they earned 75 percent as much as whites.

The median earnings of Asian men have fallen since 1988, in part because of the immigration of poorly educated Asians over the past decade. Nevertheless, the median earnings of Asian men who work full-time are second only to those of non-Hispanic white men.

✘ The earnings of black men are rising as better educated, younger generations replace older blacks in the workforce, a trend that should continue. The trend in Hispanic earnings is also likely to continue until immigrants make up a much smaller share of Hispanic men.

### Black men are earning more

*(percent change in median earnings of men working full-time by race, 1967 to 1997; in 1997 dollars)*

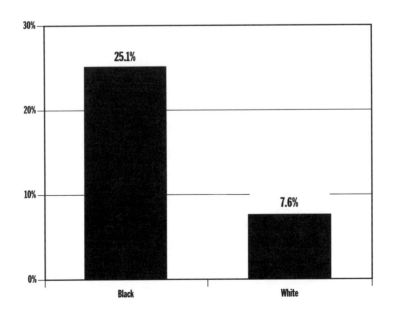

# Median Earnings of Men Who Work Full-Time, by Race and Hispanic Origin, 1967 to 1997

*(median earnings of men aged 15 or older working full-time, year-round, by race and Hispanic origin, 1967 to 1997; percent change in earnings for selected years; in 1997 dollars)*

| | total men | Asian | black | Hispanic | white | non-Hispanic white |
|---|---|---|---|---|---|---|
| 1997 | $33,674 | $34,682 | $26,432 | $21,615 | $35,193 | $36,597 |
| 1996 | 32,882 | 35,243 | 27,010 | 21,539 | 33,722 | 36,255 |
| 1995 | 33,170 | 33,252 | 25,726 | 21,462 | 33,882 | 36,230 |
| 1994 | 33,415 | 34,722 | 25,712 | 22,000 | 34,221 | 35,348 |
| 1993 | 33,774 | 34,325 | 25,568 | 22,380 | 34,531 | 35,511 |
| 1992 | 34,545 | 34,916 | 25,622 | 22,354 | 35,299 | 36,288 |
| 1991 | 34,670 | 35,540 | 26,013 | 23,298 | 35,666 | 36,586 |
| 1990 | 33,989 | 32,868 | 25,928 | 23,499 | 35,466 | 37,003 |
| 1989 | 35,376 | 36,437 | 26,438 | 23,762 | 36,942 | 38,789 |
| 1988 | 36,165 | 36,796 | 27,638 | 24,219 | 36,941 | 38,337 |
| 1987 | 36,658 | – | 27,018 | 24,632 | 37,482 | 38,393 |
| 1986 | 36,985 | – | 26,856 | 24,624 | 37,968 | – |
| 1985 | 36,090 | – | 26,072 | 25,434 | 37,383 | – |
| 1984 | 35,866 | – | 25,699 | 26,168 | 37,015 | – |
| 1983 | 35,260 | – | 26,030 | 26,055 | 36,124 | – |
| 1982 | 35,386 | – | 26,028 | 25,824 | 36,267 | – |
| 1981 | 36,090 | – | 26,234 | 26,222 | 36,885 | – |
| 1980 | 36,297 | – | 26,419 | 26,441 | 37,360 | – |
| 1979 | 36,902 | – | 27,411 | 26,851 | 37,748 | – |
| 1978 | 37,402 | – | 29,351 | 27,903 | 38,033 | – |
| 1977 | 37,144 | – | 26,526 | 27,399 | 38,246 | – |
| 1976 | 36,356 | – | 27,323 | 27,742 | 37,323 | – |
| 1975 | 36,435 | – | 27,722 | 26,882 | 37,281 | – |
| 1974 | 36,686 | – | 26,960 | 27,477 | 37,475 | – |
| 1973 | 38,037 | – | 26,795 | – | 39,159 | – |
| 1972 | 36,879 | – | 26,392 | – | 38,292 | – |
| 1971 | 35,001 | – | 24,835 | – | 35,969 | – |
| 1970 | 34,844 | – | 24,747 | – | 35,842 | – |
| 1969 | 34,442 | – | 23,953 | – | 35,587 | – |
| 1968 | 32,628 | – | 22,623 | – | 33,505 | – |
| 1967 | 31,755 | – | 21,121 | – | 32,701 | – |
| **Percent change** | | | | | | |
| 1990–97 | –0.9% | 5.5% | 1.9% | –8.0% | –0.8% | –1.1% |
| 1967*–97 | 6.0 | –5.7 | 25.1 | –21.3 | 7.6 | –4.7 |

*\* Or earliest year available.*

*Note: Earnings include wages and salaries only. (–) means data not available.*

*Source: Bureau of the Census, Internet web site, <http:// www.census.gov/hhes/income/histinc/index.html>; calculations by New Strategist*

# Incomes Have Declined for Blue-Collar Men

## But pay for managers and professionals is rising.

Since 1982, the median earnings of men working full-time have fallen nearly 5 percent, after adjusting for inflation. But men in many occupations have made gains. Managers and professionals have seen their earnings rise more than 5 percent, with a 7 percent gain for men in professional specialty occupations—which include lawyers and physicians. The earnings of technologists and protective service workers have also grown, as have the earnings of men working in farming, forestry, and fishing.

In contrast, men with blue-collar jobs have lost ground. Precision production, craft, and repair workers saw their earnings fall 10 percent, while operators, fabricators, and laborers experienced a 9 percent decline. Because one in three men with full-time jobs works in these occupations, their eroding financial well-being greatly affects trends in the earnings of all men.

✘ Men employed in the new, white-collar economy—which rewards educated specialists—are faring well, while those in traditional jobs such as sales and blue-collar work are losing ground.

## Men's fortunes vary by occupation

*(percent change in median income of men working full-time by selected occupation, 1982 to 1997; in 1997 dollars)*

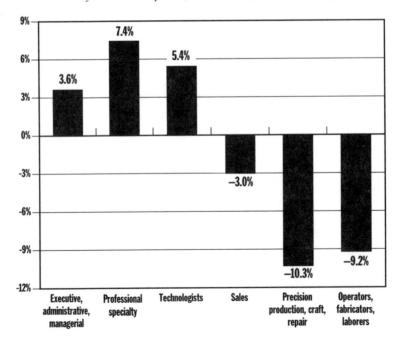

# Median Earnings of Men Working Full-Time by Occupation, 1982 to 1997

*(median earnings of men aged 15 or older working full-time, year-round by occupation of longest job held, 1982 to 1997; income in 1997 dollars)*

| | total men | managerial and professional specialty | | | technical, sales, and administrative support | | | | |
|---|---|---|---|---|---|---|---|---|---|
| | | total | executive, administrative & managerial | professional specialty | total | health technologists | technologists, except health | sales | administrative support |
| 1997 | $33,674 | $50,270 | $50,149 | $50,402 | $33,922 | $31,052 | $40,642 | $35,655 | $29,442 |
| 1996 | 32,882 | 48,682 | 47,724 | 51,160 | 34,269 | 32,992 | 39,814 | 35,909 | 31,078 |
| 1995 | 33,170 | 49,410 | 49,007 | 49,855 | 33,755 | 32,809 | 39,135 | 36,928 | 28,881 |
| 1994 | 33,415 | 50,042 | 49,757 | 50,346 | 34,044 | 27,572 | 40,295 | 35,576 | 29,104 |
| 1993 | 33,774 | 49,013 | 47,452 | 50,134 | 34,765 | 35,166 | 39,761 | 35,906 | 29,708 |
| 1992 | 34,545 | 49,360 | 48,571 | 50,277 | 34,875 | 36,075 | 38,010 | 35,725 | 30,997 |
| 1991 | 34,670 | 49,427 | 49,063 | 49,915 | 35,481 | 32,149 | 38,613 | 36,056 | 31,861 |
| 1990 | 33,989 | 50,142 | 49,791 | 50,471 | 35,153 | 37,100 | 38,337 | 36,413 | 32,164 |
| 1989 | 35,376 | 51,570 | 51,884 | 51,126 | 36,110 | 34,004 | 41,317 | 38,318 | 32,530 |
| 1988 | 36,165 | 50,363 | 49,872 | 50,863 | 36,212 | 31,551 | 41,849 | 36,661 | 33,103 |
| 1987 | 36,658 | 49,769 | 49,861 | 49,673 | 36,608 | 31,613 | 42,393 | 37,583 | 33,097 |
| 1986 | 36,985 | 50,360 | 50,191 | 50,527 | 37,715 | 32,885 | 41,882 | 39,251 | 33,269 |
| 1985 | 36,090 | 48,906 | 49,033 | 48,759 | 37,227 | 31,587 | 40,122 | 37,955 | 34,303 |
| 1984 | 35,866 | 49,115 | 49,675 | 48,541 | 36,900 | 34,284 | 41,441 | 37,156 | 34,201 |
| 1983 | 35,260 | 48,482 | 49,048 | 47,613 | 36,253 | 34,786 | 40,494 | 37,270 | 33,571 |
| 1982 | 35,386 | 47,635 | 48,385 | 46,908 | 35,928 | 31,618 | 38,557 | 36,769 | 34,430 |
| **Percent change** | | | | | | | | | |
| 1982–97 | −4.8% | 5.5% | 3.6% | 7.4% | −5.6% | −1.8% | 5.4% | −3.0% | −14.5% |

*(continued)*

*(continued from previous page)*

| | service occupations | | | farming, forestry, fishing | precision production, craft, and repair | operators, fabricators, laborers |
|---|---|---|---|---|---|---|
| | total | protective service | service except protective and household | | | |
| 1997 | $22,335 | $37,133 | $18,272 | $17,394 | $31,496 | $26,261 |
| 1996 | 21,510 | 35,142 | 18,281 | 18,543 | 31,119 | 25,933 |
| 1995 | 22,465 | 34,155 | 18,274 | 18,271 | 32,038 | 24,871 |
| 1994 | 22,739 | 35,624 | 18,658 | 17,611 | 31,978 | 25,117 |
| 1993 | 23,170 | 34,810 | 18,386 | 17,388 | 30,715 | 25,633 |
| 1992 | 23,333 | 35,108 | 18,236 | 16,943 | 32,829 | 26,022 |
| 1991 | 23,489 | 34,619 | 19,650 | 17,650 | 32,416 | 26,323 |
| 1990 | 22,779 | 33,661 | 18,898 | 17,747 | 32,549 | 27,001 |
| 1989 | 24,445 | 36,544 | 20,237 | 17,984 | 34,287 | 28,028 |
| 1988 | 25,300 | 37,488 | 20,934 | 19,401 | 34,930 | 28,609 |
| 1987 | 26,220 | 36,905 | 22,803 | 19,171 | 34,284 | 29,495 |
| 1986 | 25,381 | 35,615 | 20,981 | 15,740 | 35,557 | 29,918 |
| 1985 | 25,095 | 35,616 | 20,328 | 15,455 | 34,709 | 29,308 |
| 1984 | 24,001 | 33,971 | 20,141 | 14,774 | 34,881 | 28,782 |
| 1983 | 23,669 | 33,168 | 19,610 | 15,407 | 34,678 | 28,714 |
| 1982 | 24,275 | 34,454 | 20,160 | 15,266 | 35,110 | 28,915 |
| **Percent change** | | | | | | |
| 1982–97 | –8.0% | 7.8% | –9.4% | 13.9% | –10.3% | –9.2% |

*Source: Bureau of the Census, Internet web site, <http:// www.census.gov/hhes/income/histinc/index.html>; calculations by New Strategist*

# Men's Income, 1997

# Income Peaks among Men Aged 45 to 54

## Among full-time workers, however, income peaks in the oldest age group.

The median income of men stood at $25,212 in 1997, meaning one-half of men had incomes above that amount and the other half, below. Men's median income rises with age to a peak of $37,624 in the 45-to-54 age group. Seventy-six percent of men aged 45 to 54 work full-time.

Among full-time workers, income peaks at a much older age. Men aged 75 or older who work full-time have higher incomes than any others, a median of $49,672. Only 4 percent of men in the age group work full-time, however.

The income patterns are the same for black and Hispanic men, with incomes peaking in the 45-to-54 age group. Among black and Hispanic men who work full-time, incomes peak in the oldest age group.

✗ Among full-time workers, incomes are highest in the oldest age group because highly paid workers are the ones with the most incentive to continue working well into old age.

### Oldest full-time workers have the highest incomes

*(median income of men aged 15 or older who work full-time, year-round, by age, 1997)*

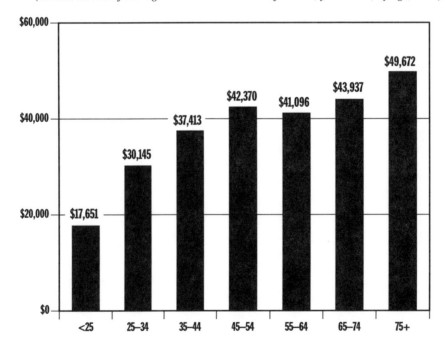

# Distribution of Men by Income and Age, 1997: Total Men

*(number and percent distribution of men aged 15 or older by income and age, 1997; median income of men with income and of men working full-time, year-round; percent working full-time, year-round; men in thousands as of 1998)*

| | total | 15–24 | 25–34 | 35–44 | 45–54 | 55–64 | aged 65 or older total | 65–74 | 75+ |
|---|---|---|---|---|---|---|---|---|---|
| **Total men** | **101,123** | **18,747** | **19,526** | **22,054** | **16,598** | **10,673** | **13,524** | **7,992** | **5,532** |
| Without income | 6,955 | 4,842 | 591 | 599 | 396 | 312 | 216 | 149 | 67 |
| With income | 94,168 | 13,905 | 18,936 | 21,456 | 16,203 | 10,361 | 13,308 | 7,843 | 5,465 |
| Under $5,000 | 8,578 | 5,201 | 880 | 886 | 599 | 516 | 495 | 258 | 236 |
| $5,000 to $9,999 | 9,598 | 2,968 | 1,291 | 1,374 | 924 | 917 | 2,124 | 1,053 | 1,070 |
| $10,000 to $14,999 | 10,695 | 1,983 | 2,138 | 1,554 | 1,044 | 1,061 | 2,916 | 1,563 | 1,352 |
| $15,000 to $19,999 | 8,866 | 1,394 | 2,031 | 1,585 | 1,046 | 808 | 2,003 | 1,125 | 877 |
| $20,000 to $24,999 | 8,934 | 936 | 2,530 | 1,861 | 1,243 | 863 | 1,501 | 907 | 594 |
| $25,000 to $29,999 | 7,625 | 569 | 2,195 | 1,933 | 1,156 | 780 | 992 | 670 | 322 |
| $30,000 to $34,999 | 7,115 | 381 | 1,943 | 2,045 | 1,281 | 778 | 686 | 439 | 248 |
| $35,000 to $39,999 | 5,829 | 172 | 1,368 | 1,759 | 1,273 | 720 | 536 | 384 | 153 |
| $40,000 to $44,999 | 4,941 | 106 | 1,091 | 1,553 | 1,179 | 674 | 338 | 222 | 116 |
| $45,000 to $49,999 | 3,597 | 29 | 821 | 1,121 | 913 | 433 | 279 | 196 | 83 |
| $50,000 to $54,999 | 3,524 | 48 | 661 | 1,099 | 1,032 | 458 | 226 | 161 | 65 |
| $55,000 to $59,999 | 2,175 | 11 | 393 | 692 | 626 | 253 | 201 | 118 | 82 |
| $60,000 to $64,999 | 2,199 | 11 | 378 | 718 | 690 | 254 | 147 | 114 | 33 |
| $65,000 to $69,999 | 1,579 | 15 | 237 | 550 | 446 | 214 | 119 | 92 | 27 |
| $70,000 to $74,999 | 1,461 | 6 | 190 | 497 | 468 | 212 | 89 | 67 | 20 |
| $75,000 to $79,999 | 1,079 | 23 | 174 | 343 | 257 | 182 | 99 | 68 | 31 |
| $80,000 to $84,999 | 965 | 11 | 124 | 276 | 301 | 168 | 86 | 70 | 16 |
| $85,000 to $89,999 | 594 | 4 | 64 | 184 | 192 | 104 | 47 | 21 | 26 |
| $90,000 to $94,999 | 490 | 1 | 67 | 161 | 141 | 82 | 39 | 25 | 15 |
| $95,000 to $99,999 | 366 | – | 22 | 115 | 128 | 69 | 33 | 19 | 13 |
| $100,000 or more | 3,957 | 38 | 337 | 1,150 | 1,262 | 815 | 355 | 272 | 83 |
| **Median income** | | | | | | | | | |
| Men with income | $25,212 | $7,468 | $25,996 | $32,851 | $37,624 | $31,157 | $17,768 | $19,651 | $15,407 |
| Men working full-time | $35,248 | $17,651 | $30,145 | $37,413 | $42,370 | $41,096 | $45,648 | $43,937 | $49,672 |
| Percent working full-time | 54.3% | 22.0% | 73.6% | 77.1% | 75.8% | 54.9% | 7.4% | 9.9% | 3.6% |
| **Percent distribution** | | | | | | | | | |
| **Total men** | **100.0%** | **100.0%** | **100.0%** | **100.0%** | **100.0%** | **100.0%** | **100.0%** | **100.0%** | **100.0%** |
| Without income | 6.9 | 25.8 | 3.0 | 2.7 | 2.4 | 2.9 | 1.6 | 1.9 | 1.2 |
| With income | 93.1 | 74.2 | 97.0 | 97.3 | 97.6 | 97.1 | 98.4 | 98.1 | 98.8 |
| Under $25,000 | 46.2 | 66.6 | 45.4 | 32.9 | 29.3 | 39.0 | 66.8 | 61.4 | 74.6 |
| $25,000 to $49,999 | 28.8 | 6.7 | 38.0 | 38.1 | 35.0 | 31.7 | 20.9 | 23.9 | 16.7 |
| $50,000 to $74,999 | 10.8 | 0.5 | 9.5 | 16.1 | 19.7 | 13.0 | 5.8 | 6.9 | 4.1 |
| $75,000 to $99,999 | 3.5 | 0.2 | 2.3 | 4.9 | 6.1 | 5.7 | 2.2 | 2.5 | 1.8 |
| $100,000 or more | 3.9 | 0.2 | 1.7 | 5.2 | 7.6 | 7.6 | 2.6 | 3.4 | 1.5 |

*Note: (–) means sample is too small to make a reliable estimate.*
*Source: Bureau of the Census, Internet web site, <http:// www.census.gov/cps/ads/sdata.htm>; calculations by New Strategist*

# Distribution of Men by Income and Age, 1997: Black Men

*(number and percent distribution of black men aged 15 or older by income and age, 1997; median income of men with income and of men working full-time, year-round; percent working full-time, year-round; men in thousands as of 1998)*

| | total | 15–24 | 25–34 | 35–44 | 45–54 | 55–64 | aged 65 or older total | 65–74 | 75+ |
|---|---|---|---|---|---|---|---|---|---|
| **Total men** | **11,283** | **2,706** | **2,389** | **2,517** | **1,636** | **968** | **1,068** | **657** | **411** |
| Without income | 1,613 | 1,044 | 170 | 200 | 97 | 65 | 36 | 24 | 12 |
| With income | 9,671 | 1,661 | 2,220 | 2,317 | 1,538 | 903 | 1,032 | 633 | 398 |
| Under $5,000 | 1,255 | 678 | 195 | 165 | 87 | 51 | 78 | 42 | 36 |
| $5,000 to $9,999 | 1,605 | 401 | 227 | 310 | 182 | 169 | 316 | 158 | 158 |
| $10,000 to $14,999 | 1,264 | 203 | 327 | 250 | 132 | 115 | 237 | 156 | 81 |
| $15,000 to $19,999 | 1,042 | 154 | 253 | 241 | 153 | 101 | 138 | 99 | 39 |
| $20,000 to $24,999 | 1,020 | 72 | 349 | 264 | 153 | 82 | 100 | 64 | 36 |
| $25,000 to $29,999 | 820 | 52 | 260 | 245 | 124 | 87 | 50 | 42 | 10 |
| $30,000 to $34,999 | 640 | 38 | 206 | 177 | 119 | 60 | 39 | 33 | 6 |
| $35,000 to $39,999 | 544 | 33 | 126 | 160 | 133 | 64 | 28 | 20 | 8 |
| $40,000 to $44,999 | 401 | 8 | 97 | 144 | 91 | 49 | 14 | 10 | 3 |
| $45,000 to $49,999 | 232 | – | 51 | 91 | 53 | 25 | 10 | – | 10 |
| $50,000 to $54,999 | 184 | 5 | 29 | 49 | 74 | 28 | – | – | – |
| $55,000 to $59,999 | 117 | – | 8 | 43 | 50 | 16 | – | – | – |
| $60,000 to $64,999 | 164 | – | 50 | 51 | 57 | 5 | – | – | – |
| $65,000 to $69,999 | 106 | – | 15 | 36 | 37 | 15 | 2 | 2 | – |
| $70,000 to $74,999 | 63 | – | 5 | 25 | 23 | 10 | – | – | – |
| $75,000 to $79,999 | 42 | – | 11 | 14 | 11 | 2 | 4 | 4 | – |
| $80,000 to $84,999 | 29 | 6 | 3 | 11 | 6 | 2 | – | – | – |
| $85,000 to $89,999 | 27 | 2 | – | 13 | 5 | 4 | 3 | – | 3 |
| $90,000 to $94,999 | 23 | – | – | 5 | 6 | 9 | 3 | – | 3 |
| $95,000 to $99,999 | 17 | – | 3 | 3 | 8 | 2 | – | – | – |
| $100,000 or more | 78 | 7 | 4 | 19 | 32 | 9 | 8 | 3 | 4 |
| **Median income** | | | | | | | | | |
| Men with income | $18,096 | $6,425 | $21,232 | $23,623 | $27,198 | $20,744 | $12,378 | $13,467 | $10,317 |
| Men working full-time | $26,897 | $16,496 | $25,354 | $28,918 | $34,569 | $30,218 | $31,921 | $30,561 | $37,446 |
| Percent working full-time | 45.8% | 18.1% | 63.9% | 63.1% | 63.9% | 47.0% | 6.3% | 7.0% | 5.1% |
| **Percent distribution** | | | | | | | | | |
| **Total men** | **100.0%** | **100.0%** | **100.0%** | **100.0%** | **100.0%** | **100.0%** | **100.0%** | **100.0%** | **100.0%** |
| Without income | 14.3 | 38.6 | 7.1 | 7.9 | 5.9 | 6.7 | 3.4 | 3.7 | 2.9 |
| With income | 85.7 | 61.4 | 92.9 | 92.1 | 94.0 | 93.3 | 96.6 | 96.3 | 96.8 |
| Under $25,000 | 54.8 | 55.7 | 56.6 | 48.9 | 43.2 | 53.5 | 81.4 | 79.0 | 85.2 |
| $25,000 to $49,999 | 23.4 | 4.8 | 31.0 | 32.5 | 31.8 | 29.4 | 13.2 | 16.0 | 9.0 |
| $50,000 to $74,999 | 5.6 | 0.2 | 4.5 | 8.1 | 14.7 | 7.6 | 0.2 | 0.3 | – |
| $75,000 to $99,999 | 1.2 | 0.3 | 0.7 | 1.8 | 2.2 | 2.0 | 0.9 | 0.6 | 1.5 |
| $100,000 or more | 0.7 | 0.3 | 0.2 | 0.8 | 2.0 | 0.9 | 0.7 | 0.5 | 1.0 |

*Note: (–) means sample is too small to make a reliable estimate.*
*Source: Bureau of the Census, Internet web site, <http:// www.census.gov/cps/ads/sdata.htm>; calculations by New Strategist*

# Distribution of Men by Income and Age, 1997: Hispanic Men

*(number and percent distribution of Hispanic men aged 15 or older by income and age, 1997; median income of men with income and of men working full-time, year-round; percent working full-time, year-round; men in thousands as of 1998)*

| | total | 15–24 | 25–34 | 35–44 | 45–54 | 55–64 | aged 65 or older total | 65–74 | 75+ |
|---|---|---|---|---|---|---|---|---|---|
| **Total men** | **10,944** | **2,890** | **2,919** | **2,365** | **1,322** | **768** | **681** | **429** | **252** |
| Without income | 1,359 | 960 | 137 | 130 | 53 | 48 | 31 | 19 | 11 |
| With income | 9,585 | 1,929 | 2,782 | 2,234 | 1,269 | 721 | 650 | 409 | 241 |
| Under $5,000 | 1,069 | 583 | 168 | 109 | 74 | 55 | 80 | 40 | 40 |
| $5,000 to $9,999 | 1,490 | 425 | 318 | 232 | 135 | 137 | 243 | 137 | 106 |
| $10,000 to $14,999 | 1,824 | 391 | 564 | 394 | 224 | 118 | 133 | 89 | 44 |
| $15,000 to $19,999 | 1,292 | 267 | 434 | 285 | 158 | 83 | 62 | 40 | 23 |
| $20,000 to $24,999 | 1,047 | 145 | 398 | 244 | 143 | 82 | 32 | 29 | 3 |
| $25,000 to $29,999 | 694 | 52 | 277 | 187 | 109 | 38 | 31 | 24 | 7 |
| $30,000 to $34,999 | 543 | 34 | 178 | 188 | 99 | 36 | 9 | 6 | 3 |
| $35,000 to $39,999 | 392 | 9 | 125 | 144 | 63 | 43 | 8 | 7 | 1 |
| $40,000 to $44,999 | 329 | 15 | 96 | 114 | 54 | 31 | 19 | 13 | 6 |
| $45,000 to $49,999 | 168 | 1 | 60 | 57 | 34 | 13 | 3 | 2 | 1 |
| $50,000 to $54,999 | 174 | 3 | 41 | 75 | 28 | 25 | 4 | 3 | 1 |
| $55,000 to $59,999 | 92 | – | 30 | 24 | 20 | 11 | 6 | 5 | 1 |
| $60,000 to $64,999 | 101 | – | 25 | 33 | 29 | 5 | 8 | 6 | 3 |
| $65,000 to $69,999 | 53 | 2 | 16 | 22 | 2 | 7 | 3 | 2 | 1 |
| $70,000 to $74,999 | 66 | – | 11 | 22 | 27 | 6 | 2 | 2 | – |
| $75,000 to $79,999 | 53 | – | 16 | 15 | 9 | 12 | – | – | – |
| $80,000 to $84,999 | 37 | – | 4 | 21 | 10 | 3 | – | – | – |
| $85,000 to $89,999 | 15 | – | 4 | 4 | 6 | – | 1 | 1 | – |
| $90,000 to $94,999 | 9 | – | – | 4 | 2 | 2 | – | – | – |
| $95,000 to $99,999 | 10 | – | – | 4 | 4 | 2 | – | – | – |
| $100,000 or more | 126 | – | 19 | 52 | 36 | 12 | 6 | 6 | – |
| **Median income** | | | | | | | | | |
| Men with income | $16,216 | $9,458 | $18,780 | $21,533 | $21,078 | $17,224 | $10,043 | $11,055 | $7,875 |
| Men working full-time | $21,799 | $15,307 | $21,279 | $26,276 | $26,185 | $25,795 | $32,105 | $23,896 | $42,230 |
| Percent working full-time | 54.6% | 28.2% | 72.6% | 70.0% | 69.8% | 51.7% | 10.0% | 12.6% | 5.6% |
| **Percent distribution** | | | | | | | | | |
| **Total men** | **100.0%** | **100.0%** | **100.0%** | **100.0%** | **100.0%** | **100.0%** | **100.0%** | **100.0%** | **100.0%** |
| Without income | 12.4 | 33.2 | 4.7 | 5.5 | 4.0 | 6.3 | 4.6 | 4.4 | 4.4 |
| With income | 87.6 | 66.7 | 95.3 | 94.5 | 96.0 | 93.9 | 95.4 | 95.3 | 95.6 |
| Under $25,000 | 61.4 | 62.7 | 64.5 | 53.4 | 55.5 | 61.8 | 80.8 | 78.1 | 85.7 |
| $25,000 to $49,999 | 19.4 | 3.8 | 25.2 | 29.2 | 27.2 | 21.0 | 10.3 | 12.1 | 7.1 |
| $50,000 to $74,999 | 4.4 | 0.2 | 4.2 | 7.4 | 8.0 | 7.0 | 3.4 | 4.2 | 2.4 |
| $75,000 to $99,999 | 1.1 | – | 0.8 | 2.0 | 2.3 | 2.5 | 0.1 | 0.2 | – |
| $100,000 or more | 1.2 | – | 0.7 | 2.2 | 2.7 | 1.6 | 0.9 | 1.4 | – |

*Note: (–) means sample is too small to make a reliable estimate.*
*Source: Bureau of the Census, Internet web site, <http:// www.census.gov/cps/ads/sdata.htm>; calculations by New Strategist*

# Distribution of Men by Income and Age, 1997: White Men

*(number and percent distribution of white men aged 15 or older by income and age, 1997; median income of men with income and of men working full-time, year-round; percent working full-time, year-round; men in thousands as of 1998)*

| | total | 15–24 | 25–34 | 35–44 | 45–54 | 55–64 | aged 65 or older total | 65–74 | 75+ |
|---|---|---|---|---|---|---|---|---|---|
| **Total men** | **85,219** | **15,157** | **15,993** | **18,465** | **14,284** | **9,258** | **12,063** | **7,109** | **4,954** |
| Without income | 4,819 | 3,480 | 349 | 354 | 275 | 226 | 134 | 88 | 46 |
| With income | 80,400 | 11,676 | 15,643 | 18,111 | 14,009 | 9,032 | 11,929 | 7,022 | 4,908 |
| Under $5,000 | 6,904 | 4,323 | 608 | 670 | 485 | 435 | 383 | 193 | 189 |
| $5,000 to $9,999 | 7,527 | 2,459 | 979 | 991 | 697 | 694 | 1,707 | 862 | 845 |
| $10,000 to $14,999 | 8,979 | 1,695 | 1,710 | 1,216 | 859 | 888 | 2,610 | 1,370 | 1,239 |
| $15,000 to $19,999 | 7,456 | 1,173 | 1,674 | 1,281 | 840 | 676 | 1,813 | 991 | 821 |
| $20,000 to $24,999 | 7,506 | 823 | 2,029 | 1,503 | 1,032 | 739 | 1,381 | 835 | 546 |
| $25,000 to $29,999 | 6,481 | 499 | 1,827 | 1,583 | 975 | 670 | 927 | 623 | 305 |
| $30,000 to $34,999 | 6,197 | 330 | 1,665 | 1,760 | 1,112 | 689 | 641 | 403 | 238 |
| $35,000 to $39,999 | 5,062 | 124 | 1,180 | 1,525 | 1,107 | 629 | 498 | 352 | 145 |
| $40,000 to $44,999 | 4,341 | 88 | 942 | 1,340 | 1,038 | 612 | 323 | 209 | 112 |
| $45,000 to $49,999 | 3,199 | 25 | 729 | 983 | 812 | 385 | 265 | 196 | 70 |
| $50,000 to $54,999 | 3,197 | 42 | 592 | 1,006 | 921 | 414 | 222 | 156 | 65 |
| $55,000 to $59,999 | 1,958 | 10 | 343 | 625 | 561 | 226 | 193 | 111 | 81 |
| $60,000 to $64,999 | 1,938 | 8 | 301 | 633 | 610 | 242 | 144 | 112 | 32 |
| $65,000 to $69,999 | 1,412 | 15 | 203 | 483 | 401 | 195 | 114 | 89 | 27 |
| $70,000 to $74,999 | 1,324 | 6 | 165 | 449 | 428 | 191 | 85 | 67 | 17 |
| $75,000 to $79,999 | 990 | 23 | 147 | 317 | 236 | 172 | 94 | 64 | 31 |
| $80,000 to $84,999 | 883 | 5 | 104 | 253 | 284 | 158 | 78 | 63 | 16 |
| $85,000 to $89,999 | 546 | 2 | 60 | 169 | 173 | 99 | 44 | 21 | 23 |
| $90,000 to $94,999 | 440 | 1 | 64 | 144 | 127 | 70 | 36 | 25 | 11 |
| $95,000 to $99,999 | 336 | – | 19 | 103 | 114 | 67 | 33 | 19 | 13 |
| $100,000 or more | 3,726 | 26 | 306 | 1,075 | 1,196 | 783 | 340 | 261 | 79 |
| **Median income** | | | | | | | | | |
| Men with income | $26,115 | $7,713 | $26,672 | $35,130 | $39,428 | $32,310 | $18,476 | $20,530 | $16,074 |
| Men working full-time | $36,118 | $18,070 | $30,597 | $38,969 | $43,903 | $42,165 | $48,401 | $46,157 | $52,108 |
| Percent working full-time | 55.4% | 23.0% | 75.5% | 79.2% | 77.1% | 55.7% | 7.4% | 10.1% | 3.5% |
| **Percent distribution** | | | | | | | | | |
| **Total men** | **100.0%** | **100.0%** | **100.0%** | **100.0%** | **100.0%** | **100.0%** | **100.0%** | **100.0%** | **100.0%** |
| Without income | 5.7 | 23.0 | 2.2 | 1.9 | 1.9 | 2.4 | 1.1 | 1.2 | 0.9 |
| With income | 94.3 | 77.0 | 97.8 | 98.1 | 98.1 | 97.6 | 98.9 | 98.8 | 99.1 |
| Under $25,000 | 45.0 | 69.1 | 43.8 | 30.7 | 27.4 | 37.1 | 65.4 | 59.8 | 73.5 |
| $25,000 to $49,999 | 29.7 | 7.0 | 39.7 | 38.9 | 35.3 | 32.2 | 22.0 | 25.1 | 17.6 |
| $50,000 to $74,999 | 11.5 | 0.5 | 10.0 | 17.3 | 20.4 | 13.7 | 6.3 | 7.5 | 4.5 |
| $75,000 to $99,999 | 3.7 | 0.2 | 2.5 | 5.3 | 6.5 | 6.1 | 2.4 | 2.7 | 1.9 |
| $100,000 or more | 4.4 | 0.2 | 1.9 | 5.8 | 8.4 | 8.5 | 2.8 | 3.7 | 1.6 |

*Note: (–) means sample is too small to make a reliable estimate.*
*Source: Bureau of the Census, Internet web site, <http:// www.census.gov/cps/ads/sdata.htm>; calculations by New Strategist*

# Distribution of Men by Income and Age, 1997: Non-Hispanic White Men

*(number and percent distribution of non-Hispanic white men aged 15 or older by income and age, 1997; median income of men with income and of men working full-time, year-round; percent working full-time, year-round; men in thousands as of 1998)*

| | total | 15–24 | 25–34 | 35–44 | 45–54 | 55–64 | aged 65 or older total | 65–74 | 75+ |
|---|---|---|---|---|---|---|---|---|---|
| **Total men** | **74,703** | **12,402** | **13,165** | **16,205** | **13,009** | **8,519** | **11,403** | **6,698** | **4,705** |
| Without income | 3,553 | 2,573 | 223 | 247 | 223 | 183 | 103 | 68 | 35 |
| With income | 71,150 | 9,828 | 12,942 | 15,957 | 12,786 | 8,337 | 11,300 | 6,630 | 4,670 |
| Under $5,000 | 5,881 | 3,765 | 450 | 568 | 411 | 382 | 304 | 154 | 150 |
| $5,000 to $9,999 | 6,086 | 2,049 | 668 | 764 | 569 | 566 | 1,472 | 731 | 741 |
| $10,000 to $14,999 | 7,217 | 1,326 | 1,161 | 833 | 641 | 773 | 2,485 | 1,290 | 1,195 |
| $15,000 to $19,999 | 6,197 | 911 | 1,251 | 1,008 | 685 | 592 | 1,750 | 952 | 798 |
| $20,000 to $24,999 | 6,489 | 680 | 1,641 | 1,269 | 890 | 660 | 1,350 | 807 | 543 |
| $25,000 to $29,999 | 5,819 | 452 | 1,559 | 1,406 | 871 | 633 | 898 | 599 | 299 |
| $30,000 to $34,999 | 5,675 | 299 | 1,495 | 1,577 | 1,016 | 654 | 633 | 398 | 235 |
| $35,000 to $39,999 | 4,685 | 115 | 1,059 | 1,385 | 1,048 | 589 | 489 | 345 | 144 |
| $40,000 to $44,999 | 4,024 | 76 | 846 | 1,225 | 991 | 583 | 304 | 196 | 108 |
| $45,000 to $49,999 | 3,037 | 24 | 671 | 930 | 780 | 372 | 262 | 193 | 69 |
| $50,000 to $54,999 | 3,028 | 39 | 551 | 935 | 894 | 391 | 218 | 153 | 64 |
| $55,000 to $59,999 | 1,871 | 10 | 315 | 602 | 541 | 214 | 187 | 107 | 80 |
| $60,000 to $64,999 | 1,845 | 8 | 277 | 604 | 584 | 237 | 135 | 106 | 29 |
| $65,000 to $69,999 | 1,360 | 13 | 187 | 461 | 399 | 187 | 111 | 87 | 25 |
| $70,000 to $74,999 | 1,262 | 6 | 153 | 428 | 403 | 187 | 83 | 66 | 17 |
| $75,000 to $79,999 | 939 | 23 | 131 | 302 | 226 | 161 | 94 | 64 | 31 |
| $80,000 to $84,999 | 848 | 5 | 99 | 232 | 277 | 155 | 78 | 63 | 16 |
| $85,000 to $89,999 | 530 | 2 | 56 | 165 | 167 | 99 | 42 | 20 | 23 |
| $90,000 to $94,999 | 431 | 1 | 64 | 140 | 124 | 68 | 36 | 25 | 11 |
| $95,000 to $99,999 | 326 | – | 19 | 99 | 110 | 65 | 33 | 19 | 13 |
| $100,000 or more | 3,600 | 26 | 287 | 1,023 | 1,160 | 770 | 334 | 256 | 79 |
| **Median income** | | | | | | | | | |
| Men with income | $27,559 | $7,375 | $28,755 | $36,548 | $41,014 | $34,011 | $18,973 | $21,097 | $16,540 |
| Men working full-time | $37,931 | $19,812 | $31,930 | $40,594 | $45,662 | $43,866 | $50,166 | $48,141 | $55,646 |
| Percent working full-time | 55.5% | 21.8% | 76.1% | 80.4% | 77.8% | 56.0% | 7.2% | 9.9% | 3.4% |
| **Percent distribution** | | | | | | | | | |
| **Total men** | **100.0%** | **100.0%** | **100.0%** | **100.0%** | **100.0%** | **100.0%** | **100.0%** | **100.0%** | **100.0%** |
| Without income | 4.8 | 20.7 | 1.7 | 1.5 | 1.7 | 2.1 | 0.9 | 1.0 | 0.7 |
| With income | 95.2 | 79.2 | 98.3 | 98.5 | 98.3 | 97.9 | 99.1 | 99.0 | 99.3 |
| Under $25,000 | 42.7 | 70.4 | 39.3 | 27.4 | 24.6 | 34.9 | 64.6 | 58.7 | 72.8 |
| $25,000 to $49,999 | 31.1 | 7.8 | 42.8 | 40.3 | 36.2 | 33.2 | 22.7 | 25.8 | 18.2 |
| $50,000 to $74,999 | 12.5 | 0.6 | 11.3 | 18.7 | 21.7 | 14.3 | 6.4 | 7.7 | 4.6 |
| $75,000 to $99,999 | 4.1 | 0.2 | 2.8 | 5.8 | 6.9 | 6.4 | 2.5 | 2.9 | 2.0 |
| $100,000 or more | 4.8 | 0.2 | 2.2 | 6.3 | 8.9 | 9.0 | 2.9 | 3.8 | 1.7 |

*Note: (–) means sample is too small to make a reliable estimate.*
*Source: Bureau of the Census, Internet web site, <http:// www.census.gov/cps/ads/sdata.htm>; calculations by New Strategist*

# Black and Hispanic Men Have Lower Incomes

**The incomes of black men are lower, in part, because fewer hold full-time jobs.**

The income differences between black, Hispanic, and non-Hispanic white men are dramatic. The $18,096 median income of black men was just 66 percent as high as the $27,559 median income of non-Hispanic white men in 1997. The $16,216 median income of Hispanic men was only 59 percent as high as the non-Hispanic white median.

The gap between the median incomes of black and non-Hispanic white men diminishes among full-time workers. The $26,897 median income of black men who work full-time was 71 percent as high as the $37,931 median of their non-Hispanic white counterparts. In contrast, the gap between Hispanic and non-Hispanic white men widens among full-time workers. The $21,799 median income of Hispanic men who work full-time was only 57 percent as high as that of non-Hispanic white men.

✘ Black men are much less likely to work full-time than non-Hispanic white men, which lowers their incomes. Hispanic men have low incomes, even if they work full-time, because many are recent immigrants with little earning power.

## Non-Hispanic white men have the highest incomes

*(median income of men aged 15 or older who work full-time,*
*year-round, by race and Hispanic origin, 1997)*

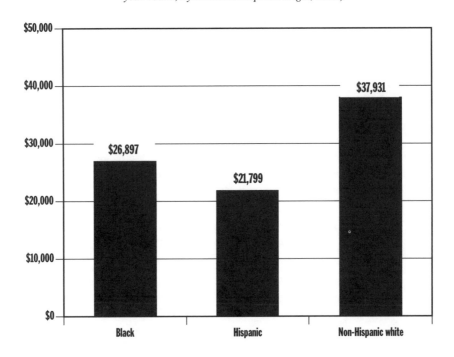

# Distribution of Men by Income, Race, and Hispanic Origin, 1997

*(number and percent distribution of men aged 15 or older by income, race, and Hispanic origin, 1997; median income of men with income and of men working full-time, year-round; percent working full-time, year-round; men in thousands as of 1998)*

| | total | white | black | Hispanic | non-Hispanic white |
|---|---|---|---|---|---|
| **Total men** | 101,123 | 85,219 | 11,283 | 10,944 | 74,703 |
| Without income | 6,955 | 4,819 | 1,613 | 1,359 | 3,553 |
| With income | 94,168 | 80,400 | 9,671 | 9,585 | 71,150 |
| Under $5,000 | 8,578 | 6,904 | 1,255 | 1,069 | 5,881 |
| $5,000 to $9,999 | 9,598 | 7,527 | 1,605 | 1,490 | 6,086 |
| $10,000 to $14,999 | 10,695 | 8,979 | 1,264 | 1,824 | 7,217 |
| $15,000 to $19,999 | 8,866 | 7,456 | 1,042 | 1,292 | 6,197 |
| $20,000 to $24,999 | 8,934 | 7,506 | 1,020 | 1,047 | 6,489 |
| $25,000 to $29,999 | 7,625 | 6,481 | 820 | 694 | 5,819 |
| $30,000 to $34,999 | 7,115 | 6,197 | 640 | 543 | 5,675 |
| $35,000 to $39,999 | 5,829 | 5,062 | 544 | 392 | 4,685 |
| $40,000 to $44,999 | 4,941 | 4,341 | 401 | 329 | 4,024 |
| $45,000 to $49,999 | 3,597 | 3,199 | 232 | 168 | 3,037 |
| $50,000 to $54,999 | 3,524 | 3,197 | 184 | 174 | 3,028 |
| $55,000 to $59,999 | 2,175 | 1,958 | 117 | 92 | 1,871 |
| $60,000 to $64,999 | 2,199 | 1,938 | 164 | 101 | 1,845 |
| $65,000 to $69,999 | 1,579 | 1,412 | 106 | 53 | 1,360 |
| $70,000 to $74,999 | 1,461 | 1,324 | 63 | 66 | 1,262 |
| $75,000 to $79,999 | 1,079 | 990 | 42 | 53 | 939 |
| $80,000 to $84,999 | 965 | 883 | 29 | 37 | 848 |
| $85,000 to $89,999 | 594 | 546 | 27 | 15 | 530 |
| $90,000 to $94,999 | 490 | 440 | 23 | 9 | 431 |
| $95,000 to $99,999 | 366 | 336 | 17 | 10 | 326 |
| $100,000 or more | 3,957 | 3,726 | 78 | 126 | 3,600 |
| **Median income** | | | | | |
| Men with income | $25,212 | $26,115 | $18,096 | $16,216 | $27,559 |
| Men working full-time | $35,248 | $36,118 | $26,897 | $21,799 | $37,931 |
| Percent working full-time | 54.3% | 55.4% | 45.8% | 54.6% | 55.5% |
| **Percent distribution** | | | | | |
| **Total men** | 100.0% | 100.0% | 100.0% | 100.0% | 100.0% |
| Without income | 6.9 | 5.7 | 14.3 | 12.4 | 4.8 |
| With income | 93.1 | 94.3 | 85.7 | 87.6 | 95.2 |
| Under $25,000 | 46.2 | 45.0 | 54.8 | 61.4 | 42.7 |
| $25,000 to $49,999 | 28.8 | 29.7 | 23.4 | 19.4 | 31.1 |
| $50,000 to $74,999 | 10.8 | 11.5 | 5.6 | 4.4 | 12.5 |
| $75,000 to $99,999 | 3.5 | 3.7 | 1.2 | 1.1 | 4.1 |
| $100,000 or more | 3.9 | 4.4 | 0.7 | 1.2 | 4.8 |

*Note: Numbers will not add to total because Hispanics may be of any race and not all races are shown.*
*Source: Bureau of the Census, Internet web site, <http:// www.census.gov/cps/ads/sdata.htm>; calculations by New Strategist*

# Incomes Are Highest for Non-Hispanic White Men in the West

## They are lowest for black men in the Northeast.

The median income of non-Hispanic white men living in the West stood at $29,815 in 1997, 18 percent greater than the median income of all men. In contrast, the median income of black men in the Northeast was just $15,593, only 62 percent as high as the median for all men and just 53 percent as high as that of non-Hispanic white men in the region. Hispanic men in the West did not fare much better, with a median income of only $15,763.

Most black men do not have full-time jobs. Only 38 percent of those in the Northeast work full-time, which explains why they have such a low median income. Among black men in the Northeast who do work full-time, the median income is a much higher $27,408—67 percent as high as the median income of their non-Hispanic white counterparts in the region.

The majority of both Hispanic men and non-Hispanic white men are full-time workers in every region. Even among Hispanic men who work full-time, median income remains relatively low, however, because many are immigrants with little earning power.

✘ Although the incomes of blacks have been rising for decades, they still remain well below those of whites. Until black men have the same educational and job opportunities as white men, their incomes will lag behind.

### Men's incomes are highest in the Northeast

*(median income of men aged 15 or older who work full-time, year-round, by region, 1997)*

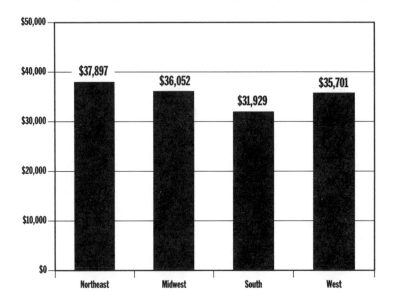

# Distribution of Men by Income and Region, 1997: Total Men

*(number and percent distribution of men aged 15 or older by income and region, 1997; median income of men with income and of men working full-time, year-round; percent working full-time, year-round; men in thousands as of 1998)*

| | total | Northeast | Midwest | South | West |
|---|---|---|---|---|---|
| **Total men** | **101,123** | **19,341** | **23,265** | **35,610** | **22,907** |
| Without income | 6,955 | 1,388 | 1,179 | 2,660 | 1,728 |
| With income | 94,168 | 17,953 | 22,086 | 32,950 | 21,179 |
| Under $5,000 | 8,578 | 1,663 | 2,042 | 2,898 | 1,977 |
| $5,000 to $9,999 | 9,598 | 1,788 | 2,024 | 3,547 | 2,239 |
| $10,000 to $14,999 | 10,695 | 1,917 | 2,300 | 3,880 | 2,597 |
| $15,000 to $19,999 | 8,866 | 1,597 | 2,003 | 3,350 | 1,916 |
| $20,000 to $24,999 | 8,934 | 1,566 | 2,057 | 3,402 | 1,909 |
| $25,000 to $29,999 | 7,625 | 1,276 | 1,922 | 2,905 | 1,522 |
| $30,000 to $34,999 | 7,115 | 1,239 | 1,920 | 2,528 | 1,428 |
| $35,000 to $39,999 | 5,829 | 1,218 | 1,438 | 1,913 | 1,260 |
| $40,000 to $44,999 | 4,941 | 966 | 1,255 | 1,698 | 1,021 |
| $45,000 to $49,999 | 3,597 | 699 | 953 | 1,137 | 808 |
| $50,000 to $54,999 | 3,524 | 769 | 900 | 1,111 | 744 |
| $55,000 to $59,999 | 2,175 | 438 | 523 | 646 | 568 |
| $60,000 to $64,999 | 2,199 | 465 | 476 | 679 | 577 |
| $65,000 to $69,999 | 1,579 | 353 | 347 | 509 | 372 |
| $70,000 to $74,999 | 1,461 | 317 | 365 | 457 | 323 |
| $75,000 to $79,999 | 1,079 | 226 | 208 | 316 | 329 |
| $80,000 to $84,999 | 965 | 211 | 191 | 306 | 258 |
| $85,000 to $89,999 | 594 | 144 | 149 | 179 | 122 |
| $90,000 to $94,999 | 490 | 112 | 127 | 130 | 122 |
| $95,000 to $99,999 | 366 | 77 | 79 | 117 | 94 |
| $100,000 or more | 3,957 | 914 | 807 | 1,243 | 993 |
| **Median income** | | | | | |
| Men with income | $25,212 | $26,378 | $26,285 | $23,896 | $24,832 |
| Men working full-time | $35,248 | $37,897 | $36,052 | $31,929 | $35,701 |
| Percent working full-time | 54.3% | 53.1% | 55.7% | 55.1% | 52.7% |
| **Percent distribution** | | | | | |
| **Total men** | **100.0%** | **100.0%** | **100.0%** | **100.0%** | **100.0%** |
| Without income | 6.9 | 7.2 | 5.1 | 7.5 | 7.5 |
| With income | 93.1 | 92.8 | 94.9 | 92.5 | 92.5 |
| Under $25,000 | 46.2 | 44.1 | 44.8 | 48.0 | 46.4 |
| $25,000 to $49,999 | 28.8 | 27.9 | 32.2 | 28.6 | 26.4 |
| $50,000 to $74,999 | 10.8 | 12.1 | 11.2 | 9.6 | 11.3 |
| $75,000 to $99,999 | 3.5 | 4.0 | 3.2 | 2.9 | 4.0 |
| $100,000 or more | 3.9 | 4.7 | 3.5 | 3.5 | 4.3 |

*Source: Bureau of the Census, Internet web site, <http:// www.census.gov/cps/ads/sdata.htm>; calculations by New Strategist*

# Distribution of Men by Income and Region, 1997: Black Men

*(number and percent distribution of black men aged 15 or older by income and region, 1997; median income of men with income and of men working full-time, year-round; percent working full-time, year-round; men in thousands as of 1998)*

| | total | Northeast | Midwest | South | West |
|---|---|---|---|---|---|
| **Total men** | **11,283** | **2,034** | **1,912** | **6,306** | **1,032** |
| Without income | 1,613 | 363 | 242 | 864 | 144 |
| With income | 9,671 | 1,671 | 1,670 | 5,442 | 888 |
| Under $5,000 | 1,255 | 260 | 253 | 665 | 75 |
| $5,000 to $9,999 | 1,605 | 322 | 264 | 908 | 111 |
| $10,000 to $14,999 | 1,264 | 231 | 229 | 694 | 109 |
| $15,000 to $19,999 | 1,042 | 148 | 135 | 685 | 73 |
| $20,000 to $24,999 | 1,020 | 163 | 190 | 549 | 117 |
| $25,000 to $29,999 | 820 | 107 | 112 | 508 | 94 |
| $30,000 to $34,999 | 640 | 98 | 119 | 362 | 60 |
| $35,000 to $39,999 | 544 | 100 | 105 | 285 | 54 |
| $40,000 to $44,999 | 401 | 40 | 74 | 248 | 39 |
| $45,000 to $49,999 | 232 | 29 | 35 | 130 | 38 |
| $50,000 to $54,999 | 184 | 42 | 47 | 75 | 20 |
| $55,000 to $59,999 | 117 | 33 | 15 | 48 | 20 |
| $60,000 to $64,999 | 164 | 37 | 19 | 82 | 25 |
| $65,000 to $69,999 | 106 | 17 | 10 | 72 | 6 |
| $70,000 to $74,999 | 63 | 10 | 14 | 35 | 3 |
| $75,000 to $79,999 | 42 | – | 11 | 21 | 10 |
| $80,000 to $84,999 | 29 | 8 | 5 | 12 | 3 |
| $85,000 to $89,999 | 27 | 5 | 2 | 13 | 7 |
| $90,000 to $94,999 | 23 | 8 | 2 | 9 | 3 |
| $95,000 to $99,999 | 17 | 3 | 2 | 12 | – |
| $100,000 or more | 78 | 9 | 25 | 28 | 17 |
| **Median income** | | | | | |
| Men with income | $18,096 | $15,593 | $18,129 | $18,023 | $23,315 |
| Men working full-time | $26,897 | $27,408 | $29,565 | $26,050 | $31,680 |
| Percent working full-time | 45.8% | 38.2% | 41.7% | 49.4% | 46.5% |
| **Percent distribution** | | | | | |
| **Total men** | **100.0%** | **100.0%** | **100.0%** | **100.0%** | **100.0%** |
| Without income | 14.3 | 17.8 | 12.7 | 13.7 | 14.0 |
| With income | 85.7 | 82.2 | 87.3 | 86.3 | 86.0 |
| Under $25,000 | 54.8 | 55.3 | 56.0 | 55.5 | 47.0 |
| $25,000 to $49,999 | 23.4 | 18.4 | 23.3 | 24.3 | 27.6 |
| $50,000 to $74,999 | 5.6 | 6.8 | 5.5 | 4.9 | 7.2 |
| $75,000 to $99,999 | 1.2 | 1.2 | 1.2 | 1.1 | 2.2 |
| $100,000 or more | 0.7 | 0.4 | 1.3 | 0.4 | 1.6 |

*Note: (–) means sample is too small to make a reliable estimate.*
*Source: Bureau of the Census, Internet web site, <http:// www.census.gov/cps/ads/sdata.htm>; calculations by New Strategist*

# Distribution of Men by Income and Region, 1997: Hispanic Men

*(number and percent distribution of Hispanic men aged 15 or older by income and region, 1997; median income of men with income and of men working full-time, year-round; percent working full-time, year-round; men in thousands as of 1998)*

| | total | Northeast | Midwest | South | West |
|---|---|---|---|---|---|
| **Total men** | **10,944** | **1,674** | **851** | **3,508** | **4,912** |
| Without income | 1,359 | 243 | 98 | 360 | 658 |
| With income | 9,585 | 1,431 | 753 | 3,148 | 4,254 |
| Under $5,000 | 1,069 | 173 | 74 | 371 | 452 |
| $5,000 to $9,999 | 1,490 | 229 | 85 | 489 | 687 |
| $10,000 to $14,999 | 1,824 | 245 | 156 | 553 | 870 |
| $15,000 to $19,999 | 1,292 | 188 | 76 | 428 | 600 |
| $20,000 to $24,999 | 1,047 | 143 | 88 | 388 | 427 |
| $25,000 to $29,999 | 694 | 108 | 74 | 248 | 263 |
| $30,000 to $34,999 | 543 | 88 | 55 | 150 | 249 |
| $35,000 to $39,999 | 392 | 73 | 39 | 99 | 181 |
| $40,000 to $44,999 | 329 | 36 | 22 | 121 | 151 |
| $45,000 to $49,999 | 168 | 27 | 19 | 50 | 72 |
| $50,000 to $54,999 | 174 | 38 | 19 | 50 | 65 |
| $55,000 to $59,999 | 92 | 6 | 8 | 38 | 40 |
| $60,000 to $64,999 | 101 | 17 | 11 | 23 | 50 |
| $65,000 to $69,999 | 53 | 12 | 5 | 20 | 15 |
| $70,000 to $74,999 | 66 | 4 | 2 | 24 | 36 |
| $75,000 to $79,999 | 53 | 3 | 5 | 18 | 25 |
| $80,000 to $84,999 | 37 | 14 | – | 13 | 11 |
| $85,000 to $89,999 | 15 | 4 | – | 6 | 4 |
| $90,000 to $94,999 | 9 | – | – | 2 | 7 |
| $95,000 to $99,999 | 10 | 1 | – | 5 | 4 |
| $100,000 or more | 126 | 20 | 13 | 49 | 44 |
| **Median income** | | | | | |
| Men with income | $16,216 | $16,307 | $18,754 | $16,459 | $15,763 |
| Men working full-time | $21,799 | $22,325 | $24,065 | $21,928 | $21,226 |
| Percent working full-time | 54.6% | 52.4% | 57.5% | 56.2% | 53.7% |
| **Percent distribution** | | | | | |
| **Total men** | **100.0%** | **100.0%** | **100.0%** | **100.0%** | **100.0%** |
| Without income | 12.4 | 14.5 | 11.5 | 10.3 | 13.4 |
| With income | 87.6 | 85.5 | 88.5 | 89.7 | 86.6 |
| Under $25,000 | 61.4 | 58.4 | 56.3 | 63.5 | 61.8 |
| $25,000 to $49,999 | 19.4 | 19.8 | 24.6 | 19.0 | 18.6 |
| $50,000 to $74,999 | 4.4 | 4.6 | 5.3 | 4.4 | 4.2 |
| $75,000 to $99,999 | 1.1 | 1.3 | 0.6 | 1.3 | 1.0 |
| $100,000 or more | 1.2 | 1.2 | 1.5 | 1.4 | 0.9 |

*Note: (–) means sample is too small to make a reliable estimate.*
*Source: Bureau of the Census, Internet web site, <http:// www.census.gov/cps/ads/sdata.htm>; calculations by New Strategist*

# Distribution of Men by Income and Region, 1997: White Men

*(number and percent distribution of white men aged 15 or older by income and region, 1997; median income of men with income and of men working full-time, year-round; percent working full-time, year-round; men in thousands as of 1998)*

|  | total | Northeast | Midwest | South | West |
|---|---|---|---|---|---|
| **Total men** | **85,219** | **16,597** | **20,767** | **28,407** | **19,450** |
| Without income | 4,819 | 944 | 871 | 1,719 | 1,285 |
| With income | 80,400 | 15,652 | 19,895 | 26,688 | 18,165 |
| Under $5,000 | 6,904 | 1,321 | 1,737 | 2,172 | 1,674 |
| $5,000 to $9,999 | 7,527 | 1,403 | 1,713 | 2,529 | 1,882 |
| $10,000 to $14,999 | 8,979 | 1,639 | 2,014 | 3,093 | 2,232 |
| $15,000 to $19,999 | 7,456 | 1,380 | 1,815 | 2,601 | 1,661 |
| $20,000 to $24,999 | 7,506 | 1,359 | 1,799 | 2,764 | 1,584 |
| $25,000 to $29,999 | 6,481 | 1,138 | 1,778 | 2,330 | 1,236 |
| $30,000 to $34,999 | 6,197 | 1,098 | 1,776 | 2,091 | 1,232 |
| $35,000 to $39,999 | 5,062 | 1,067 | 1,299 | 1,582 | 1,114 |
| $40,000 to $44,999 | 4,341 | 880 | 1,159 | 1,409 | 894 |
| $45,000 to $49,999 | 3,199 | 643 | 894 | 979 | 683 |
| $50,000 to $54,999 | 3,197 | 707 | 836 | 1,003 | 650 |
| $55,000 to $59,999 | 1,958 | 393 | 504 | 581 | 481 |
| $60,000 to $64,999 | 1,938 | 418 | 441 | 577 | 502 |
| $65,000 to $69,999 | 1,412 | 325 | 333 | 436 | 319 |
| $70,000 to $74,999 | 1,324 | 290 | 325 | 415 | 294 |
| $75,000 to $79,999 | 990 | 219 | 192 | 288 | 290 |
| $80,000 to $84,999 | 883 | 192 | 181 | 283 | 227 |
| $85,000 to $89,999 | 546 | 132 | 145 | 158 | 110 |
| $90,000 to $94,999 | 440 | 102 | 123 | 113 | 103 |
| $95,000 to $99,999 | 336 | 74 | 72 | 102 | 89 |
| $100,000 or more | 3,726 | 873 | 762 | 1,183 | 908 |
| **Median income** | | | | | |
| Men with income | $26,115 | $27,620 | $26,961 | $25,302 | $25,164 |
| Men working full-time | $36,118 | $39,481 | $36,505 | $33,677 | $36,046 |
| Percent working full-time | 55.4% | 54.9% | 56.9% | 56.2% | 53.2% |
| **Percent distribution** | | | | | |
| **Total men** | **100.0%** | **100.0%** | **100.0%** | **100.0%** | **100.0%** |
| Without income | 5.7 | 5.7 | 4.2 | 6.1 | 6.6 |
| With income | 94.3 | 94.3 | 95.8 | 93.9 | 93.4 |
| Under $25,000 | 45.0 | 42.8 | 43.7 | 46.3 | 46.4 |
| $25,000 to $49,999 | 29.7 | 29.1 | 33.3 | 29.5 | 26.5 |
| $50,000 to $74,999 | 11.5 | 12.9 | 11.7 | 10.6 | 11.5 |
| $75,000 to $99,999 | 3.7 | 4.3 | 3.4 | 3.3 | 4.2 |
| $100,000 or more | 4.4 | 5.3 | 3.7 | 4.2 | 4.7 |

*Source: Bureau of the Census, Internet web site, <http:// www.census.gov/cps/ads/sdata.htm>; calculations by New Strategist*

# Distribution of Men by Income and Region, 1997: Non-Hispanic White Men

*(number and percent distribution of non-Hispanic white men aged 15 or older by income and region, 1997; median income of men with income and of men working full-time, year-round; percent working full-time, year-round; men in thousands as of 1998)*

| | total | Northeast | Midwest | South | West |
|---|---|---|---|---|---|
| **Total men** | **74,703** | **15,125** | **19,947** | **24,987** | **14,644** |
| Without income | 3,553 | 749 | 786 | 1,367 | 650 |
| With income | 71,150 | 14,376 | 19,161 | 23,620 | 13,993 |
| Under $5,000 | 5,881 | 1,174 | 1,665 | 1,810 | 1,234 |
| $5,000 to $9,999 | 6,086 | 1,205 | 1,629 | 2,049 | 1,204 |
| $10,000 to $14,999 | 7,217 | 1,419 | 1,862 | 2,563 | 1,374 |
| $15,000 to $19,999 | 6,197 | 1,210 | 1,741 | 2,179 | 1,068 |
| $20,000 to $24,999 | 6,489 | 1,226 | 1,713 | 2,379 | 1,171 |
| $25,000 to $29,999 | 5,819 | 1,041 | 1,708 | 2,092 | 978 |
| $30,000 to $34,999 | 5,675 | 1,022 | 1,722 | 1,943 | 988 |
| $35,000 to $39,999 | 4,685 | 1,003 | 1,260 | 1,486 | 937 |
| $40,000 to $44,999 | 4,024 | 848 | 1,138 | 1,295 | 743 |
| $45,000 to $49,999 | 3,037 | 620 | 875 | 930 | 612 |
| $50,000 to $54,999 | 3,028 | 669 | 816 | 954 | 590 |
| $55,000 to $59,999 | 1,871 | 387 | 495 | 544 | 446 |
| $60,000 to $64,999 | 1,845 | 405 | 430 | 554 | 455 |
| $65,000 to $69,999 | 1,360 | 313 | 327 | 415 | 304 |
| $70,000 to $74,999 | 1,262 | 286 | 325 | 391 | 259 |
| $75,000 to $79,999 | 939 | 216 | 187 | 271 | 266 |
| $80,000 to $84,999 | 848 | 178 | 181 | 272 | 215 |
| $85,000 to $89,999 | 530 | 128 | 145 | 151 | 106 |
| $90,000 to $94,999 | 431 | 102 | 123 | 112 | 96 |
| $95,000 to $99,999 | 326 | 73 | 72 | 97 | 85 |
| $100,000 or more | 3,600 | 853 | 749 | 1,134 | 864 |
| **Median income** | | | | | |
| Men with income | $27,559 | $29,477 | $27,265 | $26,508 | $29,815 |
| Men working full-time | $37,931 | $40,944 | $36,991 | $35,799 | $41,152 |
| Percent working full-time | 55.5% | 54.9% | 56.8% | 56.2% | 53.0% |
| **Percent distribution** | | | | | |
| **Total men** | **100.0%** | **100.0%** | **100.0%** | **100.0%** | **100.0%** |
| Without income | 4.8 | 5.0 | 3.9 | 5.5 | 4.4 |
| With income | 95.2 | 95.0 | 96.1 | 94.5 | 95.6 |
| Under $25,000 | 42.7 | 41.2 | 43.2 | 43.9 | 41.3 |
| $25,000 to $49,999 | 31.1 | 30.0 | 33.6 | 31.0 | 29.1 |
| $50,000 to $74,999 | 12.5 | 13.6 | 12.0 | 11.4 | 14.0 |
| $75,000 to $99,999 | 4.1 | 4.6 | 3.5 | 3.6 | 5.2 |
| $100,000 or more | 4.8 | 5.6 | 3.8 | 4.5 | 5.9 |

*Source: Bureau of the Census, Internet web site, <http:// www.census.gov/cps/ads/sdata.htm>; calculations by New Strategist*

# Men with Highest Incomes Live in the Suburbs

## Men living in the suburbs of the largest metropolitan areas make the most.

Not surprisingly, men living outside of the central cities of the nation's major metropolitan areas (in other words, in the suburbs) have the highest incomes. Their median income stood at $30,614 in 1997. Those with full-time jobs had a median income of $40,781. Six percent of men living in the suburbs of metropolitan areas with populations of at least 1 million had incomes of $100,000 or more.

At the other extreme, men living in nonmetropolitan areas had the lowest incomes, a median of just $21,684 in 1997. Those who worked full-time had a median income of $30,475—only 75 percent as much as their suburban counterparts. The cost of living in many nonmetropolitan areas is much lower than in the suburbs, however, so the gap in spending power is probably far smaller than the gap in income.

✘ As technological advances allow more people to work from remote locations, the gap in incomes by metropolitan status is likely to diminish.

### Men in nonmetropolitan areas have the lowest incomes

*(median income of men aged 15 or older who work full-time, year-round, by metropolitan residence, 1997)*

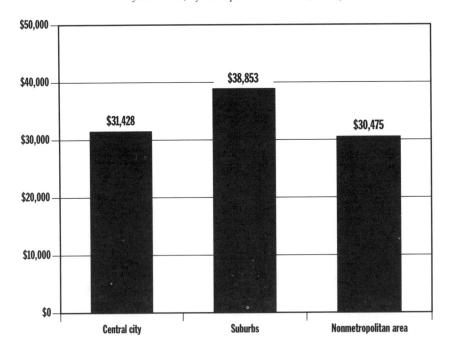

# Distribution of Men by Income and Metropolitan Residence, 1997

*(number and percent distribution of men aged 15 or older by income and metropolitan residence, 1997; median income of men with income and of men working full-time, year-round; percent working full-time, year-round; men in thousands as of 1998)*

| | | inside metropolitan areas | | | | | | | outside metropolitan areas |
|---|---|---|---|---|---|---|---|---|---|
| | | | inside central cities | | | | outside central cities | | |
| | total | total | total | 1 million or more | under 1 million | total | 1 million or more | under 1 million | |
| **Total men** | **101,123** | **81,515** | **29,770** | **19,246** | **10,523** | **51,745** | **35,493** | **16,252** | **19,608** |
| Without income | 6,955 | 5,674 | 2,587 | 1,839 | 747 | 3,087 | 2,140 | 947 | 1,281 |
| With income | 94,168 | 75,841 | 27,183 | 17,407 | 9,776 | 48,658 | 33,353 | 15,305 | 18,327 |
| Under $5,000 | 8,578 | 6,671 | 2,629 | 1,717 | 912 | 4,041 | 2,677 | 1,365 | 1,908 |
| $5,000 to $9,999 | 9,598 | 7,343 | 3,254 | 2,104 | 1,150 | 4,089 | 2,650 | 1,439 | 2,255 |
| $10,000 to $14,999 | 10,695 | 8,431 | 3,632 | 2,396 | 1,238 | 4,799 | 3,079 | 1,720 | 2,264 |
| $15,000 to $19,999 | 8,866 | 6,915 | 2,713 | 1,637 | 1,076 | 4,203 | 2,681 | 1,521 | 1,951 |
| $20,000 to $24,999 | 8,934 | 6,954 | 2,687 | 1,681 | 1,007 | 4,267 | 2,708 | 1,559 | 1,980 |
| $25,000 to $29,999 | 7,625 | 5,866 | 2,175 | 1,362 | 814 | 3,691 | 2,466 | 1,225 | 1,759 |
| $30,000 to $34,999 | 7,115 | 5,635 | 1,826 | 1,180 | 646 | 3,810 | 2,558 | 1,252 | 1,480 |
| $35,000 to $39,999 | 5,829 | 4,712 | 1,522 | 957 | 565 | 3,190 | 2,145 | 1,045 | 1,117 |
| $40,000 to $44,999 | 4,941 | 3,997 | 1,180 | 735 | 445 | 2,817 | 2,004 | 813 | 944 |
| $45,000 to $49,999 | 3,597 | 3,068 | 928 | 603 | 325 | 2,140 | 1,504 | 638 | 529 |
| $50,000 to $54,999 | 3,524 | 2,962 | 837 | 523 | 315 | 2,125 | 1,579 | 545 | 562 |
| $55,000 to $59,999 | 2,175 | 1,889 | 545 | 330 | 215 | 1,345 | 987 | 357 | 286 |
| $60,000 to $64,999 | 2,199 | 1,963 | 543 | 379 | 163 | 1,420 | 1,042 | 379 | 236 |
| $65,000 to $69,999 | 1,579 | 1,385 | 409 | 282 | 127 | 976 | 774 | 202 | 195 |
| $70,000 to $74,999 | 1,461 | 1,303 | 405 | 253 | 152 | 897 | 679 | 220 | 158 |
| $75,000 to $79,999 | 1,079 | 959 | 241 | 179 | 62 | 717 | 573 | 145 | 120 |
| $80,000 to $84,999 | 965 | 861 | 254 | 170 | 84 | 607 | 442 | 165 | 104 |
| $85,000 to $89,999 | 594 | 535 | 160 | 112 | 49 | 376 | 280 | 95 | 58 |
| $90,000 to $94,999 | 490 | 446 | 137 | 98 | 40 | 307 | 253 | 56 | 44 |
| $95,000 to $99,999 | 366 | 333 | 86 | 56 | 30 | 247 | 199 | 47 | 34 |
| $100,000 or more | 3,957 | 3,611 | 1,019 | 657 | 361 | 2,593 | 2,074 | 519 | 346 |
| **Median income** | | | | | | | | | |
| Men with income | $25,212 | $26,077 | $22,133 | $22,136 | $22,129 | $28,566 | $30,614 | $25,149 | $21,684 |
| Men working full-time | $35,248 | $36,388 | $31,428 | $31,445 | $31,392 | $38,853 | $40,781 | $35,018 | $30,475 |
| Percent working full-time | 54.3% | 55.2% | 52.0% | 52.1% | 51.9% | 57.1% | 58.3% | 54.4% | 50.7% |
| **Percent distribution** | | | | | | | | | |
| **Total men** | **100.0%** | **100.0%** | **100.0%** | **100.0%** | **100.0%** | **100.0%** | **100.0%** | **100.0%** | **100.0%** |
| Without income | 6.9 | 7.0 | 8.7 | 9.6 | 7.1 | 6.0 | 6.0 | 5.8 | 6.5 |
| With income | 93.1 | 93.0 | 91.3 | 90.4 | 92.9 | 94.0 | 94.0 | 94.2 | 93.5 |
| Under $25,000 | 46.2 | 44.5 | 50.1 | 49.5 | 51.2 | 41.4 | 38.9 | 46.8 | 52.8 |
| $25,000 to $49,999 | 28.8 | 28.6 | 25.6 | 25.1 | 26.6 | 30.2 | 30.1 | 30.6 | 29.7 |
| $50,000 to $74,999 | 10.8 | 11.7 | 9.2 | 9.2 | 9.2 | 13.1 | 14.3 | 10.5 | 7.3 |
| $75,000 to $99,999 | 3.5 | 3.8 | 2.9 | 3.2 | 2.5 | 4.4 | 4.9 | 3.1 | 1.8 |
| $100,000 or more | 3.9 | 4.4 | 3.4 | 3.4 | 3.4 | 5.0 | 5.8 | 3.2 | 1.8 |

*Source: Bureau of the Census, Internet web site, <http:// www.census.gov/cps/ads/sdata.htm>; calculations by New Strategist*

# Only Men Who Work Full-Time Make Much Money

## Men who work part-time made less than $9,000 in 1997.

Among the nation's 101 million men aged 15 or older, 55 million (54 percent) worked full-time, year-round in 1997. Only 11 million worked part-time. Among those with full-time, year-round jobs, median earnings stood at $33,674. Five percent earned at least $100,000. Among those who worked part-time, year-round, median earnings were just $8,976.

Only 46 percent of black men work full-time, year-round. Their median earnings stood at $26,432, one-quarter higher than the median earnings of all black men. Black men who worked part-time, year-round, had higher earnings than any other part-time workers—a median of $11,092. In contrast, non-Hispanic white men who worked part-time, year-round, earned only $8,848.

The majority of Hispanic men work full-time, but even they have low earnings. Hispanic men who worked full-time, year-round had median earnings of only $21,615 in 1997, just 59 percent as high as that of their non-Hispanic white counterparts.

✘ The earnings of black men will rise in the years ahead as educational attainment and job opportunities grow. The earnings of Hispanic men are not likely to rise until immigrants become a smaller share of the Hispanic population.

### Earnings of Hispanic men who work full-time are well below average

*(median earnings of men aged 15 or older who work full-time, year-round, by race and Hispanic origin, 1997)*

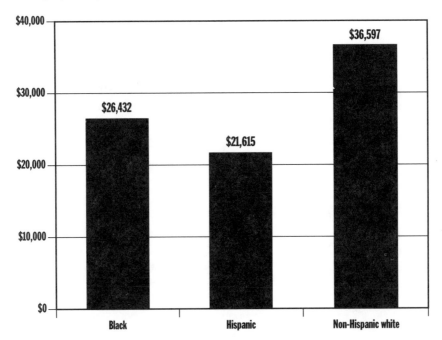

# Distribution of Men by Earnings and Work Experience, 1997: Total Men

*(number and percent distribution of men aged 15 or older by earnings and work experience, 1997; median earnings of men with earnings; men in thousands as of 1998)*

| | | worked | | | | |
| | | total | full-time | | part-time | |
| | total | total | total | year-round | total | year-round |
|---|---|---|---|---|---|---|
| **Total men** | **101,123** | **76,731** | **66,160** | **54,933** | **10,571** | **4,288** |
| Without earnings | 24,429 | 38 | 27 | 24 | 11 | 7 |
| With earnings | 76,694 | 76,694 | 66,133 | 54,909 | 10,560 | 4,281 |
| Under $5,000 | 8,503 | 8,503 | 3,180 | 774 | 5,324 | 1,051 |
| $5,000 to $9,999 | 5,871 | 5,871 | 3,506 | 1,350 | 2,366 | 1,299 |
| $10,000 to $14,999 | 6,934 | 6,934 | 5,765 | 3,982 | 1,168 | 772 |
| $15,000 to $19,999 | 6,623 | 6,623 | 6,080 | 4,841 | 542 | 383 |
| $20,000 to $24,999 | 7,141 | 7,141 | 6,807 | 5,941 | 334 | 219 |
| $25,000 to $29,999 | 6,445 | 6,445 | 6,265 | 5,614 | 180 | 124 |
| $30,000 to $34,999 | 6,357 | 6,357 | 6,206 | 5,713 | 152 | 92 |
| $35,000 to $39,999 | 5,257 | 5,257 | 5,150 | 4,821 | 107 | 70 |
| $40,000 to $44,999 | 4,590 | 4,590 | 4,546 | 4,264 | 44 | 29 |
| $45,000 to $49,999 | 3,193 | 3,193 | 3,160 | 2,937 | 32 | 20 |
| $50,000 to $54,999 | 3,294 | 3,294 | 3,261 | 3,087 | 33 | 29 |
| $55,000 to $59,999 | 1,820 | 1,820 | 1,784 | 1,680 | 36 | 20 |
| $60,000 to $64,999 | 2,057 | 2,057 | 2,030 | 1,920 | 27 | 16 |
| $65,000 to $69,999 | 1,347 | 1,347 | 1,333 | 1,277 | 14 | 3 |
| $70,000 to $74,999 | 1,245 | 1,245 | 1,217 | 1,129 | 28 | 16 |
| $75,000 to $79,999 | 910 | 910 | 897 | 861 | 12 | 8 |
| $80,000 to $84,999 | 861 | 861 | 843 | 809 | 17 | 15 |
| $85,000 to $89,999 | 402 | 402 | 397 | 385 | 4 | 4 |
| $90,000 to $94,999 | 489 | 489 | 478 | 465 | 11 | 11 |
| $95,000 to $99,999 | 254 | 254 | 249 | 235 | 6 | 6 |
| $100,000 or more | 3,102 | 3,102 | 2,979 | 2,822 | 123 | 93 |
| Median earnings of men with earnings | $26,843 | $26,843 | $30,786 | $33,674 | $4,937 | $8,976 |
| **Percent distribution** | | | | | | |
| **Total men** | **100.0%** | **100.0%** | **100.0%** | **100.0%** | **100.0%** | **100.0%** |
| Without earnings | 24.2 | 0.0 | 0.0 | 0.0 | 0.1 | 0.2 |
| With earnings | 75.8 | 100.0 | 100.0 | 100.0 | 99.9 | 99.8 |
| Under $25,000 | 34.7 | 45.7 | 38.3 | 30.7 | 92.1 | 86.8 |
| $25,000 to $49,999 | 25.6 | 33.7 | 38.3 | 42.5 | 4.9 | 7.8 |
| $50,000 to $74,999 | 9.7 | 12.7 | 14.5 | 16.6 | 1.3 | 2.0 |
| $75,000 to $99,999 | 2.9 | 3.8 | 4.3 | 5.0 | 0.5 | 1.0 |
| $100,000 or more | 3.1 | 4.0 | 4.5 | 5.1 | 1.2 | 2.2 |

*Source: Bureau of the Census, Internet web site, <http:// www.census.gov/cps/ads/sdata.htm>; calculations by New Strategist*

# Distribution of Men by Earnings and Work Experience, 1997: Black Men

*(number and percent distribution of black men aged 15 or older by earnings and work experience, 1997; median earnings of men with earnings; men in thousands as of 1998)*

| | | | worked | | | |
| | | | full-time | | part-time | |
| | total | total | total | year-round | total | year-round |
|---|---|---|---|---|---|---|
| **Total men** | **11,283** | **7,565** | **6,415** | **5,172** | **1,150** | **395** |
| Without earnings | 3,719 | 0 | 0 | 0 | 0 | 0 |
| With earnings | 7,565 | 7,565 | 6,415 | 5,172 | 1,150 | 395 |
| Under $5,000 | 1,058 | 1,058 | 400 | 72 | 659 | 73 |
| $5,000 to $9,999 | 708 | 708 | 522 | 195 | 186 | 102 |
| $10,000 to $14,999 | 858 | 858 | 741 | 564 | 117 | 80 |
| $15,000 to $19,999 | 903 | 903 | 831 | 709 | 72 | 56 |
| $20,000 to $24,999 | 879 | 879 | 841 | 753 | 38 | 31 |
| $25,000 to $29,999 | 758 | 758 | 734 | 682 | 24 | 23 |
| $30,000 to $34,999 | 564 | 564 | 548 | 511 | 16 | 16 |
| $35,000 to $39,999 | 495 | 495 | 490 | 465 | 5 | – |
| $40,000 to $44,999 | 372 | 372 | 370 | 346 | 2 | 2 |
| $45,000 to $49,999 | 214 | 214 | 214 | 202 | – | – |
| $50,000 to $54,999 | 188 | 188 | 188 | 166 | – | – |
| $55,000 to $59,999 | 96 | 96 | 85 | 79 | 12 | 6 |
| $60,000 to $64,999 | 176 | 176 | 168 | 153 | 8 | – |
| $65,000 to $69,999 | 89 | 89 | 86 | 86 | 3 | – |
| $70,000 to $74,999 | 40 | 40 | 40 | 40 | – | – |
| $75,000 to $79,999 | 34 | 34 | 34 | 32 | – | – |
| $80,000 to $84,999 | 18 | 18 | 18 | 18 | – | – |
| $85,000 to $89,999 | 12 | 12 | 12 | 10 | – | – |
| $90,000 to $94,999 | 31 | 31 | 31 | 31 | – | – |
| $95,000 to $99,999 | 8 | 8 | 5 | 5 | 3 | 3 |
| $100,000 or more | 63 | 63 | 57 | 51 | 5 | 3 |
| Median earnings of men with earnings | $21,141 | $21,141 | $23,980 | $26,432 | $3,762 | $11,092 |
| **Percent distribution** | | | | | | |
| **Total men** | **100.0%** | **100.0%** | **100.0%** | **100.0%** | **100.0%** | **100.0%** |
| Without earnings | 33.0 | 0.0 | 0.0 | 0.0 | 0.0 | 0.0 |
| With earnings | 67.0 | 100.0 | 100.0 | 100.0 | 100.0 | 100.0 |
| Under $25,000 | 39.0 | 58.2 | 52.0 | 44.3 | 93.2 | 86.6 |
| $25,000 to $49,999 | 21.3 | 31.8 | 36.7 | 42.7 | 4.1 | 10.4 |
| $50,000 to $74,999 | 5.2 | 7.8 | 8.8 | 10.1 | 2.0 | 1.5 |
| $75,000 to $99,999 | 0.9 | 1.4 | 1.6 | 1.9 | 0.3 | 0.8 |
| $100,000 or more | 0.6 | 0.8 | 0.9 | 1.0 | 0.4 | 0.8 |

*Note: (–) means samples is too small to make a reliable estimate.*
*Source: Bureau of the Census, Internet web site, <http:// www.census.gov/cps/ads/sdata.htm>; calculations by New Strategist*

# Distribution of Men by Earnings and Work Experience, 1997: Hispanic Men

*(number and percent distribution of Hispanic men aged 15 or older by earnings and work experience, 1997; median earnings of men with earnings; men in thousands as of 1998)*

| | | worked | | | | |
| | *total* | *total* | full-time | | part-time | |
| | | | *total* | *year-round* | *total* | *year-round* |
|---|---|---|---|---|---|---|
| **Total men** | **10,944** | **8,465** | **7,452** | **5,976** | **1,013** | **391** |
| Without earnings | 2,480 | 0 | 0 | 0 | 0 | 0 |
| With earnings | 8,465 | 8,465 | 7,452 | 5,976 | 1,013 | 391 |
| Under $5,000 | 950 | 950 | 438 | 95 | 511 | 86 |
| $5,000 to $9,999 | 1,049 | 1,049 | 775 | 357 | 275 | 159 |
| $10,000 to $14,999 | 1,594 | 1,594 | 1,472 | 1,171 | 122 | 80 |
| $15,000 to $19,999 | 1,202 | 1,202 | 1,152 | 970 | 49 | 36 |
| $20,000 to $24,999 | 974 | 974 | 956 | 882 | 18 | 15 |
| $25,000 to $29,999 | 651 | 651 | 639 | 590 | 12 | 12 |
| $30,000 to $34,999 | 522 | 522 | 514 | 471 | 8 | – |
| $35,000 to $39,999 | 384 | 384 | 384 | 361 | – | – |
| $40,000 to $44,999 | 299 | 299 | 296 | 290 | 4 | – |
| $45,000 to $49,999 | 160 | 160 | 160 | 153 | – | – |
| $50,000 to $54,999 | 166 | 166 | 163 | 156 | 2 | 2 |
| $55,000 to $59,999 | 90 | 90 | 88 | 86 | 2 | – |
| $60,000 to $64,999 | 87 | 87 | 87 | 80 | – | – |
| $65,000 to $69,999 | 57 | 57 | 57 | 57 | – | – |
| $70,000 to $74,999 | 57 | 57 | 57 | 55 | – | – |
| $75,000 to $79,999 | 49 | 49 | 49 | 48 | – | – |
| $80,000 to $84,999 | 35 | 35 | 35 | 35 | – | – |
| $85,000 to $89,999 | 11 | 11 | 11 | 11 | – | – |
| $90,000 to $94,999 | 10 | 10 | 10 | 9 | – | – |
| $95,000 to $99,999 | 8 | 8 | 8 | 8 | – | – |
| $100,000 or more | 107 | 107 | 97 | 91 | 10 | – |
| Median earnings of men with earnings | $17,045 | $17,045 | $19,315 | $21,615 | $4,928 | $7,687 |
| **Percent distribution** | | | | | | |
| **Total men** | **100.0%** | **100.0%** | **100.0%** | **100.0%** | **100.0%** | **100.0%** |
| Without earnings | 22.7 | 0.0 | 0.0 | 0.0 | 0.0 | 0.0 |
| With earnings | 77.3 | 100.0 | 100.0 | 100.0 | 100.0 | 100.0 |
| Under $25,000 | 52.7 | 68.2 | 64.3 | 58.1 | 96.2 | 96.2 |
| $25,000 to $49,999 | 18.4 | 23.8 | 26.7 | 31.2 | 2.4 | 3.1 |
| $50,000 to $74,999 | 4.2 | 5.4 | 6.1 | 7.3 | 0.4 | 0.5 |
| $75,000 to $99,999 | 1.0 | 1.3 | 1.5 | 1.9 | 0.0 | 0.0 |
| $100,000 or more | 1.0 | 1.3 | 1.3 | 1.5 | 1.0 | 0.0 |

*Note: (–) means sample is too small to make a reliable estimate.*
*Source: Bureau of the Census, Internet web site, <http:// www.census.gov/cps/ads/sdata.htm>; calculations by New Strategist*

# Distribution of Men by Earnings and Work Experience, 1997: White Men

*(number and percent distribution of white men aged 15 or older by earnings and work experience, 1997; median earnings of men with earnings; men in thousands as of 1998)*

| | | worked | | | | |
|---|---|---|---|---|---|---|
| | | | full-time | | part-time | |
| | total | total | total | year-round | total | year-round |
| **Total men** | **85,219** | **65,609** | **56,701** | **47,241** | **8,908** | **3,630** |
| Without earnings | 19,637 | 27 | 16 | 13 | 11 | 7 |
| With earnings | 65,582 | 65,582 | 56,685 | 47,228 | 8,897 | 3,623 |
| Under $5,000 | 7,079 | 7,079 | 2,628 | 649 | 4,451 | 920 |
| $5,000 to $9,999 | 4,841 | 4,841 | 2,776 | 1,065 | 2,065 | 1,127 |
| $10,000 to $14,999 | 5,731 | 5,731 | 4,752 | 3,223 | 980 | 644 |
| $15,000 to $19,999 | 5,382 | 5,382 | 4,954 | 3,906 | 430 | 295 |
| $20,000 to $24,999 | 5,901 | 5,901 | 5,632 | 4,891 | 269 | 172 |
| $25,000 to $29,999 | 5,401 | 5,401 | 5,255 | 4,680 | 146 | 93 |
| $30,000 to $34,999 | 5,534 | 5,534 | 5,406 | 4,973 | 128 | 72 |
| $35,000 to $39,999 | 4,561 | 4,561 | 4,468 | 4,180 | 93 | 60 |
| $40,000 to $44,999 | 4,020 | 4,020 | 3,982 | 3,733 | 37 | 27 |
| $45,000 to $49,999 | 2,837 | 2,837 | 2,807 | 2,613 | 30 | 18 |
| $50,000 to $54,999 | 2,966 | 2,966 | 2,933 | 2,787 | 33 | 29 |
| $55,000 to $59,999 | 1,648 | 1,648 | 1,622 | 1,527 | 25 | 14 |
| $60,000 to $64,999 | 1,786 | 1,786 | 1,766 | 1,673 | 19 | 16 |
| $65,000 to $69,999 | 1,190 | 1,190 | 1,179 | 1,129 | 11 | 3 |
| $70,000 to $74,999 | 1,137 | 1,137 | 1,115 | 1,026 | 23 | 11 |
| $75,000 to $79,999 | 821 | 821 | 809 | 778 | 12 | 8 |
| $80,000 to $84,999 | 802 | 802 | 785 | 758 | 17 | 15 |
| $85,000 to $89,999 | 367 | 367 | 363 | 358 | 4 | 4 |
| $90,000 to $94,999 | 439 | 439 | 428 | 416 | 11 | 11 |
| $95,000 to $99,999 | 234 | 234 | 231 | 217 | 2 | 2 |
| $100,000 or more | 2,905 | 2,905 | 2,794 | 2,645 | 111 | 83 |
| Median earnings of men with earnings | $27,731 | $27,731 | $31,456 | $35,193 | $4,996 | $8,700 |
| **Percent distribution** | | | | | | |
| **Total men** | **100.0%** | **100.0%** | **100.0%** | **100.0%** | **100.0%** | **100.0%** |
| Without earnings | 23.0 | 0.0 | 0.0 | 0.0 | 0.1 | 0.2 |
| With earnings | 77.0 | 100.0 | 100.0 | 100.0 | 99.9 | 99.8 |
| Under $25,000 | 34.0 | 44.1 | 36.6 | 29.1 | 92.0 | 87.0 |
| $25,000 to $49,999 | 26.2 | 34.1 | 38.7 | 42.7 | 4.9 | 7.4 |
| $50,000 to $74,999 | 10.2 | 13.3 | 15.2 | 17.2 | 1.2 | 2.0 |
| $75,000 to $99,999 | 3.1 | 4.1 | 4.6 | 5.3 | 0.5 | 1.1 |
| $100,000 or more | 3.4 | 4.4 | 4.9 | 5.6 | 1.2 | 2.3 |

*Source: Bureau of the Census, Internet web site, <http:// www.census.gov/cps/ads/sdata.htm>; calculations by New Strategist*

## Distribution of Men by Earnings and Work Experience, 1997: Non-Hispanic White Men

*(number and percent distribution of non-Hispanic white men aged 15 or older by earnings and work experience, 1997; median earnings of men with earnings; men in thousands as of 1998)*

| | | | worked | | | |
| | | | full-time | | part-time | |
| | total | total | total | year-round | total | year-round |
|---|---|---|---|---|---|---|
| **Total men** | **74,703** | **57,421** | **49,496** | **41,464** | **7,924** | **3,242** |
| Without earnings | 17,309 | 27 | 16 | 13 | 11 | 7 |
| With earnings | 57,394 | 57,394 | 49,480 | 41,450 | 7,914 | 3,236 |
| Under $5,000 | 6,164 | 6,164 | 2,206 | 559 | 3,958 | 833 |
| $5,000 to $9,999 | 3,818 | 3,818 | 2,021 | 719 | 1,797 | 968 |
| $10,000 to $14,999 | 4,190 | 4,190 | 3,327 | 2,091 | 863 | 565 |
| $15,000 to $19,999 | 4,217 | 4,217 | 3,838 | 2,966 | 381 | 258 |
| $20,000 to $24,999 | 4,958 | 4,958 | 4,707 | 4,037 | 252 | 157 |
| $25,000 to $29,999 | 4,774 | 4,774 | 4,638 | 4,112 | 136 | 83 |
| $30,000 to $34,999 | 5,031 | 5,031 | 4,910 | 4,518 | 120 | 72 |
| $35,000 to $39,999 | 4,191 | 4,191 | 4,099 | 3,832 | 92 | 60 |
| $40,000 to $44,999 | 3,731 | 3,731 | 3,698 | 3,453 | 33 | 27 |
| $45,000 to $49,999 | 2,684 | 2,684 | 2,654 | 2,465 | 30 | 18 |
| $50,000 to $54,999 | 2,807 | 2,807 | 2,776 | 2,636 | 30 | 26 |
| $55,000 to $59,999 | 1,560 | 1,560 | 1,537 | 1,445 | 23 | 14 |
| $60,000 to $64,999 | 1,705 | 1,705 | 1,685 | 1,600 | 19 | 16 |
| $65,000 to $69,999 | 1,135 | 1,135 | 1,124 | 1,073 | 11 | 3 |
| $70,000 to $74,999 | 1,081 | 1,081 | 1,059 | 972 | 23 | 11 |
| $75,000 to $79,999 | 773 | 773 | 761 | 732 | 12 | 8 |
| $80,000 to $84,999 | 767 | 767 | 750 | 723 | 17 | 15 |
| $85,000 to $89,999 | 356 | 356 | 352 | 347 | 4 | 4 |
| $90,000 to $94,999 | 429 | 429 | 418 | 408 | 11 | 11 |
| $95,000 to $99,999 | 226 | 226 | 223 | 209 | 2 | 2 |
| $100,000 or more | 2,798 | 2,798 | 2,697 | 2,555 | 101 | 83 |
| Median earnings of men with earnings | $30,384 | $30,384 | $33,205 | $36,597 | $4,999 | $8,848 |
| **Percent distribution** | | | | | | |
| **Total men** | **100.0%** | **100.0%** | **100.0%** | **100.0%** | **100.0%** | **100.0%** |
| Without earnings | 23.2 | 0.0 | 0.0 | 0.0 | 0.1 | 0.2 |
| With earnings | 76.8 | 100.0 | 100.0 | 100.0 | 99.9 | 99.8 |
| Under $25,000 | 31.3 | 40.7 | 32.5 | 25.0 | 91.5 | 85.8 |
| $25,000 to $49,999 | 27.3 | 35.5 | 40.4 | 44.3 | 5.2 | 8.0 |
| $50,000 to $74,999 | 11.1 | 14.4 | 16.5 | 18.6 | 1.3 | 2.2 |
| $75,000 to $99,999 | 3.4 | 4.4 | 5.1 | 5.8 | 0.6 | 1.2 |
| $100,000 or more | 3.7 | 4.9 | 5.4 | 6.2 | 1.3 | 2.6 |

*Source: Bureau of the Census, Internet web site, <http:// www.census.gov/cps/ads/sdata.htm>; calculations by New Strategist*

# Men's Earnings Rise with Education

## Those with professional degrees earn the most.

The median earnings of men with professional degrees stood at $71,459 in 1997, more than double the $31,262 median earnings of all men. Earnings rise in lock step with education—from a low of $14,826 for men who did not finish ninth grade, to $31,174 for those with some college, to $51,198 for those with a bachelor's degree or more.

One factor contributing to the higher earnings of educated men is their greater propensity to work full-time. Only 31 percent of the least educated men hold full-time jobs compared with 73 percent of men with a bachelor's degree and 76 percent of those with professional degrees.

The men with the highest earnings are those aged 55 to 64 with professional degrees who work full-time. Their median earnings stood at $90,518 in 1997, and fully 41 percent earned more than $100,000.

Education pays off almost immediately. Among men aged 25 to 34 who work full-time, the median earnings of the best educated are more than three times as high as those of the least educated—$51,417 versus $14,958 in 1997.

✗ Most of today's young men go to college, but fewer than half earn a college degree. As the financial returns to education become more evident in the years ahead, the share of young men who earn a diploma will rise.

## A college diploma pays off

*(median earnings of men aged 25 or older who work full-time, year-round, by educational attainment, 1997)*

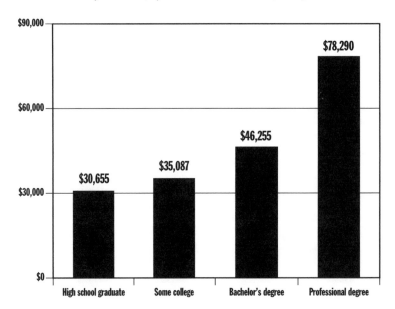

# Distribution of Men by Earnings and Education, 1997: Total Men

*(number and percent distribution of men aged 25 or older by earnings and educational attainment, 1997; median earnings of men with earnings and of men with earnings who work full-time, year-round; percent of men who work full-time, year-round; men in thousands as of 1998)*

| | total | less than 9th grade | 9th to 12th grade, no diploma | high school graduate, incl. GED | some college, no degree | associate's degree | bachelor's degree or more — total | bachelor's degree | master's degree | professional degree | doctoral degree |
|---|---|---|---|---|---|---|---|---|---|---|---|
| Total men | 82,376 | 6,159 | 8,018 | 26,575 | 14,122 | 5,670 | 21,832 | 14,090 | 4,640 | 1,749 | 1,353 |
| Without earnings | 18,083 | 3,166 | 2,915 | 5,960 | 2,583 | 667 | 2,793 | 1,752 | 644 | 201 | 195 |
| With earnings | 64,293 | 2,993 | 5,103 | 20,615 | 11,540 | 5,003 | 19,039 | 12,338 | 3,996 | 1,547 | 1,158 |
| Under $5,000 | 3,496 | 341 | 529 | 1,196 | 607 | 180 | 644 | 436 | 146 | 38 | 23 |
| $5,000 to $9,999 | 3,518 | 475 | 468 | 1,191 | 565 | 247 | 572 | 403 | 116 | 32 | 20 |
| $10,000 to $14,999 | 5,284 | 697 | 798 | 1,941 | 902 | 285 | 661 | 483 | 116 | 36 | 27 |
| $15,000 to $19,999 | 5,324 | 442 | 701 | 2,195 | 828 | 398 | 761 | 556 | 122 | 54 | 30 |
| $20,000 to $24,999 | 6,276 | 365 | 717 | 2,447 | 1,211 | 507 | 1,030 | 811 | 166 | 25 | 30 |
| $25,000 to $29,999 | 5,958 | 198 | 486 | 2,375 | 1,214 | 486 | 1,200 | 973 | 161 | 37 | 29 |
| $30,000 to $34,999 | 6,043 | 151 | 446 | 2,313 | 1,231 | 517 | 1,386 | 1,063 | 204 | 82 | 36 |
| $35,000 to $39,999 | 5,096 | 104 | 273 | 1,784 | 1,051 | 462 | 1,423 | 1,000 | 296 | 63 | 64 |
| $40,000 to $44,999 | 4,497 | 76 | 204 | 1,536 | 882 | 485 | 1,311 | 916 | 259 | 81 | 55 |
| $45,000 to $49,999 | 3,159 | 42 | 126 | 983 | 627 | 285 | 1,095 | 707 | 243 | 89 | 57 |
| $50,000 to $54,999 | 3,253 | 21 | 153 | 867 | 596 | 284 | 1,333 | 859 | 291 | 100 | 83 |
| $55,000 to $59,999 | 1,809 | 8 | 30 | 392 | 341 | 176 | 863 | 563 | 219 | 39 | 42 |
| $60,000 to $64,999 | 2,051 | 12 | 37 | 379 | 405 | 210 | 1,007 | 602 | 287 | 42 | 77 |
| $65,000 to $69,999 | 1,326 | 4 | 13 | 241 | 203 | 96 | 768 | 515 | 174 | 31 | 47 |
| $70,000 to $74,999 | 1,237 | 9 | 28 | 210 | 178 | 104 | 707 | 404 | 197 | 44 | 63 |
| $75,000 to $79,999 | 897 | 13 | 18 | 111 | 136 | 55 | 564 | 353 | 112 | 60 | 39 |
| $80,000 to $84,999 | 856 | 5 | 7 | 103 | 150 | 30 | 560 | 283 | 154 | 51 | 71 |
| $85,000 to $89,999 | 400 | — | 2 | 39 | 38 | 31 | 289 | 158 | 85 | 24 | 23 |
| $90,000 to $94,999 | 489 | 2 | 4 | 52 | 55 | 35 | 340 | 159 | 91 | 50 | 41 |
| $95,000 to $99,999 | 254 | 3 | 7 | 22 | 23 | 15 | 185 | 88 | 42 | 30 | 23 |
| $100,000 or more | 3,070 | 25 | 55 | 239 | 297 | 117 | 2,338 | 1,008 | 512 | 538 | 280 |

*(continued)*

(continued from previous page)

| | total | less than 9th grade | 9th to 12th grade, no diploma | high school graduate, incl. GED | some college, no degree | associate's degree | bachelor's degree or more | | | | |
| --- | --- | --- | --- | --- | --- | --- | --- | --- | --- | --- | --- |
| | | | | | | | total | bachelor's degree | master's degree | professional degree | doctoral degree |
| **Median earnings** | | | | | | | | | | | |
| Men with earnings | $31,262 | $14,826 | $20,314 | $27,005 | $31,174 | $33,218 | $46,736 | $41,579 | $51,813 | $71,459 | $65,593 |
| Men working full-time | $35,715 | $18,551 | $24,241 | $30,655 | $35,087 | $36,677 | $51,198 | $46,255 | $57,553 | $78,290 | $70,706 |
| Percent working full-time | 61.7% | 31.1% | 44.3% | 61.1% | 64.9% | 72.1% | 72.7% | 73.5% | 69.6% | 75.5% | 71.4% |
| **Percent distribution** | | | | | | | | | | | |
| Total men | 100.0% | 100.0% | 100.0% | 100.0% | 100.0% | 100.0% | 100.0% | 100.0% | 100.0% | 100.0% | 100.0% |
| Without earnings | 22.0 | 51.4 | 36.4 | 22.4 | 18.3 | 11.8 | 12.8 | 12.4 | 13.9 | 11.5 | 14.4 |
| With earnings | 78.0 | 48.6 | 63.6 | 77.6 | 81.7 | 88.2 | 87.2 | 87.6 | 86.1 | 88.5 | 85.6 |
| Under $25,000 | 29.0 | 37.7 | 40.1 | 33.8 | 29.1 | 28.5 | 16.8 | 19.1 | 14.4 | 10.6 | 9.6 |
| $25,000 to $49,999 | 30.0 | 9.3 | 19.1 | 33.8 | 35.4 | 39.4 | 29.4 | 33.1 | 25.1 | 20.1 | 17.8 |
| $50,000 to $74,999 | 11.7 | 0.9 | 3.3 | 7.9 | 12.2 | 15.3 | 21.4 | 20.9 | 25.2 | 14.6 | 23.1 |
| $75,000 to $99,999 | 3.5 | 0.4 | 0.5 | 1.2 | 2.8 | 2.9 | 8.9 | 7.4 | 10.4 | 12.3 | 14.6 |
| $100,000 or more | 3.7 | 0.4 | 0.7 | 0.9 | 2.1 | 2.1 | 10.7 | 7.2 | 11.0 | 30.8 | 20.7 |

Note: (–) means sample is too small to make a reliable estimate.
Source: Bureau of the Census, Internet web site, <http://www.census.gov/cps/ads/sdata/sdata.htm>; calculations by New Strategist

# Distribution of Men by Earnings and Education, 1997: Men Aged 25 to 34

*(number and percent distribution of men aged 25 to 34 by earnings and educational attainment, 1997; median earnings of men with earnings and of men with earnings who work full-time, year-round; percent who work full-time, year-round; men in thousands as of 1998)*

| | total | less than 9th grade | 9th to 12th grade, no diploma | high school graduate, incl. GED | some college, no degree | associate's degree | bachelor's degree or more | | | | |
|---|---|---|---|---|---|---|---|---|---|---|---|
| | | | | | | | total | bachelor's degree | master's degree | professional degree | doctoral degree |
| **Total men** | **19,526** | **843** | **1,736** | **6,592** | **3,657** | **1,575** | **5,124** | **3,931** | **821** | **241** | **131** |
| Without earnings | 1,158 | 116 | 211 | 415 | 187 | 56 | 174 | 118 | 51 | 4 | 1 |
| With earnings | 18,369 | 727 | 1,525 | 6,176 | 3,470 | 1,520 | 4,950 | 3,813 | 769 | 238 | 130 |
| Under $5,000 | 885 | 67 | 166 | 305 | 171 | 52 | 123 | 104 | 16 | – | 3 |
| $5,000 to $9,999 | 1,103 | 130 | 172 | 387 | 197 | 72 | 146 | 127 | 13 | 3 | 3 |
| $10,000 to $14,999 | 2,058 | 226 | 305 | 805 | 368 | 118 | 236 | 185 | 37 | 3 | 11 |
| $15,000 to $19,999 | 2,031 | 135 | 253 | 855 | 356 | 152 | 279 | 215 | 46 | 18 | – |
| $20,000 to $24,999 | 2,495 | 91 | 255 | 944 | 529 | 220 | 457 | 381 | 67 | 4 | 6 |
| $25,000 to $29,999 | 2,152 | 34 | 116 | 865 | 456 | 167 | 515 | 443 | 45 | 13 | 14 |
| $30,000 to $34,999 | 1,948 | 9 | 89 | 690 | 415 | 182 | 563 | 464 | 56 | 35 | 7 |
| $35,000 to $39,999 | 1,319 | 17 | 56 | 389 | 283 | 136 | 439 | 350 | 66 | 7 | 17 |
| $40,000 to $44,999 | 1,069 | 6 | 42 | 319 | 185 | 118 | 400 | 314 | 62 | 17 | 7 |
| $45,000 to $49,999 | 792 | 5 | 19 | 219 | 135 | 85 | 327 | 246 | 45 | 25 | 11 |
| $50,000 to $54,999 | 649 | – | 17 | 138 | 106 | 68 | 320 | 228 | 65 | 20 | 6 |
| $55,000 to $59,999 | 365 | – | 4 | 66 | 69 | 35 | 193 | 139 | 34 | 17 | 3 |
| $60,000 to $64,999 | 382 | – | 6 | 55 | 61 | 51 | 206 | 153 | 44 | 4 | 6 |
| $65,000 to $69,999 | 226 | – | – | 31 | 35 | 17 | 142 | 105 | 28 | 6 | 3 |
| $70,000 to $74,999 | 162 | 3 | 4 | 19 | 14 | 8 | 115 | 71 | 37 | 3 | 3 |
| $75,000 to $79,999 | 153 | – | 5 | 22 | 24 | 4 | 96 | 71 | 18 | 5 | 1 |
| $80,000 to $84,999 | 130 | – | 2 | 14 | 18 | 5 | 91 | 50 | 24 | 6 | 9 |
| $85,000 to $89,999 | 67 | – | 2 | 7 | 5 | 10 | 43 | 32 | 7 | – | 4 |
| $90,000 to $94,999 | 52 | – | – | – | 4 | 3 | 45 | 26 | 8 | 9 | 2 |
| $95,000 to $99,999 | 15 | 3 | – | 6 | – | – | 6 | 5 | 1 | – | – |
| $100,000 or more | 315 | 4 | 10 | 41 | 36 | 16 | 208 | 104 | 51 | 40 | 13 |

*(continued)*

(continued from previous page)

| | total | less than 9th grade | 9th to 12th grade, no diploma | high school graduate, incl. GED | some college, no degree | associate's degree | bachelor's degree or more | | | | |
| --- | --- | --- | --- | --- | --- | --- | --- | --- | --- | --- | --- |
| | | | | | | | total | bachelor's degree | master's degree | professional degree | doctoral degree |
| **Median earnings** | | | | | | | | | | | |
| Men with earnings | $26,000 | $12,612 | $16,979 | $23,578 | $25,894 | $29,086 | $36,191 | $34,801 | $42,158 | $47,695 | $43,775 |
| Men working full-time | $29,800 | $14,958 | $20,531 | $26,014 | $29,209 | $31,693 | $40,631 | $37,441 | $50,127 | $51,417 | $48,339 |
| Percent working full-time | 73.6% | 61.8% | 59.7% | 74.1% | 73.8% | 77.0% | 78.5% | 79.6% | 71.5% | 83.0% | 83.2% |
| **Percent distribution** | | | | | | | | | | | |
| **Total men** | 100.0% | 100.0% | 100.0% | 100.0% | 100.0% | 100.0% | 100.0% | 100.0% | 100.0% | 100.0% | 100.0% |
| Without earnings | 5.9 | 13.8 | 12.2 | 6.3 | 5.1 | 3.6 | 3.4 | 3.0 | 6.2 | 1.7 | 0.8 |
| With earnings | 94.1 | 86.2 | 87.8 | 93.7 | 94.9 | 96.5 | 96.6 | 97.0 | 93.7 | 98.8 | 99.2 |
| Under $25,000 | 43.9 | 77.0 | 66.3 | 50.0 | 44.3 | 39.0 | 24.2 | 25.7 | 21.8 | 11.6 | 17.6 |
| $25,000 to $49,999 | 37.3 | 8.4 | 18.5 | 37.7 | 40.3 | 43.7 | 43.8 | 46.2 | 33.4 | 40.2 | 42.7 |
| $50,000 to $74,999 | 9.1 | 0.4 | 1.8 | 4.7 | 7.8 | 11.4 | 19.0 | 17.7 | 25.3 | 20.7 | 16.0 |
| $75,000 to $99,999 | 2.1 | 0.4 | 0.5 | 0.7 | 1.4 | 1.4 | 5.5 | 4.7 | 7.1 | 8.3 | 12.2 |
| $100,000 or more | 1.6 | 0.5 | 0.6 | 0.6 | 1.0 | 1.0 | 4.1 | 2.6 | 6.2 | 16.6 | 9.9 |

Note: (–) means sample is too small to make a reliable estimate.
Source: Bureau of the Census, Internet web site, <http://www.census.gov/cps/ads/sdata.htm>; calculations by New Strategist

# Distribution of Men by Earnings and Education, 1997: Men Aged 35 to 44

*(number and percent distribution of men aged 35 to 44 by earnings and educational attainment, 1997; median earnings of men with earnings and of men with earnings who work full-time, year-round; percent of men who work full-time, year-round; men in thousands as of 1998)*

| | total | less than 9th grade | 9th to 12th grade, no diploma | high school graduate, incl. GED | some college, no degree | associate's degree | bachelor's degree or more | | | | |
| --- | --- | --- | --- | --- | --- | --- | --- | --- | --- | --- | --- |
| | | | | | | | total | bachelor's degree | master's degree | professional degree | doctoral degree |
| Total men | 22,054 | 926 | 1,946 | 7,537 | 3,895 | 1,820 | 5,929 | 3,971 | 1,174 | 474 | 311 |
| Without earnings | 1,711 | 188 | 368 | 684 | 203 | 106 | 162 | 109 | 42 | 9 | 2 |
| With earnings | 20,343 | 738 | 1,578 | 6,853 | 3,692 | 1,714 | 5,767 | 3,861 | 1,132 | 465 | 309 |
| Under $5,000 | 801 | 53 | 151 | 301 | 123 | 44 | 131 | 108 | 15 | 5 | 3 |
| $5,000 to $9,999 | 886 | 105 | 113 | 334 | 157 | 81 | 97 | 75 | 14 | 6 | 3 |
| $10,000 to $14,999 | 1,395 | 181 | 244 | 534 | 231 | 64 | 142 | 102 | 25 | 13 | 3 |
| $15,000 to $19,999 | 1,577 | 106 | 232 | 685 | 252 | 118 | 183 | 138 | 28 | 8 | 8 |
| $20,000 to $24,999 | 1,841 | 105 | 212 | 771 | 353 | 143 | 257 | 219 | 33 | – | 6 |
| $25,000 to $29,999 | 1,882 | 66 | 189 | 817 | 345 | 155 | 309 | 262 | 25 | 13 | 9 |
| $30,000 to $34,999 | 2,082 | 47 | 180 | 855 | 428 | 216 | 357 | 278 | 53 | 12 | 14 |
| $35,000 to $39,999 | 1,775 | 30 | 73 | 686 | 372 | 172 | 441 | 295 | 110 | 23 | 13 |
| $40,000 to $44,999 | 1,609 | 12 | 63 | 625 | 288 | 202 | 420 | 305 | 64 | 32 | 18 |
| $45,000 to $49,999 | 1,073 | 6 | 32 | 330 | 255 | 106 | 343 | 233 | 75 | 19 | 16 |
| $50,000 to $54,999 | 1,102 | 5 | 47 | 307 | 211 | 92 | 440 | 299 | 88 | 31 | 23 |
| $55,000 to $59,999 | 633 | 2 | 13 | 137 | 133 | 53 | 295 | 199 | 72 | 13 | 10 |
| $60,000 to $64,999 | 665 | 3 | 8 | 136 | 130 | 73 | 315 | 207 | 72 | 12 | 23 |
| $65,000 to $69,999 | 562 | – | 6 | 85 | 103 | 41 | 327 | 232 | 63 | 16 | 16 |
| $70,000 to $74,999 | 467 | – | – | 74 | 74 | 48 | 271 | 175 | 65 | 15 | 16 |
| $75,000 to $79,999 | 323 | 7 | 2 | 25 | 58 | 37 | 193 | 126 | 35 | 18 | 14 |
| $80,000 to $84,999 | 275 | 1 | – | 40 | 31 | 12 | 192 | 115 | 50 | 13 | 14 |
| $85,000 to $89,999 | 138 | – | – | 15 | 19 | 8 | 96 | 51 | 31 | 7 | 7 |
| $90,000 to $94,999 | 169 | – | 3 | 10 | 29 | 10 | 117 | 47 | 44 | 21 | 5 |
| $95,000 to $99,999 | 88 | – | – | 3 | 8 | 6 | 71 | 33 | 10 | 15 | 12 |
| $100,000 or more | 1,001 | 10 | 10 | 81 | 94 | 36 | 770 | 361 | 161 | 171 | 77 |

*(continued)*

*(continued from previous page)*

| | total | less than 9th grade | 9th to 12th grade, no diploma | high school graduate, incl. GED | some college, no degree | associate's degree | bachelor's degree or more | | | | |
| --- | --- | --- | --- | --- | --- | --- | --- | --- | --- | --- | --- |
| | | | | | | | total | bachelor's degree | master's degree | professional degree | doctoral degree |
| **Median earnings** | | | | | | | | | | | |
| Men with earnings | $33,605 | $16,033 | $20,985 | $29,855 | $33,897 | $35,798 | $51,455 | $47,277 | $56,726 | $77,194 | $66,103 |
| Men working full-time | $36,778 | $20,275 | $24,902 | $31,503 | $36,447 | $37,965 | $54,006 | $50,620 | $60,151 | $81,677 | $66,917 |
| Percent working full-time | 77.1% | 50.8 % | 59.0% | 74.1% | 80.5% | 81.2% | 87.4% | 86.5% | 87.8% | 90.7% | 91.6% |
| **Percent distribution** | | | | | | | | | | | |
| **Total men** | 100.0% | 100.0% | 100.0% | 100.0% | 100.0% | 100.0% | 100.0% | 100.0% | 100.0% | 100.0% | 100.0% |
| Without earnings | 7.8 | 20.3 | 18.9 | 9.1 | 5.2 | 5.8 | 2.7 | 2.7 | 3.6 | 1.9 | 0.6 |
| With earnings | 92.2 | 79.7 | 81.1 | 90.9 | 94.8 | 94.2 | 97.3 | 97.2 | 96.4 | 98.1 | 99.4 |
| Under $25,000 | 29.5 | 59.4 | 48.9 | 34.8 | 28.7 | 24.7 | 13.7 | 16.2 | 9.8 | 6.8 | 7.4 |
| $25,000 to $49,999 | 38.2 | 17.4 | 27.6 | 44.0 | 43.3 | 46.8 | 31.5 | 34.6 | 27.9 | 20.9 | 22.5 |
| $50,000 to $74,999 | 15.5 | 1.1 | 3.8 | 9.8 | 16.7 | 16.9 | 27.8 | 28.0 | 30.7 | 18.4 | 28.3 |
| $75,000 to $99,999 | 4.5 | 0.9 | 0.3 | 1.2 | 3.7 | 4.0 | 11.3 | 9.4 | 14.5 | 15.6 | 16.7 |
| $100,000 or more | 4.5 | 1.1 | 0.5 | 1.1 | 2.4 | 2.0 | 13.0 | 9.1 | 13.7 | 36.1 | 24.8 |

*Note: (–) means sample is too small to make a reliable estimate.*
*Source: Bureau of the Census, Internet web site, <http://www.census.gov/cps/ads/sdata.htm>; calculations by New Strategist*

# Distribution of Men by Earnings and Education, 1997: Men Aged 45 to 54

*(number and percent distribution of men aged 45 to 54 by earnings and educational attainment, 1997; median earnings of men with earnings and of men with earnings who work full-time, year-round; percent of men who work full-time, year-round; men in thousands as of 1998)*

| | total | less than 9th grade | 9th to 12th grade, no diploma | high school graduate, incl. GED | some college, no degree | associate's degree | bachelor's degree or more | | | | |
|---|---|---|---|---|---|---|---|---|---|---|---|
| | | | | | | | total | bachelor's degree | master's degree | professional degree | doctoral degree |
| **Total men** | **16,598** | **894** | **1,337** | **4,701** | **2,995** | **1,388** | **5,283** | **3,091** | **1,341** | **450** | **401** |
| Without earnings | 1,551 | 207 | 282 | 538 | 258 | 99 | 166 | 121 | 29 | 3 | 13 |
| With earnings | 15,048 | 687 | 1,055 | 4,163 | 2,737 | 1,289 | 5,117 | 2,969 | 1,313 | 447 | 388 |
| Under $5,000 | 596 | 58 | 80 | 190 | 108 | 42 | 116 | 75 | 32 | 11 | – |
| $5,000 to $9,999 | 514 | 98 | 70 | 120 | 85 | 40 | 101 | 62 | 27 | 11 | – |
| $10,000 to $14,999 | 909 | 168 | 119 | 269 | 147 | 74 | 133 | 104 | 19 | 6 | 4 |
| $15,000 to $19,999 | 960 | 107 | 133 | 369 | 127 | 95 | 127 | 96 | 20 | 4 | 7 |
| $20,000 to $24,999 | 1,196 | 78 | 158 | 424 | 228 | 122 | 187 | 129 | 44 | 6 | 7 |
| $25,000 to $29,999 | 1,192 | 55 | 104 | 424 | 265 | 106 | 237 | 178 | 53 | 5 | 1 |
| $30,000 to $34,999 | 1,288 | 43 | 98 | 452 | 274 | 87 | 332 | 243 | 63 | 17 | 10 |
| $35,000 to $39,999 | 1,238 | 16 | 86 | 406 | 258 | 121 | 352 | 240 | 81 | 16 | 15 |
| $40,000 to $44,999 | 1,208 | 22 | 41 | 381 | 291 | 132 | 341 | 207 | 93 | 23 | 18 |
| $45,000 to $49,999 | 930 | 22 | 55 | 300 | 166 | 80 | 307 | 175 | 86 | 30 | 16 |
| $50,000 to $54,999 | 991 | 4 | 57 | 274 | 194 | 86 | 376 | 227 | 97 | 25 | 28 |
| $55,000 to $59,999 | 569 | 3 | 10 | 114 | 114 | 72 | 257 | 161 | 79 | 3 | 13 |
| $60,000 to $64,999 | 706 | 4 | 14 | 114 | 159 | 64 | 352 | 180 | 132 | 14 | 25 |
| $65,000 to $69,999 | 338 | – | – | 68 | 36 | 33 | 201 | 126 | 54 | 6 | 14 |
| $70,000 to $74,999 | 419 | 3 | 5 | 91 | 50 | 40 | 229 | 122 | 66 | 20 | 21 |
| $75,000 to $79,999 | 262 | – | 2 | 42 | 32 | 13 | 172 | 106 | 31 | 14 | 22 |
| $80,000 to $84,999 | 288 | 5 | 4 | 24 | 75 | 11 | 167 | 62 | 50 | 20 | 36 |
| $85,000 to $89,999 | 128 | – | – | 11 | 11 | 5 | 101 | 45 | 39 | 10 | 7 |
| $90,000 to $94,999 | 155 | – | 1 | 20 | 15 | 13 | 106 | 48 | 25 | 11 | 21 |
| $95,000 to $99,999 | 94 | – | – | 6 | 12 | 8 | 67 | 29 | 22 | 14 | 3 |
| $100,000 or more | 1,067 | 2 | 16 | 59 | 88 | 46 | 856 | 357 | 197 | 182 | 119 |

*(continued)*

*(continued from previous page)*

| | total | less than 9th grade | 9th to 12th grade, no diploma | high school graduate, incl. GED | some college, no degree | associate's degree | bachelor's degree or more | | | | |
|---|---|---|---|---|---|---|---|---|---|---|---|
| | | | | | | | total | bachelor's degree | master's degree | professional degree | doctoral degree |
| **Median earnings** | | | | | | | | | | | |
| Men with earnings | $37,667 | $15,715 | $23,535 | $32,030 | $36,832 | $37,255 | $53,319 | $49,053 | $56,691 | $81,989 | $76,927 |
| Men working full-time | $41,127 | $19,349 | $27,792 | $35,400 | $39,573 | $40,689 | $56,529 | $51,180 | $60,602 | $82,371 | $80,224 |
| Percent working full-time | 75.8% | 52.6% | 56.9% | 74.6% | 76.6% | 77.9% | 84.5% | 84.5% | 82.8% | 90.4% | 83.3% |
| **Percent distribution** | | | | | | | | | | | |
| **Total men** | 100.0% | 100.0% | 100.0% | 100.0% | 100.0% | 100.0% | 100.0% | 100.0% | 100.0% | 100.0% | 100.0% |
| Without earnings | 9.3 | 23.2 | 21.1 | 11.4 | 8.6 | 7.1 | 3.1 | 3.9 | 2.2 | 0.7 | 3.2 |
| With earnings | 90.7 | 76.8 | 78.9 | 88.6 | 91.4 | 92.9 | 96.9 | 96.1 | 97.9 | 99.3 | 96.8 |
| Under $25,000 | 25.2 | 56.9 | 41.9 | 29.2 | 23.2 | 26.9 | 12.6 | 15.1 | 10.6 | 8.4 | 4.5 |
| $25,000 to $49,999 | 35.3 | 17.7 | 28.7 | 41.8 | 41.9 | 37.9 | 29.7 | 33.7 | 28.0 | 20.2 | 15.0 |
| $50,000 to $74,999 | 18.2 | 1.6 | 6.4 | 14.1 | 18.5 | 21.3 | 26.8 | 26.4 | 31.9 | 15.1 | 25.2 |
| $75,000 to $99,999 | 5.6 | 0.6 | 0.5 | 2.2 | 4.8 | 3.6 | 11.6 | 9.4 | 12.5 | 15.3 | 22.2 |
| $100,000 or more | 6.4 | 0.2 | 1.2 | 1.3 | 2.9 | 3.3 | 16.2 | 11.5 | 14.7 | 40.4 | 29.7 |

*Note: (–) means sample is too small to make a reliable estimate.*
*Source: Bureau of the Census, Internet web site, <http://www.census.gov/cps/ads/sdata.htm>; calculations by New Strategist*

# Distribution of Men by Earnings and Education, 1997: Men Aged 55 to 64

*(number and percent distribution of men aged 55 to 64 by earnings and educational attainment, 1997; median earnings of men with earnings and of men with earnings who work full-time, year-round; percent of men who work full-time, year-round; men in thousands as of 1998)*

| | total | less than 9th grade | 9th to 12th grade, no diploma | high school graduate, incl. GED | some college, no degree | associate's degree | bachelor's degree or more | | | | |
|---|---|---|---|---|---|---|---|---|---|---|---|
| | | | | | | | total | bachelor's degree | master's degree | professional degree | doctoral degree |
| **Total men** | **10,673** | **1,017** | **1,091** | **3,661** | **1,589** | **493** | **2,821** | **1,550** | **744** | **266** | **261** |
| Without earnings | 2,874 | 500 | 386 | 997 | 399 | 111 | 481 | 308 | 128 | 10 | 36 |
| With earnings | 7,799 | 517 | 705 | 2,664 | 1,190 | 383 | 2,339 | 1,242 | 616 | 256 | 225 |
| Under $5,000 | 576 | 69 | 59 | 211 | 91 | 26 | 120 | 70 | 38 | 9 | 3 |
| $5,000 to $9,999 | 497 | 62 | 63 | 194 | 56 | 30 | 92 | 60 | 25 | 4 | 3 |
| $10,000 to $14,999 | 563 | 80 | 87 | 206 | 88 | 23 | 79 | 54 | 23 | 1 | 2 |
| $15,000 to $19,999 | 554 | 64 | 70 | 233 | 56 | 14 | 117 | 86 | 16 | 12 | 3 |
| $20,000 to $24,999 | 608 | 78 | 82 | 260 | 82 | 20 | 85 | 54 | 20 | 8 | 4 |
| $25,000 to $29,999 | 626 | 33 | 66 | 242 | 120 | 54 | 110 | 76 | 28 | 4 | 2 |
| $30,000 to $34,999 | 638 | 46 | 71 | 291 | 93 | 28 | 108 | 62 | 29 | 13 | 4 |
| $35,000 to $39,999 | 666 | 35 | 53 | 274 | 122 | 33 | 150 | 91 | 34 | 11 | 13 |
| $40,000 to $44,999 | 495 | 19 | 45 | 185 | 96 | 31 | 118 | 65 | 38 | 4 | 11 |
| $45,000 to $49,999 | 332 | 9 | 17 | 131 | 64 | 15 | 96 | 46 | 27 | 11 | 12 |
| $50,000 to $54,999 | 413 | 4 | 31 | 121 | 67 | 26 | 164 | 88 | 39 | 16 | 21 |
| $55,000 to $59,999 | 193 | 3 | 3 | 46 | 22 | 16 | 101 | 54 | 34 | 3 | 10 |
| $60,000 to $64,999 | 268 | 5 | 9 | 68 | 51 | 21 | 112 | 50 | 34 | 6 | 21 |
| $65,000 to $69,999 | 173 | – | 4 | 57 | 22 | 3 | 88 | 44 | 29 | 2 | 12 |
| $70,000 to $74,999 | 154 | 1 | 19 | 19 | 35 | 7 | 74 | 26 | 25 | 5 | 17 |
| $75,000 to $79,999 | 131 | 3 | 6 | 22 | 19 | – | 81 | 37 | 26 | 16 | 2 |
| $80,000 to $84,999 | 149 | – | 1 | 24 | 26 | 2 | 95 | 50 | 27 | 8 | 11 |
| $85,000 to $89,999 | 63 | – | – | 6 | 2 | 8 | 47 | 29 | 8 | 6 | 3 |
| $90,000 to $94,999 | 108 | 2 | – | 22 | 7 | 9 | 67 | 33 | 14 | 9 | 11 |
| $95,000 to $99,999 | 48 | – | 4 | 6 | 3 | – | 35 | 18 | 9 | – | 8 |
| $100,000 or more | 545 | 3 | 14 | 48 | 66 | 14 | 400 | 145 | 94 | 110 | 51 |

*(continued)*

(continued from previous page)

| | total | less than 9th grade | 9th to 12th grade, no diploma | high school graduate, incl. GED | some college, no degree | associate's degree | bachelor's degree or more | | | | |
|---|---|---|---|---|---|---|---|---|---|---|---|
| | | | | | | | total | bachelor's degree | master's degree | professional degree | doctoral degree |
| **Median earnings** | | | | | | | | | | | |
| Men with earnings | $32,395 | $18,362 | $24,474 | $29,562 | $35,271 | $33,962 | $51,601 | $45,191 | $52,288 | $81,448 | $65,636 |
| Men working full-time | $37,904 | $22,784 | $28,666 | $32,395 | $38,259 | $39,920 | $60,270 | $51,860 | $61,744 | $90,518 | $70,888 |
| Percent working full-time | 54.9% | 34.1% | 47.8% | 54.3% | 56.3% | 56.0% | 65.1% | 63.0% | 60.6% | 83.1% | 72.4% |
| **Percent distribution** | | | | | | | | | | | |
| **Total men** | 100.0% | 100.0% | 100.0% | 100.0% | 100.0% | 100.0% | 100.0% | 100.0% | 100.0% | 100.0% | 100.0% |
| Without earnings | 26.9 | 49.2 | 35.4 | 27.2 | 25.1 | 22.5 | 17.1 | 19.9 | 17.2 | 3.8 | 13.8 |
| With earnings | 73.1 | 50.8 | 64.6 | 72.8 | 74.9 | 77.7 | 82.9 | 80.1 | 82.8 | 96.2 | 86.2 |
| Under $25,000 | 26.2 | 34.7 | 33.1 | 30.2 | 23.5 | 22.9 | 17.5 | 20.9 | 16.4 | 12.8 | 5.7 |
| $25,000 to $49,999 | 25.8 | 14.0 | 23.1 | 30.7 | 31.2 | 32.7 | 20.6 | 21.9 | 21.0 | 16.2 | 16.1 |
| $50,000 to $74,999 | 11.3 | 1.3 | 6.0 | 8.5 | 12.4 | 14.8 | 19.1 | 16.9 | 21.6 | 12.0 | 31.0 |
| $75,000 to $99,999 | 4.7 | 0.5 | 1.0 | 2.2 | 3.6 | 3.9 | 11.5 | 10.8 | 11.3 | 14.7 | 13.4 |
| $100,000 or more | 5.1 | 0.3 | 1.3 | 1.3 | 4.2 | 2.8 | 14.2 | 9.4 | 12.6 | 41.4 | 19.5 |

*Note: (–) means sample is too small to make a reliable estimate.*
*Source: Bureau of the Census, Internet web site, <http://www.census.gov/cps/ads/sdata.htm>; calculations by New Strategist*

# Distribution of Men by Earnings and Education, 1997: Men Aged 65 or Older

*(number and percent distribution of men aged 65 or older by earnings and educational attainment, 1997; median earnings of men with earnings and of men with earnings who work full-time, year-round; percent of men who work full-time, year-round; men in thousands as of 1998)*

| | total | less than 9th grade | 9th to 12th grade, no diploma | high school graduate, incl. GED | some college, no degree | associate's degree | bachelor's degree or more | | | | |
|---|---|---|---|---|---|---|---|---|---|---|---|
| | | | | | | | total | bachelor's degree | master's degree | professional degree | doctoral degree |
| | 13,524 | 2,478 | 1,908 | 4,084 | 1,986 | 393 | 2,675 | 1,549 | 560 | 317 | 250 |
| Total men | | | | | | | | | | | |
| Without earnings | 10,790 | 2,155 | 1,668 | 3,325 | 1,536 | 295 | 1,810 | 1,096 | 394 | 176 | 144 |
| With earnings | 2,735 | 324 | 240 | 759 | 450 | 98 | 865 | 453 | 165 | 141 | 105 |
| Under $5,000 | 638 | 95 | 73 | 188 | 113 | 15 | 153 | 80 | 45 | 14 | 13 |
| $5,000 to $9,999 | 518 | 81 | 49 | 157 | 69 | 25 | 137 | 79 | 38 | 8 | 11 |
| $10,000 to $14,999 | 358 | 42 | 43 | 126 | 69 | 8 | 70 | 38 | 12 | 12 | 7 |
| $15,000 to $19,999 | 202 | 30 | 12 | 53 | 36 | 17 | 54 | 19 | 11 | 12 | 10 |
| $20,000 to $24,999 | 137 | 12 | 10 | 49 | 20 | 2 | 46 | 28 | 3 | 7 | 6 |
| $25,000 to $29,999 | 108 | 9 | 11 | 27 | 28 | 3 | 29 | 14 | 9 | 2 | 4 |
| $30,000 to $34,999 | 89 | 6 | 8 | 25 | 21 | 4 | 25 | 16 | 4 | 5 | – |
| $35,000 to $39,999 | 99 | 7 | 5 | 30 | 16 | – | 42 | 25 | 4 | 8 | 5 |
| $40,000 to $44,999 | 116 | 20 | 12 | 25 | 22 | 4 | 34 | 25 | 1 | 7 | 2 |
| $45,000 to $49,999 | 32 | – | 1 | 2 | 7 | – | 21 | 6 | 11 | 4 | – |
| $50,000 to $54,999 | 98 | 7 | 1 | 26 | 18 | 12 | 33 | 18 | 3 | 9 | 4 |
| $55,000 to $59,999 | 50 | – | – | 28 | 3 | – | 18 | 10 | – | 2 | 6 |
| $60,000 to $64,999 | 30 | – | – | 5 | 3 | – | 22 | 12 | 6 | 4 | – |
| $65,000 to $69,999 | 26 | 4 | 3 | – | 7 | 2 | 10 | 7 | – | – | 3 |
| $70,000 to $74,999 | 35 | 2 | – | 7 | 5 | 2 | 19 | 10 | 3 | – | 6 |
| $75,000 to $79,999 | 29 | 3 | 2 | – | 3 | – | 22 | 13 | 2 | 7 | – |
| $80,000 to $84,999 | 15 | – | – | – | – | – | 15 | 6 | 3 | 4 | 1 |
| $85,000 to $89,999 | 3 | – | – | – | – | – | 3 | – | – | – | 3 |
| $90,000 to $94,999 | 4 | – | – | – | – | – | 4 | 3 | – | – | 1 |
| $95,000 to $99,999 | 9 | – | 3 | – | – | – | 6 | 3 | – | 2 | – |
| $100,000 or more | 142 | 6 | 5 | 10 | 13 | 5 | 104 | 40 | 9 | 35 | 21 |

*(continued)*

(continued from previous page)

|  | total | less than 9th grade | 9th to 12th grade, no diploma | high school graduate, incl. GED | some college, no degree | associate's degree | bachelor's degree or more | | | | |
|  |  |  |  |  |  |  | total | bachelor's degree | master's degree | professional degree | doctoral degree |
|---|---|---|---|---|---|---|---|---|---|---|---|
| **Median earnings** | | | | | | | | | | | |
| Men with earnings | $12,317 | $8,334 | $9,439 | $10,951 | $13,068 | $15,299 | $21,743 | $21,335 | $9,579 | $40,775 | $26,988 |
| Men working full-time | $35,892 | $17,488 | $21,671 | $25,404 | $31,244 | $40,976 | $51,752 | $42,011 | $49,631 | $76,491 | $66,877 |
| Percent working full-time | 7.4% | 4.3% | 4.2% | 6.3% | 7.4% | 10.7% | 13.6% | 13.0% | 8.8% | 20.2% | 20.0% |
| **Percent distribution** | | | | | | | | | | | |
| **Total men** | 100.0% | 100.0% | 100.0% | 100.0% | 100.0% | 100.0% | 100.0% | 100.0% | 100.0% | 100.0% | 100.0% |
| Without earnings | 79.8 | 87.0 | 87.4 | 81.4 | 77.3 | 75.1 | 67.7 | 70.8 | 70.4 | 55.5 | 57.6 |
| With earnings | 20.2 | 13.1 | 12.6 | 18.6 | 22.7 | 24.9 | 32.3 | 29.2 | 29.5 | 44.5 | 42.0 |
| Under $25,000 | 13.7 | 10.5 | 9.8 | 14.0 | 15.5 | 17.0 | 17.2 | 15.8 | 19.5 | 16.7 | 18.8 |
| $25,000 to $49,999 | 3.3 | 1.7 | 1.9 | 2.7 | 4.7 | 2.8 | 5.6 | 5.6 | 5.2 | 8.2 | 4.4 |
| $50,000 to $74,999 | 1.8 | 0.5 | 0.2 | 1.6 | 1.8 | 4.1 | 3.8 | 3.7 | 2.1 | 4.7 | 7.6 |
| $75,000 to $99,999 | 0.4 | 0.1 | 0.3 | 0.0 | 0.2 | 0.0 | 1.9 | 1.6 | 0.9 | 4.1 | 2.0 |
| $100,000 or more | 1.0 | 0.2 | 0.3 | 0.2 | 0.7 | 1.3 | 3.9 | 2.6 | 1.6 | 11.0 | 8.4 |

*Note: (–) means sample is too small to make a reliable estimate.*
*Source: Bureau of the Census, Internet web site, <http://www.census.gov/cps/ads/sdata.htm>; calculations by New Strategist*

# Education Boosts Earnings of Black and Hispanic Men

## The best-educated black men earn more than three times as much as the least educated.

Education lifts earnings in every racial and ethnic group. Black men with doctoral degrees who work full-time earned a median of $61,573 in 1997, more than triple the $17,118 median earnings of black men who did not finish ninth grade. Hispanic men with professional degrees who work full-time earned $57,284, more than three times the $16,198 median earnings of their least-educated counterparts. Among non-Hispanic white men with full-time jobs, those with professional degrees earned fully $81,814 in 1997 compared with median earnings of $25,905 for those with the least education.

While education is important regardless of race and ethnicity, even the best-educated black and His-panic men have far lower earnings than their non-Hispanic white counterparts. Part of the earnings gap can be explained by the younger age (and fewer years of job experience) of black and Hispanic men compared to non-Hispanic white men. Another factor is the different career choices made by blacks, Hispanics, and whites. But a large portion of the earnings gap is due to the more limited job opportunities available to blacks and Hispanics.

✘ The incomes of educated blacks and Hispanics will rise in the years ahead as they gain job experience and their career opportunities expand.

### Among the educated, black and Hispanic earnings lag

*(median earnings of men aged 25 or older with a bachelor's degree who work full-time, year-round, by race and Hispanic origin, 1997)*

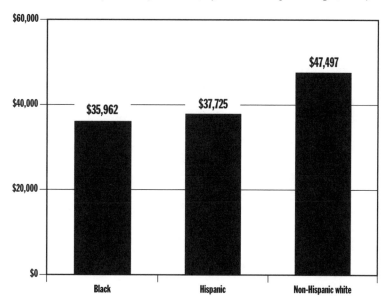

# Distribution of Men by Earnings and Education, 1997: Black Men

*(number and percent distribution of black men aged 25 or older by earnings and educational attainment, 1997; median earnings of men with earnings and of men with earnings who work full-time, year-round; percent of men who work full-time, year-round; men in thousands as of 1998)*

| | total | less than 9th grade | 9th to 12th grade, no diploma | high school graduate, incl. GED | some college, no degree | associate's degree | bachelor's degree or more | | | | |
| --- | --- | --- | --- | --- | --- | --- | --- | --- | --- | --- | --- |
| | | | | | | | total | bachelor's degree | master's degree | professional degree | doctoral degree |
| **Total men** | **8,578** | **760** | **1,369** | **3,167** | **1,628** | **458** | **1,195** | **880** | **218** | **63** | **35** |
| Without earnings | 2,364 | 519 | 599 | 764 | 271 | 75 | 136 | 94 | 31 | 5 | 7 |
| With earnings | 6,214 | 241 | 770 | 2,403 | 1,358 | 383 | 1,059 | 786 | 187 | 59 | 28 |
| Under $5,000 | 440 | 30 | 117 | 162 | 57 | 22 | 51 | 44 | 4 | 3 | – |
| $5,000 to $9,999 | 481 | 31 | 78 | 218 | 88 | 44 | 21 | 11 | 6 | 4 | – |
| $10,000 to $14,999 | 701 | 60 | 163 | 291 | 115 | 27 | 45 | 40 | 5 | – | – |
| $15,000 to $19,999 | 744 | 34 | 120 | 350 | 144 | 21 | 77 | 62 | 9 | 3 | 3 |
| $20,000 to $24,999 | 821 | 46 | 96 | 346 | 188 | 50 | 92 | 69 | 15 | 6 | 3 |
| $25,000 to $29,999 | 710 | 9 | 42 | 294 | 163 | 56 | 144 | 133 | 9 | 3 | – |
| $30,000 to $34,999 | 540 | 7 | 52 | 198 | 156 | 38 | 89 | 65 | 19 | 5 | – |
| $35,000 to $39,999 | 456 | – | 25 | 178 | 132 | 26 | 97 | 74 | 23 | – | – |
| $40,000 to $44,999 | 369 | 12 | 30 | 140 | 95 | 19 | 72 | 48 | 18 | 6 | 2 |
| $45,000 to $49,999 | 214 | – | 12 | 77 | 53 | 18 | 55 | 31 | 16 | 4 | 3 |
| $50,000 to $54,999 | 182 | – | 20 | 54 | 42 | 16 | 49 | 23 | 17 | 7 | 2 |
| $55,000 to $59,999 | 92 | – | 2 | 12 | 13 | 10 | 55 | 43 | 10 | – | 3 |
| $60,000 to $64,999 | 176 | – | 8 | 19 | 42 | 18 | 90 | 69 | 12 | 6 | 3 |
| $65,000 to $69,999 | 89 | 4 | – | 25 | 21 | 3 | 35 | 27 | 4 | – | 4 |
| $70,000 to $74,999 | 38 | – | – | 6 | 22 | – | 10 | 5 | 3 | – | 3 |
| $75,000 to $79,999 | 34 | 1 | 2 | 9 | 12 | 1 | 9 | 7 | 2 | – | – |
| $80,000 to $84,999 | 18 | 1 | – | 3 | 3 | 3 | 8 | 5 | 3 | – | – |
| $85,000 to $89,999 | 10 | – | – | 2 | 1 | 6 | – | – | – | – | – |
| $90,000 to $94,999 | 31 | – | – | 7 | 2 | 3 | 18 | 18 | – | – | – |
| $95,000 to $99,999 | 8 | 3 | – | 2 | – | – | 3 | 3 | – | – | – |
| $100,000 or more | 55 | – | – | 9 | 8 | 3 | 35 | 7 | 12 | 12 | 5 |

*(continued)*

*(continued from previous page)*

| | total | less than 9th grade | 9th to 12th grade, no diploma | high school graduate, incl. GED | some college, no degree | associate's degree | bachelor's degree or more | | | | |
| | | | | | | | total | bachelor's degree | master's degree | professional degree | doctoral degree |
|---|---|---|---|---|---|---|---|---|---|---|---|
| **Median earnings** | | | | | | | | | | | |
| Men with earnings | $24,339 | $14,766 | $15,784 | $22,174 | $26,635 | $26,569 | $35,290 | $31,631 | $40,776 | $42,282 | $60,679 |
| Men working full-time | $27,210 | $17,118 | $20,067 | $25,790 | $30,249 | $31,474 | $37,134 | $35,962 | $42,125 | $45,655 | $61,573 |
| Percent working full-time | 54.6% | 18.6% | 36.1% | 57.9% | 66.9% | 61.4% | 70.5% | 73.5% | 59.6% | 71.4% | 57.1% |
| **Percent distribution** | | | | | | | | | | | |
| **Total men** | 100.0% | 100.0% | 100.0% | 100.0% | 100.0% | 100.0% | 100.0% | 100.0% | 100.0% | 100.0% | 100.0% |
| Without earnings | 27.6 | 68.3 | 43.8 | 24.1 | 16.6 | 16.4 | 11.4 | 10.7 | 14.2 | 7.9 | 20.0 |
| With earnings | 72.4 | 31.7 | 56.2 | 75.9 | 83.4 | 83.6 | 88.6 | 89.3 | 85.8 | 93.7 | 80.0 |
| Under $25,000 | 37.2 | 26.4 | 41.9 | 43.2 | 36.4 | 35.8 | 23.9 | 25.7 | 17.9 | 25.4 | 17.1 |
| $25,000 to $49,999 | 26.7 | 3.7 | 11.8 | 28.0 | 36.8 | 34.3 | 38.2 | 39.9 | 39.0 | 28.6 | 5.7 |
| $50,000 to $74,999 | 6.7 | 0.5 | 2.2 | 3.7 | 8.6 | 10.3 | 20.0 | 19.0 | 21.1 | 20.6 | 42.9 |
| $75,000 to $99,999 | 1.2 | 0.7 | 0.1 | 0.7 | 1.1 | 2.8 | 3.2 | 3.8 | 2.3 | – | – |
| $100,000 or more | 0.6 | – | – | 0.3 | 0.5 | 0.7 | 2.9 | 0.8 | 5.5 | 19.0 | 14.3 |

*Note: (–) means sample is too small to make a reliable estimate.*
*Source: Bureau of the Census, Internet web site, <http://www.census.gov/cps/ads/sdata.htm>; calculations by New Strategist*

# Distribution of Men by Earnings and Education, 1997: Hispanic Men

*(number and percent distribution of Hispanic men aged 25 or older by earnings and educational attainment, 1997; median earnings of men with earnings and of men with earnings who work full-time, year-round; percent of men who work full-time, year-round; men in thousands as of 1998)*

| | total | less than 9th grade | 9th to 12th grade, no diploma | high school graduate, incl. GED | some college, no degree | associate's degree | bachelor's degree or more | | | | |
|---|---|---|---|---|---|---|---|---|---|---|---|
| | | | | | | | total | bachelor's degree | master's degree | professional degree | doctoral degree |
| Total men | 8,055 | 2,267 | 1,302 | 2,187 | 1,021 | 382 | 896 | 585 | 174 | 85 | 51 |
| Without earnings | 1,386 | 594 | 240 | 281 | 120 | 52 | 100 | 59 | 28 | 6 | 8 |
| With earnings | 6,669 | 1,674 | 1,063 | 1,906 | 901 | 330 | 796 | 526 | 147 | 79 | 44 |
| Under $5,000 | 402 | 134 | 83 | 109 | 48 | 8 | 20 | 14 | 6 | – | – |
| $5,000 to $9,999 | 663 | 277 | 116 | 141 | 58 | 29 | 43 | 34 | 5 | 4 | – |
| $10,000 to $14,999 | 1,234 | 502 | 227 | 320 | 104 | 36 | 46 | 40 | 4 | 2 | – |
| $15,000 to $19,999 | 940 | 301 | 178 | 287 | 86 | 38 | 49 | 27 | 12 | 11 | – |
| $20,000 to $24,999 | 833 | 194 | 141 | 269 | 120 | 37 | 73 | 59 | 9 | – | 4 |
| $25,000 to $29,999 | 609 | 92 | 99 | 220 | 100 | 38 | 60 | 46 | 3 | 8 | 4 |
| $30,000 to $34,999 | 492 | 68 | 77 | 170 | 76 | 33 | 68 | 61 | 3 | 2 | 2 |
| $35,000 to $39,999 | 372 | 39 | 59 | 108 | 79 | 26 | 63 | 35 | 17 | 2 | 8 |
| $40,000 to $44,999 | 291 | 16 | 35 | 120 | 47 | 17 | 57 | 26 | 22 | 5 | 3 |
| $45,000 to $49,999 | 159 | 14 | 18 | 49 | 40 | 12 | 26 | 18 | 3 | 4 | 2 |
| $50,000 to $54,999 | 162 | 8 | 11 | 32 | 52 | 12 | 47 | 38 | 8 | 1 | 1 |
| $55,000 to $59,999 | 90 | 3 | 2 | 24 | 16 | 10 | 35 | 21 | 11 | 3 | – |
| $60,000 to $64,999 | 87 | – | 3 | 18 | 21 | 8 | 36 | 25 | 9 | 2 | – |
| $65,000 to $69,999 | 56 | – | – | 8 | 12 | 9 | 26 | 17 | 4 | 7 | – |
| $70,000 to $74,999 | 57 | 2 | 2 | 8 | 14 | 10 | 23 | 12 | 4 | 3 | 4 |
| $75,000 to $79,999 | 49 | 5 | 5 | 3 | 7 | 1 | 28 | 18 | 5 | 2 | 2 |
| $80,000 to $84,999 | 35 | – | – | 7 | 5 | – | 23 | 12 | 7 | 3 | 1 |
| $85,000 to $89,999 | 11 | – | – | – | 3 | 2 | 6 | 3 | 2 | – | – |
| $90,000 to $94,999 | 10 | – | – | – | 2 | – | 8 | 6 | 2 | – | – |
| $95,000 to $99,999 | 8 | – | – | – | 5 | – | 3 | – | 1 | 2 | – |
| $100,000 or more | 107 | 20 | 8 | 13 | 7 | 4 | 55 | 15 | 11 | 17 | 11 |

*(continued)*

*(continued from previous page)*

| | total | less than 9th grade | 9th to 12th grade, no diploma | high school graduate, incl. GED | some college, no degree | associate's degree | bachelor's degree or more | | | | |
| --- | --- | --- | --- | --- | --- | --- | --- | --- | --- | --- | --- |
| | | | | | | | total | bachelor's degree | master's degree | professional degree | doctoral degree |
| **Median earnings** | | | | | | | | | | | |
| Men with earnings | $20,416 | $13,845 | $17,347 | $21,274 | $26,356 | $27,023 | $37,854 | $33,114 | $42,962 | $53,747 | $41,965 |
| Men working full-time | $23,272 | $16,198 | $20,877 | $24,021 | $29,569 | $30,090 | $41,511 | $37,725 | $44,702 | $57,284 | $42,082 |
| Percent working full-time | 64.1% | 51.1% | 62.0% | 69.0% | 73.2% | 72.5% | 74.2% | 73.8% | 74.1% | 76.5% | 78.4% |
| **Percent distribution** | | | | | | | | | | | |
| **Total men** | 100.0% | 100.0% | 100.0% | 100.0% | 100.0% | 100.0% | 100.0% | 100.0% | 100.0% | 100.0% | 100.0% |
| Without earnings | 17.2 | 26.2 | 18.4 | 12.8 | 11.8 | 13.6 | 11.2 | 10.1 | 16.1 | 7.1 | 15.7 |
| With earnings | 82.8 | 73.8 | 81.6 | 87.2 | 88.2 | 86.4 | 88.8 | 89.9 | 84.5 | 92.9 | 86.3 |
| Under $25,000 | 50.6 | 62.1 | 57.2 | 51.5 | 40.7 | 38.7 | 25.8 | 29.7 | 20.7 | 20.0 | 7.8 |
| $25,000 to $49,999 | 23.9 | 10.1 | 22.1 | 30.5 | 33.5 | 33.0 | 30.6 | 31.8 | 27.6 | 24.7 | 37.3 |
| $50,000 to $74,999 | 5.6 | 0.6 | 1.4 | 4.1 | 11.3 | 12.8 | 18.6 | 19.3 | 20.7 | 18.8 | 9.8 |
| $75,000 to $99,999 | 1.4 | 0.2 | 0.4 | 0.5 | 2.2 | 0.8 | 7.6 | 6.7 | 9.8 | 8.2 | 5.9 |
| $100,000 or more | 1.3 | 0.9 | 0.6 | 0.6 | 0.7 | 1.0 | 6.1 | 2.6 | 6.3 | 20.0 | 21.6 |

*Note: (–) means sample is too small to make a reliable estimate.*
*Source: Bureau of the Census, Internet web site, <http:// www.census.gov/cps/ads/sdata.htm>; calculations by New Strategist*

# Distribution of Men by Earnings and Education, 1997: White Men

*(number and percent distribution of white men aged 25 or older by earnings and educational attainment, 1997; median earnings of men with earnings and of men with earnings who work full-time, year-round; percent of men who work full-time, year-round; men in thousands as of 1998)*

| | total | less than 9th grade | 9th to 12th grade, no diploma | high school graduate, incl. GED | some college, no degree | associate's degree | bachelor's degree or more | | | | |
| --- | --- | --- | --- | --- | --- | --- | --- | --- | --- | --- | --- |
| | | | | | | | total | bachelor's degree | master's degree | professional degree | doctoral degree |
| **Total men** | **70,062** | **5,155** | **6,367** | **22,483** | **11,983** | **4,962** | **19,111** | **12,300** | **4,040** | **1,564** | **1,208** |
| Without earnings | 15,046 | 2,535 | 2,224 | 5,016 | 2,232 | 555 | 2,484 | 1,541 | 579 | 183 | 181 |
| With earnings | 55,016 | 2,621 | 4,143 | 17,467 | 9,751 | 4,407 | 16,628 | 10,759 | 3,461 | 1,381 | 1,026 |
| Under $5,000 | 2,876 | 304 | 384 | 987 | 513 | 154 | 534 | 354 | 129 | 30 | 21 |
| $5,000 to $9,999 | 2,818 | 419 | 361 | 921 | 446 | 176 | 494 | 356 | 97 | 23 | 19 |
| $10,000 to $14,999 | 4,292 | 602 | 600 | 1,550 | 731 | 245 | 564 | 408 | 98 | 36 | 22 |
| $15,000 to $19,999 | 4,305 | 392 | 572 | 1,752 | 637 | 349 | 601 | 425 | 102 | 47 | 27 |
| $20,000 to $24,999 | 5,120 | 305 | 588 | 1,982 | 964 | 436 | 846 | 673 | 137 | 16 | 20 |
| $25,000 to $29,999 | 4,975 | 176 | 429 | 2,008 | 1,006 | 404 | 950 | 765 | 136 | 25 | 25 |
| $30,000 to $34,999 | 5,254 | 133 | 382 | 2,050 | 1,026 | 461 | 1,200 | 942 | 176 | 58 | 25 |
| $35,000 to $39,999 | 4,450 | 98 | 239 | 1,558 | 896 | 420 | 1,240 | 878 | 244 | 59 | 57 |
| $40,000 to $44,999 | 3,938 | 64 | 170 | 1,359 | 769 | 455 | 1,119 | 794 | 214 | 65 | 46 |
| $45,000 to $49,999 | 2,808 | 37 | 110 | 877 | 555 | 252 | 978 | 645 | 199 | 80 | 55 |
| $50,000 to $54,999 | 2,931 | 21 | 130 | 789 | 533 | 256 | 1,203 | 788 | 248 | 92 | 75 |
| $55,000 to $59,999 | 1,641 | 7 | 28 | 360 | 320 | 166 | 760 | 487 | 194 | 39 | 38 |
| $60,000 to $64,999 | 1,783 | 10 | 29 | 344 | 358 | 182 | 859 | 506 | 253 | 36 | 65 |
| $65,000 to $69,999 | 1,168 | – | 9 | 210 | 173 | 91 | 683 | 461 | 148 | 31 | 43 |
| $70,000 to $74,999 | 1,131 | 9 | 27 | 196 | 152 | 104 | 643 | 374 | 166 | 44 | 58 |
| $75,000 to $79,999 | 808 | 12 | 16 | 101 | 121 | 51 | 506 | 318 | 96 | 55 | 38 |
| $80,000 to $84,999 | 797 | 5 | 7 | 92 | 147 | 26 | 518 | 258 | 152 | 45 | 63 |
| $85,000 to $89,999 | 367 | – | – | 35 | 37 | 25 | 270 | 147 | 81 | 24 | 19 |
| $90,000 to $94,999 | 439 | 2 | 4 | 45 | 53 | 32 | 304 | 138 | 80 | 50 | 35 |
| $95,000 to $99,999 | 234 | – | 7 | 21 | 23 | 12 | 171 | 85 | 34 | 30 | 20 |
| $100,000 or more | 2,885 | 23 | 49 | 227 | 289 | 111 | 2,185 | 955 | 478 | 497 | 256 |

*(continued)*

*(continued from previous page)*

| | total | less than 9th grade | 9th to 12th grade, no diploma | high school graduate, incl. GED | some college, no degree | associate's degree | bachelor's degree or more | | | | |
| --- | --- | --- | --- | --- | --- | --- | --- | --- | --- | --- | --- |
| | | | | | | | total | bachelor's degree | master's degree | professional degree | doctoral degree |
| **Median earnings** | | | | | | | | | | | |
| Men with earnings | $31,995 | $14,811 | $21,056 | $28,072 | $31,861 | $34,637 | $48,199 | $42,396 | $52,484 | $75,627 | $66,327 |
| Men working full-time | $36,476 | $18,590 | $25,162 | $31,195 | $35,869 | $37,164 | $51,882 | $47,220 | $60,081 | $80,951 | $71,423 |
| Percent working full-time | 62.5% | 32.8% | 45.9% | 61.5% | 64.9% | 73.3% | 72.8% | 73.6% | 69.5% | 76.2% | 71.5% |
| **Percent distribution** | | | | | | | | | | | |
| **Total men** | 100.0% | 100.0% | 100.0% | 100.0% | 100.0% | 100.0% | 100.0% | 100.0% | 100.0% | 100.0% | 100.0% |
| Without earnings | 21.5 | 49.2 | 34.9 | 22.3 | 18.6 | 11.2 | 13.0 | 12.5 | 14.3 | 11.7 | 15.0 |
| With earnings | 78.5 | 50.8 | 65.1 | 77.7 | 81.4 | 88.8 | 87.0 | 87.5 | 85.7 | 88.3 | 84.9 |
| Under $25,000 | 27.7 | 39.2 | 39.3 | 32.0 | 27.5 | 27.4 | 15.9 | 18.0 | 13.9 | 9.7 | 9.0 |
| $25,000 to $49,999 | 30.6 | 9.9 | 20.9 | 34.9 | 35.5 | 40.1 | 28.7 | 32.7 | 24.0 | 18.4 | 17.2 |
| $50,000 to $74,999 | 12.4 | 0.9 | 3.5 | 8.4 | 12.8 | 16.1 | 21.7 | 21.3 | 25.0 | 15.5 | 23.1 |
| $75,000 to $99,999 | 3.8 | 0.4 | 0.5 | 1.3 | 3.2 | 2.9 | 9.3 | 7.7 | 11.0 | 13.0 | 14.5 |
| $100,000 or more | 4.1 | 0.4 | 0.8 | 1.0 | 2.4 | 2.2 | 11.4 | 7.8 | 11.8 | 31.8 | 21.2 |

*Note: (–) means sample is too small to make a reliable estimate.*
*Source: Bureau of the Census, Internet web site, <http://www.census.gov/cps/ads/sdata.htm>; calculations by New Strategist*

# Distribution of Men by Earnings and Education, 1997: Non-Hispanic White Men

*(number and percent distribution of non-Hispanic white men aged 25 or older by earnings and educational attainment, 1997; median earnings of men with earnings and of men with earnings who work full-time, year-round; percent of men who work full-time, year-round; men in thousands as of 1998)*

| | total | less than 9th grade | 9th to 12th grade, no diploma | high school graduate, incl. GED | some college, no degree | associate's degree | bachelor's degree or more | | | | |
|---|---|---|---|---|---|---|---|---|---|---|---|
| | | | | | | | total | bachelor's degree | master's degree | professional degree | doctoral degree |
| **Total men** | **62,301** | **2,933** | **5,114** | **20,374** | **11,011** | **4,594** | **18,276** | **11,749** | **3,886** | **1,483** | **1,157** |
| Without earnings | 13,745 | 1,956 | 2,011 | 4,755 | 2,117 | 505 | 2,401 | 1,490 | 561 | 177 | 173 |
| With earnings | 48,556 | 977 | 3,103 | 15,619 | 8,893 | 4,089 | 15,874 | 10,259 | 3,326 | 1,306 | 984 |
| Under $5,000 | 2,487 | 173 | 305 | 880 | 468 | 148 | 513 | 339 | 125 | 30 | 21 |
| $5,000 to $9,999 | 2,173 | 146 | 246 | 784 | 393 | 149 | 454 | 323 | 91 | 20 | 19 |
| $10,000 to $14,999 | 3,091 | 110 | 380 | 1,243 | 627 | 211 | 520 | 370 | 93 | 34 | 22 |
| $15,000 to $19,999 | 3,393 | 97 | 396 | 1,475 | 555 | 311 | 559 | 401 | 95 | 36 | 27 |
| $20,000 to $24,999 | 4,313 | 114 | 449 | 1,726 | 850 | 399 | 776 | 614 | 132 | 16 | 15 |
| $25,000 to $29,999 | 4,388 | 89 | 332 | 1,791 | 912 | 367 | 896 | 723 | 135 | 17 | 21 |
| $30,000 to $34,999 | 4,777 | 65 | 305 | 1,885 | 955 | 429 | 1,138 | 884 | 173 | 56 | 24 |
| $35,000 to $39,999 | 4,093 | 61 | 183 | 1,452 | 824 | 395 | 1,177 | 842 | 228 | 58 | 49 |
| $40,000 to $44,999 | 3,655 | 48 | 136 | 1,239 | 730 | 439 | 1,062 | 769 | 192 | 59 | 43 |
| $45,000 to $49,999 | 2,657 | 24 | 93 | 830 | 516 | 241 | 953 | 629 | 196 | 76 | 53 |
| $50,000 to $54,999 | 2,776 | 13 | 118 | 760 | 482 | 244 | 1,159 | 752 | 242 | 90 | 74 |
| $55,000 to $59,999 | 1,553 | 5 | 26 | 336 | 304 | 155 | 728 | 470 | 184 | 36 | 38 |
| $60,000 to $64,999 | 1,702 | 10 | 26 | 328 | 338 | 172 | 826 | 484 | 244 | 34 | 65 |
| $65,000 to $69,999 | 1,114 | – | 9 | 202 | 162 | 84 | 657 | 445 | 144 | 24 | 43 |
| $70,000 to $74,999 | 1,075 | 7 | 25 | 189 | 138 | 95 | 622 | 364 | 162 | 41 | 54 |
| $75,000 to $79,999 | 760 | 7 | 11 | 98 | 114 | 50 | 480 | 300 | 90 | 54 | 36 |
| $80,000 to $84,999 | 762 | 5 | 7 | 86 | 142 | 26 | 495 | 246 | 144 | 42 | 62 |
| $85,000 to $89,999 | 356 | – | – | 35 | 34 | 23 | 264 | 144 | 78 | 24 | 19 |
| $90,000 to $94,999 | 429 | 2 | 4 | 45 | 50 | 32 | 296 | 133 | 78 | 50 | 35 |
| $95,000 to $99,999 | 226 | – | 7 | 21 | 18 | 12 | 168 | 85 | 33 | 29 | 20 |
| $100,000 or more | 2,777 | 3 | 40 | 214 | 282 | 107 | 2,130 | 939 | 466 | 479 | 245 |

*(continued)*

*(continued from previous page)*

| | total | less than 9th grade | 9th to 12th grade, no diploma | high school graduate, incl. GED | some college, no degree | associate's degree | bachelor's degree or more | | | | |
| | | | | | | | total | bachelor's degree | master's degree | professional degree | doctoral degree |
|---|---|---|---|---|---|---|---|---|---|---|---|
| **Median earnings** | | | | | | | | | | | |
| Men with earnings | $34,298 | $16,979 | $22,105 | $29,582 | $32,227 | $35,280 | $49,017 | $43,155 | $53,043 | $76,529 | $66,536 |
| Men working full-time | $37,893 | $25,905 | $26,390 | $31,727 | $36,293 | $37,662 | $52,104 | $47,497 | $60,281 | $81,814 | $71,804 |
| Percent working full-time | 62.2% | 19.0% | 41.7% | 60.7% | 64.1% | 73.3% | 72.7% | 73.5% | 69.2% | 76.1% | 71.2% |
| **Percent distribution** | | | | | | | | | | | |
| **Total men** | 100.0% | 100.0% | 100.0% | 100.0% | 100.0% | 100.0% | 100.0% | 100.0% | 100.0% | 100.0% | 100.0% |
| Without earnings | 22.1 | 66.7 | 39.3 | 23.3 | 19.2 | 11.0 | 13.1 | 12.7 | 14.4 | 11.9 | 15.0 |
| With earnings | 77.9 | 33.3 | 60.7 | 76.7 | 80.8 | 89.0 | 86.9 | 87.3 | 85.6 | 88.1 | 85.0 |
| Under $25,000 | 24.8 | 21.8 | 34.7 | 30.0 | 26.3 | 26.5 | 15.4 | 17.4 | 13.8 | 9.2 | 9.0 |
| $25,000 to $49,999 | 31.4 | 9.8 | 20.5 | 35.3 | 35.8 | 40.7 | 28.6 | 32.7 | 23.8 | 17.9 | 16.4 |
| $50,000 to $74,999 | 13.2 | 1.2 | 4.0 | 8.9 | 12.9 | 16.3 | 21.8 | 21.4 | 25.1 | 15.2 | 23.7 |
| $75,000 to $99,999 | 4.1 | 0.5 | 0.6 | 1.4 | 3.3 | 3.1 | 9.3 | 7.7 | 10.9 | 13.4 | 14.9 |
| $100,000 or more | 4.5 | 0.1 | 0.8 | 1.1 | 2.6 | 2.3 | 11.7 | 8.0 | 12.0 | 32.3 | 21.2 |

*Note: (–) means sample is too small to make a reliable estimate.*
*Source: Bureau of the Census, Internet web site, <http://www.census.gov/cps/ads/sdata.htm>; calculations by New Strategist*

# Men's Earnings Vary Widely by Occupation

## Those in the health-diagnosing occupations earn the most.

The median earnings of all men aged 15 or older who work full-time stood at $33,674 in 1997. By occupation, men's earnings vary widely. The highest-paid men are, not surprisingly, those in the health-diagnosing occupations—i.e., physicians. Their median income was more than $200,000 in 1997. Other highly paid men are lawyers and judges ($90,146), administrators in the federal government ($56,669), managers in manufacturing ($64,033), managers in the finance, insurance, and real estate industries ($66,357), engineers ($56,891), and college teachers ($52,263).

The occupation in which men's earnings are lowest is private household services—such as butlers. The median income of the handful of men who worked full-time in this occupation amounted to just $12,444 in 1997. Other low-paying occupations include food preparation workers ($15,588), farm laborers ($15,639), and cashiers ($17,206).

✘ Many of the men in low-paying occupations are young adults working their way up the career ladder. As they get older and gain job experience, they will find jobs in higher-paying occupations.

## Career choice affects earnings

*(median earnings of men aged 15 or older who work full-time, year-round, by selected occupation, 1997)*

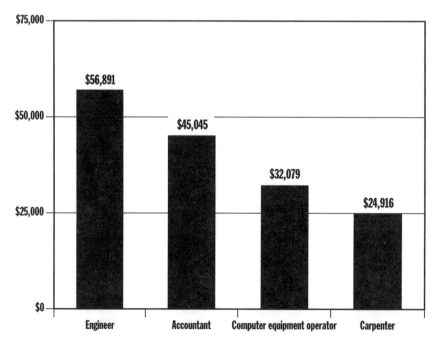

# Median Earnings of Men by Occupation, 1997

*(number and median earnings of men aged 15 or older who work full-time, year-round, by occupation of longest job held, 1997; men in thousands as of 1998)*

| | number with earnings | median earnings |
|---|---|---|
| **Total men who work full-time, year-round** | **54,909** | **$33,674** |
| Managerial and professional specialty occupations | 16,563 | 50,270 |
| Executive, administrative, and managerial | 9,046 | 50,149 |
| Administrators and officials, public | 372 | 50,112 |
| Federal | 142 | 56,669 |
| State or local | 231 | 46,278 |
| Other administrators and officials, salaried | 6,362 | 52,550 |
| Manufacturing | 1,537 | 64,033 |
| Retail trade | 736 | 33,325 |
| Finance, insurance, and real estate | 640 | 66,357 |
| Other industries | 3,449 | 51,242 |
| Other administrators and officials, self-employed | 711 | 30,654 |
| Management-related occupations | 1,601 | 44,790 |
| Accountants and auditors | 551 | 45,045 |
| Professional specialty occupations | 7,516 | 50,402 |
| Engineers, architects, and surveyors | 1,776 | 56,308 |
| Engineers | 1,629 | 56,891 |
| Natural scientists and mathematicians | 1,325 | 51,194 |
| Health-diagnosing occupations | 646 | 200,000 |
| Health-assessment and treating occupations | 354 | 44,735 |
| Teachers, postsecondary | 322 | 52,263 |
| Teachers, except postsecondary | 876 | 37,138 |
| Lawyers and judges | 561 | 90,146 |
| Other professional specialty occupations | 1,657 | 36,032 |
| Technical, sales, and administrative support | 10,734 | 33,922 |
| Health technologists and technicians, except LPNs | 253 | 31,052 |
| Licensed practical nurses (LPNs) | 15 | 25,995 |
| Technologists and technicians, except health | 1,323 | 40,642 |
| Sales occupations | 6,108 | 35,655 |
| Supervisors and proprietors, salaried | 2,234 | 37,061 |
| Supervisors and proprietors, self-employed | 378 | 28,681 |
| Sales representatives, finance and business services | 1,158 | 44,754 |
| Sales representatives, commodities, except retail | 1,037 | 41,402 |
| Sales workers, retail and personal services | 1,289 | 22,300 |
| Cashiers | 264 | 17,206 |
| Sales-related occupations | 13 | 40,386 |
| Administrative support occupations, including clerical | 3,035 | 29,442 |
| Supervisors, administrative support, including clerical | 228 | 36,140 |
| Computer equipment operators | 166 | 32,079 |

*(continued)*

*(continued from previous page)*

| | *number with earnings* | *median earnings* |
|---|---|---|
| Secretaries, stenographers, and typists | 58 | $23,843 |
| Financial record processors | 104 | 28,791 |
| Mail and message distributors | 497 | 36,275 |
| Material recording, scheduling, and distribution clerks | 828 | 25,681 |
| Other administrative support, including clerical | 1,153 | 26,758 |
| Service occupations | 4,703 | 22,335 |
| Private household occupations | 7 | 12,444 |
| Protective service occupations | 1,603 | 37,133 |
| Police and firefighters | 668 | 43,983 |
| Service, except protective and household | 3,093 | 18,272 |
| Food preparation and service occupations | 1,343 | 15,588 |
| Health service occupations | 232 | 18,862 |
| Cleaning and building service occupations, except household | 1,245 | 20,789 |
| Personal service occupations | 273 | 22,367 |
| Farming, forestry, and fishing occupations | 1,651 | 17,394 |
| Farm operators and managers | 643 | 21,020 |
| Farm occupations, except managerial | 435 | 15,639 |
| Related agricultural occupations | 515 | 18,471 |
| Forestry and fishing occupations | 58 | 17,237 |
| Precision production, craft, and repair occupations | 10,629 | 31,496 |
| Auto mechanics and repairers | 852 | 25,783 |
| Mechanics and repairers, except auto | 2,999 | 34,029 |
| Carpenters | 836 | 24,916 |
| Construction trades, except carpenters | 3,164 | 31,399 |
| Extractive occupations | 123 | 38,172 |
| Precision production occupations | 2,654 | 33,203 |
| Supervisors, production occupations | 879 | 37,354 |
| Precision metal working occupations | 851 | 35,744 |
| Plant and system operators | 219 | 40,959 |
| Other precision production occupations | 705 | 25,031 |
| Operators, fabricators, and laborers | 9,972 | 26,261 |
| Machine operators and tenders, except precision | 2,562 | 26,639 |
| Fabricators, assemblers, and hand-working occupations | 1,109 | 27,380 |
| Production inspectors, testers, samplers, and weighers | 355 | 29,164 |
| Motor vehicle operators | 2,673 | 27,585 |
| Transportation occupations, except motor vehicle | 117 | 49,960 |
| Material moving equipment operators | 851 | 27,290 |
| Handlers, equipment cleaners, helpers, and laborers | 2,304 | 21,475 |
| Construction laborers | 436 | 21,708 |
| Freight, stock, and material handlers | 814 | 21,242 |
| Hand packers and packagers | 54 | 25,577 |
| Helpers and miscellaneous manual occupations | 1,000 | 21,304 |
| Armed forces | 657 | 27,910 |

*Source: Bureau of the Census, Internet web site, <http:// www.census.gov/cps/ads/sdata.htm>*

# Three out of Four Men Receive Wage-and-Salary Income

## The majority also receive interest income.

Seventy-five percent of men received income from wages and salaries in 1997. The only other money received by the majority of men was interest income, with 53 percent receiving it. Only 8 percent of men received nonfarm self-employment income, while 10 percent received pension income and 17 percent had Social Security income. The median income of men receiving Social Security payments was just $15,673 compared to a much higher $26,388 for those receiving retirement income from pensions.

Black and Hispanic men are less likely to receive some types of income than non-Hispanic white men. While 75 percent of blacks and 84 percent of Hispanics received wage-and-salary income, only 29 and 24 percent, respectively, received interest income in 1997. Just 7 percent of blacks and 3 percent of Hispanics received income from a pension. Five percent of black men received educational assistance, however, compared with 3 percent of non-Hispanic white men.

Hispanic men are much less likely to receive Social Security income than black or non-Hispanic white men. Only 10 percent did in 1997, compared with 17 percent of blacks and 19 percent of non-Hispanic whites.

✘ When the baby-boom generation retires beginning in about ten years, the percentage of men receiving pension and Social Security income will rise.

### Wage-and-salary income is most common

*(percent of men aged 15 or older receiving income, by source, 1997)*

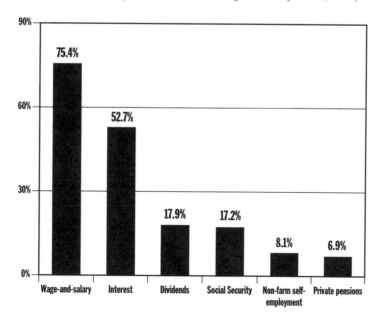

## Median Income of Men by Source of Income, 1997: Total Men

*(number and percent of men aged 15 or older with income by source of income, and median income of those with income, 1997; men in thousands as of 1998)*

|  | number | percent | median income |
|---|---|---|---|
| **Total men** | **94,168** | **100.0%** | **$25,212** |
| **Earnings** | **76,694** | **81.4** | **28,892** |
| Wages and salary | 70,995 | 75.4 | 29,311 |
| Nonfarm self-employment | 7,612 | 8.1 | 30,009 |
| Farm self-employment | 1,521 | 1.6 | 30,112 |
| **Social Security or railroad retirement** | **16,228** | **17.2** | **15,673** |
| **SSI (Supplemental Security)** | **1,967** | **2.1** | **6,902** |
| **Public assistance** | **495** | **0.5** | **5,931** |
| **Veterans payments** | **1,892** | **2.0** | **26,636** |
| **Unemployment compensation** | **3,550** | **3.8** | **22,811** |
| **Workers compensation** | **1,397** | **1.5** | **25,340** |
| **Property income** | **51,849** | **55.1** | **35,133** |
| Interest | 49,610 | 52.7 | 35,428 |
| Dividends | 16,881 | 17.9 | 46,378 |
| Rent, royalties, estates, trusts | 6,489 | 6.9 | 42,676 |
| **Retirement income** | **9,711** | **10.3** | **26,388** |
| Private pensions (includes company/union, annuities, IRA, Keough) | 6,519 | 6.9 | 23,716 |
| Military retirement | 1,041 | 1.1 | 43,481 |
| Federal employee pensions | 1,059 | 1.1 | 32,726 |
| State or local employee pensions | 1,476 | 1.6 | 29,702 |
| **Other income** | **5,132** | **5.4** | **17,295** |
| Alimony | 16 | 0.0 | 69,296 |
| Child support | 276 | 0.3 | 26,760 |
| Education assistance | 3,247 | 3.4 | 13,772 |
| All other | 1,812 | 1.9 | 22,303 |

*Source: Bureau of the Census, Internet web site, <http:// www.census.gov/cps/ads/sdata.htm>; calculations by New Strategist*

# Median Income of Men by Source of Income, 1997: Black Men

*(number and percent of black men aged 15 or older with income by source of income, and median income of those with income, by age, 1997; men in thousands as of 1998)*

| | number | percent | median income |
|---|---|---|---|
| **Total men** | **9,671** | **100.0%** | **$18,096** |
| **Earnings** | **7,565** | **78.2** | **22,004** |
| Wages and salary | 7,286 | 75.3 | 22,257 |
| Nonfarm self-employment | 435 | 4.5 | 21,607 |
| Farm self-employment | 54 | 0.6 | 24,630 |
| **Social Security or railroad retirement** | **1,611** | **16.7** | **10,408** |
| **SSI (Supplemental Security)** | **502** | **5.2** | **6,608** |
| **Public assistance** | **146** | **1.5** | **4,382** |
| **Veterans payments** | **226** | **2.3** | **22,735** |
| **Unemployment compensation** | **319** | **3.3** | **17,872** |
| **Workers compensation** | **156** | **1.6** | **20,895** |
| **Property income** | **3,012** | **31.1** | **30,171** |
| Interest | 2,813 | 29.1 | 30,221 |
| Dividends | 569 | 5.9 | 41,035 |
| Rent, royalties, estates, trusts | 321 | 3.3 | 33,298 |
| **Retirement income** | **684** | **7.1** | **22,300** |
| Private pensions (includes company/union, annuities, IRA, Keough) | 371 | 3.8 | 19,463 |
| Military retirement | 125 | 1.3 | 36,981 |
| Federal employee pensions | 84 | 0.9 | 26,879 |
| State or local employee pensions | 118 | 1.2 | 26,574 |
| **Other income** | **645** | **6.7** | **11,714** |
| Alimony | – | – | – |
| Child support | 49 | 0.5 | 24,388 |
| Education assistance | 449 | 4.6 | 10,861 |
| All other | 171 | 1.8 | 13,965 |

*Note: (–) means sample is too small to make a reliable estimate.*
*Source: Bureau of the Census, Internet web site, <http:// www.census.gov/cps/ads/sdata.htm>; calculations by New Strategist*

## Median Income of Men by Source of Income, 1997: Hispanic Men

*(number and percent of Hispanic men aged 15 or older with income by source of income, and median income of those with income, 1997; men in thousands as of 1998)*

| | number | percent | median income |
|---|---|---|---|
| **Total men** | **9,585** | **100.0%** | **$16,216** |
| **Earnings** | **8,465** | **88.3** | **17,477** |
| Wages and salary | 8,071 | 84.2 | 17,496 |
| Nonfarm self-employment | 500 | 5.2 | 19,646 |
| Farm self-employment | 54 | 0.6 | 10,771 |
| **Social Security or railroad retirement** | **918** | **9.6** | **9,741** |
| **SSI (Supplemental Security)** | **262** | **2.7** | **6,604** |
| **Public assistance** | **116** | **1.2** | **5,455** |
| **Veterans payments** | **73** | **0.8** | **21,129** |
| **Unemployment compensation** | **383** | **4.0** | **15,505** |
| **Workers compensation** | **116** | **1.2** | **17,273** |
| **Property income** | **2,447** | **25.5** | **28,517** |
| Interest | 2,300 | 24.0 | 28,864 |
| Dividends | 406 | 4.2 | 43,019 |
| Rent, royalties, estates, trusts | 282 | 2.9 | 35,693 |
| **Retirement income** | **303** | **3.2** | **20,262** |
| Private pensions (includes company/union, annuities, IRA, Keough) | 183 | 1.9 | 17,770 |
| Military retirement | 37 | 0.4 | 33,420 |
| Federal employee pensions | 43 | 0.4 | 19,602 |
| State or local employee pensions | 47 | 0.5 | 25,377 |
| **Other income** | **327** | **3.4** | **13,647** |
| Alimony | – | – | – |
| Child support | 14 | 0.1 | 15,219 |
| Education assistance | 210 | 2.2 | 12,603 |
| All other | 114 | 1.2 | 13,786 |

*Note: (–) means sample is too small to make a reliable estimate.*
*Source: Bureau of the Census, Internet web site, <http:// www.census.gov/cps/ads/sdata.htm>; calculations by New Strategist*

# Median Income of Men by Source of Income, 1997: White Men

*(number and percent of white men aged 15 or older with income by source of income, and median income of those with income, 1997; men in thousands as of 1998)*

| | number | percent | median income |
|---|---|---|---|
| **Total men** | **80,400** | **100.0%** | **$26,115** |
| **Earnings** | **65,582** | **81.6** | **30,223** |
| Wages and salary | 60,399 | 75.1 | 30,462 |
| Nonfarm self-employment | 6,852 | 8.5 | 30,483 |
| Farm self-employment | 1,417 | 1.8 | 30,186 |
| **Social Security or railroad retirement** | **14,297** | **17.8** | **16,577** |
| **SSI (Supplemental Security)** | **1,350** | **1.7** | **7,038** |
| **Public assistance** | **306** | **0.4** | **6,949** |
| **Veterans payments** | **1,623** | **2.0** | **27,374** |
| **Unemployment compensation** | **3,083** | **3.8** | **23,850** |
| **Workers compensation** | **1,202** | **1.5** | **25,480** |
| **Property income** | **46,870** | **58.3** | **35,484** |
| Interest | 44,935 | 55.9 | 35,773 |
| Dividends | 15,765 | 19.6 | 46,435 |
| Rent, royalties, estates, trusts | 5,911 | 7.4 | 43,599 |
| **Retirement income** | **8,803** | **10.9** | **26,657** |
| Private pensions (includes company/union, annuities, IRA, Keough) | 6,012 | 7.5 | 24,003 |
| Military retirement | 891 | 1.1 | 44,651 |
| Federal employee pensions | 945 | 1.2 | 33,479 |
| State or local employee pensions | 1,318 | 1.6 | 30,164 |
| **Other income** | **4,182** | **5.2** | **18,598** |
| Alimony | 16 | 0.0 | 69,296 |
| Child support | 226 | 0.3 | 26,989 |
| Education assistance | 2,603 | 3.2 | 14,320 |
| All other | 1,522 | 1.9 | 23,538 |

*Source: Bureau of the Census, Internet web site, <http:// www.census.gov/cps/ads/sdata.htm>; calculations by New Strategist*

# Median Income of Men by Source of Income, 1997: Non-Hispanic White Men

*(number and percent of non-Hispanic white men aged 15 or older with income by source of income, and median income of those with income, 1997; men in thousands as of 1998)*

|  | number | percent | median income |
|---|---|---|---|
| **Total men** | **71,150** | **100.0%** | **$27,559** |
| **Earnings** | **57,394** | **80.7** | **31,714** |
| Wages and salary | 52,599 | 73.9 | 32,032 |
| Nonfarm self-employment | 6,361 | 8.9 | 31,280 |
| Farm self-employment | 1,363 | 1.9 | 30,758 |
| **Social Security or railroad retirement** | **13,415** | **18.9** | **17,178** |
| **SSI (Supplemental Security)** | **1,099** | **1.5** | **7,154** |
| **Public assistance** | **203** | **0.3** | **7,391** |
| **Veterans payments** | **1,557** | **2.2** | **27,606** |
| **Unemployment compensation** | **2,710** | **3.8** | **25,220** |
| **Workers compensation** | **1,091** | **1.5** | **26,122** |
| **Property income** | **44,507** | **62.6** | **35,821** |
| Interest | 42,718 | 60.0 | 36,106 |
| Dividends | 15,373 | 21.6 | 46,508 |
| Rent, royalties, estates, trusts | 5,639 | 7.9 | 44,191 |
| **Retirement income** | **8,512** | **12.0** | **26,868** |
| Private pensions (includes company/union, annuities, IRA, Keough) | 5,835 | 8.2 | 24,173 |
| Military retirement | 856 | 1.2 | 45,186 |
| Federal employee pensions | 902 | 1.3 | 33,860 |
| State or local employee pensions | 1,275 | 1.8 | 30,394 |
| **Other income** | **3,875** | **5.4** | **19,270** |
| Alimony | 16 | 0.0 | 69,296 |
| Child support | 213 | 0.3 | 27,348 |
| Education assistance | 2,406 | 3.4 | 14,441 |
| All other | 1,414 | 2.0 | 24,424 |

*Source: Bureau of the Census, Internet web site, <http:// www.census.gov/cps/ads/sdata.htm>; calculations by New Strategist*

Chapter 3.

# Women's Income

Women's incomes have surged during the past three decades. Between 1967 and 1997, the median income of women rose 70 percent, after adjusting for inflation, to $13,703. Women of all ages have made income gains, with the largest increases among the oldest women as a more affluent cohort entered the older age groups.

Behind women's expanding incomes is their rising labor force participation rate. A growing percentage of women work full-time, and the educational attainment and career asipriations of those who work full-time have been increasing rapidly—thanks to the ambitions of baby boomers and younger women.

Women's incomes still lag behind men's for a variety of reasons. The average female worker is younger and less educated than the average male worker—lowering her earnings. In addition, women make different career choices than men and more often choose less demanding jobs with greater flexibility—jobs that typically pay less. Finally, many women choose to drop out of the labor force for a few years while their children are young, depressing their earnings.

✗ Among young adults, women are more educated than men. As they age, the gap between men's and women's incomes will continue to narrow.

# Women's Income Trends

# Women's Incomes Are Rising

## But the majority still have incomes below $15,000.

The percentage of women with incomes of $50,000 or more was six times greater in 1997 than in 1967, after adjusting for inflation. Never before have so many women had such lofty incomes. Nevertheless, the proportion remains well below that for men, 20 percent of whom had incomes of $50,000 or more in 1997.

The share of women with incomes below $5,000 has plunged over the past three decades as more women have gone to work. The percentage with the lowest incomes fell from 38 to 19 percent between 1967 and 1997, after adjusting for inflation.

The trends in women's incomes are the same for blacks, whites, and Hispanics. The upper-income brackets are growing while the lowest bracket is shrinking. Among black women, 4.3 percent had incomes of $50,000 or more in 1997, up from fewer than 1 percent in 1967, after adjusting for inflation. An enormous 43 percent of black women had incomes of less than $5,000 in 1967, but by 1997 only 17 percent had incomes that low. Among Hispanic women, the share in the lowest income bracket has not fallen as sharply as among blacks.

✘ Women's incomes have been rising rapidly because a growing share of women have jobs, and among those with jobs a growing proportion work full-time. Women's incomes will continue to rise as career-oriented baby boomers and younger women replace older just-a-job women in the population.

## Fewer women have very low incomes

*(percent of women aged 15 or older with incomes under $5,000, by race and Hispanic origin, 1967 and 1997; in 1997 dollars)*

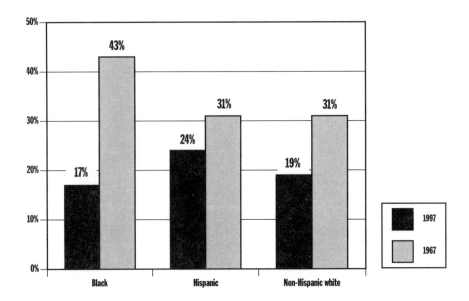

# Distribution of Women by Income, 1967 to 1997: Total Women

*(total number of women aged 15 or older, number with income, and percent distribution by income of women with income, 1967 to 1997; in 1997 dollars; women in thousands as of the following year)*

| | total women | women with income | percent distribution | | | | | | |
|---|---|---|---|---|---|---|---|---|---|
| | | | under $5,000 | $5,000 to $9,999 | $10,000 to $14,999 | $15,000 to $24,999 | $25,000 to $49,999 | $50,000 to $74,999 | $75,000 or over |
| 1997 | 108,168 | 97,447 | 19.0% | 19.6% | 14.5% | 20.0% | 20.5% | 4.5% | 2.0% |
| 1996 | 107,076 | 96,558 | 19.9 | 20.4 | 14.5 | 19.8 | 19.8 | 4.0 | 1.7 |
| 1995 | 106,031 | 96,007 | 21.0 | 20.4 | 14.5 | 19.4 | 19.5 | 3.8 | 1.5 |
| 1994 | 105,028 | 95,147 | 22.0 | 20.8 | 14.3 | 19.1 | 18.9 | 3.5 | 1.5 |
| 1993 | 104,032 | 94,417 | 22.9 | 20.7 | 14.2 | 18.9 | 18.6 | 3.5 | 1.2 |
| 1992 | 102,954 | 93,517 | 23.2 | 20.2 | 14.8 | 18.2 | 19.3 | 3.2 | 1.2 |
| 1991 | 101,483 | 92,569 | 22.9 | 20.5 | 14.3 | 19.4 | 18.6 | 3.0 | 1.2 |
| 1990 | 100,680 | 92,245 | 23.9 | 19.6 | 14.3 | 19.2 | 18.7 | 3.3 | 1.1 |
| 1989 | 99,838 | 91,399 | 23.6 | 19.7 | 13.6 | 19.6 | 19.1 | 3.3 | 1.1 |
| 1988 | 99,019 | 90,593 | 24.6 | 20.4 | 13.5 | 18.9 | 18.8 | 3.0 | 1.0 |
| 1987 | 98,225 | 89,661 | 25.2 | 20.1 | 13.8 | 18.9 | 18.3 | 2.7 | 0.9 |
| 1986 | 97,320 | 87,822 | 26.3 | 20.3 | 13.9 | 18.5 | 17.6 | 2.5 | 0.8 |
| 1985 | 96,354 | 86,531 | 27.4 | 20.5 | 14.1 | 18.2 | 16.9 | 2.2 | 0.7 |
| 1984 | 95,282 | 85,555 | 27.8 | 20.7 | 13.5 | 19.3 | 16.1 | 1.9 | 0.7 |
| 1983 | 94,269 | 83,781 | 28.9 | 21.0 | 13.2 | 19.2 | 15.4 | 1.8 | 0.6 |
| 1982 | 93,145 | 82,505 | 28.9 | 21.6 | 13.8 | 18.8 | 14.7 | 1.5 | 0.5 |
| 1981 | 92,228 | 82,139 | 29.6 | 22.1 | 13.9 | 19.0 | 13.7 | 1.4 | 0.3 |
| 1980 | 91,133 | 80,826 | 30.5 | 21.8 | 13.4 | 19.0 | 13.7 | 1.2 | 0.4 |
| 1979 | 89,914 | 79,921 | 31.6 | 20.9 | 13.2 | 19.4 | 13.4 | 1.2 | 0.4 |
| 1978 | 88,617 | 71,864 | 29.9 | 22.1 | 13.8 | 19.2 | 13.4 | 1.2 | 0.4 |
| 1977 | 87,399 | 65,407 | 27.3 | 22.9 | 14.9 | 19.5 | 14.0 | 1.1 | 0.4 |
| 1976 | 86,157 | 63,170 | 28.4 | 23.2 | 14.8 | 19.4 | 12.8 | 1.1 | 0.3 |
| 1975 | 84,982 | 60,807 | 28.5 | 23.3 | 15.4 | 18.9 | 12.8 | 0.9 | 0.2 |
| 1974 | 83,599 | 59,642 | 29.5 | 23.2 | 14.0 | 19.8 | 12.4 | 1.0 | 0.3 |
| 1973 | 82,244 | 57,029 | 30.5 | 21.4 | 14.8 | 19.1 | 12.8 | 1.1 | 0.3 |
| 1972 | 80,896 | 54,487 | 31.3 | 21.1 | 14.4 | 18.5 | 13.3 | 1.0 | 0.3 |
| 1971 | 79,565 | 52,603 | 32.9 | 20.6 | 14.6 | 18.8 | 11.9 | 0.8 | 0.3 |
| 1970 | 77,649 | 51,647 | 34.5 | 20.4 | 13.0 | 19.4 | 11.7 | 0.8 | 0.3 |
| 1969 | 76,277 | 50,224 | 35.4 | 19.3 | 13.7 | 20.0 | 10.6 | 0.7 | 0.3 |
| 1968 | 74,889 | 48,544 | 35.5 | 20.0 | 14.5 | 18.6 | 10.5 | 0.7 | 0.2 |
| 1967 | 73,584 | 46,843 | 38.4 | 19.1 | 13.9 | 18.6 | 8.9 | 0.7 | 0.4 |

*Source: Bureau of the Census,* Money Income in the United States: 1997, *Current Population Reports, P60-200, 1998*

# Distribution of Women by Income, 1967 to 1997: Black Women

*(total number of black women aged 15 or older, number with income, and percent distribution by income of black women with income, 1967 to 1997; in 1997 dollars; women in thousands as of the following year)*

| | total women | women with income | percent distribution | | | | | | |
| | | | under $5,000 | $5,000 to $9,999 | $10,000 to $14,999 | $15,000 to $24,999 | $25,000 to $49,999 | $50,000 to $74,999 | $75,000 or over |
|---|---|---|---|---|---|---|---|---|---|
| 1997 | 13,715 | 11,961 | 17.1% | 23.2% | 13.9% | 22.5% | 18.9% | 3.5% | 0.8% |
| 1996 | 13,514 | 11,817 | 19.5 | 24.4 | 13.6 | 21.2 | 18.1 | 2.6 | 0.7 |
| 1995 | 13,292 | 11,607 | 20.1 | 25.3 | 15.0 | 19.2 | 17.5 | 2.5 | 0.5 |
| 1994 | 13,097 | 11,450 | 21.2 | 24.8 | 14.5 | 19.5 | 16.2 | 2.7 | 1.0 |
| 1993 | 12,872 | 11,267 | 23.9 | 25.2 | 14.3 | 18.2 | 15.4 | 2.5 | 0.6 |
| 1992 | 12,677 | 11,076 | 24.3 | 25.8 | 14.3 | 16.1 | 16.8 | 2.4 | 0.2 |
| 1991 | 12,288 | 10,727 | 22.9 | 26.6 | 14.0 | 18.4 | 15.7 | 1.6 | 0.6 |
| 1990 | 12,124 | 10,687 | 24.7 | 25.4 | 14.3 | 17.6 | 15.5 | 2.2 | 0.4 |
| 1989 | 11,966 | 10,577 | 23.6 | 26.1 | 12.5 | 18.2 | 16.7 | 2.5 | 0.4 |
| 1988 | 11,786 | 10,380 | 24.0 | 26.6 | 13.7 | 17.0 | 16.5 | 1.8 | 0.3 |
| 1987 | 11,663 | 10,164 | 25.1 | 26.3 | 13.9 | 17.7 | 15.2 | 1.5 | 0.3 |
| 1986 | 11,447 | 9,819 | 25.6 | 26.4 | 14.6 | 17.2 | 14.2 | 1.5 | 0.4 |
| 1985 | 11,263 | 9,611 | 26.2 | 26.9 | 14.5 | 16.2 | 14.8 | 1.2 | 0.1 |
| 1984 | 11,092 | 9,460 | 25.6 | 26.8 | 14.6 | 17.9 | 13.7 | 1.2 | 0.2 |
| 1983 | 10,911 | 9,107 | 28.0 | 26.7 | 13.6 | 17.7 | 12.9 | 1.0 | 0.2 |
| 1982 | 10,687 | 8,921 | 26.9 | 27.5 | 14.1 | 18.0 | 12.6 | 0.7 | 0.1 |
| 1981 | 10,511 | 8,829 | 27.7 | 28.0 | 15.0 | 17.2 | 11.2 | 0.8 | 0.1 |
| 1980 | 10,317 | 9,596 | 26.8 | 28.5 | 13.8 | 18.3 | 11.8 | 0.6 | 0.1 |
| 1979 | 10,108 | 8,533 | 29.2 | 26.5 | 13.0 | 18.8 | 11.7 | 0.8 | 0.1 |
| 1978 | 9,902 | 7,959 | 26.9 | 28.4 | 14.1 | 18.0 | 11.9 | 0.5 | 0.1 |
| 1977 | 9,684 | 7,562 | 26.2 | 28.3 | 15.3 | 18.1 | 11.5 | 0.5 | 0.1 |
| 1976 | 9,484 | 7,188 | 25.3 | 28.4 | 16.1 | 18.7 | 10.7 | 0.7 | 0.1 |
| 1975 | 9,269 | 6,969 | 26.8 | 28.7 | 16.1 | 17.0 | 11.0 | 0.5 | – |
| 1974 | 9,047 | 6,779 | 28.4 | 28.3 | 13.9 | 19.3 | 9.7 | 0.5 | 0.1 |
| 1973 | 8,839 | 6,513 | 31.3 | 23.6 | 17.5 | 17.8 | 9.2 | 0.5 | 0.1 |
| 1972 | 8,616 | 6,274 | 31.2 | 23.7 | 16.7 | 17.1 | 10.6 | 0.6 | 0.1 |
| 1971 | 8,428 | 6,151 | 34.9 | 24.2 | 15.6 | 16.2 | 8.7 | 0.2 | – |
| 1970 | 8,041 | 5,844 | 34.8 | 24.3 | 15.4 | 16.8 | 8.3 | 0.4 | – |
| 1969 | 7,841 | 5,728 | 38.3 | 22.4 | 16.1 | 16.2 | 6.7 | 0.3 | – |
| 1968 | 7,636 | 5,629 | 39.6 | 23.5 | 15.6 | 15.2 | 6.0 | 0.1 | – |
| 1967 | 7,461 | 5,397 | 42.6 | 23.0 | 15.7 | 13.0 | 5.0 | 0.4 | 0.2 |

*Note: (–) means sample is too small to make a reliable estimate.*
*Source: Bureau of the Census,* Money Income in the United States: 1997, *Current Population Reports, P60-200, 1998*

# Distribution of Women by Income, 1972 to 1997: Hispanic Women

*(total number of Hispanic women aged 15 or older, number with income, and percent distribution by income of Hispanic women with income, 1972 to 1997; in 1997 dollars; women in thousands as of the following year)*

| | total women | women with income | percent distribution | | | | | | |
| | | | under $5,000 | $5,000 to $9,999 | $10,000 to $14,999 | $15,000 to $24,999 | $25,000 to $49,999 | $50,000 to $74,999 | $75,000 or over |
|---|---|---|---|---|---|---|---|---|---|
| 1997 | 10,485 | 8,055 | 24.4% | 24.5% | 17.2% | 17.6% | 13.8% | 1.9% | 0.8% |
| 1996 | 10,073 | 7,744 | 25.8 | 25.6 | 16.4 | 17.6 | 11.9 | 2.0 | 0.5 |
| 1995 | 9,754 | 7,478 | 26.6 | 26.2 | 15.9 | 17.2 | 12.0 | 1.5 | 0.5 |
| 1994 | 9,433 | 7,298 | 26.4 | 26.9 | 16.1 | 15.8 | 12.5 | 1.5 | 0.7 |
| 1993 | 9,146 | 7,053 | 28.7 | 26.4 | 15.2 | 16.0 | 11.6 | 1.5 | 0.5 |
| 1992 | 8,815 | 6,749 | 27.9 | 24.1 | 17.8 | 14.7 | 13.5 | 1.4 | 0.6 |
| 1991 | 7,806 | 6,084 | 28.8 | 24.8 | 16.1 | 16.8 | 11.8 | 1.3 | 0.5 |
| 1990 | 7,559 | 5,903 | 29.4 | 24.0 | 16.0 | 16.7 | 11.7 | 1.7 | 0.4 |
| 1989 | 7,323 | 5,677 | 28.5 | 21.7 | 16.5 | 17.4 | 13.8 | 1.6 | 0.5 |
| 1988 | 7,045 | 5,532 | 30.2 | 22.1 | 16.5 | 15.6 | 13.7 | 1.2 | 0.5 |
| 1987 | 6,835 | 5,357 | 29.7 | 24.3 | 14.7 | 16.5 | 12.8 | 1.3 | 0.5 |
| 1986 | 6,588 | 5,096 | 29.6 | 23.3 | 16.1 | 17.1 | 12.3 | 1.3 | 0.2 |
| 1985 | 6,366 | 4,843 | 30.4 | 24.9 | 15.5 | 16.0 | 12.0 | 0.8 | 0.2 |
| 1984 | 5,967 | 4,617 | 30.8 | 23.8 | 14.6 | 19.1 | 10.7 | 0.8 | 0.2 |
| 1983 | 5,790 | 4,098 | 31.9 | 25.0 | 14.5 | 17.4 | 10.0 | 1.0 | 0.2 |
| 1982 | 5,119 | 3,832 | 31.2 | 24.4 | 15.5 | 18.6 | 9.4 | 0.8 | 0.2 |
| 1981 | 4,955 | 3,787 | 31.8 | 23.4 | 16.7 | 18.1 | 9.2 | 0.6 | 0.1 |
| 1980 | 4,734 | 3,617 | 32.7 | 24.2 | 16.8 | 16.8 | 8.7 | 0.6 | 0.1 |
| 1979 | 4,501 | 3,495 | 31.7 | 23.1 | 17.1 | 18.5 | 8.8 | 0.7 | 0.2 |
| 1978 | 4,178 | 2,949 | 30.4 | 25.1 | 17.5 | 17.6 | 8.6 | 0.7 | 0.1 |
| 1977 | 4,212 | 2,780 | 28.9 | 24.1 | 19.0 | 18.8 | 8.7 | 0.3 | 0.1 |
| 1976 | 3,922 | 2,568 | 29.5 | 24.8 | 19.2 | 19.4 | 6.8 | 0.3 | 0.1 |
| 1975 | 3,777 | 2,380 | 30.1 | 24.5 | 20.6 | 17.8 | 6.9 | 0.2 | – |
| 1974 | 3,743 | 2,353 | 29.0 | 25.4 | 17.9 | 20.4 | 7.0 | 0.3 | – |
| 1973 | 3,752 | 2,154 | 30.0 | 23.8 | 17.2 | 20.3 | 8.0 | 0.4 | 0.2 |
| 1972 | 3,511 | 1,928 | 31.2 | 21.2 | 20.0 | 18.9 | 8.6 | 0.3 | – |

*Note: (–) means sample is too small to make a reliable estimate.*
*Source: Bureau of the Census,* Money Income in the United States: 1997, *Current Population Reports, P60-200, 1998*

# Distribution of Women by Income, 1967 to 1997: White Women

*(total number of white women aged 15 or older, number with income, and percent distribution by income of white women with income, 1967 to 1997; in 1997 dollars; women in thousands as of the following year)*

| | total women | women with income | percent distribution | | | | | | |
| --- | --- | --- | --- | --- | --- | --- | --- | --- | --- |
| | | | under $5,000 | $5,000 to $9,999 | $10,000 to $14,999 | $15,000 to $24,999 | $25,000 to $49,999 | $50,000 to $74,999 | $75,000 or over |
| 1997 | 89,489 | 81,352 | 19.1% | 19.2% | 14.6% | 19.7% | 20.7% | 4.6% | 2.1% |
| 1996 | 88,756 | 80,741 | 19.8 | 19.9 | 14.7 | 19.6 | 20.0 | 4.1 | 1.8 |
| 1995 | 88,134 | 80,608 | 21.0 | 19.8 | 14.5 | 19.5 | 19.7 | 3.9 | 1.6 |
| 1994 | 87,484 | 80,045 | 22.0 | 20.2 | 14.3 | 19.1 | 19.2 | 3.6 | 1.5 |
| 1993 | 86,765 | 79,484 | 22.6 | 20.2 | 14.2 | 19.0 | 19.0 | 3.6 | 1.3 |
| 1992 | 86,098 | 78,885 | 22.9 | 19.6 | 14.9 | 18.5 | 19.7 | 3.2 | 1.3 |
| 1991 | 85,510 | 78,721 | 22.8 | 19.8 | 14.4 | 19.5 | 19.1 | 3.2 | 1.2 |
| 1990 | 85,012 | 78,566 | 23.8 | 18.8 | 14.3 | 19.4 | 19.1 | 3.4 | 1.2 |
| 1989 | 84,508 | 77,933 | 23.6 | 18.9 | 13.8 | 19.7 | 19.4 | 3.4 | 1.1 |
| 1988 | 84,035 | 77,493 | 24.4 | 19.6 | 13.4 | 19.2 | 19.1 | 3.1 | 1.0 |
| 1987 | 83,552 | 76,940 | 25.2 | 19.4 | 13.9 | 19.0 | 18.7 | 2.9 | 1.0 |
| 1986 | 83,003 | 75,587 | 26.4 | 19.7 | 13.9 | 18.7 | 18.0 | 2.6 | 0.9 |
| 1985 | 82,345 | 74,640 | 27.5 | 19.8 | 14.1 | 18.4 | 17.1 | 2.3 | 0.8 |
| 1984 | 81,603 | 73,977 | 28.0 | 20.0 | 13.5 | 19.4 | 16.3 | 2.0 | 0.7 |
| 1983 | 80,901 | 72,643 | 29.0 | 20.3 | 13.2 | 19.4 | 15.6 | 1.9 | 0.7 |
| 1982 | 80,066 | 71,624 | 29.1 | 21.0 | 13.9 | 18.9 | 14.9 | 1.7 | 0.6 |
| 1981 | 79,591 | 71,566 | 29.9 | 21.4 | 13.8 | 19.3 | 13.9 | 1.4 | 0.3 |
| 1980 | 78,766 | 70,573 | 30.9 | 21.1 | 13.4 | 19.1 | 13.8 | 1.3 | 0.4 |
| 1979 | 77,882 | 69,839 | 31.8 | 20.3 | 13.2 | 19.4 | 13.6 | 1.2 | 0.4 |
| 1978 | 77,091 | 62,695 | 30.3 | 21.4 | 13.8 | 19.3 | 13.5 | 1.3 | 0.4 |
| 1977 | 76,194 | 56,813 | 27.4 | 22.3 | 14.9 | 19.7 | 14.3 | 1.1 | 0.4 |
| 1976 | 75,239 | 55,026 | 28.7 | 22.5 | 14.7 | 19.5 | 13.1 | 1.1 | 0.4 |
| 1975 | 74,351 | 52,936 | 28.7 | 22.7 | 15.3 | 19.1 | 13.0 | 1.0 | 0.2 |
| 1974 | 73,312 | 52,038 | 29.6 | 22.6 | 14.0 | 19.8 | 12.6 | 1.0 | 0.3 |
| 1973 | 72,248 | 49,741 | 30.4 | 21.1 | 14.5 | 19.3 | 13.3 | 1.1 | 0.3 |
| 1972 | 71,226 | 47,519 | 31.3 | 20.8 | 14.1 | 18.6 | 13.7 | 1.1 | 0.3 |
| 1971 | 70,293 | 45,941 | 32.8 | 20.2 | 14.5 | 19.2 | 12.2 | 0.9 | 0.3 |
| 1970 | 68,793 | 45,288 | 34.4 | 19.9 | 12.7 | 19.7 | 12.1 | 0.8 | 0.3 |
| 1969 | 67,680 | 44,025 | 35.1 | 18.9 | 13.4 | 20.5 | 11.1 | 0.8 | 0.3 |
| 1968 | 66,543 | 42,482 | 35.0 | 19.5 | 14.3 | 19.0 | 11.1 | 0.7 | 0.3 |
| 1967 | 66,240 | 41,045 | 37.9 | 18.6 | 13.6 | 19.3 | 9.4 | 0.8 | 0.4 |

*Source: Bureau of the Census,* Money Income in the United States: 1997, *Current Population Reports, P60-200, 1998*

# Distribution of Women by Income, 1972 to 1997: Non-Hispanic White Women

*(total number of non-Hispanic white women aged 15 or older, number with income, and percent distribution by income of non-Hispanic white women with income, 1972 to 1997; in 1997 dollars; women in thousands as of the following year)*

| | total women | women with income | percent distribution | | | | | | |
|---|---|---|---|---|---|---|---|---|---|
| | | | under $5,000 | $5,000 to $9,999 | $10,000 to $14,999 | $15,000 to $24,999 | $25,000 to $49,999 | $50,000 to $74,999 | $75,000 or over |
| 1997 | 79,502 | 73,709 | 18.5% | 18.6% | 14.3% | 20.0% | 21.5% | 4.9% | 2.3% |
| 1996 | 79,232 | 73,445 | 19.2 | 19.4 | 14.5 | 19.8 | 20.9 | 4.3 | 1.9 |
| 1995 | 78,867 | 73,506 | 20.4 | 19.2 | 14.3 | 19.7 | 20.5 | 4.2 | 1.7 |
| 1994 | 79,252 | 73,665 | 21.6 | 19.6 | 14.2 | 19.4 | 19.8 | 3.8 | 1.6 |
| 1993 | 78,477 | 73,128 | 22.1 | 19.6 | 14.1 | 19.3 | 19.7 | 3.8 | 1.3 |
| 1992 | 77,820 | 72,559 | 22.4 | 19.2 | 14.6 | 18.9 | 20.2 | 3.4 | 1.3 |
| 1991 | 78,081 | 72,959 | 22.3 | 19.4 | 14.3 | 19.7 | 19.7 | 3.4 | 1.3 |
| 1990 | 77,796 | 72,939 | 23.3 | 18.4 | 14.2 | 19.6 | 19.7 | 3.5 | 1.3 |
| 1989 | 77,500 | 72,509 | 23.2 | 18.7 | 13.6 | 19.9 | 19.8 | 3.5 | 1.2 |
| 1988 | 77,296 | 72,216 | 24.0 | 19.4 | 13.2 | 19.5 | 19.5 | 3.3 | 1.1 |
| 1987 | 76,983 | 71,817 | 24.8 | 19.1 | 13.8 | 19.2 | 19.1 | 3.0 | 1.0 |
| 1986 | 76,641 | 70,671 | 26.1 | 19.4 | 13.7 | 18.8 | 18.4 | 2.7 | 0.9 |
| 1985 | 76,199 | 69,972 | 27.2 | 19.4 | 14.0 | 18.6 | 17.5 | 2.4 | 0.9 |
| 1984 | 75,804 | 69,497 | 27.8 | 19.8 | 13.4 | 19.5 | 16.7 | 2.1 | 0.8 |
| 1983 | 75,274 | 68,380 | 28.7 | 20.0 | 13.1 | 19.5 | 16.0 | 1.9 | 0.7 |
| 1982 | 75,083 | 67,894 | 28.9 | 20.8 | 13.8 | 18.9 | 15.2 | 1.7 | 0.6 |
| 1981 | 74,787 | 67,889 | 29.8 | 21.3 | 13.6 | 19.3 | 14.2 | 1.5 | 0.3 |
| 1980 | 74,193 | 67,084 | 30.8 | 21.0 | 13.2 | 19.2 | 14.1 | 1.3 | 0.4 |
| 1979 | 73,535 | 66,447 | 31.8 | 20.2 | 13.0 | 19.5 | 13.8 | 1.3 | 0.4 |
| 1978 | 73,030 | 59,833 | 30.3 | 21.2 | 13.6 | 19.4 | 13.8 | 1.3 | 0.4 |
| 1977 | 72,104 | 54,110 | 27.3 | 22.2 | 14.7 | 19.7 | 14.6 | 1.2 | 0.4 |
| 1976 | 71,425 | 52,538 | 28.7 | 22.4 | 14.5 | 19.5 | 13.4 | 1.2 | 0.4 |
| 1975 | 70,686 | 50,628 | 28.6 | 22.6 | 15.0 | 19.2 | 13.2 | 1.0 | 0.2 |
| 1974 | 69,666 | 49,757 | 29.6 | 22.5 | 13.9 | 19.8 | 12.9 | 1.1 | 0.3 |
| 1973 | 68,605 | 47,526 | 30.5 | 21.0 | 14.3 | 19.3 | 13.5 | 1.2 | 0.3 |
| 1972 | 67,815 | 45,594 | 31.4 | 20.8 | 13.9 | 18.6 | 13.9 | 1.1 | 0.3 |

*Source: Bureau of the Census,* Money Income in the United States: 1997, *Current Population Reports, P60-200, 1998*

# Women of All Ages Have Enjoyed Growing Incomes

## The biggest gains have been for the oldest women.

During the past three decades, the median income of women rose an enormous 72 percent, after adjusting for inflation, from $7,963 to $13,703. This figure is far below the median income of men because many more women work part-time.

The biggest gain in income has been among women aged 65 or older. Since 1967 their median income has more than doubled. Despite this rapid growth, the median income of women aged 65 or older amounted to just $10,062 in 1997.

Women aged 25 to 54 have seen their median incomes grow about 50 percent over the past three decades, after adjusting for inflation. Those aged 45 to 54 had the highest incomes in both 1967 and 1997, with a median of $20,534 in 1997.

✘ Women's incomes today are showing a more distinct peak in middle age than they did in the past because career-oriented baby-boom women are replacing older just-a-job women in the middle age groups. This trend will intensify as younger boomers and Generation Xers enter middle age.

### Incomes of oldest women have doubled

*(percent change in median income of women by age, 1967 to 1997; in 1997 dollars)*

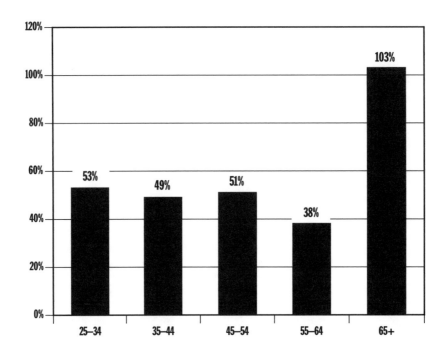

# Median Income of Women by Age, 1967 to 1997

*(median income of women aged 15 or older with income by age, 1967 to 1997; percent change in income for selected years; in 1997 dollars)*

| | total women | 15 to 24 | 25 to 34 | 35 to 44 | 45 to 54 | 55 to 64 | aged 65 or older total | 65 to 74 | 75 or older |
|---|---|---|---|---|---|---|---|---|---|
| 1997 | $13,703 | $6,342 | $17,647 | $18,706 | $20,534 | $14,376 | $10,062 | $10,141 | $9,996 |
| 1996 | 13,109 | 6,016 | 16,760 | 18,870 | 19,483 | 13,622 | 9,847 | 9,878 | 9,818 |
| 1995 | 12,775 | 5,592 | 16,384 | 18,322 | 18,665 | 13,039 | 9,852 | 9,770 | 9,928 |
| 1994 | 12,418 | 5,965 | 16,119 | 17,533 | 18,466 | 11,769 | 9,693 | 9,559 | 9,814 |
| 1993 | 12,269 | 5,944 | 15,537 | 17,598 | 18,132 | 12,028 | 9,440 | 9,604 | 9,291 |
| 1992 | 12,257 | 5,914 | 15,594 | 17,637 | 18,134 | 11,592 | 9,361 | 9,398 | 9,325 |
| 1991 | 12,345 | 6,124 | 15,277 | 17,824 | 17,351 | 11,669 | 9,650 | 9,586 | 9,711 |
| 1990 | 12,366 | 6,020 | 15,459 | 17,811 | 17,474 | 11,543 | 9,878 | 10,057 | 9,690 |
| 1989 | 12,457 | 6,134 | 15,831 | 17,869 | 17,012 | 11,860 | 9,908 | 10,288 | 9,548 |
| 1988 | 12,053 | 6,085 | 15,690 | 17,021 | 16,308 | 11,365 | 9,637 | 9,844 | 9,421 |
| 1987 | 11,720 | 6,228 | 15,512 | 16,947 | 15,913 | 10,654 | 9,743 | 9,870 | 9,605 |
| 1986 | 11,144 | 5,922 | 15,098 | 16,202 | 15,201 | 10,803 | 9,409 | – | – |
| 1985 | 10,765 | 5,655 | 14,736 | 15,327 | 14,348 | 10,700 | 9,417 | – | – |
| 1984 | 10,609 | 5,575 | 14,508 | 14,769 | 13,753 | 10,561 | 9,299 | – | – |
| 1983 | 10,183 | 5,571 | 13,702 | 14,277 | 13,222 | 9,877 | 9,022 | – | – |
| 1982 | 9,884 | 5,628 | 13,384 | 13,181 | 12,595 | 9,917 | 9,007 | – | – |
| 1981 | 9,723 | 3,556 | 13,535 | 13,121 | 12,523 | 9,575 | 8,383 | – | – |
| 1980 | 9,595 | 6,092 | 13,599 | 12,608 | 12,487 | 9,607 | 8,241 | – | – |
| 1979 | 9,439 | 6,123 | 13,773 | 12,768 | 12,137 | 9,513 | 8,157 | – | – |
| 1978 | 9,673 | 6,139 | 13,884 | 13,801 | 13,487 | 10,636 | 8,037 | – | – |
| 1977 | 10,008 | 5,813 | 14,988 | 14,064 | 14,399 | 11,512 | 7,865 | – | – |
| 1976 | 9,662 | 5,426 | 14,515 | 13,937 | 14,404 | 10,954 | 7,609 | – | – |
| 1975 | 9,667 | 5,380 | 14,428 | 13,437 | 14,468 | 11,138 | 7,708 | – | – |
| 1974 | 9,531 | 5,480 | 13,959 | 13,765 | 14,593 | 11,204 | 7,543 | – | – |
| 1973 | 9,508 | – | 14,085 | 13,976 | 14,632 | 11,667 | 7,205 | – | – |
| 1972 | 9,395 | – | 13,755 | 13,961 | 14,702 | 11,600 | 6,865 | – | – |
| 1971 | 8,967 | – | 13,201 | 13,525 | 14,594 | 11,473 | 6,353 | – | – |
| 1970 | 8,693 | – | 12,533 | 13,407 | 14,367 | 11,449 | 5,915 | – | – |
| 1969 | 8,685 | – | 12,221 | 13,186 | 14,494 | 11,369 | 5,691 | – | – |
| 1968 | 8,595 | – | 12,265 | 12,959 | 13,892 | 10,967 | 5,581 | – | – |
| 1967 | 7,963 | – | 11,567 | 12,539 | 13,623 | 10,399 | 4,965 | – | – |
| **Percent change** | | | | | | | | | |
| 1990–97 | 10.8% | 5.3% | 14.2% | 5.0% | 17.5% | 24.5% | 1.9% | 0.8% | 3.2% |
| 1967*–97 | 72.1 | 15.7 | 52.6 | 49.2 | 50.7 | 38.2 | 102.7 | 2.7 | 4.1 |

*\* Or earliest year available.*
*Note: (–) means data not available.*
*Source: Bureau of the Census, Internet web site, <http:// www.census.gov/hhes/income/histinc/index.html>; calculations by New Strategist*

# Incomes of Black Women Have Doubled

## Hispanic women have seen the slowest income growth.

Between 1967 and 1997, the median income of black women grew 102 percent, more than doubling from $6,455 to $13,048. Today, the median income of black women is 95 percent as high as that of white women, while it was just 79 percent of the white median in 1967. The incomes of black women have been growing rapidly because younger generations of better-educated, career-oriented women are taking advantage of widening opportunities and replacing older women in the workforce.

The median income of Hispanic women has grown only 7 percent since 1972, rising from $9,569 to $10,260, after adjusting for inflation. In 1972, the median income of Hispanic women surpassed that of black women by 8 percent. By 1997, black women were ahead by 27 percent. Behind the sluggish income growth of Hispanic women is the arrival in the United States over the past few decades of millions of poorly educated Hispanic immigrants with little earning power.

✘ The income gap between black and white women is likely to disappear in the next few years, as black income growth continues to outpace gains among whites.

## Black income gain surpasses white

*(percent change in median income of women by race, 1967 to 1997; in 1997 dollars)*

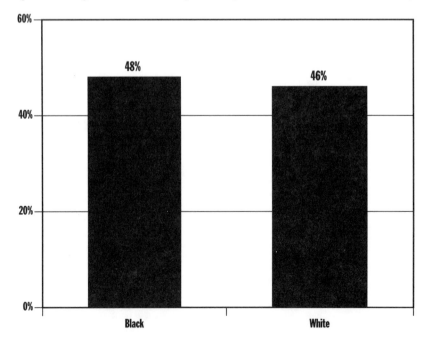

# Median Income of Women by Race and Hispanic Origin, 1967 to 1997

*(median income of women aged 15 or older with income by race and Hispanic origin, 1967 to 1997; percent change in income for selected years; in 1997 dollars)*

| | total women | Asian | black | Hispanic | white | non-Hispanic white |
|---|---|---|---|---|---|---|
| 1997 | $13,703 | $14,312 | $13,048 | $10,260 | $13,792 | $14,389 |
| 1996 | 13,109 | 14,970 | 12,042 | 9,702 | 13,258 | 13,824 |
| 1995 | 12,775 | 13,546 | 11,544 | 9,403 | 12,971 | 13,488 |
| 1994 | 12,418 | 13,388 | 11,419 | 9,328 | 12,595 | 12,936 |
| 1993 | 12,269 | 13,734 | 10,561 | 8,997 | 12,513 | 12,883 |
| 1992 | 12,257 | 13,580 | 10,167 | 9,504 | 12,541 | 12,872 |
| 1991 | 12,345 | 12,993 | 10,389 | 9,443 | 12,634 | 12,964 |
| 1990 | 12,366 | 13,614 | 10,227 | 9,249 | 12,669 | 12,993 |
| 1989 | 12,457 | 14,508 | 10,193 | 9,898 | 12,700 | 12,960 |
| 1988 | 12,053 | 12,542 | 9,971 | 9,483 | 12,350 | 12,639 |
| 1987 | 11,720 | – | 9,818 | 9,367 | 12,019 | 12,289 |
| 1986 | 11,144 | – | 9,615 | 9,281 | 11,364 | 11,556 |
| 1985 | 10,765 | – | 9,363 | 8,980 | 10,974 | 11,095 |
| 1984 | 10,609 | – | 9,522 | 9,006 | 10,735 | 10,906 |
| 1983 | 10,183 | – | 8,932 | 8,705 | 10,347 | – |
| 1982 | 9,884 | – | 8,836 | 8,629 | 10,018 | 10,317 |
| 1981 | 9,723 | – | 8,734 | 9,014 | 9,831 | 10,008 |
| 1980 | 9,595 | – | 8,932 | 8,591 | 9,648 | 9,712 |
| 1979 | 9,439 | – | 8,671 | 9,001 | 9,528 | 9,775 |
| 1978 | 9,673 | – | 8,814 | 9,007 | 9,789 | 10,222 |
| 1977 | 10,008 | – | 8,774 | 9,318 | 10,161 | 10,626 |
| 1976 | 9,662 | – | 9,181 | 9,076 | 9,743 | 10,411 |
| 1975 | 9,667 | – | 8,873 | 9,145 | 9,767 | 10,327 |
| 1974 | 9,531 | – | 8,702 | 9,302 | 9,639 | 10,122 |
| 1973 | 9,508 | – | 8,664 | 9,018 | 9,599 | 9,803 |
| 1972 | 9,395 | – | 8,835 | 9,569 | 9,456 | 9,543 |
| 1971 | 8,967 | – | 7,988 | – | 9,116 | – |
| 1970 | 8,693 | – | 8,017 | – | 8,806 | – |
| 1969 | 8,685 | – | 7,495 | – | 8,889 | – |
| 1968 | 8,595 | – | 7,020 | – | 8,851 | – |
| 1967 | 7,963 | – | 6,455 | – | 8,202 | – |
| **Percent change** | | | | | | |
| 1990–97 | 10.8% | 5.1% | 27.6% | 10.9% | 8.9% | 10.7% |
| 1967*–97 | 72.1 | 14.1 | 102.1 | 7.2 | 68.2 | 50.8 |

*\* Or earliest year available.*
*Note: (–) means data not available.*
*Source: Bureau of the Census, Internet web site, <http:// www.census.gov/hhes/income/histinc/index.html>; calculations by New Strategist*

# Incomes Grew for Women of All Educational Levels

## Those with professional degrees saw the biggest rise.

Between 1991 and 1997, the median income of women aged 25 or older grew 14 percent, after adjusting for inflation, to $15,573. By educational level, income growth was fastest for women with professional degrees (such as lawyers and physicians), up 13 percent during those years.

The slowest income growth by educational level was experienced by the least-educated women—those who did not finish 9th grade saw their median income rise just 1.6 percent between 1991 and 1997. But those with a master's degree saw their income rise only a bit faster—a 2.4 percent gain during those years.

Despite these variations in income growth by educational level, women with college degrees remain far ahead of less-educated women in economic well-being. Those with professional or doctoral degrees had a median income surpassing $45,000 in 1997. In contrast, women who stopped their education with a high school diploma had a median income of just $13,407, while high school drop-outs had a median income of less than $9,000.

✗ The higher incomes of the educated have encouraged millions of women to go to college. Women now make up the majority of college students and earn most college degrees.

### Slow growth for women with master's degrees

*(percent change in median income of women by educational attainment, 1991 to 1997; in 1997 dollars)*

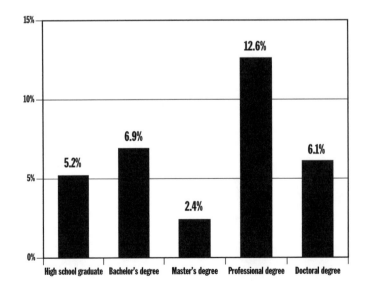

# Median Income of Women by Education, 1991 to 1997

*(median income of women aged 25 or older with income by educational attainment, 1991 to 1997; income in 1997 dollars)*

| | total women | less than 9th grade | 9th to 12th grade | high school graduate | associate's degree | some college | total | bachelor's degree | bachelor's degree or more | | |
| | | | | | | | | | master's degree | professional degree | doctoral degree |
|---|---|---|---|---|---|---|---|---|---|---|---|
| 1997 | $15,573 | $7,505 | $8,861 | $13,407 | $21,073 | $17,153 | $29,781 | $26,401 | $35,882 | $45,199 | $46,545 |
| 1996 | 15,019 | 7,443 | 8,740 | 12,993 | 20,929 | 16,628 | 28,188 | 25,770 | 34,066 | 43,024 | 43,405 |
| 1995 | 14,556 | 7,473 | 8,485 | 12,686 | 20,484 | 16,379 | 28,270 | 25,344 | 35,290 | 40,639 | 41,937 |
| 1994 | 13,826 | 7,435 | 8,250 | 12,335 | 19,444 | 15,795 | 28,415 | 25,348 | 34,731 | 38,778 | 44,179 |
| 1993 | 13,589 | 7,198 | 7,983 | 12,317 | 20,377 | 16,093 | 28,041 | 24,938 | 34,865 | 36,367 | 47,469 |
| 1992 | 13,638 | 7,249 | 8,343 | 12,470 | 19,826 | 16,474 | 28,706 | 25,606 | 34,513 | 41,915 | 44,983 |
| 1991 | 13,646 | 7,386 | 8,314 | 12,748 | 20,462 | 16,454 | 27,842 | 24,708 | 35,054 | 40,141 | 43,886 |
| **Percent change** | | | | | | | | | | | |
| 1991–97 | 14.1% | 1.6% | 6.6% | 5.2% | 3.0% | 4.2% | 7.0% | 6.9% | 2.4% | 12.6% | 6.1% |

*Source: Bureau of the Census, Internet web site, <http://www.census.gov/hhes/income/histinc/index.html>; calculations by New Strategist*

# Women in Midwest and South Saw Biggest Gains

## Regional differences in women's incomes have almost disappeared.

Between 1967 and 1997, women's median income rose more than 80 percent in the Midwest and South. Median income climbed a smaller but still substantial 59 percent in the West and 53 percent in the Northeast during those years.

The geographic variations in median income growth have erased much of the income gap by region. In both 1967 and 1997, women's median income was highest in the Northeast and lowest in the South. But in 1967, women's median income in the Northeast was 36 percent higher than that in the South. In 1997, it was only 10 percent greater.

During the 1990s, regional income growth has continued in the same pattern, with women's incomes in the Midwest and South growing faster than those in the Northeast and West. The next few years should see the income gap between regions narrow even more.

✘ Women's incomes have been growing in every region because more women are going to work, and a growing share of those with jobs are working full-time. The healthy Midwestern and Southern economies of the past decade have given women in those regions an additional boost.

### Women's incomes have grown more slowly in the Northeast and West

*(percent change in median income of women by region, 1967 to 1997; in 1997 dollars)*

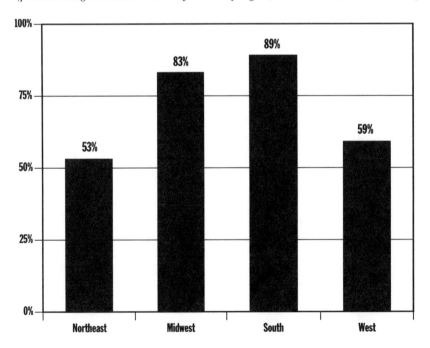

# Median Income of Women by Region, 1967 to 1997

*(median income of women aged 15 or older with income by region, 1967 to 1997; percent change in income for selected years; in 1997 dollars)*

|  | total women | Northeast | Midwest | South | West |
|---|---|---|---|---|---|
| 1997 | $13,703 | $14,333 | $13,899 | $13,036 | $14,002 |
| 1996 | 13,109 | 13,760 | 13,350 | 12,641 | 13,125 |
| 1995 | 12,775 | 13,145 | 13,038 | 12,205 | 13,119 |
| 1994 | 12,418 | 12,956 | 12,532 | 11,847 | 12,776 |
| 1993 | 12,269 | 12,635 | 12,252 | 11,726 | 12,849 |
| 1992 | 12,257 | 12,927 | 12,054 | 11,607 | 12,978 |
| 1991 | 12,345 | 13,018 | 12,019 | 11,847 | 12,934 |
| 1990 | 12,366 | 13,179 | 12,426 | 11,564 | 12,854 |
| 1989 | 12,457 | 13,646 | 11,834 | 11,713 | 13,341 |
| 1988 | 12,053 | 13,039 | 11,259 | 11,429 | 13,159 |
| 1987 | 11,720 | 12,353 | 11,057 | 11,279 | 12,631 |
| 1986 | 11,144 | 11,745 | 10,639 | 10,670 | 11,979 |
| 1985 | 10,765 | 11,251 | 10,222 | 10,136 | 12,105 |
| 1984 | 10,609 | 10,818 | 10,083 | 10,341 | 11,692 |
| 1983 | 10,183 | 10,297 | 9,611 | 9,938 | 11,206 |
| 1982 | 9,884 | 10,031 | 9,422 | 9,533 | 11,089 |
| 1981 | 9,723 | 9,799 | 9,373 | 9,293 | 10,642 |
| 1980 | 9,595 | 9,634 | 9,337 | 9,269 | 10,511 |
| 1979 | 9,439 | 9,804 | 9,205 | 8,715 | 10,231 |
| 1978 | 9,673 | 10,467 | 9,518 | 8,852 | 10,229 |
| 1977 | 10,008 | 10,689 | 9,912 | 9,163 | 10,605 |
| 1976 | 9,662 | 10,278 | 9,716 | 9,019 | 9,970 |
| 1975 | 9,667 | 10,430 | 9,670 | 8,905 | 9,987 |
| 1974 | 9,531 | 10,397 | 9,454 | 8,656 | 9,930 |
| 1973 | 9,508 | 10,337 | 9,470 | 8,572 | 10,021 |
| 1972 | 9,395 | 10,382 | 9,456 | 8,538 | 9,576 |
| 1971 | 8,967 | 10,557 | 8,908 | 7,865 | 9,097 |
| 1970 | 8,693 | 10,197 | 8,418 | 7,702 | 8,857 |
| 1969 | 8,685 | 10,066 | 8,115 | 7,797 | 9,039 |
| 1968 | 8,595 | 9,736 | 8,187 | 7,621 | 9,332 |
| 1967 | 7,963 | 9,365 | 7,592 | 6,884 | 8,825 |
| **Percent change** | | | | | |
| 1990–97 | 10.8% | 8.8% | 11.9% | 12.7% | 8.9% |
| 1967–97 | 72.1 | 53.0 | 83.1 | 89.4 | 58.7 |

*Source: Bureau of the Census, Internet web site, <http:// www.census.gov/hhes/income/histinc/index.html>; calculations by New Strategist*

# Women's Earnings Have Grown Because More Work Full-Time

## Those with full-time jobs have experienced the smallest income gain.

The rapid rise in women's earnings over the past few decades is largely due to the growing share of women with full-time, year-round jobs. Evidence of this can be seen in median income trends by work status.

Women who work full-time, year-round have experienced the slowest income growth over the past three decades. Between 1967 and 1997, women working full-time, year-round saw their median income rise 36 percent. While this is a substantial gain—particularly in comparison to men's—the rise is much smaller than the earnings growth of all women regardless of work status. Among all women with earnings, median earnings climbed fully 61 percent between 1967 and 1997. Behind this higher growth is the growing proportion of women committed to the labor force—and earning higher salaries because of it.

Women with part-time jobs also saw their earnings rise rapidly over the past three decades. The median income of women who work part-time surpasses that of their male counterparts.

✗ The rise in women's earnings is likely to slow in the coming years because most women now are in the labor force. Nevertheless, women's earnings will continue to grow faster than men's as younger, career-oriented women replace older just-a-job women in the labor force.

### Earnings have grown more slowly for women with full-time jobs

*(percent change in median earnings of women by work status, 1967 to 1997; in 1997 dollars)*

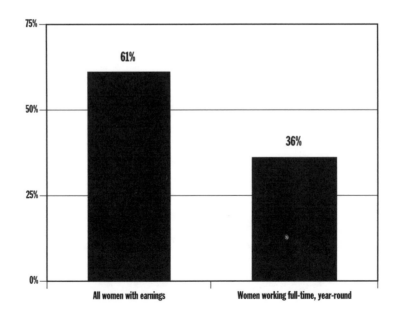

# Median Earnings of Women by Work Experience, 1967 to 1997

*(median earnings of women aged 15 or older with earnings by work experience, 1967 to 1997; percent change in earnings for selected years; in 1997 dollars)*

| | total women who worked | worked full-time | | worked part-time | |
|---|---|---|---|---|---|
| | | total | year-round | total | year-round |
| 1997 | $16,716 | $21,883 | $24,973 | $5,749 | $9,425 |
| 1996 | 16,396 | 21,671 | 24,254 | 5,644 | 9,016 |
| 1995 | 16,136 | 21,445 | 23,693 | 5,322 | 9,222 |
| 1994 | 15,512 | 21,415 | 24,048 | 5,335 | 9,337 |
| 1993 | 15,435 | 21,479 | 24,155 | 5,266 | 8,975 |
| 1992 | 15,475 | 21,439 | 24,453 | 5,334 | 8,804 |
| 1991 | 15,183 | 21,096 | 24,220 | 5,275 | 8,650 |
| 1990 | 15,043 | 20,750 | 24,341 | 5,209 | 8,808 |
| 1989 | 15,191 | 20,970 | 24,294 | 5,048 | 8,719 |
| 1988 | 15,054 | 20,950 | 23,886 | 4,915 | 8,813 |
| 1987 | 15,004 | 20,783 | 23,893 | 4,932 | 8,880 |
| 1986 | 14,668 | 19,975 | 23,770 | 4,610 | 8,923 |
| 1985 | 13,914 | 19,196 | 23,305 | 4,335 | 8,282 |
| 1984 | 13,401 | 18,815 | 22,831 | 4,234 | 8,641 |
| 1983 | 13,262 | 18,864 | 22,423 | 4,441 | 8,473 |
| 1982 | 12,904 | 18,456 | 21,849 | 4,489 | 8,326 |
| 1981 | 12,865 | 18,223 | 21,378 | 4,354 | 8,697 |
| 1980 | 12,918 | 17,973 | 21,836 | 4,353 | 8,368 |
| 1979 | 12,964 | 17,644 | 22,017 | 4,201 | 8,396 |
| 1978 | 12,481 | 17,748 | 22,232 | 3,888 | 8,139 |
| 1977 | 11,870 | 17,340 | 21,886 | 3,649 | 7,997 |
| 1976 | 11,608 | 17,093 | 21,884 | 3,664 | 8,028 |
| 1975 | 11,289 | 16,715 | 21,430 | 3,638 | 7,994 |
| 1974 | 11,019 | 16,706 | 21,555 | 3,334 | 7,802 |
| 1973 | 11,113 | 16,502 | 21,542 | 3,285 | 6,981 |
| 1972 | 11,503 | 16,610 | 21,339 | 3,145 | 7,143 |
| 1971 | 11,120 | 16,229 | 20,828 | 3,046 | 6,535 |
| 1970 | 10,609 | 15,933 | 20,686 | 2,849 | 6,758 |
| 1969 | 10,445 | 15,435 | 20,274 | 2,864 | 6,322 |
| 1968 | 10,694 | 14,947 | 18,975 | 3,427 | 6,505 |
| 1967 | 10,395 | 14,573 | 18,349 | 3,303 | 6,208 |
| **Percent change** | | | | | |
| 1990–97 | 11.1% | 5.5% | 2.6% | 10.4% | 7.0% |
| 1967–97 | 60.8 | 50.2 | 36.1 | 74.1 | 51.8 |

*Note: Earnings include wages and salaries only.*
*Source: Bureau of the Census, Internet web site, <http:// www.census.gov/hhes/income/histinc/index.html>; calculations by New Strategist*

# The Earnings of Black Women Are Growing Fastest

## Since 1990, however, the earnings of Asian women have lead growth.

The median earnings of black women with full-time jobs rose 56 percent between 1967 and 1997, after adjusting for inflation. In contrast, white women with full-time jobs saw their earnings grow a smaller 34 percent during those years. Consequently, the median earnings of black women have been approaching those of white women during most of the past three decades. Among full-time workers in 1967, black women earned only 75 percent as much as white women. By 1997, the figure was 87 percent.

Since 1990, Asian women have experienced the fastest earnings growth among women working full-time—a 6 percent gain. Black and Hispanic women, in contrast, have seen their earnings fall slightly during the 1990s, while the earnings of white and non-Hispanic white women rose. In 1997, Asian women had the highest earnings, a median of $27,781—11 percent higher than the median earnings of all women working full-time.

✘ The declining earnings of black women during the 1990s is causing the income gap between blacks and whites to widen a bit. This trend is likely to be short-lived, however, since the rising educational level of black women should continue to boost their earnings in the years ahead.

## Earnings growth faster for blacks than whites

*(percent change in median earnings of women working
full-time, year-round, by race, 1967 to 1997; in 1997 dollars)*

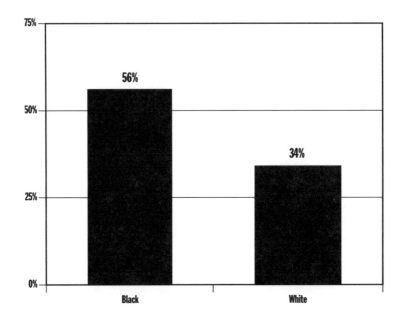

# Median Earnings of Women Who Work Full-Time, by Race and Hispanic Origin, 1967 to 1997

*(median earnings of women aged 15 or older working full-time, year-round, by race and Hispanic origin, 1967 to 1997; percent change in earnings for selected years; in 1997 dollars)*

| | total women | Asian | black | Hispanic | white | non-Hispanic white |
|---|---|---|---|---|---|---|
| 1997 | $24,973 | $27,781 | $22,035 | $18,973 | $25,331 | $25,915 |
| 1996 | 24,254 | 26,141 | 21,966 | 19,093 | 24,714 | 25,461 |
| 1995 | 23,693 | 26,199 | 21,763 | 18,091 | 24,129 | 24,920 |
| 1994 | 24,048 | 26,481 | 21,562 | 19,027 | 24,501 | 25,121 |
| 1993 | 24,155 | 27,041 | 22,010 | 18,614 | 24,462 | 24,861 |
| 1992 | 24,453 | 26,084 | 22,610 | 19,546 | 24,703 | 25,046 |
| 1991 | 24,220 | 24,952 | 22,060 | 19,142 | 24,504 | 24,857 |
| 1990 | 24,341 | 26,186 | 22,153 | 19,245 | 24,619 | 24,998 |
| 1989 | 24,294 | 27,650 | 22,508 | 20,272 | 24,492 | 24,905 |
| 1988 | 23,886 | 26,250 | 22,437 | 20,141 | 24,175 | 24,576 |
| 1987 | 23,893 | – | 22,254 | 20,522 | 24,124 | 24,386 |
| 1986 | 23,770 | – | 21,577 | 20,262 | 24,049 | – |
| 1985 | 23,305 | – | 21,342 | 19,490 | 23,562 | – |
| 1984 | 22,831 | – | 21,194 | 19,379 | 23,023 | – |
| 1983 | 22,423 | – | 20,449 | 18,796 | 22,667 | – |
| 1982 | 21,849 | – | 20,368 | 18,656 | 22,094 | – |
| 1981 | 21,378 | – | 19,949 | 19,112 | 21,569 | – |
| 1980 | 21,836 | – | 20,812 | 18,876 | 21,992 | – |
| 1979 | 22,017 | – | 20,440 | 18,312 | 22,188 | – |
| 1978 | 22,232 | – | 20,974 | 19,201 | 22,411 | – |
| 1977 | 21,886 | – | 20,563 | 19,087 | 22,023 | – |
| 1976 | 21,884 | – | 20,670 | 18,855 | 22,032 | – |
| 1975 | 21,430 | – | 20,668 | 18,366 | 21,456 | – |
| 1974 | 21,555 | – | 20,296 | 18,323 | 21,709 | – |
| 1973 | 21,542 | – | 18,658 | – | 21,878 | – |
| 1972 | 21,339 | – | 18,606 | – | 21,682 | – |
| 1971 | 20,828 | – | 18,672 | – | 21,044 | – |
| 1970 | 20,686 | – | 17,282 | – | 21,032 | – |
| 1969 | 20,274 | – | 16,331 | – | 20,686 | – |
| 1968 | 18,975 | – | 14,845 | – | 19,498 | – |
| 1967 | 18,349 | – | 14,122 | – | 18,920 | – |
| **Percent change** | | | | | | |
| 1990–97 | 2.6% | 6.1% | –0.5% | –1.4% | 2.9% | 3.7% |
| 1967*–97 | 36.1 | 5.8 | 56.0 | 3.5 | 33.9 | 6.3 |

*\* Or earliest year available.*
*Note: Earnings include wages and salaries only. (–) means data not available.*
*Source: Bureau of the Census, Internet web site, <http:// www.census.gov/hhes/income/histinc/index.html>; calculations by New Strategist*

# Women in Most Occupations Have Gained Ground

## Those in blue-collar jobs have experienced income losses.

Among women who work full-time, median earnings rose 14 percent between 1982 and 1997. Earnings in some occupations grew much faster than in others, however.

The median earnings of women managers and professionals grew 14 percent between 1982 and 1997, after adjusting for inflation. In contrast, women in administrative support occupations (including secretaries and other clerical workers) saw a much smaller 5.5 percent rise in median earnings. The few women in protective services experienced an 18.5 percent rise in median earnings, while the median earnings of the handful of women in farming, forestry, and fishing nearly doubled.

Median earnings for women in some occupations fell between 1982 and 1997. Health technologists saw a 4 percent decline in earnings as managed care limited health care spending. Women in blue-collar occupations (precision production, craft, repair and operators, fabricators, laborers) also saw their earnings decline as high-paying manufacturing jobs became harder to find.

✘ While women have enjoyed rapid earnings growth over the past few decades, they are not immune from structural changes in the economy. Because most women work in white-collar occupations, however, they are hurt less than men by the shift from manufacturing to service employment in the U.S.

### Some occupations saw little or no earnings growth

*(percent change in median earnings of women working full-time, year-round by selected occupation, 1982 to 1997; in 1997 dollars)*

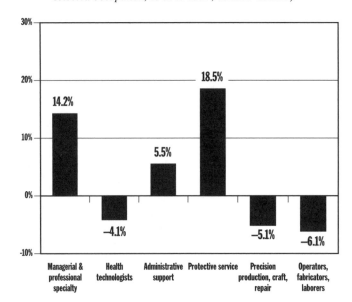

# Median Earnings of Women Who Work Full-Time by Occupation, 1982 to 1997

*(median earnings of women aged 15 or older working full-time, year-round by occupation of longest job held, 1982 to 1997; income in 1997 dollars)*

| | total women | managerial and professional specialty | | | technical, sales, and administrative support | | | | |
|---|---|---|---|---|---|---|---|---|---|
| | | total | executive, administrative & managerial | professional specialty | total | health technologists | technologists, except health | sales | administrative support |
| 1997 | $24,973 | $34,475 | $33,037 | $35,417 | $22,803 | $24,946 | $31,769 | $21,392 | $22,474 |
| 1996 | 24,254 | 33,046 | 31,924 | 35,329 | 22,641 | 25,547 | 32,214 | 21,840 | 22,257 |
| 1995 | 23,693 | 33,435 | 32,263 | 35,071 | 22,563 | 26,414 | 33,420 | 21,357 | 22,265 |
| 1994 | 24,048 | 34,070 | 32,814 | 35,004 | 22,948 | 27,698 | 32,718 | 20,562 | 22,680 |
| 1993 | 24,155 | 34,182 | 32,073 | 35,439 | 23,188 | 28,149 | 32,142 | 20,818 | 22,973 |
| 1992 | 24,453 | 34,025 | 31,380 | 35,723 | 23,267 | 26,131 | 30,803 | 20,357 | 23,196 |
| 1991 | 24,220 | 34,109 | 31,732 | 35,926 | 23,080 | 25,210 | 30,259 | 20,332 | 22,913 |
| 1990 | 24,341 | 33,502 | 31,754 | 35,834 | 23,007 | 28,053 | 32,902 | 20,859 | 22,687 |
| 1989 | 24,294 | 34,088 | 31,835 | 36,163 | 22,751 | 28,462 | 32,122 | 20,783 | 22,664 |
| 1988 | 23,886 | 33,639 | 31,688 | 34,988 | 22,743 | 27,893 | 32,738 | 20,994 | 22,625 |
| 1987 | 23,893 | 32,340 | 30,539 | 34,345 | 22,940 | 25,782 | 30,655 | 20,195 | 22,997 |
| 1986 | 23,770 | 32,731 | 31,385 | 33,793 | 22,719 | 26,427 | 33,526 | 18,973 | 22,712 |
| 1985 | 23,305 | 31,805 | 30,675 | 32,489 | 22,549 | 25,676 | 32,604 | 18,917 | 22,609 |
| 1984 | 22,831 | 31,253 | 29,134 | 32,284 | 22,064 | 27,410 | 31,176 | 18,532 | 22,271 |
| 1983 | 22,423 | 30,434 | 29,452 | 30,943 | 21,790 | 26,507 | 29,673 | 19,304 | 21,711 |
| 1982 | 21,849 | 30,198 | 29,088 | 30,930 | 21,110 | 26,004 | 29,778 | 18,471 | 21,310 |
| Percent change | | | | | | | | | |
| 1982–97 | 14.3% | 14.2% | 13.6% | 14.5% | 8.0% | –4.1% | 6.7% | 15.8% | 5.5% |

*(continued)*

*(continued from previous page)*

| | service occupations | | | farming, forestry, fishing | precision production, craft, and repair | operators, fabricators, laborers |
|---|---|---|---|---|---|---|
| | total | protective service | service except protective and household | | | |
| 1997 | $15,964 | $29,862 | $15,773 | $17,301 | $21,649 | $17,389 |
| 1996 | 15,320 | 28,392 | 15,090 | 17,647 | 21,651 | 17,743 |
| 1995 | 15,246 | 26,254 | 15,065 | 12,514 | 22,477 | 17,182 |
| 1994 | 14,640 | 26,206 | 14,506 | 11,572 | 23,433 | 17,685 |
| 1993 | 14,579 | 30,322 | 14,201 | 11,753 | 23,722 | 17,264 |
| 1992 | 14,746 | 27,904 | 14,369 | 11,508 | 21,705 | 17,981 |
| 1991 | 14,315 | 26,543 | 14,073 | 12,026 | 21,864 | 18,053 |
| 1990 | 14,907 | 27,827 | 14,799 | 12,289 | 23,012 | 17,936 |
| 1989 | 15,108 | 28,023 | 15,122 | 14,633 | 22,596 | 18,751 |
| 1988 | 14,967 | 29,973 | 14,992 | 13,467 | 22,887 | 18,028 |
| 1987 | 15,691 | 26,774 | 15,779 | 11,995 | 21,981 | 18,944 |
| 1986 | 15,182 | 25,106 | 15,226 | 11,762 | 24,617 | 18,138 |
| 1985 | 15,221 | 26,894 | 15,350 | 10,118 | 22,513 | 18,361 |
| 1984 | 14,684 | 25,464 | 14,871 | 7,861 | 21,282 | 18,308 |
| 1983 | 14,870 | 21,724 | 15,088 | 4,280 | 21,344 | 18,243 |
| 1982 | 14,380 | 25,202 | 14,568 | 8,979 | 22,818 | 18,516 |
| **Percent change** | | | | | | |
| 1982–97 | 11.0% | 18.5% | 8.3% | 92.7% | –5.1% | –6.1% |

*Source: Bureau of the Census, Internet web site, <http:// www.census.gov/hhes/income/histinc/index.html>; calculations by New Strategist*

# Women Are Closing the Gap

## Women's earnings have grown much faster than men's over the past three decades.

Between 1967 and 1997, the median earnings of women with full-time jobs rose 36 percent, after adjusting for inflation. In contrast, the median earnings of men working full-time rose just 6 percent. Consequently, the earnings gap between women and men narrowed considerably. In 1967, women earned just 58 percent of what men earned. By 1997, they earned 74 percent as much as men.

The median earnings of women who work full-time stood at $24,973 in 1997, compared to a median of $33,674 for men. Men earned $13,406 more than women in 1967, a difference that fell to just $8,701 by 1997.

✘ Women's earnings are lower than men's largely because of differences in the characteristics of male and female workers—the average male worker continues to be older and better educated than the average female worker. These differences are disappearing as younger generations replace older ones in the work-force, narrowing the earnings gap.

## Women are catching up to men

*(women's median earnings as a percentage of men's median earnings for full-time, year-round workers, 1967 to 1997)*

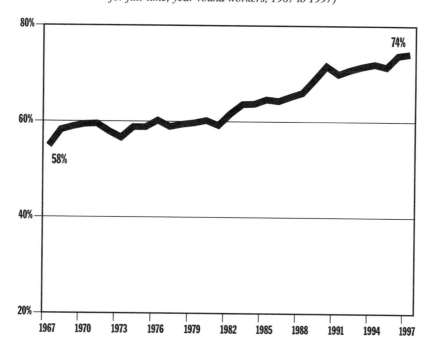

# Women's Earnings as a Percentage of Men's Earnings, 1967 to 1997

*(median earnings of people aged 15 or older working full-time, year-round by sex, and women's earnings as a percentage of men's earnings, 1967 to 1997; in 1997 dollars)*

| | men | women | women's earnings as a percentage of men's earnings |
|---|---|---|---|
| 1997 | $33,674 | $24,973 | 74.2% |
| 1996 | 32,882 | 24,254 | 73.8 |
| 1995 | 33,170 | 23,693 | 71.4 |
| 1994 | 33,415 | 24,048 | 72.0 |
| 1993 | 33,774 | 24,155 | 71.5 |
| 1992 | 34,545 | 24,453 | 70.8 |
| 1991 | 34,670 | 24,220 | 69.9 |
| 1990 | 33,989 | 24,341 | 71.6 |
| 1989 | 35,376 | 24,294 | 68.7 |
| 1988 | 36,165 | 23,886 | 66.0 |
| 1987 | 36,658 | 23,893 | 65.2 |
| 1986 | 36,985 | 23,770 | 64.3 |
| 1985 | 36,090 | 23,305 | 64.6 |
| 1984 | 35,866 | 22,831 | 63.7 |
| 1983 | 35,260 | 22,423 | 63.6 |
| 1982 | 35,386 | 21,849 | 61.7 |
| 1981 | 36,090 | 21,378 | 59.2 |
| 1980 | 36,297 | 21,836 | 60.2 |
| 1979 | 36,902 | 22,017 | 59.7 |
| 1978 | 37,402 | 22,232 | 59.4 |
| 1977 | 37,144 | 21,886 | 58.9 |
| 1976 | 36,356 | 21,884 | 60.2 |
| 1975 | 36,435 | 21,430 | 58.8 |
| 1974 | 36,686 | 21,555 | 58.8 |
| 1973 | 38,037 | 21,542 | 56.6 |
| 1972 | 36,879 | 21,339 | 57.9 |
| 1971 | 35,001 | 20,828 | 59.5 |
| 1970 | 34,844 | 20,686 | 59.4 |
| 1969 | 34,442 | 20,274 | 58.9 |
| 1968 | 32,628 | 18,975 | 58.2 |
| 1967 | 31,755 | 18,349 | 57.8 |
| **Percent change** | | | |
| 1990–97 | –0.9% | 2.6% | – |
| 1967–97 | 6.0 | 36.1 | – |

*Note: Earnings include wages and salaries only.*
*Source: Bureau of the Census, Internet web site, <http:// www.census.gov/hhes/income/histinc/index.html>; calculations by New Strategist*

# Many Wives Earn More Than Their Husbands

## More than 7 million wives are primary breadwinners.

Among the nation's 33 million dual-earner couples, 7.4 million wives earn more than their husbands—accounting for a substantial 23 percent (or nearly one in four) of all dual-earner couples. In 1997, 60 percent of all married couples were dual earners, up from 52 percent in 1981.

Only 16 percent of wives earned more than their husbands in 1981, numbering just over 4 million. The number of wives with higher earnings grew fully 82 percent between 1981 and 1997. This is much faster than the 27 percent growth in all dual-earner couples during those years.

✘ The number and proportion of wives who earn more than their husbands are likely to continue their steady climb, especially as younger generations replace older ones in the population. Today's young women are more educated than their male counterparts, suggesting higher earnings for more wives in the years ahead.

## More wives are breadwinners

*(percent of dual-earner couples in which wives earn more than husbands, 1981 to 1997)*

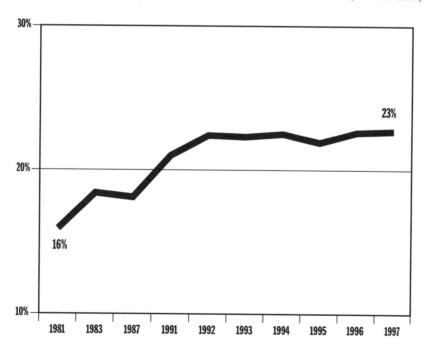

## Wives Who Earn More Than Their Husbands, 1981 to 1997

*(number of married couples, dual-earner couples, and wives who earn more than their husbands; women who earn more than their husbands as a percent of all dual-earner couples, 1981 to 1997; percent change, 1981–1997; numbers in thousands as of the following year)*

|  | total married couples | dual-earner couples | wives who earn more than their husbands | percent of dual-earner couples with wives who earn more |
|---|---|---|---|---|
| 1997 | 54,321 | 32,745 | 7,446 | 22.7% |
| 1996 | 53,604 | 32,390 | 7,327 | 22.6 |
| 1995 | 53,570 | 32,030 | 7,028 | 21.9 |
| 1994 | 53,865 | 32,093 | 7,218 | 22.5 |
| 1993 | 53,181 | 31,267 | 6,960 | 22.3 |
| 1992 | 53,171 | 31,224 | 6,979 | 22.4 |
| 1991 | 52,457 | 31,003 | 6,499 | 21.0 |
| 1987 | 51,809 | 29,079 | 5,266 | 18.1 |
| 1983 | 50,090 | 26,120 | 4,800 | 18.4 |
| 1981 | 49,630 | 25,744 | 4,088 | 15.9 |
| **Percent change** | | | | |
| 1981–97 | 9.5% | 27.2% | 82.1% | – |

*Source: Bureau of the Census, Internet web site, <http:// www.census.gov/hhes/income/histinc/index.html>; calculations by New Strategist*

# Women's Income, 1997

# Women's Incomes Peak in 45-to-54 Age Group

## Among full-time workers, however, income peaks in the 65-to-74 age group.

The incomes of women peak in the 45-to-54 age group, in part because at that age the percentage of women with full-time jobs is highest, at 53 percent. The median income of women aged 45 to 54 stood at $20,534, 50 percent higher than the $13,703 median income of all women aged 15 or older. Only 35 percent of women aged 15 or older work full-time. Among full-time workers, median income peaks for women aged 65 to 74, at $31,426. Only 5 percent of women in the age group work full-time, however.

Black women are more likely to work full-time than the average woman, and 58 percent of black women aged 45 to 54 hold full-time jobs. The median income of black women peaks in the 45-to-54 age group, at $20,064. Among black women who work full-time, the income peak is in the oldest age group, at $30,414, but fewer than 1 percent of black women aged 75 or older work full-time.

Hispanic women are less likely to work full-time than black or non-Hispanic white women. Consequently, their income does not rise with age. Among Hispanic women who work full-time, median income peaks in the 55-to-64 age group at $22,050.

✘ As women's commitment to the labor force grows, their incomes rise to a peak in middle age, just as men's incomes do. This trend should intensify as younger, career-oriented women replace older, just-a-job women in the years ahead.

### Older women make more

*(median income of women aged 15 or older, by age, 1997)*

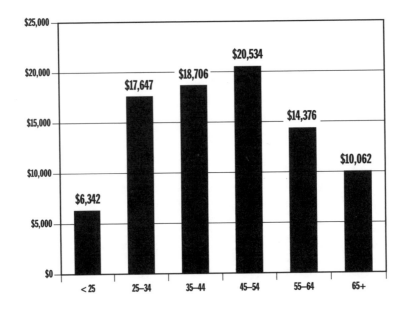

# Distribution of Women by Income and Age, 1997: Total Women

*(number and percent distribution of women aged 15 or older by income and age, 1997; median income of women with income and of women working full-time, year-round; percent working full-time, year-round; women in thousands as of 1998)*

| | total | 15–24 | 25–34 | 35–44 | 45–54 | 55–64 | aged 65 or older total | 65–74 | 75+ |
|---|---|---|---|---|---|---|---|---|---|
| **Total women** | 108,168 | 18,333 | 19,828 | 22,407 | 17,459 | 11,582 | 18,558 | 9,882 | 8,677 |
| Without income | 10,721 | 4,707 | 1,747 | 1,598 | 1,228 | 976 | 465 | 311 | 155 |
| With income | 97,447 | 13,626 | 18,081 | 20,809 | 16,231 | 10,607 | 18,093 | 9,571 | 8,522 |
| Under $5,000 | 18,456 | 5,705 | 3,004 | 3,364 | 2,249 | 1,930 | 2,205 | 1,290 | 915 |
| $5,000 to $9,999 | 19,077 | 3,331 | 2,345 | 2,657 | 1,909 | 2,049 | 6,786 | 3,438 | 3,348 |
| $10,000 to $14,999 | 14,123 | 1,918 | 2,407 | 2,606 | 1,924 | 1,476 | 3,791 | 1,760 | 2,031 |
| $15,000 to $19,999 | 10,600 | 1,179 | 2,315 | 2,250 | 1,808 | 1,144 | 1,904 | 1,044 | 860 |
| $20,000 to $24,999 | 8,872 | 677 | 2,258 | 2,176 | 1,746 | 929 | 1,088 | 628 | 459 |
| $25,000 to $29,999 | 6,387 | 308 | 1,657 | 1,783 | 1,269 | 674 | 696 | 395 | 300 |
| $30,000 to $34,999 | 5,426 | 223 | 1,396 | 1,463 | 1,268 | 666 | 411 | 267 | 144 |
| $35,000 to $39,999 | 3,595 | 92 | 807 | 1,183 | 926 | 345 | 241 | 139 | 102 |
| $40,000 to $44,999 | 2,627 | 64 | 535 | 840 | 665 | 308 | 214 | 149 | 65 |
| $45,000 to $49,999 | 1,984 | 22 | 366 | 630 | 585 | 216 | 166 | 114 | 51 |
| $50,000 to $54,999 | 1,631 | 52 | 293 | 491 | 474 | 226 | 95 | 51 | 44 |
| $55,000 to $59,999 | 1,005 | 15 | 148 | 273 | 310 | 162 | 95 | 57 | 40 |
| $60,000 to $64,999 | 768 | 10 | 133 | 246 | 224 | 85 | 70 | 51 | 19 |
| $65,000 to $69,999 | 546 | 4 | 103 | 161 | 172 | 63 | 43 | 25 | 17 |
| $70,000 to $74,999 | 400 | 10 | 38 | 105 | 131 | 56 | 59 | 29 | 30 |
| $75,000 to $79,999 | 305 | – | 41 | 85 | 123 | 32 | 24 | 18 | 6 |
| $80,000 to $84,999 | 235 | 3 | 42 | 82 | 59 | 33 | 19 | 12 | 6 |
| $85,000 to $89,999 | 193 | 2 | 29 | 71 | 47 | 23 | 21 | 11 | 11 |
| $90,000 to $94,999 | 160 | – | 23 | 44 | 43 | 32 | 16 | 10 | 5 |
| $95,000 to $99,999 | 133 | – | 19 | 27 | 40 | 16 | 32 | 15 | 16 |
| $100,000 or more | 922 | 11 | 120 | 274 | 258 | 141 | 118 | 67 | 50 |
| **Median income** | | | | | | | | | |
| Women with income | $13,703 | $6,342 | $17,647 | $18,706 | $20,534 | $14,376 | $10,062 | $10,141 | $9,996 |
| Women working full-time | $26,029 | $16,290 | $25,144 | $27,524 | $29,364 | $26,661 | $30,359 | $31,426 | $26,917 |
| Percent working full-time | 34.9% | 16.8% | 48.9% | 49.7% | 52.7% | 34.6% | 3.3% | 5.2% | 1.2% |
| **Percent distribution** | | | | | | | | | |
| **Total women** | 100.0% | 100.0% | 100.0% | 100.0% | 100.0% | 100.0% | 100.0% | 100.0% | 100.0% |
| Without income | 9.9 | 25.7 | 8.8 | 7.1 | 7.0 | 8.4 | 2.5 | 3.1 | 1.8 |
| With income | 90.1 | 74.3 | 91.2 | 92.9 | 93.0 | 91.6 | 97.5 | 96.9 | 98.2 |
| Under $25,000 | 65.8 | 69.9 | 62.2 | 58.3 | 55.2 | 65.0 | 85.0 | 82.6 | 87.7 |
| $25,000 to $49,999 | 18.5 | 3.9 | 24.0 | 26.3 | 27.0 | 19.1 | 9.3 | 10.8 | 7.6 |
| $50,000 to $74,999 | 4.0 | 0.5 | 3.6 | 5.7 | 7.5 | 5.1 | 2.0 | 2.2 | 1.7 |
| $75,000 to $99,999 | 0.9 | – | 0.8 | 1.4 | 1.8 | 1.2 | 0.6 | 0.7 | 0.5 |
| $100,000 or more | 0.9 | 0.1 | 0.6 | 1.2 | 1.5 | 1.2 | 0.6 | 0.7 | 0.6 |

*Note: (–) means sample is too small to make a reliable estimate.*
*Source: Bureau of the Census, Internet web site, <http:// www.census.gov/cps/ads/sdata.htm>; calculations by New Strategist*

# Distribution of Women by Income and Age, 1997: Black Women

*(number and percent distribution of black women aged 15 or older by income and age, 1997; median income of women with income and of women working full-time, year-round; percent working full-time, year-round; women in thousands as of 1998)*

| | total | 15–24 | 25–34 | 35–44 | 45–54 | 55–64 | aged 65 or older total | 65–74 | 75+ |
|---|---|---|---|---|---|---|---|---|---|
| **Total women** | **13,715** | **2,916** | **2,910** | **2,982** | **2,028** | **1,255** | **1,623** | **956** | **668** |
| Without income | 1,754 | 960 | 202 | 229 | 189 | 105 | 68 | 57 | 11 |
| With income | 11,961 | 1,957 | 2,708 | 2,753 | 1,838 | 1,150 | 1,555 | 898 | 657 |
| Under $5,000 | 2,046 | 785 | 362 | 331 | 155 | 164 | 248 | 138 | 111 |
| $5,000 to $9,999 | 2,779 | 569 | 466 | 439 | 239 | 311 | 754 | 398 | 355 |
| $10,000 to $14,999 | 1,661 | 238 | 402 | 338 | 254 | 163 | 266 | 156 | 110 |
| $15,000 to $19,999 | 1,497 | 168 | 436 | 415 | 267 | 129 | 82 | 62 | 19 |
| $20,000 to $24,999 | 1,201 | 92 | 388 | 315 | 223 | 100 | 83 | 60 | 22 |
| $25,000 to $29,999 | 745 | 41 | 221 | 237 | 152 | 60 | 32 | 20 | 13 |
| $30,000 to $34,999 | 663 | 35 | 169 | 231 | 145 | 60 | 24 | 12 | 11 |
| $35,000 to $39,999 | 390 | 10 | 97 | 141 | 108 | 28 | 5 | 5 | – |
| $40,000 to $44,999 | 267 | 6 | 40 | 105 | 66 | 27 | 24 | 20 | 4 |
| $45,000 to $49,999 | 201 | – | 32 | 68 | 71 | 26 | 4 | 4 | – |
| $50,000 to $54,999 | 191 | 5 | 35 | 41 | 53 | 42 | 13 | 6 | 7 |
| $55,000 to $59,999 | 91 | 6 | 8 | 31 | 35 | 7 | 3 | – | 3 |
| $60,000 to $64,999 | 55 | – | 11 | 16 | 20 | 4 | 3 | 3 | – |
| $65,000 to $69,999 | 50 | – | 14 | 11 | 17 | 3 | 6 | 6 | – |
| $70,000 to $74,999 | 27 | – | 4 | 13 | 4 | 7 | – | – | – |
| $75,000 to $79,999 | 16 | – | 3 | 5 | 2 | 6 | – | – | – |
| $80,000 to $84,999 | 16 | 3 | 3 | 3 | 6 | 1 | – | – | – |
| $85,000 to $89,999 | 21 | – | – | 8 | 8 | 5 | – | – | – |
| $90,000 to $94,999 | 2 | – | – | 1 | – | 1 | – | – | – |
| $95,000 to $99,999 | 2 | – | – | – | – | – | 2 | 2 | – |
| $100,000 or more | 41 | – | 16 | 6 | 10 | 5 | 4 | 4 | – |
| **Median income** | | | | | | | | | |
| Women with income | $13,048 | $6,254 | $16,400 | $17,681 | $20,064 | $12,447 | $7,874 | $8,433 | $7,366 |
| Women working full-time | $22,764 | $16,838 | $21,863 | $24,227 | $26,054 | $23,494 | $25,953 | $25,705 | $30,414 |
| Percent working full-time | 38.7% | 14.9% | 52.3% | 56.4% | 57.9% | 36.2% | 2.8% | 4.2% | 0.7% |
| **Percent distribution** | | | | | | | | | |
| **Total women** | **100.0%** | **100.0%** | **100.0%** | **100.0%** | **100.0%** | **100.0%** | **100.0%** | **100.0%** | **100.0%** |
| Without income | 12.8 | 32.9 | 6.9 | 7.7 | 9.3 | 8.4 | 4.2 | 6.0 | 1.6 |
| With income | 87.2 | 67.1 | 93.1 | 92.3 | 90.6 | 91.6 | 95.8 | 93.9 | 98.4 |
| Under $25,000 | 67.0 | 63.5 | 70.6 | 61.6 | 56.1 | 69.1 | 88.3 | 85.1 | 92.4 |
| $25,000 to $49,999 | 16.5 | 3.2 | 19.2 | 26.2 | 26.7 | 16.0 | 5.5 | 6.4 | 4.2 |
| $50,000 to $74,999 | 3.0 | 0.4 | 2.5 | 3.8 | 6.4 | 5.0 | 1.5 | 1.6 | 1.5 |
| $75,000 to $99,999 | 0.4 | 0.1 | 0.2 | 0.6 | 0.8 | 1.0 | 0.1 | 0.2 | – |
| $100,000 or more | 0.3 | – | 0.5 | 0.2 | 0.5 | 0.4 | 0.2 | 0.4 | – |

*Note: (–) means sample is too small to make a reliable estimate.*
*Source: Bureau of the Census, Internet web site, <http:// www.census.gov/cps/ads/sdata.htm>; calculations by New Strategist*

# Distribution of Women by Income and Age, 1997: Hispanic Women

*(number and percent distribution of Hispanic women aged 15 or older by income and age, 1997; median income of women with income and of women working full-time, year-round; percent working full-time, year-round; women in thousands as of 1998)*

| | total | 15–24 | 25–34 | 35–44 | 45–54 | 55–64 | aged 65 or older total | 65–74 | 75+ |
|---|---|---|---|---|---|---|---|---|---|
| **Total women** | **10,485** | **2,496** | **2,569** | **2,241** | **1,377** | **865** | **937** | **586** | **351** |
| Without income | 2,430 | 975 | 582 | 387 | 237 | 174 | 74 | 50 | 24 |
| With income | 8,055 | 1,520 | 1,988 | 1,854 | 1,140 | 691 | 863 | 536 | 327 |
| Under $5,000 | 1,959 | 667 | 389 | 328 | 179 | 170 | 226 | 148 | 77 |
| $5,000 to $9,999 | 1,975 | 390 | 374 | 370 | 237 | 191 | 413 | 237 | 176 |
| $10,000 to $14,999 | 1,384 | 233 | 378 | 336 | 220 | 94 | 123 | 76 | 46 |
| $15,000 to $19,999 | 826 | 120 | 253 | 224 | 136 | 54 | 38 | 24 | 15 |
| $20,000 to $24,999 | 589 | 56 | 206 | 131 | 120 | 52 | 24 | 20 | 3 |
| $25,000 to $29,999 | 384 | 20 | 128 | 126 | 51 | 39 | 18 | 15 | 3 |
| $30,000 to $34,999 | 284 | 10 | 103 | 77 | 55 | 28 | 12 | 7 | 5 |
| $35,000 to $39,999 | 218 | 13 | 56 | 80 | 49 | 17 | 4 | 4 | – |
| $40,000 to $44,999 | 132 | 5 | 33 | 54 | 23 | 13 | 3 | 3 | – |
| $45,000 to $49,999 | 91 | 2 | 18 | 50 | 16 | 6 | – | – | – |
| $50,000 to $54,999 | 58 | 2 | 14 | 21 | 14 | 6 | 2 | 2 | – |
| $55,000 to $59,999 | 42 | – | 9 | 17 | 15 | 3 | – | – | – |
| $60,000 to $64,999 | 19 | – | 1 | 9 | 8 | 1 | – | – | – |
| $65,000 to $69,999 | 18 | – | 6 | 6 | 5 | – | – | – | – |
| $70,000 to $74,999 | 13 | – | 1 | 4 | 1 | 6 | – | – | – |
| $75,000 to $79,999 | 7 | – | 1 | 3 | 3 | – | – | – | – |
| $80,000 to $84,999 | 10 | – | 4 | 4 | 1 | 2 | – | – | – |
| $85,000 to $89,999 | 2 | – | – | 1 | – | 2 | – | – | – |
| $90,000 to $94,999 | 10 | – | 7 | 1 | – | 1 | – | – | – |
| $95,000 to $99,999 | 2 | – | – | – | – | 2 | – | – | – |
| $100,000 or more | 29 | – | 8 | 12 | 5 | 3 | 1 | 1 | – |
| **Median income** | | | | | | | | | |
| Women with income | $10,260 | $5,920 | $12,363 | $12,461 | $12,923 | $9,460 | $6,859 | $6,849 | $6,873 |
| Women working full-time | $19,676 | $13,823 | $20,404 | $20,988 | $20,693 | $22,050 | $14,905 | $20,125 | $11,931 |
| Percent working full-time | 30.0% | 14.3% | 37.8% | 41.8% | 42.7% | 29.1% | 4.2% | 5.3% | 2.0% |
| **Percent distribution** | | | | | | | | | |
| **Total women** | **100.0%** | **100.0%** | **100.0%** | **100.0%** | **100.0%** | **100.0%** | **100.0%** | **100.0%** | **100.0%** |
| Without income | 23.2 | 39.1 | 22.7 | 17.3 | 17.2 | 20.1 | 7.9 | 8.5 | 6.8 |
| With income | 76.8 | 60.9 | 77.4 | 82.7 | 82.8 | 79.9 | 92.1 | 91.5 | 93.2 |
| Under $25,000 | 64.2 | 58.7 | 62.3 | 62.0 | 64.8 | 64.9 | 87.9 | 86.2 | 90.3 |
| $25,000 to $49,999 | 10.6 | 2.0 | 13.2 | 17.3 | 14.1 | 11.9 | 3.9 | 4.9 | 2.3 |
| $50,000 to $74,999 | 1.4 | 0.1 | 1.2 | 2.5 | 3.1 | 1.8 | 0.2 | 0.3 | – |
| $75,000 to $99,999 | 0.3 | – | 0.5 | 0.4 | 0.3 | 0.8 | – | – | – |
| $100,000 or more | 0.3 | – | 0.3 | 0.5 | 0.4 | 0.3 | 0.1 | 0.2 | – |

*Note: (–) means sample is too small to make a reliable estimate.*
*Source: Bureau of the Census, Internet web site, <http:// www.census.gov/cps/ads/sdata.htm>; calculations by New Strategist*

# Distribution of Women by Income and Age, 1997: White Women

*(number and percent distribution of white women aged 15 or older by income and age, 1997; median income of women with income and of women working full-time, year-round; percent working full-time, year-round; women in thousands as of 1998)*

| | total | 15–24 | 25–34 | 35–44 | 45–54 | 55–64 | aged 65 or older total | 65–74 | 75+ |
|---|---|---|---|---|---|---|---|---|---|
| **Total women** | **89,489** | **14,473** | **15,786** | **18,272** | **14,587** | **9,882** | **16,490** | **8,651** | **7,839** |
| Without income | 8,137 | 3,414 | 1,386 | 1,264 | 938 | 801 | 335 | 199 | 136 |
| With income | 81,352 | 11,059 | 14,399 | 17,007 | 13,650 | 9,081 | 16,155 | 8,452 | 7,703 |
| Under $5,000 | 15,501 | 4,639 | 2,468 | 2,860 | 1,975 | 1,676 | 1,884 | 1,105 | 779 |
| $5,000 to $9,999 | 15,597 | 2,613 | 1,772 | 2,090 | 1,582 | 1,673 | 5,867 | 2,955 | 2,911 |
| $10,000 to $14,999 | 11,889 | 1,588 | 1,895 | 2,112 | 1,548 | 1,269 | 3,478 | 1,572 | 1,906 |
| $15,000 to $19,999 | 8,727 | 977 | 1,760 | 1,740 | 1,482 | 975 | 1,792 | 958 | 834 |
| $20,000 to $24,999 | 7,333 | 563 | 1,757 | 1,782 | 1,442 | 796 | 992 | 562 | 431 |
| $25,000 to $29,999 | 5,395 | 254 | 1,368 | 1,460 | 1,085 | 589 | 640 | 361 | 279 |
| $30,000 to $34,999 | 4,503 | 183 | 1,156 | 1,168 | 1,046 | 573 | 378 | 250 | 128 |
| $35,000 to $39,999 | 3,051 | 80 | 671 | 976 | 782 | 312 | 230 | 133 | 97 |
| $40,000 to $44,999 | 2,223 | 56 | 459 | 684 | 560 | 278 | 188 | 128 | 60 |
| $45,000 to $49,999 | 1,676 | 20 | 292 | 522 | 494 | 190 | 159 | 109 | 50 |
| $50,000 to $54,999 | 1,362 | 45 | 229 | 428 | 409 | 168 | 83 | 46 | 37 |
| $55,000 to $59,999 | 881 | 9 | 132 | 231 | 268 | 153 | 88 | 52 | 36 |
| $60,000 to $64,999 | 671 | 10 | 114 | 208 | 201 | 74 | 66 | 48 | 18 |
| $65,000 to $69,999 | 458 | 3 | 80 | 139 | 145 | 57 | 36 | 20 | 17 |
| $70,000 to $74,999 | 356 | 8 | 34 | 83 | 122 | 49 | 59 | 29 | 30 |
| $75,000 to $79,999 | 276 | – | 37 | 78 | 116 | 23 | 20 | 14 | 6 |
| $80,000 to $84,999 | 206 | – | 33 | 74 | 51 | 31 | 19 | 12 | 6 |
| $85,000 to $89,999 | 150 | 2 | 18 | 53 | 38 | 18 | 21 | 11 | 11 |
| $90,000 to $94,999 | 154 | – | 23 | 43 | 43 | 29 | 16 | 10 | 5 |
| $95,000 to $99,999 | 119 | – | 10 | 27 | 36 | 16 | 29 | 13 | 16 |
| $100,000 or more | 826 | 11 | 91 | 250 | 227 | 135 | 111 | 63 | 48 |
| **Median income** | | | | | | | | | |
| Women with income | $13,792 | $6,412 | $17,876 | $18,952 | $20,688 | $14,640 | $10,403 | $10,452 | $10,362 |
| Women working full-time | $26,470 | $16,207 | $25,678 | $28,176 | $29,895 | $27,074 | $32,002 | $32,976 | $27,406 |
| Percent working full-time | 34.2% | 17.6% | 48.5% | 48.6% | 52.0% | 34.3% | 3.3% | 5.3% | 1.2% |
| **Percent distribution** | | | | | | | | | |
| **Total women** | **100.0%** | **100.0%** | **100.0%** | **100.0%** | **100.0%** | **100.0%** | **100.0%** | **100.0%** | **100.0%** |
| Without income | 9.1 | 23.6 | 8.8 | 6.9 | 6.4 | 8.1 | 2.0 | 2.3 | 1.7 |
| With income | 90.9 | 76.4 | 91.2 | 93.1 | 93.6 | 91.9 | 98.0 | 97.7 | 98.3 |
| Under $25,000 | 66.0 | 71.7 | 61.1 | 57.9 | 55.0 | 64.7 | 85.0 | 82.7 | 82.0 |
| $25,000 to $49,999 | 18.8 | 4.1 | 25.0 | 26.3 | 27.2 | 19.7 | 9.7 | 11.3 | 7.2 |
| $50,000 to $74,999 | 4.2 | 0.5 | 3.7 | 6.0 | 7.8 | 5.1 | 2.0 | 2.3 | 1.4 |
| $75,000 to $99,999 | 1.0 | – | 0.8 | 1.5 | 1.9 | 1.2 | 0.6 | 0.7 | 0.6 |
| $100,000 or more | 0.9 | 0.1 | 0.6 | 1.4 | 1.6 | 1.4 | 0.7 | 0.7 | 0.6 |

*Note: (–) means sample is too small to make a reliable estimate.*
*Source: Bureau of the Census, Internet web site, <http:// www.census.gov/cps/ads/sdata.htm>; calculations by New Strategist*

# Distribution of Women by Income and Age, 1997: Non-Hispanic White Women

*(number and percent distribution of non-Hispanic white women aged 15 or older by income and age, 1997; median income of women with income and of women working full-time, year-round; percent working full-time, year-round; women in thousands as of 1998)*

| | total | 15–24 | 25–34 | 35–44 | 45–54 | 55–64 | aged 65 or older total | 65–74 | 75+ |
|---|---|---|---|---|---|---|---|---|---|
| **Total women** | **79,502** | **12,093** | **13,347** | **16,141** | **13,289** | **9,040** | **15,592** | **8,091** | **7,501** |
| Without income | 5,793 | 2,474 | 819 | 889 | 717 | 629 | 264 | 151 | 114 |
| With income | 73,709 | 9,619 | 12,528 | 15,252 | 12,573 | 8,411 | 15,327 | 7,940 | 7,387 |
| Under $5,000 | 13,604 | 3,997 | 2,090 | 2,544 | 1,799 | 1,510 | 1,664 | 963 | 702 |
| $5,000 to $9,999 | 13,732 | 2,250 | 1,416 | 1,742 | 1,360 | 1,490 | 5,473 | 2,731 | 2,742 |
| $10,000 to $14,999 | 10,576 | 1,372 | 1,537 | 1,790 | 1,336 | 1,178 | 3,361 | 1,501 | 1,861 |
| $15,000 to $19,999 | 7,947 | 862 | 1,522 | 1,529 | 1,357 | 922 | 1,754 | 934 | 820 |
| $20,000 to $24,999 | 6,772 | 509 | 1,569 | 1,654 | 1,326 | 743 | 971 | 542 | 428 |
| $25,000 to $29,999 | 5,037 | 234 | 1,251 | 1,343 | 1,034 | 551 | 622 | 346 | 276 |
| $30,000 to $34,999 | 4,253 | 173 | 1,071 | 1,101 | 997 | 545 | 366 | 245 | 122 |
| $35,000 to $39,999 | 2,843 | 67 | 615 | 903 | 736 | 295 | 226 | 129 | 97 |
| $40,000 to $44,999 | 2,099 | 50 | 429 | 632 | 537 | 266 | 184 | 125 | 60 |
| $45,000 to $49,999 | 1,588 | 18 | 274 | 473 | 480 | 184 | 159 | 109 | 50 |
| $50,000 to $54,999 | 1,304 | 42 | 216 | 407 | 396 | 161 | 81 | 44 | 37 |
| $55,000 to $59,999 | 840 | 9 | 123 | 214 | 255 | 151 | 88 | 52 | 36 |
| $60,000 to $64,999 | 657 | 10 | 113 | 203 | 193 | 72 | 66 | 48 | 18 |
| $65,000 to $69,999 | 445 | 3 | 74 | 133 | 143 | 57 | 36 | 20 | 17 |
| $70,000 to $74,999 | 342 | 8 | 33 | 79 | 120 | 43 | 59 | 29 | 30 |
| $75,000 to $79,999 | 269 | – | 36 | 74 | 114 | 23 | 20 | 14 | 6 |
| $80,000 to $84,999 | 195 | – | 29 | 70 | 49 | 30 | 19 | 12 | 6 |
| $85,000 to $89,999 | 149 | 2 | 18 | 53 | 38 | 17 | 21 | 11 | 11 |
| $90,000 to $94,999 | 145 | – | 16 | 42 | 43 | 28 | 16 | 10 | 5 |
| $95,000 to $99,999 | 117 | – | 10 | 27 | 36 | 14 | 29 | 13 | 16 |
| $100,000 or more | 800 | 11 | 83 | 239 | 224 | 134 | 110 | 62 | 48 |
| **Median income** | | | | | | | | | |
| Women with income | $14,389 | $6,508 | $18,960 | $20,049 | $21,366 | $15,147 | $10,672 | $10,794 | $10,574 |
| Women working full-time | $27,149 | $16,542 | $26,319 | $28,997 | $30,484 | $27,449 | $33,373 | $34,019 | $28,620 |
| Percent working full-time | 34.8% | 18.3% | 50.6% | 49.6% | 52.9% | 34.8% | 3.3% | 5.3% | 1.1% |
| **Percent distribution** | | | | | | | | | |
| **Total women** | **100.0%** | **100.0%** | **100.0%** | **100.0%** | **100.0%** | **100.0%** | **100.0%** | **100.0%** | **100.0%** |
| Without income | 7.3 | 20.5 | 6.1 | 5.5 | 5.4 | 7.0 | 1.7 | 1.9 | 1.5 |
| With income | 92.7 | 79.5 | 93.9 | 94.5 | 94.6 | 93.0 | 98.3 | 98.1 | 98.5 |
| Under $25,000 | 66.2 | 74.3 | 60.9 | 57.4 | 54.0 | 64.6 | 84.8 | 82.4 | 87.4 |
| $25,000 to $49,999 | 19.9 | 4.5 | 27.3 | 27.6 | 28.5 | 20.4 | 10.0 | 11.8 | 8.1 |
| $50,000 to $74,999 | 4.5 | 0.6 | 4.2 | 6.4 | 8.3 | 5.4 | 2.1 | 2.4 | 1.8 |
| $75,000 to $99,999 | 1.1 | – | 0.8 | 1.6 | 2.1 | 1.2 | 0.7 | 0.7 | 0.6 |
| $100,000 or more | 1.0 | 0.1 | 0.6 | 1.5 | 1.7 | 1.5 | 0.7 | 0.8 | 0.6 |

*Note: (–) means sample is too small to make a reliable estimate.*

*Source: Bureau of the Census, Internet web site, <http:// www.census.gov/cps/ads/sdata.htm>; calculations by New Strategist*

# Women's Incomes Do Not Vary Much by Race

## The incomes of black women are not far below those of white women.

The median income of black women was 91 percent as high as the median income of non-Hispanic white women in 1997, $13,048 for blacks versus $14,389 for non-Hispanic whites. The median income of Hispanic women was a far lower $10,260.

Black women are more likely to work full-time than Hispanic or non-Hispanic white women, which is one reason why their median income is close to that of non-Hispanic whites. Thirty-nine percent of all black women aged 15 or older work full-time, versus 35 percent of non-Hispanic white women and just 30 percent of Hispanic women.

The income gap between black and white women is larger among full-time workers. Black women who work full-time had a median income of $22,764 in 1997, only 84 percent as high as the $27,149 median income of their non-Hispanic white counterparts. The median income of Hispanic women who work full-time stood at just $19,676 in 1997 because many are recent immigrants with little earning power.

✘ The average black woman is not as well educated as the average non-Hispanic white woman, which in part explains the income gap between them. As black women gain in educational attainment in the years ahead, the income gap should shrink.

### Hispanic women have the lowest incomes

*(median income of women aged 15 or older who work full-time, year-round, by race and Hispanic origin, 1997)*

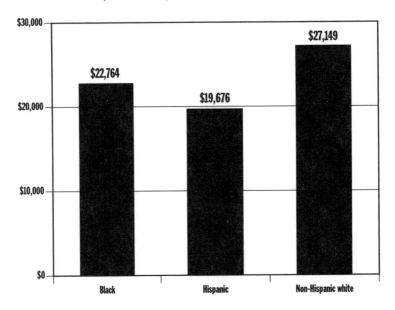

# Distribution of Women by Income, Race, and Hispanic Origin, 1997

*(number and percent distribution of women aged 15 or older by income, race, and Hispanic origin, 1997; median income of women with income and of women working full-time, year-round; percent working full-time, year-round; women in thousands as of 1998)*

| | total | white | black | Hispanic | non-Hispanic white |
|---|---|---|---|---|---|
| **Total women** | **108,168** | **89,489** | **13,715** | **10,485** | **79,502** |
| Without income | 10,721 | 8,137 | 1,754 | 2,430 | 5,793 |
| With income | 97,447 | 81,352 | 11,961 | 8,055 | 73,709 |
| Under $5,000 | 18,456 | 15,501 | 2,046 | 1,959 | 13,604 |
| $5,000 to $9,999 | 19,077 | 15,597 | 2,779 | 1,975 | 13,732 |
| $10,000 to $14,999 | 14,123 | 11,889 | 1,661 | 1,384 | 10,576 |
| $15,000 to $19,999 | 10,600 | 8,727 | 1,497 | 826 | 7,947 |
| $20,000 to $24,999 | 8,872 | 7,333 | 1,201 | 589 | 6,772 |
| $25,000 to $29,999 | 6,387 | 5,395 | 745 | 384 | 5,037 |
| $30,000 to $34,999 | 5,426 | 4,503 | 663 | 284 | 4,253 |
| $35,000 to $39,999 | 3,595 | 3,051 | 390 | 218 | 2,843 |
| $40,000 to $44,999 | 2,627 | 2,223 | 267 | 132 | 2,099 |
| $45,000 to $49,999 | 1,984 | 1,676 | 201 | 91 | 1,588 |
| $50,000 to $54,999 | 1,631 | 1,362 | 191 | 58 | 1,304 |
| $55,000 to $59,999 | 1,005 | 881 | 91 | 42 | 840 |
| $60,000 to $64,999 | 768 | 671 | 55 | 19 | 657 |
| $65,000 to $69,999 | 546 | 458 | 50 | 18 | 445 |
| $70,000 to $74,999 | 400 | 356 | 27 | 13 | 342 |
| $75,000 to $79,999 | 305 | 276 | 16 | 7 | 269 |
| $80,000 to $84,999 | 235 | 206 | 16 | 10 | 195 |
| $85,000 to $89,999 | 193 | 150 | 21 | 2 | 149 |
| $90,000 to $94,999 | 160 | 154 | 2 | 10 | 145 |
| $95,000 to $99,999 | 133 | 119 | 2 | 2 | 117 |
| $100,000 or more | 922 | 826 | 41 | 29 | 800 |
| **Median income** | | | | | |
| Women with income | $13,703 | $13,792 | $13,048 | $10,260 | $14,389 |
| Women working full-time | $26,029 | $26,470 | $22,764 | $19,676 | $27,149 |
| Percent working full-time | 34.9% | 34.2% | 38.7% | 30.0% | 34.8% |
| **Percent distribution** | | | | | |
| **Total women** | **100.0%** | **100.0%** | **100.0%** | **100.0%** | **100.0%** |
| Without income | 9.9 | 9.1 | 12.8 | 23.2 | 7.3 |
| With income | 90.1 | 90.9 | 87.2 | 76.8 | 92.7 |
| Under $25,000 | 65.8 | 66.0 | 67.0 | 64.2 | 66.2 |
| $25,000 to $49,999 | 18.5 | 18.8 | 16.5 | 10.6 | 19.9 |
| $50,000 to $74,999 | 4.0 | 4.2 | 3.0 | 1.4 | 4.5 |
| $75,000 to $99,999 | 0.9 | 1.0 | 0.4 | 0.3 | 1.1 |
| $100,000 or more | 0.9 | 0.9 | 0.3 | 0.3 | 1.0 |

*Note: Numbers will not add to total because Hispanics may be of any race and not all races are shown.*
*Source: Bureau of the Census, Internet web site, <http:// www.census.gov/cps/ads/sdata.htm>; calculations by New Strategist*

# Women in the Northeast Have the Highest Incomes

## For black women, incomes are highest in the West.

The median income of all women aged 15 or older ranges from $13,036 in the South to $14,333 in the Northeast. Among full-time workers, median income ranges from a low of $23,963 in the South to a high of $29,158 in the Northeast. Slightly more than one-third of women work full-time, a percentage that varies little by region.

By race and Hispanic origin, income patterns differ. Among black women, incomes are highest in the West. Black women in the region who work full-time had a median income of $27,635, 91 percent as high as the median income of their non-Hispanic white counterparts in the West. Incomes for black women with full-time jobs are lowest in the South, at $21,469 in 1997.

Among Hispanic women who work full-time, income peaks in the Northeast, at $23,158. This figure is only 77 percent as high as the median income of non-Hispanic white women in the region. Incomes for Hispanic women with full-time jobs are lowest in the West, at $18,798.

✘ As black women gain in educational attainment, their incomes will rise to meet those of non-Hispanic whites. The incomes of Hispanic women will not approach those of non-Hispanic whites until immigrants become a much smaller share of the Hispanic population.

### Women in the South have the lowest incomes

*(median income of women aged 15 or older who work full-time, year-round, by region, 1997)*

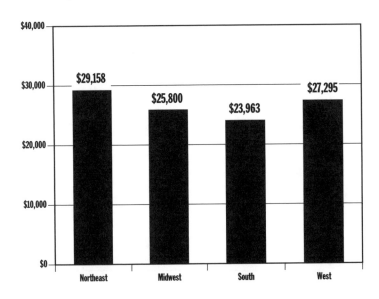

# Distribution of Women by Income and Region, 1997: Total Women

*(number and percent distribution of women aged 15 or older by income and region, 1997; median income of women with income and of women working full-time, year-round; percent working full-time, year-round; women in thousands as of 1998)*

| | total | Northeast | Midwest | South | West |
|---|---|---|---|---|---|
| **Total women** | **108,168** | **21,285** | **25,167** | **38,347** | **23,368** |
| Without income | 10,721 | 2,002 | 1,751 | 4,192 | 2,776 |
| With income | 97,447 | 19,283 | 23,417 | 34,154 | 20,592 |
| Under $5,000 | 18,456 | 3,412 | 4,434 | 6,602 | 4,008 |
| $5,000 to $9,999 | 19,077 | 3,808 | 4,491 | 7,101 | 3,678 |
| $10,000 to $14,999 | 14,123 | 2,717 | 3,389 | 4,931 | 3,085 |
| $15,000 to $19,999 | 10,600 | 1,882 | 2,744 | 3,921 | 2,053 |
| $20,000 to $24,999 | 8,872 | 1,587 | 2,210 | 3,237 | 1,838 |
| $25,000 to $29,999 | 6,387 | 1,335 | 1,556 | 2,195 | 1,302 |
| $30,000 to $34,999 | 5,426 | 1,191 | 1,245 | 1,778 | 1,212 |
| $35,000 to $39,999 | 3,595 | 754 | 804 | 1,170 | 869 |
| $40,000 to $44,999 | 2,627 | 598 | 670 | 782 | 577 |
| $45,000 to $49,999 | 1,984 | 487 | 496 | 595 | 406 |
| $50,000 to $54,999 | 1,631 | 377 | 388 | 512 | 356 |
| $55,000 to $59,999 | 1,005 | 193 | 259 | 297 | 256 |
| $60,000 to $64,999 | 768 | 234 | 164 | 200 | 170 |
| $65,000 to $69,999 | 546 | 132 | 115 | 163 | 137 |
| $70,000 to $74,999 | 400 | 97 | 95 | 86 | 123 |
| $75,000 to $79,999 | 305 | 79 | 45 | 88 | 91 |
| $80,000 to $84,999 | 235 | 47 | 42 | 87 | 59 |
| $85,000 to $89,999 | 193 | 65 | 43 | 47 | 39 |
| $90,000 to $94,999 | 160 | 29 | 36 | 43 | 50 |
| $95,000 to $99,999 | 133 | 33 | 24 | 46 | 30 |
| $100,000 or more | 922 | 227 | 169 | 273 | 253 |
| **Median income** | | | | | |
| Women with income | $13,703 | $14,333 | $13,899 | $13,036 | $14,002 |
| Women working full-time | $26,029 | $29,158 | $25,800 | $23,963 | $27,295 |
| Percent working full-time | 34.9% | 33.9% | 35.2% | 36.3% | 32.9% |
| **Percent distribution** | | | | | |
| **Total women** | **100.0%** | **100.0%** | **100.0%** | **100.0%** | **100.0%** |
| Without income | 9.9 | 9.4 | 7.0 | 10.9 | 11.9 |
| With income | 90.1 | 90.6 | 93.0 | 89.1 | 88.1 |
| Under $25,000 | 65.8 | 63.0 | 68.6 | 67.3 | 62.7 |
| $25,000 to $49,999 | 18.5 | 20.5 | 19.0 | 17.0 | 18.7 |
| $50,000 to $74,999 | 4.0 | 4.9 | 4.1 | 3.3 | 4.5 |
| $75,000 to $99,999 | 0.9 | 1.2 | 0.8 | 0.8 | 1.2 |
| $100,000 or more | 0.9 | 1.1 | 0.7 | 0.7 | 1.1 |

*Source: Bureau of the Census, Internet web site, <http:// www.census.gov/cps/ads/sdata.htm>; calculations by New Strategist*

# Distribution of Women by Income and Region, 1997: Black Women

*(number and percent distribution of black women aged 15 or older by income and region, 1997; median income of women with income and of women working full-time, year-round; percent working full-time, year-round; women in thousands as of 1998)*

| | total | Northeast | Midwest | South | West |
|---|---|---|---|---|---|
| **Total women** | **13,715** | **2,583** | **2,453** | **7,576** | **1,102** |
| Without income | 1,754 | 318 | 273 | 1,022 | 141 |
| With income | 11,961 | 2,265 | 2,180 | 6,554 | 962 |
| Under $5,000 | 2,046 | 391 | 372 | 1,177 | 106 |
| $5,000 to $9,999 | 2,779 | 514 | 548 | 1,509 | 208 |
| $10,000 to $14,999 | 1,661 | 307 | 246 | 971 | 137 |
| $15,000 to $19,999 | 1,497 | 242 | 289 | 857 | 109 |
| $20,000 to $24,999 | 1,201 | 191 | 199 | 705 | 106 |
| $25,000 to $29,999 | 745 | 155 | 145 | 385 | 59 |
| $30,000 to $34,999 | 663 | 167 | 105 | 312 | 78 |
| $35,000 to $39,999 | 390 | 67 | 84 | 207 | 32 |
| $40,000 to $44,999 | 267 | 48 | 50 | 132 | 37 |
| $45,000 to $49,999 | 201 | 48 | 45 | 85 | 24 |
| $50,000 to $54,999 | 191 | 57 | 31 | 85 | 18 |
| $55,000 to $59,999 | 91 | 13 | 20 | 51 | 6 |
| $60,000 to $64,999 | 55 | 12 | 17 | 18 | 8 |
| $65,000 to $69,999 | 50 | 14 | 12 | 15 | 9 |
| $70,000 to $74,999 | 27 | 4 | 12 | 6 | 4 |
| $75,000 to $79,999 | 16 | 5 | – | 4 | 8 |
| $80,000 to $84,999 | 16 | 1 | – | 12 | 3 |
| $85,000 to $89,999 | 21 | 13 | 3 | 5 | – |
| $90,000 to $94,999 | 2 | 1 | – | – | 1 |
| $95,000 to $99,999 | 2 | 2 | – | – | – |
| $100,000 or more | 41 | 12 | 2 | 18 | 8 |
| **Median income** | | | | | |
| Women with income | $13,048 | $13,458 | $12,947 | $12,536 | $16,295 |
| Women working full-time | $22,764 | $26,307 | $24,226 | $21,469 | $27,635 |
| Percent working full-time | 38.7% | 35.7% | 37.0% | 40.1% | 40.3% |
| **Percent distribution** | | | | | |
| **Total women** | **100.0%** | **100.0%** | **100.0%** | **100.0%** | **100.0%** |
| Without income | 12.8 | 12.3 | 11.1 | 13.5 | 12.8 |
| With income | 87.2 | 87.7 | 88.9 | 86.5 | 87.3 |
| Under $25,000 | 67.0 | 63.7 | 67.4 | 68.9 | 60.4 |
| $25,000 to $49,999 | 16.5 | 18.8 | 17.5 | 14.8 | 20.9 |
| $50,000 to $74,999 | 3.0 | 3.9 | 3.8 | 2.3 | 4.1 |
| $75,000 to $99,999 | 0.4 | 0.9 | 0.1 | 0.3 | 1.1 |
| $100,000 or more | 0.3 | 0.5 | 0.1 | 0.2 | 0.7 |

*Note: (–) means sample is too small to make a reliable estimate.*
*Source: Bureau of the Census, Internet web site, <http:// www.census.gov/cps/ads/sdata.htm>; calculations by New Strategist*

# Distribution of Women by Income and Region, 1997: Hispanic Women

*(number and percent distribution of Hispanic women aged 15 or older by income and region, 1997; median income of women with income and of women working full-time, year-round; percent working full-time, year-round; women in thousands as of 1998)*

| | total | Northeast | Midwest | South | West |
|---|---|---|---|---|---|
| **Total women** | **10,485** | **1,785** | **703** | **3,590** | **4,407** |
| Without income | 2,430 | 340 | 170 | 777 | 1,143 |
| With income | 8,055 | 1,445 | 533 | 2,813 | 3,264 |
| Under $5,000 | 1,959 | 290 | 133 | 770 | 765 |
| $5,000 to $9,999 | 1,975 | 407 | 100 | 684 | 785 |
| $10,000 to $14,999 | 1,384 | 239 | 87 | 452 | 605 |
| $15,000 to $19,999 | 826 | 140 | 72 | 282 | 332 |
| $20,000 to $24,999 | 589 | 106 | 50 | 183 | 251 |
| $25,000 to $29,999 | 384 | 70 | 32 | 122 | 160 |
| $30,000 to $34,999 | 284 | 70 | 15 | 96 | 102 |
| $35,000 to $39,999 | 218 | 40 | 9 | 81 | 87 |
| $40,000 to $44,999 | 132 | 22 | 8 | 59 | 43 |
| $45,000 to $49,999 | 91 | 14 | 10 | 30 | 37 |
| $50,000 to $54,999 | 58 | 10 | 5 | 13 | 30 |
| $55,000 to $59,999 | 42 | 9 | 2 | 13 | 20 |
| $60,000 to $64,999 | 19 | 8 | 2 | – | 10 |
| $65,000 to $69,999 | 18 | 5 | 2 | 4 | 6 |
| $70,000 to $74,999 | 13 | 4 | 1 | 3 | 4 |
| $75,000 to $79,999 | 7 | 3 | – | 1 | 2 |
| $80,000 to $84,999 | 10 | – | – | 3 | 7 |
| $85,000 to $89,999 | 2 | 1 | 2 | – | – |
| $90,000 to $94,999 | 10 | 3 | – | 1 | 6 |
| $95,000 to $99,999 | 2 | – | – | 2 | – |
| $100,000 or more | 29 | 5 | 2 | 11 | 11 |
| **Median income** | | | | | |
| Women with income | $10,260 | $10,438 | $11,394 | $9,562 | $10,517 |
| Women working full-time | $19,676 | $23,158 | $19,835 | $19,030 | $18,798 |
| Percent working full-time | 30.0% | 29.8% | 29.0% | 30.9% | 29.5% |
| **Percent distribution** | | | | | |
| **Total women** | **100.0%** | **100.0%** | **100.0%** | **100.0%** | **100.0%** |
| Without income | 23.2 | 19.0 | 24.2 | 21.6 | 25.9 |
| With income | 76.8 | 81.0 | 75.8 | 78.4 | 74.1 |
| Under $25,000 | 64.2 | 66.2 | 62.9 | 66.0 | 62.1 |
| $25,000 to $49,999 | 10.6 | 12.1 | 10.5 | 10.8 | 9.7 |
| $50,000 to $74,999 | 1.4 | 2.0 | 1.7 | 0.9 | 1.6 |
| $75,000 to $99,999 | 0.3 | 0.4 | 0.3 | 0.2 | 0.3 |
| $100,000 or more | 0.3 | 0.3 | 0.3 | 0.3 | 0.2 |

*Note: (–) means sample is too small to make a reliable estimate.*
*Source: Bureau of the Census, Internet web site, <http:// www.census.gov/cps/ads/sdata.htm>; calculations by New Strategist*

# Distribution of Women by Income and Region, 1997: White Women

*(number and percent distribution of white women aged 15 or older by income and region, 1997; median income of women with income and of women working full-time, year-round; percent working full-time, year-round; women in thousands as of 1998)*

| | total | Northeast | Midwest | South | West |
|---|---|---|---|---|---|
| **Total women** | **89,489** | **17,980** | **22,164** | **29,814** | **19,531** |
| Without income | 8,137 | 1,535 | 1,411 | 2,967 | 2,224 |
| With income | 81,352 | 16,445 | 20,752 | 26,847 | 17,308 |
| Under $5,000 | 15,501 | 2,888 | 3,954 | 5,230 | 3,428 |
| $5,000 to $9,999 | 15,597 | 3,210 | 3,879 | 5,468 | 3,039 |
| $10,000 to $14,999 | 11,889 | 2,341 | 3,072 | 3,862 | 2,616 |
| $15,000 to $19,999 | 8,727 | 1,581 | 2,406 | 2,999 | 1,741 |
| $20,000 to $24,999 | 7,333 | 1,360 | 1,959 | 2,474 | 1,539 |
| $25,000 to $29,999 | 5,395 | 1,144 | 1,385 | 1,763 | 1,103 |
| $30,000 to $34,999 | 4,503 | 982 | 1,097 | 1,424 | 999 |
| $35,000 to $39,999 | 3,051 | 672 | 709 | 943 | 727 |
| $40,000 to $44,999 | 2,223 | 531 | 607 | 624 | 462 |
| $45,000 to $49,999 | 1,676 | 419 | 442 | 487 | 329 |
| $50,000 to $54,999 | 1,362 | 309 | 352 | 410 | 289 |
| $55,000 to $59,999 | 881 | 178 | 229 | 240 | 235 |
| $60,000 to $64,999 | 671 | 209 | 147 | 176 | 139 |
| $65,000 to $69,999 | 458 | 113 | 93 | 141 | 110 |
| $70,000 to $74,999 | 356 | 93 | 80 | 74 | 108 |
| $75,000 to $79,999 | 276 | 72 | 45 | 81 | 78 |
| $80,000 to $84,999 | 206 | 39 | 42 | 75 | 49 |
| $85,000 to $89,999 | 150 | 49 | 35 | 42 | 25 |
| $90,000 to $94,999 | 154 | 28 | 36 | 41 | 49 |
| $95,000 to $99,999 | 119 | 28 | 22 | 46 | 23 |
| $100,000 or more | 826 | 200 | 161 | 246 | 219 |
| **Median income** | | | | | |
| Women with income | $13,792 | $14,432 | $13,954 | $13,175 | $13,941 |
| Women working full-time | $26,470 | $29,612 | $25,938 | $25,007 | $27,306 |
| Percent working full-time | 34.2% | 33.7% | 34.9% | 35.5% | 32.0% |
| **Percent distribution** | | | | | |
| **Total women** | **100.0%** | **100.0%** | **100.0%** | **100.0%** | **100.0%** |
| Without income | 9.1 | 8.5 | 6.4 | 10.0 | 11.4 |
| With income | 90.9 | 91.5 | 93.6 | 90.0 | 88.6 |
| Under $25,000 | 66.0 | 63.3 | 68.9 | 67.2 | 63.3 |
| $25,000 to $49,999 | 18.8 | 20.8 | 19.1 | 17.6 | 18.5 |
| $50,000 to $74,999 | 4.2 | 5.0 | 4.1 | 3.5 | 4.5 |
| $75,000 to $99,999 | 1.0 | 1.2 | 0.8 | 1.0 | 1.1 |
| $100,000 or more | 0.9 | 1.1 | 0.7 | 0.8 | 1.1 |

*Source: Bureau of the Census, Internet web site, <http:// www.census.gov/cps/ads/sdata.htm>; calculations by New Strategist*

# Distribution of Women by Income and Region, 1997: Non-Hispanic White Women

*(number and percent distribution of non-Hispanic white women aged 15 or older by income and region, 1997; median income of women with income and of women working full-time, year-round; percent working full-time, year-round; women in thousands as of 1998)*

|  | total | Northeast | Midwest | South | West |
|---|---|---|---|---|---|
| **Total women** | **79,502** | **16,442** | **21,499** | **26,324** | **15,237** |
| Without income | 5,793 | 1,232 | 1,246 | 2,217 | 1,098 |
| With income | 73,709 | 15,210 | 20,253 | 24,107 | 14,139 |
| Under $5,000 | 13,604 | 2,634 | 3,824 | 4,468 | 2,678 |
| $5,000 to $9,999 | 13,732 | 2,864 | 3,787 | 4,806 | 2,275 |
| $10,000 to $14,999 | 10,576 | 2,141 | 2,988 | 3,423 | 2,024 |
| $15,000 to $19,999 | 7,947 | 1,458 | 2,341 | 2,724 | 1,424 |
| $20,000 to $24,999 | 6,772 | 1,265 | 1,910 | 2,300 | 1,297 |
| $25,000 to $29,999 | 5,037 | 1,083 | 1,358 | 1,646 | 950 |
| $30,000 to $34,999 | 4,253 | 932 | 1,081 | 1,335 | 905 |
| $35,000 to $39,999 | 2,843 | 634 | 701 | 866 | 642 |
| $40,000 to $44,999 | 2,099 | 515 | 598 | 565 | 421 |
| $45,000 to $49,999 | 1,588 | 408 | 432 | 456 | 292 |
| $50,000 to $54,999 | 1,304 | 299 | 348 | 397 | 259 |
| $55,000 to $59,999 | 840 | 169 | 229 | 227 | 215 |
| $60,000 to $64,999 | 657 | 203 | 146 | 176 | 132 |
| $65,000 to $69,999 | 445 | 113 | 91 | 137 | 103 |
| $70,000 to $74,999 | 342 | 88 | 79 | 71 | 104 |
| $75,000 to $79,999 | 269 | 69 | 45 | 79 | 74 |
| $80,000 to $84,999 | 195 | 39 | 42 | 72 | 43 |
| $85,000 to $89,999 | 149 | 49 | 33 | 42 | 25 |
| $90,000 to $94,999 | 145 | 25 | 36 | 40 | 43 |
| $95,000 to $99,999 | 117 | 28 | 22 | 44 | 23 |
| $100,000 or more | 800 | 195 | 160 | 235 | 210 |
| **Median income** |  |  |  |  |  |
| Women with income | $14,389 | $14,904 | $14,043 | $13,855 | $15,293 |
| Women working full-time | $27,149 | $30,182 | $26,095 | $25,622 | $30,230 |
| Percent working full-time | 34.8% | 34.1% | 35.1% | 36.1% | 32.8% |
| **Percent distribution** |  |  |  |  |  |
| **Total women** | **100.0%** | **100.0%** | **100.0%** | **100.0%** | **100.0%** |
| Without income | 7.3 | 7.5 | 5.8 | 8.4 | 7.2 |
| With income | 92.7 | 92.5 | 94.2 | 91.6 | 92.8 |
| Under $25,000 | 66.2 | 63.0 | 69.1 | 67.3 | 63.6 |
| $25,000 to $49,999 | 19.9 | 21.7 | 19.4 | 18.5 | 21.1 |
| $50,000 to $74,999 | 4.5 | 5.3 | 4.2 | 3.8 | 5.3 |
| $75,000 to $99,999 | 1.1 | 1.3 | 0.8 | 1.1 | 1.4 |
| $100,000 or more | 1.0 | 1.2 | 0.7 | 0.9 | 1.4 |

*Source: Bureau of the Census, Internet web site, <http:// www.census.gov/cps/ads/sdata.htm>; calculations by New Strategist*

# Women in Nonmetropolitan Areas Have the Lowest Incomes

## Women living in the suburbs of the nation's largest metropolitan areas have the highest incomes.

Women living in nonmetropolitan areas—the countryside and small towns of America—have the lowest incomes. The median income of women in nonmetropolitan areas who work full-time stood at $21,340 in 1997. The $30,101 median income of their counterparts living in the suburbs of the nation's largest metropolitan areas was 41 percent higher. Women with full-time jobs living in the central cities of the largest metropolitan areas had a median income of $26,364.

The proportion of women who work full-time varies by metropolitan residence. Among women in nonmetropolitan areas, only 31 percent have full-time jobs, lower than the figures for women in central cities and suburbs. Among women in the suburbs of the largest metropolitan areas—those with populations of 1 million or more—37 percent work full-time.

✗ The nation's largest metropolitan areas attract the best-educated and most career-oriented women, which in part explains why women in those areas have higher incomes. As technological advances increase job opportunities for the educated and career-oriented outside of metropolitan areas, the incomes of women in nonmetropolitan areas may rise.

### Suburban women have the highest incomes

*(median income of women aged 15 or older who work full-time, year-round, by metropolitan residence, 1997)*

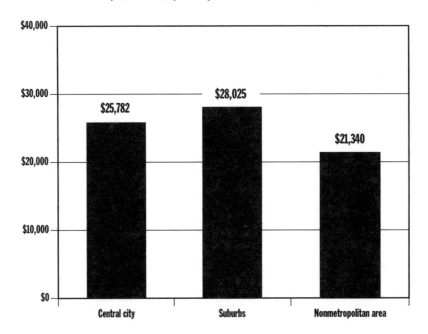

# Distribution of Women by Income and Metropolitan Residence, 1997

*(number and percent distribution of women aged 15 or older by income and metropolitan residence, 1997; median income of women with income and of women working full-time, year-round; percent working full-time, year-round; women in thousands as of 1998)*

| | | inside metropolitan areas | | | | | | | outside metropolitan areas |
|---|---|---|---|---|---|---|---|---|---|
| | | | inside central cities | | | outside central cities | | | |
| | total | total | total | 1 million or more | under 1 million | total | 1 million or more | under 1 million | |
| **Total women** | 108,168 | 86,884 | 32,535 | 21,053 | 11,482 | 54,349 | 37,343 | 17,006 | 21,284 |
| Without income | 10,721 | 8,485 | 3,619 | 2,645 | 974 | 4,865 | 3,272 | 1,593 | 2,237 |
| With income | 97,447 | 78,399 | 28,916 | 18,408 | 10,508 | 49,484 | 34,071 | 15,413 | 19,047 |
| Under $5,000 | 18,456 | 14,277 | 5,013 | 3,074 | 1,940 | 9,263 | 6,231 | 3,032 | 4,180 |
| $5,000 to $9,999 | 19,077 | 14,636 | 6,056 | 3,787 | 2,270 | 8,581 | 5,489 | 3,091 | 4,440 |
| $10,000 to $14,999 | 14,123 | 10,915 | 4,197 | 2,595 | 1,601 | 6,719 | 4,434 | 2,284 | 3,208 |
| $15,000 to $19,999 | 10,600 | 8,431 | 3,203 | 1,996 | 1,207 | 5,228 | 3,423 | 1,804 | 2,169 |
| $20,000 to $24,999 | 8,872 | 7,138 | 2,600 | 1,685 | 917 | 4,537 | 3,129 | 1,408 | 1,734 |
| $25,000 to $29,999 | 6,387 | 5,309 | 1,868 | 1,152 | 716 | 3,441 | 2,406 | 1,035 | 1,078 |
| $30,000 to $34,999 | 5,426 | 4,682 | 1,575 | 1,046 | 531 | 3,107 | 2,217 | 889 | 744 |
| $35,000 to $39,999 | 3,595 | 3,146 | 1,100 | 753 | 348 | 2,046 | 1,533 | 514 | 450 |
| $40,000 to $44,999 | 2,627 | 2,265 | 760 | 549 | 212 | 1,504 | 1,137 | 368 | 362 |
| $45,000 to $49,999 | 1,984 | 1,797 | 612 | 386 | 226 | 1,186 | 919 | 265 | 187 |
| $50,000 to $54,999 | 1,631 | 1,495 | 517 | 351 | 166 | 978 | 778 | 200 | 136 |
| $55,000 to $59,999 | 1,005 | 897 | 304 | 228 | 77 | 591 | 497 | 94 | 109 |
| $60,000 to $64,999 | 768 | 710 | 178 | 129 | 49 | 531 | 441 | 90 | 59 |
| $65,000 to $69,999 | 546 | 517 | 164 | 122 | 43 | 351 | 298 | 54 | 31 |
| $70,000 to $74,999 | 400 | 372 | 132 | 90 | 42 | 240 | 199 | 41 | 27 |
| $75,000 to $79,999 | 305 | 290 | 89 | 82 | 7 | 200 | 164 | 36 | 14 |
| $80,000 to $84,999 | 235 | 216 | 59 | 30 | 29 | 158 | 133 | 25 | 19 |
| $85,000 to $89,999 | 193 | 189 | 68 | 56 | 14 | 121 | 87 | 34 | 4 |
| $90,000 to $94,999 | 160 | 144 | 37 | 27 | 9 | 108 | 93 | 14 | 16 |
| $95,000 to $99,999 | 133 | 119 | 52 | 38 | 13 | 67 | 56 | 11 | 13 |
| $100,000 or more | 922 | 856 | 328 | 236 | 92 | 528 | 404 | 124 | 66 |
| **Median income** | | | | | | | | | |
| Women with income | $13,703 | $14,634 | $13,751 | $14,343 | $12,893 | $15,153 | $16,152 | $13,087 | $11,222 |
| Women working full-time | $26,029 | $27,094 | $25,782 | $26,364 | $24,730 | $28,025 | $30,101 | $24,818 | $21,340 |
| Percent working full-time | 34.9% | 35.8% | 35.0% | 35.8% | 33.6% | 36.3% | 37.0% | 34.8% | 31.0% |
| **Percent distribution** | | | | | | | | | |
| **Total women** | 100.0% | 100.0% | 100.0% | 100.0% | 100.0% | 100.0% | 100.0% | 100.0% | 100.0% |
| Without income | 9.9 | 9.8 | 11.1 | 12.6 | 8.5 | 9.0 | 8.8 | 9.4 | 10.5 |
| With income | 90.1 | 90.2 | 88.9 | 87.4 | 91.5 | 91.0 | 91.2 | 90.6 | 89.5 |
| Under $25,000 | 65.8 | 63.8 | 64.8 | 62.4 | 69.1 | 63.2 | 60.8 | 68.3 | 73.9 |
| $25,000 to $49,999 | 18.5 | 19.8 | 18.2 | 18.5 | 17.7 | 20.8 | 22.0 | 18.1 | 13.3 |
| $50,000 to $74,999 | 4.0 | 4.6 | 4.0 | 4.4 | 3.3 | 5.0 | 5.9 | 2.8 | 1.7 |
| $75,000 to $99,999 | 0.9 | 1.1 | 0.9 | 1.1 | 0.6 | 1.2 | 1.4 | 0.7 | 0.3 |
| $100,000 or more | 0.9 | 1.0 | 1.0 | 1.1 | 0.8 | 1.0 | 1.1 | 0.7 | 0.3 |

*Source: Bureau of the Census, Internet web site, <http:// www.census.gov/cps/ads/sdata.htm>; calculations by New Strategist*

# Women Earn Little from Part-Time Work

## Women who work part-time earn a median of less than $10,000 a year.

Sixty-three percent of the nation's 108 million women aged 15 or older worked during 1997. Fully 38 million (35 percent of total) worked full-time, year-round. Their median earnings stood at $24,973, 67 percent higher than the $16,716 median earnings of all women with earnings. The 10 million women (9 percent of all women) with part-time, year-round jobs earned a median of only $9,425.

Among black women aged 15 or older, median earnings were $16,338 in 1997. Those working full-time, year-round earned $22,035. Non-Hispanic white women who worked full-time, year-round earned more than blacks, with a median of $25,915. The earnings of Hispanic women were lower than the earnings of blacks and non-Hispanic whites. Those working full-time, year-round earned only $18,973. Only 30 percent of Hispanic women had full-time, year-round jobs in 1997 versus 39 percent of black and 35 percent of non-Hispanic white women.

✘ More women are working full-time nowadays because part-time work pays little and offers few benefits. With women's earnings becoming more important to family well-being, the percentage of women with full-time jobs will continue to grow in the years ahead.

### Among full-time workers, non-Hispanic white women have the highest earnings

*(median income of women aged 15 or older who work full-time, year-round, by race and Hispanic origin, 1997)*

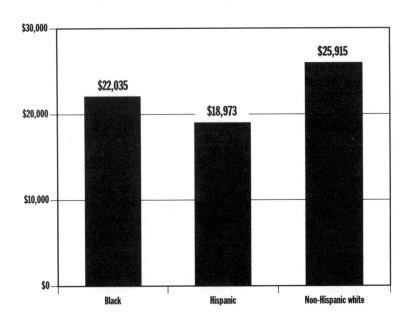

# Distribution of Women by Earnings and Work Experience, 1997: Total Women

*(number and percent distribution of women aged 15 or older by earnings and work experience, 1997; median earnings of women with earnings; women in thousands as of 1998)*

| | | | worked | | | |
| | | | *full-time* | | *part-time* | |
| | *total* | *total* | *total* | *year-round* | *total* | *year-round* |
|---|---|---|---|---|---|---|
| **Total women** | **108,168** | **67,851** | **47,817** | **37,715** | **20,034** | **9,592** |
| Without earnings | 40,432 | 115 | 39 | 32 | 76 | 31 |
| With earnings | 67,736 | 67,736 | 47,777 | 37,683 | 19,958 | 9,561 |
| Under $5,000 | 12,283 | 12,283 | 3,279 | 613 | 9,004 | 2,009 |
| $5,000 to $9,999 | 9,190 | 9,190 | 4,095 | 1,733 | 5,095 | 3,057 |
| $10,000 to $14,999 | 9,142 | 9,142 | 6,536 | 4,823 | 2,607 | 1,872 |
| $15,000 to $19,999 | 7,948 | 7,948 | 6,724 | 5,738 | 1,224 | 961 |
| $20,000 to $24,999 | 7,405 | 7,405 | 6,669 | 5,957 | 735 | 589 |
| $25,000 to $29,999 | 5,407 | 5,407 | 5,030 | 4,625 | 376 | 290 |
| $30,000 to $34,999 | 4,760 | 4,760 | 4,422 | 4,053 | 337 | 306 |
| $35,000 to $39,999 | 3,131 | 3,131 | 2,957 | 2,732 | 173 | 147 |
| $40,000 to $44,999 | 2,293 | 2,293 | 2,175 | 1,991 | 118 | 93 |
| $45,000 to $49,999 | 1,637 | 1,637 | 1,564 | 1,424 | 74 | 68 |
| $50,000 to $54,999 | 1,336 | 1,336 | 1,263 | 1,151 | 72 | 53 |
| $55,000 to $59,999 | 680 | 680 | 662 | 617 | 18 | 12 |
| $60,000 to $64,999 | 716 | 716 | 687 | 624 | 29 | 23 |
| $65,000 to $69,999 | 346 | 346 | 330 | 316 | 16 | 10 |
| $70,000 to $74,999 | 242 | 242 | 236 | 219 | 6 | 2 |
| $75,000 to $79,999 | 236 | 236 | 214 | 201 | 22 | 22 |
| $80,000 to $84,999 | 165 | 165 | 158 | 154 | 7 | 7 |
| $85,000 to $89,999 | 97 | 97 | 86 | 84 | 11 | 11 |
| $90,000 to $94,999 | 97 | 97 | 87 | 84 | 10 | 7 |
| $95,000 to $99,999 | 67 | 67 | 67 | 62 | – | – |
| $100,000 or more | 559 | 559 | 534 | 480 | 25 | 20 |
| Median earnings of women with earnings | $16,716 | $16,716 | $21,883 | $24,973 | $5,749 | $9,425 |
| **Percent distribution** | | | | | | |
| **Total women** | **100.0%** | **100.0%** | **100.0%** | **100.0%** | **100.0%** | **100.0%** |
| Without earnings | 37.4 | 0.2 | 0.1 | 0.1 | 0.4 | 0.3 |
| With earnings | 62.6 | 99.8 | 99.9 | 99.9 | 99.6 | 99.7 |
| Under $25,000 | 42.5 | 67.7 | 57.1 | 50.0 | 93.2 | 88.5 |
| $25,000 to $49,999 | 15.9 | 25.4 | 33.8 | 39.3 | 5.4 | 9.4 |
| $50,000 to $74,999 | 3.1 | 4.9 | 6.6 | 7.8 | 0.7 | 1.0 |
| $75,000 to $99,999 | 0.6 | 1.0 | 1.3 | 1.6 | 0.2 | 0.5 |
| $100,000 or more | 0.5 | 0.8 | 1.1 | 1.3 | 0.1 | 0.2 |

*Note: (–) means sample is too small to make a reliable estimate.*
*Source: Bureau of the Census, Internet web site, <http:// www.census.gov/cps/ads/sdata.htm>; calculations by New Strategist*

# Distribution of Women by Earnings and Work Experience, 1997: Black Women

*(number and percent distribution of black women aged 15 or older by earnings and work experience, 1997; median earnings of women with earnings; women in thousands as of 1998)*

| | total | worked total | full-time total | full-time year-round | part-time total | part-time year-round |
|---|---|---|---|---|---|---|
| **Total women** | **13,715** | **8,702** | **6,803** | **5,313** | **1,899** | **853** |
| Without earnings | 5,013 | 0 | 0 | 0 | 0 | 0 |
| With earnings | 8,702 | 8,702 | 6,803 | 5,313 | 1,899 | 853 |
| Under $5,000 | 1,524 | 1,524 | 554 | 87 | 970 | 204 |
| $5,000 to $9,999 | 1,213 | 1,213 | 699 | 291 | 514 | 344 |
| $10,000 to $14,999 | 1,201 | 1,201 | 1,003 | 758 | 198 | 120 |
| $15,000 to $19,999 | 1,292 | 1,292 | 1,197 | 1,046 | 95 | 82 |
| $20,000 to $24,999 | 1,016 | 1,016 | 977 | 913 | 38 | 29 |
| $25,000 to $29,999 | 693 | 693 | 669 | 630 | 24 | 19 |
| $30,000 to $34,999 | 608 | 608 | 583 | 554 | 27 | 27 |
| $35,000 to $39,999 | 361 | 361 | 357 | 332 | 4 | 4 |
| $40,000 to $44,999 | 212 | 212 | 199 | 189 | 13 | 10 |
| $45,000 to $49,999 | 184 | 184 | 181 | 160 | 2 | 2 |
| $50,000 to $54,999 | 158 | 158 | 155 | 135 | 3 | – |
| $55,000 to $59,999 | 60 | 60 | 59 | 59 | 1 | 1 |
| $60,000 to $64,999 | 74 | 74 | 74 | 71 | – | – |
| $65,000 to $69,999 | 28 | 28 | 26 | 26 | 2 | 2 |
| $70,000 to $74,999 | 14 | 14 | 14 | 12 | – | – |
| $75,000 to $79,999 | 17 | 17 | 14 | 14 | 3 | 3 |
| $80,000 to $84,999 | 11 | 11 | 11 | 11 | – | – |
| $85,000 to $89,999 | 7 | 7 | 4 | 4 | 3 | 3 |
| $90,000 to $94,999 | 3 | 3 | 3 | 3 | – | – |
| $95,000 to $99,999 | – | – | – | – | – | – |
| $100,000 or more | 24 | 24 | 24 | 18 | – | – |
| Median earnings of women with earnings | $16,338 | $16,338 | $19,741 | $22,035 | $4,875 | $8,105 |
| **Percent distribution** | | | | | | |
| **Total women** | **100.0%** | **100.0%** | **100.0%** | **100.0%** | **100.0%** | **100.0%** |
| Without earnings | 36.6 | 0.0 | 0.0 | 0.0 | 0.0 | 0.0 |
| With earnings | 63.4 | 100.0 | 100.0 | 100.0 | 100.0 | 100.0 |
| Under $25,000 | 45.5 | 71.8 | 65.1 | 58.3 | 95.6 | 91.3 |
| $25,000 to $49,999 | 15.0 | 23.6 | 29.2 | 35.1 | 3.7 | 7.3 |
| $50,000 to $74,999 | 2.4 | 3.8 | 4.8 | 5.7 | 0.3 | 0.4 |
| $75,000 to $99,999 | 0.3 | 0.4 | 0.5 | 0.6 | 0.3 | 0.7 |
| $100,000 or more | 0.2 | 0.3 | 0.4 | 0.3 | 0.0 | 0.0 |

*Note: (–) means sample is too small to make a reliable estimate.*
*Source: Bureau of the Census, Internet web site, <http:// www.census.gov/cps/ads/sdata.htm>; calculations by New Strategist*

# Distribution of Women by Earnings and Work Experience, 1997: Hispanic Women

*(number and percent distribution of Hispanic women aged 15 or older by earnings and work experience, 1997; median earnings of women with earnings; women in thousands as of 1998)*

| | | worked | | | | |
| --- | --- | --- | --- | --- | --- | --- |
| | | | full-time | | part-time | |
| | *total* | *total* | *total* | *year-round* | *total* | *year-round* |
| **Total women** | **10,485** | **5,856** | **4,273** | **3,143** | **1,583** | **746** |
| Without earnings | 4,644 | 15 | 7 | 5 | 8 | 4 |
| With earnings | 5,841 | 5,841 | 4,266 | 3,139 | 1,575 | 741 |
| Under $5,000 | 1,159 | 1,159 | 435 | 64 | 723 | 144 |
| $5,000 to $9,999 | 1,112 | 1,112 | 624 | 271 | 488 | 319 |
| $10,000 to $14,999 | 1,120 | 1,120 | 904 | 739 | 215 | 165 |
| $15,000 to $19,999 | 723 | 723 | 658 | 575 | 65 | 46 |
| $20,000 to $24,999 | 549 | 549 | 523 | 459 | 26 | 20 |
| $25,000 to $29,999 | 330 | 330 | 314 | 286 | 17 | 9 |
| $30,000 to $34,999 | 261 | 261 | 250 | 222 | 11 | 11 |
| $35,000 to $39,999 | 208 | 208 | 196 | 181 | 12 | 12 |
| $40,000 to $44,999 | 125 | 125 | 119 | 111 | 6 | 4 |
| $45,000 to $49,999 | 76 | 76 | 74 | 70 | 2 | 2 |
| $50,000 to $54,999 | 57 | 57 | 52 | 48 | 5 | 5 |
| $55,000 to $59,999 | 38 | 38 | 38 | 36 | – | – |
| $60,000 to $64,999 | 22 | 22 | 21 | 21 | 2 | 2 |
| $65,000 to $69,999 | 5 | 5 | 5 | 3 | – | – |
| $70,000 to $74,999 | 13 | 13 | 12 | 12 | 1 | – |
| $75,000 to $79,999 | 5 | 5 | 5 | 5 | – | – |
| $80,000 to $84,999 | 12 | 12 | 12 | 12 | – | – |
| $85,000 to $89,999 | – | – | – | – | – | – |
| $90,000 to $94,999 | 8 | 8 | 6 | 6 | 2 | 2 |
| $95,000 to $99,999 | – | – | – | – | – | – |
| $100,000 or more | 20 | 20 | 19 | 17 | 1 | – |
| Median earnings of women with earnings | $12,135 | $12,135 | $15,967 | $18,973 | $5,545 | $8,351 |
| **Percent distribution** | | | | | | |
| **Total women** | **100.0%** | **100.0%** | **100.0%** | **100.0%** | **100.0%** | **100.0%** |
| Without earnings | 44.3 | 0.3 | 0.2 | 0.2 | 0.5 | 0.5 |
| With earnings | 55.7 | 99.7 | 99.8 | 99.9 | 99.5 | 99.3 |
| Under $25,000 | 44.5 | 79.6 | 73.6 | 67.1 | 95.8 | 93.0 |
| $25,000 to $49,999 | 9.5 | 17.1 | 22.3 | 27.7 | 3.0 | 5.1 |
| $50,000 to $74,999 | 1.3 | 2.3 | 3.0 | 3.8 | 0.5 | 0.9 |
| $75,000 to $99,999 | 0.2 | 0.4 | 0.5 | 0.7 | 0.1 | 0.3 |
| $100,000 or more | 0.2 | 0.3 | 0.4 | 0.5 | 0.1 | 0.0 |

*Note: (–) means sample is too small to make a reliable estimate.*
*Source: Bureau of the Census, Internet web site, <http:// www.census.gov/cps/ads/sdata.htm>; calculations by New Strategist*

# Distribution of Women by Earnings and Work Experience, 1997: White Women

*(number and percent distribution of white women aged 15 or older by earnings and work experience, 1997; median earnings of women with earnings; women in thousands as of 1998)*

| | total | worked total | full-time total | full-time year-round | part-time total | part-time year-round |
|---|---|---|---|---|---|---|
| **Total women** | **89,489** | **56,028** | **38,745** | **30,606** | **17,282** | **8,366** |
| Without earnings | 33,555 | 94 | 27 | 20 | 67 | 27 |
| With earnings | 55,934 | 55,934 | 38,718 | 30,586 | 17,215 | 8,338 |
| Under $5,000 | 10,213 | 10,213 | 2,581 | 514 | 7,631 | 1,708 |
| $5,000 to $9,999 | 7,626 | 7,626 | 3,211 | 1,359 | 4,414 | 2,640 |
| $10,000 to $14,999 | 7,498 | 7,498 | 5,224 | 3,850 | 2,275 | 1,659 |
| $15,000 to $19,999 | 6,329 | 6,329 | 5,247 | 4,460 | 1,083 | 846 |
| $20,000 to $24,999 | 6,054 | 6,054 | 5,399 | 4,774 | 654 | 526 |
| $25,000 to $29,999 | 4,500 | 4,500 | 4,164 | 3,812 | 337 | 260 |
| $30,000 to $34,999 | 3,912 | 3,912 | 3,620 | 3,294 | 292 | 265 |
| $35,000 to $39,999 | 2,622 | 2,622 | 2,454 | 2,270 | 168 | 142 |
| $40,000 to $44,999 | 1,949 | 1,949 | 1,852 | 1,691 | 97 | 75 |
| $45,000 to $49,999 | 1,365 | 1,365 | 1,295 | 1,182 | 69 | 63 |
| $50,000 to $54,999 | 1,112 | 1,112 | 1,044 | 952 | 68 | 53 |
| $55,000 to $59,999 | 588 | 588 | 571 | 527 | 17 | 11 |
| $60,000 to $64,999 | 596 | 596 | 568 | 507 | 29 | 23 |
| $65,000 to $69,999 | 292 | 292 | 279 | 267 | 14 | 8 |
| $70,000 to $74,999 | 209 | 209 | 203 | 195 | 6 | 2 |
| $75,000 to $79,999 | 210 | 210 | 190 | 177 | 18 | 18 |
| $80,000 to $84,999 | 147 | 147 | 142 | 138 | 5 | 5 |
| $85,000 to $89,999 | 78 | 78 | 74 | 72 | 4 | 4 |
| $90,000 to $94,999 | 89 | 89 | 79 | 77 | 10 | 7 |
| $95,000 to $99,999 | 52 | 52 | 52 | 47 | – | – |
| $100,000 or more | 493 | 493 | 468 | 422 | 25 | 20 |
| Median earnings of women with earnings | $16,748 | $16,748 | $22,193 | $25,331 | $5,865 | $9,575 |
| **Percent distribution** | | | | | | |
| **Total women** | **100.0%** | **100.0%** | **100.0%** | **100.0%** | **100.0%** | **100.0%** |
| Without earnings | 37.5 | 0.2 | 0.1 | 0.1 | 0.4 | 0.3 |
| With earnings | 62.5 | 99.8 | 99.9 | 99.9 | 99.6 | 99.7 |
| Under $25,000 | 42.2 | 67.3 | 55.9 | 48.9 | 92.9 | 88.2 |
| $25,000 to $49,999 | 16.0 | 25.6 | 34.5 | 40.0 | 5.6 | 9.6 |
| $50,000 to $74,999 | 3.1 | 5.0 | 6.9 | 8.0 | 0.8 | 1.2 |
| $75,000 to $99,999 | 0.6 | 1.0 | 1.4 | 1.7 | 0.2 | 0.4 |
| $100,000 or more | 0.6 | 0.9 | 1.2 | 1.4 | 0.1 | 0.2 |

*Note: (–) means sample is too small to make a reliable estimate.*
*Source: Bureau of the Census, Internet web site, <http:// www.census.gov/cps/ads/sdata.htm>; calculations by New Strategist*

# Distribution of Women by Earnings and Work Experience, 1997: Non-Hispanic White Women

*(number and percent distribution of non-Hispanic white women aged 15 or older by earnings and work experience, 1997; median earnings of women with earnings; women in thousands as of 1998)*

| | | worked | | | | |
|---|---|---|---|---|---|---|
| | | | full-time | | part-time | |
| | total | total | total | year-round | total | year-round |
| **Total women** | **79,502** | **50,464** | **34,711** | **27,650** | **15,753** | **7,649** |
| Without earnings | 29,117 | 79 | 20 | 16 | 58 | 23 |
| With earnings | 50,385 | 50,385 | 34,691 | 27,634 | 15,694 | 7,626 |
| Under $5,000 | 9,095 | 9,095 | 2,164 | 450 | 6,930 | 1,570 |
| $5,000 to $9,999 | 6,568 | 6,568 | 2,621 | 1,105 | 3,946 | 2,334 |
| $10,000 to $14,999 | 6,417 | 6,417 | 4,351 | 3,133 | 2,066 | 1,500 |
| $15,000 to $19,999 | 5,650 | 5,650 | 4,629 | 3,923 | 1,020 | 801 |
| $20,000 to $24,999 | 5,536 | 5,536 | 4,908 | 4,343 | 628 | 507 |
| $25,000 to $29,999 | 4,195 | 4,195 | 3,871 | 3,547 | 323 | 253 |
| $30,000 to $34,999 | 3,675 | 3,675 | 3,394 | 3,097 | 281 | 253 |
| $35,000 to $39,999 | 2,425 | 2,425 | 2,268 | 2,099 | 156 | 130 |
| $40,000 to $44,999 | 1,831 | 1,831 | 1,740 | 1,584 | 91 | 71 |
| $45,000 to $49,999 | 1,296 | 1,296 | 1,229 | 1,120 | 67 | 61 |
| $50,000 to $54,999 | 1,057 | 1,057 | 994 | 907 | 63 | 48 |
| $55,000 to $59,999 | 554 | 554 | 537 | 495 | 17 | 11 |
| $60,000 to $64,999 | 577 | 577 | 550 | 489 | 28 | 22 |
| $65,000 to $69,999 | 288 | 288 | 275 | 264 | 14 | 8 |
| $70,000 to $74,999 | 196 | 196 | 192 | 183 | 4 | 2 |
| $75,000 to $79,999 | 204 | 204 | 186 | 173 | 18 | 18 |
| $80,000 to $84,999 | 136 | 136 | 131 | 127 | 5 | 5 |
| $85,000 to $89,999 | 78 | 78 | 74 | 72 | 4 | 4 |
| $90,000 to $94,999 | 80 | 80 | 72 | 69 | 8 | 6 |
| $95,000 to $99,999 | 52 | 52 | 52 | 47 | – | – |
| $100,000 or more | 476 | 476 | 452 | 408 | 24 | 20 |
| Median earnings of women with earnings | $17,362 | $17,362 | $23,046 | $25,915 | $5,903 | $9,753 |
| **Percent distribution** | | | | | | |
| **Total women** | **100.0%** | **100.0%** | **100.0%** | **100.0%** | **100.0%** | **100.0%** |
| Without earnings | 36.6 | 0.2 | 0.1 | 0.1 | 0.4 | 0.3 |
| With earnings | 63.4 | 99.8 | 99.9 | 99.9 | 99.6 | 99.7 |
| Under $25,000 | 41.8 | 65.9 | 53.8 | 46.8 | 92.6 | 87.8 |
| $25,000 to $49,999 | 16.9 | 26.6 | 36.0 | 41.4 | 5.8 | 10.0 |
| $50,000 to $74,999 | 3.4 | 5.3 | 7.3 | 8.5 | 0.8 | 1.2 |
| $75,000 to $99,999 | 0.7 | 1.1 | 1.5 | 1.8 | 0.2 | 0.4 |
| $100,000 or more | 0.6 | 0.9 | 1.3 | 1.5 | 0.2 | 0.3 |

*Note: (–) means sample is too small to make a reliable estimate.*
*Source: Bureau of the Census, Internet web site, <http:// www.census.gov/cps/ads/sdata.htm>; calculations by New Strategist*

# Women with Professional Degrees Earn the Most

## Those who dropped out of high school earn the least.

The more highly educated a woman, the more committed she is to the labor force and the more she earns. Fifty-two percent of women with at least a bachelor's degree have full-time jobs. They earned a median of $36,346 in 1997. Those with professional degrees earned the most, a median of $54,528. Fifteen percent of women with professional degrees had earnings of $100,000 or more. Women who ended their education with a high school diploma earned a median of $21,291 at full-time jobs, while those without a high school diploma earned less than $16,000 working full-time.

Women aged 45 to 54 with professional degrees and full-time jobs have the highest earnings, a median of $61,842 in 1997. Even the youngest women benefit from educational credentials. Women aged 25 to 34 with at least a bachelor's degree and a full-time job earned $32,100. Their counterparts who went no further than high school earned just $19,813.

✗ Among 25-to-34-year-olds, women are now better educated than men. As these well-educated and career-oriented women enter middle age, replacing older, just-a-job women in the labor force, the earnings of women with college degrees will grow.

## Women's earnings rise with education

*(median earnings of women aged 25 or older who work full-time, year-round, by education, 1997)*

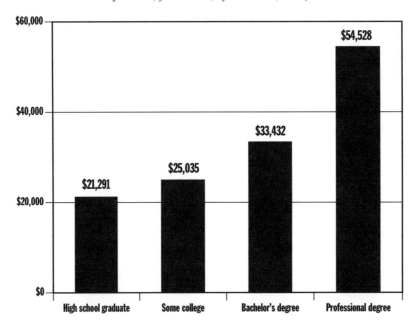

# Distribution of Women by Earnings and Education, 1997: Total Women

*(number and percent distribution of women aged 25 or older by earnings and educational attainment, 1997; median earnings of women with earnings and of women who work full-time, year-round; percent of women who work full-time, year-round; women in thousands as of 1998)*

| | total | less than 9th grade | 9th to 12th grade, no diploma | high school graduate, incl. GED | some college, no degree | associate's degree | total | bachelor's degree | master's degree | professional degree | doctoral degree |
|---|---|---|---|---|---|---|---|---|---|---|---|
| | | | | | | | | bachelor's degree or more | | | |
| **Total women** | **89,835** | **6,623** | **8,758** | **31,599** | **15,516** | **7,198** | **20,142** | **14,215** | **4,592** | **820** | **515** |
| Without earnings | 33,702 | 4,999 | 5,184 | 12,805 | 4,814 | 1,696 | 4,204 | 3,107 | 866 | 157 | 74 |
| With earnings | 56,134 | 1,624 | 3,574 | 18,794 | 10,702 | 5,502 | 15,938 | 11,108 | 3,726 | 663 | 441 |
| Under $5,000 | 7,073 | 413 | 814 | 2,675 | 1,398 | 511 | 1,261 | 967 | 247 | 22 | 25 |
| $5,000 to $9,999 | 6,521 | 397 | 798 | 2,640 | 1,180 | 475 | 1,031 | 788 | 198 | 26 | 19 |
| $10,000 to $14,999 | 7,607 | 423 | 809 | 3,217 | 1,463 | 624 | 1,071 | 812 | 219 | 30 | 9 |
| $15,000 to $19,999 | 6,992 | 215 | 457 | 3,000 | 1,494 | 703 | 1,124 | 890 | 178 | 35 | 20 |
| $20,000 to $24,999 | 6,844 | 78 | 312 | 2,670 | 1,505 | 775 | 1,505 | 1,250 | 200 | 36 | 18 |
| $25,000 to $29,999 | 5,141 | 33 | 174 | 1,713 | 1,052 | 637 | 1,533 | 1,162 | 314 | 34 | 23 |
| $30,000 to $34,999 | 4,557 | 35 | 97 | 1,131 | 904 | 585 | 1,804 | 1,337 | 384 | 54 | 28 |
| $35,000 to $39,999 | 3,066 | 17 | 36 | 666 | 565 | 352 | 1,430 | 1,021 | 333 | 41 | 35 |
| $40,000 to $44,999 | 2,244 | 8 | 45 | 431 | 333 | 306 | 1,122 | 674 | 372 | 41 | 34 |
| $45,000 to $49,999 | 1,617 | 1 | 3 | 200 | 257 | 181 | 974 | 567 | 326 | 45 | 37 |
| $50,000 to $54,999 | 1,300 | 1 | 13 | 173 | 197 | 130 | 786 | 420 | 289 | 35 | 42 |
| $55,000 to $59,999 | 672 | – | – | 64 | 99 | 44 | 465 | 267 | 176 | 9 | 11 |
| $60,000 to $64,999 | 713 | – | 4 | 68 | 64 | 70 | 507 | 286 | 136 | 38 | 47 |
| $65,000 to $69,999 | 338 | – | – | 14 | 51 | 29 | 245 | 136 | 89 | 8 | 13 |
| $70,000 to $74,999 | 240 | – | 3 | 20 | 25 | 16 | 176 | 97 | 45 | 26 | 7 |
| $75,000 to $79,999 | 236 | – | – | 25 | 37 | 11 | 162 | 90 | 43 | 20 | 9 |
| $80,000 to $84,999 | 162 | – | – | 14 | 15 | 10 | 123 | 61 | 37 | 10 | 14 |
| $85,000 to $89,999 | 97 | – | – | 4 | 11 | 2 | 80 | 39 | 18 | 11 | 12 |
| $90,000 to $94,999 | 97 | 2 | – | 3 | 8 | 6 | 78 | 48 | 11 | 14 | 4 |
| $95,000 to $99,999 | 67 | – | – | 6 | 5 | 2 | 55 | 39 | 13 | 2 | 1 |
| $100,000 or more | 548 | – | 6 | 63 | 37 | 31 | 411 | 159 | 98 | 121 | 33 |

*(continued)*

(continued from previous page)

| | total | less than 9th grade | 9th to 12th grade, no diploma | high school graduate, incl. GED | some college, no degree | associate's degree | bachelor's degree or more | | | | |
|---|---|---|---|---|---|---|---|---|---|---|---|
| | | | | | | | total | bachelor's degree | master's degree | professional degree | doctoral degree |
| **Median earnings** | | | | | | | | | | | |
| Women with earnings | $19,891 | $10,007 | $10,775 | $16,225 | $19,332 | $22,220 | $30,882 | $28,328 | $36,428 | $45,650 | $45,910 |
| Women working full-time | $25,823 | $13,447 | $15,907 | $21,291 | $25,035 | $27,206 | $36,346 | $33,432 | $41,856 | $54,528 | $50,758 |
| Percent working full-time | 38.6% | 11.9% | 20.2% | 36.3% | 42.8% | 49.2% | 51.8% | 50.5% | 53.3% | 59.5% | 61.7% |
| **Percent distribution** | | | | | | | | | | | |
| Total women | 100.0% | 100.0% | 100.0% | 100.0% | 100.0% | 100.0% | 100.0% | 100.0% | 100.0% | 100.0% | 100.0% |
| Without earnings | 37.5 | 75.5 | 59.2 | 40.5 | 31.0 | 23.6 | 20.9 | 21.9 | 18.9 | 19.1 | 14.4 |
| With earnings | 62.5 | 24.5 | 40.8 | 59.5 | 69.0 | 76.4 | 79.1 | 78.1 | 81.1 | 80.9 | 85.6 |
| Under $25,000 | 39.0 | 23.0 | 36.4 | 44.9 | 45.4 | 42.9 | 29.7 | 33.1 | 22.7 | 18.2 | 17.7 |
| $25,000 to $49,999 | 18.5 | 1.4 | 4.1 | 13.1 | 20.1 | 28.6 | 34.1 | 33.5 | 37.7 | 26.2 | 30.5 |
| $50,000 to $74,999 | 3.6 | 0.0 | 0.2 | 1.1 | 2.8 | 4.0 | 10.8 | 8.5 | 16.0 | 14.1 | 23.3 |
| $75,000 to $99,999 | 0.7 | 0.0 | – | 0.2 | 0.5 | 0.4 | 2.5 | 1.9 | 2.7 | 7.0 | 7.8 |
| $100,000 or more | 0.6 | – | 0.1 | 0.2 | 0.2 | 0.4 | 2.0 | 1.1 | 2.1 | 14.8 | 6.4 |

Note: (–) means sample is too small to make a reliable estimate.
Source: Bureau of the Census, Internet web site, <http://www.census.gov/cps/ads/sdata.htm>; calculations by New Strategist

# Distribution of Women by Earnings and Education, 1997: Women Aged 25 to 34

*(number and percent distribution of women aged 25 to 34 by earnings and educational attainment, 1997; median earnings of women with earnings who work full-time, year-round; percent of women who work full-time, year-round; women in thousands as of 1998)*

| | total | less than 9th grade | 9th to 12th grade, no diploma | high school graduate incl. GED | some college, no degree | associate's degree | bachelor's degree or more | | | | |
|---|---|---|---|---|---|---|---|---|---|---|---|
| | | | | | | | total | bachelor's degree | master's degree | professional degree | doctoral degree |
| **Total women** | **19,828** | **684** | **1,492** | **5,978** | **4,128** | **1,858** | **5,688** | **4,436** | **943** | **234** | **75** |
| Without earnings | 3,969 | 377 | 641 | 1,401 | 752 | 217 | 581 | 478 | 78 | 18 | 7 |
| With earnings | 15,859 | 307 | 851 | 4,577 | 3,376 | 1,641 | 5,107 | 3,957 | 865 | 216 | 68 |
| Under $5,000 | 2,114 | 99 | 246 | 769 | 488 | 171 | 342 | 288 | 53 | – | 2 |
| $5,000 to $9,999 | 1,828 | 86 | 195 | 676 | 416 | 144 | 310 | 237 | 54 | 16 | 4 |
| $10,000 to $14,999 | 2,182 | 84 | 184 | 810 | 529 | 208 | 367 | 282 | 70 | 15 | – |
| $15,000 to $19,999 | 2,193 | 16 | 106 | 847 | 558 | 255 | 410 | 333 | 61 | 7 | 8 |
| $20,000 to $24,999 | 2,166 | 9 | 66 | 620 | 524 | 304 | 643 | 560 | 68 | 11 | 5 |
| $25,000 to $29,999 | 1,569 | 4 | 28 | 388 | 350 | 189 | 609 | 481 | 106 | 13 | 9 |
| $30,000 to $34,999 | 1,357 | 5 | 12 | 225 | 215 | 171 | 728 | 576 | 114 | 33 | 4 |
| $35,000 to $39,999 | 770 | – | 7 | 107 | 115 | 61 | 480 | 377 | 86 | 15 | 2 |
| $40,000 to $44,999 | 505 | 2 | 4 | 49 | 47 | 54 | 350 | 255 | 75 | 14 | 6 |
| $45,000 to $49,999 | 316 | – | – | 21 | 48 | 26 | 219 | 141 | 60 | 12 | 7 |
| $50,000 to $54,999 | 264 | – | – | 27 | 31 | 22 | 185 | 134 | 35 | 8 | 8 |
| $55,000 to $59,999 | 123 | – | – | 9 | 14 | 3 | 95 | 62 | 27 | 5 | 1 |
| $60,000 to $64,999 | 125 | – | – | 10 | 6 | 16 | 94 | 60 | 17 | 12 | 5 |
| $65,000 to $69,999 | 86 | – | – | 2 | 16 | 13 | 54 | 38 | 11 | 3 | 2 |
| $70,000 to $74,999 | 31 | – | 3 | – | – | – | 28 | 20 | 3 | 3 | 2 |
| $75,000 to $79,999 | 34 | – | – | 3 | 2 | – | 28 | 25 | – | 4 | – |
| $80,000 to $84,999 | 33 | – | – | – | – | – | 33 | 16 | 7 | 7 | 2 |
| $85,000 to $89,999 | 22 | – | – | – | 2 | – | 20 | 14 | – | 7 | – |
| $90,000 to $94,999 | 24 | 2 | – | 3 | 3 | 1 | 14 | 12 | – | 3 | – |
| $95,000 to $99,999 | 19 | – | – | – | – | – | 19 | 13 | 6 | – | – |
| $100,000 or more | 99 | – | 1 | 10 | 10 | – | 79 | 37 | 11 | 28 | 3 |

*(continued)*

(continued from previous page)

|  | total | less than 9th grade | 9th to 12th grade, no diploma | high school graduate, incl. GED | some college, no degree | associate's degree | bachelor's degree or more | | | | |
|  |  |  |  |  |  |  | total | bachelor's degree | master's degree | professional degree | doctoral degree |
|---|---|---|---|---|---|---|---|---|---|---|---|
| **Median earnings** |  |  |  |  |  |  |  |  |  |  |  |
| Women with earnings | $19,019 | $8,170 | $9,510 | $15,182 | $17,080 | $20,570 | $28,711 | $27,443 | $30,581 | $39,077 | $42,841 |
| Women working full-time | $24,421 | $12,068 | $15,083 | $19,813 | $21,930 | $24,083 | $32,100 | $31,408 | $35,936 | $49,304 | $47,132 |
| Percent working full-time | 48.9% | 18.6% | 26.2% | 44.7% | 48.5% | 57.4% | 60.2% | 60.6% | 59.0% | 63.2% | 50.7% |
| **Percent distribution** |  |  |  |  |  |  |  |  |  |  |  |
| **Total women** | 100.0% | 100.0% | 100.0% | 100.0% | 100.0% | 100.0% | 100.0% | 100.0% | 100.0% | 100.0% | 100.0% |
| Without earnings | 20.0 | 55.1 | 43.0 | 23.4 | 18.2 | 11.7 | 10.2 | 10.8 | 8.3 | 7.7 | 9.3 |
| With earnings | 80.0 | 44.9 | 57.0 | 76.6 | 81.8 | 88.3 | 89.8 | 89.2 | 91.7 | 92.3 | 90.7 |
| Under $25,000 | 52.9 | 43.0 | 53.4 | 62.3 | 60.9 | 58.2 | 36.4 | 38.3 | 32.4 | 20.9 | 25.3 |
| $25,000 to $49,999 | 22.8 | 1.6 | 3.4 | 13.2 | 18.8 | 27.0 | 41.9 | 41.3 | 46.8 | 37.2 | 37.3 |
| $50,000 to $74,999 | 3.2 | – | 0.2 | 0.8 | 1.6 | 2.9 | 8.0 | 7.1 | 9.9 | 13.2 | 24.0 |
| $75,000 to $99,999 | 0.7 | 0.3 | – | 0.1 | 0.2 | 0.1 | 2.0 | 1.8 | 1.4 | 9.0 | 2.7 |
| $100,000 or more | 0.5 | – | 0.1 | 0.2 | 0.2 | 0.0 | 1.4 | 0.8 | 1.2 | 12.0 | 4.0 |

Note: (–) means sample is too small to make a reliable estimate.
Source: Bureau of the Census, Internet web site, <http://www.census.gov/cps/ads/sdata.htm>; calculations by New Strategist

# Distribution of Women by Earnings and Education, 1997: Women Aged 35 to 44

*(number and percent distribution of women aged 35 to 44 by earnings and educational attainment, 1997; median earnings of women with earnings and of women with earnings who work full-time, year-round; percent of women who work full-time, year-round; women in thousands as of 1998)*

| | total | less than 9th grade | 9th to 12th grade, no diploma | high school graduate, incl. GED | some college, no degree | associate's degree | bachelor's degree or more | | | | |
|---|---|---|---|---|---|---|---|---|---|---|---|
| | | | | | | | total | bachelor's degree | master's degree | professional degree | doctoral degree |
| **Total women** | **22,407** | **831** | **1,624** | **7,599** | **4,252** | **2,326** | **5,775** | **4,185** | **1,204** | **226** | **159** |
| Without earnings | 4,588 | 402 | 602 | 1,601 | 827 | 343 | 811 | 638 | 133 | 29 | 12 |
| With earnings | 17,820 | 429 | 1,022 | 5,998 | 3,425 | 1,983 | 4,963 | 3,548 | 1,071 | 197 | 147 |
| Under $5,000 | 1,970 | 92 | 228 | 729 | 394 | 153 | 376 | 310 | 51 | 7 | 8 |
| $5,000 to $9,999 | 2,034 | 114 | 206 | 872 | 364 | 160 | 318 | 261 | 51 | 6 | – |
| $10,000 to $14,999 | 2,401 | 129 | 273 | 1,023 | 441 | 238 | 296 | 256 | 36 | 3 | 1 |
| $15,000 to $19,999 | 2,139 | 63 | 122 | 930 | 426 | 236 | 362 | 297 | 51 | 7 | 7 |
| $20,000 to $24,999 | 2,134 | 11 | 82 | 883 | 497 | 243 | 416 | 338 | 59 | 19 | 2 |
| $25,000 to $29,999 | 1,686 | 12 | 46 | 573 | 346 | 230 | 480 | 376 | 81 | 17 | 6 |
| $30,000 to $34,999 | 1,437 | 5 | 39 | 375 | 295 | 228 | 494 | 361 | 122 | 6 | 6 |
| $35,000 to $39,999 | 1,087 | 1 | 8 | 235 | 236 | 146 | 460 | 346 | 93 | 9 | 12 |
| $40,000 to $44,999 | 806 | 2 | 12 | 168 | 152 | 126 | 346 | 204 | 121 | 9 | 12 |
| $45,000 to $49,999 | 592 | – | 2 | 84 | 77 | 77 | 353 | 226 | 104 | 15 | 9 |
| $50,000 to $54,999 | 415 | – | – | 47 | 104 | 50 | 214 | 122 | 74 | 7 | 10 |
| $55,000 to $59,999 | 225 | – | – | 24 | 17 | 23 | 161 | 102 | 50 | 4 | 5 |
| $60,000 to $64,999 | 247 | – | – | 16 | 28 | 27 | 174 | 111 | 39 | 5 | 20 |
| $65,000 to $69,999 | 111 | – | – | 5 | 6 | 5 | 95 | 49 | 40 | 1 | 6 |
| $70,000 to $74,999 | 85 | – | – | 7 | 6 | 8 | 63 | 42 | 8 | 10 | 2 |
| $75,000 to $79,999 | 76 | – | – | 9 | 11 | 4 | 52 | 21 | 18 | 8 | 5 |
| $80,000 to $84,999 | 66 | – | – | 8 | 8 | 4 | 46 | 21 | 16 | 2 | 7 |
| $85,000 to $89,999 | 47 | – | – | – | 6 | 2 | 38 | 16 | 11 | 3 | 9 |
| $90,000 to $94,999 | 35 | – | – | – | 2 | 4 | 28 | 19 | 5 | 2 | 2 |
| $95,000 to $99,999 | 10 | – | – | – | – | – | 10 | 7 | 3 | 2 | – |
| $100,000 or more | 218 | 2 | 2 | 10 | 8 | 17 | 181 | 65 | 41 | 57 | 18 |

*(continued)*

*(continued from previous page)*

| | total | less than 9th grade | 9th to 12th grade, no diploma | high school graduate, incl. GED | some college, no degree | associate's degree | bachelor's degree or more | | | | |
|---|---|---|---|---|---|---|---|---|---|---|---|
| | | | | | | | total | bachelor's degree | master's degree | professional degree | doctoral degree |
| **Median earnings** | | | | | | | | | | | |
| Women with earnings | $20,641 | $10,245 | $11,024 | $16,580 | $20,647 | $23,941 | $31,827 | $29,083 | $39,249 | $50,522 | $57,672 |
| Women working full-time | $26,428 | $12,791 | $15,070 | $21,417 | $26,057 | $29,158 | $38,080 | $35,574 | $44,599 | $60,876 | $61,199 |
| Percent working full-time | 49.7% | 26.2% | 32.0% | 49.5% | 51.4% | 55.0% | 54.9% | 51.9% | 60.4% | 71.7% | 69.2% |
| **Percent distribution** | | | | | | | | | | | |
| Total women | 100.0% | 100.0% | 100.0% | 100.0% | 100.0% | 100.0% | 100.0% | 100.0% | 100.0% | 100.0% | 100.0% |
| Without earnings | 20.5 | 48.4 | 37.1 | 21.1 | 19.4 | 14.7 | 14.0 | 15.2 | 11.0 | 12.8 | 7.5 |
| With earnings | 79.5 | 51.6 | 62.9 | 78.9 | 80.6 | 85.3 | 85.9 | 84.8 | 89.0 | 87.2 | 92.5 |
| Under $25,000 | 47.7 | 49.2 | 56.1 | 58.4 | 49.9 | 44.3 | 30.6 | 34.9 | 20.6 | 18.6 | 11.3 |
| $25,000 to $49,999 | 25.0 | 2.4 | 6.6 | 18.9 | 26.0 | 34.7 | 36.9 | 36.2 | 43.3 | 24.8 | 28.3 |
| $50,000 to $74,999 | 4.8 | – | – | 1.3 | 3.8 | 4.9 | 12.2 | 10.2 | 17.5 | 11.9 | 27.0 |
| $75,000 to $99,999 | 1.0 | – | – | 0.2 | 0.6 | 0.6 | 3.0 | 2.0 | 4.4 | 7.5 | 14.5 |
| $100,000 or more | 1.0 | – | 0.1 | 0.1 | 0.2 | 0.7 | 3.1 | 1.6 | 3.4 | 25.2 | 11.3 |

*Note: (–) means sample is too small to make a reliable estimate.*
*Source: Bureau of the Census, Internet web site, <http://www.census.gov/cps/ads/sdata.htm>; calculations by New Strategist*

# Distribution of Women by Earnings and Education, 1997: Women Aged 45 to 54

*(number and percent distribution of women aged 45 to 54 by earnings and educational attainment, 1997; median earnings of women with earnings and of women with earnings who work full-time, year-round; percent of women who work full-time, year-round; women in thousands as of 1998)*

| | total | less than 9th grade | 9th to 12th grade, no diploma | high school graduate, incl. GED | some college, no degree | associate's degree | bachelor's degree or more | | | | |
| --- | --- | --- | --- | --- | --- | --- | --- | --- | --- | --- | --- |
| | | | | | | | total | bachelor's degree | master's degree | professional degree | doctoral degree |
| Total women | 17,459 | 852 | 1,256 | 6,242 | 3,070 | 1,520 | 4,519 | 2,858 | 1,301 | 185 | 175 |
| Without earnings | 3,790 | 415 | 497 | 1,513 | 591 | 213 | 561 | 405 | 119 | 25 | 12 |
| With earnings | 13,670 | 437 | 759 | 4,729 | 2,480 | 1,307 | 3,958 | 2,453 | 1,182 | 161 | 162 |
| Under $5,000 | 1,312 | 88 | 104 | 519 | 244 | 103 | 254 | 199 | 44 | 5 | 6 |
| $5,000 to $9,999 | 1,291 | 87 | 174 | 489 | 222 | 93 | 226 | 157 | 53 | – | 16 |
| $10,000 to $14,999 | 1,706 | 131 | 168 | 733 | 322 | 110 | 239 | 160 | 65 | 7 | 8 |
| $15,000 to $19,999 | 1,718 | 70 | 123 | 794 | 343 | 155 | 231 | 174 | 40 | 16 | – |
| $20,000 to $24,999 | 1,688 | 30 | 84 | 772 | 334 | 157 | 311 | 247 | 49 | 5 | 9 |
| $25,000 to $29,999 | 1,259 | 6 | 52 | 478 | 247 | 159 | 317 | 225 | 81 | 3 | 6 |
| $30,000 to $34,999 | 1,181 | 15 | 21 | 362 | 251 | 132 | 400 | 283 | 100 | 4 | 12 |
| $35,000 to $39,999 | 859 | 7 | 13 | 212 | 157 | 123 | 345 | 203 | 109 | 17 | 15 |
| $40,000 to $44,999 | 652 | 1 | 15 | 136 | 101 | 97 | 301 | 156 | 123 | 11 | 11 |
| $45,000 to $49,999 | 533 | – | – | 62 | 95 | 59 | 317 | 152 | 138 | 9 | 18 |
| $50,000 to $54,999 | 411 | – | – | 69 | 37 | 43 | 262 | 133 | 100 | 11 | 20 |
| $55,000 to $59,999 | 231 | – | – | 23 | 43 | 15 | 150 | 80 | 69 | – | 2 |
| $60,000 to $64,999 | 241 | – | 3 | 30 | 16 | 22 | 171 | 84 | 59 | 12 | 15 |
| $65,000 to $69,999 | 120 | – | – | – | 29 | 8 | 82 | 44 | 30 | 4 | 4 |
| $70,000 to $74,999 | 95 | – | – | 12 | 6 | 6 | 72 | 24 | 32 | 13 | 3 |
| $75,000 to $79,999 | 99 | – | – | 13 | 12 | 7 | 66 | 33 | 24 | 5 | 4 |
| $80,000 to $84,999 | 46 | – | – | 5 | 1 | 1 | 39 | 21 | 14 | 1 | 3 |
| $85,000 to $89,999 | 16 | – | – | – | – | – | 16 | 6 | 5 | 2 | 3 |
| $90,000 to $94,999 | 26 | – | – | – | 3 | – | 24 | 12 | 2 | 7 | 2 |
| $95,000 to $99,999 | 21 | – | – | 3 | 2 | – | 15 | 13 | 2 | – | – |
| $100,000 or more | 165 | – | 2 | 16 | 14 | 15 | 118 | 46 | 39 | 29 | 5 |

*(continued)*

*(continued from previous page)*

| | total | less than 9th grade | 9th to 12th grade, no diploma | high school graduate, incl. GED | some college, no degree | associate's degree | bachelor's degree or more | | | | |
| --- | --- | --- | --- | --- | --- | --- | --- | --- | --- | --- | --- |
| | | | | | | | total | bachelor's degree | master's degree | professional degree | doctoral degree |
| **Median earnings** | | | | | | | | | | | |
| Women with earnings | $21,867 | $11,194 | $12,256 | $18,739 | $21,184 | $25,787 | $34,991 | $30,702 | $41,351 | $50,798 | $41,775 |
| Women working full-time | $27,249 | $13,702 | $16,636 | $22,340 | $26,974 | $30,374 | $40,476 | $36,328 | $45,776 | $61,842 | $47,486 |
| Percent working full-time | 52.7% | 29.5% | 34.8% | 51.3% | 53.8% | 59.4% | 60.9% | 59.3% | 62.4% | 66.5% | 69.1% |
| **Percent distribution** | | | | | | | | | | | |
| **Total women** | 100.0% | 100.0% | 100.0% | 100.0% | 100.0% | 100.0% | 100.0% | 100.0% | 100.0% | 100.0% | 100.0% |
| Without earnings | 21.7 | 48.7 | 39.6 | 24.2 | 19.3 | 14.0 | 12.4 | 14.2 | 9.1 | 13.5 | 6.9 |
| With earnings | 78.3 | 51.3 | 60.4 | 75.8 | 80.8 | 86.0 | 87.6 | 85.8 | 90.9 | 87.0 | 92.6 |
| Under $25,000 | 44.2 | 47.7 | 52.0 | 53.0 | 47.7 | 40.7 | 27.9 | 32.8 | 19.3 | 17.8 | 22.3 |
| $25,000 to $49,999 | 25.7 | 3.4 | 8.0 | 20.0 | 27.7 | 37.5 | 37.2 | 35.7 | 42.4 | 23.8 | 35.4 |
| $50,000 to $74,999 | 6.3 | – | 0.2 | 2.1 | 4.3 | 6.2 | 16.3 | 12.8 | 22.3 | 21.6 | 25.1 |
| $75,000 to $99,999 | 1.2 | – | – | 0.3 | 0.6 | 0.5 | 3.5 | 3.0 | 3.6 | 8.1 | 6.9 |
| $100,000 or more | 0.9 | – | 0.2 | 0.3 | 0.5 | 1.0 | 2.6 | 1.6 | 3.0 | 15.7 | 2.9 |

*Note: (–) means sample is too small to make a reliable estimate.*
*Source: Bureau of the Census, Internet web site, <http://www.census.gov/cps/ads/sdata.htm>; calculations by New Strategist*

# Distribution of Women by Earnings and Education, 1997: Women Aged 55 to 64

*(number and percent distribution of women aged 55 to 64 by earnings and educational attainment, 1997; median earnings of women with earnings and of women with earnings who work full-time, year-round; percent of women who work full-time, year-round; women in thousands as of 1998)*

| | total | less than 9th grade | 9th to 12th grade, no diploma | high school graduate, incl. GED | some college, no degree | associate's degree | bachelor's degree or more | | | | |
| --- | --- | --- | --- | --- | --- | --- | --- | --- | --- | --- | --- |
| | | | | | | | total | bachelor's degree | master's degree | professional degree | doctoral degree |
| Total women | 11,582 | 931 | 1,519 | 4,650 | 1,737 | 669 | 2,077 | 1,340 | 601 | 78 | 58 |
| Without earnings | 4,985 | 661 | 841 | 2,033 | 630 | 214 | 607 | 450 | 128 | 15 | 14 |
| With earnings | 6,597 | 270 | 678 | 2,617 | 1,108 | 455 | 1,470 | 890 | 473 | 63 | 44 |
| Under $5,000 | 846 | 52 | 140 | 315 | 134 | 49 | 155 | 106 | 41 | 3 | 5 |
| $5,000 to $9,999 | 874 | 51 | 147 | 400 | 119 | 39 | 117 | 83 | 32 | 2 | – |
| $10,000 to $14,999 | 1,003 | 59 | 137 | 491 | 143 | 53 | 120 | 84 | 36 | – | – |
| $15,000 to $19,999 | 822 | 58 | 93 | 375 | 147 | 56 | 95 | 67 | 21 | 4 | 2 |
| $20,000 to $24,999 | 773 | 25 | 65 | 356 | 141 | 69 | 116 | 91 | 22 | 1 | 2 |
| $25,000 to $29,999 | 550 | 9 | 43 | 247 | 90 | 53 | 108 | 64 | 43 | – | 1 |
| $30,000 to $34,999 | 510 | 9 | 23 | 151 | 127 | 43 | 157 | 102 | 41 | 8 | 6 |
| $35,000 to $39,999 | 304 | 3 | 4 | 98 | 56 | 22 | 120 | 85 | 29 | 2 | 5 |
| $40,000 to $44,999 | 241 | 1 | 11 | 75 | 31 | 27 | 98 | 44 | 44 | 6 | 2 |
| $45,000 to $49,999 | 149 | – | 1 | 32 | 29 | 12 | 73 | 41 | 21 | 7 | 4 |
| $50,000 to $54,999 | 192 | 1 | 13 | 27 | 23 | 12 | 114 | 29 | 76 | 6 | 3 |
| $55,000 to $59,999 | 81 | – | – | 8 | 17 | 3 | 54 | 22 | 29 | – | 3 |
| $60,000 to $64,999 | 84 | – | 1 | 7 | 14 | 6 | 56 | 24 | 19 | 10 | 3 |
| $65,000 to $69,999 | 23 | – | – | 7 | – | 2 | 14 | 5 | 6 | – | 2 |
| $70,000 to $74,999 | 22 | – | – | 1 | 9 | – | 12 | 11 | 2 | – | – |
| $75,000 to $79,999 | 24 | – | – | – | 13 | – | 13 | 7 | – | – | – |
| $80,000 to $84,999 | 17 | – | – | 2 | 6 | 6 | 4 | 3 | – | 4 | 1 |
| $85,000 to $89,999 | 10 | – | – | 4 | 3 | – | 3 | 2 | 1 | – | – |
| $90,000 to $94,999 | 7 | – | – | – | – | – | 7 | 3 | 4 | – | – |
| $95,000 to $99,999 | 13 | – | – | – | 3 | 2 | 8 | 6 | 2 | – | – |
| $100,000 or more | 53 | – | – | 21 | 5 | – | 27 | 9 | 4 | 8 | 5 |

*(continued)*

(continued from previous page)

| | total | less than 9th grade | 9th to 12th grade, no diploma | high school graduate, incl. GED | some college, no degree | associate's degree | bachelor's degree or more | | | | |
| | | | | | | | total | bachelor's degree | master's degree | professional degree | doctoral degree |
|---|---|---|---|---|---|---|---|---|---|---|---|
| **Median earnings** | | | | | | | | | | | |
| Women with earnings | $18,203 | $11,675 | $11,351 | $16,192 | $20,345 | $21,251 | $30,643 | $25,746 | $35,296 | $48,397 | $41,450 |
| Women working full-time | $24,602 | $16,013 | $17,248 | $21,513 | $26,077 | $29,039 | $37,862 | $34,191 | $41,836 | $49,636 | $46,082 |
| Percent working full-time | 34.6% | 18.0% | 23.0% | 34.9% | 40.2% | 39.2% | 43.7% | 39.1% | 49.1% | 61.5% | 69.0% |
| **Percent distribution** | | | | | | | | | | | |
| **Total women** | 100.0% | 100.0% | 100.0% | 100.0% | 100.0% | 100.0% | 100.0% | 100.0% | 100.0% | 100.0% | 100.0% |
| Without earnings | 43.0 | 71.0 | 55.4 | 43.7 | 36.3 | 32.0 | 29.2 | 33.6 | 21.3 | 19.2 | 24.1 |
| With earnings | 57.0 | 29.0 | 44.6 | 56.3 | 63.8 | 68.0 | 70.8 | 66.4 | 78.7 | 80.8 | 75.9 |
| Under $25,000 | 37.3 | 26.3 | 38.3 | 41.7 | 39.4 | 39.8 | 29.0 | 32.2 | 25.3 | 12.8 | 15.5 |
| $25,000 to $49,999 | 15.1 | 2.4 | 5.4 | 13.0 | 19.2 | 23.5 | 26.8 | 25.1 | 29.6 | 29.5 | 31.0 |
| $50,000 to $74,999 | 3.5 | 0.1 | 0.9 | 1.1 | 3.6 | 3.4 | 12.0 | 6.8 | 22.0 | 20.5 | 19.0 |
| $75,000 to $99,999 | 0.6 | – | – | 0.1 | 1.4 | 1.2 | 1.7 | 1.6 | 1.2 | 5.1 | 1.7 |
| $100,000 or more | 0.5 | – | – | 0.5 | 0.3 | – | 1.3 | 0.7 | 0.7 | 10.3 | 8.6 |

*Note: (–) means sample is too small to make a reliable estimate.*
*Source: Bureau of the Census, Internet web site, <http://www.census.gov/cps/ads/sdata.htm>; calculations by New Strategist*

# Distribution of Women by Earnings and Education, 1997: Women Aged 65 or Older

*(number and percent distribution of women aged 65 or older by earnings and educational attainment, 1997; median earnings of women with earnings and of women with earnings who work full-time, year-round; percent of women who work full-time, year-round; women in thousands as of 1998)*

| | total | less than 9th grade | 9th to 12th grade, no diploma | high school graduate, incl. GED | some college, no degree | associate's degree | bachelor's degree or more | | | | |
|---|---|---|---|---|---|---|---|---|---|---|---|
| | | | | | | | total | bachelor's degree | master's degree | professional degree | doctoral degree |
| **Total women** | **18,558** | **3,325** | **2,867** | **7,131** | **2,328** | **825** | **2,083** | **1,396** | **544** | **96** | **47** |
| Without earnings | 16,370 | 3,144 | 2,603 | 6,258 | 2,014 | 709 | 1,643 | 1,136 | 409 | 70 | 28 |
| With earnings | 2,188 | 181 | 264 | 873 | 313 | 117 | 440 | 260 | 135 | 27 | 18 |
| Under $5,000 | 830 | 82 | 98 | 344 | 139 | 35 | 134 | 64 | 57 | 8 | 4 |
| $5,000 to $9,999 | 495 | 59 | 78 | 201 | 59 | 38 | 60 | 48 | 9 | 2 | – |
| $10,000 to $14,999 | 315 | 21 | 47 | 159 | 28 | 14 | 47 | 29 | 12 | 5 | 1 |
| $15,000 to $19,999 | 120 | 7 | 12 | 54 | 20 | 1 | 26 | 19 | 3 | – | 4 |
| $20,000 to $24,999 | 84 | 1 | 16 | 39 | 9 | 3 | 18 | 15 | 3 | – | – |
| $25,000 to $29,999 | 76 | 2 | 4 | 27 | 19 | 6 | 20 | 15 | 4 | 1 | – |
| $30,000 to $34,999 | 73 | – | 3 | 18 | 18 | 10 | 25 | 14 | 8 | 3 | – |
| $35,000 to $39,999 | 48 | 5 | 4 | 13 | – | – | 26 | 9 | 17 | – | – |
| $40,000 to $44,999 | 39 | 2 | 3 | 3 | 4 | 1 | 26 | 16 | 8 | – | 3 |
| $45,000 to $49,999 | 29 | 1 | – | 1 | 8 | 7 | 12 | 7 | 2 | 3 | – |
| $50,000 to $54,999 | 18 | – | – | 4 | – | 2 | 11 | 3 | 6 | 3 | – |
| $55,000 to $59,999 | 12 | – | – | – | 8 | – | 5 | 2 | 2 | – | – |
| $60,000 to $64,999 | 18 | – | – | 5 | – | – | 14 | 7 | 2 | – | 5 |
| $65,000 to $69,999 | – | – | – | – | – | – | – | – | – | – | – |
| $70,000 to $74,999 | 5 | – | – | – | 3 | 2 | – | – | – | – | – |
| $75,000 to $79,999 | 3 | – | – | – | – | – | 3 | 3 | – | 3 | – |
| $80,000 to $84,999 | – | – | – | – | – | – | – | – | – | – | – |
| $85,000 to $89,999 | 2 | – | – | – | – | – | 2 | 2 | – | – | – |
| $90,000 to $94,999 | 5 | – | – | – | – | – | 5 | 3 | – | 2 | – |
| $95,000 to $99,999 | 3 | – | 2 | 2 | – | – | 1 | – | – | – | 1 |
| $100,000 or more | 13 | 1 | 6 | 6 | – | – | 6 | 2 | 2 | – | 2 |

*(continued)*

(continued from previous page)

| | total | less than 9th grade | 9th to 12th grade, no diploma | high school graduate, incl. GED | some college, no degree | associate's degree | bachelor's degree or more | | | | |
|---|---|---|---|---|---|---|---|---|---|---|---|
| | | | | | | | total | bachelor's degree | master's degree | professional degree | doctoral degree |
| **Median earnings** | | | | | | | | | | | |
| Women with earnings | $7,272 | $5,539 | $6,933 | $7,172 | $6,257 | $7,106 | $11,882 | $12,086 | $10,197 | $13,353 | $40,741 |
| Women working full-time | $21,717 | $10,896 | $13,228 | $16,362 | $26,879 | $31,093 | $35,822 | $32,043 | $36,190 | $45,962 | $60,815 |
| Percent working full-time | 3.3% | 0.8% | 2.4% | 3.1% | 4.2% | 3.3% | 8.4% | 7.2% | 10.7% | 8.3% | 17.0% |
| **Percent distribution** | | | | | | | | | | | |
| Total women | 100.0% | 100.0% | 100.0% | 100.0% | 100.0% | 100.0% | 100.0% | 100.0% | 100.0% | 100.0% | 100.0% |
| Without earnings | 88.2 | 94.6 | 90.8 | 87.8 | 86.5 | 85.9 | 78.9 | 81.4 | 75.2 | 72.9 | 59.6 |
| With earnings | 11.8 | 5.4 | 9.2 | 12.2 | 13.4 | 14.2 | 21.1 | 18.6 | 24.8 | 28.1 | 38.3 |
| Under $25,000 | 9.9 | 5.1 | 8.8 | 11.2 | 11.0 | 11.0 | 13.7 | 12.5 | 15.4 | 15.6 | 19.1 |
| $25,000 to $49,999 | 1.4 | 0.3 | 0.5 | 0.9 | 2.1 | 2.9 | 5.2 | 4.4 | 7.2 | 7.3 | 6.4 |
| $50,000 to $74,999 | 0.3 | – | – | 0.1 | 0.5 | 0.5 | 1.4 | 0.9 | 1.8 | 3.1 | 10.6 |
| $75,000 to $99,999 | 0.1 | – | – | 0.0 | – | – | 0.5 | 0.6 | – | 2.1 | 2.1 |
| $100,000 or more | 0.1 | – | 0.0 | 0.1 | – | – | 0.3 | 0.1 | 0.4 | – | 4.3 |

Note: (–) means sample is too small to make a reliable estimate.
Source: Bureau of the Census, Internet web site, <http://www.census.gov/cps/ads/sdata.htm>; calculations by New Strategist

# Education Boosts Earnings of Black, Hispanic, and White Women

### Non-Hispanic white women with professional degrees earn the most.

The earnings of women vary dramatically depending on their education and their race and Hispanic origin. Among full-time workers, those with the highest earnings are non-Hispanic white women with professional degrees. Their median income stood at $60,337 in 1997. The women with the lowest earnings were Hispanics with less than a ninth grade education—a median of just $12,421.

The earnings gap between non-Hispanic white women and black or Hispanic women is due, in large part, to their differing educational attainment. Only 13 percent of non-Hispanic white women do not have a high school diploma compared with 23 percent of black women and fully 45 percent of Hispanic women. Whereas 24 percent of non-Hispanic white women aged 25 or older have a bachelor's degree, the figure is 15 percent among blacks and only 11 percent among Hispanics.

✘ The educational attainment of black women is rising, and their earnings will approach those of non-Hispanic white women in the years ahead. The educational attainment of Hispanic women will not rise much until immigrants become a smaller share of the Hispanic population.

### Earnings of educated black, white, and Hispanic women are nearly the same

*(median earnings of women aged 25 or older with a bachelor's degree who work full-time, year-round, by race and Hispanic origin, 1997)*

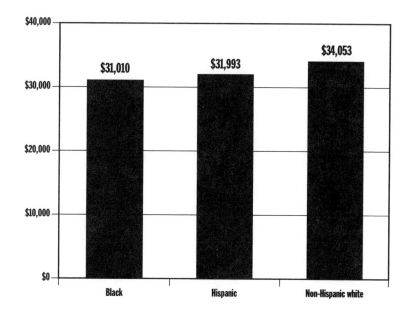

# Distribution of Women by Earnings and Education, 1997: Black Women

*(number and percent distribution of black women aged 25 or older by earnings and educational attainment, 1997; median earnings of women with earnings and of women with earnings who work full-time, year-round; percent of women who work full-time, year-round; women in thousands as of 1998)*

| | total | less than 9th grade | 9th to 12th grade, no diploma | high school graduate, incl. GED | some college, no degree | associate's degree | bachelor's degree or more | | | | |
| --- | --- | --- | --- | --- | --- | --- | --- | --- | --- | --- | --- |
| | | | | | | | total | bachelor's degree | master's degree | professional degree | doctoral degree |
| **Total women** | **10,798** | **804** | **1,708** | **3,805** | **2,069** | **752** | **1,661** | **1,121** | **452** | **51** | **38** |
| Without earnings | 3,617 | 647 | 916 | 1,232 | 463 | 99 | 259 | 163 | 87 | 4 | 4 |
| With earnings | 7,181 | 156 | 792 | 2,573 | 1,605 | 652 | 1,403 | 957 | 365 | 47 | 34 |
| Under $5,000 | 854 | 39 | 197 | 359 | 146 | 50 | 63 | 47 | 7 | 5 | 4 |
| $5,000 to $9,999 | 841 | 30 | 162 | 340 | 161 | 69 | 80 | 57 | 22 | – | – |
| $10,000 to $14,999 | 1,001 | 49 | 190 | 396 | 198 | 77 | 92 | 78 | 7 | 2 | 4 |
| $15,000 to $19,999 | 1,163 | 29 | 126 | 534 | 271 | 77 | 126 | 95 | 21 | 5 | 5 |
| $20,000 to $24,999 | 957 | 2 | 56 | 391 | 249 | 109 | 152 | 126 | 22 | – | 5 |
| $25,000 to $29,999 | 647 | 4 | 29 | 226 | 191 | 56 | 140 | 101 | 35 | 4 | – |
| $30,000 to $34,999 | 585 | 5 | 27 | 137 | 137 | 82 | 198 | 137 | 48 | 9 | 4 |
| $35,000 to $39,999 | 351 | – | 3 | 83 | 108 | 45 | 113 | 76 | 30 | 7 | – |
| $40,000 to $44,999 | 209 | – | 3 | 34 | 38 | 28 | 108 | 66 | 39 | 1 | 2 |
| $45,000 to $49,999 | 184 | – | – | 25 | 53 | 10 | 96 | 59 | 33 | 2 | 2 |
| $50,000 to $54,999 | 155 | – | – | 32 | 19 | 17 | 87 | 36 | 47 | 3 | 1 |
| $55,000 to $59,999 | 56 | – | – | 2 | 16 | 5 | 32 | 18 | 14 | – | – |
| $60,000 to $64,999 | 74 | – | – | 3 | 5 | 14 | 52 | 26 | 18 | 2 | 5 |
| $65,000 to $69,999 | 28 | – | – | 2 | 8 | 6 | 12 | 9 | 2 | – | – |
| $70,000 to $74,999 | 14 | – | – | – | – | 2 | 12 | 7 | 4 | – | 2 |
| $75,000 to $79,999 | 17 | – | – | 3 | 3 | 3 | 11 | 8 | 3 | – | – |
| $80,000 to $84,999 | 8 | – | – | – | – | – | 8 | – | 8 | – | – |
| $85,000 to $89,999 | 7 | – | – | – | 1 | – | 6 | 2 | 4 | – | – |
| $90,000 to $94,999 | 3 | – | – | 3 | – | – | – | – | – | – | – |
| $95,000 to $99,999 | – | – | – | – | – | – | – | – | – | – | – |
| $100,000 or more | 24 | – | – | 5 | – | 3 | 16 | 9 | – | 7 | 1 |

*(continued)*

*(continued from previous page)*

| | total | less than 9th grade | 9th to 12th grade, no diploma | high school graduate, incl. GED | some college, no degree | associate's degree | bachelor's degree or more | | | | |
|---|---|---|---|---|---|---|---|---|---|---|---|
| | | | | | | | total | bachelor's degree | master's degree | professional degree | doctoral degree |
| **Median earnings** | | | | | | | | | | | |
| Women with earnings | $18,600 | $10,627 | $10,692 | $16,525 | $20,405 | $22,064 | $30,864 | $28,648 | $36,763 | $32,444 | $24,626 |
| Women working full-time | $22,595 | $13,604 | $15,084 | $19,993 | $23,769 | $26,758 | $32,369 | $31,010 | $40,589 | $36,419 | $40,342 |
| Percent working full-time | 45.2% | 9.5% | 24.1% | 45.4% | 54.9% | 58.9% | 65.4% | 67.4% | 61.9% | 60.8% | 52.6% |
| **Percent distribution** | | | | | | | | | | | |
| **Total women** | 100.0% | 100.0% | 100.0% | 100.0% | 100.0% | 100.0% | 100.0% | 100.0% | 100.0% | 100.0% | 100.0% |
| Without earnings | 33.5 | 80.5 | 53.6 | 32.4 | 22.4 | 13.2 | 15.6 | 14.5 | 19.2 | 7.8 | 10.5 |
| With earnings | 66.5 | 19.4 | 46.4 | 67.6 | 77.6 | 86.7 | 84.5 | 85.4 | 80.8 | 92.2 | 89.5 |
| Under $25,000 | 44.6 | 18.5 | 42.8 | 53.1 | 49.5 | 50.8 | 30.9 | 36.0 | 17.5 | 23.5 | 47.4 |
| $25,000 to $49,999 | 18.3 | 1.1 | 3.6 | 13.3 | 25.5 | 29.4 | 39.4 | 39.2 | 40.9 | 45.1 | 21.1 |
| $50,000 to $74,999 | 3.0 | – | – | 1.0 | 2.3 | 5.9 | 11.7 | 8.6 | 18.8 | 9.8 | 21.1 |
| $75,000 to $99,999 | 0.3 | – | – | 0.1 | 0.2 | 0.4 | 1.5 | 0.9 | 3.3 | – | – |
| $100,000 or more | 0.2 | – | – | 0.1 | – | 0.4 | 1.0 | 0.8 | – | 13.7 | 2.6 |

*Note: (–) means sample is too small to make a reliable estimate.*
*Source: Bureau of the Census, Internet web site, <http:// www.census.gov/cps/ads/sdata.htm>; calculations by New Strategist*

# Distribution of Women by Earnings and Education, 1997: Hispanic Women

*(number and percent distribution of Hispanic women aged 25 or older by earnings and educational attainment, 1997; median earnings of women with earnings and of women with earnings who work full-time, year-round; percent of women who work full-time, year-round; women in thousands as of 1998)*

| | total | less than 9th grade | 9th to 12th grade, no diploma | high school graduate, incl. GED | some college, no degree | associate's degree | bachelor's degree or more | | | | |
|---|---|---|---|---|---|---|---|---|---|---|---|
| | | | | | | | total | bachelor's degree | master's degree | professional degree | doctoral degree |
| **Total women** | **7,989** | **2,322** | **1,252** | **2,116** | **998** | **429** | **872** | **670** | **129** | **45** | **28** |
| Without earnings | 3,376 | 1,431 | 667 | 765 | 258 | 85 | 169 | 130 | 23 | 11 | 5 |
| With earnings | 4,614 | 891 | 585 | 1,351 | 740 | 344 | 703 | 540 | 106 | 34 | 23 |
| Under $5,000 | 628 | 195 | 121 | 166 | 75 | 25 | 44 | 37 | 1 | 1 | 5 |
| $5,000 to $9,999 | 806 | 247 | 168 | 221 | 82 | 40 | 49 | 40 | 6 | 1 | – |
| $10,000 to $14,999 | 924 | 265 | 152 | 272 | 129 | 29 | 76 | 58 | 12 | 4 | 3 |
| $15,000 to $19,999 | 617 | 109 | 68 | 228 | 127 | 44 | 41 | 38 | 2 | 1 | – |
| $20,000 to $24,999 | 503 | 39 | 39 | 179 | 103 | 73 | 70 | 63 | 3 | 2 | 2 |
| $25,000 to $29,999 | 312 | 11 | 21 | 91 | 78 | 36 | 77 | 57 | 14 | 2 | 4 |
| $30,000 to $34,999 | 248 | 8 | 7 | 75 | 45 | 41 | 71 | 61 | 8 | 2 | – |
| $35,000 to $39,999 | 203 | 7 | 2 | 54 | 43 | 10 | 87 | 72 | 12 | 2 | – |
| $40,000 to $44,999 | 119 | 4 | 3 | 30 | 16 | 14 | 52 | 32 | 18 | 1 | – |
| $45,000 to $49,999 | 76 | 1 | 1 | 13 | 18 | 14 | 29 | 18 | 10 | 1 | – |
| $50,000 to $54,999 | 55 | 1 | – | 7 | 11 | 4 | 32 | 15 | 10 | 4 | 4 |
| $55,000 to $59,999 | 38 | – | – | 4 | 1 | 5 | 28 | 18 | 8 | 1 | 1 |
| $60,000 to $64,999 | 22 | – | – | 2 | 3 | 2 | 15 | 10 | 3 | – | 2 |
| $65,000 to $69,999 | 5 | – | – | – | – | 1 | 3 | 2 | 1 | – | – |
| $70,000 to $74,999 | 13 | – | – | 4 | 1 | 2 | 6 | 4 | – | 1 | – |
| $75,000 to $79,999 | 5 | – | – | – | 3 | – | 2 | 2 | – | – | – |
| $80,000 to $84,999 | 12 | – | – | 2 | – | 3 | 7 | 4 | – | 2 | 2 |
| $85,000 to $89,999 | – | – | – | – | – | – | – | – | – | – | – |
| $90,000 to $94,999 | 8 | 2 | – | – | 2 | – | 4 | 3 | 1 | – | – |
| $95,000 to $99,999 | – | – | – | – | – | – | – | – | – | – | – |
| $100,000 or more | 20 | – | 2 | 3 | 2 | 2 | 11 | 4 | – | 7 | – |

*(continued)*

*(continued from previous page)*

| | total | less than 9th grade | 9th to 12th grade, no diploma | high school graduate, incl. GED | some college, no degree | associate's degree | bachelor's degree or more | | | | |
| --- | --- | --- | --- | --- | --- | --- | --- | --- | --- | --- | --- |
| | | | | | | | total | bachelor's degree | master's degree | professional degree | doctoral degree |
| **Median earnings** | | | | | | | | | | | |
| Women with earnings | $14,577 | $10,048 | $10,072 | $15,276 | $18,056 | $22,085 | $29,503 | $27,598 | $37,397 | $37,309 | $27,559 |
| Women working full-time | $20,267 | $12,421 | $13,850 | $19,247 | $22,932 | $24,322 | $35,191 | $31,993 | $41,554 | $50,535 | $55,956 |
| Percent working full-time | 34.9% | 19.9% | 22.9% | 41.0% | 45.9% | 56.9% | 53.7% | 53.9% | 54.3% | 62.2% | 28.6% |
| **Percent distribution** | | | | | | | | | | | |
| **Total women** | 100.0% | 100.0% | 100.0% | 100.0% | 100.0% | 100.0% | 100.0% | 100.0% | 100.0% | 100.0% | 100.0% |
| Without earnings | 42.3 | 61.6 | 53.3 | 36.2 | 25.9 | 19.8 | 19.4 | 19.4 | 17.8 | 24.4 | 17.9 |
| With earnings | 57.8 | 38.4 | 46.7 | 63.8 | 74.1 | 80.2 | 80.6 | 80.6 | 82.2 | 75.6 | 82.1 |
| Under $25,000 | 43.5 | 36.8 | 43.8 | 50.4 | 51.7 | 49.2 | 32.1 | 35.2 | 18.6 | 20.0 | 35.7 |
| $25,000 to $49,999 | 12.0 | 1.3 | 2.7 | 12.4 | 20.0 | 26.8 | 36.2 | 35.8 | 48.1 | 17.8 | 14.3 |
| $50,000 to $74,999 | 1.7 | 0.0 | – | 0.8 | 1.6 | 3.3 | 9.6 | 7.3 | 17.1 | 13.3 | 25.0 |
| $75,000 to $99,999 | 0.3 | 0.1 | – | 0.1 | 0.5 | 0.7 | 1.5 | 1.3 | 0.8 | 4.4 | 7.1 |
| $100,000 or more | 0.3 | – | 0.2 | 0.1 | 0.2 | 0.5 | 1.3 | 0.6 | – | 15.6 | – |

*Note: (–) means sample is too small to make a reliable estimate.*
*Source: Bureau of the Census, Internet web site, <http://www.census.gov/cps/ads/sdata.htm>; calculations by New Strategist*

# Distribution of Women by Earnings and Education, 1997: White Women

*(number and percent distribution of white women aged 25 or older by earnings and educational attainment, 1997; median earnings of women with earnings and of women with earnings who work full-time, year-round; percent of women who work full-time, year-round; women in thousands as of 1998)*

| | total | less than 9th grade | 9th to 12th grade, no diploma | high school graduate, incl. GED | some college, no degree | associate's degree | bachelor's degree or more | | | | |
|---|---|---|---|---|---|---|---|---|---|---|---|
| | | | | | | | total | bachelor's degree | master's degree | professional degree | doctoral degree |
| Total women | 75,016 | 5,392 | 6,726 | 26,738 | 12,909 | 6,159 | 17,092 | 12,088 | 3,879 | 694 | 432 |
| Without earnings | 28,683 | 4,061 | 4,123 | 11,164 | 4,172 | 1,532 | 3,631 | 2,711 | 716 | 143 | 61 |
| With earnings | 46,333 | 1,331 | 2,603 | 15,574 | 8,736 | 4,627 | 13,462 | 9,377 | 3,163 | 551 | 371 |
| Under $5,000 | 5,924 | 346 | 581 | 2,245 | 1,203 | 444 | 1,107 | 845 | 224 | 19 | 21 |
| $5,000 to $9,999 | 5,433 | 353 | 598 | 2,187 | 998 | 399 | 897 | 699 | 164 | 24 | 10 |
| $10,000 to $14,999 | 6,224 | 326 | 573 | 2,675 | 1,221 | 521 | 908 | 686 | 190 | 26 | 5 |
| $15,000 to $19,999 | 5,531 | 166 | 323 | 2,362 | 1,174 | 593 | 912 | 734 | 144 | 19 | 15 |
| $20,000 to $24,999 | 5,571 | 66 | 236 | 2,175 | 1,205 | 631 | 1,258 | 1,037 | 172 | 35 | 13 |
| $25,000 to $29,999 | 4,291 | 29 | 130 | 1,457 | 828 | 553 | 1,293 | 976 | 271 | 23 | 23 |
| $30,000 to $34,999 | 3,732 | 19 | 65 | 950 | 719 | 479 | 1,500 | 1,124 | 323 | 34 | 19 |
| $35,000 to $39,999 | 2,569 | 17 | 34 | 577 | 434 | 290 | 1,218 | 871 | 287 | 31 | 28 |
| $40,000 to $44,999 | 1,903 | 7 | 35 | 375 | 281 | 264 | 942 | 564 | 311 | 36 | 31 |
| $45,000 to $49,999 | 1,344 | 1 | 3 | 172 | 199 | 163 | 804 | 457 | 273 | 43 | 31 |
| $50,000 to $54,999 | 1,081 | 1 | 13 | 137 | 169 | 110 | 651 | 354 | 231 | 31 | 36 |
| $55,000 to $59,999 | 584 | – | – | 59 | 83 | 38 | 404 | 227 | 157 | 8 | 11 |
| $60,000 to $64,999 | 594 | – | 4 | 65 | 52 | 50 | 422 | 238 | 109 | 36 | 38 |
| $65,000 to $69,999 | 286 | – | – | 12 | 41 | 23 | 210 | 116 | 77 | 5 | 13 |
| $70,000 to $74,999 | 209 | – | 3 | 20 | 25 | 15 | 148 | 80 | 38 | 25 | 5 |
| $75,000 to $79,999 | 210 | – | – | 25 | 34 | 8 | 141 | 72 | 40 | 20 | 9 |
| $80,000 to $84,999 | 147 | – | 13 | 13 | 15 | 10 | 109 | 58 | 29 | 8 | 14 |
| $85,000 to $89,999 | 78 | – | – | 4 | 10 | 2 | 62 | 25 | 14 | 11 | 12 |
| $90,000 to $94,999 | 89 | 2 | – | – | 7 | 4 | 76 | 46 | 11 | 14 | 4 |
| $95,000 to $99,999 | 52 | – | – | 6 | 3 | 2 | 42 | 30 | 9 | 2 | 1 |
| $100,000 or more | 482 | – | 6 | 58 | 34 | 25 | 358 | 138 | 87 | 101 | 32 |

*(continued)*

*(continued from previous page)*

| | total | less than 9th grade | 9th to 12th grade, no diploma | high school graduate, incl. GED | some college, no degree | associate's degree | bachelor's degree or more | | | | |
|---|---|---|---|---|---|---|---|---|---|---|---|
| | | | | | | | total | bachelor's degree | master's degree | professional degree | doctoral degree |
| **Median earnings** | | | | | | | | | | | |
| Women with earnings | $20,038 | $9,544 | $10,775 | $16,228 | $18,965 | $22,218 | $30,850 | $28,144 | $36,298 | $46,973 | $47,642 |
| Women working full-time | $26,207 | $13,339 | $16,254 | $21,602 | $25,140 | $27,195 | $36,623 | $33,896 | $41,884 | $60,003 | $52,653 |
| Percent working full-time | 37.4% | 11.8% | 18.5% | 35.0% | 40.8% | 47.6% | 50.4% | 48.7% | 52.6% | 59.1% | 61.6% |
| **Percent distribution** | | | | | | | | | | | |
| **Total women** | 100.0% | 100.0% | 100.0% | 100.0% | 100.0% | 100.0% | 100.0% | 100.0% | 100.0% | 100.0% | 100.0% |
| Without earnings | 38.2 | 75.3 | 61.3 | 41.8 | 32.3 | 24.9 | 21.2 | 22.4 | 18.5 | 20.6 | 14.1 |
| With earnings | 61.8 | 24.7 | 38.7 | 58.2 | 67.7 | 75.1 | 78.8 | 77.6 | 81.5 | 79.4 | 85.9 |
| Under $25,000 | 38.2 | 23.3 | 34.4 | 43.5 | 44.9 | 42.0 | 29.7 | 33.1 | 23.0 | 17.7 | 14.8 |
| $25,000 to $49,999 | 18.4 | 1.4 | 4.0 | 13.2 | 19.1 | 28.4 | 33.7 | 33.0 | 37.8 | 24.1 | 30.6 |
| $50,000 to $74,999 | 3.7 | 0.0 | 0.3 | 1.1 | 2.9 | 3.8 | 10.7 | 8.4 | 15.8 | 15.1 | 23.8 |
| $75,000 to $99,999 | 0.8 | 0.0 | – | 0.2 | 0.5 | 0.4 | 2.5 | 1.9 | 2.7 | 7.9 | 9.3 |
| $100,000 or more | 0.6 | – | 0.1 | 0.2 | 0.3 | 0.4 | 2.1 | 1.1 | 2.2 | 14.6 | 7.4 |

*Note: (–) means sample is too small to make a reliable estimate.*
*Source: Bureau of the Census, Internet web site, <http:// www.census.gov/cps/ads/sdata.htm>; calculations by New Strategist*

# Distribution of Women by Earnings and Education, 1997: Non-Hispanic White Women

*(number and percent distribution of non-Hispanic white women aged 25 or older by earnings and educational attainment, 1997; median earnings of women with earnings and of women with earnings who work full-time, year-round; percent of women who work full-time, year-round; women in thousands as of 1998)*

| | total | less than 9th grade | 9th to 12th grade, no diploma | high school graduate, incl. GED | some college, no degree | associate's degree | bachelor's degree or more | | | | |
|---|---|---|---|---|---|---|---|---|---|---|---|
| | | | | | | | total | bachelor's degree | master's degree | professional degree | doctoral degree |
| **Total women** | **67,409** | **3,148** | **5,530** | **24,742** | **11,953** | **5,762** | **16,274** | **11,457** | **3,761** | **652** | **404** |
| Without earnings | 25,447 | 2,685 | 3,487 | 10,439 | 3,922 | 1,448 | 3,467 | 2,582 | 697 | 132 | 55 |
| With earnings | 41,962 | 464 | 2,043 | 14,303 | 8,031 | 4,313 | 12,807 | 8,874 | 3,064 | 520 | 349 |
| Under $5,000 | 5,320 | 154 | 463 | 2,090 | 1,130 | 420 | 1,065 | 809 | 222 | 18 | 15 |
| $5,000 to $9,999 | 4,663 | 111 | 436 | 1,977 | 921 | 360 | 856 | 663 | 161 | 23 | 10 |
| $10,000 to $14,999 | 5,328 | 63 | 426 | 2,419 | 1,094 | 493 | 834 | 630 | 178 | 23 | 3 |
| $15,000 to $19,999 | 4,952 | 65 | 261 | 2,152 | 1,050 | 551 | 875 | 699 | 143 | 17 | 15 |
| $20,000 to $24,999 | 5,098 | 29 | 198 | 2,006 | 1,106 | 571 | 1,188 | 974 | 168 | 33 | 11 |
| $25,000 to $29,999 | 4,001 | 19 | 113 | 1,369 | 760 | 522 | 1,218 | 920 | 257 | 21 | 19 |
| $30,000 to $34,999 | 3,509 | 10 | 58 | 883 | 677 | 441 | 1,439 | 1,072 | 317 | 31 | 19 |
| $35,000 to $39,999 | 2,377 | 9 | 31 | 524 | 395 | 281 | 1,136 | 803 | 276 | 29 | 28 |
| $40,000 to $44,999 | 1,790 | 3 | 33 | 347 | 264 | 252 | 891 | 532 | 294 | 36 | 31 |
| $45,000 to $49,999 | 1,276 | – | 2 | 160 | 182 | 151 | 782 | 443 | 266 | 42 | 31 |
| $50,000 to $54,999 | 1,029 | – | 13 | 129 | 159 | 106 | 621 | 340 | 221 | 28 | 33 |
| $55,000 to $59,999 | 551 | – | – | 55 | 82 | 33 | 379 | 213 | 149 | 7 | 10 |
| $60,000 to $64,999 | 575 | – | 4 | 62 | 49 | 49 | 409 | 228 | 108 | 36 | 36 |
| $65,000 to $69,999 | 282 | – | – | 12 | 41 | 22 | 208 | 114 | 77 | 5 | 13 |
| $70,000 to $74,999 | 196 | – | 3 | 16 | 24 | 13 | 142 | 76 | 38 | 24 | 5 |
| $75,000 to $79,999 | 204 | – | – | 25 | 31 | 8 | 139 | 70 | 40 | 20 | 9 |
| $80,000 to $84,999 | 136 | – | – | 11 | 15 | 8 | 103 | 55 | 29 | 6 | 12 |
| $85,000 to $89,999 | 78 | – | – | 4 | 10 | 2 | 62 | 25 | 14 | 11 | 12 |
| $90,000 to $94,999 | 80 | – | – | – | 5 | 4 | 71 | 43 | 9 | 14 | 4 |
| $95,000 to $99,999 | 52 | – | 6 | 6 | 3 | 2 | 42 | 30 | 9 | 2 | 1 |
| $100,000 or more | 465 | – | 4 | 55 | 32 | 23 | 350 | 134 | 87 | 96 | 32 |

*(continued)*

*(continued from previous page)*

| | total | less than 9th grade | 9th to 12th grade, no diploma | high school graduate, incl. GED | some college, no degree | associate's degree | bachelor's degree or more | | | | |
|---|---|---|---|---|---|---|---|---|---|---|---|
| | | | | | | | total | bachelor's degree | master's degree | professional degree | doctoral degree |
| **Median earnings** | | | | | | | | | | | |
| Women with earnings | $20,535 | $8,486 | $11,068 | $16,336 | $19,097 | $22,269 | $30,927 | $28,225 | $36,234 | $47,131 | $48,281 |
| Women working full-time | $26,732 | $16,548 | $16,996 | $21,766 | $25,335 | $27,429 | $36,757 | $34,053 | $41,932 | $60,337 | $52,456 |
| Percent working full-time | 37.7% | 6.0% | 17.6% | 34.6% | 40.4% | 47.1% | 50.2% | 48.5% | 52.5% | 59.0% | 63.9% |
| **Percent distribution** | | | | | | | | | | | |
| **Total women** | 100.0% | 100.0% | 100.0% | 100.0% | 100.0% | 100.0% | 100.0% | 100.0% | 100.0% | 100.0% | 100.0% |
| Without earnings | 37.8 | 85.3 | 63.1 | 42.2 | 32.8 | 25.1 | 21.3 | 22.5 | 18.5 | 20.2 | 13.6 |
| With earnings | 62.2 | 14.7 | 36.9 | 57.8 | 67.2 | 74.9 | 78.7 | 77.5 | 81.5 | 79.8 | 86.4 |
| Under $25,000 | 37.6 | 13.4 | 32.3 | 43.0 | 44.3 | 41.6 | 29.6 | 32.9 | 23.2 | 17.5 | 13.4 |
| $25,000 to $49,999 | 19.2 | 1.3 | 4.3 | 13.3 | 19.1 | 28.6 | 33.6 | 32.9 | 37.5 | 24.4 | 31.7 |
| $50,000 to $74,999 | 3.9 | – | 0.4 | 1.1 | 3.0 | 3.9 | 10.8 | 8.5 | 15.8 | 15.3 | 24.0 |
| $75,000 to $99,999 | 0.8 | – | – | 0.2 | 0.5 | 0.4 | 2.6 | 1.9 | 2.7 | 8.1 | 9.4 |
| $100,000 or more | 0.7 | – | 0.1 | 0.2 | 0.3 | 0.4 | 2.2 | 1.2 | 2.3 | 14.7 | 7.9 |

*Note: (–) means sample is too small to make a reliable estimate.*
*Source: Bureau of the Census, Internet web site, <http://www.census.gov/cps/ads/sdata.htm>; calculations by New Strategist*

# In Some Occupations, Women Earn More Than Men

## Among full-time workers, women earn 74 percent as much as men.

There are many reasons for the earnings gap between men and women. On average, working men are older and have more job experience than working women, and the average male worker is better educated—all of these factors boost men's earnings. The different career choices of men and women also contribute to the gap.

Among full-time workers, women's median earnings range from a high of $184,299 for women in health-diagnosing occupation (i.e., physicians) to just $12,648 for those in private household occupations, such as nannies. Women's earnings as a percentage of men's range from a high of 154 percent for those in the extractive occupations (meaning the few women in those occupations make 54 percent more than the men) to a low of 44 percent for women in sales-related occupations. Women executives, administrators, and managers make 66 percent as much as their male counterparts. Women elementary and secondary school teachers earn 85 percent as much as their male counterparts, while women in the armed forces make 90 percent as much as men.

✗ Women's earnings will approach those of men in many occupations as better-educated, career-oriented women replace older, just-a-job women.

## Women's earnings vary by occupation

*(median earnings of women aged 15 or older who work full-time, year-round, by selected occupation, 1997)*

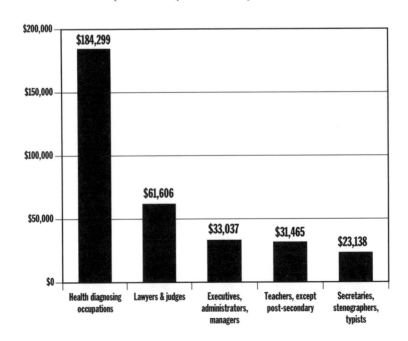

# Median Earnings of Women by Occupation, 1997

*(number and median earnings of women aged 15 or older who work full-time, year-round by occupation of longest job held, and women's earnings as a percentage of men's earnings, 1997; women in thousands as of 1998)*

| | number with earnings | median earnings | women's earnings as a percentage of men's earnings |
|---|---|---|---|
| **Total women who work full-time, year-round** | **37,683** | **$24,973** | **74.2%** |
| Managerial and professional specialty occupations | 13,289 | 34,475 | 68.6 |
| Executive, administrative, and managerial | 6,611 | 33,037 | 65.9 |
| Administrators and officials, public | 248 | 35,399 | 70.6 |
| Federal | 88 | 46,085 | 81.3 |
| State or local | 160 | 28,196 | 60.9 |
| Other administrators and officials, salaried | 4,083 | 35,834 | 68.2 |
| Manufacturing | 504 | 40,559 | 63.3 |
| Retail trade | 449 | 24,967 | 74.9 |
| Finance, insurance, and real estate | 604 | 33,985 | 51.2 |
| Other industries | 2,526 | 37,358 | 72.9 |
| Other administrators and officials, self-employed | 206 | 17,172 | 56.0 |
| Management-related occupations | 2,074 | 31,071 | 69.4 |
| Accountants and auditors | 723 | 31,501 | 69.9 |
| Professional specialty occupations | 6,679 | 35,417 | 70.3 |
| Engineers, architects, and surveyors | 186 | 45,725 | 81.2 |
| Engineers | 169 | 46,479 | 81.7 |
| Natural scientists and mathematicians | 524 | 46,302 | 90.4 |
| Health-diagnosing occupations | 192 | 184,299 | 92.1 |
| Health-assessment and treating occupations | 1,549 | 39,645 | 88.6 |
| Teachers, postsecondary | 157 | 46,036 | 88.1 |
| Teachers, except postsecondary | 2,254 | 31,465 | 84.7 |
| Lawyers and judges | 193 | 61,606 | 68.3 |
| Other professional specialty occupations | 1,624 | 28,894 | 80.2 |
| Technical, sales, and administrative support | 15,602 | 22,803 | 67.2 |
| Health technologists and technicians, except LPNs | 706 | 24,946 | 80.3 |
| Licensed practical nurses (LPNs) | 404 | 27,424 | 105.5 |
| Technologists and technicians, except health | 626 | 31,769 | 78.2 |
| Sales occupations | 4,077 | 21,392 | 60.0 |
| Supervisors and proprietors, salaried | 1,334 | 24,364 | 65.7 |
| Supervisors and proprietors, self-employed | 148 | 12,577 | 43.9 |
| Sales representatives, finance and business services | 771 | 31,298 | 69.9 |
| Sales representatives, commodities, except retail | 324 | 40,411 | 97.6 |
| Sales workers, retail and personal services | 1,485 | 14,655 | 65.7 |
| Cashiers | 812 | 12,832 | 74.6 |
| Sales-related occupations | 15 | 17,680 | 43.8 |
| Administrative support occupations, including clerical | 9,790 | 22,474 | 76.3 |
| Supervisors, administrative support, including clerical | 352 | 30,578 | 84.6 |
| Computer equipment operators | 132 | 26,650 | 83.1 |

*(continued)*

*(continued from previous page)*

| | number with earnings | median earnings | women's earnings as a percentage of men's earnings |
|---|---|---|---|
| Secretaries, stenographers, and typists | 2,418 | $23,138 | 97.0% |
| Financial record processors | 1,449 | 22,528 | 78.2 |
| Mail and message distributors | 296 | 32,770 | 90.3 |
| Material recording, scheduling, and distribution clerks | 620 | 21,748 | 84.7 |
| Other administrative support, including clerical | 4,523 | 21,607 | 80.7 |
| Service occupations | 4,807 | 15,964 | 71.5 |
| Private household occupations | 225 | 12,648 | 101.6 |
| Protective service occupations | 290 | 29,862 | 80.4 |
| Police and firefighters | 86 | 40,499 | 92.1 |
| Service, except protective and household | 4,292 | 15,773 | 86.3 |
| Food preparation and service occupations | 1,154 | 13,570 | 87.1 |
| Health service occupations | 1,206 | 17,344 | 92.0 |
| Cleaning and building service occupations, except household | 790 | 15,536 | 74.7 |
| Personal service occupations | 1,143 | 16,169 | 72.3 |
| Farming, forestry, and fishing occupations | 223 | 17,301 | 99.5 |
| Farm operators and managers | 96 | 20,235 | 96.3 |
| Farm occupations, except managerial | 50 | 14,750 | 94.3 |
| Related agricultural occupations | 75 | 17,880 | 96.8 |
| Forestry and fishing occupations | 1 | 24,256 | 140.7 |
| Precision production, craft, and repair occupations | 865 | 21,649 | 68.7 |
| Auto mechanics and repairers | 1 | 36,250 | 140.6 |
| Mechanics and repairers, except auto | 153 | 32,654 | 96.0 |
| Carpenters | 5 | 37,525 | 150.6 |
| Construction trades, except carpenters | 42 | 24,914 | 79.3 |
| Extractive occupations | 2 | 58,750 | 153.9 |
| Precision production occupations | 662 | 19,629 | 59.1 |
| Supervisors, production occupations | 200 | 27,107 | 72.6 |
| Precision metal working occupations | 47 | 20,730 | 58.0 |
| Plant and system operators | 6 | 40,351 | 98.5 |
| Other precision production occupations | 408 | 17,000 | 67.9 |
| Operators, fabricators, and laborers | 2,802 | 17,389 | 66.2 |
| Machine operators and tenders, except precision | 1,333 | 16,873 | 63.3 |
| Fabricators, assemblers, and hand-working occupations | 460 | 19,188 | 70.1 |
| Production inspectors, testers, samplers, and weighers | 298 | 20,101 | 68.9 |
| Motor vehicle operators | 190 | 20,052 | 72.7 |
| Transportation occupations, except motor vehicle | 10 | 36,615 | 73.3 |
| Material moving equipment operators | 46 | 22,792 | 83.5 |
| Handlers, equipment cleaners, helpers, and laborers | 465 | 15,774 | 73.5 |
| Construction laborers | 12 | 16,105 | 74.2 |
| Freight, stock, and material handlers | 186 | 15,559 | 73.2 |
| Hand packers and packagers | 89 | 15,587 | 60.9 |
| Helpers and miscellaneous manual occupations | 178 | 15,944 | 74.8 |
| Armed forces | 94 | 25,156 | 90.1 |

*Source: Bureau of the Census, Internet web site, <http:// www.census.gov/cps/ads/sdata.htm>; calculations by New Strategist*

# Two-Thirds of Women Receive Wage-and-Salary Income

## More than one in five receives Social Security checks.

Only two sources of income are received by the majority of women. Fully 66 percent receive wage-and-salary income, and 55 percent receive interest income. Twenty-two percent of women receive Social Security payments, while 16 percent get dividends. About 5 percent of women receive child support. The median income of women receiving Social Security was just $9,840, while the median of those receiving child support was $19,184.

Black women are more likely to receive wage-and-salary income than non-Hispanic white women (71 versus 65 percent). Blacks are less likely to receive Social Security (18 versus 25 percent) or dividends (5 versus 20 percent). Hispanic women are less likely to receive Social Security than either blacks or non-Hispanic whites, with only 14 percent having income from this source.

✘ When the baby-boom generation begins to retire, the proportion of women with Social Security and private pension income will rise in every racial and ethnic group.

### Few women receive private pension income

*(percent of women aged 15 or older receiving income, by source of income, 1997)*

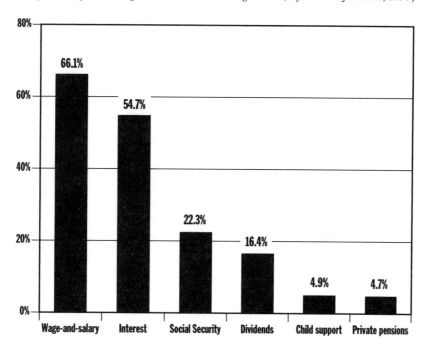

## Median Income of Women by Source of Income, 1997: Total Women

*(number and percent of women aged 15 or older with income by source of income, and median income of those with income, by age, 1997; women in thousands as of 1998)*

|  | number | percent | median income |
|---|---|---|---|
| **Total women** | **97,447** | **100.0%** | **$13,703** |
| **Earnings** | **67,736** | **69.5** | **18,738** |
| Wages and salary | 64,421 | 66.1 | 19,041 |
| Nonfarm self-employment | 4,689 | 4.8 | 15,498 |
| Farm self-employment | 591 | 0.6 | 19,975 |
| **Social Security or railroad retirement** | **21,737** | **22.3** | **9,840** |
| **SSI (Supplemental Security)** | **3,145** | **3.2** | **6,815** |
| **Public assistance** | **3,263** | **3.3** | **6,454** |
| **Veterans payments** | **460** | **0.5** | **15,018** |
| **Unemployment compensation** | **2,493** | **2.6** | **14,579** |
| **Workers compensation** | **944** | **1.0** | **16,739** |
| **Property income** | **55,371** | **56.8** | **18,359** |
| Interest | 53,323 | 54.7 | 18,485 |
| Dividends | 16,004 | 16.4 | 24,648 |
| Rent, royalties, estates, trusts | 6,298 | 6.5 | 22,874 |
| **Retirement income** | **6,972** | **7.2** | **17,594** |
| Private pensions (includes company/union, annuities, IRA, Keough) | 4,594 | 4.7 | 16,300 |
| Military retirement | 175 | 0.2 | 20,481 |
| Federal employee pensions | 704 | 0.7 | 22,333 |
| State or local employee pensions | 1,756 | 1.8 | 21,314 |
| **Other income** | **11,433** | **11.7** | **14,673** |
| Alimony | 393 | 0.4 | 27,656 |
| Child support | 4,758 | 4.9 | 19,184 |
| Education assistance | 4,570 | 4.7 | 11,854 |
| All other | 2,579 | 2.6 | 13,357 |

*Source: Bureau of the Census, Internet web site, <http:// www.census.gov/cps/ads/sdata.htm>; calculations by New Strategist*

# Median Income of Women by Source of Income, 1997: Black Women

*(number and percent of black women aged 15 or older with income by source of income, and median income of those with income, by age, 1997; women in thousands as of 1998)*

| | number | percent | median income |
|---|---|---|---|
| **Total women** | **11,961** | **100.0%** | **$13,048** |
| **Earnings** | **8,702** | **72.8** | **17,497** |
| Wages and salary | 8,517 | 71.2 | 17,503 |
| Nonfarm self-employment | 271 | 2.3 | 19,002 |
| Farm self-employment | 34 | 0.3 | 31,398 |
| **Social Security or railroad retirement** | **2,197** | **18.4** | **8,113** |
| **SSI (Supplemental Security)** | **838** | **7.0** | **6,909** |
| **Public assistance** | **1,118** | **9.3** | **6,379** |
| **Veterans payments** | **65** | **0.5** | **17,862** |
| **Unemployment compensation** | **499** | **4.2** | **12,273** |
| **Workers compensation** | **99** | **0.8** | **13,245** |
| **Property income** | **3,592** | **30.0** | **21,802** |
| Interest | 3,426 | 28.6 | 21,957 |
| Dividends | 622 | 5.2 | 31,744 |
| Rent, royalties, estates, trusts | 285 | 2.4 | 30,674 |
| **Retirement income** | **621** | **5.2** | **16,473** |
| Private pensions (includes company/union, annuities, IRA, Keough) | 384 | 3.2 | 14,913 |
| Military retirement | 9 | 0.1 | 7,159 |
| Federal employee pensions | 88 | 0.7 | 21,163 |
| State or local employee pensions | 153 | 1.3 | 21,299 |
| **Other income** | **1,674** | **14.0** | **12,818** |
| Alimony | 16 | 0.1 | 23,054 |
| Child support | 752 | 6.3 | 15,374 |
| Education assistance | 689 | 5.8 | 10,851 |
| All other | 324 | 2.7 | 10,618 |

*Source: Bureau of the Census, Internet web site, <http:// www.census.gov/cps/ads/sdata.htm>; calculations by New Strategist*

# Median Income of Women by Source of Income, 1997: Hispanic Women

*(number and percent of Hispanic women aged 15 or older with income by source of income, and median income of those with income, by age, 1997; women in thousands as of 1998)*

| | number | percent | median income |
|---|---|---|---|
| **Total women** | **8,055** | **100.0%** | **$10,260** |
| **Earnings** | **5,841** | **72.5** | **13,174** |
| Wages and salary | 5,669 | 70.4 | 13,372 |
| Nonfarm self-employment | 248 | 3.1 | 10,758 |
| Farm self-employment | 24 | 0.3 | 20,748 |
| **Social Security or railroad retirement** | **1,107** | **13.7** | **7,135** |
| **SSI (Supplemental Security)** | **471** | **5.8** | **6,626** |
| **Public assistance** | **693** | **8.6** | **6,229** |
| **Veterans payments** | **15** | **0.2** | **12,169** |
| **Unemployment compensation** | **290** | **3.6** | **11,862** |
| **Workers compensation** | **97** | **1.2** | **12,616** |
| **Property income** | **2,575** | **32.0** | **15,635** |
| Interest | 2,450 | 30.4 | 15,658 |
| Dividends | 387 | 4.8 | 29,537 |
| Rent, royalties, estates, trusts | 259 | 3.2 | 20,253 |
| **Retirement income** | **193** | **2.4** | **14,056** |
| Private pensions (includes company/union, annuities, IRA, Keough) | 136 | 1.7 | 14,051 |
| Military retirement | 5 | 0.1 | 19,383 |
| Federal employee pensions | 19 | 0.2 | 23,317 |
| State or local employee pensions | 33 | 0.4 | 11,137 |
| **Other income** | **919** | **11.4** | **10,963** |
| Alimony | 22 | 0.3 | 20,753 |
| Child support | 435 | 5.4 | 12,908 |
| Education assistance | 328 | 4.1 | 9,608 |
| All other | 188 | 2.3 | 10,509 |

*Source: Bureau of the Census, Internet web site, <http://www.census.gov/cps/ads/sdata.htm>; calculations by New Strategist*

# Median Income of Women by Source of Income, 1997: White Women

*(number and percent of white women aged 15 or older with income by source of income, and median income of those with income, by age, 1997; women in thousands as of 1998)*

| | number | percent | median income |
|---|---|---|---|
| **Total women** | **81,352** | **100.0%** | **$13,792** |
| **Earnings** | **55,934** | **68.8** | **18,955** |
| Wages and salary | 52,965 | 65.1 | 19,327 |
| Nonfarm self-employment | 4,201 | 5.2 | 15,141 |
| Farm self-employment | 541 | 0.7 | 19,575 |
| **Social Security or railroad retirement** | **19,117** | **23.5** | **10,110** |
| **SSI (Supplemental Security)** | **2,138** | **2.6** | **6,778** |
| **Public assistance** | **1,982** | **2.4** | **6,495** |
| **Veterans payments** | **384** | **0.5** | **15,134** |
| **Unemployment compensation** | **1,879** | **2.3** | **15,155** |
| **Workers compensation** | **788** | **1.0** | **17,082** |
| **Property income** | **49,652** | **61.0** | **17,969** |
| Interest | 47,877 | 58.9 | 18,103 |
| Dividends | 14,830 | 18.2 | 23,995 |
| Rent, royalties, estates, trusts | 5,787 | 7.1 | 22,339 |
| **Retirement income** | **6,220** | **7.6** | **17,718** |
| Private pensions (includes company/union, annuities, IRA, Keough) | 4,128 | 5.1 | 16,442 |
| Military retirement | 164 | 0.2 | 21,482 |
| Federal employee pensions | 601 | 0.7 | 22,483 |
| State or local employee pensions | 1,568 | 1.9 | 21,321 |
| **Other income** | **9,269** | **11.4** | **15,278** |
| Alimony | 367 | 0.5 | 28,323 |
| Child support | 3,913 | 4.8 | 20,240 |
| Education assistance | 3,642 | 4.5 | 12,151 |
| All other | 2,076 | 2.6 | 13,794 |

*Source: Bureau of the Census, Internet web site, <http:// www.census.gov/cps/ads/sdata.htm>; calculations by New Strategist*

# Median Income of Women by Source of Income, 1997: Non-Hispanic White Women

*(number and percent of non-Hispanic white women aged 15 or older with income by source of income, and median income of those with income, by age, 1997; women in thousands as of 1998)*

| | number | percent | median income |
|---|---|---|---|
| **Total women** | **73,709** | **100.0%** | **$14,389** |
| **Earnings** | **50,385** | **68.4** | **19,812** |
| Wages and salary | 47,580 | 64.6 | 20,159 |
| Nonfarm self-employment | 3,961 | 5.4 | 15,425 |
| Farm self-employment | 517 | 0.7 | 19,385 |
| **Social Security or railroad retirement** | **18,062** | **24.5** | **10,376** |
| **SSI (Supplemental Security)** | **1,696** | **2.3** | **6,842** |
| **Public assistance** | **1,357** | **1.8** | **6,661** |
| **Veterans payments** | **369** | **0.5** | **15,225** |
| **Unemployment compensation** | **1,600** | **2.2** | **15,665** |
| **Workers compensation** | **695** | **0.9** | **18,103** |
| **Property income** | **47,208** | **64.0** | **18,109** |
| Interest | 45,556 | 61.8 | 18,248 |
| Dividends | 14,473 | 19.6 | 23,852 |
| Rent, royalties, estates, trusts | 5,533 | 7.5 | 22,528 |
| **Retirement income** | **6,042** | **8.2** | **17,806** |
| Private pensions (includes company/union, annuities, IRA, Keough) | 4,007 | 5.4 | 16,494 |
| Military retirement | 159 | 0.2 | 21,615 |
| Federal employee pensions | 581 | 0.8 | 22,443 |
| State or local employee pensions | 1,535 | 2.1 | 21,559 |
| **Other income** | **8,410** | **11.4** | **16,038** |
| Alimony | 347 | 0.5 | 28,532 |
| Child support | 3,505 | 4.8 | 21,192 |
| Education assistance | 3,345 | 4.5 | 12,353 |
| All other | 1,897 | 2.6 | 14,163 |

*Source: Bureau of the Census, Internet web site, <http:// www.census.gov/cps/ads/sdata.htm>; calculations by New Strategist*

Chapter 4.

# Discretionary Income

BY THOMAS G. EXTER AND VLADISLAV BALABAN,
COMPUSEARCH MICROMARKETING DATA AND SYSTEMS

Fully 82 percent of American households had at least some discretionary income in 1999, averaging $17,441 in uncommitted dollars per household. In the aggregate, consumers controlled nearly $1.5 trillion in discretionary income—amounting to about one-fourth of all income accruing to the household sector.

Discretionary income is the money that remains for spending or saving after people pay their taxes and buy necessities. Many businesses depend on discretionary spending for sales and profits. This dependency makes discretionary income statistics important for marketing strategy. Despite this importance, however, discretionary income statistics can be hard to find because no government agency is charged with producing them. This chapter contains estimates of discretionary income for 1999.

## Estimating Discretionary Income

The estimates of discretionary income shown here were produced in three steps. The first step was to create a two-year database of household spending using the Bureau of Labor Statistics' Consumer Expenditure Survey (CEX). The CEX is the only ongoing national survey of American household spending. It tracks the dollars Americans spend by detailed category of goods and services. Some dollars, of course, are spent on taxes. We subtracted tax expenditures from estimates of before-tax income, including federal and state income taxes, payroll taxes including FICA, and local property taxes. What remains after subtracting taxes from income is "disposable" or after-tax income. We converted all figures to 1999 dollars using the standard Consumer Price Index deflator.

In the second step, we subtracted necessary household expenses—the basics—from disposable income. We defined basic expenses to include spending on food, housing (except for spending on "other lodging," which includes hotel and motel expenses), apparel and apparel services (except for "other apparel products," which includes jewelry), transportation (except for "public transportation," which includes spending on airline and ship fares), and health care. These necessary expenses were subtracted from after-tax income after controlling for age of householder, household size, and household income. In all, we calculated average spending on necessities for 150 types of households—six age groups by five income levels by five household sizes.

No definition of basic expenses can be exact. All are likely to include at least some discretionary items. Similarly, some nondiscretionary items are included in discretionary spending as well. One reason for this overlap is that the categories of expenses in the Consumer Expenditure Survey sometimes include both discretionary and nondiscretionary items. Another problem is that discretionary spending to one person may be a necessary expense to another. Defining basic expenses is a judgment call. Some of the food spending we define as basic is discretionary, for example, such as a birthday dinner at an expensive restaurant. But most food spending is not discretionary, which is why we included all food spending under basic expenses. While some might argue that spending on any restaurant food is discretionary, it's likely that most Americans would strongly disagree. Restaurant and carry-out meals have become a necessary expense for today's busy two-earner households. The small amount of discretionary spending included in such basic items as food spending is likely to be canceled out by some nondiscretionary spending included in items classified as discretionary. We defined spending on personal care products and services, for example, as discretionary. But there are some nondiscretionary items included in the category, such as spending on toothpaste, shaving products, and shampoo.

In the third and final step, we accounted for spending above and beyond the basics that may be considered necessary by some households. To do this, we multiplied by 75 percent any income remaining after subtracting taxes and basic expenses. In other words, we trimmed our estimates of discretionary income by 25 percent to arrive at the conservative figures shown on the following pages.

For more information about how the estimates were derived, contact Tom Exter at Compusearch; telephone (716) 624-7390; e-mail tge@frontiernet.net.

# Most Households Have Discretionary Income

**Only among households with incomes below $15,000 are those with discretionary income in the minority.**

Eighty-two percent of American households have money left over after they pay their taxes and buy necessities. The average amount of discretionary income available per household stood at a substantial $17,441 in 1999. With household affluence at a record high, and with the economy experiencing an unprecedented boom, it's little wonder that so many households have fun money to spend.

A 49 percent minority of households with incomes below $15,000 have discretionary income. Above that income threshold, more than 90 percent of households have money left over after paying taxes and buying necessities. The proportion of households with discretionary income does not vary much above the $15,000 income level, but the average amount of discretionary income available rises steadily with income. Households with incomes of $75,000 or more had fully $43,760 in discretionary income in 1999, or $14,208 per household member.

✘ The discretionary income available to households should continue to rise during the next few years because the large, baby-boom generation is entering its peak earning years.

### Discretionary income rises with household income

*(average discretionary income per household, by household income, 1999)*

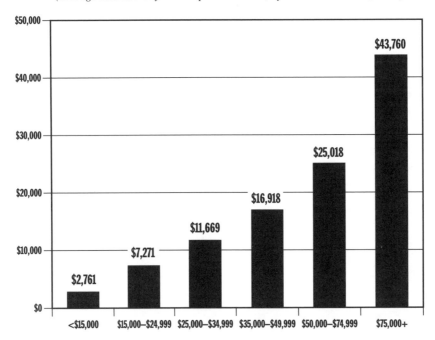

# Households with Discretionary Income by Household Income, 1999

*(total number of households, number and percent with discretionary income, and amount of discretionary income by before-tax household income, 1999; households in thousands)*

| | total households | households with discretionary income | percent with discretionary income | discretionary income | | | |
|---|---|---|---|---|---|---|---|
| | | | | average amount | aggregate amount (billions) | percent distribution of aggregate | per household member |
| **Total households** | **103,000** | **84,872** | **82.4%** | **$17,441** | **$1,480.2** | **100.0%** | **$6,867** |
| Under $15,000 | 24,451 | 11,973 | 49.0 | 2,761 | 33.1 | 2.2 | 1,267 |
| $15,000 to $24,999 | 18,338 | 17,005 | 92.7 | 7,271 | 123.6 | 8.4 | 3,081 |
| $25,000 to $34,999 | 14,671 | 13,618 | 92.8 | 11,669 | 158.9 | 10.7 | 4,649 |
| $35,000 to $49,999 | 16,810 | 15,619 | 92.9 | 16,918 | 264.2 | 17.9 | 5,999 |
| $50,000 to $74,999 | 15,282 | 14,199 | 92.9 | 25,018 | 355.2 | 24.0 | 8,149 |
| $75,000 or more | 13,448 | 12,458 | 92.6 | 43,760 | 545.2 | 36.8 | 14,208 |

*Note: For definition of discretionary income, see chapter introduction or glossary.*
*Source: Balaban, V. and Exter, T.,* Putting Dollars on the Map: The Many Shades of Consumer Income, *Business Geographics Conference paper, Chicago, 1999*

# Discretionary Income Peaks among Older Householders

**Householders aged 55 to 64 have more discretionary income per capita than those younger or older.**

At least 80 percent of householders aged 25 or older have discretionary income. Those aged 45 to 54 had the highest average amount, fully $21,428 in 1999. But after adjusting for household size, householders aged 55 to 64 have the most discretionary income per capita—$7,892 per household member in 1999. Not only are these householders done with the expenses of raising children, but most have already put their children through college, leaving them with extra cash.

With the baby-boom generation spanning the ages of 35 to 53, there are more householders in the 35-to-54 age group than in any other. This explains why householders aged 35 to 54 control 52 percent of the nation's discretionary income, or more than $775 billion in fun money in 1999.

✘ As boomers age, the share of discretionary income controlled by Americans aged 55 or older will rise.

## Per capita discretionary income peaks in the 55-to-64 age group

*(average discretionary income per household member, by age of householder, 1999)*

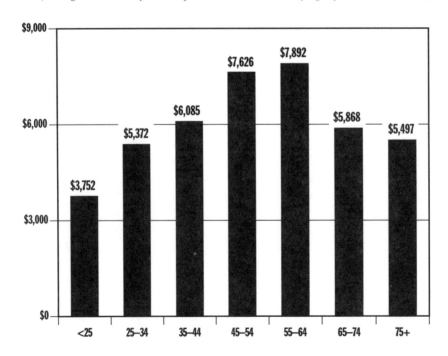

# Households with Discretionary Income by Age of Householder, 1999

*(total number of households, number and percent with discretionary income, and amount of discretionary income by age of householder, 1999; households in thousands)*

| | total households | households with discretionary income | percent with discretionary income | discretionary income | | | |
| | | | | average amount | aggregate amount (billions) | percent distribution of aggregate | per household member |
|---|---|---|---|---|---|---|---|
| **Total households** | **103,000** | **84,872** | **82.4%** | **$17,441** | **$1,480.2** | **100.0%** | **$6,867** |
| under age 25 | 7,294 | 5,395 | 74.0 | 7,317 | 43.3 | 2.9 | 3,752 |
| Age 25 to 34 | 20,122 | 16,774 | 83.4 | 14,934 | 274.5 | 18.5 | 5,372 |
| Age 35 to 44 | 22,637 | 18,826 | 83.2 | 19,716 | 406.8 | 27.5 | 6,085 |
| Age 45 to 54 | 18,864 | 15,707 | 83.3 | 21,428 | 368.8 | 24.9 | 7,626 |
| Age 55 to 64 | 12,325 | 9,905 | 80.4 | 17,441 | 189.3 | 12.8 | 7,892 |
| Age 65 to 74 | 12,073 | 10,221 | 84.7 | 10,974 | 122.9 | 8.3 | 5,868 |
| Age 75 or older | 9,684 | 8,044 | 83.1 | 8,466 | 74.6 | 5.0 | 5,497 |

*Note: For definition of discretionary income, see chapter introduction or glossary.*
*Source: Balaban, V. and Exter, T.,* Putting Dollars on the Map: The Many Shades of Consumer Income, *Business Geographics Conference paper, Chicago, 1999.*

# Empty Nesters Have the Most Discretionary Income

## Single parents have the smallest amount of discretionary income.

More than 80 percent of households, regardless of household type, have money left over after paying taxes and buying necessities. Married couples with children under age 18 at home have the largest amount of discretionary income, a total of $24,593 in 1999. Single parents with children under age 18 at home had only $8,719 in discretionary income.

After adjusting for household size, married couples without children under age 18 at home (empty nesters) have the most money to play with, an average of $8,582 in 1999—over $2,000 more than is available to married couples with kids at home. Single parents with children under age 18 had only $2,976 in discretionary income per capita.

Married couples with children at home control 39 percent of the nation's discretionary income, while those without children at home control 32 percent. Combined, married couples with or without children control 71 percent of the nation's discretionary income, a total of more than $1 trillion in 1999.

✘ As the children of the baby-boom generation grow up in the decade ahead, the share of discretionary income controlled by empty nesters will surpass the share controlled by parents, changing the nation's discretionary spending patterns.

### Married couples control the most discretionary income

*(percent of discretionary income accruing to households, by type, 1999)*

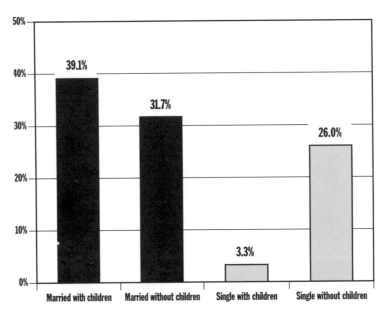

# Households with Discretionary Income by Household Type, 1999

*(total number of households, number and percent with discretionary income, and amount of discretionary income by household type and presence of children at home, 1999; households in thousands)*

| | total households | households with discretionary income | percent with discretionary income | discretionary income | | | |
| --- | --- | --- | --- | --- | --- | --- | --- |
| | | | | average amount | aggregate amount (billions) | percent distribution of aggregate | per household member |
| **Total households** | **103,000** | **84,872** | **82.4%** | **$17,441** | **$1,480.2** | **100.0%** | **$6,867** |
| Married | | | | | | | |
| With children < 18 | 27,838 | 23,524 | 84.5 | 24,593 | 578.5 | 39.1 | 6,226 |
| Without children < 18 | 26,572 | 22,109 | 83.2 | 21,198 | 468.7 | 31.7 | 8,582 |
| Single | | | | | | | |
| With children < 18 | 6,833 | 5,583 | 81.7 | 8,719 | 48.7 | 3.3 | 2,976 |
| Without children < 18 | 41,757 | 33,657 | 80.6 | 11,421 | 384.4 | 26.0 | 7,274 |

*Note: For definition of discretionary income, see chapter introduction or glossary.*
*Source: Balaban, V. and Exter, T.,* Putting Dollars on the Map: The Many Shades of Consumer Income, *Business Geographics Conference paper, Chicago, 1999.*

# Discretionary Income Is Highest in the West

## Households in the Midwest and South have the smallest amount of discretionary income.

Fully 88 percent of households in the West have money left over after paying taxes and buying necessities. The average amount of discretionary income available to households in the West stood at $18,500 in 1999. A smaller 80 percent of households in the Midwest have discretionary income, and those that do had an average of $16,708 available.

After adjusting for household size, households in the Northeast have the most discretionary income available per household member, an average of $7,366 in 1999. In the West, per capita discretionary income stood at $7,007. The figure was smallest in the South, at $6,995.

Households in the West control a larger share of discretionary income than those in the Northeast or Midwest—24 percent of the nation's $1.5 trillion in discretionary spending power was in the hands of western residents in 1999. The largest share of discretionary income (33.5 percent) is controlled by the South, however, because it is the most populous region.

✘ Regional differences in discretionary spending power may shrink in the years ahead as technological advances erode regional differences in income.

### The South has the largest share of discretionary income

*(percent of discretionary income accruing to households, by region, 1999)*

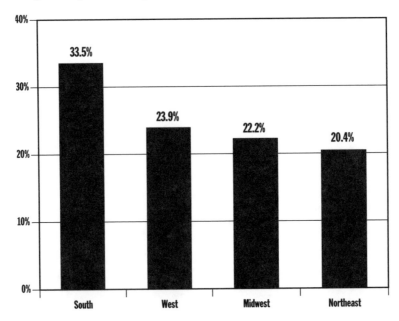

# Households with Discretionary Income by Region, 1999

*(total number of households, number and percent with discretionary income, and amount of discretionary income by region, 1999; households in thousands)*

| | total households | households with discretionary income | percent with discretionary income | discretionary income | | | |
| --- | --- | --- | --- | --- | --- | --- | --- |
| | | | | average amount | aggregate amount (billions) | percent distribution of aggregate | per household member |
| **Total households** | **103,000** | **84,872** | **82.4%** | **$17,441** | **$1,480.2** | **100.0%** | **$6,867** |
| Northeast | 20,387 | 16,353 | 80.2 | 18,488 | 302.3 | 20.4 | 7366 |
| Midwest | 24,642 | 19,668 | 79.8 | 16,708 | 328.6 | 22.2 | 6710 |
| South | 36,174 | 29,738 | 82.2 | 16,669 | 495.7 | 33.5 | 6695 |
| West | 21,797 | 19,113 | 87.7 | 18,500 | 353.6 | 23.9 | 7007 |

*Note: For definition of discretionary income, see chapter introduction or glossary.*
*Source: Balaban, V. and Exter, T.,* Putting Dollars on the Map: The Many Shades of Consumer Income, *Business Geographics Conference paper, Chicago, 1999.*

# Asian Households Are Most Likely to Have Discretionary Income

## The great majority of black, white and Hispanic households have discretionary income as well.

More than 80 percent of African American, American Indian, Asian, Hispanic, and white households have discretionary income—money left over after taxes are paid and necessities are purchased. The proportion of households with discretionary income peaks at 90 percent among Asians. The average amount of discretionary income enjoyed by Asian householders is greater than that of other racial or ethnic groups, standing at $19,484 in 1999. American Indians have the smallest average amount of discretionary income, just $9,688 per household.

After adjusting for household size, white householders have the most discretionary income per capita, with $7,254 per household member in 1999. American Indians have the smallest per capita amount, only $3,628.

Because the great majority of households are headed by whites, they control 90 percent of the nation's discretionary income—$1.3 trillion in spending money in 1999. Blacks control $107.5 billion, while Hispanics control $86 billion and Asians $40 billion.

✗ Minorities are growing as a percentage of the U.S. population, boosting their share of discretionary spending power in the future.

### American Indian households have the smallest amount of discretionary income

*(average discretionary income per household, by race and Hispanic origin of householder, 1999)*

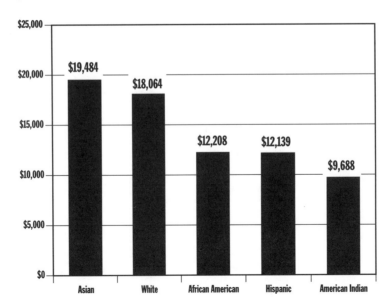

# Households with Discretionary Income by Race and Hispanic Origin, 1999

*(total number of households, number and percent with discretionary income, and amount of discretionary income by race and Hispanic origin of householder, 1999; households in thousands)*

| | total households | households with discretionary income | percent with discretionary income | discretionary income | | | |
| --- | --- | --- | --- | --- | --- | --- | --- |
| | | | | average amount | aggregate amount (billions) | percent distribution of aggregate | per household member |
| **Total households** | **103,000** | **84,872** | **82.4%** | **$17,441** | **$1,480.2** | **100.0%** | **$6,867** |
| White | 89,369 | 73,516 | 82.3 | 18,064 | 1,328.0 | 89.7 | 7,254 |
| African American | 10,761 | 8,808 | 81.9 | 12,208 | 107.5 | 7.3 | 4,360 |
| Asian or Pacific Islander | 2,278 | 2,048 | 89.9 | 19,484 | 39.9 | 2.7 | 6,495 |
| American Indian, Aleut, Eskimo | 593 | 500 | 84.3 | 9,688 | 4.8 | 0.3 | 3,628 |
| Hispanic* | 8,284 | 7,121 | 86.0 | 12,139 | 86.4 | 5.8 | 4,875 |

*\* Numbers will not add to total because Hispanics may be of any race.*
*Note: For definition of discretionary income, see chapter introduction or glossary.*
*Source: Balaban, V. and Exter, T., Putting Dollars on the Map: The Many Shades of Consumer Income, Business Geographics Conference paper, Chicago, 1999.*

# The College Educated Control Most Discretionary Income

## Just 10 percent is controlled by those who did not graduate from high school.

If you want to know where the money is, look no further than the college educated. People with at least some college experience control 61 percent of the nation's $1.5 trillion in discretionary income—the money that remains once taxes are paid and necessities are purchased. People who went no further than high school control 28 percent of discretionary income, while those without a high school diploma account for only 10 percent of discretionary spending power.

Regardless of educational level, most households have at least some discretionary income. The largest amount is available to the most educated householders. Those with a graduate degree have an average of $26,911 in discretionary income, while college graduates have $22,687. Householders with a high school diploma had an average of $14,125 in discretionary income in 1999.

The pattern is the same after adjusting for household size, with the most educated householders having the most discretionary income per capita. Householders with a graduate degree averaged more than $10,000 in discretionary income per household member in 1999.

✗ The rising educational level of the American population is boosting incomes and discretionary spending power. As educated householders control more of the nation's fun money, businesses must become more sophisticated to capture the dollars of these savvy consumers.

### Discretionary income rises with education

*(average discretionary income per household, by educational attainment of householder, 1999)*

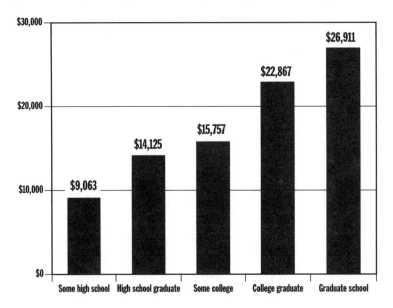

# Households with Discretionary Income by Education, 1999

*(total number of households, number and percent with discretionary income, and amount of discretionary income by educational attainment of householder, 1999; households in thousands)*

| | total households | households with discretionary income | percent with discretionary income | discretionary income | | | |
| --- | --- | --- | --- | --- | --- | --- | --- |
| | | | | average amount | aggregate amount (billions) | percent distribution of aggregate | per household member |
| **Total households** | **103,000** | **84,872** | **82.4%** | **$17,441** | **$1,480.2** | **100.0%** | **$ 6,867** |
| Never attended school | 332 | 263 | 79.3 | 7,513 | 2.2 | 0.2 | 2,538 |
| Elementary only | 8,724 | 7,247 | 83.1 | 7,190 | 57.3 | 3.9 | 2,899 |
| Some high school | 12,391 | 9,860 | 79.6 | 9,063 | 98.2 | 6.6 | 3,446 |
| High school diploma | 32,874 | 27,014 | 82.2 | 14,125 | 419.4 | 28.3 | 5,391 |
| Some college | 24,023 | 19,909 | 82.9 | 15,757 | 344.8 | 23.3 | 6,354 |
| College graduate | 13,908 | 11,318 | 81.4 | 22,867 | 284.5 | 19.2 | 9,296 |
| Graduate school | 10,747 | 9,261 | 86.2 | 26,911 | 273.9 | 18.5 | 10,851 |

*Note: For definition of discretionary income, see chapter introduction or glossary.*
*Source: Balaban, V. and Exter, T.,* Putting Dollars on the Map: The Many Shades of Consumer Income, *Business Geographics Conference paper, Chicago, 1999.*

# Single-Person Households Have the Most Discretionary Income

**One- and two-person households control nearly half the nation's fun money.**

The percentage of households with discretionary income does not vary much by household size. More than 80 percent of households—ranging in size from just one person to seven or more persons—have at least some money left over after they pay taxes and buy necessities.

Not surprisingly, the average amount of discretionary income per household is greatest for the largest households. Those with seven or more people averaged $21,778 in discretionary income in 1999. But after adjusting for household size, the largest households have the least discretionary per household member— only $2,796. In contrast, single-person households average $9,114 in discretionary income per household member.

One- and two-person households control 48 percent of the nation's discretionary income, amounting to more than $700 billion in 1999. Three- and four-person households control another 38 percent, while households with five or more persons account for just 14 percent of discretionary spending power.

✘ As single-person households become a larger share of all households with the aging of the baby-boom generation, they will control a growing share of discretionary income.

## Small households control the most

*(percent of discretionary income accruing to households by size, 1999)*

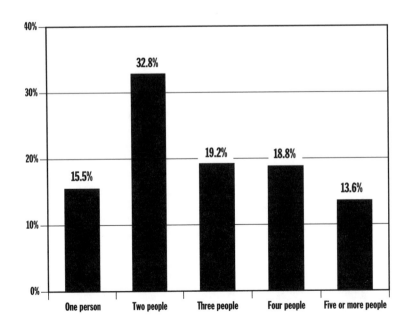

## Households with Discretionary Income by Household Size, 1999

*(total number of households, number and percent with discretionary income, and amount of discretionary income by household size, 1999; households in thousands)*

| | total households | households with discretionary income | percent with discretionary income | discretionary income | | | |
| | | | | average amount | aggregate amount (billions) | percent distribution of aggregate | per household member |
|---|---|---|---|---|---|---|---|
| **Total households** | **103,000** | **84,872** | **82.4%** | **$17,441** | **$1,480.2** | **100.0%** | **$6,867** |
| One person | 28,890 | 23,141 | 80.1 | 9,114 | 229.5 | 15.5 | 9,114 |
| Two people | 31,402 | 25,907 | 82.5 | 17,206 | 485.1 | 32.8 | 8,603 |
| Three people | 16,329 | 13,880 | 85.0 | 18,794 | 283.9 | 19.2 | 6,265 |
| Four people | 15,073 | 12,571 | 83.4 | 20,370 | 278.7 | 18.8 | 5,093 |
| Five people | 6,657 | 5,585 | 83.9 | 19,823 | 120.5 | 8.1 | 3,965 |
| Six people | 2,261 | 1,834 | 81.1 | 18,153 | 36.2 | 2.4 | 3,026 |
| Seven or more people | 2,387 | 1,954 | 81.9 | 21,778 | 46.3 | 3.1 | 2,796 |

*Note: For definition of discretionary income, see chapter introduction or glossary.*
*Source: Balaban, V. and Exter, T.,* Putting Dollars on the Map: The Many Shades of Consumer Income, *Business Geographics Conference paper, Chicago, 1999.*

**Chapter 5.**

# Wealth

The stock market is reaching record highs with regularity. The economy is growing at an unprecedented pace. The wealth of American households should be skyrocketing, it seems. Unfortunately, no one knows for sure. The last time the wealth of Americans was examined in detail by the federal government was in 1995—and those data are presented in this chapter. In that year, the average household had a relatively low net worth, few financial assets, and plenty of debt.

Whether a full-employment economy and stock market gains have changed the picture remains to be seen. The next examination of the wealth of American households—the Survey of Consumer Finances—will be released late in 1999 or early 2000 by the Federal Reserve, examining wealth accumulation through 1998. Keep tabs on their web site for the latest weath data, <http://www.bog.frb.fed.us/pubs/oss/oss2/scfindex.html>.

✘ With boomers in their peak earning years and beginning to build wealth, it's likely that the net worth of American households is rising.

# Net Worth Rises with Age, Income, Education

## Net worth peaks in the 55-to-64 age group.

The median net worth of American households stood at $56,400 in 1995 (the latest data available). Net worth, which is one of the most important measures of wealth, is what remains after a household's debts are subtracted from its assets.

Net worth rises with age, income, and education. The youngest householders, those under age 35, had a net worth of just $11,400 in 1995. People in this age group are buying homes, starting careers, and having children. Most take on debt to achieve these goals—educational loans, mortgages, and credit card charges. Net worth rises in middle age as people pay off their debts. The median net worth of householders aged 45 to 54 is nearly double that of 35-to-44-year-olds—$90,500 versus $48,500 in 1995.

Median net worth peaks in the 55-to-64 age group at $110,800. At this age, many people own their homes free and clear. At the peak of their earnings, they can buy cars and other necessities without taking on debt. They have accumulated retirement savings as well. After age 65, net worth slowly declines as people spend their wealth in retirement.

✘ For most households, homeownership is the single largest component of net worth. Because older people are much more likely to own a home than younger adults, and because they have had more time to build equity in their homes, their net worth is much greater.

## Net worth is highest for richest households

*(median net worth of households by income, 1995)*

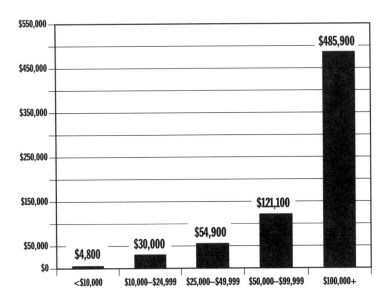

# Net Worth of Households, 1995

*(median net worth of households by selected characteristics of householders, 1995)*

|  | median net worth |
|---|---|
| **Total households** | **$56,400** |
| **Income** | |
| Under $10,000 | 4,800 |
| $10,000 to $24,999 | 30,000 |
| $25,000 to $49,999 | 54,900 |
| $50,000 to $99,999 | 121,100 |
| $100,000 or more | 485,900 |
| **Age of householder** | |
| Under age 35 | 11,400 |
| Aged 35 to 44 | 48,500 |
| Aged 45 to 54 | 90,500 |
| Aged 55 to 64 | 110,800 |
| Aged 65 to 74 | 104,100 |
| Aged 75 or older | 95,000 |
| **Education of householder** | |
| No high school diploma | 26,300 |
| High school diploma | 50,000 |
| Some college | 43,200 |
| College degree | 104,100 |
| **Race or ethnicity of householder** | |
| Non-Hispanic white | 73,900 |
| Nonwhite or Hispanic | 16,500 |

*Source: Federal Reserve Board,* Family Finances in the U.S.: Recent Evidence from the Survey of Consumer Finances, *Federal Reserve Bulletin, January 1997*

# Americans Have Few Financial Assets

## The financial assets of young adults are far below average.

The median value of the financial assets held by householders aged 55 to 64 was $32,300 in 1995 (the latest data available), about two and one-half times the $13,000 median for the average household. The youngest householders have the fewest financial assets, with a median value of only $5,300.

At all ages, the most commonly held financial asset is a transaction account, such as checking and savings accounts and money market mutual funds. But nearly one in five households headed by people under age 35 does not have any type of transaction account. Most households without transaction accounts have relatively low incomes.

Among households headed by people under age 65, the second most commonly held financial asset is a retirement account. Over half the people aged 35 to 54 have retirement accounts. The median value of retirement accounts rises during the prime working years, from $12,000 for householders aged 35 to 44 to $25,000 for those aged 45 to 54 and $32,800 for householders aged 55 to 64.

✗ As boomers and younger generations save for retirement, the financial assets of Americans will grow more rapidly than their nonfinancial assets.

### Most households with incomes of $25,000 or more own retirement accounts

*(percent of households owning retirement accounts by household income, 1995)*

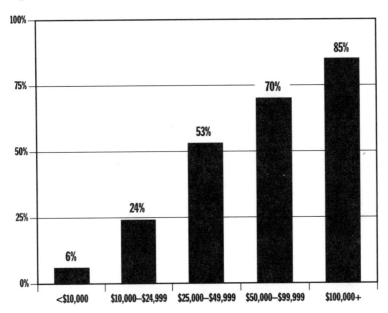

# Ownership of Financial Assets, 1995

*(percent of households owning financial assets, and median value of asset for owners, by selected characteristics of households and type of asset, 1995)*

| | any financial asset | transaction accounts | CDs | savings bonds | bonds | stocks | mutual funds | retirement accounts | life insurance | other managed | other financial |
|---|---|---|---|---|---|---|---|---|---|---|---|
| **PERCENT OWNING ASSET** | | | | | | | | | | | |
| **Total households** | 90.8% | 87.1% | 14.1% | 22.9% | 3.0% | 15.3% | 12.0% | 43.0% | 31.4% | 3.8% | 11.0% |
| **Income** | | | | | | | | | | | |
| Under $10,000 | 68.1 | 61.1 | 7.2 | 5.9 | – | 2.5 | 1.8 | 5.9 | 15.8 | – | 8.9 |
| $10,000 to $24,999 | 87.6 | 82.3 | 16.0 | 11.8 | – | 9.2 | 4.9 | 24.2 | 25.2 | 3.2 | 8.6 |
| $25,000 to $49,999 | 97.8 | 94.7 | 13.7 | 27.4 | 3.2 | 14.3 | 12.4 | 52.6 | 33.1 | 4.2 | 13.2 |
| $50,000 to $99,999 | 99.5 | 98.6 | 15.6 | 39.9 | 4.8 | 26.0 | 20.9 | 69.8 | 42.5 | 5.3 | 11.3 |
| $100,000 or more | 100.0 | 100.0 | 21.1 | 36.3 | 14.5 | 45.2 | 38.0 | 84.6 | 54.1 | 8.0 | 15.2 |
| **Age of householder** | | | | | | | | | | | |
| Under age 35 | 87.0 | 80.8 | 7.1 | 21.1 | 0.5 | 11.1 | 8.8 | 39.2 | 22.3 | 1.6 | 13.5 |
| Aged 35 to 44 | 92.0 | 87.4 | 8.2 | 31.0 | 1.6 | 14.5 | 10.5 | 51.5 | 28.9 | 3.4 | 10.5 |
| Aged 45 to 54 | 92.4 | 88.9 | 12.5 | 25.1 | 4.6 | 17.5 | 16.0 | 54.3 | 37.5 | 2.9 | 13.0 |
| Aged 55 to 64 | 90.5 | 88.2 | 16.2 | 19.6 | 2.9 | 14.9 | 15.2 | 47.2 | 37.5 | 7.1 | 9.0 |
| Aged 65 to 74 | 92.0 | 91.1 | 23.9 | 17.0 | 5.1 | 18.0 | 13.7 | 35.0 | 37.0 | 5.6 | 10.4 |
| Aged 75 or older | 93.8 | 93.0 | 34.1 | 15.3 | 7.0 | 21.3 | 10.4 | 16.5 | 35.1 | 5.7 | 5.3 |
| **Race and ethnicity of householder** | | | | | | | | | | | |
| Non-Hispanic white | 94.7 | 92.4 | 16.5 | 26.2 | 3.7 | 18.2 | 14.5 | 47.0 | 33.5 | 4.7 | 11.7 |
| Nonwhite or Hispanic | 77.4 | 69.1 | 5.9 | 11.3 | 0.6 | 5.5 | 3.5 | 29.2 | 24.4 | 1.0 | 8.5 |

*(continued)*

(continued from previous page)

## MEDIAN VALUE OF ASSET FOR OWNERS

| | any financial asset | transaction accounts | CDs | savings bonds | bonds | stocks | mutual funds | retirement accounts | life insurance | other managed | other financial |
|---|---|---|---|---|---|---|---|---|---|---|---|
| **Total households** | **$13,000** | **$2,100** | **$10,000** | **$1,000** | **$26,200** | **$8,000** | **$19,000** | **$15,600** | **$5,000** | **$30,000** | **$3,000** |
| **Income** | | | | | | | | | | | |
| Under $10,000 | 1,200 | 700 | 7,000 | 400 | – | 2,000 | 25,000 | 3,500 | 1,500 | – | 2,000 |
| $10,000 to $24,999 | 5,400 | 1,400 | 10,000 | 800 | – | 5,700 | 8,000 | 6,000 | 3,000 | 19,700 | 2,000 |
| $25,000 to $49,999 | 12,100 | 2,000 | 10,000 | 700 | 29,000 | 6,900 | 12,500 | 10,000 | 5,000 | 25,000 | 2,500 |
| $50,000 to $99,999 | 40,700 | 4,500 | 13,000 | 1,200 | 9,400 | 5,700 | 15,000 | 23,000 | 7,000 | 35,000 | 3,000 |
| $100,000 or more | 214,500 | 15,800 | 15,600 | 1,500 | 58,000 | 30,000 | 48,000 | 85,000 | 12,000 | 62,500 | 23,000 |
| **Age of householder** | | | | | | | | | | | |
| Under age 35 | 5,300 | 1,200 | 6,000 | 500 | 2,000 | 3,700 | 5,000 | 5,200 | 3,400 | 3,800 | 1,000 |
| Aged 35 to 44 | 11,600 | 2,000 | 6,000 | 1,000 | 11,000 | 4,000 | 10,000 | 12,000 | 5,000 | 10,800 | 2,000 |
| Aged 45 to 54 | 24,800 | 2,700 | 12,000 | 1,000 | 17,000 | 10,000 | 17,500 | 25,000 | 6,500 | 43,000 | 5,000 |
| Aged 55 to 64 | 32,300 | 3,000 | 14,000 | 1,100 | 10,000 | 17,000 | 55,000 | 32,800 | 6,000 | 42,000 | 9,000 |
| Aged 65 to 74 | 19,100 | 3,000 | 17,000 | 1,500 | 58,000 | 15,000 | 50,000 | 28,500 | 5,000 | 26,000 | 9,000 |
| Aged 75 or older | 20,900 | 5,000 | 11,000 | 4,000 | 40,000 | 25,000 | 50,000 | 17,500 | 5,000 | 100,000 | 35,000 |
| **Race and ethnicity of householder** | | | | | | | | | | | |
| Non-Hispanic white | 16,900 | 2,500 | 10,000 | 1,000 | 26,200 | 8,600 | 20,000 | 17,500 | 5,000 | 30,000 | 4,000 |
| Nonwhite or Hispanic | 5,200 | 1,500 | 10,000 | 500 | 27,000 | 5,000 | 7,800 | 9,600 | 5,000 | 1,800 | 1,500 |

*Note: (–) means sample is too small to make a reliable estimate.*
*Source: Federal Reserve Board, Family Finances in the U.S.: Recent Evidence from the Survey of Consumer Finances, Federal Reserve Bulletin, January 1997*

# Value of Nonfinancial Assets Peaks in 45-to-54 Age Group

## The youngest householders have few nonfinancial assets.

The median value of the nonfinancial assets of the average American household amounted to $83,000 in 1995 (the latest data available). But there are substantial differences by age in the value of nonfinancial assets.

The youngest householders, those under age 35, had a median of $21,500 in nonfinancial assets in 1995. The low value of the nonfinancial assets of these households is due to their low rate of homeownership. Owned homes account for the largest share of the nonfinancial assets of the average household. But among householders under age 35, vehicles are the primary nonfinancial asset. Fully 84 percent of the youngest householders own vehicles, but only 38 percent own a home.

Households headed by people aged 45 to 54 have the most nonfinancial assets, a median of $111,700 in 1995. Three-quarters of them own their home and one-quarter have investments in other real estate.

The value of nonfinancial assets is substantially lower among older households. Householders aged 65 to 74 had nonfinancial assets valued at a median of $93,500, while those aged 75 or older had $79,000 in nonfinancial assets.

✗ Homeownership will always account for the largest share of the average American's nonfinancial assets. As today's young adults age and become homeowners, the value of their nonfinancial assets will grow.

### Housing value rises sharply with income

*(median value of primary residence for homeowners by income, 1995)*

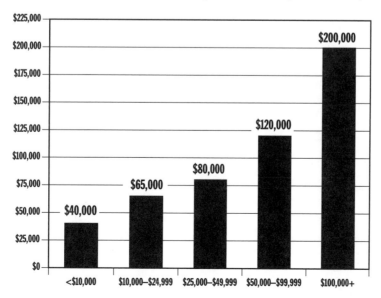

# Ownership of Nonfinancial Assets, 1995

*(percent of households owning nonfinancial assets, and median value of assets for owners, by selected characteristics of households and type of asset, 1995)*

| | any nonfinancial asset | vehicles | primary residence | investment real estate | business | other non-financial |
|---|---|---|---|---|---|---|
| **PERCENT OWNING ASSET** | | | | | | |
| **Total households** | **91.1%** | **84.2%** | **64.7%** | **17.5%** | **11.0%** | **9.0%** |
| **Income** | | | | | | |
| Under $10,000 | 69.8 | 57.7 | 37.6 | 6.9 | 4.8 | 3.8 |
| $10,000 to $24,999 | 89.4 | 82.7 | 55.4 | 11.5 | 6.2 | 6.2 |
| $25,000 to $49,999 | 96.6 | 92.2 | 68.4 | 16.5 | 9.8 | 9.6 |
| $50,000 to $99,999 | 99.1 | 93.3 | 84.4 | 24.9 | 17.5 | 11.5 |
| $100,000 or more | 99.4 | 90.2 | 91.1 | 52.3 | 32.1 | 22.6 |
| **Age of householder** | | | | | | |
| Under age 35 | 87.6 | 83.9 | 37.9 | 7.2 | 9.3 | 7.6 |
| Aged 35 to 44 | 90.9 | 85.1 | 64.6 | 14.4 | 13.9 | 10.2 |
| Aged 45 to 54 | 93.7 | 88.2 | 75.4 | 23.9 | 14.8 | 10.7 |
| Aged 55 to 64 | 94.0 | 88.7 | 82.1 | 26.9 | 11.7 | 9.8 |
| Aged 65 to 74 | 92.5 | 82.0 | 79.0 | 26.5 | 7.9 | 8.9 |
| Aged 75 or older | 90.2 | 72.8 | 73.0 | 16.6 | 3.8 | 5.4 |
| **Race and ethnicity of householder** | | | | | | |
| Non-Hispanic white | 94.9 | 88.1 | 69.4 | 19.7 | 12.6 | 10.5 |
| Nonwhite or Hispanic | 78.1 | 71.1 | 48.2 | 10.2 | 5.4 | 3.5 |
| **MEDIAN VALUE OF ASSET FOR OWNERS** | | | | | | |
| **Total households** | **$83,000** | **$10,000** | **$90,000** | **$50,000** | **$41,000** | **$10,000** |
| **Income** | | | | | | |
| Under $10,000 | 13,100 | 3,600 | 40,000 | 16,200 | 50,600 | 2,500 |
| $10,000 to $24,999 | 44,500 | 6,100 | 65,000 | 30,000 | 30,000 | 8,000 |
| $25,000 to $49,999 | 81,500 | 11,100 | 80,000 | 40,000 | 26,300 | 6,000 |
| $50,000 to $99,999 | 145,200 | 16,200 | 120,000 | 57,300 | 30,000 | 14,000 |
| $100,000 or more | 319,300 | 22,800 | 200,000 | 130,000 | 300,000 | 20,000 |
| **Age of householder** | | | | | | |
| Under age 35 | 21,500 | 9,000 | 80,000 | 33,500 | 20,000 | 5,000 |
| Aged 35 to 44 | 95,600 | 10,700 | 95,000 | 45,000 | 35,000 | 9,000 |
| Aged 45 to 54 | 111,700 | 12,400 | 100,000 | 55,000 | 60,000 | 12,000 |
| Aged 55 to 64 | 107,000 | 11,900 | 85,000 | 82,500 | 75,000 | 10,000 |
| Aged 65 to 74 | 93,500 | 8,000 | 80,000 | 55,000 | 100,000 | 16,000 |
| Aged 75 or older | 79,000 | 5,300 | 80,000 | 20,000 | 30,000 | 15,000 |
| **Race and ethnicity of householder** | | | | | | |
| Non-Hispanic white | 93,000 | 10,800 | 92,000 | 50,000 | 45,000 | 10,000 |
| Nonwhite or Hispanic | 42,100 | 7,700 | 70,000 | 33,500 | 26,300 | 8,000 |

*Source: Federal Reserve Board,* Family Finances in the U.S.: Recent Evidence from the Survey of Consumer Finances, *Federal Reserve Bulletin, January 1997*

# Most Households Have Some Debt

## Only among householders aged 75 or older is the majority free of debt.

Overall, 75 percent of householders have debt, owing a median of $22,500 in 1995 (the latest data available). Only 30 percent of householders aged 75 or older have debt. Among those who do, the median amount owed is only $2,000. The debt of the oldest householders is lower primarily because they have paid off their home mortgages.

In every age group, the largest debts are mortgages. The median amount owed on mortgage and home equity debt was $51,000 in 1995. Younger householders have the highest mortgage and equity debt because their loans are relatively recent. After age 45, the median amount owed for mortgages and home equity loans drops sharply.

Over half the households headed by people under age 45 have installment debt. Car loans are the primary example of this type of debt. As is the case with other types of debt, the proportion of Americans owing installment debt falls with age.

More than half the householders under age 45 have credit card debt. Households headed by people aged 45 to 54 owed the most on their credit cards—a median of $2,000 in 1995.

✘ Until households pay down their debts, their net worth will remain low.

### Percent with debt peaks among middle-income households

*(percent of households with debt by household income, 1995)*

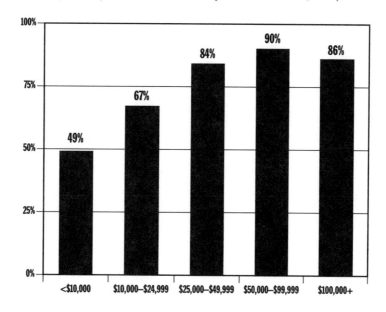

# Households with Debt, 1995

*(percent of households with debt, and median value of debt for those with debt, by selected characteristics of households and type of debt, 1995)*

| | any debt | mortgage and home equity | installment | other lines of credit | credit card | investment real estate | other debt |
|---|---|---|---|---|---|---|---|
| **PERCENT WITH DEBT** | | | | | | | |
| **Total households** | 75.2% | 41.1% | 46.5% | 1.9% | 47.8% | 6.3% | 9.0% |
| **Income** | | | | | | | |
| Under $10,000 | 48.5 | 8.9 | 25.9 | – | 25.4 | 1.6 | 6.6 |
| $10,000 to $24,999 | 67.3 | 24.8 | 41.3 | 1.4 | 41.9 | 2.5 | 8.7 |
| $25,000 to $49,999 | 83.9 | 47.3 | 54.3 | 2.0 | 56.7 | 5.8 | 8.5 |
| $50,000 to $99,999 | 89.9 | 68.7 | 60.7 | 3.2 | 62.8 | 9.5 | 10.0 |
| $100,000 or more | 86.4 | 73.6 | 37.0 | 4.0 | 37.0 | 27.9 | 15.8 |
| **Age of householder** | | | | | | | |
| Under age 35 | 83.8 | 32.9 | 62.2 | 2.6 | 55.4 | 2.6 | 7.8 |
| Aged 35 to 44 | 87.2 | 54.1 | 60.7 | 2.2 | 55.8 | 6.5 | 11.1 |
| Aged 45 to 54 | 86.5 | 61.9 | 54.0 | 2.3 | 57.3 | 10.4 | 14.1 |
| Aged 55 to 64 | 75.2 | 45.8 | 36.0 | 1.4 | 43.4 | 12.5 | 7.5 |
| Aged 65 to 74 | 54.2 | 24.8 | 16.7 | 1.3 | 31.3 | 5.0 | 5.5 |
| Aged 75 or older | 30.1 | 7.1 | 9.6 | – | 18.3 | 1.5 | 3.6 |
| **Race and ethnicity of householder** | | | | | | | |
| Non-Hispanic white | 75.8 | 43.5 | 46.4 | 2.1 | 47.5 | 6.9 | 9.1 |
| Nonwhite or Hispanic | 73.1 | 32.7 | 46.9 | 1.3 | 48.8 | 4.4 | 8.5 |
| **MEDIAN VALUE OF DEBT FOR DEBTOR HOUSEHOLDS** | | | | | | | |
| **Total households** | $22,500 | $51,000 | $6,100 | $3,500 | $1,500 | $28,000 | $2,000 |
| **Income** | | | | | | | |
| Under $10,000 | 2,600 | 14,000 | 2,900 | – | 600 | 15,000 | 2,000 |
| $10,000 to $24,999 | 9,200 | 26,000 | 3,900 | 3,000 | 1,200 | 18,300 | 1,200 |
| $25,000 to $49,999 | 23,400 | 46,000 | 6,600 | 3,000 | 1,400 | 25,000 | 1,500 |
| $50,000 to $99,999 | 65,000 | 68,000 | 9,000 | 2,200 | 2,200 | 34,000 | 2,500 |
| $100,000 or more | 112,200 | 103,400 | 8,500 | 19,500 | 3,000 | 36,800 | 7,000 |
| **Age of householder** | | | | | | | |
| Under age 35 | 15,200 | 63,000 | 7,000 | 1,400 | 1,400 | 22,800 | 1,500 |
| Aged 35 to 44 | 37,600 | 60,000 | 5,600 | 2,000 | 1,800 | 30,000 | 1,700 |
| Aged 45 to 54 | 41,000 | 48,000 | 7,000 | 5,700 | 2,000 | 28,100 | 2,500 |
| Aged 55 to 64 | 25,800 | 36,000 | 5,900 | 3,500 | 1,300 | 26,000 | 4,000 |
| Aged 65 to 74 | 7,700 | 19,000 | 4,900 | 3,800 | 800 | 36,000 | 2,000 |
| Aged 75 or older | 2,000 | 15,900 | 3,900 | – | 400 | 8,000 | 3,000 |
| **Race and ethnicity of householder** | | | | | | | |
| Non-Hispanic white | 27,200 | 54,000 | 6,400 | 3,500 | 1,500 | 29,000 | 2,000 |
| Nonwhite or Hispanic | 12,200 | 36,500 | 5,000 | 800 | 1,200 | 25,000 | 1,500 |

*Note: (–) means sample is too small to make a reliable estimate.*
*Source: Federal Reserve Board,* Family Finances in the U.S.: Recent Evidence from the Survey of Consumer Finances, *Federal Reserve Bulletin, January 1997*

# Chapter 6.

# Poverty

The poverty rate dropped slightly during the past few years, thanks to the booming economy. During the 1990s, the percentage of people in poverty peaked at 15.1 in 1993 and fell to 13.3 by 1997. In the past 40 years, however, the poverty rate has never fallen below 11.1 percent.

The poverty population has changed dramatically since 1959. Among age groups, the elderly were once most likely to be poor. Today, children have the highest poverty rate. Among household types, married couples once accounted for the majority of poor families. Today, female-headed families dominate the poor. Blacks once outnumbered Hispanics among the poor by two to one, now they are almost equal in number because poverty rates have fallen for blacks and climbed for Hispanics.

Marriage, a college education, and full-time work are the most certain escape routes from poverty. With the poverty population increasingly dominated by female-headed families and their children, it has become more difficult than ever to signficantly reduce the poverty rate.

✗ Poverty rates will not fall much below their current levels until marriage regains its popularity and college becomes more affordable to those with low incomes.

# Poverty Trends

# Most Poor Families Are Now Headed by Women

## Married couples once accounted for the majority of poor families.

In 1997, 55 percent of the nation's poor families were headed by women, up from 45 percent in 1973. Married couples accounted for only 39 percent of poor families in 1997, down from the 51 percent majority in 1973. Few poor families are headed by men, although the proportion has more than doubled. Male-headed families accounted for 7 percent of the poor in 1997, up from 3 percent in 1973.

Several factors account for the changing face of the nation's poor. During the 1970s, divorce became more common and the number of single-parent families expanded. At the same time, women poured into the workforce. Dual-earners became the majority of married couples, making it easier for couples to avoid poverty. Consequently, female-headed families became more numerous than married couples among the nation's poor.

✗ Poverty is more difficult to combat when female-headed families dominate the poor. Most female-headed families have one or no earners, while most married couples are dual earners—making it easier for them to climb out of poverty.

### Married couples are now a minority of poor families

*(percent of poor families by family type, 1973 to 1997)*

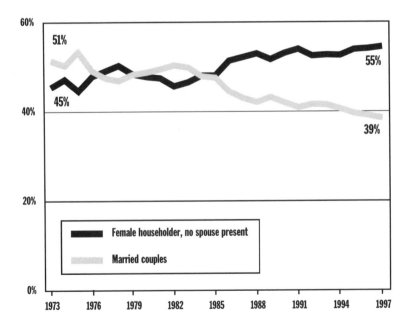

# Percent Distribution of Families below Poverty Level by Family Type, 1973 to 1997

*(number of families below poverty level and percent distribution by family type, 1973 to 1997; families in thousands as of the following year)*

| | total families in poverty | | married couples | female householder, no spouse present | male householder, no spouse present |
|---|---|---|---|---|---|
| | number | percent | | | |
| 1997 | 7,324 | 100.0% | 38.5% | 54.5% | 6.9% |
| 1996 | 7,708 | 100.0 | 39.1 | 54.1 | 6.9 |
| 1995 | 7,532 | 100.0 | 39.6 | 53.9 | 6.5 |
| 1994 | 8,053 | 100.0 | 40.6 | 52.6 | 6.8 |
| 1993 | 8,393 | 100.0 | 41.5 | 52.7 | 5.8 |
| 1992 | 8,144 | 100.0 | 41.6 | 52.5 | 5.9 |
| 1991 | 7,712 | 100.0 | 40.9 | 54.0 | 5.1 |
| 1990 | 7,098 | 100.0 | 42.0 | 53.1 | 4.9 |
| 1989 | 6,784 | 100.0 | 43.2 | 51.7 | 5.1 |
| 1988 | 6,874 | 100.0 | 42.1 | 53.0 | 4.9 |
| 1987 | 7,005 | 100.0 | 43.0 | 52.2 | 4.9 |
| 1986 | 7,023 | 100.0 | 44.5 | 51.4 | 4.1 |
| 1985 | 7,223 | 100.0 | 47.6 | 48.1 | 4.3 |
| 1984 | 7,277 | 100.0 | 47.9 | 48.1 | 4.0 |
| 1983 | 7,647 | 100.0 | 49.9 | 46.6 | 3.5 |
| 1982 | 7,512 | 100.0 | 50.4 | 45.7 | 3.9 |
| 1981 | 6,851 | 100.0 | 49.5 | 47.5 | 3.0 |
| 1980 | 6,217 | 100.0 | 48.8 | 47.8 | 3.4 |
| 1979 | 5,461 | 100.0 | 48.3 | 48.4 | 3.2 |
| 1978 | 5,280 | 100.0 | 46.9 | 50.3 | 2.9 |
| 1977 | 5,311 | 100.0 | 47.5 | 49.1 | 3.3 |
| 1976 | 5,311 | 100.0 | 49.1 | 47.9 | 3.1 |
| 1975 | 5,450 | 100.0 | 53.3 | 44.6 | 2.1 |
| 1974 | 4,922 | 100.0 | 50.3 | 47.2 | 2.5 |
| 1973 | 4,828 | 100.0 | 51.4 | 45.4 | 3.2 |

*Source: Bureau of the Census,* Poverty in the United States: 1997, *Current Population Reports, P60-201, 1998; calculations by New Strategist*

# Poverty Rate Is Down for Black Families

## Hispanic families are more likely to be poor.

The proportion of the nation's families who are poor has remained remarkably stable over the past few decades. In 1997, 10 percent of families had incomes that placed them below poverty level, up slightly from 9 percent in 1973. Married couples and female-headed families are no more likely to be poor today than they were in 1973, however.

Poverty rates have changed considerably for blacks and Hispanics. Among blacks, the poverty rate has fallen. In 1997, 24 percent of black families were poor, down from 28 percent in 1973. The steepest decline was for black female-headed families. In 1973, the 53 percent majority were poor. By 1997, only 40 percent lived below poverty level.

The trend runs in the opposite direction for Hispanics. Twenty-five percent of Hispanic families were poor in 1997, up from 20 percent in 1973. While Hispanic female-headed families are slightly less likely to be poor today than they were in 1973, Hispanic couples are more likely to be poor.

✗ Poorly-educated and unskilled Hispanic immigrants arriving in the U.S. by the millions over the past few decades have boosted the poverty rate for Hispanics.

### Less poverty for black families

*(poverty rate of families by race and Hispanic origin, 1973 and 1997)*

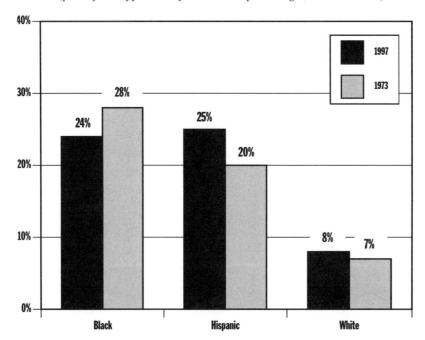

# Number and Percent of Families below Poverty Level by Family Type, 1973 to 1997: Total Families

*(number and percent of families below poverty level by family type, 1973 to 1997; families in thousands as of the following year)*

|  | total families | | married couples | | female householder, no spouse present | | male householder, no spouse present | |
|---|---|---|---|---|---|---|---|---|
|  | number | percent | number | percent | number | percent | number | percent |
| 1997 | 7,324 | 10.3% | 2,821 | 5.2% | 3,995 | 31.6% | 508 | 13.0% |
| 1996 | 7,708 | 11.0 | 3,010 | 5.6 | 4,167 | 32.6 | 531 | 13.8 |
| 1995 | 7,532 | 10.8 | 2,982 | 5.6 | 4,057 | 32.4 | 493 | 14.0 |
| 1994 | 8,053 | 11.6 | 3,272 | 6.1 | 4,232 | 34.6 | 549 | 17.0 |
| 1993 | 8,393 | 12.3 | 3,481 | 6.5 | 4,424 | 35.6 | 488 | 16.8 |
| 1992 | 8,144 | 11.9 | 3,385 | 6.4 | 4,275 | 35.4 | 484 | 15.8 |
| 1991 | 7,712 | 11.5 | 3,158 | 6.0 | 4,161 | 35.6 | 393 | 13.0 |
| 1990 | 7,098 | 10.7 | 2,981 | 5.7 | 3,768 | 33.4 | 349 | 12.0 |
| 1989 | 6,784 | 10.3 | 2,931 | 5.6 | 3,504 | 32.2 | 348 | 12.1 |
| 1988 | 6,874 | 10.4 | 2,897 | 5.6 | 3,642 | 33.4 | 336 | 11.8 |
| 1987 | 7,005 | 10.7 | 3,011 | 5.8 | 3,654 | 34.2 | 340 | 12.0 |
| 1986 | 7,023 | 10.9 | 3,123 | 6.1 | 3,613 | 34.6 | 287 | 11.4 |
| 1985 | 7,223 | 11.4 | 3,438 | 6.7 | 3,474 | 34.0 | 311 | 12.9 |
| 1984 | 7,277 | 11.6 | 3,488 | 6.9 | 3,498 | 34.5 | 292 | 13.1 |
| 1983 | 7,647 | 12.3 | 3,815 | 7.6 | 3,564 | 36.0 | 268 | 13.2 |
| 1982 | 7,512 | 12.2 | 3,789 | 7.6 | 3,434 | 36.3 | 290 | 14.4 |
| 1981 | 6,851 | 11.2 | 3,394 | 6.8 | 3,252 | 34.6 | 205 | 10.3 |
| 1980 | 6,217 | 10.3 | 3,032 | 6.2 | 2,972 | 32.7 | 213 | 11.0 |
| 1979 | 5,461 | 9.2 | 2,640 | 5.4 | 2,645 | 30.4 | 176 | 10.2 |
| 1978 | 5,280 | 9.1 | 2,474 | 5.2 | 2,654 | 31.4 | 152 | 9.2 |
| 1977 | 5,311 | 9.3 | 2,524 | 5.3 | 2,610 | 31.7 | 177 | 11.1 |
| 1976 | 5,311 | 9.4 | 2,606 | 5.5 | 2,543 | 33.0 | 162 | 10.8 |
| 1975 | 5,450 | 9.7 | 2,904 | 6.1 | 2,430 | 32.5 | 116 | 8.0 |
| 1974 | 4,922 | 8.8 | 2,474 | 5.3 | 2,324 | 32.1 | 125 | 8.9 |
| 1973 | 4,828 | 8.8 | 2,482 | 5.3 | 2,193 | 32.2 | 154 | 10.7 |

*Source: Bureau of the Census,* Poverty in the United States: 1997, *Current Population Reports, P60-201, 1998*

# Number and Percent of Families below Poverty Level by Family Type, 1973 to 1997: Black Families

*(number and percent of black families below poverty level by family type, 1973 to 1997; families in thousands as of the following year)*

| | total families | | married couples | | female householder, no spouse present | | male householder, no spouse present | |
|---|---|---|---|---|---|---|---|---|
| | number | percent | number | percent | number | percent | number | percent |
| 1997 | 1,985 | 23.6% | 312 | 8.0% | 1,563 | 39.8% | 110 | 19.6% |
| 1996 | 2,206 | 26.1 | 352 | 9.1 | 1,724 | 43.7 | 130 | 19.8 |
| 1995 | 2,127 | 26.4 | 314 | 8.5 | 1,701 | 45.1 | 112 | 19.5 |
| 1994 | 2,212 | 27.3 | 336 | 8.7 | 1,715 | 46.2 | 161 | 30.1 |
| 1993 | 2,499 | 31.3 | 458 | 12.3 | 1,908 | 49.9 | 133 | 29.6 |
| 1992 | 2,484 | 31.1 | 490 | 13.0 | 1,878 | 50.2 | 116 | 24.8 |
| 1991 | 2,343 | 30.4 | 399 | 11.0 | 1,834 | 51.2 | 110 | 21.9 |
| 1990 | 2,193 | 29.3 | 448 | 12.6 | 1,648 | 48.1 | 97 | 20.6 |
| 1989 | 2,077 | 27.8 | 443 | 11.8 | 1,524 | 46.5 | 110 | 24.7 |
| 1988 | 2,089 | 28.2 | 421 | 11.3 | 1,579 | 49.0 | 88 | 18.9 |
| 1987 | 2,117 | 29.4 | 439 | 11.9 | 1,577 | 51.1 | 101 | 23.4 |
| 1986 | 1,987 | 28.0 | 403 | 10.8 | 1,488 | 50.1 | 96 | 24.9 |
| 1985 | 1,983 | 28.7 | 447 | 12.2 | 1,452 | 50.5 | 84 | 22.9 |
| 1984 | 2,094 | 30.9 | 479 | 13.8 | 1,533 | 51.7 | 82 | 23.8 |
| 1983 | 2,161 | 32.3 | 535 | 15.5 | 1,541 | 53.7 | 85 | 24.0 |
| 1982 | 2,158 | 33.0 | 543 | 15.6 | 1,535 | 56.2 | 79 | 25.6 |
| 1981 | 1,972 | 30.8 | 543 | 15.4 | 1,377 | 52.9 | 52 | 19.1 |
| 1980 | 1,826 | 28.9 | 474 | 14.0 | 1,301 | 49.4 | 52 | 17.7 |
| 1979 | 1,722 | 27.8 | 453 | 13.2 | 1,234 | 49.4 | 35 | 13.7 |
| 1978 | 1,622 | 27.5 | 366 | 11.3 | 1,208 | 50.6 | 48 | 17.6 |
| 1977 | 1,637 | 28.2 | 429 | 13.1 | 1,162 | 51.0 | 46 | 17.1 |
| 1976 | 1,617 | 27.9 | 450 | 13.2 | 1,122 | 52.2 | 45 | 18.2 |
| 1975 | 1,513 | 27.1 | 479 | 14.3 | 1,004 | 50.1 | 30 | 13.0 |
| 1974 | 1,479 | 26.9 | 435 | 13.0 | 1,010 | 52.2 | 35 | 17.4 |
| 1973 | 1,527 | 28.1 | – | – | 974 | 52.7 | – | – |

*Note: (–) means data not available.*
*Source: Bureau of the Census,* Poverty in the United States: 1997, *Current Population Reports, P60-201, 1998*

## Number and Percent of Families below Poverty Level by Family Type, 1973 to 1997: Hispanic Families

*(number and percent of Hispanic families below poverty level by family type, 1973 to 1997; families in thousands as of the following year)*

| | total families | | married couples | | female householder, no spouse present | | male householder, no spouse present | |
|---|---|---|---|---|---|---|---|---|
| | number | percent | number | percent | number | percent | number | percent |
| 1997 | 1,721 | 24.7% | 836 | 17.4% | 767 | 47.6% | 118 | 21.7% |
| 1996 | 1,748 | 26.4 | 815 | 18.0 | 823 | 50.9 | 110 | 22.3 |
| 1995 | 1,695 | 27.0 | 803 | 18.9 | 792 | 49.4 | 100 | 22.9 |
| 1994 | 1,724 | 27.8 | 827 | 19.5 | 773 | 52.1 | 124 | 25.8 |
| 1993 | 1,625 | 27.3 | 770 | 19.1 | 772 | 51.6 | 83 | 20.2 |
| 1992 | 1,529 | 26.7 | 743 | 18.8 | 664 | 49.3 | 122 | 27.4 |
| 1991 | 1,372 | 26.5 | 674 | 19.1 | 627 | 49.7 | 71 | 18.5 |
| 1990 | 1,244 | 25.0 | 605 | 17.5 | 573 | 48.3 | 66 | 19.4 |
| 1989 | 1,133 | 23.4 | 549 | 16.2 | 530 | 47.5 | 54 | 16.3 |
| 1988 | 1,141 | 23.7 | 547 | 16.1 | 546 | 49.1 | 48 | 15.2 |
| 1987 | 1,168 | 25.5 | 556 | 17.4 | 565 | 52.2 | 47 | 15.8 |
| 1986 | 1,085 | 24.7 | 518 | 16.6 | 528 | 51.2 | 39 | 15.5 |
| 1985 | 1,074 | 25.5 | 505 | 17.0 | 521 | 53.1 | 48 | 18.4 |
| 1984 | 991 | 25.2 | 469 | 16.6 | 483 | 53.4 | 39 | 18.4 |
| 1983 | 981 | 25.9 | 437 | 17.7 | 454 | 52.8 | 40 | 22.6 |
| 1982 | 916 | 27.2 | 465 | 19.0 | 425 | 55.4 | 26 | 17.0 |
| 1981 | 792 | 24.0 | 366 | 15.1 | 399 | 53.2 | 27 | 19.2 |
| 1980 | 751 | 23.2 | 363 | 15.3 | 362 | 51.3 | 26 | 16.0 |
| 1979 | 614 | 20.3 | 298 | 13.1 | 300 | 49.2 | 16 | 11.8 |
| 1978 | 559 | 20.4 | 248 | 11.9 | 288 | 53.1 | 23 | 20.9 |
| 1977 | 591 | 21.4 | 280 | 13.3 | 301 | 53.6 | 10 | 10.1 |
| 1976 | 598 | 23.1 | 312 | 15.8 | 275 | 53.1 | 11 | 12.5 |
| 1975 | 627 | 25.1 | 335 | 17.7 | 279 | 53.6 | 13 | 16.0 |
| 1974 | 526 | 21.2 | 278 | 14.4 | 229 | 49.6 | 19 | 21.6 |
| 1973 | 468 | 19.8 | 239 | 12.7 | 211 | 51.4 | 18 | 23.1 |

*Source: Bureau of the Census,* Poverty in the United States: 1997, *Current Population Reports, P60-201, 1998*

# Number and Percent of Families below Poverty Level by Family Type, 1973 to 1997: White Families

*(number and percent of white families below poverty level by family type, 1973 to 1997; families in thousands as of the following year)*

| | total families | | married couples | | female householder, no spouse present | | male householder, no spouse present | |
|---|---|---|---|---|---|---|---|---|
| | *number* | *percent* | *number* | *percent* | *number* | *percent* | *number* | *percent* |
| 1997 | 4,990 | 8.4% | 2,312 | 4.8% | 2,305 | 27.7% | 373 | 11.9% |
| 1996 | 5,059 | 8.6 | 2,416 | 5.1 | 2,276 | 27.3 | 367 | 12.5 |
| 1995 | 4,994 | 8.5 | 2,443 | 5.1 | 2,200 | 26.6 | 351 | 12.9 |
| 1994 | 5,312 | 9.1 | 2,629 | 5.5 | 2,329 | 29.0 | 354 | 14.1 |
| 1993 | 5,452 | 9.4 | 2,757 | 5.8 | 2,376 | 29.2 | 319 | 13.9 |
| 1992 | 5,255 | 9.1 | 2,677 | 5.7 | 2,245 | 28.5 | 333 | 13.8 |
| 1991 | 5,022 | 8.8 | 2,573 | 5.5 | 2,192 | 28.4 | 257 | 10.8 |
| 1990 | 4,622 | 8.1 | 2,386 | 5.1 | 2,010 | 26.8 | 226 | 9.9 |
| 1989 | 4,409 | 7.8 | 2,329 | 5.0 | 1,858 | 25.4 | 223 | 9.7 |
| 1988 | 4,471 | 7.9 | 2,294 | 4.9 | 1,945 | 26.5 | 231 | 10.2 |
| 1987 | 4,567 | 8.1 | 2,382 | 5.1 | 1,961 | 26.9 | 224 | 9.8 |
| 1986 | 4,811 | 8.6 | 2,591 | 5.6 | 2,041 | 28.2 | 179 | 8.8 |
| 1985 | 4,983 | 9.1 | 2,815 | 6.1 | 1,950 | 27.4 | 218 | 11.2 |
| 1984 | 4,925 | 9.1 | 2,858 | 6.3 | 1,878 | 27.1 | 189 | 10.4 |
| 1983 | 5,220 | 9.7 | 3,125 | 6.9 | 1,926 | 28.3 | 168 | 10.4 |
| 1982 | 5,118 | 9.6 | 3,104 | 6.9 | 1,813 | 27.9 | 201 | 12.2 |
| 1981 | 4,670 | 8.8 | 2,712 | 6.0 | 1,814 | 27.4 | 145 | 8.8 |
| 1980 | 4,195 | 8.0 | 2,437 | 5.4 | 1,609 | 25.7 | 149 | 9.4 |
| 1979 | 3,581 | 6.9 | 2,099 | 4.7 | 1,350 | 22.3 | 132 | 9.2 |
| 1978 | 3,523 | 6.9 | 2,033 | 4.7 | 1,391 | 23.5 | 99 | 7.3 |
| 1977 | 3,540 | 7.0 | 2,028 | 4.7 | 1,400 | 24.0 | 112 | 8.8 |
| 1976 | 3,560 | 7.1 | 2,071 | 4.8 | 1,379 | 25.2 | 110 | 9.0 |
| 1975 | 3,838 | 7.7 | 2,363 | 5.5 | 1,394 | 25.9 | 81 | 6.9 |
| 1974 | 3,352 | 6.8 | 1,977 | 4.6 | 1,289 | 24.8 | 86 | 7.3 |
| 1973 | 3,219 | 6.6 | 2,306 | 5.3 | 1,190 | 24.5 | – | – |

*Note: (–) means data not available.*
*Source: Bureau of the Census,* Poverty in the United States: 1997, *Current Population Reports, P60-201, 1998*

# Female-Headed Families with Children Are Less Likely to Be Poor

## Poverty rate has fallen the most for black female-headed families with children.

Sixteen percent of families with children under age 18 were poor in 1997, up from 12 percent in 1974. Behind this increase is the changing composition of American families, with a growing share headed by single parents, who are more likely to be poor. Despite the increase in poverty among all families, the poverty rate of married couples with children rose only slightly between 1974 and 1997, while it fell for single-parent families headed by women.

Black female-headed single-parent families saw the biggest percentage point decline in the poverty rate. In 1974, the 59 percent majority had incomes that placed them below poverty level. By 1997, only 47 percent were poor—marking the first time the share dropped below 50 percent.

The poverty rate for Hispanic female-headed single-parent families also fell slightly during the past two decades, from 57 to 54 percent. But the poverty rate remained stable among Hispanic couples with children, at about one in five.

✘ The poverty rate has fallen for black female-headed families with children because of blacks' rising educational levels and growing job opportunities.

### Poor are now a minority of black female-headed families with children

*(poverty rate of black female-headed families with children under age 18, 1974 to 1997)*

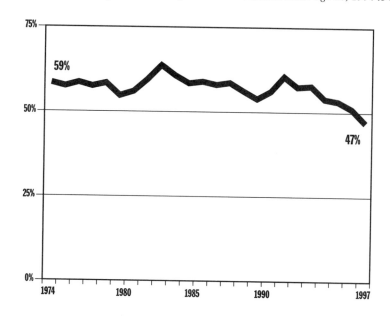

# Number and Percent of Families with Children below Poverty Level by Family Type, 1974 to 1997: Total Families

*(number and percent of families with related children under age 18 below poverty level by family type, 1974 to 1997; families in thousands as of the following year)*

|  | total families | | married couples | | female householder, no spouse present | | male householder, no spouse present | |
|---|---|---|---|---|---|---|---|---|
|  | *number* | *percent* | *number* | *percent* | *number* | *percent* | *number* | *percent* |
| 1997 | 5,884 | 15.7% | 1,863 | 7.1% | 3,614 | 41.0% | 407 | 18.7% |
| 1996 | 6,131 | 16.5 | 1,964 | 7.5 | 3,755 | 41.9 | 412 | 20.0 |
| 1995 | 5,976 | 16.3 | 1,961 | 7.5 | 3,634 | 41.5 | 381 | 19.7 |
| 1994 | 6,408 | 17.4 | 2,197 | 8.3 | 3,816 | 44.0 | 395 | 22.6 |
| 1993 | 6,751 | 18.5 | 2,363 | 9.0 | 4,034 | 46.1 | 354 | 22.5 |
| 1992 | 6,457 | 18.0 | 2,237 | 8.6 | 3,867 | 46.2 | 353 | 22.5 |
| 1991 | 6,170 | 17.7 | 2,106 | 8.3 | 3,767 | 47.1 | 297 | 19.6 |
| 1990 | 5,676 | 16.4 | 1,990 | 7.8 | 3,426 | 44.5 | 260 | 18.8 |
| 1989 | 5,308 | 15.5 | 1,872 | 7.3 | 3,190 | 42.8 | 246 | 18.1 |
| 1988 | 5,373 | 15.7 | 1,847 | 7.2 | 3,294 | 44.7 | 232 | 18.0 |
| 1987 | 5,465 | 16.1 | 1,963 | 7.7 | 3,281 | 45.5 | 221 | 16.8 |
| 1986 | 5,516 | 16.3 | 2,050 | 8.0 | 3,264 | 46.0 | 202 | 17.8 |
| 1985 | 5,586 | 16.7 | 2,258 | 8.9 | 3,131 | 45.4 | 197 | 17.1 |
| 1984 | 5,662 | 17.2 | 2,344 | 9.4 | 3,124 | 45.7 | 194 | 18.1 |
| 1983 | 5,871 | 17.9 | 2,557 | 10.1 | 3,122 | 47.1 | 192 | 20.2 |
| 1982 | 5,712 | 17.5 | 2,470 | 9.8 | 3,059 | 47.8 | 184 | 20.6 |
| 1981 | 5,191 | 15.9 | 2,199 | 8.7 | 2,877 | 44.3 | 115 | 14.0 |
| 1980 | 4,822 | 14.7 | 1,974 | 7.7 | 2,703 | 42.9 | 144 | 18.0 |
| 1979 | 4,081 | 12.6 | 1,573 | 6.1 | 2,392 | 39.6 | 116 | 15.5 |
| 1978 | 4,060 | 12.8 | 1,495 | 5.9 | 2,462 | 42.2 | 103 | 14.7 |
| 1977 | 4,081 | 12.9 | 1,602 | 6.3 | 2,384 | 41.8 | 95 | 14.8 |
| 1976 | 4,060 | 12.9 | 1,623 | 6.4 | 2,343 | 44.1 | 94 | 15.4 |
| 1975 | 4,172 | 13.3 | 1,855 | 7.2 | 2,252 | 44.0 | 65 | 11.7 |
| 1974 | 3,789 | 12.1 | 1,558 | 6.0 | 2,147 | 43.7 | 84 | 15.4 |

*Source: Bureau of the Census,* Poverty in the United States: 1997, *Current Population Reports, P60-201, 1998*

# Number and Percent of Families with Children below Poverty Level by Family Type, 1974 to 1997: Black Families

*(number and percent of black families with related children under age 18 below poverty level by family type, 1974 to 1997; families in thousands as of the following year)*

| | total families | | married couples | | female householder, no spouse present | | male householder, no spouse present | |
|---|---|---|---|---|---|---|---|---|
| | number | percent | number | percent | number | percent | number | percent |
| 1997 | 1,721 | 30.5% | 205 | 9.0% | 1,436 | 46.9% | 80 | 25.6% |
| 1996 | 1,941 | 34.1 | 239 | 11.0 | 1,593 | 51.0 | 109 | 27.2 |
| 1995 | 1,821 | 34.1 | 209 | 9.9 | 1,533 | 53.2 | 79 | 23.4 |
| 1994 | 1,954 | 35.9 | 245 | 11.4 | 1,591 | 53.9 | 118 | 34.6 |
| 1993 | 2,171 | 39.3 | 298 | 13.9 | 1,780 | 57.7 | 93 | 31.6 |
| 1992 | 2,132 | 39.1 | 343 | 15.4 | 1,706 | 57.4 | 83 | 33.5 |
| 1991 | 2,016 | 39.2 | 263 | 12.4 | 1,676 | 60.5 | 77 | 31.7 |
| 1990 | 1,887 | 37.2 | 301 | 14.3 | 1,513 | 56.1 | 73 | 27.3 |
| 1989 | 1,783 | 35.4 | 291 | 13.3 | 1,415 | 53.9 | 77 | 33.8 |
| 1988 | 1,802 | 36.0 | 272 | 12.5 | 1,452 | 56.2 | 78 | 31.7 |
| 1987 | 1,788 | 36.6 | 290 | 13.2 | 1,437 | 58.6 | 61 | 27.5 |
| 1986 | 1,699 | 35.4 | 257 | 11.5 | 1,384 | 58.0 | 58 | 31.5 |
| 1985 | 1,670 | 36.0 | 281 | 12.9 | 1,336 | 58.9 | 53 | 29.0 |
| 1984 | 1,758 | 39.0 | 331 | 16.6 | 1,364 | 58.4 | 62 | 35.5 |
| 1983 | 1,789 | 39.9 | 369 | 18.0 | 1,362 | 60.7 | 58 | 31.1 |
| 1982 | 1,819 | 40.7 | 360 | 17.2 | 1,401 | 63.7 | 58 | 32.7 |
| 1981 | 1,652 | 37.1 | 357 | 16.2 | 1,261 | 59.5 | 34 | 25.0 |
| 1980 | 1,583 | 35.5 | 333 | 15.5 | 1,217 | 56.0 | 34 | 24.0 |
| 1979 | 1,441 | 33.5 | 286 | 13.7 | 1,129 | 54.7 | 26 | 18.4 |
| 1978 | 1,431 | 34.4 | 247 | 12.0 | 1,144 | 58.4 | 40 | 25.5 |
| 1977 | 1,406 | 34.2 | 295 | 14.1 | 1,081 | 57.5 | 30 | 21.3 |
| 1976 | 1,382 | 34.2 | 311 | 14.5 | 1,043 | 58.6 | 28 | 23.3 |
| 1975 | 1,314 | 33.9 | 349 | 16.5 | 949 | 57.5 | 16 | 14.8 |
| 1974 | 1,293 | 33.0 | 317 | 14.5 | 949 | 58.5 | 27 | 26.2 |

*Source: Bureau of the Census,* Poverty in the United States: 1997, *Current Population Reports, P60-201, 1998*

# Number and Percent of Families with Children below Poverty Level by Family Type, 1974 to 1997: Hispanic Families

*(number and percent of Hispanic families with related children under age 18 below poverty level by family type, 1974 to 1997; families in thousands as of the following year)*

| | total families | | married couples | | female householder, no spouse present | | male householder, no spouse present | |
|---|---|---|---|---|---|---|---|---|
| | number | percent | number | percent | number | percent | number | percent |
| 1997 | 1,492 | 30.4% | 692 | 21.0% | 701 | 54.2% | 99 | 30.5% |
| 1996 | 1,549 | 33.0 | 687 | 22.0 | 760 | 59.7 | 102 | 35.1 |
| 1995 | 1,470 | 33.2 | 657 | 22.6 | 735 | 57.3 | 78 | 32.9 |
| 1994 | 1,497 | 34.2 | 698 | 23.9 | 700 | 59.2 | 99 | 36.4 |
| 1993 | 1,424 | 34.3 | 652 | 23.7 | 706 | 60.5 | 66 | 27.6 |
| 1992 | 1,302 | 32.9 | 615 | 22.9 | 598 | 57.7 | 89 | 38.2 |
| 1991 | 1,219 | 33.7 | 575 | 23.5 | 584 | 60.1 | 60 | 29.4 |
| 1990 | 1,085 | 31.0 | 501 | 20.8 | 536 | 58.2 | 48 | 28.1 |
| 1989 | 986 | 29.8 | 453 | 19.6 | 491 | 57.9 | 42 | 26.8 |
| 1988 | 988 | 29.7 | 445 | 19.0 | 510 | 59.2 | 33 | 26.4 |
| 1987 | 1,022 | 31.9 | 460 | 20.9 | 527 | 60.9 | 35 | 25.2 |
| 1986 | 949 | 30.8 | – | – | 489 | 59.5 | – | – |
| 1985 | 955 | 32.1 | – | – | 493 | 64.0 | – | – |
| 1984 | 872 | 31.3 | – | – | 447 | 62.8 | – | – |
| 1983 | 867 | 21.1 | – | – | 418 | 63.4 | – | – |
| 1982 | 802 | 32.6 | – | – | 391 | 63.8 | – | – |
| 1981 | 692 | 28.5 | – | – | 374 | 60.0 | – | – |
| 1980 | 655 | 27.2 | – | – | – | – | – | – |
| 1979 | 544 | 24.6 | – | – | 288 | 57.3 | – | – |
| 1978 | 483 | 24.1 | – | – | – | – | – | – |
| 1977 | 520 | 25.3 | – | – | – | – | – | – |
| 1976 | 517 | 27.2 | – | – | – | – | – | – |
| 1975 | 550 | 29.1 | – | – | – | – | – | – |
| 1974 | 462 | 25.2 | – | – | – | – | – | – |

*Note: (–) means data not available.*
*Source: Bureau of the Census,* Poverty in the United States: 1997, *Current Population Reports, P60-201, 1998*

# Number and Percent of Families with Children below Poverty Level by Family Type, 1974 to 1997: White Families

*(number and percent of white families with related children under age 18 below poverty level by family type, 1974 to 1997; families in thousands as of the following year)*

| | total families | | married couples | | female householder, no spouse present | | male householder, no spouse present | |
|---|---|---|---|---|---|---|---|---|
| | number | percent | number | percent | number | percent | number | percent |
| 1997 | 3,895 | 13.0% | 1,516 | 6.7% | 2,069 | 37.6% | 310 | 17.5% |
| 1996 | 3,863 | 13.0 | 1,548 | 6.8 | 2,032 | 36.9 | 283 | 18.0 |
| 1995 | 3,839 | 12.9 | 1,583 | 7.0 | 1,980 | 35.6 | 276 | 18.4 |
| 1994 | 4,025 | 13.6 | 1,708 | 7.5 | 2,064 | 38.3 | 253 | 19.2 |
| 1993 | 4,226 | 14.5 | 1,868 | 8.2 | 2,123 | 39.6 | 235 | 19.5 |
| 1992 | 4,020 | 14.0 | 1,753 | 7.8 | 2,021 | 39.6 | 246 | 19.7 |
| 1991 | 3,880 | 13.7 | 1,715 | 7.7 | 1,969 | 39.6 | 196 | 16.5 |
| 1990 | 3,553 | 12.6 | 1,572 | 7.1 | 1,814 | 37.9 | 167 | 16.0 |
| 1989 | 3,290 | 11.8 | 1,457 | 6.5 | 1,671 | 36.1 | 162 | 15.0 |
| 1988 | 3,321 | 11.9 | 1,434 | 6.4 | 1,740 | 38.2 | 147 | 14.5 |
| 1987 | 3,433 | 12.3 | 1,538 | 6.9 | 1,742 | 38.3 | 153 | 14.6 |
| 1986 | 3,637 | 13.0 | 1,692 | 7.5 | 1,812 | 39.8 | 132 | 14.5 |
| 1985 | 3,695 | 13.3 | 1,827 | 8.2 | 1,730 | 38.7 | 138 | 14.9 |
| 1984 | 3,679 | 13.4 | 1,879 | 8.5 | 1,682 | 38.8 | 117 | 13.6 |
| 1983 | 3,859 | 14.1 | 2,060 | 9.2 | 1,676 | 39.8 | 123 | 16.8 |
| 1982 | 3,709 | 13.7 | 2,005 | 9.0 | 1,584 | 39.3 | 120 | 17.4 |
| 1981 | 3,362 | 12.4 | 1,723 | 7.7 | 1,564 | 36.9 | 75 | 11.6 |
| 1980 | 3,078 | 11.2 | 1,544 | 6.8 | 1,433 | 35.9 | 100 | 16.0 |
| 1979 | 2,509 | 9.2 | 1,216 | 5.3 | 1,211 | 31.3 | 82 | 14.1 |
| 1978 | 2,513 | 9.3 | 1,185 | 5.2 | 1,268 | 33.5 | 60 | 11.4 |
| 1977 | 2,572 | 9.6 | 1,256 | 5.5 | 1,261 | 33.8 | 55 | 11.3 |
| 1976 | 2,566 | 9.6 | 1,242 | 5.4 | 1,260 | 36.4 | 64 | 13.2 |
| 1975 | 2,776 | 10.3 | 1,456 | 6.3 | 1,272 | 37.3 | 48 | 11.0 |
| 1974 | 2,430 | 9.0 | – | – | 1,180 | 36.4 | – | – |

*Note: (–) means data not available.*

*Source: Bureau of the Census,* Poverty in the United States: 1997, *Current Population Reports, P60-201, 1998*

# Little Change in Poverty Rates for Men and Women

## Females account for the majority of poor, a proportion that has not changed in three decades.

In 1997, females accounted for the 57 percent majority of the nation's 36 million poor. This proportion has not changed much in the past 30 years. Similarly, poverty rates for males and females have changed little despite three decades of effort at combatting poverty.

Among females, 16 percent were poor in 1967. This figure fell slightly to 15 percent in 1997. Males have always been less likely to be poor than females. In 1967, 12.5 percent of the nation's males were poor. By 1997, the figure had fallen slightly to just under 12 percent.

✗ Females have a higher poverty rate than males because they are more likely to be raising children, which limits their ability to work full-time.

### Males are slightly less likely to be poor than females

*(poverty rate of people by sex, 1967 and 1997)*

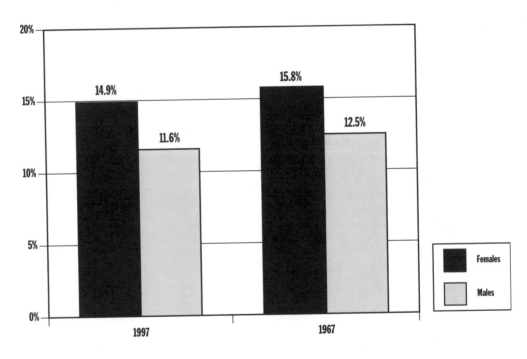

# Number and Percent of People below Poverty Level by Sex, 1967 to 1997

*(number and percent of people below poverty level by sex, and female share of poor people, 1967 to 1997; people in thousands as of the following year)*

| | male | | female | | percent of poor who are female |
|---|---|---|---|---|---|
| | number | percent | number | percent | |
| 1997 | 15,187 | 11.6% | 20,387 | 14.9% | 57.3% |
| 1996 | 15,611 | 12.0 | 20,918 | 15.4 | 57.3 |
| 1995 | 15,683 | 12.2 | 20,742 | 15.4 | 56.9 |
| 1994 | 16,316 | 12.8 | 21,744 | 16.3 | 57.1 |
| 1993 | 16,900 | 13.3 | 22,365 | 16.9 | 57.0 |
| 1992 | 16,222 | 12.9 | 21,792 | 16.6 | 57.3 |
| 1991 | 15,082 | 12.3 | 20,626 | 16.0 | 57.8 |
| 1990 | 14,211 | 11.7 | 19,373 | 15.2 | 57.7 |
| 1989 | 13,366 | 11.2 | 18,162 | 14.4 | 57.6 |
| 1988 | 13,599 | 11.5 | 18,146 | 14.5 | 57.2 |
| 1987 | 14,029 | 12.0 | 18,518 | 15.0 | 56.9 |
| 1986 | 13,721 | 11.8 | 18,649 | 15.2 | 57.6 |
| 1985 | 14,140 | 12.3 | 18,923 | 15.6 | 57.2 |
| 1984 | 14,537 | 12.8 | 19,163 | 15.9 | 56.9 |
| 1983 | 15,182 | 13.5 | 20,084 | 16.8 | 57.0 |
| 1982 | 14,842 | 13.4 | 19,556 | 16.5 | 56.9 |
| 1981 | 13,360 | 12.1 | 18,462 | 15.8 | 58.0 |
| 1980 | 12,207 | 11.2 | 17,065 | 14.7 | 58.3 |
| 1979 | 10,535 | 10.0 | 14,810 | 13.2 | 58.4 |
| 1978 | 10,017 | 9.6 | 14,480 | 13.0 | 59.1 |
| 1977 | 10,340 | 10.0 | 14,381 | 13.0 | 58.2 |
| 1976 | 10,373 | 10.1 | 14,603 | 13.4 | 58.5 |
| 1975 | 10,908 | 10.7 | 14,970 | 13.8 | 57.8 |
| 1974 | 10,313 | 10.2 | 13,881 | 12.9 | 57.4 |
| 1973 | 9,642 | 9.6 | 13,316 | 12.5 | 58.0 |
| 1972 | 10,190 | 10.2 | 14,258 | 13.4 | 58.3 |
| 1971 | 10,708 | 10.8 | 14,841 | 14.1 | 58.1 |
| 1970 | 10,879 | 11.1 | 14,632 | 14.0 | 57.4 |
| 1969 | 10,292 | 10.6 | 13,978 | 13.6 | 57.6 |
| 1968 | 10,793 | 11.3 | 14,578 | 14.3 | 57.5 |
| 1967 | 11,813 | 12.5 | 15,951 | 15.8 | 57.5 |

*Source: Bureau of the Census, Internet web site, <http:// www.census.gov/hhes/income/histinc/index.html>; calculations by New Strategist*

# A Growing Share of Poor People Are Aged 18 to 64

## Older Americans are a much smaller share of the poor than they once were.

Most of the nation's 36 million poor are aged 18 to 64. In 1997, 51 percent of the poor were in this working-age group, up from 39 percent in 1966. In contrast, children are a smaller share of the poor than they once were. The percentage of poor under age 18 fell from 44 to 40 percent between 1966 and 1997. Similarly, the share of poor aged 65 or older fell from 18 percent in 1966 to just 9.5 percent in 1997.

The poverty rate has dropped sharply among older Americans over the years. In 1959, 35 percent of people aged 65 or older had incomes that placed them below poverty level. By 1997, only 10.5 percent were poor. The poverty rate among children declined from 27 to 20 percent between 1959 and 1997. The poverty rate of working-aged adults barely changed during those years.

✗ The poverty rate among the elderly has fallen because a better educated and more affluent generation has entered the age group, and because of the expansion of Social Security benefits.

### Poverty rate has dropped among the elderly

*(poverty rate of people aged 65 or older, 1959 to 1997)*

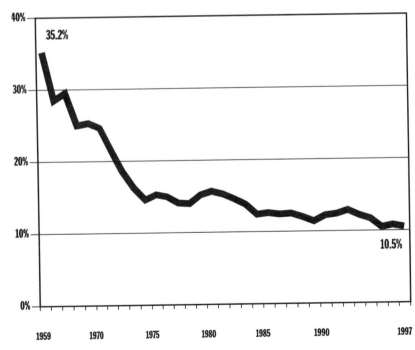

# Percent Distribution of People below Poverty Level by Age, 1966 to 1997

*(number of people below poverty level and percent distribution by age, 1966 to 1997; people in thousands as of the following year)*

| | total people | | | | |
|---|---|---|---|---|---|
| | number | percent | under age 18 | aged 18 to 64 | aged 65 or older |
| 1997 | 35,574 | 100.0% | 39.7% | 50.8% | 9.5% |
| 1996 | 36,529 | 100.0 | 39.6 | 51.0 | 9.4 |
| 1995 | 36,425 | 100.0 | 40.3 | 50.6 | 9.1 |
| 1994 | 38,059 | 100.0 | 40.2 | 50.2 | 9.6 |
| 1993 | 39,265 | 100.0 | 40.1 | 50.4 | 9.6 |
| 1992 | 38,014 | 100.0 | 40.2 | 49.4 | 10.3 |
| 1991 | 35,708 | 100.0 | 40.2 | 49.2 | 10.6 |
| 1990 | 33,585 | 100.0 | 40.0 | 49.1 | 10.9 |
| 1989 | 31,528 | 100.0 | 39.9 | 49.4 | 10.7 |
| 1988 | 31,745 | 100.0 | 39.2 | 49.8 | 11.0 |
| 1987 | 32,221 | 100.0 | 39.9 | 49.1 | 11.1 |
| 1986 | 32,370 | 100.0 | 39.8 | 49.5 | 10.7 |
| 1985 | 33,064 | 100.0 | 39.3 | 50.2 | 10.5 |
| 1984 | 33,700 | 100.0 | 39.8 | 50.3 | 9.9 |
| 1983 | 35,303 | 100.0 | 39.4 | 50.3 | 10.3 |
| 1982 | 34,398 | 100.0 | 39.7 | 49.4 | 10.9 |
| 1981 | 31,822 | 100.0 | 39.3 | 48.6 | 12.1 |
| 1980 | 29,272 | 100.0 | 39.4 | 47.3 | 13.2 |
| 1979 | 26,072 | 100.0 | 39.8 | 46.1 | 14.1 |
| 1978 | 24,497 | 100.0 | 40.5 | 46.3 | 13.2 |
| 1977 | 24,720 | 100.0 | 41.6 | 45.8 | 12.9 |
| 1976 | 24,975 | 100.0 | 41.1 | 45.6 | 13.3 |
| 1975 | 25,877 | 100.0 | 42.9 | 44.3 | 12.8 |
| 1974 | 23,370 | 100.0 | 43.5 | 43.4 | 13.2 |
| 1973 | 22,973 | 100.0 | 42.0 | 43.4 | 14.6 |
| 1972 | 24,460 | 100.0 | 42.0 | 42.7 | 15.3 |
| 1971 | 25,559 | 100.0 | 41.3 | 42.0 | 16.7 |
| 1970 | 25,420 | 100.0 | 41.1 | 40.1 | 18.9 |
| 1969 | 24,147 | 100.0 | 40.1 | 40.0 | 19.8 |
| 1968 | 25,389 | 100.0 | 43.1 | 38.6 | 18.2 |
| 1967 | 27,769 | 100.0 | 42.0 | 38.6 | 19.4 |
| 1966 | 28,510 | 100.0 | 43.5 | 38.6 | 17.9 |

*Source: Bureau of the Census,* Poverty in the United States: 1997, *Current Population Reports, P60-201, 1998; calculations by New Strategist*

# Number and Percent of People below Poverty Level by Age, 1959 to 1997

*(number and percent of people below poverty level by age, 1959 to 1997; people in thousands as of the following year)*

|  | total people | | under age 18 | | aged 18 to 64 | | aged 65 or older | |
|---|---|---|---|---|---|---|---|---|
|  | *number* | *percent* | *number* | *percent* | *number* | *percent* | *number* | *percent* |
| 1997 | 35,574 | 13.3% | 14,113 | 19.9% | 18,084 | 10.9% | 3,376 | 10.5% |
| 1996 | 36,529 | 13.7 | 14,463 | 20.5 | 18,638 | 11.4 | 3,428 | 10.8 |
| 1995 | 36,425 | 13.8 | 14,665 | 20.8 | 18,442 | 11.4 | 3,318 | 10.5 |
| 1994 | 38,059 | 14.5 | 15,289 | 21.8 | 19,107 | 11.9 | 3,663 | 11.7 |
| 1993 | 39,265 | 15.1 | 15,727 | 22.7 | 19,781 | 12.4 | 3,755 | 12.2 |
| 1992 | 38,014 | 14.8 | 15,294 | 22.3 | 18,793 | 11.9 | 3,928 | 12.9 |
| 1991 | 35,708 | 14.2 | 14,341 | 21.8 | 17,585 | 11.4 | 3,781 | 12.4 |
| 1990 | 33,585 | 13.5 | 13,431 | 20.6 | 16,496 | 10.7 | 3,658 | 12.2 |
| 1989 | 31,528 | 12.8 | 12,590 | 19.6 | 15,575 | 10.2 | 3,363 | 11.4 |
| 1988 | 31,745 | 13.0 | 12,455 | 19.5 | 15,809 | 10.5 | 3,481 | 12.0 |
| 1987 | 32,221 | 13.4 | 12,843 | 20.3 | 15,815 | 10.6 | 3,563 | 12.5 |
| 1986 | 32,370 | 13.6 | 12,876 | 20.5 | 16,017 | 10.8 | 3,477 | 12.4 |
| 1985 | 33,064 | 14.0 | 13,010 | 20.7 | 16,598 | 11.3 | 3,456 | 12.6 |
| 1984 | 33,700 | 14.4 | 13,420 | 21.5 | 16,952 | 11.7 | 3,330 | 12.4 |
| 1983 | 35,303 | 15.2 | 13,911 | 22.3 | 17,767 | 12.4 | 3,625 | 13.8 |
| 1982 | 34,398 | 15.0 | 13,647 | 21.9 | 17,000 | 12.0 | 3,751 | 14.6 |
| 1981 | 31,822 | 14.0 | 12,505 | 20.0 | 15,464 | 11.1 | 3,853 | 15.3 |
| 1980 | 29,272 | 13.0 | 11,543 | 18.3 | 13,858 | 10.1 | 3,871 | 15.7 |
| 1979 | 26,072 | 11.7 | 10,377 | 16.4 | 12,014 | 8.9 | 3,682 | 15.2 |
| 1978 | 24,497 | 11.4 | 9,931 | 15.9 | 11,332 | 8.7 | 3,233 | 14.0 |
| 1977 | 24,720 | 11.6 | 10,288 | 16.2 | 11,316 | 8.8 | 3,177 | 14.1 |
| 1976 | 24,975 | 11.8 | 10,273 | 16.0 | 11,389 | 9.0 | 3,313 | 15.0 |
| 1975 | 25,877 | 12.3 | 11,104 | 17.1 | 11,456 | 9.2 | 3,317 | 15.3 |
| 1974 | 23,370 | 11.2 | 10,156 | 15.4 | 10,132 | 8.3 | 3,085 | 14.6 |
| 1973 | 22,973 | 11.1 | 9,642 | 14.4 | 9,977 | 8.3 | 3,354 | 16.3 |
| 1972 | 24,460 | 11.9 | 10,284 | 15.1 | 10,438 | 8.8 | 3,738 | 18.6 |
| 1971 | 25,559 | 12.5 | 10,551 | 15.3 | 10,735 | 9.3 | 4,273 | 21.6 |
| 1970 | 25,420 | 12.6 | 10,440 | 15.1 | 10,187 | 9.0 | 4,793 | 24.6 |
| 1969 | 24,147 | 12.1 | 9,691 | 14.0 | 9,669 | 8.7 | 4,787 | 25.3 |
| 1968 | 25,389 | 12.8 | 10,954 | 15.6 | 9,803 | 9.0 | 4,632 | 25.0 |
| 1967 | 27,769 | 14.2 | 11,656 | 16.6 | 10,725 | 10.0 | 5,388 | 29.5 |
| 1966 | 28,510 | 14.7 | 12,389 | 17.6 | 11,007 | 10.5 | 5,114 | 28.5 |
| 1965 | 33,185 | 17.3 | 14,676 | 21.0 | – | – | – | – |
| 1964 | 36,055 | 19.0 | 16,051 | 23.0 | – | – | – | – |
| 1963 | 36,436 | 19.5 | 16,005 | 23.1 | – | – | – | – |
| 1962 | 38,625 | 21.0 | 16,963 | 25.0 | – | – | – | – |
| 1961 | 39,628 | 21.9 | 16,909 | 25.6 | – | – | – | – |
| 1960 | 39,851 | 22.2 | 17,634 | 26.9 | – | – | – | – |
| 1959 | 34,490 | 22.4 | 17,552 | 27.3 | 16,457 | 17.0 | 5,481 | 35.2 |

*Note: (–) means data not available.*
*Source: Bureau of the Census,* Poverty in the United States: 1997, *Current Population Reports, P60-201, 1998*

# Blacks Account for Only One in Four of the Nation's Poor

## Nearly seven out of ten poor people are white.

In 1973, blacks accounted for 32 percent of the poverty population. Today, the figure has fallen to 26 percent. In contrast, the Hispanic share of the poor more than doubled during those years, rising from 10 to 23 percent. The white share also grew, rising from 66 to 69 percent. Only 4 percent of poor Americans are Asian.

During the past 25 years, the black poverty rate declined while the Hispanic rate increased. In 1973, 31 percent of blacks were poor, a rate that fell to 26.5 percent by 1997. In contrast, the percentage of Hispanics living below the poverty level rose from 22 to 27 percent during those years. The poverty rate also rose for whites—in part because most Hispanics are white and the rising poverty rate of Hispanics boosted the rate for whites. Between 1987 and 1997, the poverty rate of Asians fell slightly, from 16 to 14 percent.

✘ The black poverty rate has fallen because blacks are better educated and have more job opportunities than they once did. The Hispanic poverty rate has increased because a growing share of Hispanics are immigrants with little education and few job skills.

### Poverty rate is down for blacks, up for Hispanics

*(poverty rate of people by race and Hispanic origin, 1973 and 1997)*

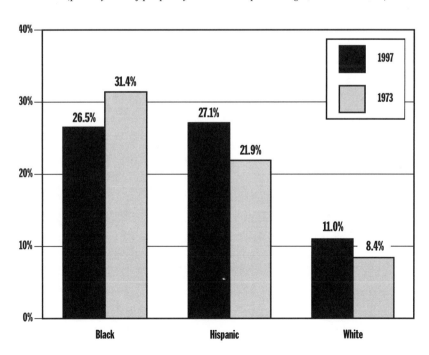

## Percent Distribution of People below Poverty Level by Race and Hispanic Origin, 1973 to 1997

*(number of people below poverty level and percent distribution by race and Hispanic origin, 1973 to 1997; people in thousands as of the following year)*

| | total people number | total people percent | Asians | blacks | Hispanics | whites |
|---|---|---|---|---|---|---|
| 1997 | 35,574 | 100.0% | 4.1% | 25.6% | 23.4% | 68.6% |
| 1996 | 36,529 | 100.0 | 4.0 | 26.5 | 23.8 | 67.5 |
| 1995 | 36,425 | 100.0 | 3.9 | 27.1 | 23.5 | 67.1 |
| 1994 | 38,059 | 100.0 | 2.6 | 26.8 | 22.1 | 66.7 |
| 1993 | 39,265 | 100.0 | 2.9 | 27.7 | 20.7 | 66.8 |
| 1992 | 38,014 | 100.0 | 2.6 | 28.5 | 20.0 | 66.4 |
| 1991 | 35,708 | 100.0 | 2.8 | 28.7 | 17.8 | 66.5 |
| 1990 | 33,585 | 100.0 | 2.6 | 29.3 | 17.9 | 66.5 |
| 1989 | 31,528 | 100.0 | 3.0 | 29.5 | 17.2 | 65.9 |
| 1988 | 31,745 | 100.0 | 3.5 | 29.5 | 16.9 | 65.3 |
| 1987 | 32,221 | 100.0 | 3.2 | 29.5 | 16.8 | 65.8 |
| 1986 | 32,370 | 100.0 | – | 27.8 | 15.8 | 68.5 |
| 1985 | 33,064 | 100.0 | – | 27.0 | 15.8 | 69.1 |
| 1984 | 33,700 | 100.0 | – | 28.2 | 14.3 | 68.1 |
| 1983 | 35,303 | 100.0 | – | 28.0 | 13.1 | 67.9 |
| 1982 | 34,398 | 100.0 | – | 28.2 | 12.5 | 68.4 |
| 1981 | 31,822 | 100.0 | – | 28.8 | 11.7 | 67.7 |
| 1980 | 29,272 | 100.0 | – | 29.3 | 11.9 | 67.3 |
| 1979 | 26,072 | 100.0 | – | 30.9 | 11.2 | 66.0 |
| 1978 | 24,497 | 100.0 | – | 31.1 | 10.6 | 66.4 |
| 1977 | 24,720 | 100.0 | – | 31.3 | 10.9 | 66.4 |
| 1976 | 24,975 | 100.0 | – | 30.4 | 11.1 | 66.9 |
| 1975 | 25,877 | 100.0 | – | 29.2 | 11.6 | 68.7 |
| 1974 | 23,370 | 100.0 | – | 30.7 | 11.0 | 67.3 |
| 1973 | 22,973 | 100.0 | – | 32.2 | 10.3 | 65.9 |

*Note: Numbers will not add to 100 because Hispanics may be of any race and not all races are shown. (–) means data not available.*
*Source: Bureau of the Census,* Poverty in the United States: 1997, *Current Population Reports, P60-201, 1998; calculations by New Strategist*

# Number and Percent of People below Poverty Level by Race and Hispanic Origin, 1973 to 1997

*(number and percent of people below poverty level by race and Hispanic origin, 1973 to 1997; people in thousands as of the following year)*

| | total people | | Asians | | blacks | | Hispanics | | whites | |
|---|---|---|---|---|---|---|---|---|---|---|
| | *number* | *percent* | *number* | *percent* | *number* | *percent* | *number* | *percent* | *number* | *percent* |
| 1997 | 35,574 | 13.3% | 1,468 | 14.0% | 9,116 | 26.5% | 8,308 | 27.1% | 24,396 | 11.0% |
| 1996 | 36,529 | 13.7 | 1,454 | 14.5 | 9,694 | 28.4 | 8,697 | 29.4 | 24,650 | 11.2 |
| 1995 | 36,425 | 13.8 | 1,411 | 14.6 | 9,872 | 29.3 | 8,574 | 30.3 | 24,423 | 11.2 |
| 1994 | 38,059 | 14.5 | 974 | 14.6 | 10,196 | 30.6 | 8,416 | 30.7 | 25,379 | 11.7 |
| 1993 | 39,265 | 15.1 | 1,134 | 15.3 | 10,877 | 33.1 | 8,126 | 30.6 | 26,226 | 12.2 |
| 1992 | 38,014 | 14.8 | 985 | 12.7 | 10,827 | 33.4 | 7,592 | 29.6 | 25,259 | 11.9 |
| 1991 | 35,708 | 14.2 | 996 | 13.8 | 10,242 | 32.7 | 6,339 | 28.7 | 23,747 | 11.3 |
| 1990 | 33,585 | 13.5 | 858 | 12.2 | 9,837 | 31.9 | 6,006 | 28.1 | 22,326 | 10.7 |
| 1989 | 31,528 | 12.8 | 939 | 14.1 | 9,302 | 30.7 | 5,430 | 26.2 | 20,785 | 10.0 |
| 1988 | 31,745 | 13.0 | 1,117 | 17.3 | 9,356 | 31.3 | 5,357 | 26.7 | 20,715 | 10.1 |
| 1987 | 32,221 | 13.4 | 1,021 | 16.1 | 9,520 | 32.4 | 5,422 | 28.0 | 21,195 | 10.4 |
| 1986 | 32,370 | 13.6 | – | – | 8,983 | 31.1 | 5,117 | 27.3 | 22,183 | 11.0 |
| 1985 | 33,064 | 14.0 | – | – | 8,926 | 31.3 | 5,236 | 29.0 | 22,860 | 11.4 |
| 1984 | 33,700 | 14.4 | – | – | 9,490 | 33.8 | 4,806 | 28.4 | 22,955 | 11.5 |
| 1983 | 35,303 | 15.2 | – | – | 9,882 | 35.7 | 4,633 | 28.0 | 23,984 | 12.1 |
| 1982 | 34,398 | 15.0 | – | – | 9,697 | 35.6 | 4,301 | 29.9 | 23,517 | 12.0 |
| 1981 | 31,822 | 14.0 | – | – | 9,173 | 34.2 | 3,713 | 26.5 | 21,553 | 11.1 |
| 1980 | 29,272 | 13.0 | – | – | 8,579 | 32.5 | 3,491 | 25.7 | 19,699 | 10.2 |
| 1979 | 26,072 | 11.7 | – | – | 8,050 | 31.0 | 2,921 | 21.8 | 17,214 | 9.0 |
| 1978 | 24,497 | 11.4 | – | – | 7,625 | 30.6 | 2,607 | 21.6 | 16,259 | 8.7 |
| 1977 | 24,720 | 11.6 | – | – | 7,726 | 31.3 | 2,700 | 22.4 | 16,416 | 8.9 |
| 1976 | 24,975 | 11.8 | – | – | 7,595 | 31.1 | 2,783 | 24.7 | 16,713 | 9.1 |
| 1975 | 25,877 | 12.3 | – | – | 7,545 | 31.3 | 2,991 | 26.9 | 17,770 | 9.7 |
| 1974 | 23,370 | 11.2 | – | – | 7,182 | 30.3 | 2,575 | 23.0 | 15,736 | 8.6 |
| 1973 | 22,973 | 11.1 | – | – | 7,388 | 31.4 | 2,366 | 21.9 | 15,142 | 8.4 |

*Note: Numbers will not add to 100 because Hispanics may be of any race and not all races are shown. (–) means data not available.*
*Source: Bureau of the Census,* Poverty in the United States: 1997, *Current Population Reports, P60-201, 1998*

# Poverty Has Grown in the West

## The South has seen poverty rate fall over the past few decades.

Until the early 1980s, fewer poor lived in the West than in any other region. Today, the West is second only to the South in the number of poor. One in four poor Americans lives in the West, up from only 16 percent in 1971. A shrinking share of the poor live in the South. In 1971, the South was home to fully 44 percent of poor Americans, a figure that had fallen to 39 percent by 1997.

Between 1971 and 1997, poverty rates grew in the West and Northeast, while they fell in the South. The poverty rate in the Midwest remained about the same during those years. In 1971, the South had the highest poverty rate among the four regions. Today, the West's poverty rate matches that of the South, at 14.6 percent. The poverty rate in the Northeast rose from 9 to 13 percent between 1971 and 1997.

✘ Behind the growing number of poor in the West is the immigration of millions of poorly educated and unskilled Hispanics into the region. The poverty rate has declined in the South because the region's economy has grown steadily and the fortunes of blacks have improved.

### One in four poor Americans lives in the West

*(percent of poor people who live in the West, 1971 to 1997)*

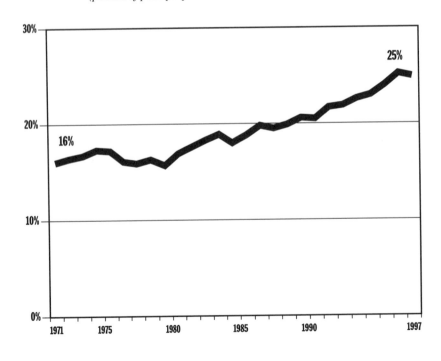

# Percent Distribution of People below Poverty Level by Region, 1971 to 1997

*(number of people below poverty level and percent distribution by region, 1971 to 1997; people in thousands as of the following year)*

| | total people | | | | | |
| | number | percent | Northeast | Midwest | South | West |
|---|---|---|---|---|---|---|
| 1997 | 35,574 | 100.0% | 18.2% | 18.3% | 38.6% | 24.9% |
| 1996 | 36,529 | 100.0 | 18.0 | 18.2 | 38.6 | 25.2 |
| 1995 | 36,425 | 100.0 | 17.7 | 18.6 | 39.7 | 24.0 |
| 1994 | 38,059 | 100.0 | 17.3 | 20.9 | 38.7 | 23.0 |
| 1993 | 39,265 | 100.0 | 17.4 | 20.8 | 39.2 | 22.6 |
| 1992 | 38,014 | 100.0 | 16.9 | 21.2 | 40.0 | 21.9 |
| 1991 | 35,708 | 100.0 | 17.3 | 22.4 | 38.6 | 21.7 |
| 1990 | 33,585 | 100.0 | 17.3 | 22.2 | 40.1 | 20.5 |
| 1989 | 31,528 | 100.0 | 16.1 | 22.3 | 41.1 | 20.6 |
| 1988 | 31,745 | 100.0 | 16.0 | 21.4 | 42.6 | 19.9 |
| 1987 | 32,221 | 100.0 | 17.0 | 23.3 | 41.2 | 19.5 |
| 1986 | 32,370 | 100.0 | 16.1 | 23.6 | 40.5 | 19.8 |
| 1985 | 33,064 | 100.0 | 17.4 | 24.8 | 39.1 | 18.8 |
| 1984 | 33,700 | 100.0 | 19.4 | 24.6 | 38.0 | 18.0 |
| 1983 | 35,303 | 100.0 | 18.6 | 24.2 | 38.2 | 18.9 |
| 1982 | 34,398 | 100.0 | 18.5 | 22.6 | 40.6 | 18.3 |
| 1981 | 31,822 | 100.0 | 18.3 | 22.4 | 41.7 | 17.6 |
| 1980 | 29,272 | 100.0 | 18.3 | 22.5 | 42.2 | 16.9 |
| 1979 | 26,072 | 100.0 | 19.3 | 21.5 | 40.8 | 15.7 |
| 1978 | 24,497 | 100.0 | 20.6 | 21.2 | 41.9 | 16.3 |
| 1977 | 24,720 | 100.0 | 20.0 | 22.6 | 41.5 | 15.9 |
| 1976 | 24,975 | 100.0 | 19.8 | 22.7 | 41.5 | 16.1 |
| 1975 | 25,877 | 100.0 | 19.0 | 21.1 | 42.7 | 17.2 |
| 1974 | 23,370 | 100.0 | 19.1 | 21.4 | 46.0 | 17.3 |
| 1973 | 22,973 | 100.0 | 18.3 | 21.2 | 43.8 | 16.7 |
| 1972 | 24,460 | 100.0 | 17.4 | 21.5 | 44.7 | 16.4 |
| 1971 | 25,559 | 100.0 | 17.7 | 22.6 | 43.7 | 16.0 |

*Source: Bureau of the Census, Internet web site, <http:// www.census.gov/hhes/income/histinc/index.html>; calculations by New Strategist*

## Number and Percent of People below Poverty Level by Region, 1971 to 1997

*(number and percent of people below poverty level by region, 1971 to 1997; people in thousands as of the following year)*

| | total people | | Northeast | | Midwest | | South | | West | |
|---|---|---|---|---|---|---|---|---|---|---|
| | number | percent | number | percent | number | percent | number | percent | number | percent |
| 1997 | 35,574 | 13.3% | 6,474 | 12.6% | 6,493 | 10.4% | 13,748 | 14.6% | 8,858 | 14.6% |
| 1996 | 36,529 | 13.7 | 6,558 | 12.7 | 6,654 | 10.7 | 14,098 | 15.1 | 9,219 | 15.4 |
| 1995 | 36,425 | 13.8 | 6,445 | 12.5 | 6,785 | 11.0 | 14,458 | 15.7 | 8,736 | 14.9 |
| 1994 | 38,059 | 14.5 | 6,597 | 12.9 | 7,965 | 13.0 | 14,729 | 16.1 | 8,768 | 15.3 |
| 1993 | 39,265 | 15.1 | 6,839 | 13.3 | 8,172 | 13.4 | 15,375 | 17.1 | 8,879 | 15.6 |
| 1992 | 38,014 | 14.8 | 6,414 | 12.6 | 8,060 | 13.3 | 15,198 | 17.1 | 8,343 | 14.8 |
| 1991 | 35,708 | 14.2 | 6,177 | 12.2 | 7,989 | 13.2 | 13,783 | 16.0 | 7,759 | 14.3 |
| 1990 | 33,585 | 13.5 | 5,794 | 11.4 | 7,458 | 12.4 | 13,456 | 15.8 | 6,877 | 13.0 |
| 1989 | 31,528 | 12.8 | 5,061 | 10.0 | 7,043 | 11.9 | 12,943 | 15.4 | 6,481 | 12.5 |
| 1988 | 31,745 | 13.0 | 5,089 | 10.1 | 6,804 | 11.4 | 13,530 | 16.1 | 6,322 | 12.7 |
| 1987 | 32,221 | 13.4 | 5,476 | 11.0 | 7,499 | 12.7 | 13,287 | 16.1 | 6,285 | 12.6 |
| 1986 | 32,370 | 13.6 | 5,211 | 10.5 | 7,641 | 13.0 | 13,106 | 16.1 | 6,412 | 13.2 |
| 1985 | 33,064 | 14.0 | 5,751 | 11.6 | 8,191 | 13.9 | 12,921 | 16.0 | 6,201 | 13.0 |
| 1984 | 33,700 | 14.4 | 6,531 | 13.2 | 8,303 | 14.1 | 12,792 | 16.2 | 6,074 | 13.1 |
| 1983 | 35,303 | 15.2 | 6,561 | 13.4 | 8,536 | 14.6 | 13,484 | 17.2 | 6,684 | 14.7 |
| 1982 | 34,398 | 15.0 | 6,364 | 13.0 | 7,772 | 13.3 | 13,967 | 18.1 | 6,296 | 14.1 |
| 1981 | 31,822 | 14.0 | 5,815 | 11.9 | 7,142 | 12.3 | 13,256 | 17.4 | 5,609 | 12.7 |
| 1980 | 29,272 | 13.0 | 5,369 | 11.1 | 6,592 | 11.4 | 12,363 | 16.5 | 4,958 | 11.4 |
| 1979 | 26,072 | 11.7 | 5,029 | 10.4 | 5,594 | 9.7 | 10,627 | 15.0 | 4,095 | 10.0 |
| 1978 | 24,497 | 11.4 | 5,050 | 10.4 | 5,192 | 9.1 | 10,255 | 14.7 | 4,000 | 10.0 |
| 1977 | 24,720 | 11.6 | 4,956 | 10.2 | 5,589 | 9.8 | 10,249 | 14.8 | 3,927 | 10.1 |
| 1976 | 24,975 | 11.8 | 4,949 | 10.2 | 5,657 | 9.9 | 10,354 | 15.2 | 4,015 | 10.5 |
| 1975 | 25,877 | 12.3 | 4,904 | 10.2 | 5,459 | 9.7 | 11,059 | 16.2 | 4,454 | 11.7 |
| 1974 | 23,370 | 11.2 | 4,473 | 9.3 | 4,990 | 8.8 | 10,761 | 16.1 | 4,036 | 10.7 |
| 1973 | 22,973 | 11.1 | 4,207 | 8.6 | 4,864 | 8.6 | 10,061 | 15.3 | 3,841 | 10.5 |
| 1972 | 24,460 | 11.9 | 4,266 | 8.7 | 5,258 | 9.3 | 10,928 | 16.9 | 4,008 | 11.1 |
| 1971 | 25,559 | 12.5 | 4,512 | 9.3 | 5,764 | 10.3 | 11,182 | 17.5 | 4,101 | 11.4 |

*Source: Bureau of the Census, Internet web site, <http:// www.census.gov/hhes/income/histinc/index.html>*

# Some States Have Seen Poverty Rate Decline Sharply

## Other states have experienced rising poverty rate.

Between 1980 and 1997, the poverty rate fell in 27 states. The steepest decline was in Mississippi, where the rate was down more than 7 percentage points, falling from 24 to 17 percent during those years. In Alabama and Tennessee, poverty rates fell more than 5 percentage points between 1980 and 1997. In contrast, California and Hawaii saw their poverty rates rise by more than 5 percentage points during those years.

Nationally and in many states, the poverty rate rose between 1980 and 1990, making the contrast between 1997 and 1990 starker than the one between 1980 and 1997. Since 1990, poverty rates fell in 30 states. Some states have seen a sharp rise in poverty during those seven years, however, and Rhode Island's poverty rate rose more than 5 percentage points, from 7.5 to 12.7 percent.

✘ The economic downturn at the end of the 1980s and in the early 1990s boosted poverty in many states, while the recovery of the mid-1990s lowered poverty rates.

### Gains and losses in poverty

*(percentage point change in poverty rates in selected states, 1980 to 1997)*

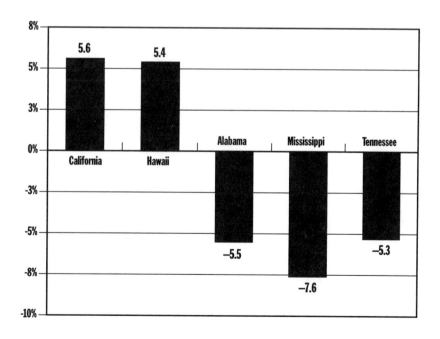

# Poverty Rates by State, 1980 to 1997

*(percent of people below poverty level by state, selected years 1980 to 1997; percentage point change, 1980–97 and 1990–97)*

| | | | | percentage point change | |
| | 1997 | 1990 | 1980 | 1980–97 | 1990–97 |
|---|---|---|---|---|---|
| **Total U.S.** | **13.3%** | **13.5%** | **13.0%** | **0.3** | **–0.2** |
| Alabama | 15.7 | 19.2 | 21.2 | –5.5 | –3.5 |
| Alaska | 8.8 | 11.4 | 9.6 | –0.8 | –2.6 |
| Arizona | 17.2 | 13.7 | 12.8 | 4.4 | 3.5 |
| Arkansas | 19.7 | 19.6 | 21.5 | –1.8 | 0.1 |
| California | 16.6 | 13.9 | 11.0 | 5.6 | 2.7 |
| Colorado | 8.2 | 13.7 | 8.6 | –0.4 | –5.5 |
| Connecticut | 8.6 | 6.0 | 8.3 | 0.3 | 2.6 |
| Delaware | 9.6 | 6.9 | 11.8 | –2.2 | 2.7 |
| D.C. | 21.8 | 21.1 | 20.9 | 0.9 | 0.7 |
| Florida | 14.3 | 14.4 | 16.7 | –2.4 | –0.1 |
| Georgia | 14.5 | 15.8 | 13.9 | 0.6 | –1.3 |
| Hawaii | 13.9 | 11.0 | 8.5 | 5.4 | 2.9 |
| Idaho | 14.7 | 14.9 | 14.7 | 0.0 | –0.2 |
| Illinois | 11.2 | 13.7 | 12.3 | –1.1 | –2.5 |
| Indiana | 8.8 | 13.0 | 11.8 | –3.0 | –4.2 |
| Iowa | 9.6 | 10.4 | 10.8 | –1.2 | –0.8 |
| Kansas | 9.7 | 10.3 | 9.4 | 0.3 | –0.6 |
| Kentucky | 15.9 | 17.3 | 19.3 | –3.4 | –1.4 |
| Louisiana | 16.3 | 23.6 | 20.3 | –4.0 | –7.3 |
| Maine | 10.1 | 13.1 | 14.6 | –4.5 | –3.0 |
| Maryland | 8.4 | 9.9 | 9.5 | –1.1 | –1.5 |
| Massachusetts | 12.2 | 10.7 | 9.5 | 2.7 | 1.5 |
| Michigan | 10.3 | 14.3 | 12.9 | –2.6 | –4.0 |
| Minnesota | 9.6 | 12.0 | 8.7 | 0.9 | –2.4 |
| Mississippi | 16.7 | 25.7 | 24.3 | –7.6 | –9.0 |
| Missouri | 11.8 | 13.4 | 13.0 | –1.2 | –1.6 |
| Montana | 15.6 | 16.3 | 13.2 | 2.4 | –0.7 |
| Nebraska | 9.8 | 10.3 | 13.0 | –3.2 | –0.5 |
| Nevada | 11.0 | 9.8 | 8.3 | 2.7 | 1.2 |
| New Hampshire | 9.1 | 6.3 | 7.0 | 2.1 | 2.8 |
| New Jersey | 9.3 | 9.2 | 9.0 | 0.3 | 0.1 |
| New Mexico | 21.2 | 20.9 | 20.6 | 0.6 | 0.3 |
| New York | 16.5 | 14.3 | 13.8 | 2.7 | 2.2 |
| North Carolina | 11.4 | 13.0 | 15.0 | –3.6 | –1.6 |
| North Dakota | 13.6 | 13.7 | 15.5 | –1.9 | –0.1 |
| Ohio | 11.0 | 11.5 | 9.8 | 1.2 | –0.5 |
| Oklahoma | 13.7 | 15.6 | 13.9 | –0.2 | –1.9 |
| Oregon | 11.6 | 9.2 | 11.5 | 0.1 | 2.4 |

*(continued)*

*(continued from previous page)*

| | 1997 | 1990 | 1980 | percentage point change | |
| | | | | 1980–97 | 1990–97 |
|---|---|---|---|---|---|
| Pennsylvania | 11.2% | 11.0% | 9.8% | 1.4 | 0.2 |
| Rhode Island | 12.7 | 7.5 | 10.7 | 2.0 | 5.2 |
| South Carolina | 13.1 | 16.2 | 16.8 | −3.7 | −3.1 |
| South Dakota | 16.5 | 13.3 | 18.8 | −2.3 | 3.2 |
| Tennessee | 14.3 | 16.9 | 19.6 | −5.3 | −2.6 |
| Texas | 16.7 | 15.9 | 15.7 | 1.0 | 0.8 |
| Utah | 8.9 | 8.2 | 10.0 | −1.1 | 0.7 |
| Vermont | 9.3 | 10.9 | 12.0 | −2.7 | −1.6 |
| Virginia | 12.7 | 11.1 | 12.4 | 0.3 | 1.6 |
| Washington | 9.2 | 8.9 | 12.7 | −3.5 | 0.3 |
| West Virginia | 16.4 | 18.1 | 15.2 | 1.2 | −1.7 |
| Wisconsin | 8.2 | 9.3 | 8.5 | −0.3 | −1.1 |
| Wyoming | 13.5 | 11.0 | 10.4 | 3.1 | 2.5 |

*Source: Bureau of the Census, Internet web site, <http:// www.census.gov/hhes/income/histinc/index.html>; calculations by New Strategist*

# Growing Share of Poor Live in Metropolitan Areas

## Most of the poor once lived in nonmetropolitan areas.

Three decades ago, slightly more than half the nation's poor lived in nonmetropolitan areas. But as a growing share of Americans became metropolitan residents, the poverty population in metro areas expanded. Today, only 23 percent of the poor live in nonmetropolitan areas. Central cities are home to 42 percent of the nation's poor, up from 31 percent in 1967. The share of the poor living in the suburbs of metropolitan areas has nearly doubled, rising from 19 percent in 1967 to 34 percent in 1997.

The poverty rate among metropolitan residents has grown slightly, rising from 10 percent in 1971 to 13 percent in 1997. The biggest increase has been in the central cities, where the poverty rate climbed from 14 to 19 percent during those years. In the suburbs the rate rose from 7 to 9 percent. The poverty rate fell slightly in nonmetropolitan areas, dropping from 17 to 16 percent between 1971 and 1997.

✘ The largest share of the poor were once rural residents. Today, the largest share live in central cities. This change affects not only the needs of the poor, but also how services are delivered to them.

### Metropolitan areas are home to most of the poor

*(percent of poor people who live in metropolitan areas, 1967 to 1997)*

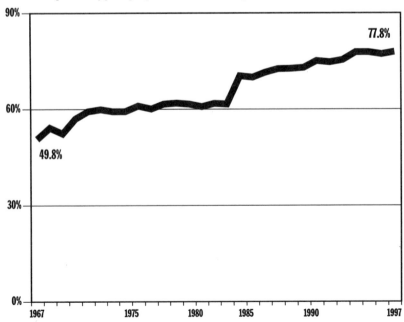

# Percent Distribution of People below Poverty Level by Metropolitan Residence, 1967 to 1997

*(number of people below poverty level and percent distribution by metropolitan residence, 1967 to 1997; people in thousands as of the following year)*

| | total people | | metropolitan area | | | nonmetropolitan area |
|---|---|---|---|---|---|---|
| | number | percent | total | central cities | suburbs | |
| 1997 | 35,574 | 100.0% | 77.9% | 42.2% | 34.4% | 23.3% |
| 1996 | 36,529 | 100.0 | 77.2 | 42.8 | 34.4 | 22.8 |
| 1995 | 36,425 | 100.0 | 77.8 | 44.7 | 33.1 | 22.2 |
| 1994 | 38,059 | 100.0 | 77.8 | 42.3 | 35.5 | 22.2 |
| 1993 | 39,265 | 100.0 | 75.4 | 42.8 | 32.6 | 24.6 |
| 1992 | 38,014 | 100.0 | 74.7 | 43.0 | 31.7 | 25.3 |
| 1991 | 35,708 | 100.0 | 75.1 | 42.9 | 32.2 | 24.9 |
| 1990 | 33,585 | 100.0 | 73.0 | 42.4 | 30.5 | 27.0 |
| 1989 | 31,528 | 100.0 | 72.7 | 43.1 | 29.6 | 27.3 |
| 1988 | 31,745 | 100.0 | 72.6 | 42.9 | 29.7 | 27.4 |
| 1987 | 32,221 | 100.0 | 71.5 | 42.5 | 29.0 | 28.5 |
| 1986 | 32,370 | 100.0 | 70.0 | 41.1 | 28.9 | 30.0 |
| 1985 | 33,064 | 100.0 | 70.4 | 42.9 | 27.5 | 29.6 |
| 1984 | 33,700 | 100.0 | – | – | – | – |
| 1983 | 35,303 | 100.0 | 61.6 | 36.5 | 25.1 | 38.3 |
| 1982 | 34,398 | 100.0 | 61.8 | 36.9 | 24.9 | 38.2 |
| 1981 | 31,822 | 100.0 | 60.8 | 35.3 | 25.5 | 39.2 |
| 1980 | 29,272 | 100.0 | 61.6 | 36.4 | 25.2 | 38.4 |
| 1979 | 26,072 | 100.0 | 61.9 | 37.3 | 24.6 | 38.1 |
| 1978 | 24,497 | 100.0 | 61.6 | 37.9 | 23.7 | 38.4 |
| 1977 | 24,720 | 100.0 | 60.1 | 37.2 | 22.9 | 39.9 |
| 1976 | 24,975 | 100.0 | 61.0 | 38.0 | 23.0 | 39.0 |
| 1975 | 25,877 | 100.0 | 59.3 | 35.1 | 24.2 | 40.7 |
| 1974 | 23,370 | 100.0 | 59.3 | 35.8 | 23.4 | 40.7 |
| 1973 | 22,973 | 100.0 | 59.9 | 37.4 | 22.5 | 40.1 |
| 1972 | 24,460 | 100.0 | 59.3 | 37.5 | 21.8 | 40.7 |
| 1971 | 25,559 | 100.0 | 57.0 | 34.9 | 22.1 | 43.0 |
| 1970 | 25,420 | 100.0 | 52.4 | 31.9 | 20.5 | 47.6 |
| 1969 | 24,147 | 100.0 | 54.2 | 33.1 | 21.1 | 45.8 |
| 1968 | 25,389 | 100.0 | 50.7 | 30.5 | 20.2 | 49.3 |
| 1967 | 27,769 | 100.0 | 49.8 | 31.1 | 18.7 | 50.2 |

*Note: (–) means data not available.*
*Note: The suburbs are the portion of a metropolitan area that is outside the central city.*
*Source: Bureau of the Census, Internet web site, <http:// www.census.gov/hhes/income/histinc/index.html>; calculations by New Strategist*

# Number and Percent of People below Poverty Level by Metropolitan Residence, 1971 to 1997

*(number and percent of people below poverty level by metropolitan residence, 1971 to 1997; people in thousands as of the following year)*

| | total people | | metropolitan total | | central cities | | suburbs | | nonmetropolitan | |
|---|---|---|---|---|---|---|---|---|---|---|
| | *number* | *percent* | *number* | *percent* | *number* | *percent* | *number* | *percent* | *number* | *percent* |
| 1997 | 35,574 | 13.3% | 27,723 | 12.6% | 15,018 | 18.8% | 12,255 | 9.0% | 8,301 | 15.9% |
| 1996 | 36,529 | 13.7 | 28,211 | 13.2 | 15,645 | 19.6 | 12,566 | 9.4 | 8,318 | 15.9 |
| 1995 | 36,425 | 13.8 | 28,342 | 13.4 | 16,269 | 20.6 | 12,072 | 9.1 | 8,083 | 15.6 |
| 1994 | 38,059 | 14.5 | 29,610 | 14.2 | 16,098 | 20.9 | 13,511 | 10.3 | 8,449 | 16.0 |
| 1993 | 39,265 | 15.1 | 29,615 | 14.6 | 16,805 | 21.5 | 12,810 | 10.3 | 9,650 | 17.2 |
| 1992 | 38,014 | 14.8 | 28,380 | 14.2 | 16,346 | 20.9 | 12,034 | 9.9 | 9,634 | 16.9 |
| 1991 | 35,708 | 14.2 | 26,827 | 13.7 | 15,314 | 20.2 | 11,513 | 9.6 | 8,881 | 16.1 |
| 1990 | 33,585 | 13.5 | 24,510 | 12.7 | 14,254 | 19.0 | 10,255 | 8.7 | 9,075 | 16.3 |
| 1989 | 31,528 | 12.8 | 22,917 | 12.0 | 13,592 | 18.1 | 9,326 | 8.0 | 8,611 | 15.7 |
| 1988 | 31,745 | 13.0 | 23,059 | 12.2 | 13,615 | 18.1 | 9,444 | 8.3 | 8,686 | 16.0 |
| 1987 | 32,221 | 13.4 | 23,054 | 12.3 | 13,697 | 18.3 | 9,357 | 8.3 | 9,167 | 17.0 |
| 1986 | 32,370 | 13.6 | 22,657 | 12.3 | 13,295 | 18.0 | 9,362 | 8.4 | 9,712 | 18.1 |
| 1985 | 33,064 | 14.0 | 23,275 | 12.7 | 14,177 | 19.0 | 9,097 | 8.4 | 9,789 | 18.3 |
| 1984 | 33,700 | 14.4 | – | – | – | – | – | – | – | – |
| 1983 | 35,303 | 15.2 | 21,750 | 13.8 | 12,872 | 19.8 | 8,878 | 9.6 | 13,516 | 18.3 |
| 1982 | 34,398 | 15.0 | 21,247 | 13.7 | 12,696 | 19.9 | 8,551 | 9.3 | 13,152 | 17.8 |
| 1981 | 31,822 | 14.0 | 19,347 | 12.6 | 11,231 | 18.0 | 8,116 | 8.9 | 12,475 | 17.0 |
| 1980 | 29,272 | 13.0 | 18,021 | 11.9 | 10,644 | 17.2 | 7,377 | 8.2 | 11,251 | 15.4 |
| 1979 | 26,072 | 11.7 | 16,135 | 10.7 | 9,720 | 15.7 | 6,415 | 7.2 | 9,937 | 13.8 |
| 1978 | 24,497 | 11.4 | 15,090 | 10.4 | 9,285 | 15.4 | 5,805 | 6.8 | 9,407 | 13.5 |
| 1977 | 24,720 | 11.6 | 14,859 | 10.4 | 9,203 | 15.4 | 5,657 | 6.8 | 9,861 | 13.9 |
| 1976 | 24,975 | 11.8 | 15,229 | 10.7 | 9,482 | 15.8 | 5,747 | 6.9 | 9,746 | 14.0 |
| 1975 | 25,877 | 12.3 | 15,348 | 10.8 | 9,090 | 15.0 | 6,259 | 7.6 | 10,529 | 15.4 |
| 1974 | 23,370 | 11.2 | 13,851 | 9.7 | 8,373 | 13.7 | 5,477 | 6.7 | 9,519 | 14.2 |
| 1973 | 22,973 | 11.1 | 13,759 | 9.7 | 8,594 | 14.0 | 5,165 | 6.4 | 9,214 | 14.0 |
| 1972 | 24,460 | 11.9 | 14,508 | 10.3 | 9,179 | 14.7 | 5,329 | 6.8 | 9,952 | 15.3 |
| 1971 | 25,559 | 12.5 | 14,561 | 10.4 | 8,912 | 14.2 | 5,649 | 7.2 | 10,999 | 17.2 |

*Note: (–) means data not available.*
*Source: Bureau of the Census, Internet web site, <http:// www.census.gov/hhes/income/histinc/index.html>*

# The Ranks of the Working Poor Are Rising

## Growing numbers are in poverty despite working full-time.

Many people have incomes that place them below the poverty level despite having jobs. In 1997, 41.5 percent of poor people aged 16 or older worked for at least part of the year. This figure was up from 39 percent in 1978. The number of poor people with jobs climbed from 6.6 million in 1978 to 9.4 million in 1997.

A substantial share of the poor have full-time jobs—yet their incomes remain below poverty level. In 1997, 10 percent of poor people worked full-time, year-round. This was up from 8 percent in 1978. The number of poor who worked full-time, year-round climbed from 1.3 million in 1978 to 2.3 million in 1997.

✘ Falling wages for uneducated, low-skilled workers have increased the number of working poor. The only way this group can climb out of poverty is to get more training and better jobs.

### Number of poor who work full-time has grown by 1 million

*(number of poor people who work full-time, year-round, 1978 to 1997)*

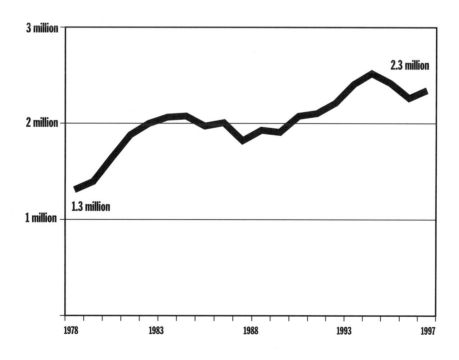

## People below Poverty Level by Work Status, 1978 to 1997

*(number of people aged 16 or older below poverty level by work status, and percent of poor who work, 1978 to 1997; people in thousands as of the following year)*

| | total poor aged 16 or older | worked | | worked full-time, year-round | |
|---|---|---|---|---|---|
| | | number | percent of poor | number | percent of poor |
| 1997 | 22,754 | 9,444 | 41.5% | 2,345 | 10.3% |
| 1996 | 23,472 | 9,586 | 40.8 | 2,263 | 9.6 |
| 1995 | 23,077 | 9,484 | 41.1 | 2,418 | 10.5 |
| 1994 | 24,108 | 9,829 | 40.8 | 2,520 | 10.5 |
| 1993 | 24,832 | 10,144 | 40.8 | 2,408 | 9.7 |
| 1992 | 23,951 | 9,739 | 40.6 | 2,211 | 9.2 |
| 1991 | 22,530 | 9,208 | 40.9 | 2,103 | 9.3 |
| 1990 | 21,242 | 8,716 | 41.0 | 2,076 | 9.8 |
| 1989 | 19,952 | 8,376 | 42.0 | 1,908 | 9.6 |
| 1988 | 20,323 | 8,363 | 41.2 | 1,929 | 9.5 |
| 1987 | 20,546 | 8,258 | 40.2 | 1,821 | 8.9 |
| 1986 | 20,688 | 8,743 | 42.3 | 2,007 | 9.7 |
| 1985 | 21,243 | 9,008 | 42.4 | 1,972 | 9.3 |
| 1984 | 21,541 | 8,999 | 41.8 | 2,076 | 9.6 |
| 1983 | 22,741 | 9,329 | 41.0 | 2,064 | 9.1 |
| 1982 | 22,100 | 9,013 | 40.8 | 1,999 | 9.0 |
| 1981 | 20,571 | 8,524 | 41.4 | 1,881 | 9.1 |
| 1980 | 18,892 | 7,674 | 40.6 | 1,644 | 8.7 |
| 1979 | 16,803 | 6,601 | 39.3 | 1,394 | 8.3 |
| 1978 | 16,914 | 6,599 | 39.0 | 1,309 | 7.7 |

*Source: Bureau of the Census, Internet web site, <http:// www.census.gov/hhes/income/histinc/index.html>*

# Poverty, 1997

# Few Households with Two Workers Are Poor

## Single-earner households are much more vulnerable to poverty.

Today, it takes two incomes to achieve a middle-class lifestyle. Only 3 percent of families with two or more workers have incomes that place them below poverty level, with the proportion ranging from just 2 percent of white families to 8 percent of Hispanic families. But among families with only one worker, 18 percent are poor. The poverty rate for these families ranges from 16 percent among whites to 37 percent among Hispanics.

Among married couples in which both husband and wife work full-time, poverty is practically nonexistent. It ranges from just 0.7 percent of whites to 2.7 percent of Hispanics. But for single-earner married couples, the poverty rate climbs as high as 33 percent among Hispanics.

The poverty rate is higher for female-headed families because most (54 percent) have only one worker. One-third of female-headed families with one worker are poor. If that worker has a full-time job, the poverty rate falls to 9.5 percent.

✘ Whites have lower poverty rates than blacks or Hispanics largely because white households have more workers.

### Two incomes have become a necessity

*(percent of families in poverty by number of workers, 1997)*

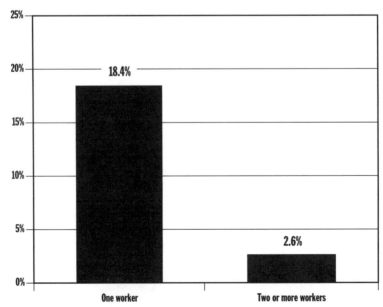

# Families below Poverty Level by Work Status, Race, and Hispanic Origin, 1997

*(number and percent of families below poverty level by work status, race, and Hispanic origin, 1997; numbers in thousands)*

| | total | black | Hispanic | white |
|---|---|---|---|---|
| **Number of families in poverty** | **7,324** | **1,985** | **1,721** | **4,990** |
| With no workers | 2,504 | 751 | 536 | 1,637 |
| With one or more workers | 4,819 | 1,234 | 1,185 | 3,353 |
| One | 3,752 | 1,056 | 886 | 2,530 |
| Two or more | 1,067 | 178 | 299 | 824 |
| With one or more full-time, year-round workers | 1,630 | 324 | 558 | 1,219 |
| One | 1,512 | 296 | 518 | 1,132 |
| Two or more | 118 | 27 | 40 | 86 |
| **Percent of families in poverty** | **10.3%** | **23.6%** | **24.7%** | **8.4%** |
| With no workers | 25.5 | 62.5 | 65.8 | 19.6 |
| With one or more workers | 7.9 | 17.1 | 19.3 | 6.6 |
| One | 18.4 | 31.1 | 36.5 | 15.6 |
| Two or more | 2.6 | 4.7 | 8.0 | 2.4 |
| With one or more full-time, year-round workers | 3.2 | 5.9 | 11.4 | 2.9 |
| One | 4.9 | 8.5 | 17.1 | 4.4 |
| Two or more | 0.6 | 1.4 | 2.2 | 0.5 |

*Note: Numbers will not add to total because Hispanics may be of any race and not all races are shown.*
*Source: Bureau of the Census, Internet web site, <http:// www.census.gov/cps/ads/sdata.htm>*

## Married Couples below Poverty Level by Work Status, Race, and Hispanic Origin, 1997

*(number and percent of married couples below poverty level by work status, race, and Hispanic origin, 1997; numbers in thousands)*

| | total | black | Hispanic | white |
|---|---|---|---|---|
| **Number of married couples in poverty** | **2,821** | **312** | **836** | **2,312** |
| With no workers | 845 | 133 | 160 | 653 |
| With one or more workers | 1,976 | 180 | 676 | 1,658 |
| One | 1,265 | 114 | 462 | 1,062 |
| Two or more | 710 | 65 | 213 | 596 |
| With one or more year-round, full-time workers | 968 | 78 | 385 | 824 |
| Husband worked year-round, full-time | 702 | 63 | 275 | 594 |
| Wife worked year-round, full-time | 124 | 17 | 35 | 105 |
| Wife did not work year-round, full-time | 578 | 46 | 240 | 489 |
| **Percent of married couples in poverty** | **5.2%** | **8.0%** | **17.4%** | **4.8%** |
| With no workers | 11.6 | 31.5 | 43.3 | 9.8 |
| With one or more workers | 4.2 | 5.1 | 15.2 | 4.0 |
| One | 10.9 | 14.8 | 33.3 | 10.4 |
| Two or more | 2.0 | 2.4 | 7.0 | 1.9 |
| With one or more year-round, full-time workers | 2.4 | 2.5 | 10.3 | 2.3 |
| Husband worked year-round, full-time | 2.2 | 2.6 | 9.5 | 2.1 |
| Wife worked year-round, full-time | 0.7 | 1.1 | 2.7 | 0.7 |
| Wife did not work year-round, full-time | 3.9 | 5.7 | 15.3 | 3.7 |

*Note: Numbers will not add to total because Hispanics may be of any race and not all races are shown.*
*Source: Bureau of the Census, Internet web site, <http:// www.census.gov/cps/ads/sdata.htm>*

## Female-Headed Families below Poverty Level by Work Status, Race, and Hispanic Origin, 1997

*(number and percent of female-headed families below poverty level by work status, race, and Hispanic origin, 1997; numbers in thousands)*

| | total | black | Hispanic | white |
|---|---|---|---|---|
| **Number of female-headed families in poverty** | **3,995** | **1,563** | **767** | **2,305** |
| With no workers | 1,525 | 576 | 355 | 899 |
| With one or more workers | 2,470 | 987 | 412 | 1,405 |
| One | 2,160 | 889 | 335 | 1,209 |
| Two or more | 310 | 98 | 77 | 197 |
| With one or more full-time, year-round workers | 547 | 228 | 135 | 302 |
| One | 539 | 223 | 134 | 300 |
| Two or more | 8 | 6 | 2 | 2 |
| **Percent of female-headed families in poverty** | **31.6%** | **39.8%** | **47.6%** | **27.7%** |
| With no workers | 69.1 | 80.9 | 86.9 | 63.4 |
| With one or more workers | 23.6 | 30.7 | 34.2 | 20.4 |
| One | 31.9 | 38.8 | 42.9 | 28.1 |
| Two or more | 8.5 | 10.6 | 18.3 | 7.6 |
| With one or more full-time, year-round workers | 8.0 | 11.2 | 17.9 | 6.6 |
| One | 9.5 | 13.2 | 22.1 | 7.8 |
| Two or more | 0.7 | 1.6 | 1.0 | 0.3 |

*Note: Numbers will not add to total because Hispanics may be of any race and not all races are shown.*
*Source: Bureau of the Census, Internet web site, <http:// www.census.gov/cps/ads/sdata.htm>*

# Poverty Rate Surpasses 66 Percent for Some Hispanic Families

## Central city families living in the Northeast are most likely to be poor.

The percentage of families living in poverty is higher in the nation's central cities than in the suburbs or nonmetropolitan areas. It is higher in the Northeast than in the other regions. It is higher for Hispanic families than for black or white families. It is higher for female-headed families than for married couples, and it is higher for families with children than for those without children.

Families who match all of the above characteristics are almost guaranteed to be poor. Hispanic female-headed families with children who live in a Northeastern central city have the highest poverty rate in the nation. In 1997, 67 percent were poor. Their white and black counterparts do not fare much better, with a poverty rate of 57 and 49 percent, respectively. Interestingly, the black poverty rate is lower than the white rate for this household type. Behind this is the fact that most Hispanics are white. The extremely high poverty rate of Hispanics drives up the white rate.

The lowest poverty rate for female-headed families with children is found among whites in the suburbs of the Midwest—a still substantial 26 percent.

✘ Female-headed families with children are especially likely to be poor because most have no or only one earner in the household.

### Families in central cities are most likely to be poor

*(percent of families in poverty by metropolitan status, 1997)*

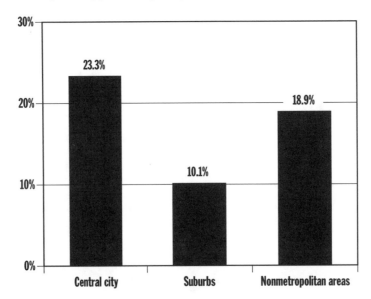

# Families below Poverty Level by Region, Metropolitan Status, Race, and Hispanic Origin, 1997

*(number and percent of families below poverty level by region, metropolitan status, race, and Hispanic origin, 1997; numbers in thousands)*

| | total | | black | | Hispanic | | white | |
|---|---|---|---|---|---|---|---|---|
| | number | percent | number | percent | number | percent | number | percent |
| **Total families in poverty** | **7,324** | **10.3%** | **1,985** | **23.6%** | **1,721** | **24.7%** | **4,990** | **8.4%** |
| Metropolitan | 5,495 | 9.8 | 1,652 | 22.8 | 1,529 | 24.2 | 3,560 | 7.7 |
| Central city | 3,035 | 15.5 | 1,211 | 26.6 | 984 | 29.5 | 1,647 | 11.9 |
| Suburbs | 2,460 | 6.7 | 441 | 16.4 | 545 | 18.4 | 1,913 | 5.9 |
| Nonmetropolitan | 1,829 | 12.6 | 334 | 28.6 | 192 | 29.4 | 1,431 | 10.9 |
| **Northeast** | **1,319** | **9.9** | **389** | **25.9** | **347** | **30.8** | **868** | **7.6** |
| Metropolitan | 1,168 | 9.9 | 385 | 25.9 | 343 | 30.8 | 723 | 7.3 |
| Central city | 743 | 20.3 | 313 | 29.2 | 282 | 37.7 | 383 | 16.4 |
| Suburbs | 426 | 5.2 | 72 | 17.2 | 61 | 16.7 | 340 | 4.5 |
| Nonmetropolitan | 150 | 9.7 | 3 | – | 4 | – | 145 | 9.4 |
| **Midwest** | **1,323** | **8.0** | **377** | **25.7** | **111** | **20.5** | **903** | **6.1** |
| Metropolitan | 923 | 7.6 | 361 | 25.8 | 94 | 19.2 | 534 | 5.1 |
| Central city | 579 | 14.3 | 305 | 29.8 | 76 | 25.2 | 256 | 8.8 |
| Suburbs | 344 | 4.2 | 56 | 14.9 | 18 | 9.6 | 278 | 3.7 |
| Nonmetropolitan | 399 | 9.0 | 16 | – | 17 | – | 369 | 8.6 |
| **South** | **2,987** | **11.6** | **1,077** | **22.8** | **519** | **22.2** | **1,834** | **9.0** |
| Metropolitan | 1,994 | 10.4 | 768 | 21.0 | 426 | 21.2 | 1,171 | 7.8 |
| Central city | 989 | 15.0 | 502 | 24.3 | 262 | 26.3 | 452 | 10.4 |
| Suburbs | 1,006 | 8.0 | 266 | 16.7 | 163 | 16.1 | 719 | 6.7 |
| Nonmetropolitan | 992 | 15.2 | 309 | 28.9 | 94 | 28.4 | 663 | 12.4 |
| **West** | **1,696** | **11.1** | **143** | **19.9** | **744** | **25.2** | **1,385** | **10.7** |
| Metropolitan | 1,409 | 10.6 | 137 | 19.5 | 667 | 24.8 | 1,132 | 10.2 |
| Central city | 725 | 13.6 | 90 | 22.6 | 364 | 28.2 | 555 | 12.9 |
| Suburbs | 685 | 8.7 | 47 | 15.4 | 303 | 21.6 | 577 | 8.5 |
| Nonmetropolitan | 287 | 14.1 | 5 | – | 77 | 30.2 | 253 | 13.5 |

*Note: The suburbs is the portion of a metropolitan area that is outside the central city. (–) means sample is too small to make a reliable estimate. Numbers will not add to total because Hispanics may be of any race and not all races are shown.*
*Source: Bureau of the Census, Internet web site, <http:// www.census.gov/cps/ads/sdata.htm>*

## Families with Children below Poverty Level by Region, Metropolitan Status, Race, and Hispanic Origin, 1997

*(number and percent of families with related children under age 18 at home below poverty level by region, metropolitan status, race, and Hispanic origin, 1997; numbers in thousands)*

| | total | | black | | Hispanic | | white | |
|---|---|---|---|---|---|---|---|---|
| | number | percent | number | percent | number | percent | number | percent |
| **Total families with children in poverty** | **5,884** | **15.7%** | **1,721** | **30.5%** | **1,492** | **30.4%** | **3,895** | **13.0%** |
| Metropolitan | 4,482 | 14.9 | 1,420 | 29.6 | 1,336 | 30.1 | 2,848 | 12.0 |
| Central city | 2,554 | 23.3 | 1,044 | 33.9 | 859 | 36.5 | 1,373 | 19.0 |
| Suburbs | 1,928 | 10.1 | 376 | 21.8 | 478 | 22.9 | 1,475 | 9.0 |
| Nonmetropolitan | 1402 | 18.9 | 302 | 35.8 | 156 | 33.1 | 1,047 | 16.4 |
| **Northeast** | **1,047** | **15.4** | **329** | **35.1** | **302** | **38.3** | **667** | **12.0** |
| Metropolitan | 944 | 15.6 | 327 | 35.2 | 299 | 38.4 | 569 | 11.7 |
| Central city | 630 | 31.2 | 268 | 38.2 | 244 | 46.4 | 323 | 27.4 |
| Suburbs | 314 | 7.8 | 59 | 26.1 | 55 | 21.8 | 246 | 6.7 |
| Nonmetropolitan | 103 | 13.9 | 2 | – | 3 | – | 99 | 13.6 |
| **Midwest** | **1,091** | **12.4** | **339** | **32.5** | **95** | **24.2** | **722** | **9.6** |
| Metropolitan | 772 | 11.8 | 323 | 32.7 | 84 | 23.7 | 429 | 8.0 |
| Central city | 498 | 21.7 | 271 | 37.5 | 68 | 30.9 | 213 | 14.3 |
| Suburbs | 275 | 6.5 | 52 | 19.8 | 16 | 11.9 | 216 | 5.6 |
| Nonmetropolitan | 319 | 14.2 | 16 | – | 11 | – | 293 | 13.6 |
| **South** | **2,352** | **17.5** | **933** | **29.2** | **433** | **28.1** | **1,359** | **13.7** |
| Metropolitan | 1,596 | 15.8 | 655 | 26.9 | 357 | 27.3 | 897 | 12.2 |
| Central city | 814 | 22.3 | 431 | 31.3 | 221 | 33.4 | 355 | 16.4 |
| Suburbs | 781 | 12.1 | 224 | 21.3 | 136 | 21.1 | 542 | 10.5 |
| Nonmetropolitan | 756 | 22.5 | 279 | 36.2 | 76 | 32.4 | 462 | 18.1 |
| **West** | **1,394** | **16.6** | **120** | **25.8** | **661** | **30.3** | **1,146** | **16.2** |
| Metropolitan | 1,171 | 16.0 | 114 | 25.1 | 596 | 29.8 | 953 | 15.6 |
| Central City | 612 | 20.5 | 73 | 26.5 | 326 | 34.4 | 482 | 20.1 |
| Suburbs | 558 | 12.9 | 41 | 23.0 | 271 | 25.7 | 471 | 12.7 |
| Nonmetropolitan | 224 | 20.8 | 5 | – | 65 | 35.0 | 193 | 19.7 |

*Note: The suburbs is the portion of a metropolitan area that is outside the central city. (–) means sample is too small to make a reliable estimate. Numbers will not add to total because Hispanics may be of any race and not all races are shown.*
*Source: Bureau of the Census, Internet web site, <http:// www.census.gov/cps/ads/sdata.htm>*

# Married Couples below Poverty Level by Region, Metropolitan Status, Race, and Hispanic Origin, 1997

*(number and percent of married couples below poverty level by region, metropolitan status, race, and Hispanic origin, 1997; numbers in thousands)*

| | total | | black | | Hispanic | | white | |
|---|---|---|---|---|---|---|---|---|
| | *number* | *percent* | *number* | *percent* | *number* | *percent* | *number* | *percent* |
| **Married couples in poverty** | **2,821** | **5.2%** | **312** | **8.0%** | **836** | **17.4%** | **2,312** | **4.8%** |
| Metropolitan | 1,974 | 4.6 | 249 | 7.5 | 724 | 16.8 | 1,552 | 4.2 |
| Central city | 930 | 7.1 | 151 | 8.2 | 447 | 21.2 | 658 | 6.4 |
| Suburbs | 1,044 | 3.5 | 98 | 6.6 | 277 | 12.5 | 894 | 3.3 |
| Nonmetropolitan | 847 | 7.3 | 63 | 10.5 | 112 | 23.1 | 760 | 7.1 |
| **Northeast** | **426** | **4.2** | **64** | **9.9** | **82** | **14.1** | **331** | **3.7** |
| Metropolitan | 348 | 4.0 | 63 | 9.8 | 80 | 14.0 | 255 | 3.3 |
| Central city | 183 | 8.6 | 48 | 12.0 | 64 | 19.1 | 110 | 7.0 |
| Suburbs | 165 | 2.5 | 15 | 6.2 | 16 | 6.8 | 145 | 2.3 |
| Nonmetropolitan | 78 | 6.1 | 1 | – | 2 | – | 76 | 6.1 |
| **Midwest** | **433** | **3.3** | **46** | **7.0** | **61** | **15.3** | **370** | **3.1** |
| Metropolitan | 253 | 2.7 | 44 | 7.3 | 50 | 14.0 | 198 | 2.3 |
| Central city | 125 | 4.7 | 31 | 8.4 | 39 | 18.8 | 84 | 3.8 |
| Suburbs | 129 | 1.9 | 13 | 5.6 | 11 | 7.3 | 114 | 1.8 |
| Nonmetropolitan | 179 | 5.0 | 2 | – | 11 | – | 173 | 4.9 |
| **South** | **1,202** | **6.2** | **170** | **7.5** | **297** | **17.2** | **986** | **5.9** |
| Metropolitan | 739 | 5.1 | 114 | 6.6 | 241 | 16.3 | 593 | 4.9 |
| Central city | 315 | 7.1 | 62 | 6.7 | 152 | 21.5 | 232 | 6.8 |
| Suburbs | 424 | 4.3 | 52 | 6.4 | 89 | 11.6 | 360 | 4.1 |
| Nonmetropolitan | 462 | 9.1 | 57 | 10.8 | 56 | 22.6 | 393 | 8.8 |
| **West** | **761** | **6.4** | **32** | **8.9** | **396** | **18.9** | **624** | **6.1** |
| Metropolitan | 634 | 6.2 | 29 | 8.3 | 352 | 18.4 | 506 | 5.8 |
| Central city | 307 | 8.0 | 10 | 7.1 | 191 | 22.3 | 232 | 7.3 |
| Suburbs | 327 | 5.1 | 18 | 9.1 | 161 | 15.3 | 274 | 5.0 |
| Nonmetropolitan | 128 | 8.0 | 3 | – | 43 | 23.6 | 118 | 7.8 |

*Note: The suburbs is the portion of a metropolitan area that is outside the central city. (–) means sample is too small to make a reliable estimate. Numbers will not add to total because Hispanics may be of any race and not all races are shown.*
*Source: Bureau of the Census, Internet web site, <http:// www.census.gov/cps/ads/sdata.htm>*

## Married Couples with Children below Poverty Level by Region, Metropolitan Status, Race, and Hispanic Origin, 1997

*(number and percent of married couples with related children under age 18 at home below poverty level by region, metropolitan status, race, and Hispanic origin, 1997; numbers in thousands)*

| | total | | black | | Hispanic | | white | |
|---|---|---|---|---|---|---|---|---|
| | number | percent | number | percent | number | percent | number | percent |
| **Married couples with children in poverty** | **1,863** | **7.1%** | **205** | **9.0%** | **692** | **21.0%** | **1,516** | **6.7%** |
| Metropolitan | 1,341 | 6.4 | 157 | 8.3 | 611 | 20.6 | 1,058 | 5.9 |
| Central city | 658 | 10.1 | 90 | 8.7 | 376 | 25.9 | 477 | 9.6 |
| Suburbs | 682 | 4.7 | 67 | 7.7 | 236 | 15.6 | 580 | 4.5 |
| Nonmetropolitan | 523 | 9.8 | 48 | 12.7 | 81 | 24.5 | 458 | 9.4 |
| **Northeast** | **268** | **5.6** | **44** | **12.9** | **62** | **16.2** | **198** | **4.7** |
| Metropolitan | 226 | 5.3 | 44 | 13.1 | 61 | 16.2 | 157 | 4.3 |
| Central city | 139 | 13.6 | 38 | 17.2 | 49 | 22.8 | 78 | 11.2 |
| Suburbs | 87 | 2.7 | 6 | 5.3 | 12 | 7.2 | 79 | 2.6 |
| Nonmetropolitan | 41 | 7.5 | 0 | – | 1 | – | 41 | 7.5 |
| **Midwest** | **260** | **4.1** | **32** | **7.9** | **53** | **18.4** | **220** | **3.8** |
| Metropolitan | 155 | 3.3 | 31 | 8.2 | 48 | 18.5 | 118 | 2.8 |
| Central city | 81 | 6.0 | 20 | 9.4 | 38 | 25.0 | 55 | 5.2 |
| Suburbs | 74 | 2.2 | 10 | 6.7 | 11 | 9.6 | 63 | 2.0 |
| Nonmetropolitan | 105 | 6.3 | 2 | – | 5 | – | 102 | 6.3 |
| **South** | **775** | **8.4** | **105** | **8.0** | **230** | **21.2** | **637** | **8.4** |
| Metropolitan | 488 | 7.1 | 62 | 6.2 | 190 | 20.7 | 402 | 7.2 |
| Central city | 200 | 9.3 | 24 | 4.8 | 119 | 26.4 | 159 | 10.1 |
| Suburbs | 288 | 6.1 | 37 | 7.8 | 71 | 15.2 | 244 | 6.1 |
| Nonmetropolitan | 287 | 12.2 | 44 | 13.2 | 40 | 23.7 | 235 | 11.8 |
| **West** | **561** | **9.3** | **23** | **11.5** | **347** | **22.6** | **460** | **8.9** |
| Metropolitan | 472 | 8.9 | 20 | 10.3 | 312 | 22.1 | 380 | 8.5 |
| Central city | 239 | 12.0 | 8 | 8.7 | 170 | 26.8 | 185 | 11.3 |
| Suburbs | 233 | 7.1 | 12 | 11.6 | 142 | 18.4 | 194 | 6.9 |
| Nonmetropolitan | 89 | 11.9 | 3 | – | 34 | 27.4 | 80 | 11.4 |

*Note: The suburbs is the portion of a metropolitan area that is outside the central city. (–) means sample is too small to make a reliable estimate. Numbers will not add to total because Hispanics may be of any race and not all races are shown.*
*Source: Bureau of the Census, Internet web site, <http:// www.census.gov/cps/ads/sdata.htm>*

# Female-Headed Families below Poverty Level by Region, Metropolitan Status, Race, and Hispanic Origin, 1997

*(number and percent of female-headed families below poverty level by region, metropolitan status, race, and Hispanic origin, 1997; numbers in thousands)*

| Female-headed | total | | black | | Hispanic | | white | |
|---|---|---|---|---|---|---|---|---|
| | number | percent | number | percent | number | percent | number | percent |
| **families in poverty** | **3,995** | **31.6%** | **1,563** | **39.8%** | **767** | **47.6%** | **2,305** | **27.7%** |
| Metropolitan | 3,153 | 30.3 | 1,316 | 38.2 | 706 | 47.1 | 1,741 | 26.4 |
| Central city | 1,920 | 36.8 | 1,007 | 41.3 | 482 | 50.6 | 864 | 33.3 |
| Suburbs | 1,233 | 23.8 | 309 | 30.6 | 224 | 41.2 | 876 | 21.8 |
| Nonmetropolitan | 843 | 37.4 | 246 | 51.5 | 61 | 53.4 | 564 | 33.1 |
| **Northeast** | **805** | **31.5** | **300** | **40.6** | **243** | **55.9** | **473** | **27.2** |
| Metropolitan | 743 | 31.8 | 299 | 40.7 | 241 | 55.7 | 415 | 27.2 |
| Central city | 520 | 41.5 | 247 | 42.1 | 201 | 61.1 | 253 | 41.2 |
| Suburbs | 223 | 20.6 | 52 | 35.0 | 40 | 38.8 | 162 | 17.8 |
| Nonmetropolitan | 62 | 28.5 | 2 | – | 2 | – | 58 | 27.6 |
| **Midwest** | **793** | **29.5** | **314** | **42.9** | **40** | **46.3** | **459** | **24.1** |
| Metropolitan | 605 | 28.9 | 299 | 41.8 | 36 | 44.7 | 291 | 21.8 |
| Central city | 410 | 37.9 | 259 | 44.2 | 31 | – | 145 | 30.3 |
| Suburbs | 195 | 19.2 | 40 | 30.9 | 5 | – | 147 | 17.1 |
| Nonmetropolitan | 188 | 31.5 | 14 | – | 4 | – | 168 | 29.7 |
| **South** | **1,597** | **32.7** | **848** | **39.4** | **190** | **40.5** | **726** | **27.3** |
| Metropolitan | 1,138 | 30.3 | 620 | 36.5 | 165 | 39.6 | 501 | 25.0 |
| Central city | 626 | 35.5 | 426 | 40.9 | 99 | 41.4 | 189 | 26.9 |
| Suburbs | 512 | 25.7 | 195 | 29.5 | 66 | 37.2 | 312 | 23.9 |
| Nonmetropolitan | 459 | 40.6 | 228 | 50.1 | 25 | – | 225 | 34.3 |
| **West** | **801** | **31.7** | **100** | **33.5** | **293** | **47.3** | **647** | **32.2** |
| Metropolitan | 667 | 30.1 | 98 | 32.9 | 264 | 46.5 | 533 | 30.7 |
| Central city | 364 | 32.6 | 75 | 33.8 | 150 | 47.0 | 278 | 34.7 |
| Suburbs | 303 | 27.6 | 23 | – | 114 | 45.7 | 256 | 27.3 |
| Nonmetropolitan | 134 | 43.5 | 2 | – | 29 | – | 113 | 41.6 |

*Note: The suburbs is the portion of a metropolitan area that is outside the central city. (–) means sample is too small to make a reliable estimate. Numbers will not add to total because Hispanics may be of any race and not all races are shown.*
*Source: Bureau of the Census, Internet web site, <http:// www.census.gov/cps/ads/sdata.htm>*

## Female-Headed Families with Children below Poverty Level by Region, Metropolitan Status, Race, and Hispanic Origin, 1997

*(number and percent of female-headed families with related children under age 18 below poverty level by region, metropolitan status, race, and Hispanic origin, 1997; numbers in thousands)*

| Female-headed families | total | | black | | Hispanic | | white | |
|---|---|---|---|---|---|---|---|---|
| | number | percent | number | percent | number | percent | number | percent |
| **with children in poverty** | **3,614** | **41.0%** | **1,436** | **46.9%** | **701** | **54.2%** | **2,069** | **37.6%** |
| Metropolitan | 2,853 | 39.5 | 1,205 | 45.2 | 644 | 53.9 | 1,568 | 36.0 |
| Central city | 1,757 | 45.9 | 922 | 48.1 | 440 | 58.3 | 791 | 43.8 |
| Suburbs | 1,096 | 32.2 | 282 | 37.6 | 204 | 46.4 | 777 | 30.4 |
| Nonmetropolitan | 761 | 47.8 | 231 | 59.0 | 57 | 58.1 | 500 | 43.8 |
| **Northeast** | **712** | **43.3** | **270** | **48.7** | **223** | **63.3** | **417** | **39.9** |
| Metropolitan | 656 | 43.5 | 268 | 48.9 | 220 | 63.2 | 365 | 39.8 |
| Central city | 463 | 52.9 | 218 | 48.8 | 181 | 66.9 | 230 | 56.8 |
| Suburbs | 193 | 30.6 | 51 | 49.2 | 39 | 50.4 | 136 | 26.5 |
| Nonmetropolitan | 56 | 40.7 | 2 | – | 2 | – | 52 | 40.0 |
| **Midwest** | **748** | **39.6** | **295** | **49.9** | **36** | **–** | **437** | **34.6** |
| Metropolitan | 566 | 38.5 | 281 | 48.7 | 32 | – | 273 | 31.5 |
| Central city | 382 | 47.0 | 242 | 51.1 | 28 | – | 133 | 40.8 |
| Suburbs | 184 | 28.0 | 38 | 37.3 | 5 | – | 140 | 25.9 |
| Nonmetropolitan | 183 | 43.3 | 14 | – | 4 | – | 164 | 41.4 |
| **South** | **1,423** | **41.3** | **780** | **46.5** | **171** | **47.4** | **621** | **36.0** |
| Metropolitan | 1,016 | 38.3 | 568 | 43.4 | 148 | 46.6 | 431 | 32.9 |
| Central city | 578 | 43.9 | 397 | 48.4 | 92 | 50.0 | 170 | 35.4 |
| Suburbs | 438 | 32.7 | 171 | 34.9 | 56 | 42.0 | 261 | 31.4 |
| Nonmetropolitan | 407 | 51.2 | 213 | 57.6 | 24 | – | 189 | 45.9 |
| **West** | **730** | **39.7** | **90** | **38.2** | **271** | **53.6** | **594** | **40.5** |
| Metropolitan | 615 | 38.4 | 88 | 37.6 | 243 | 52.9 | 498 | 39.5 |
| Central city | 334 | 40.5 | 65 | 36.6 | 139 | 56.5 | 258 | 43.5 |
| Suburbs | 281 | 36.2 | 23 | – | 104 | 48.8 | 240 | 35.9 |
| Nonmetropolitan | 115 | 48.5 | 2 | – | 27 | – | 96 | 46.6 |

*Note: The suburbs is the portion of a metropolitan area that is outside the central city. (–) means sample is too small to make a reliable estimate. Numbers will not add to total because Hispanics may be of any race and not all races are shown.*
*Source: Bureau of the Census, Internet web site, <http:// www.census.gov/cps/ads/sdata.htm>*

# One-Fourth of Americans Live in Households That Receive Poverty Assistance

## More than 60 percent of black and Hispanic children live in households that participate in low-income programs.

Twenty-four percent of all Americans live in households that receive means-tested assistance. These households have incomes so low that they receive cash, food stamps, Medicaid benefits (government-subsidized health care for the poor), or government-subsidized housing.

The proportion of people living in households that receive means-tested assistance varies not only by race and Hispanic origin, but also by age. Only 20.5 percent of whites live in households that receive means-tested assistance compared with 49 percent of Hispanics and 48 percent of blacks. Thirty-seven percent of children under age 18 live in households that participate in low-income programs, a proportion that bottoms out at 15 percent among people aged 55 to 59.

Fully 64 percent of black and Hispanic children live in households that receive means-tested assistance. Among white children, 31 percent live in participating households.

✗ The majority of black children live in households that receive means-tested assistance because most are being raised by single mothers. Among Hispanic children, public assistance is common because many Hispanic adults are poorly educated immigrants with little earning power.

### Nearly half the blacks and Hispanics live in households receiving assistance

*(percent of people living in households receiving means-tested assistance, by race and Hispanic origin, 1997)*

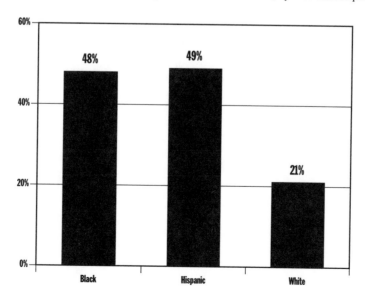

## Program Participation Status of Household by Sex and Age of Person, 1997: Total People

*(total number of people and percent in households participating in poverty programs, by sex and age, 1997; numbers in thousands)*

| | total | percent in households receiving means-tested assistance | percent in households receiving means-tested cash assistance | percent in households receiving food stamps | percent in households with one or more persons covered by Medicaid | percent living in public or subsidized housing |
|---|---|---|---|---|---|---|
| **Total people** | **268,480** | **24.3%** | **8.6%** | **8.7%** | **16.2%** | **4.2%** |
| Under age 18 | 71,069 | 37.0 | 12.3 | 15.3 | 23.8 | 6.6 |
| Aged 18 to 24 | 25,201 | 26.0 | 9.4 | 9.4 | 18.8 | 5.0 |
| Aged 25 to 34 | 39,354 | 23.5 | 7.6 | 8.5 | 15.5 | 3.7 |
| Aged 35 to 44 | 44,462 | 20.5 | 6.6 | 6.4 | 12.7 | 2.9 |
| Aged 45 to 54 | 34,057 | 15.1 | 6.2 | 4.5 | 10.8 | 2.2 |
| Aged 55 to 59 | 12,190 | 14.9 | 7.1 | 4.1 | 11.3 | 1.9 |
| Aged 60 to 64 | 10,065 | 16.2 | 8.2 | 5.1 | 12.7 | 2.8 |
| Aged 65 or older | 32,082 | 16.5 | 6.8 | 4.0 | 12.1 | 4.2 |
| Aged 65 to 74 | 17,874 | 16.0 | 6.5 | 3.9 | 12.0 | 3.4 |
| Aged 75 or older | 14,209 | 17.3 | 7.2 | 4.1 | 12.3 | 5.2 |
| **Total females** | **137,105** | **25.6** | **9.4** | **9.7** | **17.4** | **4.9** |
| Under age 18 | 34,702 | 36.9 | 12.2 | 15.4 | 24.0 | 6.7 |
| Aged 18 to 24 | 12,568 | 29.5 | 11.6 | 12.1 | 22.6 | 6.0 |
| Aged 25 to 34 | 19,828 | 27.2 | 9.3 | 11.3 | 17.9 | 5.3 |
| Aged 35 to 44 | 22,407 | 22.4 | 7.4 | 7.6 | 13.7 | 3.6 |
| Aged 45 to 54 | 17,459 | 16.3 | 7.2 | 5.4 | 12.0 | 2.6 |
| Aged 55 to 59 | 6,321 | 16.2 | 7.8 | 5.1 | 12.4 | 2.3 |
| Aged 60 to 64 | 5,261 | 17.4 | 9.0 | 5.8 | 13.7 | 3.8 |
| Aged 65 or older | 18,558 | 18.6 | 7.9 | 5.0 | 13.4 | 5.4 |
| Aged 65 to 74 | 9,882 | 18.0 | 7.8 | 5.0 | 13.5 | 4.3 |
| Aged 75 or older | 8,677 | 19.2 | 7.9 | 5.1 | 13.3 | 6.6 |
| **Total males** | **131,376** | **22.8** | **7.8** | **7.6** | **15.0** | **3.5** |
| Under age 18 | 36,367 | 37.1 | 12.4 | 15.2 | 23.6 | 6.5 |
| Aged 18 to 24 | 12,633 | 22.6 | 7.2 | 6.8 | 15.0 | 4.0 |
| Aged 25 to 34 | 19,526 | 19.8 | 5.8 | 5.5 | 13.1 | 2.2 |
| Aged 35 to 44 | 22,054 | 18.6 | 5.9 | 5.1 | 11.7 | 2.2 |
| Aged 45 to 54 | 16,598 | 13.7 | 5.1 | 3.6 | 9.4 | 1.8 |
| Aged 55 to 59 | 5,869 | 13.5 | 6.5 | 3.0 | 10.0 | 1.4 |
| Aged 60 to 64 | 4,804 | 14.9 | 7.2 | 4.2 | 11.6 | 1.7 |
| Aged 65 or older | 13,524 | 13.7 | 5.4 | 2.6 | 10.3 | 2.6 |
| Aged 65 to 74 | 7,992 | 13.4 | 4.9 | 2.7 | 10.2 | 2.3 |
| Aged 75 or older | 5,532 | 14.2 | 6.2 | 2.5 | 10.6 | 2.9 |

*Source: Bureau of the Census, Internet web site, <http:// www.census.gov/cps/ads/sdata.htm>*

# Program Participation Status of Household by Sex and Age of Person, 1997: Blacks

*(total number of blacks and percent in households participating in poverty programs, by sex and age, 1997; numbers in thousands)*

| | total | percent in households receiving means-tested assistance | percent in households receiving means-tested cash assistance | percent in households receiving food stamps | percent in households with one or more persons covered by Medicaid | percent living in public or subsidized housing |
|---|---|---|---|---|---|---|
| **Total people** | **34,458** | **47.7%** | **20.0%** | **21.4%** | **31.4%** | **12.4%** |
| Under age 18 | 11,367 | 64.3 | 26.9 | 32.2 | 42.4 | 18.0 |
| Aged 18 to 24 | 3,715 | 48.0 | 21.2 | 22.5 | 33.7 | 13.1 |
| Aged 25 to 34 | 5,299 | 41.1 | 16.2 | 16.9 | 25.6 | 11.1 |
| Aged 35 to 44 | 5,499 | 40.6 | 15.4 | 17.1 | 24.2 | 9.1 |
| Aged 45 to 54 | 3,663 | 30.8 | 14.5 | 10.4 | 19.8 | 5.9 |
| Aged 55 to 59 | 1,220 | 31.3 | 14.3 | 11.6 | 21.3 | 6.2 |
| Aged 60 to 64 | 1,003 | 36.3 | 17.4 | 14.2 | 27.1 | 9.1 |
| Aged 65 or older | 2,691 | 39.6 | 17.6 | 13.4 | 29.7 | 9.7 |
| Aged 65 to 74 | 1,613 | 37.1 | 15.3 | 12.5 | 27.0 | 8.2 |
| Aged 75 or older | 1,078 | 43.4 | 21.1 | 14.7 | 33.7 | 12.0 |
| **Total females** | **18,382** | **49.9** | **21.4** | **23.6** | **33.8** | **14.0** |
| Under age 18 | 5,588 | 62.9 | 26.0 | 32.2 | 42.6 | 18.4 |
| Aged 18 to 24 | 1,995 | 54.7 | 26.5 | 28.8 | 41.7 | 16.6 |
| Aged 25 to 34 | 2,910 | 49.8 | 20.2 | 23.8 | 31.4 | 15.5 |
| Aged 35 to 44 | 2,982 | 43.6 | 17.1 | 19.6 | 26.5 | 10.6 |
| Aged 45 to 54 | 2,028 | 32.8 | 15.6 | 12.5 | 22.6 | 6.8 |
| Aged 55 to 59 | 685 | 33.1 | 14.7 | 13.6 | 23.1 | 7.0 |
| Aged 60 to 64 | 570 | 36.4 | 17.3 | 15.1 | 24.8 | 10.0 |
| Aged 65 or older | 1,623 | 44.4 | 21.2 | 15.9 | 33.8 | 12.0 |
| Aged 65 to 74 | 956 | 41.5 | 18.9 | 14.7 | 31.1 | 10.2 |
| Aged 75 or older | 668 | 48.4 | 24.5 | 17.7 | 37.7 | 14.4 |
| **Total males** | **16,076** | **45.2** | **18.4** | **18.8** | **28.6** | **10.5** |
| Under age 18 | 5,779 | 65.6 | 27.8 | 32.3 | 42.3 | 17.5 |
| Aged 18 to 24 | 1,720 | 40.1 | 15.0 | 15.2 | 24.5 | 9.0 |
| Aged 25 to 34 | 2,389 | 30.5 | 11.3 | 8.5 | 18.6 | 5.7 |
| Aged 35 to 44 | 2,517 | 37.0 | 13.4 | 14.1 | 21.5 | 7.3 |
| Aged 45 to 54 | 1,636 | 28.3 | 13.1 | 7.9 | 16.5 | 4.9 |
| Aged 55 to 59 | 535 | 29.0 | 13.7 | 9.0 | 18.8 | 5.2 |
| Aged 60 to 64 | 433 | 36.3 | 17.7 | 13.0 | 30.2 | 7.9 |
| Aged 65 or older | 1,068 | 32.3 | 12.1 | 9.5 | 23.5 | 6.4 |
| Aged 65 to 74 | 657 | 30.5 | 9.9 | 9.4 | 21.1 | 5.4 |
| Aged 75 or older | 411 | 35.1 | 15.6 | 9.7 | 27.3 | 8.0 |

*Source: Bureau of the Census, Internet web site, <http:// www.census.gov/cps/ads/sdata.htm>*

# Program Participation Status of Household by Sex and Age of Person, 1997: Hispanics

*(total number of Hispanics and percent in households participating in poverty programs, by sex and age, 1997; numbers in thousands)*

| | total | percent in households receiving means-tested assistance | percent in households receiving means-tested cash assistance | percent in households receiving food stamps | percent in households with one or more persons covered by Medicaid | percent living in public or subsidized housing |
|---|---|---|---|---|---|---|
| **Total people** | **30,637** | **48.6%** | **15.2%** | **17.4%** | **29.8%** | **7.9%** |
| Under age 18 | 10,802 | 63.5 | 19.0 | 25.3 | 37.5 | 10.7 |
| Aged 18 to 24 | 3,791 | 42.6 | 13.9 | 14.3 | 29.0 | 7.8 |
| Aged 25 to 34 | 5,488 | 42.9 | 10.6 | 13.2 | 25.6 | 5.5 |
| Aged 35 to 44 | 4,606 | 41.9 | 11.6 | 12.6 | 22.6 | 5.7 |
| Aged 45 to 54 | 2,700 | 34.4 | 12.4 | 11.2 | 22.5 | 5.7 |
| Aged 55 to 59 | 930 | 32.5 | 14.3 | 11.6 | 22.8 | 5.2 |
| Aged 60 to 64 | 703 | 34.5 | 16.6 | 10.5 | 26.6 | 7.9 |
| Aged 65 or older | 1,617 | 40.3 | 22.7 | 16.3 | 32.9 | 9.8 |
| Aged 65 to 74 | 1,015 | 39.2 | 19.8 | 16.1 | 31.8 | 9.7 |
| Aged 75 or older | 603 | 42.1 | 27.5 | 16.7 | 34.8 | 9.9 |
| **Total females** | **14,968** | **50.5** | **16.9** | **19.4** | **31.7** | **8.6** |
| Under age 18 | 5,215 | 62.5 | 18.3 | 25.1 | 37.5 | 10.2 |
| Aged 18 to 24 | 1,763 | 45.9 | 17.6 | 18.4 | 34.1 | 7.7 |
| Aged 25 to 34 | 2,569 | 50.1 | 14.5 | 18.3 | 29.5 | 8.0 |
| Aged 35 to 44 | 2,241 | 45.1 | 12.7 | 14.9 | 23.7 | 6.9 |
| Aged 45 to 54 | 1,377 | 34.7 | 13.6 | 12.8 | 23.2 | 6.7 |
| Aged 55 to 59 | 522 | 33.5 | 17.5 | 13.9 | 25.6 | 5.5 |
| Aged 60 to 64 | 343 | 38.6 | 22.9 | 11.8 | 31.6 | 9.7 |
| Aged 65 or older | 937 | 43.6 | 26.6 | 18.9 | 36.2 | 11.2 |
| Aged 65 to 74 | 586 | 42.9 | 24.5 | 18.6 | 35.6 | 11.3 |
| Aged 75 or older | 351 | 44.6 | 30.3 | 19.6 | 37.3 | 11.2 |
| **Total males** | **15,670** | **46.7** | **13.5** | **15.5** | **28.0** | **7.3** |
| Under age 18 | 5,588 | 64.4 | 19.6 | 25.6 | 37.5 | 11.1 |
| Aged 18 to 24 | 2,027 | 39.6 | 10.7 | 10.7 | 24.5 | 8.0 |
| Aged 25 to 34 | 2,919 | 36.7 | 7.1 | 8.7 | 22.0 | 3.4 |
| Aged 35 to 44 | 2,365 | 38.9 | 10.6 | 10.4 | 21.5 | 4.4 |
| Aged 45 to 54 | 1,322 | 34.0 | 11.1 | 9.5 | 21.8 | 4.6 |
| Aged 55 to 59 | 408 | 31.3 | 10.2 | 8.7 | 19.1 | 4.9 |
| Aged 60 to 64 | 361 | 30.7 | 10.6 | 9.1 | 21.8 | 6.1 |
| Aged 65 or older | 681 | 35.7 | 17.2 | 12.7 | 28.3 | 7.8 |
| Aged 65 to 74 | 429 | 34.0 | 13.5 | 12.8 | 26.7 | 7.7 |
| Aged 75 or older | 252 | 38.7 | 23.6 | 12.6 | 31.2 | 8.1 |

*Source: Bureau of the Census, Internet web site, <http:// www.census.gov/cps/ads/sdata.htm>*

# Program Participation Status of Household by Sex and Age of Person, 1997: Whites

*(total number of whites and percent in households participating in poverty programs, by sex and age, 1997; numbers in thousands)*

| | total | percent in households receiving means-tested assistance | percent in households receiving means-tested cash assistance | percent in households receiving food stamps | percent in households with one or more persons covered by Medicaid | percent living in public or subsidized housing |
|---|---|---|---|---|---|---|
| **Total people** | **221,200** | **20.5%** | **6.7%** | **6.6%** | **13.7%** | **2.9%** |
| Under age 18 | 55,863 | 31.4 | 9.2 | 11.8 | 19.8 | 4.2 |
| Aged 18 to 24 | 20,259 | 22.2 | 7.2 | 7.0 | 16.1 | 3.5 |
| Aged 25 to 34 | 31,778 | 21.0 | 6.2 | 7.2 | 14.0 | 2.6 |
| Aged 35 to 44 | 36,736 | 17.3 | 5.3 | 4.8 | 10.8 | 1.9 |
| Aged 45 to 54 | 28,871 | 12.9 | 5.1 | 3.7 | 9.4 | 1.7 |
| Aged 55 to 59 | 10,458 | 12.9 | 6.3 | 3.3 | 9.9 | 1.4 |
| Aged 60 to 64 | 8,681 | 13.6 | 6.8 | 4.0 | 10.7 | 2.0 |
| Aged 65 or older | 28,553 | 13.9 | 5.5 | 3.1 | 10.0 | 3.6 |
| Aged 65 to 74 | 15,760 | 13.5 | 5.4 | 3.0 | 10.2 | 2.9 |
| Aged 75 or older | 12,793 | 14.4 | 5.6 | 3.2 | 9.7 | 4.5 |
| **Total females** | **112,154** | **21.5** | **7.3** | **7.4** | **14.6** | **3.4** |
| Under age 18 | 27,201 | 31.5 | 9.2 | 11.9 | 20.1 | 4.2 |
| Aged 18 to 24 | 9,937 | 24.6 | 8.7 | 8.8 | 19.0 | 3.8 |
| Aged 25 to 34 | 15,786 | 23.6 | 7.4 | 9.3 | 15.8 | 3.6 |
| Aged 35 to 44 | 18,272 | 18.7 | 5.7 | 5.7 | 11.4 | 2.4 |
| Aged 45 to 54 | 14,587 | 13.8 | 6.0 | 4.4 | 10.4 | 2.0 |
| Aged 55 to 59 | 5,383 | 14.1 | 6.9 | 4.1 | 11.0 | 1.7 |
| Aged 60 to 64 | 4,499 | 14.6 | 7.5 | 4.6 | 11.9 | 2.9 |
| Aged 65 or older | 16,490 | 15.6 | 6.3 | 3.9 | 11.0 | 4.7 |
| Aged 65 to 74 | 8,651 | 15.0 | 6.3 | 3.8 | 11.2 | 3.6 |
| Aged 75 or older | 7,839 | 16.2 | 6.2 | 4.1 | 10.8 | 5.9 |
| **Total males** | **109,047** | **19.4** | **6.0** | **5.8** | **12.8** | **2.4** |
| Under age 18 | 28,662 | 31.4 | 9.1 | 11.7 | 19.6 | 4.2 |
| Aged 18 to 24 | 10,322 | 19.8 | 5.9 | 5.4 | 13.3 | 3.1 |
| Aged 25 to 34 | 15,993 | 18.4 | 5.0 | 5.1 | 12.2 | 1.6 |
| Aged 35 to 44 | 18,465 | 15.9 | 4.8 | 3.8 | 10.2 | 1.5 |
| Aged 45 to 54 | 14,284 | 11.9 | 4.2 | 3.0 | 8.4 | 1.3 |
| Aged 55 to 59 | 5,076 | 11.6 | 5.7 | 2.4 | 8.8 | 1.0 |
| Aged 60 to 64 | 4,182 | 12.5 | 6.0 | 3.3 | 9.4 | 1.1 |
| Aged 65 or older | 12,063 | 11.6 | 4.5 | 1.9 | 8.7 | 2.1 |
| Aged 65 to 74 | 7,109 | 11.7 | 4.3 | 2.0 | 9.1 | 2.0 |
| Aged 75 or older | 4,954 | 11.5 | 4.7 | 1.7 | 8.1 | 2.4 |

*Source: Bureau of the Census, Internet web site, <http:// www.census.gov/cps/ads/sdata.htm>*

# Poverty Rate Is Highest among Children

**Hispanic and black children are equally likely to be poor.**

Fully 20 percent of the nation's children under age 18 live below poverty level—a higher poverty rate than in any other age group. Young adults aged 18 to 24 are close behind, with a poverty rate of 17.5 percent. The poverty rate of the elderly stood at 10.5 percent in 1997. People aged 45 to 54 are least likely to be poor, with a poverty rate of 7.2 percent. At all ages, females are more likely to be poor than males.

Thirty-seven percent of black and Hispanic children are poor. Among white children, only 16 percent live below poverty level. The poverty rate among blacks and Hispanics is lowest for those aged 45 to 54, at 13 and 16 percent, respectively. Among whites, the poverty rate bottoms out in the same age group at 6 percent.

✘ Black children have a much higher poverty rate than white children because most are being raised by single mothers. The poverty rate of Hispanic children is high because many have parents who are recent immigrants with little earning power.

## Poverty rates are lowest among the middle-aged

*(percent of people in poverty by age, 1997)*

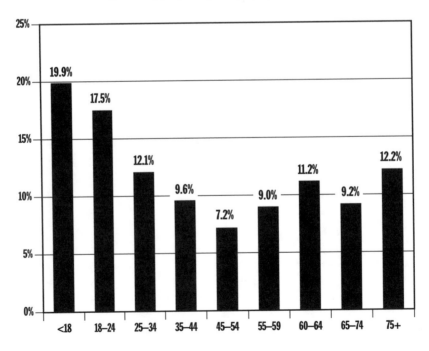

# People below Poverty Level by Age and Sex, 1997: Total People

*(number and percent of people below poverty level by age and sex, 1997; numbers in thousands)*

|  | *total* | *females* | *males* |
|---|---|---|---|
| **Number in poverty** | **35,574** | **20,387** | **15,187** |
| Under age 18 | 14,113 | 6,934 | 7,179 |
| Aged 18 to 24 | 4,416 | 2,657 | 1,760 |
| Aged 25 to 34 | 4,759 | 3,063 | 1,696 |
| Aged 35 to 44 | 4,251 | 2,566 | 1,686 |
| Aged 45 to 54 | 2,439 | 1,373 | 1,066 |
| Aged 55 to 59 | 1,092 | 723 | 370 |
| Aged 60 to 64 | 1,127 | 648 | 479 |
| Aged 65 or older | 3,376 | 2,423 | 953 |
| Aged 65 to 74 | 1,641 | 1,105 | 536 |
| Aged 75 or older | 1,735 | 1,318 | 417 |
| **Percent in poverty** | **13.3%** | **14.9%** | **11.6%** |
| Under age 18 | 19.9 | 20.0 | 19.7 |
| Aged 18 to 24 | 17.5 | 21.1 | 13.9 |
| Aged 25 to 34 | 12.1 | 15.4 | 8.7 |
| Aged 35 to 44 | 9.6 | 11.5 | 7.6 |
| Aged 45 to 54 | 7.2 | 7.9 | 6.4 |
| Aged 55 to 59 | 9.0 | 11.4 | 6.3 |
| Aged 60 to 64 | 11.2 | 12.3 | 10.0 |
| Aged 65 or older | 10.5 | 13.1 | 7.0 |
| Aged 65 to 74 | 9.2 | 11.2 | 6.7 |
| Aged 75 or older | 12.2 | 15.2 | 7.5 |

*Source: Bureau of the Census, Internet web site, <http:// www.census.gov/cps/ads/sdata.htm>*

## People below Poverty Level by Age and Sex, 1997: Blacks

*(number and percent of blacks below poverty level by age and sex, 1997; numbers in thousands)*

|  | total | females | males |
|---|---|---|---|
| **Number in poverty** | **9,116** | **5,317** | **3,799** |
| Under age 18 | 4,225 | 2,086 | 2,139 |
| Aged 18 to 24 | 1,041 | 680 | 361 |
| Aged 25 to 34 | 1,106 | 804 | 302 |
| Aged 35 to 44 | 1,063 | 700 | 363 |
| Aged 45 to 54 | 489 | 273 | 215 |
| Aged 55 to 59 | 270 | 175 | 96 |
| Aged 60 to 64 | 222 | 133 | 89 |
| Aged 65 or older | 700 | 467 | 233 |
| Aged 65 to 74 | 383 | 257 | 126 |
| Aged 75 or older | 316 | 209 | 107 |
| **Percent in poverty** | **26.5%** | **28.9%** | **23.6%** |
| Under age 18 | 37.2 | 37.3 | 37.0 |
| Aged 18 to 24 | 28.0 | 34.1 | 21.0 |
| Aged 25 to 34 | 20.9 | 27.6 | 12.6 |
| Aged 35 to 44 | 19.3 | 23.5 | 14.4 |
| Aged 45 to 54 | 13.3 | 13.5 | 13.2 |
| Aged 55 to 59 | 22.2 | 25.5 | 17.9 |
| Aged 60 to 64 | 22.1 | 23.4 | 20.5 |
| Aged 65 or older | 26.0 | 28.8 | 21.8 |
| Aged 65 to 74 | 23.8 | 26.9 | 19.2 |
| Aged 75 or older | 29.3 | 31.4 | 26.0 |

*Source: Bureau of the Census, Internet web site, <http:// www.census.gov/cps/ads/sdata.htm>*

# People below Poverty Level by Age and Sex, 1997: Hispanics

*(number and percent of Hispanics below poverty level by age and sex, 1997; numbers in thousands)*

|  | total | females | males |
|---|---|---|---|
| **Number in poverty** | **8,308** | **4,463** | **3,845** |
| Under age 18 | 3,972 | 1,933 | 2,039 |
| Aged 18 to 24 | 979 | 546 | 433 |
| Aged 25 to 34 | 1,201 | 723 | 479 |
| Aged 35 to 44 | 992 | 559 | 433 |
| Aged 45 to 54 | 427 | 241 | 185 |
| Aged 55 to 59 | 191 | 130 | 61 |
| Aged 60 to 64 | 161 | 85 | 76 |
| Aged 65 or older | 384 | 246 | 138 |
| Aged 65 to 74 | 214 | 130 | 84 |
| Aged 75 or older | 170 | 116 | 54 |
| **Percent in poverty** | **27.1%** | **29.8%** | **24.5%** |
| Under age 18 | 36.8 | 37.1 | 36.5 |
| Aged 18 to 24 | 25.8 | 31.0 | 21.3 |
| Aged 25 to 34 | 21.9 | 28.1 | 16.4 |
| Aged 35 to 44 | 21.5 | 24.9 | 18.3 |
| Aged 45 to 54 | 15.8 | 17.5 | 14.0 |
| Aged 55 to 59 | 20.5 | 24.8 | 15.0 |
| Aged 60 to 64 | 22.9 | 24.8 | 21.2 |
| Aged 65 or older | 23.8 | 26.3 | 20.3 |
| Aged 65 to 74 | 21.1 | 22.2 | 19.5 |
| Aged 75 or older | 28.2 | 33.0 | 21.5 |

*Source: Bureau of the Census, Internet web site, <http:// www.census.gov/cps/ads/sdata.htm>*

# People below Poverty Level by Age and Sex, 1997: Whites

*(number and percent of whites below poverty level by age and sex, 1997; numbers in thousands)*

|  | total | females | males |
|---|---|---|---|
| **Number in poverty** | **24,396** | **13,944** | **10,452** |
| Under age 18 | 8,990 | 4,387 | 4,602 |
| Aged 18 to 24 | 3,131 | 1,831 | 1,301 |
| Aged 25 to 34 | 3,327 | 2,073 | 1,255 |
| Aged 35 to 44 | 2,928 | 1,724 | 1,204 |
| Aged 45 to 54 | 1,817 | 1,024 | 793 |
| Aged 55 to 59 | 778 | 529 | 249 |
| Aged 60 to 64 | 857 | 488 | 369 |
| Aged 65 or older | 2,569 | 1,889 | 680 |
| Aged 65 to 74 | 1,198 | 812 | 386 |
| Aged 75 or older | 1,370 | 1,077 | 294 |
| **Percent in poverty** | **11.0%** | **12.4%** | **9.6%** |
| Under age 18 | 16.1 | 16.1 | 16.1 |
| Aged 18 to 24 | 15.5 | 18.4 | 12.6 |
| Aged 25 to 34 | 10.5 | 13.1 | 7.8 |
| Aged 35 to 44 | 8.0 | 9.4 | 6.5 |
| Aged 45 to 54 | 6.3 | 7.0 | 5.5 |
| Aged 55 to 59 | 7.4 | 9.8 | 4.9 |
| Aged 60 to 64 | 9.9 | 10.8 | 8.8 |
| Aged 65 or older | 9.0 | 11.5 | 5.6 |
| Aged 65 to 74 | 7.6 | 9.4 | 5.4 |
| Aged 75 or older | 10.7 | 13.7 | 5.9 |

*Source: Bureau of the Census, Internet web site, <http:// www.census.gov/cps/ads/sdata.htm>*

# Most College Graduates Escape Poverty

## High school drop-outs account for a large share of the poor.

In 1977, only 3 percent of the nation's college graduates had incomes that placed them below the poverty level. In contrast, one in four high school drop-outs was poor. Among the 17 million poor people aged 25 or older, fully 43 percent were high school drop-outs.

A college degree almost guarantees a life free of poverty, regardless of race or Hispanic origin. The proportion of college graduates who are poor ranges from 3 percent among whites to 8 percent among Hispanics. Even some college experience elevates incomes. Among people with some college, the poverty rate ranges from 6 percent for whites to 12 percent for blacks.

More than one-third of blacks who dropped out of high school are poor, while the poverty rate among Hispanic high school drop-outs is just below the one-third level. Two out of three poor Hispanics lacks a high-school diploma.

✘ As blacks have gained in educational attainment, their poverty rate has fallen. The Hispanic poverty rate has been rising because a growing share of the Hispanic population has little education.

### Few college graduates are poor

*(percent of people in poverty by educational attainment, 1997)*

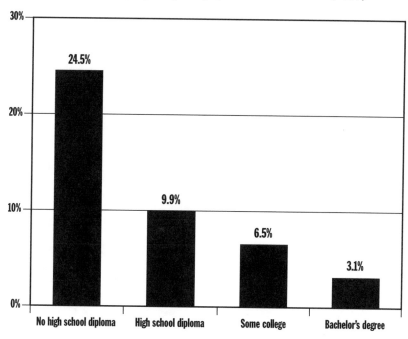

## People below Poverty Level by Education, Race, and Hispanic Origin, 1997

*(number and percent of people aged 25 or older below poverty level by educational attainment, race, and Hispanic origin, 1997; numbers in thousands)*

|  | total | black | Hispanic | white |
|---|---|---|---|---|
| **Number in poverty** | **17,044** | **3,849** | **3,357** | **12,275** |
| No high school diploma | 7,244 | 1,693 | 2,272 | 5,218 |
| High school diploma, no college | 5,769 | 1,412 | 647 | 4,107 |
| Some college, no bachelor's degree | 2,747 | 572 | 302 | 2,018 |
| Bachelor's degree or more | 1,284 | 173 | 136 | 932 |
| **Percent in poverty** | **9.9%** | **19.9%** | **20.9%** | **8.5%** |
| No high school diploma | 24.5 | 36.5 | 31.8 | 22.1 |
| High school diploma, no college | 9.9 | 20.2 | 15.0 | 8.3 |
| Some college, no bachelor's degree | 6.5 | 11.7 | 10.7 | 5.6 |
| Bachelor's degree or more | 3.1 | 6.0 | 7.7 | 2.6 |

*Note: Numbers will not add to total because Hispanics may be of any race and not all races are shown.*
*Source: Bureau of the Census, Internet web site, <http:// www.census.gov/cps/ads/sdata.htm>*

# Among Young Adults, Poverty Rate Is Highest in the West

## Among the nation's elderly, however, those in the West are least likely to be poor.

The poverty rate in the West has increased over the past few decades as minorities have become a larger share of the population. Nearly half the Western residents under age 35 are black, Hispanic, Asian, or Native American, driving up the poverty rate of the region's young adults. Twenty-two percent of Western residents aged 18 to 24 are poor. This surpasses the 19 percent poverty rate among 18-to-24-year-olds in the South and is far higher than the 14 to 15 percent poverty rate among young adults in the Midwest and Northeast.

The situation is reversed in the older age groups. Among people aged 65 or older, those in the West have the lowest poverty rate—only 8 percent are poor. Poverty rates are low among the elderly in the West because the great majority are non-Hispanic white.

✘ The poverty rate in the West will continue to rise as minorities become an ever-larger share of the population.

### Many young adults in the West are poor

*(percent of people aged 18 to 24 in poverty by region, 1997)*

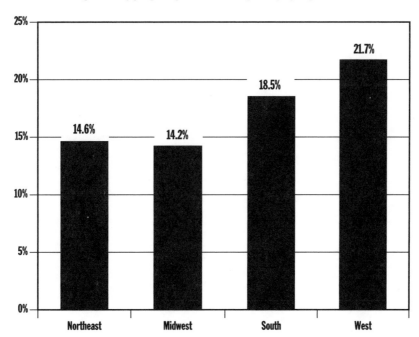

## People below Poverty Level by Age and Region, 1997: Total People

*(number and percent of people below poverty level by age and region, 1997; numbers in thousands)*

|  | Northeast | Midwest | South | West |
|---|---|---|---|---|
| **Number in poverty** | **6,474** | **6,493** | **13,748** | **8,858** |
| Under age 18 | 2,494 | 2,577 | 5,303 | 3,739 |
| Aged 18 to 24 | 674 | 850 | 1,635 | 1,257 |
| Aged 25 to 34 | 851 | 836 | 1,777 | 1,294 |
| Aged 35 to 44 | 800 | 714 | 1,647 | 1,089 |
| Aged 45 to 54 | 496 | 401 | 991 | 551 |
| Aged 55 to 59 | 220 | 228 | 457 | 187 |
| Aged 60 to 64 | 230 | 229 | 443 | 225 |
| Aged 65 or older | 709 | 657 | 1,494 | 516 |
| Aged 65 to 74 | 347 | 317 | 721 | 256 |
| Aged 75 or older | 362 | 340 | 773 | 260 |
| **Percent in poverty** | **12.6%** | **10.4%** | **14.6%** | **14.6%** |
| Under age 18 | 19.7 | 15.2 | 21.6 | 22.1 |
| Aged 18 to 24 | 14.6 | 14.2 | 18.5 | 21.7 |
| Aged 25 to 34 | 11.6 | 9.4 | 12.7 | 14.3 |
| Aged 35 to 44 | 9.3 | 7.0 | 10.8 | 10.5 |
| Aged 45 to 54 | 7.4 | 5.2 | 8.1 | 7.5 |
| Aged 55 to 59 | 9.2 | 8.4 | 10.4 | 6.9 |
| Aged 60 to 64 | 10.4 | 10.0 | 12.5 | 11.2 |
| Aged 65 or older | 10.6 | 8.6 | 13.1 | 8.2 |
| Aged 65 to 74 | 9.4 | 7.6 | 11.2 | 7.2 |
| Aged 75 or older | 12.0 | 9.7 | 15.5 | 9.5 |

*Source: Bureau of the Census, Internet web site, <http:// www.census.gov/cps/ads/sdata.htm>*

# People below Poverty Level by Age and Region, 1997: Blacks

*(number and percent of blacks below poverty level by age and region, 1997; numbers in thousands)*

| | Northeast | Midwest | South | West |
|---|---|---|---|---|
| **Number in poverty** | **1,788** | **1,696** | **4,895** | **738** |
| Under age 18 | 775 | 814 | 2,264 | 372 |
| Aged 18 to 24 | 210 | 197 | 569 | 65 |
| Aged 25 to 34 | 243 | 213 | 549 | 101 |
| Aged 35 to 44 | 226 | 174 | 573 | 89 |
| Aged 45 to 54 | 108 | 88 | 262 | 30 |
| Aged 55 to 59 | 58 | 43 | 160 | 10 |
| Aged 60 to 64 | 50 | 42 | 108 | 21 |
| Aged 65 or older | 116 | 125 | 408 | 50 |
| Aged 65 to 74 | 77 | 81 | 209 | 17 |
| Aged 75 or older | 39 | 45 | 200 | 33 |
| **Percent in poverty** | **28.5%** | **27.4%** | **25.7%** | **24.9%** |
| Under age 18 | 39.7 | 37.1 | 36.2 | 38.2 |
| Aged 18 to 24 | 28.8 | 31.6 | 27.1 | 25.0 |
| Aged 25 to 34 | 25.7 | 23.9 | 18.2 | 22.2 |
| Aged 35 to 44 | 24.1 | 18.3 | 18.9 | 15.6 |
| Aged 45 to 54 | 15.7 | 14.0 | 12.7 | 10.7 |
| Aged 55 to 59 | 24.5 | 23.3 | 23.6 | 7.9 |
| Aged 60 to 64 | 21.8 | 20.2 | 23.0 | 23.3 |
| Aged 65 or older | 21.3 | 23.7 | 29.0 | 23.5 |
| Aged 65 to 74 | 22.3 | 24.0 | 25.4 | 15.6 |
| Aged 75 or older | 19.6 | 23.3 | 34.2 | 32.0 |

*Source: Bureau of the Census, Internet web site, <http:// www.census.gov/cps/ads/sdata.htm>*

## People below Poverty Level by Age and Region, 1997: Hispanics

*(number and percent of Hispanics below poverty level by age and region, 1997; numbers in thousands)*

| | Northeast | Midwest | South | West |
|---|---|---|---|---|
| **Number in poverty** | **1,533** | **532** | **2,500** | **3,744** |
| Under age 18 | 743 | 267 | 1,102 | 1,859 |
| Aged 18 to 24 | 162 | 74 | 296 | 446 |
| Aged 25 to 34 | 209 | 81 | 353 | 559 |
| Aged 35 to 44 | 164 | 55 | 289 | 484 |
| Aged 45 to 54 | 83 | 20 | 135 | 188 |
| Aged 55 to 59 | 55 | 13 | 64 | 58 |
| Aged 60 to 64 | 37 | 14 | 64 | 46 |
| Aged 65 or older | 78 | 8 | 197 | 102 |
| Aged 65 to 74 | 46 | 5 | 97 | 66 |
| Aged 75 or older | 32 | 2 | 99 | 36 |
| **Percent in poverty** | **31.8%** | **23.4%** | **25.3%** | **27.4%** |
| Under age 18 | 46.9 | 31.8 | 33.3 | 36.7 |
| Aged 18 to 24 | 25.7 | 22.4 | 25.9 | 26.5 |
| Aged 25 to 34 | 24.1 | 18.9 | 20.6 | 22.5 |
| Aged 35 to 44 | 22.8 | 17.3 | 19.8 | 23.0 |
| Aged 45 to 54 | 19.2 | 11.7 | 14.6 | 16.1 |
| Aged 55 to 59 | 29.1 | 19.5 | 19.9 | 16.6 |
| Aged 60 to 64 | 26.6 | 30.1 | 22.6 | 19.8 |
| Aged 65 or older | 30.7 | 10.2 | 26.6 | 18.5 |
| Aged 65 to 74 | 29.2 | 9.2 | 22.1 | 18.3 |
| Aged 75 or older | 33.1 | 13.8 | 33.3 | 19.0 |

*Source: Bureau of the Census, Internet web site, <http:// www.census.gov/cps/ads/sdata.htm>*

# People below Poverty Level by Age and Region, 1997: Whites

*(number and percent of whites below poverty level by age and region, 1997; numbers in thousands)*

|  | Northeast | Midwest | South | West |
|---|---|---|---|---|
| **Number in poverty** | **4,373** | **4,546** | **8,473** | **7,004** |
| Under age 18 | 1,586 | 1,645 | 2,893 | 2,865 |
| Aged 18 to 24 | 444 | 604 | 1,027 | 1,057 |
| Aged 25 to 34 | 563 | 585 | 1,154 | 1,025 |
| Aged 35 to 44 | 514 | 527 | 1,022 | 866 |
| Aged 45 to 54 | 365 | 295 | 705 | 452 |
| Aged 55 to 59 | 156 | 183 | 284 | 155 |
| Aged 60 to 64 | 175 | 184 | 325 | 173 |
| Aged 65 or older | 571 | 523 | 1,064 | 412 |
| Aged 65 to 74 | 260 | 232 | 494 | 212 |
| Aged 75 or older | 311 | 291 | 570 | 200 |
| **Percent in poverty** | **10.2%** | **8.3%** | **11.7%** | **13.8%** |
| Under age 18 | 15.6 | 11.6 | 16.5 | 20.5 |
| Aged 18 to 24 | 11.8 | 11.8 | 15.8 | 21.7 |
| Aged 25 to 34 | 9.4 | 7.6 | 11.0 | 13.6 |
| Aged 35 to 44 | 7.1 | 5.8 | 8.7 | 10.0 |
| Aged 45 to 54 | 6.3 | 4.3 | 7.1 | 7.3 |
| Aged 55 to 59 | 7.5 | 7.4 | 7.9 | 6.7 |
| Aged 60 to 64 | 9.2 | 8.9 | 10.8 | 10.1 |
| Aged 65 or older | 9.4 | 7.3 | 10.8 | 7.5 |
| Aged 65 to 74 | 7.9 | 6.1 | 8.9 | 6.8 |
| Aged 75 or older | 11.2 | 8.9 | 13.1 | 8.3 |

*Source: Bureau of the Census, Internet web site, <http:// www.census.gov/cps/ads/sdata.htm>*

# In Every Region, Poverty Is Higher for Women

## In some age groups, however, men are poorer than women.

Among Americans aged 18 or older, women are far more likely to be poor than men. In some segments, the gap is extremely wide. Among 18-to-24-year-olds in the Midwest, for example, only 10 percent of men were poor in 1997 versus 19 percent of women—nearly twice as many.

In some age groups, women's poverty rate is lower than men's, especially among blacks and Hispanics in some regions. Among blacks aged 55 to 59 living in the Northeast, 28 percent of men are poor versus a smaller 22 percent of women. Among Hispanics aged 60 to 64 in the West, 26 percent of men are poor versus only 14 percent of women. Hispanic men aged 65 or older in the Midwest are poorer than their female counterparts.

✗ Women's poverty rate is higher than men's because many women are single parents, making it more difficult for them to work full-time.

### Men are less likely to be poor

*(percent of people in poverty by sex and region, 1997)*

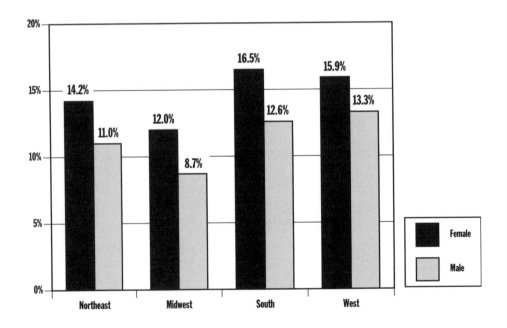

# People below Poverty Level by Age, Sex, and Region, 1997: Total People

*(number and percent of people below poverty level by age, region, and sex, 1997; numbers in thousands)*

|  | Northeast | | Midwest | | South | | West | |
|---|---|---|---|---|---|---|---|---|
|  | *females* | *males* | *females* | *males* | *females* | *males* | *females* | *males* |
| **Number in poverty** | **3,751** | **2,723** | **3,826** | **2,668** | **7,989** | **5,759** | **4,821** | **4,037** |
| Under age 18 | 1,234 | 1,260 | 1,251 | 1,326 | 2,642 | 2,661 | 1,807 | 1,932 |
| Aged 18 to 24 | 372 | 302 | 561 | 289 | 975 | 660 | 748 | 508 |
| Aged 25 to 34 | 594 | 257 | 546 | 290 | 1,150 | 627 | 771 | 523 |
| Aged 35 to 44 | 502 | 298 | 446 | 269 | 1,020 | 627 | 598 | 492 |
| Aged 45 to 54 | 279 | 217 | 243 | 157 | 553 | 439 | 298 | 253 |
| Aged 55 to 59 | 128 | 92 | 162 | 66 | 303 | 154 | 129 | 57 |
| Aged 60 to 64 | 141 | 89 | 108 | 121 | 275 | 168 | 125 | 100 |
| Aged 65 or older | 501 | 208 | 507 | 150 | 1,071 | 423 | 345 | 172 |
| Aged 65 to 74 | 238 | 109 | 234 | 82 | 478 | 243 | 155 | 101 |
| Aged 75 or older | 263 | 99 | 272 | 68 | 593 | 180 | 190 | 70 |
| **Percent in poverty** | **14.2%** | **11.0%** | **12.0%** | **8.7%** | **16.5%** | **12.6%** | **15.9%** | **13.3%** |
| Under age 18 | 19.7 | 19.6 | 15.4 | 15.1 | 21.7 | 21.5 | 22.1 | 22.0 |
| Aged 18 to 24 | 16.1 | 13.1 | 18.6 | 9.8 | 22.4 | 14.8 | 26.0 | 17.4 |
| Aged 25 to 34 | 15.9 | 7.1 | 12.2 | 6.6 | 16.0 | 9.2 | 17.5 | 11.2 |
| Aged 35 to 44 | 11.6 | 7.1 | 8.5 | 5.4 | 13.3 | 8.3 | 11.6 | 9.4 |
| Aged 45 to 54 | 8.1 | 6.7 | 6.2 | 4.1 | 8.7 | 7.4 | 7.9 | 7.1 |
| Aged 55 to 59 | 10.4 | 7.9 | 11.3 | 5.1 | 13.6 | 7.2 | 9.1 | 4.5 |
| Aged 60 to 64 | 11.9 | 8.7 | 9.2 | 10.7 | 14.6 | 10.2 | 12.2 | 10.1 |
| Aged 65 or older | 12.5 | 7.7 | 11.3 | 4.7 | 16.1 | 8.9 | 10.1 | 6.0 |
| Aged 65 to 74 | 11.4 | 6.8 | 10.2 | 4.4 | 13.2 | 8.6 | 8.3 | 6.0 |
| Aged 75 or older | 13.7 | 9.1 | 12.6 | 5.1 | 19.5 | 9.3 | 12.2 | 6.0 |

*Source: Bureau of the Census, Internet web site, <http:// www.census.gov/cps/ads/sdata.htm>*

# People below Poverty Level by Age, Sex, and Region, 1997: Blacks

*(number and percent of blacks below poverty level by age, region, and sex, 1997; numbers in thousands)*

| | Northeast | | Midwest | | South | | West | |
|---|---|---|---|---|---|---|---|---|
| | females | males | females | males | females | males | females | males |
| **Number in poverty** | **1,037** | **751** | **1,001** | **695** | **2,874** | **2,021** | **405** | **332** |
| Under age 18 | 402 | 374 | 391 | 423 | 1,113 | 1,151 | 180 | 192 |
| Aged 18 to 24 | 123 | 86 | 149 | 48 | 356 | 214 | 52 | 13 |
| Aged 25 to 34 | 177 | 66 | 149 | 64 | 419 | 130 | 59 | 42 |
| Aged 35 to 44 | 134 | 93 | 116 | 59 | 400 | 174 | 50 | 39 |
| Aged 45 to 54 | 67 | 42 | 63 | 25 | 133 | 130 | 11 | 19 |
| Aged 55 to 59 | 27 | 31 | 31 | 12 | 107 | 53 | 10 | – |
| Aged 60 to 64 | 26 | 25 | 19 | 23 | 72 | 36 | 16 | 5 |
| Aged 65 or older | 82 | 34 | 83 | 42 | 274 | 134 | 27 | 22 |
| Aged 65 to 74 | 53 | 24 | 50 | 30 | 143 | 66 | 11 | 6 |
| Aged 75 or older | 29 | 10 | 33 | 12 | 131 | 68 | 16 | 16 |
| **Percent in poverty** | **30.4%** | **26.2%** | **30.4%** | **23.9%** | **28.3%** | **22.8%** | **26.6%** | **23.1%** |
| Under age 18 | 41.8 | 37.6 | 38.0 | 36.4 | 35.9 | 36.6 | 36.2 | 40.3 |
| Aged 18 to 24 | 32.2 | 25.0 | 43.8 | 16.9 | 31.7 | 21.9 | 35.0 | 11.7 |
| Aged 25 to 34 | 32.5 | 16.5 | 29.1 | 17.0 | 25.8 | 9.4 | 25.8 | 18.6 |
| Aged 35 to 44 | 25.4 | 22.4 | 22.0 | 13.8 | 24.1 | 12.6 | 18.7 | 12.8 |
| Aged 45 to 54 | 16.7 | 14.3 | 16.9 | 9.8 | 12.0 | 13.6 | 7.4 | 14.3 |
| Aged 55 to 59 | 21.5 | 27.8 | 27.4 | 16.7 | 28.2 | 17.8 | 14.6 | – |
| Aged 60 to 64 | 19.7 | 24.4 | 18.3 | 22.0 | 26.4 | 18.2 | 26.1 | 17.5 |
| Aged 65 or older | 23.9 | 16.8 | 27.8 | 18.5 | 31.3 | 25.3 | 25.7 | 21.2 |
| Aged 65 to 74 | 26.7 | 16.3 | 27.9 | 19.5 | 27.7 | 21.5 | 18.3 | 12.2 |
| Aged 75 or older | 20.1 | 18.2 | 27.6 | 16.2 | 36.6 | 30.3 | 35.4 | 29.2 |

*Note: (–) means sample is too small to make a reliable estimate.*
*Source: Bureau of the Census, Internet web site, <http:// www.census.gov/cps/ads/sdata.htm>*

# People below Poverty Level by Age, Sex, and Region, 1997: Hispanics

*(number and percent of Hispanics below poverty level by age, region, and sex, 1997; numbers in thousands)*

|  | Northeast | | Midwest | | South | | West | |
|---|---|---|---|---|---|---|---|---|
|  | *females* | *males* | *females* | *males* | *females* | *males* | *females* | *males* |
| **Number in poverty** | **867** | **666** | **281** | **251** | **1,329** | **1,171** | **1,987** | **1,757** |
| Under age 18 | 345 | 398 | 137 | 130 | 521 | 582 | 930 | 929 |
| Aged 18 to 24 | 86 | 76 | 37 | 37 | 164 | 132 | 258 | 188 |
| Aged 25 to 34 | 154 | 56 | 44 | 37 | 192 | 160 | 333 | 226 |
| Aged 35 to 44 | 108 | 56 | 34 | 21 | 177 | 112 | 240 | 244 |
| Aged 45 to 54 | 56 | 27 | 10 | 11 | 72 | 62 | 104 | 85 |
| Aged 55 to 59 | 38 | 17 | 12 | 1 | 37 | 27 | 42 | 16 |
| Aged 60 to 64 | 24 | 13 | 4 | 11 | 41 | 22 | 16 | 31 |
| Aged 65 or older | 55 | 23 | 4 | 4 | 123 | 74 | 65 | 37 |
| Aged 65 to 74 | 29 | 17 | 3 | 3 | 57 | 40 | 42 | 24 |
| Aged 75 or older | 26 | 7 | 1 | 1 | 66 | 33 | 23 | 13 |
| **Percent in poverty** | **35.4%** | **28.0%** | **26.7%** | **20.5%** | **26.9%** | **23.6%** | **30.4%** | **24.7%** |
| Under age 18 | 45.1 | 48.7 | 34.5 | 29.3 | 33.0 | 33.5 | 37.6 | 35.8 |
| Aged 18 to 24 | 29.1 | 22.7 | 23.9 | 21.1 | 29.7 | 22.3 | 34.1 | 20.3 |
| Aged 25 to 34 | 35.1 | 13.0 | 24.4 | 14.8 | 22.5 | 18.7 | 30.3 | 16.3 |
| Aged 35 to 44 | 30.7 | 15.1 | 22.8 | 12.6 | 24.0 | 15.5 | 23.9 | 22.1 |
| Aged 45 to 54 | 24.0 | 13.6 | 12.4 | 11.1 | 15.8 | 13.3 | 17.0 | 15.2 |
| Aged 55 to 59 | 33.2 | 22.6 | 29.4 | 4.9 | 20.2 | 19.5 | 23.1 | 9.7 |
| Aged 60 to 64 | 29.8 | 22.0 | 34.3 | 28.8 | 30.6 | 15.2 | 13.5 | 25.8 |
| Aged 65 or older | 33.5 | 25.7 | 8.9 | 11.9 | 28.3 | 24.1 | 21.7 | 14.8 |
| Aged 65 to 74 | 29.7 | 28.4 | 7.7 | 11.2 | 23.0 | 20.9 | 20.1 | 15.9 |
| Aged 75 or older | 39.1 | 20.7 | 13.2 | 14.5 | 35.5 | 29.6 | 25.4 | 13.2 |

*Source: Bureau of the Census, Internet web site, <http:// www.census.gov/cps/ads/sdata.htm>*

# People below Poverty Level by Age, Sex, and Region, 1997: Whites

*(number and percent of whites below poverty level by age, region, and sex, 1997; numbers in thousands)*

| | Northeast | | Midwest | | South | | West | |
|---|---|---|---|---|---|---|---|---|
| | *females* | *males* | *females* | *males* | *females* | *males* | *females* | *males* |
| **Number in poverty** | **2,534** | **1,838** | **2,677** | **1,869** | **4,917** | **3,556** | **3,816** | **3,188** |
| Under age 18 | 755 | 831 | 787 | 858 | 1,456 | 1,438 | 1,389 | 1,476 |
| Aged 18 to 24 | 239 | 205 | 383 | 221 | 597 | 430 | 611 | 446 |
| Aged 25 to 34 | 392 | 172 | 378 | 207 | 688 | 466 | 615 | 410 |
| Aged 35 to 44 | 332 | 182 | 320 | 207 | 598 | 424 | 474 | 392 |
| Aged 45 to 54 | 203 | 162 | 171 | 125 | 404 | 301 | 247 | 205 |
| Aged 55 to 59 | 96 | 60 | 131 | 51 | 191 | 93 | 111 | 44 |
| Aged 60 to 64 | 112 | 62 | 87 | 97 | 196 | 129 | 92 | 81 |
| Aged 65 or older | 406 | 164 | 419 | 104 | 787 | 276 | 277 | 135 |
| Aged 65 to 74 | 177 | 83 | 182 | 50 | 326 | 168 | 127 | 85 |
| Aged 75 or older | 229 | 82 | 237 | 54 | 462 | 108 | 149 | 50 |
| **Percent in poverty** | **11.5%** | **8.8%** | **9.6%** | **6.9%** | **13.3%** | **10.0%** | **15.2%** | **12.5%** |
| Under age 18 | 15.1 | 16.1 | 11.5 | 11.6 | 16.8 | 16.3 | 20.8 | 20.2 |
| Aged 18 to 24 | 12.8 | 10.8 | 14.8 | 8.6 | 19.1 | 12.7 | 25.9 | 17.8 |
| Aged 25 to 34 | 13.1 | 5.7 | 9.9 | 5.4 | 12.9 | 9.0 | 17.0 | 10.5 |
| Aged 35 to 44 | 9.1 | 5.0 | 6.9 | 4.6 | 10.4 | 7.1 | 11.1 | 9.0 |
| Aged 45 to 54 | 6.9 | 5.7 | 5.0 | 3.6 | 8.0 | 6.2 | 7.8 | 6.7 |
| Aged 55 to 59 | 9.0 | 5.8 | 10.1 | 4.4 | 10.6 | 5.2 | 9.1 | 4.1 |
| Aged 60 to 64 | 11.1 | 7.0 | 8.3 | 9.6 | 12.5 | 9.0 | 10.7 | 9.5 |
| Aged 65 or older | 11.3 | 6.7 | 10.1 | 3.5 | 13.8 | 6.6 | 9.2 | 5.5 |
| Aged 65 to 74 | 9.6 | 5.8 | 8.6 | 2.9 | 10.6 | 6.8 | 7.8 | 5.7 |
| Aged 75 or older | 13.1 | 8.0 | 11.6 | 4.3 | 17.4 | 6.4 | 10.7 | 5.0 |

*Source: Bureau of the Census, Internet web site, <http:// www.census.gov/cps/ads/sdata.htm>*

# One-Third of Hispanic Central City Residents Are Poor

## Black poverty rate is higher in nonmetropolitan areas than in central cities.

Nationally, poverty rates are higher in the nation's central cities than in the suburbs or nonmetropolitan areas. In 1997, 19 percent of central city residents were poor. In the suburbs, the poverty rate was just 9 percent, while 16 percent of nonmetropolitan residents were poor.

Among Hispanics in the central cities, 32 percent are poor. Forty-three percent of Hispanic children in the central cities lived below poverty level in 1997. At 31 percent, the poverty rate for Hispanics in nonmetropolitan areas is almost as high. Even in the suburbs, the Hispanic poverty rate is above 20 percent.

Among blacks, poverty rates are higher in nonmetropolitan areas than in central cities. Thirty-two percent of blacks living in nonmetropolitan areas are poor, versus 28 percent of those living in central cities. In the suburbs, 21 percent of blacks are poor.

The poverty rate of whites is lowest in the suburbs, where only 8 percent live below poverty level. In the central cities, 15 percent of whites are poor.

✘ Poverty rates are lower in the suburbs than in the central cities because two-earner married couples account for a large share of suburban households. In the central cities, single-parents account for a disproportionately large share of households.

### In central cities, the white poverty rate is half the Hispanic rate

*(percent of central city residents who are poor, by race and Hispanic origin, 1997)*

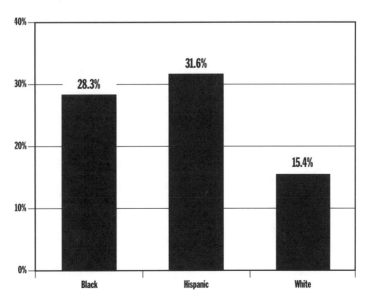

# People below Poverty Level by Sex, Age, Race, and Hispanic Origin, 1997: Total Metropolitan Residents

*(number and percent of people below poverty level in metropolitan areas by sex, age, race, and Hispanic origin, 1997; numbers in thousands)*

| | number | | | | percent | | | |
|---|---|---|---|---|---|---|---|---|
| | *total* | *black* | *Hispanic* | *white* | *total* | *black* | *Hispanic* | *white* |
| **Total people in poverty** | **27,273** | **7,509** | **7,426** | **18,050** | **12.6%** | **25.5%** | **26.7%** | **10.3%** |
| Under age 18 | 10,904 | 3,421 | 3,552 | 6,749 | 19.1 | 36.0 | 36.8 | 15.3 |
| Aged 18 to 24 | 3,526 | 891 | 854 | 2,427 | 17.1 | 27.9 | 24.9 | 14.8 |
| Aged 25 to 34 | 3,726 | 944 | 1,096 | 2,509 | 11.4 | 20.3 | 21.8 | 9.6 |
| Aged 35 to 44 | 3,350 | 916 | 911 | 2,214 | 9.2 | 19.2 | 21.5 | 7.5 |
| Aged 45 to 54 | 1,757 | 386 | 383 | 1,257 | 6.4 | 12.3 | 15.5 | 5.5 |
| Aged 55 to 59 | 772 | 211 | 158 | 526 | 8.0 | 20.3 | 19.0 | 6.4 |
| Aged 60 to 64 | 789 | 189 | 127 | 564 | 10.1 | 21.6 | 20.3 | 8.6 |
| Aged 65 or older | 2,450 | 551 | 345 | 1,805 | 9.9 | 24.3 | 23.1 | 8.3 |
| Aged 65 to 74 | 1,184 | 298 | 191 | 837 | 8.6 | 21.9 | 20.4 | 7.0 |
| Aged 75 or older | 1,265 | 253 | 154 | 968 | 11.6 | 28.0 | 27.7 | 9.9 |
| **Females in poverty** | **15,594** | **4,377** | **3,997** | **10,283** | **14.1** | **27.8** | **29.5** | **11.6** |
| Under age 18 | 5,323 | 1,697 | 1,721 | 3,250 | 19.2 | 36.3 | 37.0 | 15.2 |
| Aged 18 to 24 | 2,113 | 589 | 476 | 1,404 | 20.7 | 34.7 | 29.9 | 17.7 |
| Aged 25 to 34 | 2,375 | 674 | 655 | 1,544 | 14.4 | 26.3 | 27.8 | 12.0 |
| Aged 35 to 44 | 2,020 | 587 | 515 | 1,314 | 11.1 | 22.8 | 25.0 | 9.0 |
| Aged 45 to 54 | 1,017 | 221 | 223 | 728 | 7.2 | 12.5 | 17.6 | 6.3 |
| Aged 55 to 59 | 528 | 136 | 110 | 374 | 10.3 | 23.6 | 23.2 | 8.7 |
| Aged 60 to 64 | 468 | 118 | 71 | 330 | 11.5 | 22.6 | 22.9 | 9.8 |
| Aged 65 or older | 1,751 | 356 | 226 | 1,337 | 12.2 | 26.3 | 26.0 | 10.6 |
| Aged 65 to 74 | 798 | 192 | 118 | 577 | 10.5 | 24.2 | 21.6 | 8.8 |
| Aged 75 or older | 953 | 164 | 108 | 760 | 14.2 | 29.3 | 33.4 | 12.6 |
| **Males in poverty** | **11,679** | **3,132** | **3,429** | **7,768** | **11.0** | **22.8** | **24.2** | **9.0** |
| Under age 18 | 5,581 | 1,725 | 1,831 | 3,500 | 19.1 | 35.7 | 36.6 | 15.4 |
| Aged 18 to 24 | 1,413 | 302 | 378 | 1,022 | 13.5 | 20.2 | 20.6 | 12.1 |
| Aged 25 to 34 | 1,350 | 270 | 442 | 965 | 8.3 | 12.9 | 16.5 | 7.3 |
| Aged 35 to 44 | 1,331 | 329 | 396 | 899 | 7.4 | 15.0 | 18.2 | 6.0 |
| Aged 45 to 54 | 741 | 165 | 160 | 529 | 5.6 | 12.0 | 13.3 | 4.7 |
| Aged 55 to 59 | 243 | 75 | 48 | 151 | 5.3 | 16.3 | 13.4 | 3.9 |
| Aged 60 to 64 | 321 | 72 | 56 | 234 | 8.6 | 20.0 | 17.8 | 7.3 |
| Aged 65 or older | 699 | 194 | 119 | 468 | 6.8 | 21.4 | 19.1 | 5.1 |
| Aged 65 to 74 | 387 | 106 | 73 | 260 | 6.3 | 18.7 | 18.7 | 4.8 |
| Aged 75 or older | 312 | 89 | 46 | 208 | 7.4 | 25.9 | 19.7 | 5.6 |

*Note: Numbers will not add to total because Hispanics may be of any race and not all races are shown.*
*Source: Bureau of the Census, Internet web site, <http:// www.census.gov/cps/ads/sdata.htm>*

# People below Poverty Level by Sex, Age, Race, and Hispanic Origin, 1997: Central City Residents

*(number and percent of people below poverty level in central city areas by sex, age, race, and Hispanic origin, 1997; numbers in thousands)*

| | number | | | | percent | | | |
|---|---|---|---|---|---|---|---|---|
| | total | black | Hispanic | white | total | black | Hispanic | white |
| **Total people in poverty** | **15,018** | **5,311** | **4,652** | **8,630** | **18.8%** | **28.3%** | **31.6%** | **15.4%** |
| Under age 18 | 6,146 | 2,383 | 2,231 | 3,270 | 28.9 | 39.0 | 43.2 | 23.9 |
| Aged 18 to 24 | 2,077 | 656 | 534 | 1,317 | 24.4 | 32.0 | 28.9 | 22.2 |
| Aged 25 to 34 | 2,011 | 635 | 696 | 1,207 | 15.2 | 21.8 | 25.2 | 13.0 |
| Aged 35 to 44 | 1,844 | 641 | 549 | 1,056 | 14.4 | 21.9 | 26.3 | 11.7 |
| Aged 45 to 54 | 928 | 294 | 218 | 587 | 10.1 | 15.3 | 17.6 | 8.8 |
| Aged 55 to 59 | 424 | 173 | 108 | 232 | 13.2 | 26.7 | 24.0 | 9.6 |
| Aged 60 to 64 | 390 | 132 | 84 | 235 | 14.8 | 22.8 | 24.5 | 12.5 |
| Aged 65 or older | 1,198 | 397 | 232 | 727 | 12.9 | 24.4 | 28.5 | 10.0 |
| Aged 65 to 74 | 576 | 223 | 119 | 316 | 11.8 | 22.9 | 23.6 | 8.6 |
| Aged 75 or older | 622 | 174 | 113 | 410 | 14.2 | 26.7 | 36.5 | 11.4 |
| **Females in poverty** | **8,643** | **3,166** | **2,535** | **4,875** | **21.0** | **31.2** | **35.0** | **17.2** |
| Under age 18 | 3,024 | 1,205 | 1,082 | 1,551 | 29.4 | 40.0 | 43.6 | 23.8 |
| Aged 18 to 24 | 1,264 | 432 | 294 | 766 | 29.0 | 39.0 | 33.1 | 25.8 |
| Aged 25 to 34 | 1,307 | 490 | 428 | 723 | 19.9 | 29.2 | 33.7 | 16.4 |
| Aged 35 to 44 | 1,103 | 415 | 317 | 618 | 17.3 | 26.6 | 31.4 | 14.2 |
| Aged 45 to 54 | 563 | 164 | 135 | 367 | 11.6 | 15.1 | 20.6 | 10.8 |
| Aged 55 to 59 | 293 | 107 | 77 | 178 | 16.6 | 29.8 | 29.0 | 13.5 |
| Aged 60 to 64 | 245 | 80 | 52 | 149 | 17.3 | 23.5 | 28.6 | 15.1 |
| Aged 65 or older | 843 | 272 | 150 | 523 | 15.2 | 27.2 | 30.8 | 12.0 |
| Aged 65 to 74 | 363 | 144 | 67 | 196 | 13.0 | 24.9 | 22.3 | 9.3 |
| Aged 75 or older | 480 | 128 | 84 | 327 | 17.4 | 30.3 | 44.3 | 14.5 |
| **Males in poverty** | **6,375** | **2,145** | **2,116** | **3,755** | **16.4** | **24.9** | **28.4** | **13.5** |
| Under age 18 | 3,122 | 1,177 | 1,149 | 1,718 | 28.4 | 38.0 | 42.8 | 24.0 |
| Aged 18 to 24 | 812 | 224 | 241 | 551 | 19.5 | 23.8 | 25.1 | 18.5 |
| Aged 25 to 34 | 704 | 146 | 269 | 484 | 10.6 | 11.7 | 18.0 | 9.9 |
| Aged 35 to 44 | 741 | 225 | 231 | 438 | 11.5 | 16.5 | 21.5 | 9.4 |
| Aged 45 to 54 | 364 | 130 | 83 | 220 | 8.4 | 15.7 | 14.2 | 6.8 |
| Aged 55 to 59 | 131 | 66 | 31 | 54 | 9.0 | 22.8 | 16.9 | 4.9 |
| Aged 60 to 64 | 145 | 52 | 32 | 87 | 11.9 | 21.8 | 19.8 | 9.7 |
| Aged 65 or older | 355 | 125 | 81 | 204 | 9.6 | 19.9 | 24.9 | 7.0 |
| Aged 65 to 74 | 213 | 79 | 52 | 120 | 10.3 | 19.8 | 25.4 | 7.7 |
| Aged 75 or older | 142 | 46 | 29 | 83 | 8.7 | 20.0 | 24.2 | 6.2 |

*Note: Numbers will not add to total because Hispanics may be of any race and not all races are shown.*
*Source: Bureau of the Census, Internet web site, <http:// www.census.gov/cps/ads/sdata.htm>*

# People below Poverty Level by Sex, Age, Race, and Hispanic Origin, 1997: Suburban Residents

*(number and percent of people below poverty level in suburban areas by sex, age, race, and Hispanic origin, 1997; numbers in thousands)*

| | number | | | | percent | | | |
|---|---|---|---|---|---|---|---|---|
| | total | black | Hispanic | white | total | black | Hispanic | white |
| **Total people in poverty** | **12,255** | **2,197** | **2,774** | **9,420** | **9.0%** | **20.6%** | **21.3%** | **7.9%** |
| Under age 18 | 4,758 | 1,038 | 1,321 | 3,480 | 13.3 | 30.5 | 29.5 | 11.4 |
| Aged 18 to 24 | 1,449 | 234 | 320 | 1,109 | 11.9 | 20.4 | 20.3 | 10.7 |
| Aged 25 to 34 | 1,715 | 308 | 400 | 1,302 | 8.8 | 17.8 | 17.6 | 7.8 |
| Aged 35 to 44 | 1,506 | 275 | 362 | 1,157 | 6.4 | 15.0 | 16.8 | 5.6 |
| Aged 45 to 54 | 829 | 92 | 164 | 670 | 4.6 | 7.5 | 13.4 | 4.2 |
| Aged 55 to 59 | 347 | 38 | 50 | 294 | 5.4 | 9.7 | 13.1 | 5.1 |
| Aged 60 to 64 | 399 | 57 | 43 | 329 | 7.7 | 19.1 | 15.3 | 7.0 |
| Aged 65 or older | 1,252 | 154 | 113 | 1,078 | 8.1 | 24.2 | 16.7 | 7.5 |
| Aged 65 to 74 | 608 | 75 | 72 | 521 | 6.8 | 19.6 | 16.7 | 6.3 |
| Aged 75 or older | 643 | 79 | 41 | 557 | 9.8 | 31.3 | 16.7 | 9.1 |
| **Females in poverty** | **6,951** | **1,211** | **1,462** | **5,407** | **10.1** | **21.7** | **23.1** | **9.0** |
| Under age 18 | 2,299 | 491 | 639 | 1,698 | 13.2 | 29.4 | 29.5 | 11.4 |
| Aged 18 to 24 | 848 | 157 | 182 | 638 | 14.5 | 26.5 | 26.0 | 12.9 |
| Aged 25 to 34 | 1,068 | 184 | 227 | 822 | 10.8 | 20.8 | 20.9 | 9.7 |
| Aged 35 to 44 | 917 | 171 | 197 | 696 | 7.7 | 17.0 | 18.8 | 6.8 |
| Aged 45 to 54 | 453 | 57 | 88 | 361 | 4.9 | 8.5 | 14.4 | 4.5 |
| Aged 55 to 59 | 235 | 29 | 33 | 197 | 7.0 | 13.3 | 15.9 | 6.6 |
| Aged 60 to 64 | 223 | 38 | 19 | 182 | 8.4 | 20.9 | 14.8 | 7.6 |
| Aged 65 or older | 908 | 84 | 76 | 814 | 10.3 | 23.8 | 19.8 | 9.9 |
| Aged 65 to 74 | 435 | 48 | 51 | 382 | 9.0 | 22.4 | 20.8 | 8.5 |
| Aged 75 or older | 473 | 36 | 24 | 432 | 11.9 | 26.1 | 18.2 | 11.5 |
| **Males in poverty** | **5,304** | **987** | **1,313** | **4,013** | **7.9** | **19.4** | **19.5** | **6.8** |
| Under age 18 | 2,459 | 547 | 682 | 1,781 | 13.5 | 31.6 | 29.4 | 11.5 |
| Aged 18 to 24 | 601 | 78 | 138 | 471 | 9.6 | 14.0 | 15.7 | 8.7 |
| Aged 25 to 34 | 647 | 124 | 173 | 481 | 6.7 | 14.7 | 14.6 | 5.8 |
| Aged 35 to 44 | 590 | 104 | 165 | 462 | 5.1 | 12.5 | 14.9 | 4.5 |
| Aged 45 to 54 | 376 | 35 | 77 | 309 | 4.2 | 6.4 | 12.4 | 3.9 |
| Aged 55 to 59 | 112 | 9 | 17 | 98 | 3.6 | 5.2 | 9.7 | 3.5 |
| Aged 60 to 64 | 176 | 20 | 24 | 147 | 7.0 | 16.4 | 15.7 | 6.4 |
| Aged 65 or older | 344 | 70 | 37 | 264 | 5.2 | 24.8 | 12.6 | 4.3 |
| Aged 65 to 74 | 174 | 27 | 21 | 139 | 4.3 | 16.0 | 11.2 | 3.7 |
| Aged 75 or older | 170 | 43 | 17 | 125 | 6.6 | 37.7 | 15.0 | 5.2 |

*Note: The suburbs is the portion of a metropolitan area that is outside the central city. Numbers will not add to total because Hispanics may be of any race and not all races are shown.*
*Source: Bureau of the Census, Internet web site, <http:// www.census.gov/cps/ads/sdata.htm>*

## People below Poverty Level by Sex, Age, Race, and Hispanic Origin, 1997: Nonmetropolitan Residents

*(number and percent of people below poverty level in nonmetropolitan areas by sex, age, race, and Hispanic origin, 1997; numbers in thousands)*

| | number | | | | percent | | | |
|---|---|---|---|---|---|---|---|---|
| | total | black | Hispanic | white | total | black | Hispanic | white |
| **Total people in poverty** | **8,301** | **1,607** | **882** | **6,346** | **15.9%** | **32.0%** | **30.7%** | **13.8%** |
| Under age 18 | 3,209 | 804 | 420 | 2,240 | 22.7 | 43.2 | 36.4 | 19.0 |
| Aged 18 to 24 | 890 | 151 | 125 | 705 | 19.6 | 29.1 | 33.9 | 18.0 |
| Aged 25 to 34 | 1,033 | 162 | 105 | 818 | 15.7 | 25.1 | 23.0 | 14.2 |
| Aged 35 to 44 | 901 | 147 | 81 | 714 | 11.0 | 19.9 | 22.3 | 9.9 |
| Aged 45 to 54 | 682 | 103 | 44 | 560 | 10.1 | 19.6 | 19.0 | 9.2 |
| Aged 55 to 59 | 321 | 59 | 32 | 252 | 12.7 | 32.6 | 33.8 | 11.0 |
| Aged 60 to 64 | 338 | 33 | 34 | 293 | 14.9 | 26.1 | 43.8 | 13.9 |
| Aged 65 or older | 927 | 149 | 39 | 764 | 12.5 | 34.7 | 31.3 | 11.1 |
| Aged 65 to 74 | 457 | 85 | 23 | 361 | 11.1 | 33.6 | 29.6 | 9.5 |
| Aged 75 or older | 470 | 63 | 16 | 403 | 14.4 | 36.3 | 34.2 | 13.1 |
| **Females in poverty** | **4,792** | **940** | **466** | **3,661** | **17.8** | **35.4** | **33.3** | **15.5** |
| Under age 18 | 1,611 | 389 | 212 | 1,137 | 23.1 | 42.7 | 37.3 | 19.6 |
| Aged 18 to 24 | 544 | 91 | 70 | 426 | 23.0 | 30.8 | 40.4 | 21.2 |
| Aged 25 to 34 | 687 | 130 | 68 | 528 | 20.4 | 37.7 | 31.9 | 18.1 |
| Aged 35 to 44 | 546 | 113 | 44 | 409 | 13.2 | 27.3 | 24.2 | 11.2 |
| Aged 45 to 54 | 356 | 53 | 19 | 296 | 10.5 | 19.8 | 16.5 | 9.7 |
| Aged 55 to 59 | 195 | 39 | 19 | 154 | 16.0 | 35.8 | 40.6 | 14.1 |
| Aged 60 to 64 | 180 | 16 | 14 | 158 | 15.0 | 30.7 | 43.1 | 13.9 |
| Aged 65 or older | 672 | 110 | 20 | 552 | 16.0 | 41.1 | 29.7 | 14.2 |
| Aged 65 to 74 | 307 | 65 | 12 | 235 | 13.6 | 40.2 | 30.8 | 11.4 |
| Aged 75 or older | 365 | 45 | 8 | 317 | 18.7 | 42.4 | 28.2 | 17.4 |
| **Males in poverty** | **3,509** | **667** | **415** | **2,684** | **13.8** | **28.2** | **28.1** | **11.9** |
| Under age 18 | 1,598 | 415 | 208 | 1,103 | 22.4 | 43.6 | 35.5 | 18.5 |
| Aged 18 to 24 | 346 | 60 | 54 | 278 | 15.9 | 26.8 | 28.1 | 14.6 |
| Aged 25 to 34 | 346 | 32 | 37 | 290 | 10.7 | 10.7 | 15.2 | 10.2 |
| Aged 35 to 44 | 355 | 34 | 37 | 305 | 8.8 | 10.6 | 20.4 | 8.5 |
| Aged 45 to 54 | 325 | 50 | 26 | 264 | 9.7 | 19.4 | 21.4 | 8.7 |
| Aged 55 to 59 | 126 | 20 | 13 | 97 | 9.7 | 27.8 | 27.1 | 8.2 |
| Aged 60 to 64 | 157 | 17 | 20 | 135 | 14.8 | 23.0 | 44.3 | 13.9 |
| Aged 65 or older | 254 | 38 | 19 | 212 | 8.0 | 24.0 | 33.2 | 7.1 |
| Aged 65 to 74 | 149 | 20 | 11 | 126 | 8.0 | 22.0 | 28.4 | 7.3 |
| Aged 75 or older | 105 | 18 | 8 | 86 | 8.0 | 26.7 | 42.6 | 6.9 |

*Note: Numbers will not add to total because Hispanics may be of any race and not all races are shown.*
*Source: Bureau of the Census, Internet web site, <http:// www.census.gov/cps/ads/sdata.htm>*

# Among Workers, Poverty Rate Is Highest for Young Adults

## One in eight workers aged 18 to 24 is poor.

While the poverty rate is relatively low for people with jobs, a substantial number of workers are poor despite getting a paycheck. Among all workers aged 16 or older, 7 percent had incomes that placed them below poverty level. The poverty rate among workers is highest in the young-adult age group—13 percent of 18-to-24-year-old workers are poor. Even among young adults who work full-time, 5 percent are poor. Many young adults make minimum wage in entry-level jobs. Eventually, they will move up the career ladder, particularly if they have some college experience.

Among black workers, a substantial 12 percent were poor in 1997, including 4 percent of those with full-time jobs. Fully 23 percent of employed blacks aged 18 to 24 lived in poverty, but only 9 percent of those with full-time jobs were poor.

Fourteen percent of Hispanic workers are poor, including 8 percent of those with full-time jobs. This compares with a poverty rate of just 6 percent for white workers, and 2 percent for white workers with full-time jobs.

✗ The poverty rate is lower for white workers in part because they are more likely than black or Hispanic workers to live in households with more than one earner.

### Hispanic workers are most likely to be poor

*(percent of full-time, year-round workers aged 16 or older in poverty, by race and Hispanic origin, 1997)*

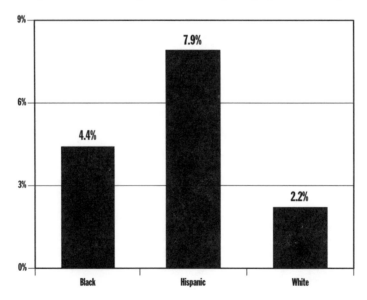

# Number and Percent of Workers below Poverty Level by Sex, Age, and Work Status, 1997: Total People

*(number and percent of workers aged 16 or older below poverty level by sex, age, and work status, 1997; numbers in thousands)*

| | total workers | | full-time, year-round workers | |
|---|---|---|---|---|
| | *number* | *percent* | *number* | *percent* |
| **Total workers in poverty** | **9,444** | **6.6%** | **2,345** | **2.5%** |
| Aged 16 to 17 | 335 | 9.7 | 2 | 2.6 |
| Aged 18 to 24 | 25,449 | 12.8 | 370 | 5.2 |
| Aged 25 to 34 | 2,710 | 7.9 | 815 | 3.4 |
| Aged 35 to 54 | 3,130 | 4.7 | 1,012 | 2.0 |
| Aged 55 to 64 | 580 | 4.0 | 131 | 1.3 |
| Aged 65 or older | 140 | 2.8 | 15 | 1.0 |
| **Men in poverty** | **4,163** | **5.4** | **1,381** | **2.5** |
| Aged 16 to 17 | 179 | 10.1 | 2 | – |
| Aged 18 to 24 | 1,048 | 10.2 | 205 | 5.1 |
| Aged 25 to 34 | 1,182 | 6.4 | 489 | 3.4 |
| Aged 35 to 54 | 1,414 | 4.0 | 592 | 2.0 |
| Aged 55 to 64 | 271 | 3.5 | 80 | 1.4 |
| Aged 65 or older | 68 | 2.5 | 12 | 1.2 |
| **Women in poverty** | **5,281** | **7.8** | **964** | **2.6** |
| Aged 16 to 17 | 155 | 9.2 | – | – |
| Aged 18 to 24 | 1,501 | 15.5 | 165 | 5.4 |
| Aged 25 to 34 | 1,528 | 9.6 | 326 | 3.4 |
| Aged 35 to 54 | 1,716 | 5.4 | 420 | 2.1 |
| Aged 55 to 64 | 308 | 4.7 | 51 | 1.3 |
| Aged 65 or older | 72 | 3.3 | 3 | 0.5 |

*Note: (–) means sample is too small to make a reliable estimate.*
*Source: Bureau of the Census,* Poverty in the United States: 1997, *Current Population Reports, P60-201, 1998*

## Number and Percent of Workers below Poverty Level by Sex, Age, and Work Status, 1997: Blacks

*(number and percent of black workers aged 16 or older below poverty level by sex, age, and work status, 1997; numbers in thousands)*

| | total workers | | full-time, year-round workers | |
|---|---|---|---|---|
| | number | percent | number | percent |
| **Total workers in poverty** | **2,011** | **12.4%** | **464** | **4.4%** |
| Aged 16 to 17 | 78 | 21.6 | – | – |
| Aged 18 to 24 | 566 | 22.9 | 85 | 9.3 |
| Aged 25 to 34 | 602 | 13.5 | 161 | 5.3 |
| Aged 35 to 54 | 639 | 8.8 | 189 | 3.4 |
| Aged 55 to 64 | 103 | 8.0 | 29 | 3.2 |
| Aged 65 or older | 23 | 6.4 | – | – |
| **Men in poverty** | **677** | **9.0** | **181** | **3.5** |
| Aged 16 to 17 | 40 | 23.4 | – | – |
| Aged 18 to 24 | 200 | 17.3 | 38 | 8.0 |
| Aged 25 to 34 | 187 | 8.9 | 64 | 4.2 |
| Aged 35 to 54 | 202 | 6.0 | 61 | 2.3 |
| Aged 55 to 64 | 35 | 6.0 | 18 | 4.0 |
| Aged 65 or older | 12 | 7.3 | – | – |
| **Women in poverty** | **1,335** | **15.4** | **283** | **5.3** |
| Aged 16 to 17 | 38 | 20.0 | – | – |
| Aged 18 to 24 | 366 | 27.7 | 46 | 10.7 |
| Aged 25 to 34 | 415 | 17.6 | 97 | 6.4 |
| Aged 35 to 54 | 437 | 11.1 | 128 | 4.5 |
| Aged 55 to 64 | 68 | 9.7 | 11 | 2.5 |
| Aged 65 or older | 11 | 5.5 | – | – |

*Note: (–) means sample is too small to make a reliable estimate.*
*Source: Bureau of the Census,* Poverty in the United States: 1997, *Current Population Reports, P60-201, 1998*

# Number and Percent of Workers below Poverty Level by Sex, Age, and Work Status, 1997: Hispanics

*(number and percent of Hispanic workers aged 16 or older below poverty level by sex, age, and work status, 1997; numbers in thousands)*

| | total workers | | full-time, year-round workers | |
|---|---|---|---|---|
| | number | percent | number | percent |
| **Total workers in poverty** | **1,999** | **14.0%** | **720** | **7.9%** |
| Aged 16 to 17 | 77 | 26.6 | – | – |
| Aged 18 to 24 | 476 | 17.7 | 100 | 8.7 |
| Aged 25 to 34 | 617 | 14.1 | 280 | 9.0 |
| Aged 35 to 54 | 728 | 12.6 | 319 | 7.8 |
| Aged 55 to 64 | 91 | 9.7 | 21 | 3.2 |
| Aged 65 or older | 10 | 4.5 | 1 | 0.9 |
| **Men in poverty** | **1,109** | **13.1** | **503** | **8.4** |
| Aged 16 to 17 | 46 | 25.5 | – | – |
| Aged 18 to 24 | 241 | 15.1 | 82 | 10.2 |
| Aged 25 to 34 | 368 | 13.6 | 208 | 9.8 |
| Aged 35 to 54 | 394 | 12.1 | 202 | 7.8 |
| Aged 55 to 64 | 53 | 9.7 | 12 | 3.0 |
| Aged 65 or older | 8 | 5.6 | – | – |
| **Women in poverty** | **890** | **15.2** | **217** | **6.9** |
| Aged 16 to 17 | 31 | 28.3 | – | – |
| Aged 18 to 24 | 236 | 21.4 | 72 | 5.2 |
| Aged 25 to 34 | 249 | 15.1 | 117 | 7.4 |
| Aged 35 to 54 | 334 | 13.3 | 9 | 7.7 |
| Aged 55 to 64 | 38 | 9.8 | 1 | 3.5 |
| Aged 65 or older | 2 | 2.8 | 39 | – |

*Note: (–) means sample is too small to make a reliable estimate.*
*Source: Bureau of the Census,* Poverty in the United States: 1997, *Current Population Reports, P60-201, 1998*

## Number and Percent of Workers below Poverty Level by Sex, Age, and Work Status, 1997: Whites

*(number and percent of white workers aged 16 or older below poverty level by sex, age, and work status, 1997; numbers in thousands)*

| | total workers | | full-time, year-round workers | |
| --- | --- | --- | --- | --- |
| | number | percent | number | percent |
| **Total workers in poverty** | **6,945** | **5.7%** | **1,751** | **2.2%** |
| Aged 16 to 17 | 245 | 8.2 | 2 | – |
| Aged 18 to 24 | 1,871 | 11.2 | 274 | 4.6 |
| Aged 25 to 34 | 1,940 | 6.9 | 599 | 3.0 |
| Aged 35 to 54 | 2,322 | 4.1 | 763 | 1.8 |
| Aged 55 to 64 | 452 | 3.6 | 98 | 1.1 |
| Aged 65 or older | 114 | 2.6 | 15 | 1.1 |
| **Men in poverty** | **3,237** | **5.0** | **1,096** | **2.3** |
| Aged 16 to 17 | 137 | 8.7 | 2 | – |
| Aged 18 to 24 | 803 | 9.2 | 161 | 4.7 |
| Aged 25 to 34 | 907 | 6.0 | 380 | 3.1 |
| Aged 35 to 54 | 1,116 | 3.7 | 482 | 1.9 |
| Aged 55 to 64 | 221 | 3.2 | 58 | 1.1 |
| Aged 65 or older | 53 | 2.1 | 12 | 1.4 |
| **Women in poverty** | **3,708** | **6.6** | **654** | **2.1** |
| Aged 16 to 17 | 109 | 7.6 | – | – |
| Aged 18 to 24 | 1,068 | 13.5 | 112 | 4.4 |
| Aged 25 to 34 | 1,033 | 8.1 | 219 | 2.9 |
| Aged 35 to 54 | 1,206 | 4.6 | 281 | 1.7 |
| Aged 55 to 64 | 231 | 4.1 | 40 | 1.2 |
| Aged 65 or older | 61 | 3.1 | 3 | 0.5 |

*Note: (–) means sample is too small to make a reliable estimate.*
*Source: Bureau of the Census,* Poverty in the United States: 1997, *Current Population Reports, P60-201, 1998*

# For More Information

The federal government is a rich source of accurate and reliable data about almost every aspect of American life. Below are the web site addresses of the agencies collecting demographic and economic data as well as the phone numbers of agencies and subject specialists, organized alphabetically by topic. Also below is a list of State Data Centers and Small Business Development Centers where researchers can go for help in tracking down economic information.

## Web site addresses

| | |
|---|---|
| Bureau of the Census | <http://www.census.gov> |
| Bureau of Labor Statistics | <http://www.bls.gov> |
| Current Population Survey home page | <http://www.bls.census.gov/cps> |
| Consumer Expenditure Survey home page | <http://www.bls.gov/csxhome.htm> |
| Federal Reserve Board | <http://www.bog.frb.fed.us> |

## Subject Specialists

| | |
|---|---|
| Absences from work, Staff | 202-606-6378 |
| Aging population, Staff | 301-457-2422 |
| Ancestry, Staff | 301-457-2403 |
| Apportionment, Ed Byerly | 301-457-2381 |
| Census, 1990 tabulations, Staff | 301-457-2422 |
| Census, 2000 plans, Arthur Cresce | 301-457-8358 |
| Census Bureau customer services | 301-457-4100 |
| Child care, Martin O'Connell/Kristin Smith | 301-457-2465 |
| Children, Staff | 301-457-2465 |
| Citizenship, Staff | 301-457-2403 |
| College graduate job outlook, Mark Mittelhauser | 202-606-5707 |
| Commuting, Phil Salopek/Celia Boertlein | 301-457-2454 |
| Consumer Expenditure Survey, Staff | 202-606-6900 |
| Contingent workers, Sharon Cohany | 202-606-6378 |
| County population, Staff | 301-457-2422 |
| Crime, Marilyn Monahan | 301-457-3925 |
| Current employment analysis, Philip Rones | 202-606-6378 |
| Current Population Survey (general information), Staff | 301-457-4100 |
| Demographic surveys (general information), Staff | 301-457-3773 |
| Disability, Jack McNeil | 301-457-3225 |
| Discouraged workers, Staff | 202-606-6378 |
| Displaced workers, Steve Hipple | 202-606-6378 |

Economic Censuses, 1997

- Accommodations, Fay Dorsett .......................................................................................301-457-2700
- Census promotions, Herb Gerardi .................................................................................301-457-2989
- Communications industry, Jack Moody .........................................................................301-457-2689
- Construction, Pat Horning ..............................................................................................301-457-4680
- Financial and insurance, Laurie Torene .......................................................................301-457-2780
- Food services, Fay Dorsett .............................................................................................301-457-2700
- General information, Robert Marske ..............................................................................301-457-2547
- Internet dissemination, Paul Zeisset ..............................................................................301-457-4151
- Manufacturing, durable goods, Kenneth Hansen .........................................................301-457-4755
- Manufacturing, nondurable goods, Robert Reinard .....................................................301-457-4810
- Mining, Pat Horning .......................................................................................................301-457-4680
- Minority/women-owned businesses, Valerie Strang .....................................................301-457-3316
- North American Industry Class. Sys., Bruce Goldhirsch ..............................................301-457-2559
- Puerto Rico, outlying areas, territories, Eddie Salyers .................................................301-457-3318
- Real estate and rental/leasing, Steve Roman ...............................................................301-457-2780
- Retail trade and accomodations, Fay Dorsett ...............................................................301-457-2700
- Services, Jack Moody ......................................................................................................301-457-2689
- Transportation and utilities, establishments, Jim Poyer ..............................................301-457-2811
- Vehicle Inventory and Use Survey, Kim Moore ............................................................301-457-2797
- Wholesale trade, John Trimble ......................................................................................301-457-2725

Education, training statistics, Alan Eck ...........................................................................202-606-5705
Education surveys, Steve Tourkin.....................................................................................301-457-3791
Educational attainment, Staff ..........................................................................................301-457-2464
Emigration/illegal immigrants, Staff ...............................................................................301-457-2438
Employee benefits, Staff ..................................................................................................202-606-6222
Employee tenure, Jennifer Martel ....................................................................................202-606-6378
Employment and unemployment , Staff ..........................................................................301-457-3242
Employment and Earnings periodical, Gloria P. Green ...............................202-606-6373 x255
Employment and unemployment trends, Staff................................................................202-606-6378
Employment Situation News Release, Staff ....................................................................202-606-6378
Equal employment opportunity data, Staff.....................................................................301-457-3242
Fertility, Amara Bachu ....................................................................................................301-457-2449
Flexitime and shift work, Thomas Beers .........................................................................202-606-6378
Foreign born, Staff ...........................................................................................................301-457-2403
Group quarters population, Denise Smith.......................................................................301-457-2378
Health surveys, Adrienne Oneto......................................................................................301-457-3879
Hispanic statistics, Staff ..................................................................................................301-457-2403
Home-based work, Staff ...................................................................................................202-606-6378
Homeless, Audrian Gray ..................................................................................................301-457-3977
Household wealth, Staff ...................................................................................................301-457-3242
Households and families, Staff ........................................................................................301-457-2465

Housing

- Affordability, Peter Fronczek/Howard Savage ..................................................................301-457-3199
- American Housing Survey, Staff ..........................................................................................301-457-3235
- Census, Staff .........................................................................................................................301-457-3237
- Components of inventory change, Barbara Williams ........................................................301-457-3235
- Homeownership and vacancy data, Linda Cavanaugh ......................................................301-457-3199
- Market absorption, Alan Friedman ....................................................................................301-457-3199
- Residential finance, Howard Savage ..................................................................................301-457-3199

Immigrants, Jay Meisenheimer ............................................................................................202-606-6378

Immigration, (general information), Staff ...........................................................................301-457-2422

Income statistics, Staff .........................................................................................................301-457-3242

Industry

- Business expenditures, Sheldon Ziman ..............................................................................301-457-3315
- Business investment, Charles Funk ....................................................................................301-457-3324
- Characteristics of business owners, Valerie Strang ..........................................................301-457-3316
- County business patterns, Paul Hanczaryk ........................................................................301-457-2600
- Economic studies, Arnold Reznek ......................................................................................301-457-1856
- Enterprise statistics, Eddie Salyers ....................................................................................301-457-3318
- Industry and commodity classification, James Kristoff ....................................................301-457-2813
- Mineral industries, Pat Horning ........................................................................................301-457-4680
- Minority/women-owned businesses, Valerie Strang ........................................................301-457-3316
- North American Industry Class. Sys., Bruce Goldhirsch ..................................................301-457-2559
- Puerto Rico and outlying areas, Irma Harahush ................................................................301-457-3314
- Quarterly Financial Report, Ronald Lee ............................................................................301-457-3343
- Statistics of U.S. Businesses, Mike Mashburn ..................................................................301-457-8641

Job mobility and tenure, Alan Eck .......................................................................................202-606-5705

Journey to work, Phil Salopek/Gloria Swieczkowski .........................................................301-457-2454

Labor force concepts, Staff ...................................................................................................202-606-6378

Labor force demographics, Howard Fullerton .....................................................................202-606-5711

Language, Staff ......................................................................................................................301-457-2464

Longitudinal surveys, Sarah Higgins ...................................................................................301-457-3801

Marital and family characteristics of workers, Staff ...........................................................202-606-6378

Marital status and living arrangements, Staff .....................................................................301-457-2422

Metropolitan areas, Staff ......................................................................................................301-457-2422

Migration, Kristin Hansen/Carol Faber ..............................................................................301-457-2454

Minimum wage data, Steven Haugen ..................................................................................202-606-6378

Minority workers, Staff .........................................................................................................202-606-6378

Multiple jobholders, John Stinson ...............................................................................202-606-6373 x263

National estimates and projections, Staff ............................................................................301-457-2422

Occupational data, Staff .......................................................................................................202-606-6378

Occupational Outlook Quarterly, Kathleen Green ..............................................................202-606-5717

## Census Regional Offices

| | |
|---|---|
| Atlanta, GA | 404-730-3833/3964 (TDD) |
| Boston, MA | 617-424-0510/0565 (TDD) |
| Charlotte, NC | 704-344-6144/6548 (TDD) |
| Chicago, IL | 708-562-1723/1791 (TDD) |
| Dallas, TX | 214-640-4470/4434 (TDD) |
| Denver, CO | 303-969-7750/6769 (TDD) |
| Detroit, MI | 313-259-1875/5169 (TDD) |
| Kansas City, KS | 913-551-6711/5839 (TDD) |
| Los Angeles, CA | 818-904-6339/6249 (TDD) |
| New York, NY | 212-264-4730/3863 (TDD) |
| Philadelphia, PA | 215-597-8313/8864 (TDD) |
| Seattle, WA | 206-553-5837/5859 (TDD) |

## State Data Centers and Business/Industry Data Centers

Below are listed the State Data Center and Business/Industry Data Center (BIDC) lead agency contacts only. Lead data centers are usually state government agencies, universities, or libraries that head up a network of affiliate centers. Every state has a State Data Center. The asterisks (*) identify states that also have Business/Industry Data Centers. In some states, one agency serves as the lead for both the State Data Centers and the Business/Industry Data Centers. The Business/Industry Data Center is listed separately if there is a separate agency serving as the lead.

| | |
|---|---|
| Alabama, Annette Watters, University of Alabama | 205-348-6191 |
| Alaska, Kathryn Lizik, Department of Labor | 907-465-2437 |
| American Samoa, Vaitoelav Filiga, Dept. of Commerce | 684-633-5155 |
| *Arizona, Betty Jeffries, Department of Security | 602-542-5984 |
| Arkansas, Sarah Breshears, University of Arkansas at Little Rock | 501-569-8530 |
| California, Linda Gage, Department of Finance | 916-323-4086 |
| Colorado, Rebecca Picaso, Department of Local Affairs | 303-866-2156 |
| Connecticut, Bill Kraynak, Office of Policy & Management | 860-418-6230 |
| *Delaware, Vacant, Development Office | 302-739-4271 |
| District of Columbia, Herb Bixhorn, Mayor's Office of Planning | 202-442-7603 |
| *Florida, Pam Schenker, Dept. of Labor & Employment Security | 850-488-1048 |
| Georgia, Robert Giacomini, Georgia Institute of Technology | 404-656-0911 |
| Guam, Rose Deaver, Department of Commerce | 011-671-475-0325/6 |
| Hawaii, Jan Nakamoto, Dept. of Business, Econ. Dev., & Tourism | 808-586-2493 |
| Idaho, Alan Porter, Department of Commerce | 208-334-2470 |
| Illinois, Suzanne Ebetsch, Bureau of the Budget | 217-782-1381 |
| *Indiana, Sylvia Andrews, State Library | 317-232-3733 |
| Indiana BIDC, Carol Rogers, Business Research Center | 317-274-2205 |
| Iowa, Beth Henning, State Library | 515-281-4350 |
| Kansas, Marc Galbraith, State Library | 913-296-3296 |
| *Kentucky, Ron Crouch, University of Louisville | 502-852-7990 |

Louisiana, Karen Paterson, Office of Planning & Budget ...................................................... ....225-342-7410

*Maine, Richard Sherwood, State Planning Office .......................................................... ....207-342-7410

*Maryland, Jane Traynham, Office of Planning ................................................................ 410-767-4450

*Massachusetts, John Gaviglio, Mass. Inst. for Social and Econ. Res ......................... ....413-545-3460

Michigan, Carolyn Lauer, Dept. of Management & Budget ......................................... ..517-373-7910

*Minnesota, David Birkholz, State Demographer's Office ........................................... ....651-296-2557

Minnesota BIDC, David Rademacher, State Dem. Office ............................................ 651-297-3255

*Mississippi, Rachael McNeely, University of Mississippi ............................................ ...601-232-7288

Mississippi BIDC, Deloise Tate, Dept. of Econ. & Comm. Dev ................................ ...601-359-3593

*Missouri, Debra Pitts, State Library ................................................................................ 573-526-7648

Missouri BIDC, Jackie Brown, Small Business Dev. Centers ..................................... ....573-882-0344

*Montana, Patricia Roberts, Department of Commerce ................................................ 406-444-2896

Nebraska, Jerome Deichert, University of Nebraska-Omaha ..................................... ..402-595-2311

Nevada, Linda Nary, State Library & Archives ............................................................. 775-687-8326

New Hampshire, Thomas Duffy, Office of State Planning ........................................... ...603-271-2155

*New Jersey, Doug Moore, Department of Labor ........................................................... ...........609-984-2595

*New Mexico, Kevin Kargacin, University of New Mexico .......................................... ....505-277-6626

*New York, Staff, Department of Economic Development .......................................... .......518-474-1141

*North Carolina, Staff, State Library .............................................................................. 919-733-3270

North Dakota, Richard Rathge, State University ......................................................... ...........701-231-8621

Northern Mariana Islands, Juan Borja, Dept. of Commerce ..................................... ......011-670-664-3034

*Ohio, Barry Bennett, Department of Development .................................................... ............614-466-2115

*Oklahoma, Jeff Wallace, Department of Commerce ................................................... ............405-815-5184

Oregon, George Hough, Portland State Univ .................................. ..503-725-5159 / 1-800-547-8887x5159

*Pennsylvania, Diane Shoop, Penns. State Univ. at Harrisburg .................................. ....717-948-6336

Puerto Rico, Lillian Torres Aguirre, Planning Bd ...................................787-728-4430 / 723-6200x2502

Rhode Island, Mark Brown, Department of Administration ...................................... ............401-222-6183

South Carolina, Mike MacFarlane, Budget & Control Board .................................... ...803-734-3780

South Dakota, Theresa Bendert, Univ. of South Dakota ........................................... .............605-677-5287

Tennessee, Don Waller, State Planning Office ............................................ .................615-741-1676

Texas, Steve Murdock, Texas A&M University.......... .......... 409-845-5115 / 5332

*Utah, David Abel, Office of Planning & Budget ....................................... .................801-538-1036

Vermont, Sybil McShane, Department of Libraries ..................................................... 802-828-3261

*Virginia, Don Lillywhite, Virginia Employment Commission ................................... ...804-786-8026

Virgin Islands, Frank Mills, Univ. of the Virgin Islands .............................................. 809-693-1027

*Washington, Yi Zhao, Office of Financial Management ............................................. 360-586-2504

*West Virginia, Delphine Coffey, Office of Comm. & Industrial Dev ..................................304-558-4010

West Virginia BIDC, Randy Childs, Center for Econ. Research ............................... 304-293-7832

*Wisconsin, Robert Naylor, Department of Administration ....................................... ....608-266-1927

Wisconsin BIDC, Ed Wallender, Univ. of Wisconsin-Madison ............................... 608-262-3097

Wyoming, Wenlin Liu, Dept. of Administration & Fiscal Control ...................................... ....307-777-7504

# Glossary

**adjusted for inflation** Income or a change in income that has been adjusted for the rise in the cost of living, or the consumer price index (CPI-U-XI). In this book any year-to-year changes in income or spending are shown in inflation-adjusted dollars.

**Asian** In this book, the term "Asian" includes both Asians and Pacific Islanders.

**baby boom** Americans born between 1946 and 1964.

**baby bust** Americans born between 1965 and 1976, also known as Generation X.

**central cities** The largest city in a metropolitan area is called the central city. The balance of the metropolitan area outside the central city is regarded as the "suburbs."

**dual-earner couple** A married couple in which both the householder and the householder's spouse are in the labor force.

**earnings** One type of income. *See also* Income.

**educational attainment** The highest grade or degree completed by a person or householder.

**employed** All civilians who did any work as a paid employee or farmer/self-employed worker, or who worked 15 hours or more as an unpaid farm worker or in a family-owned business, during the reference period. All those who have jobs but who are temporarily absent from their jobs due to illness, bad weather, vacation, labor management dispute, or personal reasons are considered employed.

**family** A group of two or more people (one of whom is the householder) related by birth, marriage, or adoption and living in the same household.

**family household** A household maintained by a householder who lives with one or more people related to him or her by blood, marriage, or adoption.

**female/male householder** A woman or man who maintains a household without a spouse present. May head family or nonfamily households.

**full-time, year-round** Indicates 50 or more weeks of full-time employment during the previous calendar year.

**geographic regions** The four major regions and nine census divisions of the United States are the state groupings as shown below:

*Northeast:*
• New England: Connecticut, Maine, Massachusetts, New Hampshire, Rhode Island, and Vermont
• Middle Atlantic: New Jersey, New York, and Pennsylvania

*Midwest:*
• East North Central: Illinois, Indiana, Michigan, Ohio, and Wisconsin
• West North Central: Iowa, Kansas, Minnesota, Missouri, Nebraska, North Dakota, and South Dakota

*South:*
• South Atlantic: Delaware, District of Columbia, Florida, Georgia, Maryland, North Carolina, South Carolina, Virginia, and West Virginia

• East South Central: Alabama, Kentucky, Mississippi, and Tennessee
• West South Central: Arkansas, Louisiana, Oklahoma, and Texas

*West:*
• Mountain: Arizona, Colorado, Idaho, Montana, Nevada, New Mexico, Utah, and Wyoming
• Pacific: Alaska, California, Hawaii, Oregon, and Washington

**Generation X** Americans born between 1965 and 1976, also known as the baby-bust generation.

**Hispanic** Persons or householders who identify their origin as Mexican, Puerto Rican, Central or South American, or some other Hispanic origin. Persons of Hispanic origin may be of any race. In other words, there are black Hispanics, white Hispanics, Asian Hispanics, and Native American Hispanics.

**household** All the persons who occupy a housing unit. A household includes the related family members and all the unrelated persons, if any, such as lodgers, foster children, wards, or employees who share the housing unit. A person living alone is counted as a household. A group of unrelated people who share a housing unit as roommates or unmarried partners is also counted as a household. Households do not include group quarters such as college dormitories, prisons, or nursing homes.

**household, race/ethnicity of** Households are categorized according to the race or ethnicity of the householder only.

**householder** The householder is the person (or one of the persons) in whose name the housing unit is owned or rented or, if there is no such person, any adult member. With married couples, the householder may be either the husband or wife. The householder is the reference person for the household.

**householder, age of** The age of the householder is used to categorize households into age groups such as those used in this book. Married couples, for example, are classified according to the age of either the husband or wife, depending on which one identified him or herself as the householder.

**income** Money received in the preceding calendar year by each person aged 15 or older from each of the following sources: (1) earnings from longest job (or self-employment); (2) earnings from jobs other than longest job; (3) unemployment compensation; (4) workers' compensation; (5) Social Security; (6) Supplemental Security income; (7) public assistance; (8) veterans' payments; (9) survivor benefits; (10) disability benefits; (11) retirement pensions; (12) interest; (13) dividends; (14) rents and royalties or estates and trusts; (15) educational assistance; (16) alimony; (17) child support; (18) financial assistance from outside the household, and other periodic income. Income is reported in several ways in this book. Household income is the combined income of all household members. Income of persons is all income accruing to a person from all sources. Earnings is the amount of money a person receives from his or her job.

**income fifths or quintiles** Where the total number of households are divided into fifths based on household income. One-fifth of households fall into the lowest income quintile, one-fifth into the second income quintile, and so on. This is a useful way to compare the characteristics of low-, middle-, and high-income households.

**married couples with or without children under age 18** Refers to married couples with or without own children under age 18 living in the same household. Couples

without children under age 18 may be parents of grown children who live elsewhere, or they could be childless couples.

**means-tested assistance** Government benefits received by persons or households whose incomes fall below a certain threshhold. Some means-tested assistance is non-cash, such as food stamps, Medicaid, and housing subsidies.

**median** The median is the amount that divides the population or households into two equal portions: one below and one above the median. Medians can be calculated for income, age, and many other characteristics.

**median income** The amount that divides the income distribution into two equal groups, half having incomes above the median, half having incomes below the median. The medians for households or families are based on all households or families. The median for persons are based on all persons aged 15 or older with income.

**metropolitan area** An area qualifies for recognition as a metropolitan area if: (1) it includes a city of at least 50,000 population, or (2) it includes a Census Bureau-defined urbanized area of at least 50,000 with a total metropolitan population of at least 100,000 (75,000 in New England). In addition to the county containing the main city or urbanized area, a metropolitan area may include other counties having strong commuting ties to the central county.

**Millennial generation** Americans born between 1997 and 1994.

**nonfamily household** A household maintained by a householder who lives alone or who lives with people to whom he or she is not related.

**nonfamily householder** A householder who lives alone or with nonrelatives.

**non-Hispanic** People who do not identify themselves as Hispanic on the Current Population Survey or the 1990 Census are classified as non-Hispanic. Non-Hispanics may be of any race.

**nonmeans-tested assistance** Government benefits received regardless of a person's or household's income level. Examples are Social Security and Medicare.

**nonmetropolitan area** Counties that are not classified as metropolitan areas.

**occupation** Occupational classification is based on the kind of work a person did at his or her job during the previous calendar year. If a person changed jobs during the year, the data refer to the occupation of the job held the longest during that year.

**outside central city** The portion of a metropolitan county or counties that falls outside of the central city or cities; generally regarded as the suburbs.

**part-time or full-time employment** Part-time is less than 35 hours of work per week in a majority of the weeks worked during the year. Full-time is 35 or more hours of work per week during a majority of the weeks worked.

**percent change** The change (either positive or negative) in a measure that is expressed as a proportion of the starting measure. When median income changes from $20,000 to $25,000, for example, this is a 25 percent increase.

**percentage point change** The change (either positive or negative) in a value which is already expressed as a percentage. When a labor force participation rate changes from 70 percent of 75 percent, for example, this is a 5 percentage point increase.

**poverty level** The official income threshold below which families and people are classified as living in poverty. The threshold rises each year with inflation and varies depending on family size, age of householder, and number of children under age 18 in the household. According to the Census Bureau, the poverty threshholds in 1997 by household size are as follows:

| Household size | Poverty threshhold |
| --- | --- |
| One person | $8,183 |
| Two people | 10,473 |
| Three people | 12,802 |
| Four people | 16,400 |
| Five people | 19,380 |
| Six people | 21,886 |
| Seven people | 24,802 |
| Eight people | 27,593 |
| Nine or more people | 32,566 |

**proportion or share** The value of a part expressed as a percentage of the whole. If there are 4 million people aged 25 and 3 million of them are white, then the white proportion is 75 percent.

**race** Race is self-reported and appears in four categories in this book: white, black, Native American, and Asian. A household is assigned the race of the householder.

**rounding** Percentages are rounded to the nearest tenth of a percent; therefore, the percentages in a distribution do not always add exactly to 100.0 percent. The totals, however, are always shown as 100.0. Moreover, individual figures are rounded to the nearest thousand without being adjusted to group totals, which are independently rounded; percentages are based on the unrounded numbers.

**sex ratio** The number of men per 100 women.

**suburbs** *See* Outside central city.

**unemployed** Unemployed people are those who, during the survey period, had no employment but were available and looking for work. Those who were laid off from their jobs and were waiting to be recalled are also classified as unemployed.

**work experience** Work experience is based on work for pay or work without pay on a family-operated farm or business at any time during the previous year, on a part-time or full-time basis.

# Index

accountants:
    men's median earnings, 1997, 183;
    women's median earnings, 1997, 265;
    women's median earnings, 1997, as a percentage of
        men's earnings, 265

administrative support occupations:
    men's median earnings, 1982–97, 134–35;
    men's median earnings, 1997, 183–84;
    women's median earnings, 1982–97, 212–13;
    women's median earnings, 1997, 265–66;
    women's median earnings, 1997, as a percentage of
        men's earnings, 265

affluence. *See also* wealth, 3, 6–7, 45, 50, 80, 86

Alabama:
    median household income, 1987–97, 37;
    people below poverty level, 1980–97, 327–329

Alaska:
    median household income, 1987–97, 37;
    people below poverty level, 1980–97, 327–329

alimony:
    source of men's 1997 income, by race and Hispanic
        origin, 185–90;
    source of women's 1997 income, by race and Hispanic
        origin, 267–72

American Indian, Aleut or Eskimo, discretionary
    income of households, 1999, 284–85

Arizona:
    median household income, 1987–97, 37;
    people below poverty level, 1980–97, 327–329

Arkansas:
    median household income, 1987–97, 37;
    people below poverty level, 1980–97, 327–329

armed forces:
    men's median earnings, 1997, 183;
    women's median earnings, 1997, 265;
    women's median earnings, 1997, as a percentage of
        men's earnings, 265

Asian Americans:
    discretionary income of households, 1999, 284–85;
    female full-time workers' median earnings, 1967–97,
        210–211;
    household median income, 1988–97, 22–23;

male full-time worker's median earnings, 1988–97,
    132–33;
    people below poverty level, 1973–97, 321–23;
    women's median income, 1988–97, 203–04

assets, financial, 294–96:
    households owning asset, 294, 296;
    median value of asset for holder, 294–95

assets, nonfinancial, 297–98:
    households owning asset, 297–98;
    median value of asset for holder, 297–98

auto mechanics:
    men's median earnings, 1997, 184;
    women's median earnings, 1997, 266;
    women's median earnings, 1997, as a percentage of
        men's earnings, 266

baby-boom generation. *See also* income categories
    analyzed by age:
    changes in family type, 30, 40, 45, 55, 65, 75, 267;
    discretionary income, 278–79;
    women's income, 200

bachelor's degree. *See* college education.

Black American men:
    full-time worker's median earnings, 1967–97, 132–33;
    income, 1997, by educational attainment, 173–75;
    income, 1997, by work experience, 154,156;
    income, 1967–97, 118;
    income, 1997, 145–46;
    income, 1997, by age, 138, 140;
    income, 1997, by work status and U.S. region,
        145–148;
    median income, 1997, by work status and age,
        138, 140;
    median income, 1967–97, 124–25;
    median income, 1997, by source of income, 185, 187;
    median income, 1997, by work status and educational
        attainment, 173–75;
    with earnings median income, 1997, by work
        experience, 154, 156;
    with earnings median income, 1997, by educational
        attainment, 173–75

Black American women:
    full-time workers' median earnings, 1967–97,
        210–211;

carpenters:
men's median earnings, 1997, 184;
women's median earnings, 1997, 266;
women's median earnings, 1997, as a percentage of
men's earnings, 266

cashiers:
men's median earnings, 1997, 183;
women's median earnings, 1997, 265;
women's median earnings, 1997, as a percentage of
men's earnings, 265

CDs (Certificates of Deposit):
households owning asset, 295;
median value of asset for holder, 296

Census divisions of the U.S. *See also* specific division,
100–04

central cities:
families below poverty level, 1997, by presence of
children, type of family, U.S. region, metropolitan
residence, and race and Hispanic origin, 336, 346;
families below poverty level, 1997, by type of family,
U.S. region, and race and Hispanic origin, 336, 345;
household income, 1997, inside and outside central
city, 110–11;
men's income, 1997, 152–53;
men's median income, 1997, by work status, 152–53;
people below poverty level, 1967–97, 330–332;
people below poverty level, 1997, by age, sex, and
race and Hispanic origin, 369, 371;
women's income 1997, 234–35;
women's median 1997 income by work status, 234–35

child support:
source of men's 1997 income, by race and Hispanic
origin, 185–90;
source of women's 1997 income, by race and Hispanic
origin, 267–72

college education, value of, 24–25, 167–172, 204–05,
242–263, 286–87

Colorado:
median household income, 1987–97, 37;
people below poverty level, 1980–97, 327–329
computer equipment operators:
men's median earnings, 1997, 183;
women's median earnings, 1997, 266;
women's median earnings, 1997, as a percentage of
men's earnings, 266

Connecticut:
median household income, 1987–97, 37;
people below poverty level, 1980–97, 327–329

construction trades:
men's median earnings, 1997, 184;
women's median earnings, 1997, 266;
women's median earnings, 1997, as a percentage of
men's earnings, 266

Consumer Expenditure Survey, 273–74

credit card debt, 299–300:
households having debt, 295;
median value of debt, 296

Current Population Survey, 2

debt, household, by type of debt and household
characteristics, 299–300:
held by households, 299–300;
median value of debt, 299–300

Delaware:
median household income, 1987–97, 37;
people below poverty level, 1980–97, 327–329
discretionary household income, 1999, 273–289:
by age of householder, 278–79;
by educational attainment, 286–87;
by race and Hispanic origin, 284–85;
by size of household, 288–89;
by total household income, 276–77;
by type of household and presence of children,
280–81;
by U.S. region, 282–83;
calculation, 273–274;
definition, 273

District of Columbia:
median household income, 1987–97, 37;
people below poverty level, 1980–97, 327–329

doctoral degrees, value of, 126–27, 160–172, 173–181,
204–05, 242–63, 286–87

dualeearner couples see two-earner couples

earnings *See* specific categories of earners.

East South Central division of the U.S., household
income, 1997, 100, 103

East North Central division of the U.S., household
income, 1997, 100, 102

education assistance:
source of men's 1997 income, 185–90;
source of women's 1997 income, 267–72

educational attainment:
and discretionary income of households, 286–87;
and household income, 24–25;

self-employed:
    men's earnings, 1997, 185–190;
    women's earnings, 1997, 267–272

service occupations, not protective services:
    men's median earnings, 1982–97, 134, 136;
    men's median earnings, 1997, 184;
    women's median earnings, 1982–97, 212, 214;
    women's median earnings, 1997, 266;
    women's median earnings, 1997, as a percentage of
        men's earnings, 266

Social Security:
    source of men's 1997 income, 185–90;
    source of women's 1997 income, 267–72

South Atlantic division of the U.S., household income,
    1997, 100, 103

South Carolina:
    median household income, 1987–97, 38;
    people below poverty level, 1980–97, 327–329

South Dakota:
    median household income, 1987–97, 38;
    people below poverty level, 1980–97, 327–329

South region of the U.S.:
    discretionary income of households, 1999, 282–83;
    families below poverty level, 1997, by family type,
        metropolitan residence, race and Hispanic origin,
        340, 343, 345;
    families below poverty level, 1997, by metropolitan
        residence and race and Hispanic origin, 340–41;
    families below poverty level, 1997, by presence of
        children, family type, metropolitan residence, and
        race and Hispanic origin, 340, 344, 346;
    families below poverty level, 1997, by presence of
        children, metropolitan residence, and race and
        Hispanic origin, 340, 342;
    household income, 1997, 100, 103;
    household income, 1997, by race and Hispanic origin,
        105, 108;
    household median income, 1975–1997, 34–35;
    men's median income, 1967–97, 128–29;
    men's median income, 1997, by work status, race and
        Hispanic origin, 146–51;
    people below poverty level, 1971–97, 324–26;
    people below poverty level, 1997, by age and sex,
        364–368;
    people below poverty level, 1997, by age and race and
        Hispanic origin, 359–63;
    women's income, 1997, by race and Hispanic origin,
        228–233;

women's median income, 1967–97, 206–07;
    women's median income, 1997, by work status and
        race and Hispanic origin, 228–233

SSI (Supplemental Security):
    source of men's 1997 income, 185–90;
    source of women's 1997 income, 267–72

states of the U.S. *See also* specific states:
    median household income, 37–38;
    people below poverty level, 327–29

stocks:
    households owning asset, 295;
    median value of asset for holder, 296

suburbs:
    families below poverty level, 1997, by presence of
        children, type of family, U.S. region, and race and
        Hispanic origin, 336, 346;
    families below poverty level, 1997, by U.S. region,
        type of family, and race and Hispanic origin, 336,
        345;
    household income, 1997, 110–11;
    men's income, 1997, 152–53;
    men's median income, 1997, by work status, 152–53;
    people below poverty level, 1967–97, 330–332;
    people below poverty level, 1997, by age, sex and
        race and Hispanic origin, 369, 372;
    women by 1997 income, 234–35;
    women's median 1997 income by work status, 234–35

Survey of Consumer Finances, 291

teachers:
    men's median earnings, 1997, 183;
    women's median earnings, 1997, 265;
    women's median earnings, 1997, as a percentage of
        men's earnings, 265

technologists, not health-related:
    men's median earnings, 1982–97, 134–35;
    men's median earnings, 1997, 183;
    women's median earnings, 1982–97, 212–13;
    women's median earnings, 1997, 265;
    women's median earnings, 1997, as a percentage of
        men's earnings, 265

Tennessee:
    median household income, 1987–97, 38;
    people below poverty level, 1980–97, 327–329

Texas:
    median household income, 1987–97, 38;
    people below poverty level, 1980–97, 327–329